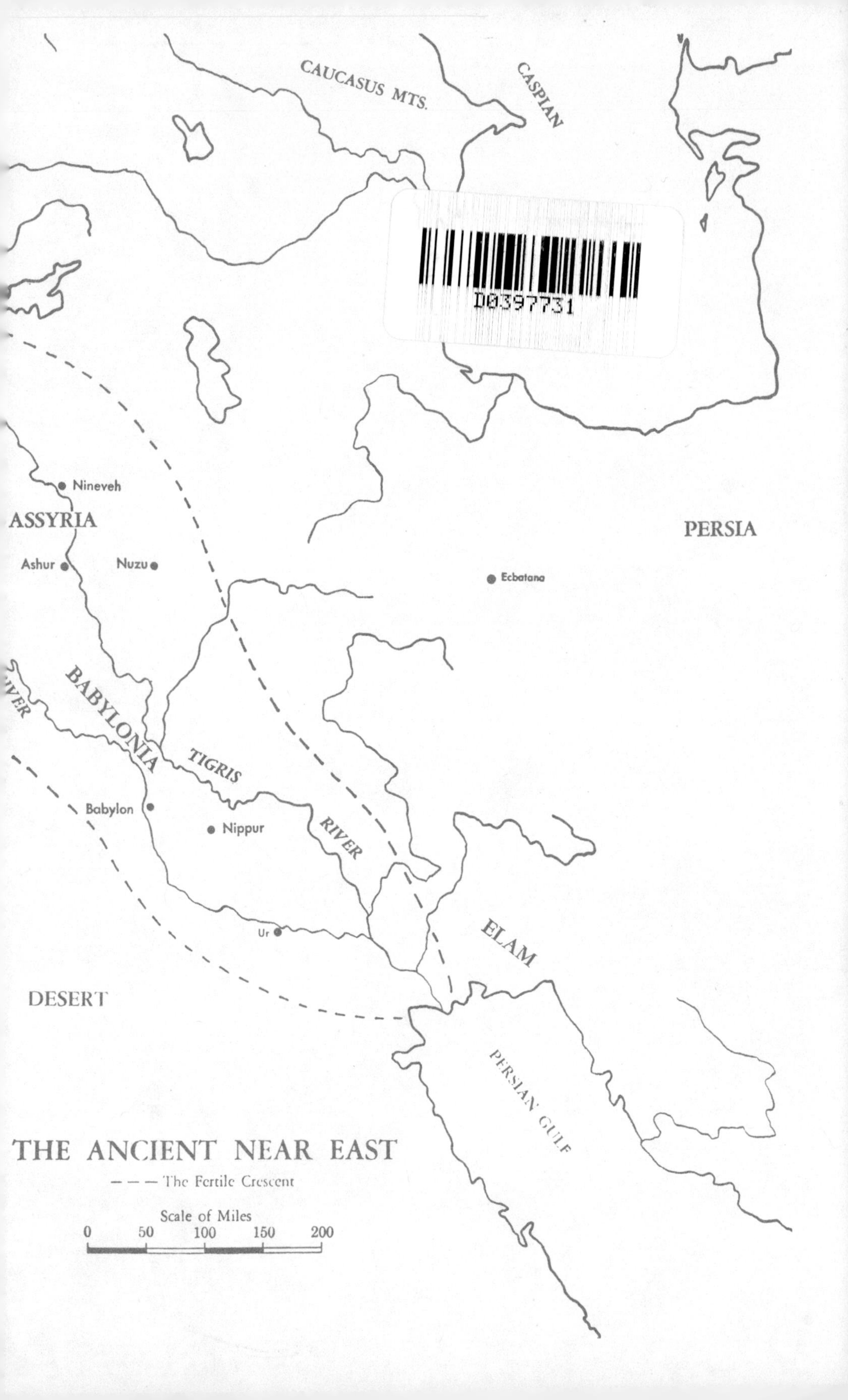
CAUCASUS MTS.
CASPIAN
D0397731
Nineveh
ASSYRIA
Ashur
Nuzu
PERSIA
Ecbatana
BABYLONIA
TIGRIS
RIVER
Babylon
Nippur
ELAM
Ur
DESERT
PERSIAN GULF
THE ANCIENT NEAR EAST
The Fertile Crescent
Scale of Miles
0
50
100
150
200

THE OLD TESTAMENT SPEAKS

FOURTH EDITION

Samuel J. Schultz

THE OLD TESTAMENT SPEAKS

FOURTH EDITION

1817

Harper & Row, Publishers, San Francisco

New York, Grand Rapids, Philadelphia, St. Louis
London, Singapore, Sydney, Tokyo, Toronto

To My Wife EYLA JUNE

All Scripture quotations, unless otherwise noted, are from the American Standard Version of the Bible.

 For information address Harper & Row, Publishers, Inc., 10 East 53rd Street, New York, NY 10022.

Library of Congress Cataloging-in-Publication Data

Schultz, Samuel J.
The Old Testament speaks : a complete survey of Old Testament history and literature / Samuel J. Schultz. — 4th ed.
p. cm.
Includes bibliographical references.
ISBN 0-06-250767-2 :
1. Bible. O.T.—History of Biblical events. 2. Bible. O.T.—Introductions. I. Title.
BS1197.S33 1990
221.9'5—dc20 89-46250
CIP

90 91 92 93 94 HAD 10 9 8 7 6 5 4 3 2 1

This edition is printed on acid-free paper that meets the American National Standards Institute Z39.48 Standard.

Contents

CHARTS

MAPS

Preface

The Bible lives today. The God who spoke and acted in times past confronts men of this generation with the written word as preserved in the Old Testament. Our knowledge of ancient cultures in which this record originated has been greatly increased through archaeological discoveries and the advancing frontiers of biblical scholarship. The preparation of this survey, designed to introduce the liberal arts student and lay reader to the history and literature of the Old Testament, has been prompted by more than a decade of classroom experience. In this volume I endeavor to offer an outline of the entire Old Testament in the light of contemporary developments.

In my graduate studies I was exposed to a wide range of Old Testament interpretation under the late Dr. Robert H. Pfeiffer at Harvard University as well as Drs. Allan A. MacRae and R. Laird Harris at Faith Theological Seminary. To these men I am indebted for a critical understanding of the basic problems confronting the Old Testament scholar. It is not without an awareness of the conflict in contemporary religious thought regarding the authority of the Scriptures that the biblical view of revelation and authority is projected as the basis for a proper understanding of the Old Testament (see Introduction). Since this analysis is based on the literary form of the Old Testament as it has been transmitted to us, questions of authorship are only occasionally noted and pertinent facts of literary criticism are mentioned in passing.

Charts are provided to aid the reader in a chronological integration of Old Testament developments. Dates for the earlier periods are still subject to reappraisal. Any dates before Davidic times should be regarded as approximate. For the Divided Kingdom I have followed the chronological scheme of Edwin H. Thiele. Since the names for the kings of Judah and Israel constitute a problem for the average reader, I have given the variants as used in this book on pages 160–162.

Maps are designed to aid the reader in a better understanding of the geographical factors as they affected contemporary history. Boundaries changed frequently. Cities were destroyed and rebuilt in accordance with the varying fortunes of the kingdoms which rose and fell.

It is a pleasure to acknowledge my debt of gratitude to Dr. Dwight Wayne Young of Brandeis University for reading this manuscript in its entirety and offering helpful criticism throughout. I wish also to express my appreciation to Dr. Burton Goddard and William Lane of Gordon Divinity School, and to Dr. John Graybill of Barrington Bible College, who read earlier versions. Special thanks is due my friend, George F. Bennett, whose concern and counsel were a continual source of encouragement.

I wish to express my thanks to the administration of Wheaton College for granting me leave of absence to complete the manuscript, to the Wheaton College Alumni Association for a research grant, and to the South Shore Baptist Church of Hingham, Massachusetts, for providing facilities to do research and writing. I am grateful for the interest and encouragement of my colleagues in the Bible and Philosophy Department of Wheaton College, especially Dr. Kenneth S. Kantzer, who assumed chairmanship responsibilities in my absence.

To Elaine Noon I am thankful for her exacting care in typing the entire manuscript. Likewise the helpful aid of librarians at Andover-Harvard and Zion Research libraries is greatly appreciated. I am indebted to Carl Lindgren of Scripture Press for the maps in this volume.

Above all this project could not have been accomplished without the willing co-operation of my family. My wife, Eyla June, read and reread every word, offering invaluable criticism, while Linda and David graciously accepted the changes this endeavor imposed upon our family life.

S. J. S.

Wheaton College
Wheaton, Illinois
January, 1960

Preface to the Fourth Edition

For three decades this volume has provided an introductory guide to the reading and study of the Old Testament for college and seminary students, laity, and Bible-study groups, as well as for various centers for biblical education by extension. Translated into many languages—Japanese, Spanish, Portuguese, Chinese, Swedish, German, Croatian, Bulgarian, Arabic, Urdu, and others—it has had a global ministry. This has been most gratifying.

The limited revisions in this edition, primarily in the Poetical Books and Minor Prophets, reflect the interpretations and insights published in recent volumes, as indicated in the footnotes. Selected readings and bibliographies offer pastors, as well as laity, guidance for further study of the Old Testament as God's Word.

S. J. S.

Lexington, Massachusetts
October 1989

Introduction: The Old Testament

Interest in the Old Testament is universal. Millions of people turn to its pages to trace the beginnings of Judaism, Christianity, or Islam. Countless others are allured by its literary excellence. Scholars diligently study the Old Testament for the archaeological, historical, geographical, and linguistic contribution it makes toward a better understanding of the Near East culture preceding the Christian Era.

In world literature the place of the Old Testament is unique. No book—ancient or modern—has had such world-wide appeal, been transmitted with such exacting care, and been accorded such extensive distribution. Acclaimed by statesman and servitor, learned and illiterate, rich and poor, the Old Testament comes to us as a living book. Poignantly it speaks to each generation.

Origin and Contents

From a literary standpoint the thirty-nine books constituting the Old Testament as used by Protestants may be divided into three groups. The first seventeen—Genesis through Esther—give an account of Israel's historical development down to the latter part of the fifth century B.C. Other nations enter the picture only as they have a bearing on Israel's history. The historical narrative breaks off long before the time of Christ, so that an interval of four centuries separates the Old and New Testaments. The apocryphal literature, embraced by the Catholic Church, was developed during this period but was never recognized by the Jews as part of their accepted books or "canon."

Five books—Job, Psalms, Proverbs, Ecclesiastes, and the Song of Solomon—are classified as wisdom literature and poetry. Being rather general in nature they are not closely related to any particular incidents in the history of Israel. At the most only a few psalms can be associated with events related in the historical books.

The remaining seventeen books record the messages of the prophets, who arose in Israel from time to time to declare God's word. The general background and, frequently, specific details given in the historical books serve as a key to the proper interpretation of these prophetic messages. Conversely, the utterances of the prophets contribute much to the understanding of Israel's history.

The arrangement of the Old Testament books has been a matter of historical development. In the modern Hebrew Bible the five books of the Law are followed by eight books called "Prophets"—Joshua, Judges, I and II Samuel, I and II Kings, Isaiah, Jeremiah, Ezekiel, and the Twelve (the Minor Prophets). The last eleven books are designated as "Writings" or Hagiographa—Psalms, Job, Proverbs, Ruth, Song of Solomon, Ecclesiastes, Lamentations, Esther, Daniel, Ezra-Nehemiah, and I and II Chronicles. The sequence of the books varied for several centuries after the completion of the Old Testament. The use of the codex, or book-form, introduced during the second century of the Christian Era, necessitated a definite order in arrangement. As long as they were kept on individual scrolls the order of the books was not of primary importance. But as the codex replaced the scrolls standard arrangements, such as are reflected in our Hebrew and English Bibles, gradually came into common use.

According to internal evidence, the Old Testament was written during a period of approximately a thousand years (*cc.* 1400–400 B.C.) by at least thirty different authors. The authorship of a number of books is unknown. The original language for most of the Old Testament was Hebrew, a branch of the great family of Semitic languages, including Phoenician, Assyrian, Babylonian, Arabic, and other tongues. Down to exilic times Hebrew continued as the spoken language of Palestine. In the course of time Aramaic became the lingua franca of the Fertile Crescent so that parts of Ezra (4:8–6:18; 7:12–26), Jeremiah (10:11), and Daniel (2:4–7:28) were written in this language.

Transmission of the Hebrew Text

Vellum, which is prepared from skins of animals, was the most frequently employed material in the writing of the Hebrew Old Testament. Because of its durability the Jews continued its use through Greek and Roman times, though papyrus was more plentiful and commercially acceptable as the standard writing material. An average leather scroll measured about thirty feet in length and approximately ten inches in height. Peculiar to ancient texts is the fact that in the original state only the consonants were written, appearing in a continuous line with very little word separation. With the beginning of the Christian Era the Jewish scribes were extremely conscious of the need for accuracy in transmitting the Hebrew text. The scholars peculiarly devoted to this task in subsequent centuries were known as Masoretes. They copied the text with great care and in time even numbered the verses, words, and letters of each book.[1] Their greatest contribution was the insertion of vowel symbols in the text as an aid in reading.

Until 1488, when the first Hebrew Bible appeared in print in Soncino, Italy, every copy was handwritten. Although private copies had appeared both on vellum and in book-form, synagogue texts were usually restricted to leather scrolls and copied with extreme care.

Until the discovery of the Dead Sea Scrolls, the earliest Hebrew manuscripts extant dated back to about A.D. 900. In the scrolls of the Qumran community, which was dispersed shortly before the destruction of Jerusalem in A.D. 70, every Old Testament book except Esther is represented. Evidence from these recent discoveries has confirmed the viewpoint that the Hebrew text preserved by the Masoretes was handed down without serious changes from the first century B.C.

The Versions[2]

The Septuagint (LXX), a Greek translation of the Old Testament, began to circulate in Egypt in the days of Ptolemy Philadelphos (285–246 B.C.). There was a demand among the Greek-speaking Jews to have copies of the Old Testament made available for private and synagogue use in the lingua franca of the East Mediterranean area. Very likely an official copy was placed in the famous library in Alexandria.

Not only was this version used by Greek-speaking Jews but it was also adopted by the Christian Church. In all likelihood it was a Greek Old Testament that Paul and other apostles used in pressing the claim that Jesus was the Messiah (Acts 17:2–4). Contemporaneously the New Testament was written in Greek and became a part of the Scriptures accepted by the Christians. Charging that the Greek Old Testament translation was inaccurate and affected by Christian belief, the Jews tenaciously adhered to the text in the original language. This Hebrew text, as we have already noted, was carefully transmitted by the Jewish scribes and Masoretes in subsequent centuries.

By virtue of these developments the Christian Church became the custodian of the Greek version. Aside from such noted scholars as Origen and Jerome, few Christians had any regard for the Old Testament in its original

[1] Since verse divisions appear in the Hebrew text in the tenth century A.D., the verse divisions in the Old Testament apparently were made by the Masoretes. Our chapter divisions began with Bishop Stephen Langton in the thirteenth century (d. 1228).

[2] For the story of how the Scriptures came to us see Sir Frederic Kenyon, *Our Bible and Ancient Manuscripts,* revised by A. W. Adams (New York: Harper & Brothers, 1958).

language until the Renaissance. Various Greek translations, however, were circulated among the Christians.

During the second century the codex-form—our modern book-form, with leaves arranged for binding—came into use. Papyrus was already the chief writing material throughout the Mediterranean world. Replacing the leather scrolls, which had been the accepted medium for the transmission of the Hebrew text, the papyri codices became the standard for Greek copies of the Scriptures. By the fourth century papyrus was replaced by vellum (parchment). Earliest copies of the Septuagint now existing date back to the first half of the fourth century. Recently some papyri, most notably the Chester Beatty collection, have provided portions of the Septuagint that antedate the vellum codices noted above.

The need for another translation developed when Latin replaced Greek as the official and common language of the Mediterranean world. Although an Old Latin version of the Septuagint had been circulated earlier in Africa, it was through the scholarly efforts of Jerome that a Latin translation of the Hebrew Old Testament appeared near the end of the fourth century. For the next millennium this version, better known as the Vulgate, was the most popular edition of the Old Testament. To this day the Vulgate, with the addition of the apocryphal books which Jerome rejected, remains the accepted translation of the Roman Catholic Church.

The Renaissance had a decisive influence on the transmission and circulation of the Scriptures. Not only did the revival of learning stimulate multiplication of copies of the Vulgate, but it also aroused a new interest in the study of the original languages of the Bible. A fresh impetus came with the fall of Constantinople, which forced numerous Greek scholars into Western Europe. Coupled with this renewed interest in Greek and Hebrew was a keen desire to make the Bible available to the layman. As a result vernacular translations appeared. Antedating the monumental work of Martin Luther's German Bible in 1522 were German, French, Italian, and English versions. Of prime importance in England was Wycliffe's translation near the end of the fourteenth century. Confined to manuscript Bibles, the availability of this early English version was quite circumscribed. With the invention of the printing press in the next century, a new era dawned for the circulation of the Scriptures.

William Tyndale is recognized as the true father of the English Bible. By 1525, the birth year of the printed Bible in English, his translation began to appear. Unlike Wycliffe, who translated from the Latin, Tyndale turned to the original languages for his version of the Scriptures. In 1536, with his task still unfinished, Tyndale was condemned to die. In his dying moments, enveloped by flames, he uttered his last prayer: "Lord, open the king of England's eyes."

The sudden turn of events soon vindicated Tyndale and his work. In 1537 Matthew's Bible was published, incorporating Tyndale's translation as supplemented by Coverdale's version (1535). Under Cromwell's orders the Great Bible (1541) was placed in every church in England. Although this was primarily a Bible for church use, some copies were made available for private study. As its counterpart, the Geneva Bible came into circulation in 1560 to become the Bible of the home. For half a century it was the most popular English Bible for private reading. In 1586 the Great Bible was revised and printed as the Bishop's Bible for official use in the churches of England.

The Authorized Version of the English Bible was published in 1611. Representing the work of Greek and Hebrew scholars who were concerned with producing the best possible translation of the Scriptures, this "King James Version" gained an undisputed place in the English-speaking world by the middle of the seventeenth century. Among noteworthy revisions are the Revised Standard Version 1952 and the New American Bible 1971. The New International Version 1978 represents a completely new translation from the best available Hebrew, Aramic and Greek texts.[3]

Meaning

Does the Old Testament come to us simply as a narrative of secular history or culture? Does it have value merely as the national literature of the Jews? The Old Testament itself purports to be more than the historical record of the Jewish nation. To Jews and Christians alike, it is the sacred history that discloses God's revelation of himself to man. Therein is recorded not only what God has done in the past, but the divine plan for mankind's future as well.

Throughout the fortunes and misfortunes of Israel, God, the creator of the universe as well as of man, ordered the course of his chosen people in the international arena of ancient cultures. God is not only the God of Israel but the supreme ruler who controls the affairs of all nations. Consequently the Old Testament does record natural events, but also interwoven throughout this history are the activities of God in a supernatural manner. This distinctive feature of the Old Testament—the disclosure of God in historical events and messages—raises it above the level of secular literature and history. Only as sacred history can the Old Testament be understood in its full significance. Recognition that both the natural and the supernatural are vital factors throughout the Bible is indispensable to a full-orbed comprehension of its contents.

[3]The NIV was sponsored by the New York International Bible Society and published by Zondervan Publishers, Grand Rapids, MI.

Unique as sacred history, the Old Testament claims distinction as Holy Writ. Such it was to Jews, to whom these writings were entrusted, as well as to the Christians (Rom. 3:2). Coming through the natural medium of human authors, the final written product had the divine stamp of approval. Surely the Spirit of God employed the attention, the investigation, the memory, the imagination, the logic—all the faculties of the writers of the Old Testament. In contrast to mechanical means, God's guidance was manifested through free exercise of the author's historical, literary, and theological capabilities. The written record as received by Jews and Christians constituted a divine-human product inerrant in its original writing. As such it contained the truth for the entire human race.

Such was the attitude of Jesus Christ and the apostles. Jesus, the God-Man, accepted the authority of the entire body of literature known as the Old Testament and freely used these Scriptures as the basis of appeal in his teaching (Cf. John 10:34–35; Matt. 22:29, 43–45; Luke 16:17; 24:25). So did the apostles in the initial period of the Christian Church (II Tim. 3:16; II Pet. 1:20–21). Recorded by man under divine guidance, the Old Testament was accepted as entirely reliable.

In our day it is just as essential to let the Old Testament constitute the ultimate authority as it did in New Testament times for the Jews and Christians.[4] As a reasonably reliable record—allowing for errors of transmission that need careful consideration by the scientific use of correct principles of textual criticism—the Old Testament speaks authoritatively in the language of the layman of two or more millennia ago. What it enunciates it declares truthfully—whether it employs figurative language or literal, whether it deals with ethics or with the natural world of science. The words of the biblical writers—properly interpreted in their total context and in their natural sense according to the usage of their day—teach the truth without error. As such let the Old Testament speak to the reader.

This volume offers a survey of the entire Old Testament. As archaeology, history, and other fields of study are related to the content of the Old Testament, may they be the means of gaining a better understanding of the Bible's message. But only to the extent that the reader allows the Bible to speak for itself will this book accomplish its purpose.

SELECTED READING

ARCHER, GLEASON. *Survey of Old Testament Introduction.* Chicago: Moody Press, 1974.

[4] For a discussion of the biblical view of revelation, inspiration, and authority by scholars who recognize the Holy Scriptures as the word of God to men, revealed to and through His prophets and apostles, see *The Bible—The Living Word of Revelation,* M. C. Tenney, ed. (Grand Rapids: Zondervan, 1968). See also articles published in the *Journal* of the Evangelical Theological Society.

Boice, James M. (ed.) *Foundations of Biblical Authority.* Grand Rapids: Zondervan Publishing House, 1978.

Bright, John. *The Authority of the Old Testament.* Nashville: Abingdon Press, 1967.

Bromily, G. W. (ed.) *The International Standard Bible Encyclopedia.* Fully revised. Vols. I–IV. Grand Rapids: Wm. B. Eerdmans Publishing Co., 1979–1988.

Buswell, J. Oliver, Jr. *A Systematic Theology of the Christian Religion.* Grand Rapids: Zondervan Publishing House, 1962.

Carpenter, Charles W. (ed.) *Wesleyan Bible Commentary.* Grand Rapids: Wm. B. Eerdmans Publishing Co., 1967.

Davidson, Francis, et al. (eds.) *The New Bible Commentary.* Grand Rapids: Wm. B. Eerdmans Publishing Co., 1953.

Douglas, J. D. (ed.) *The New Bible Dictionary.* London: Inter-Varsity Fellowship; Grand Rapids: Wm. B. Eerdmans Publishing Co., 1962.

Elwell, Walter A. (ed.) *Baker Encyclopedia of the Bible.* 2 vols. Grand Rapids: Baker Book House, 1988.

Gaebelein, Frank E. *The Expositor's Bible Commentary.* Vols. 1–12. Grand Rapids: Zondervan Publishing House, 1979–.

Guthrie, Donald, and J. A. Motyer (eds.) *The New Bible Commentary Revised.* Grand Rapids: Wm. B. Eerdmans Publishing Co., 1970.

Harrison, R. K. *Introduction to the Old Testament.* Grand Rapids: Wm. B. Eerdmans Publishing Co., 1969.

Hasel, Gerhard F. *Old Testament Theology.* Grand Rapids: Wm. B. Eerdmans Publishing Co., 1975.

Henry, Carl F. H. *God, Revelation and Authority,* Vols. I–V. Waco: Word Books, 1976, 1979.

———. (ed.) *Revelation, and the Bible.* Philadelphia: Presbyterian and Reformed Publishing Co., 1958.

Inch, Morris, and Schultz, Samuel J. (eds.) *Interpreting the Word of God.* Chicago: Moody Press, 1976.

Inch, Morris, and Youngblood, Ronald (eds.) *The Living and Active Word of God: Studies in Honor of Samuel J. Schultz.* Winona Lake, IN: Eisenbrauns, 1983.

Kaiser, Walter J., Jr. *Toward an Old Testament Theology.* Grand Rapids: Zondervan Publishing House, 1979.

———. *Toward Rediscovering the Old Testament.* Grand Rapids: Zondervan Publishing House, 1987.

Kitchen, Kenneth A. *Ancient Orient and Old Testament.* Chicago: Inter-Varsity Press, 1966.

Kline, Meredith. *The Structure of Biblical Authority.* Grand Rapids: Wm. B. Eerdmans Publishing Co., 1973.

Packer, James I. *Fundamentalism and the Word of God.* London: Inter-Varsity Fellowship, 1958.

———. *God Speaks to Man.* Philadelphia: Westminster Press, 1966.

PAYNE, J. BARTON (ed.) *New Perspectives on the Old Testament.* Waco: Word Books, 1971.

PFEIFFER, CHARLES F. *The Wycliffe Bible Commentary.* Chicago: Moody Press, 1962.

PINNOCK, CLARK. *Biblical Revelation.* Chicago: Moody Press, 1976.

PREUSS, ROBERT. *The Inspiration of Scripture.* Edinburgh: Oliver & Boyd, 1955.

SCHULTZ, SAMUEL J. *The Prophets Speak.* New York: Harper & Row, 1968.

———. *The Gospel of Moses.* New York: Harper & Row, 1974. Chicago: Moody Press, 1979.

SKILTON, JOHN H. (ed.) *The Law and the Prophets: Old Testament Studies in Honor of Oswald T. Allis.* Ventnor: Presbyterian and Reformed Publishing Co., 1974.

TENNEY, MERRILL C. (ed.) *The Bible—The Living Word of Revelation.* Grand Rapids: Zondervan Publishing House, 1968.

———. (ed.) *The Zondervan Pictorial Encyclopedia of the Bible.* 5 vols. Grand Rapids: Zondervan Publishing House, 1975.

VOS, GERHARDUS. *Biblical Theology: Old Testament and New Testament.* Grand Rapids: Wm. B. Eerdmans Publishing Co., 1975.

WALVOORD, JOHN W. (ed.) *Inspiration and Interpretation.* Grand Rapids: Wm. B. Eerdmans Publishing Co., 1957.

WALVOORD, JOHN W., AND ROY B. ZUCK. *The Bible Knowledge Commentary: Old Testament.* Wheaton: Scripture Press, 1985.

WARFIELD, B. B. *Biblical Foundations.* Grand Rapids: Wm. B. Eerdmans Publishing Co., 1958.

———. *The Inspiration and Authority of the Bible.* London: Presbyterian and Reformed Publishing Co., 1959.

WENHAM, JOHN W. *Our Lord's View of the Old Testament.* London: Tyndale Press, 1955.

———. *Christ and the Bible.* Downers Grove: Inter-Varsity Press, 1973.

———. *The Goodness of God.* Downers Grove: Inter-Varsity Press, 1974.

WILLIS, JOHN T. (ed.) *A Living Word Commentary on the Old Testament.* Austin: Sweet Publishing Co., 1979.

THE OLD TESTAMENT SPEAKS

Chapter I

The Period of Beginnings

Queries concerning the origin of life and of things have always had a part in man's thinking. Discovery of the past, as exhibited by the Dead Sea Scrolls, not only challenges the scholar but fascinates the layman.

The Old Testament provides an answer to man's inquiry into the past. Unfolded in the first eleven chapters of Genesis are the essential facts regarding the creation of this universe and of man. In the written record of God's dealings with man these chapters extend into the past beyond that which has definitely been established or corroborated by historical investigations. With reasonable assurance, nevertheless, the evangelical unequivocally accepts this part of the Bible as the "first" (and the only authentic) account of God's creation of the universe.[1]

The opening chapters of the canon are basic to the entire revelation unfolded in the Old and New Testaments. Throughout the Bible there are references[2] to creation and the early history of mankind as portrayed in these introductory chapters.

How shall we interpret this account of the beginning of man and his world? Is it mythology, allegory, a contradictory combination of documents, or a single man's idea of the origin of things? Other biblical writers recognize it as a straightforward narration of God's activity in creating the earth, the heavens, and man. But the modern reader must guard against reading into the narrative, interpreting it in scientific terms, or assuming it to be a storehouse of information bearing upon recently developed olo-

[1] For a discussion of "firsts" in recorded history see S. N. Kramer, *From the Tablets of Sumer* (Indian Hills, Colo.: The Falcon's Wing Press, 1956), 293 pp. Most of the events in Gen. 1–11 precede the Sumerian civilization, where writing appeared near the end of the fourth millennium B.C.

[2] Cf. Is. 40–50; Rom. 5:14; I Cor. 15:45; I Tim. 2:13–14, and others.

gies. In interpreting this section of the Bible—or any other text, for that matter—it is important to accept it on its own terms. Without question the author made normal use of symbols, allegory, figures of speech, poetry, and/or other literary devices. To him it apparently constituted a sensible, unified record of the beginning of all things as made known to him by God through human and divine means.

The time covered by this period of beginnings is nowhere indicated in the Scriptures. Whereas the terminal point—the time of Abraham—is related to the first half of the second millennium, the other events of this era cannot be dated with exactness. Attempts to interpret the genealogical references as a complete and exact chronology do not seem reasonable in the light of secular history. Although the narrative generally is in chronological sequence, the author of Genesis by no means suggests a date for creation.

Neither are the geographical details of this period known to us. It is improbable that the exact location of Eden, and of some of the rivers and countries mentioned, will ever be identified. What geographical changes occurred with man's expulsion from Eden and with the Flood are not indicated. In all likelihood they are beyond the limits of man's investigation.

In reading the first eleven chapters of the Old Testament one can think of questions that remain unanswered in the narrative. These queries deserve further study. More important, however, is the consideration of that which is stated; for this material provides the foundation and background for God's greater and fuller revelation as it is progressively unfolded in subsequent chapters.

The first part of Genesis falls neatly into the following subdivisions:

I. The account of creation	1:1–2:25
A. The universe and its contents	1:1–2:3
B. Man and his habitat	2:4–25
II. The fall of man and its consequences	3:1–6:10
A. Man's disobedience and expulsion	3:1–24
B. Cain and Abel	4:1–24
C. The generation of Adam	4:25–6:10
III. The Flood: God's judgment on man	6:11–8:19
A. Preparation for the Flood	6:11–22
B. The deluge	7:1–8:19
IV. Man's new beginning	8:20–11:32
A. The covenant with Noah	8:20–9:19
B. Noah and his sons	9:20–10:32
C. The tower of Babel	11:1–9
D. Shem and his descendants	11:10–32

The Account of Creation—1:1–2:25

"In the beginning" introduces the developments in preparation of the universe for the creation of man. Whether this dateless date refers to God's original creation[3] or to God's initial act in getting the world ready for man is a matter of interpretation.[4] In either case the narrator begins with God as the creator in this brief introductory paragraph or clause (1:1–2) in accounting for the existence of man and the universe.

Sequence and progression mark the era of creation and organization (1:3–2:3). In a period designated as six days order prevailed in the universe relative to the earth.[5] On the first day light and darkness were ordained to provide periods of day and night. On the second day the firmament was set apart to be the expanse of the earth's atmosphere. Next in order came the separation of land and water, so that vegetation appeared in due time. On the fourth day the luminaries in the heavens began to function in their respective places to determine the length, seasons, years, and days for the earth. The fifth day brought into existence living creatures to populate the bodies of water below and the sky above. Climactic in this series of creative events was the sixth day.[6] Land animals and man were ordained for the occupation of the earth. The latter was distinguished from the former and entrusted with responsibility to have dominion over all animal life. Vegetation was God's provision for their livelihood. On the seventh day God finished his creative acts and sanctified it as a period of rest.

Man is immediately distinguished as the most important of God's en-

[3] Estimates for the age of the universe vary so much that it is impossible to suggest an acceptable date. Einstein suggested ten billion years as the age of the earth. Computations for the age of the galaxies of stars vary from two to ten billion years. (Cf. *Modern Science and Christian Faith* [Wheaton, Ill.: Van Kampen Press, 1948], p. 30.) For dating the past 50,000 years by the "carbon 14" method see W. F. Libby, *Radiocarbon Dating* (2nd ed.; University of Chicago Press, 1955). Cf. also R. Laird Harris, *Inspiration and Canonicity of the Bible* (Grand Rapids: Zondervan, 1957), n. 24, p. 285.

[4] For 1:1 as a dependent clause see E. A. Speiser, *Genesis,* and others. Supporting 1:1 as an independent clause, E. J. Young, *Studies in Genesis One* (Grand Rapids: Baker Book House, 1964) asserts that the construct followed by a finite verb exemplifies genuine Semitic usage. Cf. Lev. 14:46, I Sam. 5:9; 25:15; Ps. 16:3; 58:9; 81:6; Isa. 29:1; Hos. 1:2. He concludes "The first verse of Genesis therefore stands as a simple declaration of the fact of absolute creation."

[5] The length of these creative days is not stated. Some suggest 24-hour days on the basis of Gen. 1:14; Ex. 20:11, and other references. These days may have been long extended eras since "day" is used in this sense in Gen. 2:4. Cf. Augustine, *Confessions,* Books XI, XII and XIII, and J. Oliver Buswell, "The Length of Creative Days" (unpublished material, Wheaton College, Wheaton, Ill.). Evening and morning would then be used in a figurative sense. For a summary discussion see Bernard Ramm, *The Christian View of Science and Scripture* (Grand Rapids: Eerdmans, 1955), pp. 171–229. This account does not provide the data to ascertain conclusively the length of this period of creative days.

[6] By using the genealogies of Gen. 5 and 11 to calculate time Bishop Ussher (1654) dated the creation of man at 4004 B.C. This date is untenable since genealogies did not represent a complete chronology. Cf. W. H. Green, *The Unity of Genesis* (New York: Charles Scribner's Sons, 1910), pp. 49–50.

tire creation (2:4b–25).[7] Created in the image of God, he becomes the focal point of interest as the narrative proceeds. More details are given here about his creation. God formed man out of the dust of the earth and breathed into him the breath of life, making him a living being. Man not only was entrusted with responsibility to care for the animals but was also commissioned to name them. The distinction between man and animals is further apparent in the fact that man found no satisfactory companionship until God created Eve as his helpmeet. For man's habitat God prepared a garden in Eden. Charged with the care of this garden, man was entrusted with the full enjoyment of all things abundantly provided by God. There was only one restriction—man was not to eat of the tree of the knowledge of good and evil.

The Fall of Man and Its Consequences—3:1–6:10

Most crucial in man's relationship with God is the drastic change that was precipitated by disobedience (3:1–24). As the most tragic development in the history of the human race it is a recurrent theme in the Bible.

Confronted with a serpent who spoke, Eve began to doubt God's prohibition and deliberately disobeyed.[8] Adam in turn yielded to Eve's persuasion. Immediately they were conscious of their deception by the serpent and their disobedience to God. With aprons of fig leaves they tried to conceal their shame. Face to face with the Lord God all parties involved in this transgression were solemnly judged. The serpent was cursed above all animals (3:14). Enmity was to be the perpetual relationship between the seed of the serpent, who represented more than the particular reptile present, and the seed of the woman.[9] In regard to Adam and Eve God preceded judgment with mercy by assuring ultimate victory to man through the woman's seed (3:15).[10] But woman was consigned to sorrow in childbearing and man was subjected to the consequences of a cursed earth. God provided skins for their clothing, which involved the killing of animals in behalf of sinful man. Conscious of the knowledge of good and evil, Adam and Eve were immediately expelled from the Garden of Eden lest they also partake of the tree of life and live forever. Banished from the habitat of bliss, man faced the consequences of the curse with only the promise of eventual relief through the seed of the woman to mitigate his fate.

[7] For a discussion of the unique manner in which God created man and theistic evolution, see J. Murray and D. A. Young as listed under selected reading.

[8] Note that the only other instance in Scripture where an animal spoke was God's use of Balaam's ass (Num. 22:28).

[9] Cf. the New Testament interpretation in John 8:44; Rom. 16:20; II Cor. 11:3; Rev. 12:9, 20:2, etc.

[10] Note the hope based on this promise in Gen. 4:1, 25; 5:29, and the Messianic promises throughout the Old Testament.

Of the children born to Adam and Eve only three are mentioned by name. The experiences of Cain and Abel reveal the condition of man in his changed state. Both worshiped God by bringing offerings. While Abel's animal sacrifice was accepted, Cain's offering of vegetables was rejected. Angered by this, Cain killed his brother. Since he had been warned by God, Cain displayed an attitude of deliberate disobedience and became the first murderer. It is not unreasonable to conclude that this same attitude prevailed when he brought his offering, which God rejected.

The civilization of Cain and his descendants is reflected in a genealogy that undoubtedly represents a very long period of time (4:17–24). Cain himself established a city. Urban society in antiquity, of course, went hand in hand with the raising of flocks and herds. Arts developed with the invention and production of musical instruments. With the use of iron and bronze came the science of metallurgy. This advanced culture apparently gave the people a false sense of security. This was reflected in an attitude of scoffing and boasting by Lamech, the first polygamist. He prided himself on the use of superior weapons to destroy life. Conspicuously absent, by contrast, was any recognition of God by Cain's progeny.

Following the loss of Abel and their disappointment in Cain as a murderer, the first parents expressed a new hope in the birth of Seth (4:25 ff.). It was in the days of Seth's son, Enos, that men began to turn to God. With the passing of numerous generations and many centuries another sign of godly concern was exemplified in the man Enoch. This remarkable figure did not experience death; his life of fellowship with God ended with his assumption. With the birth of Noah hope was revived once more. Lamech, a descendant of Seth, anticipated that through this son mankind would be relieved from the curse under which it had suffered since man's expulsion from Eden.

In the days of Noah the increasing godlessness of civilization reached a crisis. God, who had created man and his habitat, was disappointed in the prevailing culture. Intermarriage between the sons of God and the daughters of men was displeasing to him.[11] Corruption, wickedness, and violence increased to the extent that all man's plans and schemings were characterized by evil. God's attitude of regret in having created mankind was apparent in the plan to withdraw his spirit from man.[12] A period of a hundred and

[11] For translating "sons of God" as "the sons of the gods," cf. M. Kline on Gen. 6:1-4 in *The New Bible Commentary: Revised* (Grand Rapids: Wm. B. Eerdmans Publishing Co., 1970). "Nephilim" and "heroes of renown" may identify people who, with political dominance and known for their tyrannical injustice, married any they chose.

[12] For a discussion of the Hebrew word in Gen. 6:3 translated as "strive" (AV and ASV), "abide" (RSV), "remain" (Berkeley and NIV), and "rule" (LXX, Vulgate, and Syriac), see E. A. Speiser, "YDWN, Gen. 6:3," *Journal of Biblical Literature,* LXXV (1956), 126-129, who renders this word as "expiate, answer for, shield, protect." Cf. also

twenty years of warning preceded the pending judgment of the human race. Only Noah found favor in the eyes of the Lord. Blameless and righteous, he maintained an acceptable relationship with God.

The Flood: God's Judgment on Man—6:11–8:19

Noah was a man of obedience. When commanded to build the ark he followed instructions (6:11–22). The measurements of the ark still represent the basic proportions used in modern shipbuilding. Not a vessel designed for speed, the ark was constructed to accommodate all life that was to be spared during the crisis of world judgment. Ample room was provided to shelter Noah, his wife, his three sons and their wives, a representation of every basic kind of animal and bird life, and provender for all.[13]

For approximately one year Noah was confined to the ark while the world was subjected to divine judgment.[14] God's purpose to destroy the sinful human race was accomplished. Whether the Flood was local or worldwide is of secondary importance to the fact that the deluge extended far enough to include all mankind. Incessant rains and waters from subterranean sources raised the water level beyond the highest mountain peaks. In due time the water subsided. The ark rested on Mount Ararat. Bidden to leave the ark, man faced a new opportunity in a renovated world.[15]

Man's New Beginning—8:20–11:32

Civilization after the Flood began with sacrificial offerings. In response God made a covenant with Noah and his descendants. Never again would all life be destroyed with a flood. The rainbow in the sky became the perpetual sign of God's everlasting covenant. Blessing Noah, God commissioned him to populate and possess the whole earth. Properly slaughtered animals, as well as vegetation, were ordained for food. Man, however, was held strictly accountable to God—in whose image he had been created—for the shedding of human blood.

Turning to an agrarian pursuit, Noah planted a vineyard. His indul-

---

E. F. Kevan, "Genesis," *The New Bible Commentary,* F. Davidson, ed. (London: 1954, Inter-Varsity Fellowship), p. 83.

[13] Taking a cubit as 18 inches the measurements of the ark were 450 by 75 by 45 feet. Three decks would allow for a displacement of approximately 40,000 to 50,000 tons.

[14] For a chronology of this year see E. F. Kevan, *op. cit.*, pp. 84-85.

[15] Ussher's date for the Flood was 2348 B.C. S. R. Driver in his commentary on Genesis (1904) alleged 2501 B.C. as the biblical date for the Flood. In the light of a continuous civilization in Egypt since about 3000 B. C. these dates seem untenable. Neither are they supported by a proper exegesis of Scripture. The Flood may have been as early as 10,000 B.C. For relative chronologies see R. W. Errich, *Chronologies in Old World Archaelogy* (U. of Chicago Press), 1965. For continuous Indian culture in America see R. M. Underhill, *Red Man's America* (Chicago, 1953), pp. 8-9.

gence in intoxicating wine resulted in a breach of modesty to which Ham, and probably his son Canaan, responded with disrespect. This incident became the occasion for paternal utterances of curse and blessing by Noah (9:20–28). Noah's verdict was prophetic in scope. He anticipated the sinful attitude of Ham reflected in the line of Canaan, one of Ham's four sons.[16] Centuries later the wicked Canaanites were subjected to severe judgment with the occupation of their land by the Israelites. Shem and Japheth, the other sons of Noah, received their father's blessing.

Being a racial and linguistic unit, the human race remained in one location for an indefinite period (11:1–9). On the plain of Shinar they undertook a tremendous building project. The construction of the Tower of Babel represented pride in human achievement as well as defiance of God's commission to populate the earth. God, who had continuously taken an interest in man since his creation, could not ignore him now. Apparently the tower was not destroyed, but God terminated the endeavor by linguistic confusion. This resulted in the willing dispersion of the human race.

The geographical distribution of Noah's descendants is given in a brief summary (10:1–32). This genealogy, which represents a long era, merely suggests areas to which the various families migrated. Japheth and his sons settled in the vicinity of the Black and Caspian seas extending westward to Spain (10:2–5). Very likely the Greek, Indo-Germanic people and other related groups descended from Japheth.

Three sons of Ham went down into Africa (10:6–14). Subsequently they spread northward to the land of Shinar and Assyria, building such cities as Nineveh, Calah, Babel, Akkad, and others. Canaan, the fourth son of Ham, settled along the Mediterranean, extending from Sidon down to Gaza and eastward. Though Hamitic in racial origin, the Canaanites used a language closely related to that of the Semites.

Shem and his descendants occupied the area north of the Persian Gulf (10:21–31). Elam, Ashur, Aram, and other place names were associated with the Semites. After 2000 B.C. such cities as Mari and Nahor became leading centers of Semitic culture.

To conclude the period of beginnings, the scope of developments is narrowed down to the Semites (11:10–32). By means of a genealogical framework using ten generations, the record finally focuses upon Terah, who migrated from Ur to Haran. The climax is the introduction of Abram, later known as Abraham (Gen. 17:5), who embodies the beginning of a chosen nation—the nation of Israel which occupies the center of interest throughout the rest of the Old Testament.[17]

[16] H. C. Leupold, *Exposition of Genesis* (Grand Rapids: Baker, 1950), Vol. I, pp. 349–352.

[17] Nowhere do the Scriptures indicate how much time elapsed in Gen. 1–11. Con-

SELECTED READING

CASSUTO, UMBERTO. *A Commentary on the Book of Genesis.* Translated by Israel Abrahams. 2 vols. Jerusalem: Magnes Press, 1961.

HAMILTON, VICTOR P. *Handbook on the Pentateuch.* Grand Rapids: Baker Book House, 1982.

HARRIS, R. L. *Man: God's Eternal Creation.* Chicago: Moody Press, 1971.

KIDNER, DEREK. *Genesis.* Downers Grove: Inter-Varsity Press, 1967.

KLINE, M. "Genesis," in *The New Bible Commentary.* Rev. ed. D. Guthrie (ed.). Grand Rapids: Wm. B. Eerdmans Publishing Co., 1970.

LEUPOLD, H. C. *Exposition of Genesis.* 2 vols. Grand Rapids: Baker Book House, 1949.

MIXTER, RUSSELL L. (ed.) *Evolution and Christian Thought Today.* Grand Rapids: Wm. B. Eerdmans Publishing Co., 1959.

MORRIS, HENRY M. *Evolution and the Modern Christian.* Philadelphia: Presbyterian and Reformed Publishing Co., 1967.

MURRAY, JOHN. "The Origin of Man" in *The Law and the Prophets.* J. H. Skilton (ed.). Philadelphia: Presbyterian and Reformed Publishing Co., 1974.

NEWMAN, R. C. AND H. J. ECKELMAN, JR. *Genesis and the Origin of the Earth.* Downers Grove: Inter-Varsity Press, 1977.

PUN, PATTLE P. T. *Evolution—Nature and Scripture in Conflict?* Grand Rapids: Zondervan Publishing House, 1982.

ROSS, ALLEN P. "Genesis" in *Bible Knowledge Commentary.* Wheaton: Scripture Press Publications, 1985.

SCHAEFFER, FRANCIS. *Genesis in Time and Space.* Downers Grove: Inter-Varsity Press, 1972.

SMITH, A. E. WILDER. *Man's Origin, Man's Destiny (A Critical Survey of the Principles of Evolution and Christianity).* Wheaton: Harold Shaw Publishers, 1968.

SPEISER, E. A. *Genesis.* The Anchor Bible. Garden City: Doubleday, 1964.

STIGERS, HAROLD G. *A Commentary on Genesis.* Grand Rapids: Zondervan Publishing House, 1976.

WOOD, LEON J. *Genesis: A Study Guide Commentary.* Grand Rapids: Zondervan Publishing House, 1975.

YOUNG, DAVIS A. *Creation and the Flood.* Grand Rapids: Baker Book House, 1977.

---

sequently, this remains a problem for investigation. Byron Nelson points out that regardless of what date man may approximate for the beginning of the human race it is still within the scope of the scriptural account. For this "limitless view" see his book, *Before Abraham: Prehistoric Man in Biblical Light* (Minneapolis: Augsburg Publishing House, 1948). For a recent discussion of the chronology of the ancient Near East see R. K. Harrison, *Introduction to the Old Testament* (Grand Rapids: Wm. B. Eerdmans Publishing Co., 1969), pp. 145–198.

Chapter II

The Patriarchal Age

The world of the patriarchs has been the focal point of intensive study in recent decades. New discoveries have illuminated the biblical narratives by providing extensive knowledge of the contemporary cultures in the Near East.

Geographically the world of the patriarchs is identified as the Fertile Crescent.[1] Stretching north from the Persian Gulf along the Tigris and Euphrates basin and then southwestward through Canaan to the fertile Nile Valley, this area was the cradle for prehistoric civilizations. When the patriarchs come on the scene in the second millennium B.C. the Mesopotamian and Egyptian cultures already boasted of a millennial past. With Canaan as the geographic center for the beginnings of a new nation, the Genesis account is interrelated with the milieu of the two early civilizations beginning with Abraham in Mesopotamia and ending with Joseph in Egypt (Gen. 12–50).

The World of the Patriarchs

The beginnings of history coincide with the development of writing in Egypt and Mesopotamia (*ca.* 3500–3000 B.C.). Archaeological discoveries have given us an insight into the cultures that prevailed during the third millennium B.C. The period 4000–3300 B.C., or the Chalcolithic age, is usually regarded as a preliterate civilization yielding little in written materials. Stratified cities of those times indicate the existence of organized society. Consequently the fourth millennium B.C., which reveals the first creation of great buildings, marks the bounds of history in terms of the historian. What is known of the preceding civilizations is often designated as prehistorical.

[1] For geographical survey see J. McKee Adams, *Biblical Backgrounds* (8th printing; Nashville: Broadman Press, 1934)

Chart I CIVILIZATIONS IN PATRIARCHAL TIMES*

Egypt—Nile Valley	Palestine and Syria	Tigris-Euphrates Valley Asia Minor
Prehistoric—before 3200		
Early period—3200–2800 Egypt united under Dynasties I and II		
Old Kingdom—2800–2250 Dynasties IV–VI —great pyramids —religious texts		Sumerian culture—2800–2400 —first literature in Asia —royal tombs —power extended to Mediterranean Sea
Decline and recovery—2250–2000 Dynasties VII–X Dynasty XI —centralized power at Thebes	2100 B.C.	Akkadian Supremacy—2360–2160 —Sargon the great king —Guti invasion—*ca.* 2080
Middle Kingdom—2000–1780 Dynasty XII —powerful central government with capitals in Memphis and the Fayyum Classical literature (Dynasties X–XII)	Patriarchs in Canaan	Third Dynasty of Ur—2070–1950 —Hurrian pressure from north
Decline and Occupation—1780–1546 Dynasties XIII–XIV —obscurity Dynasties XV–XVI —Hyksos invaders occupy Egypt with horse and chariot Dynasty XVII —Hyksos expelled by Theban kings	1700 B.C.	First Babylonian Dynasty—1800–1500 (Amorites or Western Semites, 1750) —Zimri-Lim king at Mari (Shamshi-Adad I at Nineveh) Hammurapi—greatest king—1700
New Kingdom—1546–1085 Dynasty XVIII–XX (Amarna Age—1400–1350)	Israelites in Egypt	Decline of Babylonia a. Old Hittite Empire—1600–1500 b. Mitanni Kingdom—1500–1370 c. New Hittite Empire—1375–1200 d. Rise of Assyria—1350–1200

* All dates should be regarded as approximate for this era.

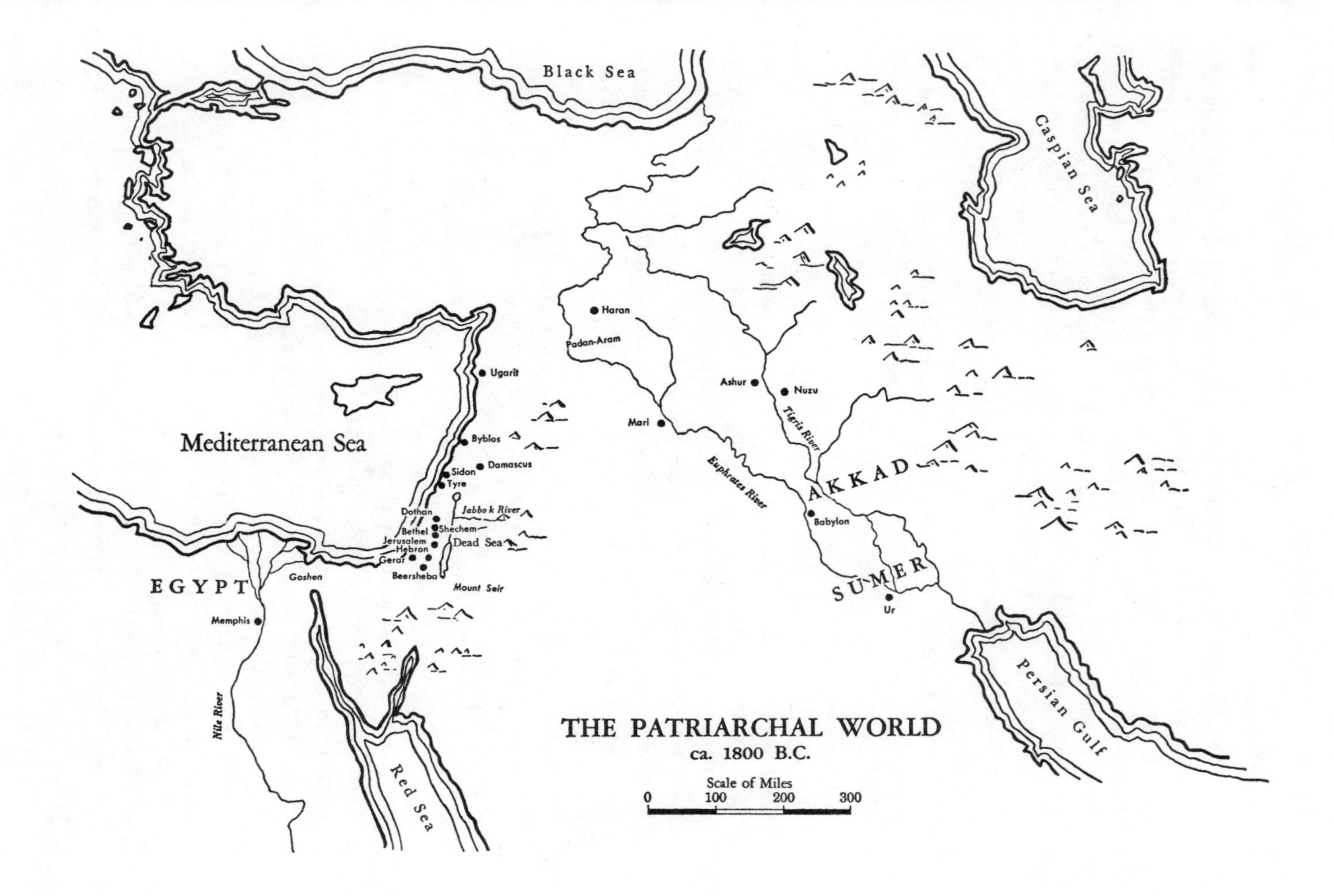

THE PATRIARCHAL WORLD
ca. 1800 B.C.

Mesopotamia

The Sumerians, a non-Semitic people, controlled the lower Euphrates area, or Sumer, during the Early Dynastic period, *ca.* 2800–2400 B.C. These Sumerians gave us the first literature in Asia. For the cuneiform world Sumerian became the classical language and flourished in writing throughout Babylonian and Assyrian cultures until about the first century A.D., although it was discontinued as a spoken language about 1800 B.C. The origin of the Sumerian script is still shrouded in obscurity. It may have been borrowed from an earlier literate people concerning whom no discernible texts are available.[2]

The advanced Sumerian culture of the First Dynasty of Ur, the last phase of the Early Dynastic period, has been uncovered in a cemetery excavated by C. Leonard Woolley.[3] The wooden coffins of the common people, in which food, drink, weapons, tools, necklaces, vanity cases, and bracelets were found, suggest the idea that these people anticipated a life after death. Royal tombs made ample provision for the afterlife by including musical instruments, jewelry, clothing, wagons, and even servants, who apparently drank quietly of the particular drug provided and then lay down to sleep. In King Abargi's tomb sixty-five victims were found. Evidently it was considered religiously essential to sacrifice human beings in the burial of sacred persons such as kings and queens, hoping thereby to assure them of servants in the afterlife.

In the field of metallurgy, as well as in the crafts of goldsmiths and gem cutters, the Sumerians were second to none in antiquity. Commercial records preserved on clay tablets reveal a detailed analysis of their economic life. A wooden panel (22″ x 9″) in one of the tombs depicts scenes from both peace and war. Chariots were already in use for javelin throwers in battle. The phalanx, which was so effectively utilized by Alexander the Great many centuries later, was known to the Sumerians. The basic principles of construction, utilized by the modern architect, were familiar to them. Successful in agriculture and prosperous in extensive trade, the Sumerian civilization reached an advanced stage of culture (*ca.* 2400 B.C.) that undoubtedly developed over a period of several centuries. Their last great king, Lugal-zaggisi, extended Sumerian power as far west as the Mediterranean.

In the meantime a Semitic people, known as Akkadians, founded the city of Agade or Akkad north of Ur on the Euphrates. Beginning with Sargon, this Semitic dynasty overpowered the Sumerians and thus held supremacy for about two centuries. After overthrowing Lugal-zaggisi, Sargon

[2] Cf. Samuel N. Kramer, *From Tablets of Sumer* (Indian Hills, Colo.: The Falcon's Wing Press, 1956).

[3] Leonard Woolley, *Ur of the Chaldees* (New York: Charles Scribner's Sons, 1930), pp. 45–68; *Ur Excavations II The Royal Cemetery*, p. 42.

appointed his own daughter as high priestess at Ur in recognition of the moon-god Nannar. Thus he extended his domain throughout Babylonia so that Finegan speaks of him as the "most powerful monarch" who had ever ruled Mesopotamia.[4] His domain extended into Asia Minor.

That the Akkadians had no cultural hostility seems to be reflected in the fact that they adopted the culture of the Sumerians. Their writing was adopted for the Semitic Babylonian tongue. Tablets uncovered at Gasur, which was later known as Nuzu in the time of the Hurrians, the biblical Horites, indicate that this Old Akkadian period was a time of prosperity in which the installment plan was used commercially throughout the empire. A clay map among the records is the oldest known to man.[5]

Under Naram-Sin, the grandson of Sargon, the Akkadian power reached its height. His stela of victory can be seen in the Louvre at Paris. It bears witness to his successful campaign in the Zagros Mountains. The supremacy of this great Semitic kingdom declined under subsequent rulers.

The Gutian invasion from the north (*ca.* 2080 B.C.) terminated the power of the Akkadian dynasty. Although little is known about these Caucasian invaders, they occupied Babylonia for about a century. A ruler at Erech in Sumer broke the power of the Gutians and paved the way for a revival of Sumerian culture, which came into full bloom under the Third Dynasty of Ur. The founder of the dynasty, Ur Nammu, erected a great ziggurat at Ur. Brick after brick excavated from this great structure (200 by 150 feet at the base, reaching a height of 80 feet) has inscribed on it the name of King Ur Nammu with the title "king of Sumer and Akkad." Here Nannar, the moon-god, and his consort, Nin-Gal, the moon-goddess, were worshiped during the golden age of Ur.

After a century of supremacy this Neo-Sumerian dynasty collapsed and the land of Sumer reverted to the old system of city-states. This afforded the Amorites, or western Semites, who had been gradually infiltrating Mesopotamia, an opportunity to gain the ascendancy. Virtually all of Mesopotamia was soon absorbed by the Semites. Zimri-Lim, whose capital was Mari on the Euphrates, extended his influence (*ca.* 1750 B.C.) from the middle Euphrates into Canaan as ruler of the most important state. The magnificent palace at Mari had nearly three hundred rooms spread over a fifteen-acre site; from the debris archaeologists have recovered some 20,000 cuneiform tablets. These clay documents, revealing the commercial and political interests of the Amorite rulers, portray an efficient administration of the far-flung empire.

[4] Jack Finegan, *Light from the Ancient Past* (Princeton University Press, 1946), pp. 38–40.

[5] For accounts of Nuzu life see Edward Chiera, *They Wrote on Clay* (8th printing; University of Chicago Press, 1956).

About 1700 B.C. Hammurapi, who had developed the small village of Babylon into a great commercial center, was able to conquer Mari with its extensive domain.[6] Not only did he dominate the upper Euphrates but he also subjugated the kingdom of Shamshi-Adad I, whose capital was at Ashur on the Tigris River. Marduk, the chief god of Babylon, gained prominent recognition in the empire. Most significant of Hammurapi's achievements was his code of law discovered in 1901 at Susa, where it had been taken by the Elamites when Hammurapi's kingdom fell. Since old Sumerian customs were incorporated in these laws, it is likely that they represent the culture that prevailed in Mesopotamia in patriarchal times. Many of Hammurapi's letters have been discovered which indicate that he was a very efficient ruler, issuing his orders with clarity and with attention to detail. The First Dynasty of Babylon (*ca.* 1800–1500 B.C.) was at its height under Hammurapi. His successors yielded gradually to the invading Cassites, who conquered Babylon *ca.* 1500 B.C.

Egypt

When Abraham came to Egypt, this land could boast of a culture more than a thousand years old. The beginning of history in Egypt is usually traced to King Menes (*ca.* 3000 B.C.), who united two kingdoms—one in the Delta and another in the Nile Valley.[7] The rulers of the first two dynasties had their capital in Upper Egypt near Thebes.[8] The royal tombs excavated in Abydos have yielded stone vases, jewelry, copper vessels, and other objects buried with the kings, which reflect a high level of civilization during this early period. This was the first era of international commerce in historical times.

The classical age of Egyptian civilization, known as the Old Kingdom period (*ca.* 2700–2200 B.C.) and comprising Dynasties III–VI, witnessed a number of notable achievements. Huge pyramids, the wonders of centuries to follow, provide ample testimony to the advanced culture of these early rulers. The Step Pyramid at Saqqara, the earliest large structure made of stone, was built as a royal mausoleum by Imhotep, an architect who also gained renown as a priest, author of proverbs, and magician. The Great Pyramid at Giza towered 481 feet from a thirteen-acre base. The gigantic

[6] For dating of Hammurapi see Finegan, *op. cit.*, p. 47. For a more recent discussion see M. B. Rowton, "The Date of Hammurapi," *Journal of Near Eastern Studies,* XVII, No. 2 (April, 1958), 97–111.

[7] The Hebrew name for Egypt is Mizraim which bespeaks two kingdoms by its dual ending.

[8] Manetho, a priest in Egypt under Ptolemy Philadelphus, *ca.* 285–246, made a study and analysis of Egyptian history. His division of Egyptian history into thirty dynasties is preserved in the writings of Josephus, A.D. 95, Sextus Julius Africanus, *ca.* A.D. 221, and Eusebius. For a complete list of these dynasties see Steindorff and Seele, *When Egypt Ruled the East* (rev. ed.; University of Chicago Press, 1957), pp. 274–275.

Sphinx representing King Khafre of the Fourth Dynasty is another work which has never been duplicated. The "Pyramid Texts," inscribed during the Fifth and Sixth Dynasties on the walls of chambers and halls, indicate that the Egyptians in their sun worship anticipated a hereafter. The proverbs of Ptahhotep, who served as grand vizier under a Pharaoh of the Fifth Dynasty, are noteworthy for their practical advice.[9]

The next five dynasties that ruled Egypt (*ca.* 2200–2000 B.C.) arose during a period of decadence. Centralized government decreased. The capital shifted from Memphis to Herakleopolis. Classical literature from this period reflects a weak and changing government. Toward the end of this period the Eleventh Dynasty, under the aggressive Intefs and Mentuhoteps, built a strong state at Thebes.

The Middle Kingdom (*ca.* 2000–1780 B.C.) marks the reappearance of a powerful centralized government. Although native to Thebes, the Twelfth Dynasty established its capital near Memphis. The wealth of Egypt was enhanced by an irrigation project which opened the fertile Fayum valley for agriculture. Building activities went on apace at Karnak near Thebes and elsewhere in the land. Besides promoting copper mining operations in the Sinaitic peninsula, the rulers also built a canal connecting the Red Sea and the Nile River; this enabled them to maintain better trade relations with the Somali coast of eastern Africa. To the south, Nubia was annexed as far as the third cataract on the Nile and a fortified trading colony was maintained there. Egyptian objects found by archaeologists in Syria-Palestine and on Crete attest the vigorous trading activities of Egyptians in the eastern Mediterranean sphere.

While the Old Kingdom was remembered for its originality and genius in art, the Middle Kingdom made its contribution in classical literature. Palace schools trained officials in reading and writing during the prosperous reigns of the Amenemhets and Sen-userts of the Twelfth Dynasty. Although the masses were in poverty, it was possible for the average individual in that age of feudalism to enter government service by means of education, training, and special ability. Texts of instruction inscribed in the coffins of others than royalty indicate that many more people now enjoyed the prospect of an afterlife. "The Tale of Sinuhe" is the finest example of literature from ancient Egypt designed to entertain. "The Song of the Harper," another masterpiece from the Middle Kingdom, enjoins men to enjoy the pleasures of life.[10]

Two centuries of disintegration, decline, and invasion followed the Mid-

[9] For the history of Egypt prior to 1600 B.C. see W. C. Hayes, *The Scepter of Egypt*, part I (New York: Harper & Brothers, 1953).

[10] For translation see James B. Pritchard, *Ancient Near Eastern Texts Relating to the Old Testament* (Princeton University Press, 1955), p. 467.

dle Kingdom; consequently this period is quite obscure to the historian. The feeble Thirteenth and Fourteenth Dynasties gave way to the Hyksos or Amurrite people. These bold intruders, who probably came from Asia Minor, overpowered the Egyptians by means of horse-drawn chariotry and the composite bow, both of which were unknown to the Egyptian troops. The Hyksos established Avaris in the Delta as their capital. However, the Egyptians were allowed to maintain a semblance of authority at Thebes. Shortly after 1600 B.C. the Theban rulers became powerful enough to expel this foreign power and to establish the Eighteenth Dynasty, introducing the New Kingdom.

Canaan

The name "Canaan" applies to the land lying between Gaza in the south and Hamath in the north along the eastern coast of the Mediterranean (Gen. 10:15–19). The Greeks in their trade with Canaan during the first millennium B.C. referred to the inhabitants as Phoenicians, a name which probably had its origin in the Greek word for "purple" designating the crimson color of a textile dye developed in Canaan. As early as the fifteenth century B.C. the name "Canaan" was applied in general to the Egyptian province in Syria or at least to the Phoenician coast, the center of the purple industry.[11] Consequently the words "Canaanite" and "Phoenician" have the same cultural, geographical, and historical origin. Later this area came to be known as Syria and Palestine. The designation "Palestine" had its origin in the name "Philistia."

With the migration of Abraham into Canaan, this land becomes the focal point of interest in the historical and geographical developments of Bible times. Being strategically located between the two great centers that cradled the earliest civilizations, Canaan served as a natural bridge linking Egypt and Mesopotamia. Consequently it is not surprising to find a mixed population in the land.[12] Cities in Canaan, such as Jericho, Dothan, and others, were occupied centuries before patriarchal times.[13] With the first great Semitic (Amorite) movement into Mesopotamia, it seems probable that Amorites extended settlements down through Palestine. During the Middle Kingdom the Egyptians advanced their political and commercial interests as far north as Syria.[14] Long before 1500 B.C. Caphtor people settled on the Mari-

[11] Cf. Merrill F. Unger, *Israel and the Aramaeans of Damascus* (London: James Clarke & Co., 1957), p. 19.

[12] Cf. Gen. 12:6; 14:13; 15:16, 19–21; 21:34; 23:3, and others. Here are noted the Canaanites, Amorites, Kenites, Kenizzites, Jebusites, Philistines, and others.

[13] Dothan began *ca.* 3000 B.C. Cf. Joseph P. Free, "The First Season of Excavation at Dothan," *Bulletin of the American Schools of Oriental Research*, No. 131, October, 1953, pp. 16–20. For dating Jericho back to the sixth or seventh millennium B.C. see Kathleen M. Kenyon, *Digging up Jericho* (London: Ernest Benn, 1957), pp. 51–76.

[14] Sinuhe, an Egyptian official during the Middle Kingdom, reflects contacts with

time Plain.[15] Not least among the invaders were the Hittites, who penetrated Canaan from the north and appeared as well-established citizens when Abraham purchased the cave of Machpelah (Gen. 23). The Rephaim, a people hitherto obscure beyond the scriptural reference, have recently been identified in Ugaritic literature.[16] Little is known about other inhabitants noted in the Genesis account. The designation "Canaanite" very likely embraced the composite mixture of people occupying the land in the patriarchal era.

Geography[17]

Extending in length 150 miles from Beersheba north to Dan, Palestine has an area of 6,000 square miles between the Mediterranean Sea and the Jordan River. The average width is 40 miles with a maximum of 54 miles from Gaza to the Dead Sea, narrowing down to 28 miles at the Sea of Galilee. With the addition of 4,000 square miles east of Jordan, which area often is called Transjordan, this land comprises about 10,000 square miles, being slightly larger than the state of Vermont.

Besides having a central and strategic location relative to the centers of civilization and great nations of Old Testament times, Palestine also has a varied topography that had a significant effect upon the historical developments. Because of its location Palestine was subject to invaders, with its neutrality usually yielding to the stronger power. The local developments not infrequently arise from factors of topography.

For an analysis of its physical features, Palestine may be divided into four main areas: the Maritime Plain, the Hill Country, the Jordan Valley, and the Eastern Plateau.

The Maritime Plain consists of the coastal area on the Mediterranean Sea. The coast line is unsuitable for harbor facilities; consequently commerce as a whole was directed to Sidon and Tyre in the north. Even Gaza, which was one of the greatest trading centers of ancient Palestine and located just three miles from the Mediterranean, did not have any permanent port facilities. This rich land along the coast may easily be divided into three areas: The Plain of Accho, or Acre, extended north from the foothills of Mount

---

Egyptian traders and residents in Palestine. For a translation of this popular Egyptian classic by John A. Wilson see James B. Pritchard, *Ancient Near Eastern Texts, op. cit.*, pp. 18–22.

[15] Cyrus H. Gordon, *The World of the Old Testament* (Garden City: Doubleday & Co., 1958), pp. 121–122. These non-Semitic people also included the Philistines.

[16] *Ibid.*, pp. 97–98.

[17] For an excellent study in historical geography see Dennis Baly, *The Geography of the Bible* (New York: Harper & Brothers, 1957). Cf. also George Adam Smith, *The Historical Geography of the Holy Land* (25th ed.; London: Hodder & Stoughton, 1931), and G. Ernest Wright and Floyd V. Filson, *The Westminster Historical Atlas to the Bible* (Philadelphia: Westminster Press, 1956), pp. 15–20, and J. McKee Adams, *op. cit.* For a topographical map of Palestine see the back end paper in this volume.

Carmel for about 20 miles with a width varying from two to ten miles. South of Mount Carmel is the Plain of Sharon, approximately 50 miles in length, reaching a maximum width of 12 miles. The Plain of Philistia begins five miles north of Joppa, stretches 70 miles south and expands to a 25-mile width toward Beersheba.

The Hill Country, located between the Jordan Valley and the Maritime Plain, is the most important section of Palestine. The three main areas—Galilee, Samaria, and Judea—have an approximate elevation varying from 2,000 to 4,000 feet above sea level. Galilee extends south from the Leontes River immediately east of Phoenicia and the Plain of Acre. It provides fertile soil for the growing of grapes, olives, nuts, and other crops, as well as some grazing areas. One of the most productive and picturesque farming valleys in Palestine separates the hills of Galilee and Samaria. Known as the Valley of Jezreel, or Esdraelon, this area is vitally important in its strategic location throughout Bible times as well as today. Southeast of Mount Carmel, this fertile plain extends about 40 miles in length to Mount Moreh, from where it divides into two valleys and continues on to the Jordan River. In Old Testament times the Hebrews distinguished between the eastern and western areas, known respectively as the valleys of Jezreel and Esdraelon. The city of Jezreel, about fifteen miles from the Jordan, marked the entrance to this famous valley. The western section was known also as the Plain of Megiddo, since the famous mountain pass at Megiddo was of crucial importance to invaders. From the Hill of Moreh in the Vale of Jezreel this fertile plain can be viewed with Mount Carmel in the west, Mount Tabor to the north, and Mount Gilboa to the south. The geographical center of Palestine, the hill country of Samaria, rises abruptly, beginning with Mount Gilboa, and continues south to Bethel. The broken hills and valleys of this fertile elevation offered a paradise to the herdsman as well as to the agriculturist. Shechem, Dothan, Bethel, and other cities in this area were frequented by the patriarchs. The highlands of Judea extend south from Bethel about 60 miles to Beersheba with an elevation of about 2,500 feet at Jerusalem, reaching a peak of over 3,000 feet near Hebron. Beginning in the vicinity of Beersheba, the hills of Judea sprawl out into the rolling plains of the great wilderness often referred to as the Negeb, or Southland, with Kadesh-barnea marking its southern extremity. To the east of the Judean hills is the wasteland aptly designated as the "Wilderness of Judah." To the west of this Judean watershed is the Shephelah, known as the lowlands. In this area—strategically important for defense and economically valuable for farming—were located such fortified cities as Lachish, Debir, and Libnah.

The Jordan Valley represents one of the most fascinating areas in the world. Beyond it, some 40 miles to the north of the Sea of Galilee, towers Mount Hermon with an altitude of 9,166 feet. To the south the Jordan

Valley reaches its lowest point at the Dead Sea, about 1,275 feet below sea level. Four streams of water—one from a westward plain and three from Mount Hermon—combine to form the Jordan River about ten miles north of Lake Huleh. From Lake Huleh,[18] which was about four miles long at seven feet above sea level, the River Jordan descends in a twenty-mile course to 685 feet below sea level into the Sea of Galilee. This body of water, approximately 15 miles in length, was also known as the Sea of Chinnereth in Old Testament times. In a distance of 60 miles the Jordan, with an average width of 90 to 100 feet, zigzags south in a 200-mile course to the Dead Sea, dropping nearly 600 feet more. The valley area, which is actually a great natural ditch between two ranges of mountains, is sometimes known as Ghor. Beginning with a four-mile width at the Sea of Galilee, it widens to seven miles at Beth-shan, narrowing down to a two-mile width before it expands to 14 miles at Jericho, within five miles of the Dead Sea. In biblical times this lake was called the "Salt Sea," since its water has a 25 per cent salt content. Most likely the Vale of Siddim in the southern end of the 46-mile long sea was the location of Sodom and Gomorrah in the days of Abraham.[19] South of the Dead Sea extends the barren and waste region known as the Arabah. In the 65-mile distance to Petra, this desert land rises 1,967 feet, sloping down to sea level 50 miles beyond, at the Gulf of Aqaba.

The Eastern Plateau may generally be divided into four main areas: Bashan, Gilead, Ammon, and Moab. Bashan, with its rich soil, extends south of Mount Hermon to the River Yarmuk in a 45-mile width at an elevation of about 2,000 feet above sea level. Below this is the well-known area called Gilead, with its main River Jabbok. Extending northeast of the Dead Sea to the upper reaches of the Jabbok is the territory of Ammon. Directly east of the Dead Sea and south of the Arnon River is Moab, whose domain extended farther north at various times.

The Biblical Account—Genesis 12–50

Current consensus of scholarship accords the patriarchs a place in the history of the Fertile Crescent in the first half of the second millennium B.C. The assertion that the biblical account consists of nothing more than fabricated legends has been replaced by a general respect for the historic quality of Gen. 12–50.[20] Largely responsible for this revolutionary change was the

[18] Lake Huleh has recently been drained and reclaimed for agricultural usage.

[19] See Nelson Glueck, *The Other Side of the Jordan* (New Haven: American Society of Oriental Research, 1940), p. 114.

[20] J. Wellhausen, *Prolegomena to the History of Israel* (3rd ed.; Edinburgh), p. 331 According to the Graf-Wellhausen theory, Abraham, Isaac, and Jacob did not actually exist as historical individuals but were mythological characters created by literary geniuses between 950 and 400 B.C. Moses may have been a historical individual with whom Israel's history began. Cf. Robert H. Pfeiffer, *Introduction to the Old Testament* (New York:

discovery and publication of the Nuzu tablets, as well as other archaeological information that has come to light since 1925. Although no concrete evidence is available to identify any specific names or events from external sources with those mentioned in the Genesis account, it is easy to recognize that the cultural milieu is the same for both. The sole evidence for the existence of Abraham comes from the Hebrew narrative, but many Old Testament scholars now recognize him for his place in the beginnings of Hebrew history.[21]

The chronology for the patriarchs still remains a moot point. Within this general period the date advocated for Abraham varies from the twenty-first to the fifteenth century. With the chronologies for this era in a state of flux, it is well to take note of several views on dating the patriarchs.

On the basis of certain chronological notations given in the Scriptures, the entrance of Abraham into Canaan is calculated to have taken place in 2091 B.C. This allows 215 years for patriarchal life in Canaan, 430 years for Egyptian bondage, and an early date for the exodus from Egypt (1447 B.C.).[22]

More illumination of the cultural, historical, and chronological context of pre-patriarchal times may come from the excavation of Tell Mardikh, which has been identified as Ebla. Located about 44 miles (*ca.* 70 kilometers) south of Aleppo, Tell Mardikh is among the largest in the Middle East—about 140 acres (56 hectares) at an elevation of about 50 feet (15 meters).[23]

Excavations from 1964–1973 yielded information about an Amorite dynasty city dated in Middle Bronze I and II, *ca.* 2000–1600 B.C. An Akkadian cuneiform inscription on the torso of a male figure carved in basalt, indicating that the statue had been dedicated to the goddess Ishtar by King Ibbit-Lim, lord of the city of Ebla, provided evidence for identifying Tell Mardikh as Ebla. The name Ebla had previously been known to scholars from references in Old Akkadian as well as Sumerian texts, and was thought

Harper & Brothers, 1941). Elmer W. K. Mould, *Essentials of Bible History* (New York: Ronald Press Co., 1951), p. 92, represents the patriarchal records as tribal stories that contain but a "little history" in modern terminology. According to Mould, only the Rachel tribes migrated into Egypt and later entered Palestine to be united with the tribes who never migrated to Egypt. W. F. Albright, *From Stone Age to Christianity* (2nd ed.; Baltimore: Johns Hopkins Press, 1940), accords greater recognition to the beginning of Israel with the patriarchs.

[21] H. H. Rowley, "Recent Discoveries and the Patriarchal Age," in *The Servant of the Lord and other Essays on the Old Testament* (London: Lutterworth Press, 1952), pp. 269–305. Cf. also W. F. Albright, *The Biblical Period* (Pittsburgh, 1950), p. 6: "But as a whole the picture in Genesis is historical, and there is no reason to doubt the general accuracy of the biographical details and the sketches of personality which make the Patriarchs come alive."

[22] For a representative calculation of the biblical references and interpretation see Merrill F. Unger, *Archeology and the Old Testament* (Grand Rapids: Zondervan, 1954), pp. 105–107.

[23] Ebla was excavated by the Italian Archaeological Mission of the University of Rome under the direction of Dr. Paolo Matthiae. The chief epigrapher of the Ebla excavations is Alfonso Archi. For further study, see the second edition of the Italian publication of Ebla, *Un impero ritrovato* by Giulio Einaudi (Torino, Italy, 1989).

[24] For an interpretation by K. A. Kitchen of the Ebla material as given in the official, firsthand reports by Profs. Matthiae and Pettinato, see "Ebla—Queen of Ancient Syria" in

to have been located on the Euphrates River north of Carchemish.

Since 1974, a royal palace was uncovered with approximately seventeen thousand tablets written in Sumerian and Eblaic, including the earliest bilingual vocabularies yet known. A variety of administrative records, religious literature, business and commercial accounts, and personal names and places will provide further knowledge about this ancient city and its extended contacts.

Ebla appears to have been a very important center in Northern Syria, where four or five kings of one dynasty ruled during the Early Bronze era (*ca.* 2400 to 2200 B.C.). With an advanced culture and a well-defined language, this kingdom had extended influence in the Fertile Crescent from the highlands of Mesopotamia reaching south into the Syrian frontier until Ebla was destroyed by Naram-Sin of Akkad.[24]

As more information becomes available from these vast resources in ancient Ebla, it may be possible to correlate the Genesis accounts with the culture preceding patriarchal times.[25]

On the basis of the leading characters the narratives of the patriarchal age may conveniently be divided as follows: Abraham—Gen. 12:1–25:18; Isaac and Jacob—Gen. 25:19–36:43; Joseph—Gen. 37:1–50:26.

Abraham (Gen. 12:1–25:18)

I. Abraham established in Canaan	12:1–14:24
Transition from Haran to Shechem, Bethel and the South Country	12:1–9
Sojourn in Egypt	12:10–20
Separation of Abraham and Lot	13:1–13
The land promised	13:14–18
Lot rescued	14:1–16
Abraham blessed by Melchizedek	14:17–24
II. Abraham awaits the promised son	15:1–22:24
The son promised	15:1–21
The birth of Ishmael	16:1–16
The promise renewed—The covenant and its sign	17:1–27
Abraham the intecessor—Lot rescued	18:1–19:38
Abraham delivered from Abimelech	20:1–18
Isaac born—Ishmael expelled	21:1–21
Abraham dwells at Beersheba	21:22–34
The covenant confirmed in obedience	22:1–24

The Bible in its World (Downers Grove: Inter-Varsity Press, 1977), pp. 37–55.

[25] Especially interesting is the question of the relationship of the word Eber (Gen. 10:24) to the word Ebrum or Ibrium, who apparently was a high palace functionary. Although the name Sodom is not found within the Ebla texts as was previously suggested, there are references to cities mentioned in the Genesis narratives such as Harran.

III. Abraham provides for posterity	23:1-25:18
Abraham acquires a burial plot	23:1-20
The bride for the promised son	24:1-67
Isaac designated as heir—death of Abraham	25:1-18

Mesopotamia, the land between the two rivers, was the homeland of Abraham (Gen. 12:6; 24:10, and Acts 7:2). Located on the Balikh, a tributary of the Euphrates River, Haran constituted the center of culture where he lived with his relatives. Names of Abraham's kinsfolk—Terah, Nahor, Peleg, Serug, and others—are attested in Mari and Assyrian documents as names of cities in this area.[26] In obedience to God's command to leave homeland and kindred, Abraham left Haran to establish a new home in the land of Canaan.

Abraham had lived in Ur of the Chaldees before he came to Haran (Gen. 11:28-31). The most generally accepted identification of Ur is modern Tell el-Muqayyar, which is located nine miles west of Nasiriyeh on the Euphrates river in southern Iraq. Some consideration has been given to contemporary geographic notations in Abraham's time to a city called Ur located in northern Mesopotamia.[27] The southern site of Ur (*Uri*) was excavated in 1922-34 by the joint British Museum and University Museum, Philadelphia, under the direction of Sir Leonard Woolley. He traced the history of Ur from the fourth millennium B.C. to 300 B.C., when this city was abandoned. At this site were found the ruins of the ziggurat which had been built by the prosperous Neo-Sumerian king Ur Nammu who ruled shortly before 2000 B.C. This city continued to be the great capital of the Third Dynasty of Ur. The Moon-god Nannar which was worshiped in Ur was also the principal deity in Haran.[28]

The life of Abraham lends itself to a variety of treatments. Geographically one can trace his movements beginning with the highly civilized city of Haran. Leaving his relatives but accompanied by Lot, his nephew, he traveled some 400 miles to the land of Canaan, where he stopped at Shechem, about 30 miles north of Jerusalem. In addition to an excursion to Egypt which was necessitated by famine, Abraham halted at such well-known places as Bethel, Hebron, Gerar, and Beersheba. Sodom and Gomorrah, the cities of the plain to which Lot migrated, were directly east of the South Country, or Negeb, where Abraham settled.

[26] This land was also known as Padan-aram so that the name "Aramaean" was applied to Abraham and his relatives. Cf. Gen. 25:20; 28:5; 31:20, 24, and Deut. 26:5. Also, Laban spoke Aramaic, Gen. 31:47.

[27] Gordon, *op. cit.*, p. 132. Cf. also Nuzu citations in an unpublished thesis by Loren Fisher at Brandeis University, *Nuzu Geographical Names*.

[28] G. E. Wright, *op. cit.*, p. 41, observes: "In any event, we are safe in saying that the home with which the Patriarchs were most closely connected was Haran, and there is little evidence of any south Mesopotamian influence upon their traditions."

Frequent references indicate that Abraham was a man of considerable wealth and prestige. Far from being a wandering nomad in the Bedouin sense, he exhibited mercantile interests. Although the evaluation of his possessions is modestly summed up in a simple statement—"all their substance that they had gathered, and the souls that they had gotten in Haran" (12:5) —it is likely that his wealth was represented by a large caravan when he migrated to Palestine. A force of 318 servants used subsequently to deliver Lot (14:14) and a caravan of ten camels (24:10) signify but a token of Abraham's material resources.[29] Servants were added by purchase, gift, and birth (16:1; 17:23; 27; 20:14). Increasing flocks and herds, silver and gold, and servants to care for his extensive possessions indicate that Abraham was a man of great means. Palestinian chieftains recognized Abraham as a prince with whom they made alliances and concluded treaties (Gen. 14:13; 21:22; 23:6).

From the standpoint of social institutions, the Genesis account of Abraham is a fascinating study. Abraham's plans to make Eliezer heir of his possessions, since he did not have a son (Gen. 15:2), reflects the laws of Nuzu which provided that a childless couple could adopt anyone they chose as a son who would have full legal rights and who would be rewarded with the inheritance in return for constant care and proper burial at death. Marital customs from Nuzu as well as the code of Hammurapi provided that, if a man's wife had no children, the son of a handmaid could be recognized as the legal heir. Hagar's relationship to Abraham and Sarah is typical of the customs that prevailed in Mesopotamia. Abraham's concern for Hagar's welfare may also be explained by the fact that legally a handmaid who bore a son could not be sold into slavery.

A devotional study of Abraham also can be rewarding. The sixfold promise made to the patriarch has far-reaching implications in history. God's promise to make him a great nation is realized in subsequent Old Testament developments. "I will bless you" soon became a reality in his personal experience. Abraham's name has been made "great" not only as the father of the Israelites and Mohammedans but also as the great example of faith for Christian believers in the New Testament writings of Romans, Galatians, Hebrews, and James. In addition, man's attitude toward Abraham and his descendants would have a direct bearing on God's blessing or curse on mankind; this assured Abraham of a unique place in the providential design for the human race. Indeed, the promise that Abraham would be a blessing was literally fulfilled during his life as well as in subsequent times. Finally, the promise to bless all the families of the earth unfolds into a world-wide scope when Matthew opens his account of the life of Jesus Christ by stating that he is the "son of Abraham."

[29] Gordon, *op. cit.*, p. 124.

The covenant plays an important role in Abraham's experience. Note the successive revelations of God after the initial promise to which Abraham responded in obedience. As God enlarged this promise, Abraham exercised faith which was reckoned to him as righteousness (Gen. 15). In this covenant the land of Canaan was specifically pledged to the descendants of Abraham. With the promise of the son, circumcision was made the sign of the covenant (Gen. 17). This covenant promise was finally sealed in Abraham's act of obedience when he demonstrated his willingness to sacrifice his only son Isaac (Gen. 22).

The religion of Abraham is a vital theme in the patriarchal accounts. From a polytheistic background where the moon-god Nannar was recognized as the major god in Babylonian culture, Abraham came into Canaan. That his family served other gods is clearly stated in Josh. 24:2. In Canaan, in the midst of a heathen environment, the mark of Abraham was that he "built an altar to the Lord." After he had rescued Lot and the king of Sodom, he refused a reward, acknowledging that he was wholly devoted to God, the "maker of heaven and earth." The intimate communion and fellowship that existed between God and Abraham is beautifully portrayed in chapter 18 where he intercedes for Sodom and Gomorrah. Perhaps it is on the basis of Is. 41:8 and James 2:23 that the Septuagint reading had inserted the words "my friend" in 18:17. Down through the centuries the southern gate of Jerusalem, leading toward Hebron and Beersheba, has been referred to as the "gate of friendship" in memory of this relationship between God and Abraham.

Isaac, the promised son, was the heir of all that Abraham possessed. Other sons of Abraham, such as Ishmael, from whom the Arabs descended, and Midian, the father of the Midianites, received gifts as they departed from Canaan, leaving this territory to Isaac. Before his death Abraham provided Rebekah as a wife for Isaac. Abraham also purchased the cave of Machpelah,[30] which became the sepulcher of Abraham, Isaac, and Jacob and their wives.

Isaac and Jacob (Gen. 25:19–36:43)

I. The family of Isaac	25:19-34
Rebekah the mother of twins	25:19-26
Esau and Jacob exchange birthrights	25:27-34
II. Isaac established in Canaan	26:1-33
The covenant confirmed to Isaac	26:1-5

[30] "Ephron the Hittite" (Gen. 23:4) and his people known as Hittites (23:7) were a group of people living in the hills in southern Palestine, who according to H. A. Hoffner, were of a different ethnic background than the Hittites in Asia Minor and Syria. Cf. his chapter "The Hittites and the Hurrians" in *Peoples in Old Testament Times*, D. J. Wiseman (ed.) (Oxford: Clarendon Press, 1973), pp. 197-228.

Troubles with Abimelech	26:6-22
God's blessing on Isaac	26:23-33
III. The patriarchal blessing	26:34-28:9
Isaac favors Esau	26:34-27:4
Blessing stolen—immediate consequences	27:5-28:9
IV. Jacob's adventures with Laban	28:10-32:2
The dream at Bethel	28:10-22
Family and wealth	29:1-30:43
Parting with Laban	31:1-32:2
V. Jacob returns to Canaan	32:3-35:21
Esau and Jacob reconciled	32:3-33:17
Troubles at Shechem	33:18-34:31
Worship at Bethel	35:1-15
Rachel buried at Bethlehem	35:16-21
VI. Descendants of Isaac	35:22-36:43
The sons of Jacob	35:22-26
Burial of Isaac	35:27-29
Esau and his clan in Edom	36:1-43

The character of Isaac as portrayed in Genesis is somewhat obscured by the eventful lives of both his father and his son. With the notation of Abraham's death the reader is immediately introduced to Jacob, who emerges as the link in the patriarchal succession. Perhaps many of Isaac's experiences were similar to those of Abraham, so that relatively little of the narrative is devoted to the former.

Although Isaac inherited his father's wealth and continued the same pattern of life, it is interesting to note that he engaged in agriculture near Gerar (26:12). Abraham on occasion had stopped at Gerar in Philistine territory but spent much of his time around Hebron. When Isaac began to till the soil he raised crops that produced a hundredfold. This unusual success in farming excited the envy of the Philistines at Gerar so that Isaac found it necessary to move to Beersheba in order to maintain peaceful relations.

The presence of the Philistines in Canaan during patriarchal times has been considered an anachronism. The Caphtorian settlement in Canaan around 1200 B.C. represented a late migration of the Sea People who had made previous settlements over a long period of time. The Philistines had thus established themselves in smaller numbers long before 1500 B.C. In time they became amalgamated with other inhabitants of Canaan, but the name "Palestine" (Philistia) continues to bear witness to their presence in Canaan. Caphtorian pottery throughout southern and central Palestine, as well as literary references, testify to the superiority of the Philistines in arts and crafts. In the days of Saul they monopolized metalwork in Palestine.[31]

Controversial in behavior, Jacob emerged as the inheritor of the covenant. In line with Nuzu customs he negotiated with Esau to secure inheritance rights. His bargaining ability is readily apparent in his acquisition of first-born rights for the meager price of a dish of lentils. Esau's unrealistic sense of true values may have been due to temporary fatigue and exhaustion from a fruitless hunting expedition. In addition, Jacob gained the deathbed blessing through trickery and deception instigated by his mother, Rebekah. The significance of this acquisition is better understood by comparison with contemporary laws which made such oral blessings legally binding. Noteworthy, however, is the fact that the biblical account emphasizes the place of leadership above material blessing.

Fearing Jacob's probable marriage to Hittite women as well as Esau's revenge, Rebekah engineers a plan to send her favorite son to Padan-aram. En route Jacob responds to a dream at Bethel with a conditional promise to serve God and a tentative commitment to tithe his income. Having been afforded a cordial reception in his ancestral homeland, Jacob enters into an agreement with Laban, Rebekah's brother. According to Nuzu custom, this may have been more than a simple labor contract for marriage. Apparently Laban did not have a son at this time, so Jacob was made legal heir. Typical of the times was Laban's gift of a handmaid to each of his daughters, Rachel and Leah. Laban's wife later gave birth to sons, so that Jacob was no longer the chief heir. This turn of affairs was not to Jacob's liking; he wanted to leave but was dissuaded by a new contract which opened the way for him to gain wealth through Laban's flocks. In the course of time Jacob became so prosperous, in spite of Laban's readjustment of the contract, that the relationship between father and son-in-law became strained.

Encouraged by God to return to the land of his fathers, Jacob gathered all his possessions and departed at an opportune time when Laban was away on a sheep-shearing mission. Three days later Laban learned of Jacob's trek and set out in hot pursuit. After seven days he overtook him in the hill country of Gilead. Laban was greatly perturbed over the disappearance of his household gods. The teraphim, which Rachel successfully hid while Laban searched all of Jacob's possessions, may have had more legal than religious significance for Laban.[32] According to Nuzu law, a son-in-law who possessed the household idols might claim the family inheritance in court. Thus Rachel was trying to obtain some advantage for her husband by stealing the idols.

[31] Gordon, *op. cit.*, pp. 121–123.

[32] Laban distinguished between the gods of Nahor and the God of Abraham (Gen. 31:29–30). Whereas Jacob was a monotheist, Laban was a polytheist.

But Laban nullified any such benefit by a covenant with Jacob before they separated.

Continuing toward Canaan, Jacob anticipated the dreaded meeting with Esau. Fear overwhelmed him even though every crisis in the past had terminated to his advantage. At the point of no return Jacob faced a crucial experience (32:1–32). Dividing all his possessions at the River Jabbok in preparation for meeting Esau, he turned to God in prayer. He humbly acknowledged that he was unworthy of all the blessings that God had bestowed upon him. But in the face of danger he pleaded for deliverance. During the loneliness of the night he wrestled with a man. In this strange experience, which he recognized as a divine encounter, his name was changed from "Jacob" to "Israel." Thereafter Jacob was not the deceiver; instead he was subjected to deception and grief by his own sons.

When Esau arrived, Jacob prostrated himself seven times—another ancient custom mentioned in Amarna and Ugaritic documents—and was granted pardon by his brother. Courteously declining the generous assistance offered by Esau, Jacob proceeded slowly to Succoth while Esau returned to Seir.

En route to Hebron Jacob encamped at Shechem, Bethel, and Bethlehem. Although he did purchase some land at Shechem, the scandal and perfidy of Levi and Simeon made it impractical to remain in that area (34:1–31). This incident, as well as Reuben's offensive act (35:22), had a bearing on Jacob's final blessings for his sons (49).

When he was instructed by God to move on to Bethel, Jacob prepared for his return to this sacred spot by removing idolatry from his household. At Bethel he built an altar. Here God renewed his covenant with the assurance that not only one nation but a company of nations and kings should emanate from Israel (35:9–15).

Along the way south Rachel died while giving birth to Benjamin. She was buried in the vicinity of Bethlehem at a place called Ephratha. Journeying onward with his sons and possessions, Jacob finally arrived in Hebron, the home of his father Isaac. When Isaac died, Esau returned from Seir to join Jacob in the burial of their father.

The Edomites apparently had an illustrious history. Little is known about them beyond this summary account (Gen. 36:1–43) which indicates that they had several kings even before any king reigned in Israel. In this way the Genesis narrative disposes of the collateral line before resuming the patriarchal account.

Joseph (*Gen. 37:1–50:26*)

I. Joseph the favorite son	37:1–36
Hatred by his brethren	37:1–24

Sold to Egypt	37:25–36
II. Judah and Tamar	38:1–30
III. Joseph—a slave and a ruler	39:1–41:57
Joseph demoted to prison	39:1–20
Interpreting dreams	39:21–41:36
Ruler next to Pharaoh	41:37–57
IV. Joseph and his brothers	42:1–45:28
The first trip—Simeon kept as hostage	42:1–38
Second trip includes Benjamin—Joseph identifies himself	43:1–45:28
V. Joseph's family established in Egypt	46:1–50:26
Goshen allotted to the Israelites	46:1–47:28
The patriarchal blessings	47:29–49:27
Jacob's burial in Canaan	49:28–50:14
Joseph's hope for Israel	50:15–26

In one of the most dramatic narratives in world literature the experiences of Joseph entwine patriarchal life with Egypt. Whereas former contacts had been primarily with the Mesopotamian milieu, the transition to Egypt resulted in a blending of customs from these two foremost centers of civilization. In this narrative we note the continuity of former influence, the adaptation to the Egyptian environment, and above all the controlling guidance of God in the fascinating fortunes of Joseph and his people.

Joseph, the son of Rachel, was Jacob's pride and joy. To show his favoritism, Jacob garbed him with a tunic, apparently the distinctive mark of a tribal chief.[33] His brothers, who already resented Joseph for his evil reports concerning them, were incited by this to greater hatred. The matter came to a head when Joseph related to them two dreams foretokening his exaltation.[34] The older brothers gave vent to their feelings by getting rid of Joseph at the first opportunity.

Sent by his father to Shechem, Joseph could not find his brothers until he came to Dothan, approximately eighty miles north of Hebron.[35] After

[33] "Coat of many colors" according to the Septuagint and Targum Jonathan, or a tunic reaching to the ankles. For the Bene Hassan tomb painting showing Semite tribal leaders appearing in Egypt *ca.* 1900 B.C. with coats of many colors, see J. B. Pritchard, *Ancient Near Eastern Texts in Pictures* (Princeton University Press, 1954), Fig. 3.

[34] Although duplexity of dreams was typical in ancient Near East literature, they had added divine import in the life of Joseph.

[35] Even today shepherds bring their livestock from southern Palestine to the well at Dothan, according to J. P. Free, who has excavated Dothan since 1953. On the upper slope of the mound, levels 3 and 4 represent the Middle Bronze Age cities (2000–1600 B.C.), dating to the period of Joseph and the early patriarchs. The lowest level dated back to 3000 B.C. Cf. *Bulletin of the American Schools of Oriental Research,* Nos. 135 and 139. During the 1959 season the upper level, only six inches below the surface, indicated a rebuilding after an Assyrian destruction in 722 (cf. II Kings 17:5–6). A second level

subjecting him to ridicule and abuse, the brothers sold him to Midianite and Ishmaelite traders who subsequently disposed of him as a slave to Potiphar in Egypt. Confronted with Joseph's bloodstained coat, Jacob mourned the loss of his favorite son in the belief that he had been torn by wild beasts (37:1–36).

The reader is left in suspense as to the welfare of Joseph with the episode of Judah and Tamar (38:1–30). This account has historical significance in that it furnishes the genealogical background for the Davidic line (Gen. 38:29; Ruth 4:18–22; Matt. 1:1). Furthermore, in spite of Judah's unexemplary behavior, the practice of levirate marriage is maintained. Judah's demand that Tamar be burned for harlotry may reflect a custom brought into Canaan by Indo-Europeans such as Hittites and Philistines. Ugaritic and Mesopotamian sources attest the use of three articles to signify personal identification. Tamar established Judah's guilt for her impregnation by using his signet, belt, and staff as proof. Since Hittite law allowed a father to fulfill levirate obligations by marrying a widowed daughter-in-law, Tamar was not subject to punishment under local law for her deception in circumventing Judah's plan to ignore her marriage rights. In Mosaic legislation provision was made for levirate marriage (Deut. 25).[36]

The setting for Joseph's experiences in the land of the Nile has been shown to be authentic in many details (39–50). Egyptian names and titles occur, as could be expected. Potiphar is designated as "captain of the guard" or "chief of executioners," which was used as the title for the king's bodyguard. Asenath (an Egyptian name), the daughter of a priest of On (Heliopolis), becomes the wife of Joseph. Important officials in the Egyptian court are appropriately identified as "chief of butlers" and "chief of bakers." Egyptian customs are likewise reflected. Being a Semite Joseph wore a beard, but for his appearance before Pharaoh he was shaved in conformity to Egyptian ways. The fine linen robe, the golden necklace, and the signet ring adorned Joseph in typical Egyptian fashion when he assumed administrative command under Pharaoh. "Abrech," probably an Egyptian word meaning "to take note," is the order to all Egyptians upon the inauguration of Joseph (Gen. 41:43). The embalmment of Jacob and the mummification of Joseph also followed the Egyptian pattern of caring for the deceased.

Parallels in the life of Joseph and in Egyptian literature also are noteworthy. Joseph's transition from slave to ruler bears resemblance to the Egyptian classic, "The Eloquent Peasant." The seven lean years of plenty, in Pharaoh's dreams, bear similarity to an ancient Egyptian tradition.[37]

---

may be the restoration after the Assyrian invasion in 733, while a third level suggests an earlier devastation, probably by the Syrians. Cf. *BASOR* for Dec. 1959.

[36] For further discussion see Cyrus H. Gordon, *op. cit.*, pp. 136–137. Also his article "Indo-European and Hebrew Epic," *Eretz-Israel,* V (1958), 10–15.

[37] For translation by John A. Wilson see J. B. Pritchard, *Ancient Near Eastern Texts,* pp. 31–32.

Throughout these years of adversity, suffering, and success the human-divine relationship is clearly apparent. Tempted by Potiphar's wife, Joseph did not yield. He did not want to sin against God (39:9). In prison Joseph frankly confessed that the interpretation of dreams belonged to God (40:8). When he appeared before Pharaoh, Joseph acknowledged that God used dreams to reveal the future (41:25–36). Even in the naming of his son, Manasseh, Joseph recognized God as the source of his promotion and his relief from sorrow (41:51). He also took God into consideration in his interpretation of history: in revealing his identity to his brothers he humbly credited God for bringing him to Egypt. Not in the least did he call them to account for selling him into slavery (45:4–15). After Jacob's death Joseph reassured them once more that he would not seek revenge. God had ordered the events of history for the good of all (50:15–21).

Joseph's magnification of God through many vicissitudes was rewarded by his own elevation. In Potiphar's house he was so trustworthy and efficient that he was promoted to overseer. Thrown into prison on false charges, Joseph was soon entrusted with supervisory responsibilities which he used wisely to help his fellow prisoners. Through the butler, who for two years failed to remember his aid, Joseph was suddenly brought before Pharaoh to interpret the king's dreams. This was indeed an opportune time—the Egyptian ruler was in need of a man of wisdom such as Joseph proved himself to be. As chief administrator he not only guided Egypt through the crucial years of plenty and famine but was instrumental in saving his own family. Joseph's position and prestige made it possible for him to allot the land of Goshen to the Israelites when they migrated to Egypt. This was quite advantageous for them because of their pastoral interests.

Jacob's blessings form a fitting conclusion to the patriarchal age in the Genesis account. On his deathbed he uttered his last will and testament. Even though he was in Egypt, this blessing reflects the custom of the Mesopotamian homeland, where oral pronouncements were recognized as binding when contested in court. In keeping with the divine promises made to the patriarchs Jacob's blessing, given in poetic form, had prophetic significance.

SELECTED READING

AHARONI, Y. and M. AVI-YONAH. *The Macmillan Bible Atlas.* New York: The Macmillan Company, 1967.

ALBRIGHT, WILLIAM F. *Archaeology of Palestine.* Baltimore: Penguin Books, 1960.

AVI-YONAH, M. (ed.) *Encyclopedia of Archaeological Excavations in the Holy Land.* London: Oxford University Press, 1976.

BEEK, M. A. *Atlas of Mesopotamia.* New York: Thomas Nelson & Sons, 1962.

BEITZEL, BARRY J. *The Moody Atlas of the Bible.* Chicago: Moody Press, 1984.

BIMSON, J. J. and J. P. KANE. *The New Bible Atlas.* London: Tyndale Press, 1985.

BRIGHT, JOHN. *A History of Israel.* 3rd ed. Philadelphia: Westminster Press, 1980.

BUSH, GEORGE. *Notes, Critical and Practical, on Genesis.* 2 vols. New York: Ivinson, Phinney & Co., 1857. Reprint. Minneapolis: Klock & Klock Christian Publishers, 1981.

DAVIS, JOHN D. *Genesis and Semitic Tradition.* Grand Rapids: Baker Book House, 1980.

DELITZSCH, FRANZ. *A New Commentary on Genesis.* Translated by Sophia Taylor. 2 vols. Edinburgh: T. & T. Clark, 1899. Reprint. Minneapolis: Klock & Klock Christian Publishers, 1978.

DEVAUX, ROLAND. *Ancient Israel, Its Life and Institutions.* Translated by J. McHugh. New York: McGraw-Hill, 1961.

FINEGAN, JACK. *Light From the Ancient Past.* 2nd ed. Princeton: Princeton University Press, 1959.

FREE, JOSEPH P. Archaeology and Bible History. 5th ed., rev. Wheaton: Scripture Press, 1956.

GLUECK, NELSON. *The Other Side of Jordan.* New Haven: ASOR, 1940.

GORDON, CYRUS H. *The World of the Old Testament.* Garden City: Doubleday, 1958.

HUNT, I. *The World of the Patriarchs.* Englewood Cliffs: Prentice-Hall, Inc., 1966.

KIDNER, F. D. *Genesis.* Downers Grove: Inter-Varsity Press, 1968.

KITCHEN, KENNETH A. *Ancient Orient and Old Testament.* Chicago: Inter-Varsity Press, 1966.

———. *The Bible in its World.* Downers Grove: Inter-Varsity Press, 1978.

KRAMER, SAMUEL NOAH. *From the Tablets of Sumer.* Indian Hills: The Falcon's Wing Press, 1956.

———. *The Sumerians.* Chicago: University of Chicago Press, 1964.

LIVINGSTON, G. HERBERT. *The Pentateuch in Its Cultural Environment.* Grand Rapids: Baker Book House, 1974.

OPPENHEIM, A. LEO. *Ancient Mesopotamia.* Chicago: University of Chicago Press, 1964.

———. *Letters From Mesopotamia.* Chicago: University of Chicago Press, 1967.

PALLIS, SVEND AAGE. *The Antiquity of Iraq (A Handbook of Assyriology).* Copenhagen: Ejnar Munksgaard, 1956.

PARROT, A. *Abraham and His Times.* Translated by J. H. Farley. Philadelphia: Fortress Press, 1968.

PAYNE, J. BARTON. *An Outline of Hebrew History.* Grand Rapids: Baker Book House, 1954.

PFEIFFER, CHARLES F. *Bible Atlas.* Grand Rapids: Baker Book House, 1961.

———. (ed.) *The Biblical World: A Dictionary of Biblical Archaeology.* Grand Rapids: Baker Book House, 1966.

———. *Old Testament History.* Grand Rapids: Baker Book House, 1973.

PFEIFFER, CHARLES F. and HOWARD F. VOS. *The Wycliffe Historical Geography of the Bible.* Chicago: Moody Press, 1967.

SCHWANTES, S.J. *A Short History of the Ancient Near East.* Grand Rapids: Baker Book House, 1965.

SMICK, ELMER. *Archaeology of the Jordan Valley.* Grand Rapids: Baker Book House, 1973.

SPEISER, E. A. *Genesis.* Garden City: Doubleday, 1964.

STIGERS, J. *A Commentary on Genesis.* Grand Rapids: Zondervan Publishing House, 1975.

THOMAS, D. W. (ed.) *Archaeology and Old Testament Study.* New York: Oxford University Press, 1957.

THOMPSON, J. A. *Archaeology and the Old Testament.* Grand Rapids: Wm. B. Eerdmans Publishing Co., 1960.

TURNER, GEORGE A. *Historical Geography of the Holy Land.* Grand Rapids: Zondervan Publishing House, 1973.

UNGER, MERRILL F. *Archaeology and the Old Testament.* Grand Rapids: Zondervan Publishing House, 1954.

WILSON, MARVIN R. *Our Father Abraham: Jewish Roots of the Christian Faith.* Grand Rapids: Wm. B. Eerdmans Publishing Co., and Dayton: Center for Judaic-Christian Studies, 1989.

WISEMAN, D.J. (ed.) *Peoples of Old Testament Times.* New York: Oxford University Press, 1973.

WOOD, LEON. *A Survey of Israel's History.* Grand Rapids: Zondervan Publishing House, 1970.

WOOLLEY, C. L. *Ur of the Chaldees.* London: Ernest Benn, 1930.

WRIGHT, G. E. *Biblical Archaeology.* Rev. ed. Philadelphia: Westminster Press, 1962.

YADIN, Y. *The Art of Warfare in Biblical Lands.* New York: McGraw-Hill, 1963.

———. *Everyday Life in Bible Times.* Washington: National Geographic Society, 1967.

YAMAUCHI, E. *The Stones and the Scriptures.* Philadelphia: Lippincott, 1972.

Chapter ***III***

Emancipation of Israel

Centuries pass in silence from the death of Joseph to the dawn of national consciousness under Moses. Sacred history, however, takes on new and exciting dimensions with the unique transition of the Israelites from the Pharaonic clutches of slavery to the status of an independent nation as God's chosen people. In less than a lifetime they undergo a miraculous deliverance from the mightiest emperor of the day, receive a divine revelation that makes them conscious of being God's covenant people, and have imparted to them a code of laws in preparation for occupying the land of patriarchal promise. It is not surprising that this remarkable experience was retold and relived annually in the observance of the Passover. Repeatedly the prophets and psalmists acclaim Israel's deliverance from Egypt as the most significant miracle in their history.

So meaningful was this emancipation and so vital was this involvement between God and Israel for coming generations that four fifths of the Pentateuch or more than one sixth of the entire Old Testament is devoted to this short period in Israel's history. Beyond the years of Egyptian oppression, which receive brief consideration in the introductory chapters, the events of these four books—Exodus, Leviticus, Numbers, and Deuteronomy—are confined to less than five decades. A summary of the material is provided in the following outline:

From Egypt to Mount Sinai	Ex. 1–18
Encampment at Mount Sinai	Ex. 19–Num. 10
Wilderness wanderings	Num. 10–21
Encampment before Canaan	Num. 22–Deut. 34

Contemporary Events

There is no disagreement among scholars, who accept the historicity of Israel's bondage in Egypt, that the Exodus occurred during the New Kingdom era. Since the closing chapters of Genesis already account for Israel's migration to Goshen, the contemporary events in Egypt are of primary importance.

The Hyksos Invasion

The powerful Twelfth Dynasty or Middle Kingdom in Egypt was followed (*ca.* 1790 B.C.) by two weak dynasties under whom the government disintegrated. Semite invaders from Asia known as Hyksos, people using the horse and chariot, which were unknown to the Egyptians, occupied Egypt by about 1700 B.C. Very little is known about these people, but Manetho assigned Dynasties Fifteen and Sixteen to these foreign rulers who controlled Lower Egypt for about a century and a half. In the course of time Theban rivals mastered the use of the horse and chariot in battle, and under Ahmose of the Seventeenth Dynasty they were able to expel the Hyksos from the country (1550 B.C.). This gave opportunity for the rise of a powerful government known as the New Kingdom. It is understandable that the Egyptians did not leave a written record of this great humiliation by the Hyksos rulers. Consequently our knowledge of this period is very limited.

The New Kingdom (ca. 1546–1085 B.C.)

Three dynasties reigned in Egypt during this period. Under the first three rulers of the Eighteenth Dynasty, Amen-hotep I and Thut-mose I and II (*ca.* 1550–1500 B.C.), Egypt became well established as an empire. Although Thut-mose III was ruler from 1504 to 1450 B.C., he was overshadowed during the first twenty-two years of his reign by Queen Hatshepsut, who took full control of the government. Because of her powerful and brilliant leadership she was recognized by both Lower and Upper Egypt. Not least among her impressive building projects was a white limestone temple. This mortuary was built in colonnaded terraces with the imposing cliff at Deir el-Bahri as background. One of her two great obelisks (containing 180 cubic yards of granite and towering nearly one hundred feet in height) is still standing at Karnak.

Thut-mose III, whose ambitions had been thwarted for many years, gained undisputed possession of the crown when Hatshepsut died. He established the absolute power of Egypt by asserting himself as the greatest military leader in Egyptian history. In eighteen campaigns he extended the control of his kingdom to the Euphrates, marching his armies through Palestine or sailing the Mediterranean Sea to the Phoenician coast. As a military man and empire builder he is often compared with Alexander the Great and Napoleon. Since these campaigns were executed in summer, he usually promoted large-scale building projects during the winter, beautifying and enlarging the great temple at Karnak, which had been erected to Amun during the Middle Kingdom. Obelisks erected by him may be seen today in London, New York, the Lateran, and Constantinople.

Thut-mose III was followed by Amen-hotep II (1450–1425), who was a great sportsman, Thut-mose IV (1425–1417), who excavated the sphinx and married a Mitannian princess, and Amen-hotep III (1417–1379). Amen-hotep IV, or Akh-en-Aton (1379–1362), is best known for effecting a revolution in religion. It is probable that the Pharaohs were becoming increasingly annoyed by the growing strength of the Amun priesthood at Thebes. Thut-mose IV had previously ascribed his royal ascendancy to the ancient sun-god Re, rather than to Amun, but Amen-hotep IV went further by actually attempting to negate the oppressive power of the Theban priests. He championed the worship of Aton, who was represented by the solar disk. Building a temple at Thebes to his new god while he was still coregent with his father, he proclaimed himself the first priest of Aton. Not satisfied with erecting temples in various cities throughout his empire, he selected the new site of Amarna for the precinct of his god. From this capital, located about midway between Thebes and Memphis, he established the worship of Aton as the state religion. Before long he admonished all subjects everywhere to serve only this god. So devoted was he to Aton that he and his votaries were oblivious to appeals for aid from various parts of the kingdom. The archives of Amarna, discovered in 1887, bear witness to this.[1] When Akh-en-Aton died the newly established capital was abandoned. His son-in-law, Tut-ankh-Amon, secured his throne by renouncing Aton and restoring the former Theban god. The tomb of Tut-ankh-Amon, discovered in 1922, provided abundant evidence of his devotion to Amun. With the short-lived reign of Ay the Eighteenth Dynasty terminated in 1348 B.C.

The two greatest kings of the next dynasty, which lasted until 1200 B.C., were Seti I (1318–1304) and Ramses II (1304–1237). The former began to reconquer the Asiatic empire, which had been lost during the days of Akh-en-Aton, and moved the capital to the eastern Delta. The latter continued this attempt to reconquer Syria but eventually signed a peace treaty with the Hittite king, who sealed this agreement by giving his daugher in marriage to Ramses II. This is the earliest nonaggression pact between nations known today. In addition to the extensive building projects at or near

[1] Most of these letters were written in Akkadian by Canaanite scribes in Palestine, Phoenicia, and southern Syria to Amen-hotep III and Akh-en-Aton. For a translation of some of these cuneiform texts by W. F. Albright see Pritchard, *Ancient Near Eastern Texts,* pp. 483–490.

Thebes, Ramses II also beautified Tanis, the Delta capital, which the Hyksos rulers had used centuries before.

During the remainder of the Nineteenth and Twentieth Dynasties the Egyptian rulers struggled to retain their kingdom. As the central power decreased, the local priesthood of Amun gained enough strength to establish the Twenty-first Dynasty about 1085 B.C. and Egypt never recovered sufficiently from the resultant decline to regain her position as a world power.

Religion in Egypt[2]

Egypt was a land of many gods. With local deities as the basis of religion, Egyptian gods became numerous. Nature gods were commonly represented by animals and birds. Eventually cosmic divinities, which were personified in the forces of nature, were elevated above the local gods and were theoretically considered as national or universal deities. These were so plentiful that they came to be grouped in families of triads and enneads.

Temples likewise were numerous throughout Egypt. With the provision of a home or temple for each god came the priesthood, the offerings, the festivals, rites, and ceremonies for worship. In return for these accommodations the people looked to their gods as their benefactors. Fertility of land and animals, victory or defeat, the flooding of the Nile Valley, in fact, every factor affecting welfare in this life was ascribed to some god.

The national prominence accorded any one god was closely related to politics. The falcon god, Horus, rose from a local to a state deity when King Menes united Lower and Upper Egypt at the dawn of Egyptian history. When the Fifth Dynasty patronized the sun-god of Heliopolis, Re became the head of the Egyptian pantheon. The nearest approximation to a national god in Egypt was the recognition given to Amun during the Middle and New Kingdoms. The magnificent temples at Karnak and Luxor, in the vicinity of Thebes, still bear witness to the royal patronage of this god. In the Eighteenth Dynasty the Amun cult with its Theban priesthood became so strong that the Pharaonic challenge of its power was successfully squelched upon Akh-en-Aton's death. Despite the prominence of the national gods, at no time were they worshiped exclusively by the Egyptian populace. To an Egyptian peasant the local god was all-important.

Egyptians believed in a life after death. A blameless record here on earth entitled man to immortality. This accounts for the royal burials represented by the pyramids and other tombs, in which adequate provision, such as food, drink, and the luxuries of life, was made for the hereafter. In early times even servants were slain and placed beside their master's body. Like

[2] Cf. W. C. Hayes, *The Scepter of Egypt;* vol. I (New York: Harper & Brothers, 1953), chap. VI, "The Religion and Funerary Beliefs in Ancient Egypt," pp. 75-83.

Osiris, the divine symbol of immortality, the deceased Egyptian anticipated trial before a tribunal of the underworld with the hope of being morally fit for the bliss of eternal life.

Extreme tolerance in the Egyptian religion accounts for the endless addition and recognition of so many gods. None were ever eliminated. Since the modern student finds it difficult to make a logical analysis of the multitudinous unrelated elements of this religion, it is doubtful that any native Egyptian did. Confusion results from any attempt to correlate the host of deities with their respective cults and rituals. Neither can the host of myths and beliefs be rationalized.

The Date of the Exodus

That Israel left the land of bondage during the latter half of the second millennium B.C. hardly remains subject to question. Very few scholars would date the Exodus beyond a span of two and a half centuries (1450–1200). Since no references or incidents in the Book of Exodus can be definitely correlated with Egyptian history, the absolute dating bears further investigation.

Concerning a more specific date for the Mosaic era, two kinds of evidence warrant careful examination: archaeological and biblical. So far neither has provided a suitable answer to gain the unanimous support of Old Testament scholars.

The fall of Jericho, which occurred within half a century after the Exodus, is still subject to an archaeological date range of about two centuries (1400–1200). Recent excavations have subjected former findings and conclusions to reexamination. Garstang, who excavated Jericho (1930–1936), reasoned that Joshua's invasion is best dated about 1400 B.C.[3] Miss Kathleen Kenyon maintains that the findings on which these conclusions were based date back to the Early Bronze Age (third millennium) and that virtually nothing remains of the centuries during which the Israelite occupation is dated (1500–1200). Consequently she asserts that her recent excavations (1952–1956) shed no light on Joshua's destruction of Jericho. Whereas Garstang dated the latest pottery from the Bronze Age occupation not later than 1385 B.C., Kenyon prefers a later date—*ca.* 1350–1325 B.C.[4] Since this represents the latest Bronze Age occupation, she dates the destruction of

[3] John Garstang, *Joshua Judges* (London: Constable, 1931), p. 146. Cf. also *The Story of Jericho* (new rev. ed.; London: Marshall, Morgan, and Scott, 1948), pp. xiv, 126-127. See also J. P. Free, *Archaeology and Bible History* (5th ed., rev.; Wheaton: Scripture Press Book Division, 1956), pp. 131-132, 137.

[4] Recently J. J. Bimson, *Redating the Exodus and Conquest* (Sheffield, 1978) has offered a reconstructed chronology dating the Exodus in the first half of the fifteenth century during the reign of Thutmose III.

Jericho by the Israelites in the third quarter of the fourteenth century.[5] Albright, Vincent, de Vaux, and Rowley favor the latter half of the thirteenth century for the fall of Jericho under Joshua.[6]

Surface examinations of the pottery in the Arabah and Transjordan have indicated that the Moabite, Ammonite, and Edomite kingdoms were not established until the thirteenth century.[7] These have not been confirmed by extensive excavations, so that pottery dating for this area may yet be subject to chronological adjustments.[8] Comparatively little is known about the living conditions of the people whom the Israelites encountered on their way to Canaan. Although Glueck found no evidence of dwellings in Transjordan for the period before the thirteenth century, it is possible that people were living there in tent cities and would in that case leave no ruins.[9]

Neither has the identification of Pithom and Ramses provided conclusive evidence for dating Israel's departure from Egypt.[10] These cities may have been built by the Israelites, but rebuilt and renamed by Ramses during his reign. Consequently archaeological evidence, which at present is subject to various interpretations, does not offer conclusive evidence for precise dating of the Exodus.

The biblical record provides limited data for establishing a definite date for the time of Israel's Egyptian bondage. Only one chronological reference specifically links the Solomonic era[11]—which has well-established dates—with the Exodus. The assumption, that the 480 years noted in I Kings 6:1 provide a basis for exact dating, yields a date for the Exodus near 1450 B.C.[12] Although other references[13] and the account of intervening developments point to a long era between the deliverance from Egypt and the kingdom era in Israel, none of the biblical passages involved warrant precise dating.

[5] Kathleen Kenyon, *Digging up Jericho* (London: Ernest Benn, 1957), pp. 262–263.

[6] Vincent and de Vaux suggest 1250–1200 B.C. For a survey of this problem with a conclusion favoring this late date see H. H. Rowley, *From Joseph to Joshua* (London: Oxford University Press, 1950).

[7] Nelson Glueck, *The Other Side of the Jordan* (New Haven, 1940), pp. 125–147.

[8] Such was the case with pottery chronology for Palestine. Cf. Free, *op. cit.*, p. 99.

[9] Dwight Wayne Young of Brandeis University points out that such was the case with the Midianites in the days of Gideon, Judg. 6–7.

[10] This name Pi-Ramses came into use in the 19th Dynasty for the site previously known as Avaris. From the 22nd Dynasty onward this city was known as Tanis. The use in Gen. 47:11 and Ex. 1:11 may represent geographical name modernization in the Hebrew text.

[11] Acceptable dates for the end of Solomon's reign are now confined to a variable period of ten years. Representative dates are: Albright, 922; Thiele, 931.

[12] According to Thiele, Solomon began building the Temple in 967 B.C. The date for the Exodus on this calculation is 967 plus 480, or *ca.* 1447 B.C. For a discussion of diverse theories see Rowley, *op. cit.*, pp. 74–98. Using round numbers and allotting 25 instead of 40 years to a generation, Wright, *op. cit.*, pp. 83–84, reduces 480 to about 300 years dating the Exodus after 1300 B.C.

[13] Cf. Judg. 11:26 and Acts 13:19; certainly the latter is a total attained by adding up round numbers. Allowance for Moses, Joshua, the judges, Saul, and David points to a longer period than a late date of the Exodus suggests.

More numerous are the biblical notations approximating the period preceding the Exodus. Even though problems of interpretation are yet unsolved, they convey the impression that the Israelites spent several centuries in Egypt.[14] Genealogical references may suggest a comparatively short period of time between Joseph and Moses, but the use of a genealogy as a basis for time approximation is still subject to question.[15] Genealogies often have long gaps which make them unsuitable for fixing a chronology.[16] The increase of the Israelites from seventy to a great multitude which threatened Egyptian rule likewise favored the lapse of centuries for Israel's residence in the land of the Nile.

Biblical considerations bespeak longer chronologies before and after the Exodus. On this basis it is reasonable to consider *ca.* 1450 as a date for the Exodus and allow for the migration of Jacob and his sons in the Hyksos era of supremacy in Egypt.

The Biblical Account

Israel's dramatic deliverance from Egyptian bondage is vividly portrayed in Ex. 1:1–19:2. Beginning with a brief reference to Joseph and the adverse fortunes of Israel, the histrionic developments center around Moses, culminating in the emancipation of Israel. This narrative lends itself to the following subdivisions:

I. Israel freed from slavery	1:1–13:19
Conditions in Egypt	1:1–22
Moses—birth, education, and call	2:1–4:31
The contest with Pharaoh	5:1–11:10
The Passover	12:1–13:19
II. From Egypt to Mount Sinai	13:20–19:2
Divine deliverance	13:20–15:21
En route to the Sinaitic encampment	15:22–19:2

Oppression under Pharaoh

In the days of Joseph the Israelites, who had pastoral interests, were granted the most fertile areas in the Nile Delta. The Hyksos invaders, also

[14] Cf. Ex. 12:40, 41 (Hebrew text reads 430; LXX reads 215), Gen. 15:13, and Gal. 3:17 mention 400 years. These seem to be round numbers and leave the scope of this period in question. Did this period begin with Abraham, the birth of Isaac, or with the migration of Jacob and his sons to Egypt? Rabbinic tradition dates the 400 years from the birth of Isaac. Cf. *The Soncino Chumash,* ed. A. Cohen (Hindhead, Surrey: The Soncino Press, 1947), p. 397.

[15] Cf. Rowley, *op. cit.,* pp. 71 ff. See his discussion of Num. 26:59 and other passages.

[16] For example in Matt. 1 where several well-known kings are omitted. Cf. also the study by W. H. Green in *Bibliotheca Sacra,* April, 1890.

shepherd people, very likely were favorably disposed toward the Israelites. With the expulsion of the Hyksos the Egyptian rulers assumed more power and in time began the oppression of the Israelites. A new ruler, unfamiliar with Joseph, had no personal interest in Israel but introduced policies that were designed to alleviate his fears of an Israelite rebellion. Consequently the chosen people were consigned to hard labor in building treasure cities such as Pithom and Ramses (Ex. 1:11). A royal edict instructed the Egyptians to drown at birth all male children born to Israelites. This was Pharaoh's design to counteract God's blessing upon Israel as the people increased and prospered (Ex. 1:15–22). Years later, when Moses challenged the power of Pharaoh, the oppression was intensified by withholding from Israelite slaves the straw so useful in their production of bricks (Ex. 5:1–21).

Preparation of a Leader

Moses was born in perilous times. He was adopted by Pharaoh's daughter and given educational advantages in the foremost center of civilization. Although not mentioned in Exodus, Stephen in addressing the Sanhedrin in Jerusalem refers to Moses as having been instructed in Egyptian wisdom (Acts 7:22). Extensive educational facilities at the Egyptian court were used during the New Kingdom period for training royal heirs of tributary princes. Although kept as hostages to ensure collection of tribute, they were handsomely treated in this princely prison. If a distant prince died, a son who had been exposed to Egyptian culture was designated to the throne with the hope that he would be a loyal vassal of Pharaoh.[17] It is highly probable that Moses received his Egyptian training along with royal heirs from Syria and other lands.

Moses' valiant attempt to help his people ended in failure. Fearing the vengeance of Pharaoh, he fled into the land of Midian, where he spent the next forty years. Here he was favorably received in the home of Reuel, a priest of Midian, who was also known as Jethro.[18] In the course of time Moses married Reuel's daughter Zipporah and settled down to a shepherd's life in the Midian wilderness. Through experience gained from shepherding flocks in the area surrounding the Gulf of Aqaba, Moses undoubtedly acquired a thorough knowledge of this territory. Without being conscious of its relevance he received excellent preparation for leading Israel through this desert many years later.

The call of Moses is indeed significant in the light of his background and training (Ex. 3–4). In the court of Pharaoh he realized that he would

[17] Steindorff and Seele, *When Egypt Ruled the East,* p. 105.

[18] Pronunciation in Hebrew is *Reuel* (Ex. 2:18) and in Greek is *Reguel* (Num. 10:29 in AV and ASV). Elsewhere in Exodus he is called Jethro. Cf. *The New Bible Commentary* in discussion on Num. 10:29.

have to contend with authority. Not without reason was he reluctant to ask for Israel's release. God assured Moses of divine aid and provided three miracles to accredit him before the Israelites—the rod which became a serpent, the leprous hand, and water turning to blood. This furnished a reasonable basis for the Israelites to believe that Moses had been commissioned by the God of the patriarchs. Having been assured that Aaron would be his spokesman, Moses complied with God's call and returned to Egypt.

The Contest with Pharaoh

During the New Kingdom period the power of Pharaoh was unsurpassed among contemporary nations. His domain at times extended as far as the Euphrates. Moses' appearance at the royal court demanding the release of his people Israel presented a challenge to Pharaoh's power.

The plagues, occurring during a relatively short period, demonstrate the power of Israel's God not only to Pharaoh and the Egyptians but also to the Israelites. Pharaoh's attitude from the very beginning is that of defiance expressed in the question, "Who is the Lord, that I should obey his voice to let Israel go?" (Ex. 5:2) When confronted with the opportunity of complying with God's will, Pharaoh resisted, hardening his heart in the course of these developments.[19] The three different Hebrew words adverting to Pharaoh's attitude—as stated ten times in Ex. 7:13–13:15—denote the intensification of an already existing condition. God permitted Pharaoh to live and endowed him with the ability to resist the divine overtures (Ex. 9:16). In this way God hardened his heart as is indicated in the two predictive references (Ex. 4:21 and 7:23) as well as the narrative (9:12–14:17). The purpose of the plagues—clearly stated in Ex. 9:16—is to show Pharaoh the power of God on behalf of Israel. The ruler of Egypt was challenged by supernatural might.

How extensively the Egyptians were affected through the plagues is not fully stated. The last plague was designed to bring judgment on all the gods of Egypt (Ex. 12:12). The inability of Pharaoh and his people to counteract these plagues must have demonstrated to the Egyptians the superiority of Israel's God in comparison to the gods they worshiped. This caused some Egyptians to acknowledge the God of Israel (Ex. 9:20).

Israel likewise became conscious of divine intervention. Having been in bondage for several generations, the Israelites had not witnessed a demonstration of God's power in their day. Each succeeding plague brought a greater manifestation of the supernatural, so that with the death of the firstborn the Israelites realized that they were being delivered by One who is omnipotent.

The plagues are best explained as a manifestation of God's power

[19] Cf. Free, *op. cit.*, pp. 93–94, for further discussion.

through natural phenomena. Neither the natural nor the supernatural element should be excluded. All the plagues had elements commonly known to the Egyptians, such as the frogs, the insects, and the inundation of the Nile. But the intensification of those things that were natural, the exact prediction of the coming and departure of the plagues, as well as the discrimination whereby the Israelites were excluded from certain plagues were developments that should have caused the naturalist to recognize the supernatural.

The Passover

Specific instructions were given to the Israelites by Moses before the execution of the last plague (Ex. 12:1–51). The death of the first-born did not affect those who complied with the divine requirements.

A year-old male lamb or goat without blemish was selected on the tenth day of Abib. The animal was slain on the fourteenth day toward evening and its blood applied to the doorposts and the lintel of each home. With preparations for departure completed, the Israelites ate the Passover meal consisting of meat, unleavened bread, and bitter herbs. They left Egypt immediately after the first-born in every Egyptian home had been slain.

For Israel the exodus from Egypt was the greatest event in Old Testament times. When Pharaoh realized that the first-born in every Egyptian home had been slain he was willing to allow Israel's departure. The observance of the Passover was an annual reminder that God had freed them from bondage. The month Abib, later known as Nisan, thereafter marked the beginning of their religious year.

The Route to Mount Sinai

Israel's journey to Canaan via the Sinaitic peninsula was divinely ordered. No doubt the direct route—a well-traveled road used for military and commercial purposes—would have brought them to the promised land in a fortnight. For a disorganized multitude of liberated slaves the Sinaitic detour not only had a military advantage but also provided time and opportunity for organization.

Increased archaeological and topographical knowledge has dispelled former questions about the historicity[20] of this southward course, even though some geographical identifications are still uncertain. The imprecise meanings of such place names as Succoth, Etham, Pi-hahiroth, Migdol, and Baal-zephon allow for various theories concerning the exact route.[21] The Bitter

[20] Albright points out that the Egyptologist Alan Gardiner, who rejected the historicity of the Exodus route, withdrew his objections in 1933. Cf. *From Stone Age to Christianity,* p. 194.

[21] Succoth means "tabernacles" and is used more than once as a place name. Etham refers to "wall" or "rampart"; Pi-hahiroth means "house of marshes"; migdol designates a "fort." Cf. L. H. Grollenberg, *Atlas of the Bible* (New York: Nelson & Sons, 1956), p. 48.

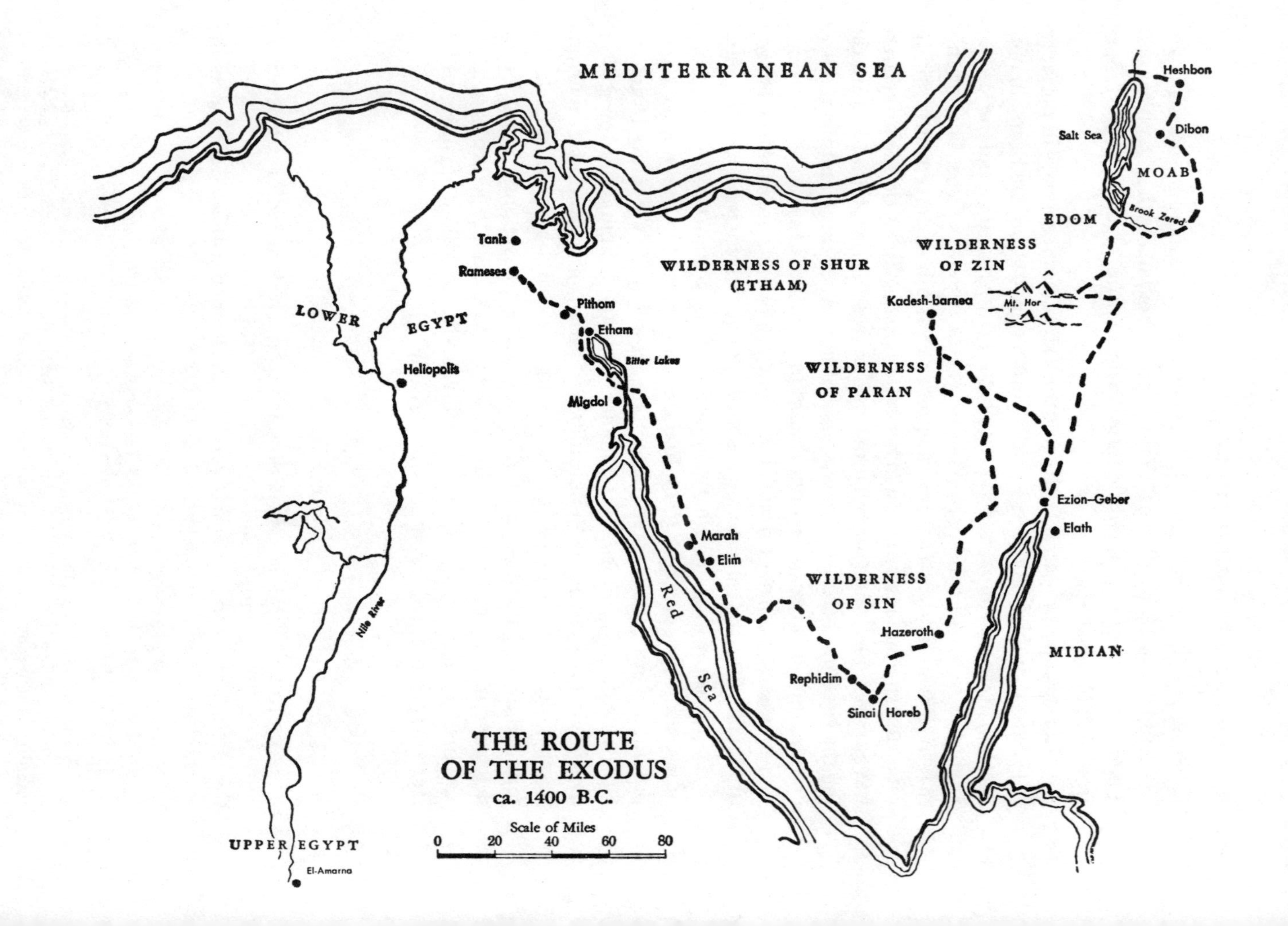
THE ROUTE
OF THE EXODUS
ca. 1400 B.C.
Scale of Miles
0
20
40
60
80
MEDITERRANEAN SEA
Heshbon
Dibon
Salt Sea
MOAB
Brook Zered
EDOM
WILDERNESS
OF ZIN
Mt. Hor
Kadesh-barnea
Tanis
Rameses
WILDERNESS OF SHUR
(ETHAM)
Pithom
Etham
Bitter Lakes
LOWER
EGYPT
Heliopolis
Migdol
WILDERNESS
OF PARAN
Ezion-Geber
Elath
Marah
Elim
Red
Sea
WILDERNESS
OF SIN
Hazeroth
MIDIAN
Rephidim
Sinai
Horeb
Nile River
UPPER
EGYPT
El-Amarna

Lakes may have been linked with the Gulf of Suez, so that this marshy channel could be the "Sea of Reeds" (Yam Suph).[22] Very likely the Egyptians had a line of fortifications roughly identical with the Suez Canal to protect them from Asiatic invaders.

The exact point of Israel's crossing the waters is of secondary importance to the fact that this body of water, in addition to drowning the Egyptian pursuers, provided an impassable barrier between the Israelites and the land of Egypt. A strong east wind parted the waters for Israel's passage. Though this may have been similar to natural phenomena,[23] the time element clearly indicates supernatural intervention in her behalf (Ex. 14:21 ff.). Divine protection was apparent also when the pillar of cloud barred the Egyptians from attacking the Israelites before the waters were parted. After this triumphant deliverance Israel had reason to offer thanks to God (Ex. 15).

A three-day journey through the wilderness of Shur brought Israel down to Marah, where bitter waters were made sweet. Advancing south the wanderers encamped at Elim, where they enjoyed the comfort of twelve springs of water and seventy palm trees. In the wilderness of Sin God miraculously provided manna, which served as their daily food until they entered Canaan. Quails also were supplied in abundance when the Israelites hankered after the fleshpots of Egypt. At Rephidim three things of significance occurred: water gushed forth when Moses struck the rock with his rod; Amalek was repulsed by the Israelite army under Joshua when Moses prayed; and Moses delegated his administrative duties to elders according to Jethro's advice.[24]

In less than three months the Israelites arrived at Mount Sinai (Horeb).[25] Here they encamped for approximately one year.

SELECTED READING

Bimson, John J. *Redating the Exodus and Conquest.* Journal for the Study of the Old Testament, Series 5. Sheffield, 1978.

Cassuto, Umberto. *A Commentary on the Book of Exodus.* Translated by Israel Abrahams. Jerusalem: Magnes Press, 1967.

[22] M. F. Unger, *Archaeology and Old Testament,* pp. 137–138.

[23] For reference to subsequent observations of similar events see Free, *op. cit.,* pp. 100–101.

[24] For the availability of supplies of manna, quails, and even water from a rock in the Sinaitic peninsula see G. E. Wright, *Biblical Archaeology,* pp. 64–65. The time element and abundant supply are indicative of supernatural provisions for such a large nation.

[25] Although a number of scholars locate Mount Sinai in Midian, east of the Gulf of Aqaba, the traditional site, Jebel Musa, is regarded as the area of Israel's encampment. At the apex of the Sinaitic peninsula (a triangle 150 miles wide at its northern border and extending south 260 miles) the granite mountains rise to a peak of nearly 8,000 feet. Cf. Wright, *op. cit.,* pp. 62–64, and Grollenberg, *op. cit.,* p. 48.

CHILDS, BREVARD. *The Book of Exodus.* Philadelphia: Westminster Press, 1974.

COLE, R. ALAN. *Exodus: An Introduction and Commentary.* Tyndale Old Testament Commentaries. Downers Grove: Inter-Varsity Press, 1973.

DAVIES, G. I. *The Way of the Wilderness.* Cambridge: Cambridge University Press, 1979.

FAKHRY, AHMED. *The Pyramids.* Chicago: University of Chicago Press, 1961.

HANNAH, JOHN D. "Exodus" in *Bible Knowledge Commentary.* Wheaton: Scripture Press, 1985.

HONEYCUTT, ROY L., JR. "Exodus" in *The Broadman Bible Commentary,* vol. 1. Nashville: Broadman Press, 1969.

HUEY, F. B., JR. *Exodus: A Study Guide Commentary.* Grand Rapids: Zondervan Publishing House, 1977.

HYATT, J. PHILLIP. *Exodus.* New Century Bible. Greenwood: Attic Press, 1971. Reprint. Grand Rapids: Wm. B. Eerdmans Publishing Co., 1980.

KITCHEN, KENNETH A. "Egypt" pp. 337–354, and "Moses" pp. 843–850, in *The New Bible Dictionary.* J. G. Douglas (ed.). London: Inter-Varsity Press, 1960.

RAMM, B. *His Way Out.* Glendale, Calif.: Gospel Light Publications, 1974.

STEINDORFF, GEORGE, and STEELE, KEITH C. *When Egypt Ruled the East.* Chicago: University of Chicago Press, 1957.

VAN SETERS, JOHN. *The Hyksos: A New Investigation.* New Haven: Yale University Press, 1966.

WALTKE, BRUCE. "Palestinian Artifactual Evidence Supporting the Early Date for the Exodus" in *Bibliotheca Sacra,* 129, 1972, pp. 33–47.

WENHAM, J. W. "Large Numbers in the Old Testament" in *Tyndale,* Bulletin 18, pp. 19–53, 1967.

WILSON, J. A. *The Culture of Ancient Egypt.* Chicago: University of Chicago Press, 1951.

YOUNGBLOOD, RONALD F. *Exodus.* Chicago: Moody Press, 1983.

Chart II THE ANNUAL CALENDAR

Sacred year	Hebrew months	Civil year	Modern equivalent	Babylonian month	Farm season
1	Abib (Nisan) 1—New Moon 14—Passover 15—Sabbath—holy convocation 16—week of unleavened bread 21—holy convocation	7	March/April	Nisanu	later spring rain beginning of barley harvest
2	Iyyar (Ziv) 1—New Moon	8	April/May	Aiaru	barley harvest
3	Sivan 1—New Moon 6–7 Feast of Weeks	9	May/June	Simanu	wheat harvest
4	Tammuz 1—New Moon	10	June/July	Duzu	
5	Ab 1—New Moon	11	July/Aug.	Abu	figs and olives ripen
6	Elul 1—New Moon	12	Aug./Sept.	Ululu	vintage season
7	Tishri (Ethanim) 1—New Moon New Year's Day Feast of Trumpets 10—Day of Atonement 15–22 Feast of Tabernacles	1	Sept./Oct.	Tashritu	former early rains plowing time
8	Heshvan 1—New Moon	2	Oct./Nov.	Arahsamnu	seeding time for wheat and barley
9	Kislev (Chislev) 1—New Moon	3	Nov./Dec.	Kislimu	
10	Tebeth	4	Dec./Jan.	Tebetu	
11	Shebat	5	Jan./Feb.	Shabatu	
12	Adar	6	Feb./March	Addaru	almond trees blossom

Chapter IV

The Religion of Israel

Israel's encampment at Mount Sinai was purposeful. In less than a year's time God's covenant people became a nation. The covenant expanded in the Decalogue and laws for holy living, construction of the tabernacle, organization of the priesthood, the institution of offerings, and observances of feasts and seasons—these enabled Israel to serve God effectively (Ex. 19:1–Num. 10:10).

The religion of Israel was a revealed religion. For centuries the Israelites had known that God had made a covenant with Abraham, Isaac, and Jacob but they had not been experientially conscious of his power and manifestation on their behalf. God was mindful of this covenant in delivering Israel out of Egyptian bondage and slavery (Ex. 6:2–9). It was here at Mount Sinai that God revealed himself to Israel.

Israel's experience and God's revelation at this encampment is recorded in Ex. 19 through Lev. 27. The following subdivisions may serve as a guide for further consideration:

I. God's covenant with Israel		19:3–24:8
Preparation for meeting God		19:3–25
The Decalogue		20:1–17
Ordinances for Israel		20:18–23:33
Ratification of the covenant		24:1–8
II. The place of worship		24:9–40:38
Preparation for construction		24:10–31:18
Idolatry and judgment		32:1–34:35
Building of the tabernacle		35:1–40:38
III. Instructions for holy living	Leviticus	1:1–27:34
The offerings		1:1–7:38

The priesthood	8:1–10:20
Laws of purification	11:1–15:33
The Day of Atonement	16:1–34
Heathen customs forbidden	17:1–18:30
Laws of holiness	19:1–22:33
Feasts and seasons	23:1–25:55
Conditions for God's blessings	26:1–27:34

The Covenant

Having been in bondage in an idolatrous environment, Israel now was to be a people wholly devoted to God. By an act unprecedented in history nor duplicated since, it was suddenly changed from the status of slavery to that of an independent nation. Here at Sinai, on the basis of this deliverance, God made a covenant with it to be his holy nation.

Israel was instructed to prepare three days for the establishment of this covenant. Through Moses God revealed the Decalogue, other laws, and instructions for observing sacred feasts. Under the leadership of Aaron, two of his sons, and seventy elders, the people worshiped God with burnt and peace offerings. After Moses read the book of the covenant they responded by accepting the terms. The sprinkling of the blood upon the altar and upon the people sealed the agreement. Israel was assured that it would be brought into the land of Canaan in due time. The condition of the covenant was obedience. Individual members of the nation could forfeit their rights under the covenant by disobedience. On the plains of Moab Moses led the Israelites in a public renewal of this before his death (Deut. 29:1).

The Decalogue[1]

The ten words or ten commandments constitute the introduction to the covenant. The most common enumerations of the decalogue as used at present are:

Most Protestants and Greek Catholic Church (Josephus' order)	Lutherans and Roman Catholic Church (Augustine's order)
1. Foreign gods, Ex. 20:2–3	1. Foreign gods and images, Ex. 20:2–6
2. Images, 20:4–6	2. Name of God
3. Name of God	3. Sabbath
4. Sabbath	4. Parents
5. Parents	5. Murder

[1] For helpful discussions of the Decalogue, the law, the tabernacle, the priesthood, offerings, and the feasts and seasons see the commentary on Exodus and Leviticus by Keil and Delitzsch.

6. Murder
7. Adultery
8. Theft
9. False witness
10. Coveting

6. Adultery
7. Theft
8. False witness
9. Coveting neighbor's house
10. Coveting neighbor's other property or wife

The Jews differ from Josephus by using Ex. 20:2 as the first commandment and verses 3–6 as the second. The division used by the Jews since the early Christian centuries sets verse 2 apart as the first commandment and combines verses 3–6 as the second. Augustine's enumeration differed slightly from the list above in that the ninth commandment dealt with covetousness toward a neighbor's wife while property was grouped under the tenth commandment, following the order in Deuteronomy.

In allotting the Ten Commandments to two tablets the Jews, from Philo to the present, divide them into two groups of five each. Since the first pentad is four times as long as the second, this division may be subject to question. Augustine apportioned three to the first tablet and seven to the second, beginning the latter with the command to honor parents. Calvin and many others who follow Josephus' enumeration use the same twofold division, with four on the first tablet and six on the second. This twofold division by Augustine and Calvin assigns all the duties toward God to the first tablet. The duties toward men are on the second. When Jesus reduced the commandments to two in Matt. 22:34–40 he may have alluded to such a division.

The distinctive feature of the Decalogue is evident in the first two commandments. In Egypt many gods were worshiped. The plagues had been directed against Egyptian gods. The inhabitants of Canaan also were polytheistic. Israel was to be distinct and unique as God's own people, characterized by a singular devotion to God and God alone. Not even an image or likeness of God was permissible. Consequently idolatry was one of the worst offenses in the religion of Israel.

God gave Moses the first copy of the Decalogue on Mount Sinai. Moses broke these tables of stone on which the ten words were written by the finger of God when he realized that his people were worshiping a molten calf. After Israel had been duly punished, but saved from annihilation through the intercessory prayer of Moses, God commanded him to furnish two tables of stone (Deut. 10:2, 4). On these God once more wrote the Decalogue. These tablets were later placed in the ark of the covenant.

Laws for Holy Living

Expansion of the moral laws and additional regulations for holy living were designed to guide the Israelites in their conduct as God's holy people

(Ex. 20–24; Lev. 11–26). Simple obedience to these moral, civil, and ceremonial laws would distinguish them from the surrounding nations.

These laws for Israel can better be understood in the light of the contemporary cultures in Egypt and Canaan. Marriage of brother and sister, which was common in Egypt, was forbidden. Regulations regarding motherhood and childbirth not only reminded them that man is a sinful creature but stood in contrast to sex perversion, prostitution, and child sacrifice associated with the religious rites and ceremonies of the Canaanites. Pure food laws and restrictions concerning the slaughter of animals were designed to keep the Israelites from conforming to some of the Egyptian customs associated with idolatrous rituals. It was fitting that the Israelites, having vivid memories of slavery, should be instructed to leave gleanings for the poor at harvest time, provide for the helpless, honor the aged, and constantly render righteous judgment in all their relationships. As more knowledge becomes available concerning the contemporary religious milieu of Egypt and Canaan, it is likely that many of the restrictions for the Israelites will seem more reasonable to the modern mind.

The moral laws were permanent, but many of the civil and ceremonial laws were temporary in nature. The law limiting the slaughter of animals for food to the central sanctuary was abrogated when Israel entered Canaan (cf. Lev. 17 and Deut. 12:20–24).

The Sanctuary

Up to this time the altar had been the place of sacrifice and worship. One of the marks of the patriarchs was that they erected altars wherever they went. Here at Sinai Moses built an altar, with twelve pillars representing the twelve tribes, on which the young men of Israel offered sacrifices for the ratification of the covenant (Ex. 24:4 ff.). A "tent of meeting" mentioned in Ex. 33 was erected "outside the camp." This temporarily served not only as the meeting place for all Israel but also as the place of divine revelation. Since no priesthood had been organized, Joshua was the sole minister. Immediately following the ratification of the covenant Israel was commanded to construct a tabernacle so that God might "dwell in their midst" (Ex. 25:8). In contrast to the many temples in Egypt, Israel had only one sanctuary. Detailed instructions are given in Ex. 25–40.

Bezalel of the tribe of Judah was appointed chief foreman in charge of construction. Working closely with him was Oholiab of the tribe of Dan. These men were especially filled with the "Spirit of God" and "ability and intelligence" to supervise the building of the place of worship (Ex. 31, 35–36). Assisting them were many men who were divinely motivated and endowed with ability to perform their particular tasks. Freewill offerings of the people provided more than enough building material.

The enclosure for the tabernacle was commonly called the court (Ex. 27:9–18; 38:9–20). With a perimeter of 300 cubits (450 feet), this enclosure was marked by a curtain of fine twined linen hung on bronze pillars with silver hooks. These pillars were seven and a half feet high and spaced seven and a half feet apart. The only entrance (30 feet in width) was at the east end.

The eastern half of this court was the worshiper's square. Here the Israelite made his offering at the altar of sacrifice (Ex. 27:1–8; 38:1–7). This brazen altar (7½ feet square and 4½ feet high), with horns on each corner, was built of acacia or shittim wood covered with bronze. The altar was portable, equipped with staves and rings. Beyond the altar stood the laver (Ex. 30:17–21; 38:8; 40:30), which also was constructed of bronze. Here the priests washed their feet in preparation for officiating at the altar of sacrifice or in the tabernacle.

In the western half of this court stood the tabernacle proper. With a length of 45 feet and a width of 15 feet, it was divided into two parts. The single entrance opened from the east into the holy place (30 ft. long) which was accessible to the priests. Beyond the veil was the holy of holies (15 x 15) where the high priest was permitted to enter on the Day of Atonement.

The tabernacle itself was made of 48 planks (15 feet high and 2¼ feet wide) with twenty on each side and eight on the west end. Made of acacia wood overlaid with gold (Ex. 26:1–37; 36:20–38), these planks were held together by means of bars and silver sockets. The ceiling consisted of a curtain of fine twined linen in colors of blue, purple, and scarlet figured with cherubim. The main external covering was made of goats' hair, which served as a protection for the linen. Two more coverings, one made of rams' skins and one of goatskins, were provided to protect the first two. Two veils of the same material as the first covering were used for the east end of the tabernacle and also for the entrance into the most holy place. The exact construction of the tabernacle cannot be determined, however, since not enough details are given in the scriptural account.

Three pieces of furniture were set in the holy place: the table of shewbread on the north side, the golden candlestick (lampstand) on the south side, and the altar of incense before the veil separating the holy place from the holy of holies (Ex. 40:22–28).

The table of shewbread was made of acacia wood, overlaid with gold, with a golden rim around the top. One ring was attached to each of the four legs so that it could easily be carried with staves (Ex. 25:23–30; 37:10–16). Plates and dishes for incense, as well as flagons and bowls for pouring libations, were placed on this table. Twelve flat cakes of unleavened bread were provided for this table every Sabbath. These were eaten by the priests (Lev. 24:5–9).

The golden candlestick or lampstand was made of one piece of pure beaten or hammered gold (Ex. 25:31–39; 37:17–24). The shape and measurements of the pedestal are uncertain. With one central stem, specifically called the candlestick, and three curving branches on each side, this lampstand had seven lamps. Ornamentation on each of the branches consisted of three cups while the stem had four. The snuffers and trays also were made of pure gold. Every evening the priests filled these lamps with olive oil, furnished by the Israelites, to provide light throughout the night (Ex. 27:20–21; 30:7–8).

The golden altar, primarily used for the burning of incense, stood in the holy place before the entrance into the holy of holies. Made of acacia wood overlaid with gold, this altar was three feet high and one and a half feet square. It had a border of gold around the top, and a horn and a ring on each corner so that it could conveniently be carried with staves (Ex. 30:1–10, 28, 34–37). Each morning and evening as the priests came in to attend to the candlestick they would burn incense, using fire from the brazen altar.

The ark of the covenant or testimony was the most sacred object in the religion of Israel. This and this alone had its special place in the holy of holies. Made of acacia wood and overlaid within and without with pure gold, this chest was three feet nine inches long with a depth and breadth of two feet three inches (Ex. 25:10–22; 37:1–9). With golden rings and staves on each side, the priests could easily carry it. The cover of this chest was called the mercy seat. Two cherubim of gold stood on the lid facing each other with their wings overshadowing the center of the mercy seat. This cover with its cherubim was made of one solid piece of gold. The mercy seat represented the presence of God. Unlike the heathen, there was no material object to represent the God of Israel in this space between the cherubim. The Decalogue clearly forbade any image or likeness of God. Nevertheless, this mercy seat was the place where God and man met (Ex. 30:6), where God spoke to man (Ex. 25:22; Num. 7:89), and where the high priest appeared on the Day of Atonement to sprinkle the blood for the nation of Israel (Lev. 16:14). Within the ark itself were deposited the Decalogue (Ex. 25:21; 31:18; Deut. 10:3–5), a pot of manna (Ex. 16:32–34), and Aaron's rod that blossomed (Num. 17:10). Before Israel entered Canaan the book of the law was placed next to the ark (Deut. 31:26).

The Priesthood

Prior to Mosaic times offerings were usually made by the head of a household, who officially represented his family in the recognition and worship of God. Except for the reference to Melchizedek as priest in Gen. 14:18, the official office of a priest is not mentioned. But now that Israel has been redeemed out of Egypt the priestly office becomes significantly important.

God desired Israel to be a holy nation (Ex. 19:6). For orderly ministration and effective worship, God designated Aaron to serve as high priest during Israel's sojourn in the wilderness. Assisting him were his four sons: Nadab, Abihu, Eleazar, and Ithamar. The former two were later smitten in judgment for bringing unholy fire into the tabernacle (Lev. 8:10; Num. 10:2–4). By virtue of having escaped death in Egypt the first-born of every family belonged to God. Chosen as substitutes for the oldest son in each family, the Levites assisted the priests in their ministration (Num. 3:5–13; 8:17). In this way the entire nation was represented in the priestly ministry.

The functions of the priests were several. Their primary responsibility was to mediate between God and man. By officiating in the prescribed offerings they led the people in securing atonement for sin (Ex. 28:1–43; Lev. 16:1–34). The discernment of God's will for the people was a most solemn obligation (Num. 27:21; Deut. 33:8). Being custodians of the law they were also commissioned to instruct the laity. The care and ministration of the tabernacle also was under their jurisdiction. Consequently, the Levites were assigned to assist the priests in the performance of the many responsibilities allotted to them.

The sanctity of the priests is apparent in the requirements for holy living as well as in the prerequisites for service (Lev. 21:1–22:10). Exemplary in conduct, the priests were under obligation to exercise special care in matters of marriage and family discipline. While physical blemishes barred them permanently from priestly service, ceremonial uncleanness resulting from leprosy, a bodily issue, or forbidden contacts disqualified them temporarily from ministration. Heathen customs, profanation of holy things, and defilement—these were to be avoided by the priests at all times. For the high priest the restrictions were even more exacting (Lev. 21:1–15).

The holiness peculiar to the priests was also indicated by the garments they were instructed to wear. Made of the choicest material and the best in workmanship, these vestments adorned the priests in beauty and dignity. The priest wore a coat, a girdle, a cap, and breeches—all made of fine linen (Ex. 28:40–43; 39:27–29). The coat was a long white seamless tunic with sleeves reaching almost to the feet. The girdle or belt, although nowhere described in particular, was worn above the tunic. According to Ex. 39:29, blue, purple, and scarlet were worked into the white linen of the girdle with a needle, corresponding to the materials and colors used in the veil and furnishings of the tabernacle. The priest's cap was a plain, close-fitting bonnet. Underneath the coat he was to wear linen breeches whenever he entered the sanctuary (Ex. 28:42).

The high priest was distinguished by additional garments consisting of a robe, an ephod, a breastplate, and a special headdress (Ex. 28:4–39). The robe, extending from the neck to below the knees, was blue in color and very plain except for pomegranates and bells alternately attached to the bottom. The former—in colors of blue, purple, and scarlet—were for ornamental purposes. The bells, made of gold, were designed to convey to the waiting congregation every movement of the high priest as he went into the holy of holies on the Day of Atonement.

The ephod consisted of two pieces of linen made of gold, blue, purple, and scarlet joined together with shoulder straps. At the hips one piece extended into a waistband holding both in place. On each shoulder piece of the ephod the high priest wore a precious stone with the names of six tribes engraved in order of their birth. To make the count even, the Levites were omitted, since they assisted the priests, or possibly Joseph stood for Ephraim and Manasseh. In this way the high priest represented the whole nation of Israel in his ministry of mediation. Adorning the ephod were two golden borders and two small chains of pure gold.

The breastplate, a pouch nine inches square, was the most luxurious, magnificent, and mysterious part of the high priest's apparel. Chains of pure gold linked it to the shoulder strap of the ephod. The bottom was tied with blue lace to the waistband. Twelve stones engraved with the tribal names were mounted in gold on the breastplate, serving as a visible reminder that the priest represented his nation before God. The Urim and Thummim, meaning "lights" and "perfection," were placed in the fold of the breastplate (Ex. 28:30; Lev. 8:8). Little is known about their function or the prescribed procedure of the officiating priest, but the important fact remains—this provided a means of discerning God's will.

Equally significant was the headdress or turban of the high priest. Extending across the forehead and attached to the turban was a plate of pure gold on which was inscribed "Holiness to the Lord." This was a constant reminder that holiness is the essence of God's nature. Through expiatory provision the high priest presented his people as holy unto God. By means of holy garments the high priest, as well as the ordinary priests, manifested not only the glory of this ministry of mediation between God and Israel but also the beauty in worship by the blending of their colorful garments with the sanctuary.

In an elaborate ceremony of consecration the priests were set apart for their ministry (Ex. 29:1–37; 40:12–15; Lev. 8:1–36). After being washed with water, Aaron and his sons were clothed in the priestly garments and anointed with oil. With Moses officiating as mediator, a young ox was offered as a sin offering to make atonement not only for Aaron and his sons but also for the purification of the altar from the sins associated with their service. This was followed by a burnt offering in which a ram was sacrificed in accordance with the usual ritual. Another ram was then presented as a peace offering in a special ceremony. Moses applied the blood to the right thumb, the right ear, and the large toe on the right foot of each priest. He then took the fat, the right leg, and three pieces of pastry, which was normally allotted to the officiating priest, and presented them to Aaron and his sons, who made this a wave offering before it was consumed on the altar. After being presented as a wave offering, the breast was boiled and eaten by Moses and the priests. Preceding this sacrificial meal, Moses sprinkled the anointing oil and the blood upon the priests and their garments. This impressive ordination ceremony was repeated on each of seven successive days, sanctifying the priests for their ministration at the tabernacle. In this way the entire congregation became conscious of God's holiness when the people came to the priests with their offerings.

The Offerings

The sacrificial laws and instructions given at Mount Sinai do not imply the absence of offerings prior to this time. Whether or not the various kinds of offerings were clearly distinguished and known to the Israelites may be debatable, but the practice of making sacrifices was undoubtedly familiar to them from the records concerning Cain, Abel, Noah, and the patriarchs. When appealing to Pharaoh for Israel's release, Moses anticipated the offering of sacrifices and did so after the departure from Egypt (Ex. 5:1–3; 18:12, and 24:5).

Now that Israel was a free nation and in covenant relationship with God, specific instructions were given concerning the various kinds of offerings. By bringing these offerings as prescribed the Israelites had the opportunity to serve God in an acceptable manner (Lev. 1–7).

Four kinds of offerings involved the shedding of blood: the burnt offering, the peace offering, the sin offering, and the guilt or trespass offering. Animals deemed acceptable for sacrifice were clean tame animals whose flesh could be eaten, such as sheep, goats, or oxen, male or female, old or young. In case of extreme poverty, the substitution of pigeons was permissible.

General rules for making the sacrifice were as follows:

1. presentation of the animal at the altar
2. the offerer's hand placed on the victim
3. slaying of the animal

4. sprinkling of the blood on the altar
5. burning the sacrifice.

When a sacrifice was offered for the nation the priest officiated. When an individual sacrificed for himself he would bring the animal, place his hand on it, and slay it. The priest then sprinkled the blood and burned the sacrifice. He who offered could not eat of the sacrifice except in the case of a peace offering. When several offerings were presented at the same time, the sin offering preceded the burnt and peace offerings.

Burnt Offering

The distinctive feature about the burnt offering was the fact that the entire sacrifice was consumed on the altar (Lev. 1:5–17; 6:8–13). Expiation was not excluded, since atonement was part of every blood sacrifice. The offerer's complete consecration to God was signified by the consumption of the whole sacrifice. Perhaps Paul had reference to this offering in his appeal for complete consecration (Rom. 12:1). Israel was commanded to maintain a continual, day-and-night burnt offering by means of a fire on the brazen altar. A lamb was offered each morning and evening, thereby reminding Israel of her devotion to God (Ex. 29:38–42; Num. 28:3–8).

Peace or Fellowship Offering

The peace offering was entirely voluntary. Whereas representation and expiation were included, the primary feature of this offering was the sacrificial meal (Lev. 3:1–17; 7:11–34; 19:5–8; 22:21–25). This represented living communion and fellowship between man and God. Family and friends were permitted to join the offerer in this sacrificial meal (Deut. 12:6–7, 17–18). Since this was a voluntary sacrifice, any animal, except a bird, was acceptable regardless of age or sex. After the slaying of the victim and the sprinkling of the blood to make atonement for sin, the fat of the animal was burned on the altar. Through the rites of waving the hands of the offerer, who held the thigh and breast, the officiating priest dedicated this portion of the animal to God. The remainder of the offering provided a feast for the offerer and his invited guests. This joyous fellowship signified the bond of friendship between God and man.

There were three kinds of peace offerings. These varied according to the motive of the offerer. When the sacrifice was made in recognition of unmerited or unexpected blessings, it was called a thank or praise offering. If the offering was made in payment of a vow, it was designated as a votive offering. If the offering was motivated by an expression of love for God, it was called a freewill offering. Each of these offerings was accompanied by a prescribed meal offering. The thank offering lasted one day, while the other two were extended to two days, with the provision that anything left over was to be consumed by fire on the third day. In this way the Israelite was privileged to enter into practical enjoyment of his covenant relationship with God.

Sin Offering

Sins of ignorance committed inadvertently required a sin offering (Lev. 4:1–35; 6:24–30). The violation of negative commands punishable by excision could be rectified by a prescribed sacrifice. Although God has only one standard of morality, the offering varied with the responsibility of the individual. No religious or civil leader was so prominent that his sin was condoned, nor any man so insignificant that his sin was ignored. There was gradation in the required offerings: a young bullock for the high priest or the congregation; a male goat for a ruler; a young doe for a private citizen. The ritual also varied. For the priest or the congregation, the blood was sprinkled seven times before the entrance of the holy of holies. For the ruler and layman, the blood was applied to the horns of the altar. Since it was an offering of expiation, the guilty party was not allowed to eat any part of the animal. Consequently this sacrifice was either consumed on the altar or burned outside the camp, with one exception—the priest received a portion when officiating on behalf of a ruler or layman.

The sin offering was also required for specific sins such as refusal to testify, ceremonial defilement, and idle swearing (Lev. 5:1–13). Even though these sins may be regarded as intentional, they do not represent a calculated defiance of God punishable by death (Num. 15:27–31). Expiation was available for any repentant sinner regardless of his economic status. If he could not afford a sheep or goat, he could substitute a turtledove or pigeon. In cases of extreme poverty even a small portion of fine flour—the equivalent of a day's food ration—would assure the guilty party of acceptance by God. (For other occasions requiring a sin offering see Lev. 12:6–8; 14:19–31; 15:25–30; and Num. 6:10–14.)

Trespass or Guilt Offering

The legal rights of a person and his property, in situations involving God as well as one's fellow man, were clearly set forth in the requirements for the trespass offering (Lev. 5:14–6:7; 7:1–7). Failure to recognize God by neglecting to bring the first-fruits, the tithe, or other required offerings necessitated not only restitution but also a sacrifice. In addition to paying six fifths of the required dues, the offender also sacrificed a ram in order to obtain forgiveness. This costly sacrifice made him conscious of the price of sin. When this wrong was committed against a fellow man, the additional fifth also was required to make amends. If restitution could not be made to the one offended or a near relative, these reparations were paid to the priest (Num. 5:5–10). Infringement on the rights of another person also represented an offense against God. Consequently a sacrifice was necessary.

Grain Offering[2]

This is the only offering which did not involve the life of an animal but consisted primarily of the products of the soil, which represented the fruits of man's labor (Lev. 2:1–16; 6:14–23). This offering could be presented in three different ways, always mixed with oil, frankincense, and salt but without leaven or honey. If an offering consisted of first-fruits, the ears of new grain were parched in the fire. After grinding the grain it might be presented to the priest as fine flour or as unleavened bread, cakes, or wafers prepared in the oven. It seems that a subordinate part of this offering was a suitable quantity of wine for a drink offering (Ex. 39:40; Lev. 23:13; Num. 15:5, 10). A justifiable inference is that the grain offering was never brought by itself. Primarily it was an accompaniment to the burnt and peace offerings. For these two it seemed to be the necessary and proper supplement (Num. 15:1–13). Such was the case with the daily burnt offering (Lev. 6:14–23, Num. 4:16). When offered by the priest for the congregation the entire offering was consumed. In the case of an individual offering the officiating priest presented only a handful at the altar of burnt offering and retained the remainder for the tabernacle. Neither in the offering itself nor in the ritual is there any suggestion that it provided atonement or expiation for sin. By means of this offering the Israelite presented the fruit of his labor, thus signifying the dedication of his gifts to God.

Appointed Feasts and Seasons

Through appointed feasts and seasons Israelites were constantly reminded that they were God's holy people. In the covenant which Israel ratified at Mount Sinai the faithful observance of stated periods was a part of the committal (Ex. 20–24).

Sabbath

First, foremost, and most frequent was the observance of the Sabbath. Although seven-day periods are referred to in Genesis, the Sabbath is first mentioned in Ex. 16:23–30. In the Decalogue (Ex. 20:8–11) the Israelites are reminded to "remember the sabbath day" indicating that this was not

[2] The grain offering is identified as the "meat offering" in the AV, the "meal offering" in the ASV, the "cereal offering" in the RSV, and "food offering" in the Berkeley Version.

the beginning of its observance. By rest or cessation from work the Israelites were reminded that God rested from his creative work on the seventh day. Observance of the Sabbath was a reminder that God had redeemed Israel from Egyptian bondage and sanctified her as his holy people (Ex. 31:13; Deut. 5:12–15). Having been freed from bondage and servitude, Israel was able to devote one day of each week to God, which undoubtedly was not possible as long as the people served Egyptian masters. Even their servants were included in Sabbath observance. Extreme punishment was prescribed for anyone who deliberately disregarded the Sabbath (Ex. 35:3; Num. 15:32–36). Whereas the daily sacrifice for Israel was one lamb, two lambs were offered on the Sabbath (Num. 28:9, 19). This was also the day when twelve loaves of bread were placed on the table in the holy place (Lev. 24:5–8).

New Moon and Feast of Trumpets

Trumpet blasts officially proclaimed the beginning of a new month (Num. 10:10). The New Moon was also observed by sacrificing sin and burnt offerings with appropriate meat and drink provisions (Num. 28: 11–15). The seventh month, with the Day of Atonement and the Feast of Weeks, marked the climax of the religious year, or the year's end (Ex. 34:22). On the first day of this month the New Moon was designated as the Feast of Trumpets and additional offerings were presented (Lev. 23: 23–25; Num. 29:1–6). This also was the beginning of the civil year.

Sabbatical Year

Closely related to the Sabbath was the Sabbath year, applicable to the Israelites when they entered Canaan (Ex. 23:10–11; Lev. 25:1–7). Observing it as a year of rest for the land, they left the field unseeded and the vineyard unpruned every seventh year. Whatever they raised that year was to be shared alike by the owner, servants, and strangers as well as the beasts. Creditors were instructed to cancel the debts incurred by the poor during the six preceding years (Deut. 15:1–11). Since slaves were freed every six years, probably this was also the year of their emancipation (Ex. 21:2–6; Deut. 15:12–18). Thus the Israelites were reminded of their deliverance from Egyptian bondage.

Mosaic instructions also provided for the public reading of the law (Deut. 31:10–31). In this way the Sabbatical year became significant to old and young, to master as well as to servant.

Year of Jubilee

After seven observances of the sabbatical year came the Year of Jubilee. This was ushered in by the blowing of the trumpet on the tenth day of

Tishri, the seventh month. According to the instructions given in Lev. 25: 8–55, this marked a year of liberty in which family inheritance was restored to those who had had the misfortune of losing it, Hebrew slaves were restored to freedom, and land was left uncultivated.

In the possession of land the Israelite was to acknowledge God as the giver. Consequently it was to be kept in the family and passed on as an inheritance. In case of necessity only the right to the products of this land could be sold. Since every fifty years this land reverted to the original owner, the price was directly related to the number of years remaining before the Year of Jubilee. At any time during this period the land was subject to redemption by the owner or a near kinsman. Houses in walled cities, excepting Levitical cities, were not included under the provisions of the Year of Jubilee.

Slaves were released during this year regardless of their length of service. Six years was the maximum period of servitude for any Hebrew slave without the option of freedom (Ex. 21:1). Consequently he could not be reduced to a perpetual state of slavery even though he might find it necessary to sell himself to another as a hired servant when financially pressed. Even non-Hebrew slaves could not be regarded as absolute property. Death as a result of cruelty by the owner was subject to punishment (Ex. 21:20–21). In case of severe mistreatment a slave might claim his freedom (Ex. 21: 26–27). By the periodic release of Hebrew slaves and the demonstration of love and kindness to strangers in the land (Lev. 19:33–34) the Israelites were to remind themselves that once they had been bondmen in Egypt.

Even though the Year of Jubilee followed the sabbatical year, the Israelites were not allowed to cultivate the soil during this period. God promised that they would receive such an abundant crop in the sixth year that they would have sufficient for the seventh and eighth years, which were times of rest for the land. In this way the Israelites were reminded that the land they possessed, as well as the crops they received, were a gift from God.

Annual Feasts

The three annual observances celebrated as feasts were: (1) the Passover and Feast of Unleavened Bread; (2) the Feast of Weeks, First-fruits, or Harvest; (3) the Feast of Tabernacles, or Ingathering. So significant were these festivals that all Israelite men were required to attend (Ex. 23:14–17).

Passover and Feast of Unleavened Bread

Historically the Passover was first observed in Egypt when the families of Israel were excluded from the death of the first-born by killing the paschal lamb (Ex. 12:1–13:10). The lamb was selected on the tenth day of the month of Abib and killed on the fourteenth. During the seven days following only unleavened bread was to be eaten. This month of Abib, later known as

Nisan, was designated as the "beginning of months" or the beginning of the religious year (Ex. 12:2). The second Passover was observed on the fourteenth day of Abib one year after Israel left Egypt (Num. 9:1–5). Since no uncircumcised person was to partake of the Passover (Ex. 12:48), Israel did not observe this festival during the remainder of the wilderness wanderings (Josh. 5:6). Not until the people entered Canaan forty years after leaving Egypt did they observe the third Passover.

The stated purpose of the Passover observance was to remind the Israelites annually of God's miraculous intervention in their behalf (Ex. 13:3–4; 34:18; Deut. 16:1). It marked the opening of the religious year.

The Passover ritual undoubtedly underwent some changes from the original observance when Israel had no priesthood or tabernacle. Rites of temporary character were: the slaying of the lamb by the head of each family, the sprinkling of the blood on the doorposts and lintels, and possibly also the posture in which they partook of the lamb. With the establishment of the tabernacle, Israel had one central sanctuary at which the men were to congregate three times a year beginning with the Passover season (Ex. 23:17; Deut. 16:13). The fifteenth and twenty-first days were days of holy convocation. Throughout the entire week only unleavened bread was eaten by the Israelites. Since the Passover was the principal event of the week, pilgrims were allowed to return home on the morning following this feast (Deut. 16:7). Meanwhile throughout the week additional daily offerings were made for the nation, consisting of two young bulls, one ram, and seven male lambs for a burnt offering, with the prescribed meal offering, and one male goat for a sin offering (Num. 28:19–23; Lev. 23:8). In addition to this the Israelite was instructed to bring a sheaf of the first-fruits to the Lord (Lev. 23:9–14). Accompanying the ritual in which the priest waved the sheaf before the Lord was the presentation of a burnt offering consisting of one male lamb plus a meal offering of fine flour mingled with oil and a drink offering of wine. No grain was to be used from the new crop until public acknowledgment had been made that these material blessings came from God. Consequently, in the observance of the Passover week the Israelites were not only conscious of their historic deliverance from Egypt but also recognized that God's blessing was continually evident in material provisions.

So significant was the Passover celebration that special provision was made for those who were unable to participate at the appointed time to observe it one month later (Num. 9:9–12). Anyone who refused to observe the Passover was ostracized from Israel. Even the stranger in Israel was welcome to participate in this annual celebration (Num. 9:13–14).

Thus the Passover was the most significant of all the feasts and observances in Israel. It commemorated the greatest of all miracles that the Lord had performed for Israel. This is indicated by many references in the Psalms and the prophetical books. Although the Passover was observed at the tabernacle, every family was vividly reminded of its significance by the eating of unleavened bread. No Israelite was excused from participation. This served as an annual reminder that Israel was God's chosen nation.

Feast of Weeks

Whereas the Passover and Feast of Unleavened Bread was observed at the beginning of barley harvest, the Feast of Weeks took place fifty days later, after the wheat harvest (Deut. 16:9).[3] Although a very important occasion, the feast was observed for only one day. On this day of rest a special meal offering consisting of two loaves of leavened bread was presented to the Lord for use at the tabernacle, signifying that even the daily bread was provided by God (Lev. 23:15–20). Prescribed sacrifices were presented with this offering. On this joyous occasion the Israelite was not to forget the less fortunate, leaving the gleanings in the field for the poor and needy (Lev. 23:22).

Feast of Tabernacles

The final festival of the year was the Feast of Tabernacles[4]—a seven-day period during which the Israelites lived in tents (Ex. 23:16; 34:22; Lev. 23:40–41). This feast not only marked the end of the harvest season but when once settled in Canaan it reminded them annually of their wilderness sojourn when they had lived in tents.

The festivities of this week found expression in the largest burnt offerings ever presented, sacrificing a total of seventy bulls. Offering thirteen on the first day, which was a holy convocation, the number was daily decreased by one. Each day an additional burnt offering was sacrificed. This offering consisted of fourteen lambs and two rams with proportional meat and drink offerings. A holy convocation on the eighth day brought to a conclusion the activities of the religious year.

Every seventh year was peculiarly significant in the celebration of the Feast of Tabernacles. This was the year for the public reading of the law. Although pilgrims were required to attend the Passover or the Feast of Weeks only one day, they normally spent the entire week at the Feast of Tabernacles. This provided ample opportunity for the reading of the law in accordance with Moses' command (Deut. 31:9–13).

Day of Atonement

The most solemn occasion of the whole year was the Day of Atonement

[3] This was also known as the Feast of Firstfruits (Num. 28:26) or the Feast of Harvest (Ex. 23:16). Based on the Greek word for "fifty," this was called Pentecost in New Testament times.

[4] Also known as Feast of Ingathering (Ex. 23:16; 34:22; Lev. 23:39; Deut. 16:13–15). It was observed on the fifteenth day of Tishri when the olives, grapes, and grain harvests were completed.

(Lev. 16:1–34; 23:26–32; Num. 29:7–11). This was observed on the tenth day of Tishri with a holy convocation and fasting. No work was permitted on this day. This was the only fast required by the law of Moses.

The main purpose of this observance was to make atonement. In its elaborate and unique ceremony propitiation was made for Aaron and his house, the holy place, the tent of meeting, the altar of the burnt offering, and for the congregation of Israel.

Only the high priest could officiate on this day. The other priests were not even allowed in the sanctuary but were identified with the congregation. For this occasion the high priest laid aside his special garments and dressed in white linen. The prescribed offerings for the day were as follows: two rams as burnt offerings for himself and the congregation, a bullock for his own sin offering, and two goats as a sin offering for the people.

While the two goats remained standing at the altar the high priest offered his sin offering, making atonement for himself. Sacrificing one goat at the altar, he made atonement for the congregation. In both cases he applied the blood to the mercy seat. In a similar manner he sanctified the inner sanctuary, the holy place, and the altar of burnt offering. In this way the three divisions of the tabernacle were properly cleansed on the Day of Atonement for the nation. Placing his hand upon the live goat the high priest confessed the sins of the nation. Then the goat was taken into the wilderness to carry away the sins of the congregation.[5]

Having confessed the sins of the people, the high priest returned to the tabernacle to cleanse himself and change into his official attire. Once more he returned to the altar in the outer court. Here he concluded the Day of Atonement ritual with two burnt offerings, one for himself and another for the congregation of Israel.

The distinctive features of Israel's revealed religion formed a contrast to the religious milieu of Egypt and Canaan. Instead of many idols they were to worship God alone. In place of multiple shrines the Israelites had only one sanctuary. By means of prescribed offerings and consecrated priests provision was made for the laity to approach God without fear. The law guided them into a pattern of behavior that distinguished Israel as God's covenant nation in contrast to the surrounding heathen cultures. To the extent that the Israelites practiced this divinely revealed religion were they assured of God's favor as expressed in the priestly formula for blessing the congregation of Israel (Num. 6:24–26):

> The Lord bless thee, and keep thee:
> The Lord make his face shine upon thee, and be gracious unto thee:
> The Lord lift up his countenance upon thee, and give thee peace.

[5] The person who led this goat into the wilderness was permitted to return to the camp only after he had cleansed himself and washed his clothes.

SELECTED READING

ALBRIGHT, WILLIAM L. *Archaeology and the Religion of Israel.* Baltimore: The Johns Hopkins Press, 1942.

ALLIS, O. T. "Leviticus" in *The New Bible Commentary: Revised.* D. Guthrie (ed.). Grand Rapids: Wm. B. Eerdmans Publishing Co., 1970.

BONAR, A. A. *A Commentary on the Book of Leviticus.* Grand Rapids: Zondervan Publishing House, (1851) 1959.

CERNY, J. *Ancient Egyptian Religion.* London: Hutchinson's University Library, 1952.

CLEMENTS, RONALD E. "Leviticus" in *The Broadman Bible Commentary.* Vol. 2. Nashville: Broadman Press, 1970.

DOUGLAS, MARY. *Purity and Danger.* London: Routledge and Kegan, 1966, 1978.

ERDMAN, CHARLES R. *The Book of Leviticus.* Westwood: Revell, 1951.

FERM, V. (ed.) *Forgotten Religions.* New York: Philosophical Library, 1950.

FRANKFORT, H. *The Problem of Similarity in Ancient Near Eastern Religions.* New York: Oxford University Press, 1951.

GOLDBERG, LOUIS. *Leviticus: A Study Guide Commentary.* Grand Rapids: Zondervan Publishing House, 1979.

GORDON, ROBERT P. "Leviticus" in *The New Layman's Bible Commentary.* Grand Rapids: Zondervan Publishing House, 1979.

HARRISON, R. K. *Leviticus: An Introduction and Commentary.* Tyndale Old Testament Commentaries. Downers Grove: Inter-Varsity Press, 1980.

KAUFMANN, Y. *The Religion of Israel.* Chicago: University of Chicago Press, 1960.

KEIL, C. F., AND F. DELITZSCH. *Commentary on the Old Testament.* Edinburgh, 1866. Reprint, Vol. II, pp. 88–486. Grand Rapids: Wm. B. Eerdmans Publishing Co., 1949.

KELLOGG, S. H. *The Book of Leviticus.* London: Hodder & Stoughton, 1899.

LINDSEY, F. DUANE. "Leviticus" in *Bible Knowledge Commentary.* Wheaton: Scripture Press, 1985.

MERRILL, EUGENE H. "Numbers" in *Bible Knowledge Commentary.* Wheaton: Scripture Press, 1985.

NOORDTZIJ, A. *Leviticus.* Grand Rapids: Zondervan Publishing House, 1982.

PFEIFFER, C. F. *The Book of Leviticus, A Study Manual.* Grand Rapids: Baker Book House, 1957.

PORTER, J. R. *Leviticus.* London: Cambridge University Press, 1976.

RAVEN, J. H. *The History of the Religion of Israel.* New Brunswick: N. B. Theological Seminary, 1933.

SCHULTZ, S. J. "Hermeneutical Principles for Interpreting The Pentateuch" in *Literature and Meaning of Scripture,* M. Inch and H. Bullock (eds.). Grand Rapids: Baker Book House, 1981.

———. *Leviticus.* Chicago: Moody Press, 1983.

WENHAM, GORDON. *The Book of Leviticus.* Grand Rapids: Wm. B. Eerdmans Publishing Co., 1979.

Chapter V

Preparation for Nationhood

In the environs of Mount Sinai Israel celebrated the first anniversary of her emancipation. Approximately a month later the people broke camp, looking forward to immediate occupation of the promised land. An eleven-day march brought them to Kadesh, where a crisis precipitated the divine verdict of prolonged wilderness wanderings. It was not until thirty-eight years later that they proceeded to the Plains of Moab (Num. 33:38) and thence into Canaan.

Organization of Israel[1]

While still stationed at Mount Sinai the Israelites received detailed instructions (Num. 1:1–10:10), many of which were directly related to their preparation for continuing the journey to Canaan. In the Bible this material is presented in a logical, rather than chronological, arrangement, as can be seen from the following outline:

I. The numbering of Israel	1:1–4:49
The military census	1:1–54
Camp assignments	2:1–34
Levites and their duties	3:1–4:49
II. Camp regulations	5:1–6:21
Restrictions of evil practices	5:1–31
Nazarite vows	6:1–21
III. Religious life of Israel	6:22–9:14
Tabernacle worship instituted	6:22–8:26
The second Passover	9:1–14

[1] For an excellent brief commentary on the book of Numbers see A. A. MacRae, "Numbers," in *The New Bible Commentary* (London, 1953), pp. 162–194.

IV. Provisions for guidance	9:15–10:10
Divine manifestations	9:15–23
Human responsibility	10:1–10

Instructions in the opening chapters pertain largely to organizational matters. Very likely the census dated in the month of Israel's departure from Mount Sinai represents a tabulation of the count taken previously (Ex. 30:11 ff.; 38:26). Whereas formerly Moses was concerned about the collection of dues for the building of the tabernacle, now he is instructed to ascertain the manpower available for military service. Excluding women, children, and Levites, the count was over 600,000. Almost four decades later, when the rebellious generation had perished in the wilderness, the figures were approximately the same (Num. 26).

The passage of so great a host of people through the wilderness transcends ordinary history.[2] Not only did this require a supernatural supply of material provisions in manna, quails, and water, but careful organization was necessary. Whether in camp or on the march, law and order was essential to Israel's national welfare.

Levites were numbered separately. Substituted for the first-born in each family, the Levites were assigned to serve under the supervision of Aaron and his sons, who had already been designated as priests. As assistants to the Aaronic priests they were given various responsibilities. Mature Levites between the ages of thirty and fifty were entrusted with special assignments in the tabernacle itself. The lower age limit, given as twenty-five in Num. 8:23–26, may have provided for a five-year period of apprenticeship.

The camp of Israel was carefully planned, with the tabernacle and its court occupying the central place. Surrounding the court were the assigned places for the Levites, while Moses and the Aaronic priests were located at the eastern end before the entrance. Beyond the Levites were four camps headed by Judah, Reuben, Ephraim, and Dan. Two additional tribes were assigned to each camp. Care and efficiency in camp organization are indicated by the assignments made to the various families of Levites: Aaron and his sons had supervision over the whole tabernacle and its court; the Gershonites cared for the curtains and coverings; the Kohathites had charge of the furniture; the Merarites were responsible for the boards and pillars. The following diagram indicates the position of each group in Israel's encampment:

[2] In a recent study of contemporary customs and an examination of the census lists in Numbers, G. E. Mendenhall suggests that " 'elef," the Hebrew word usually translated as "thousand," is a designation of some subsection of a tribe. According to this theory, Israel had nearly 600 units, furnishing an army of approximately 5,500 men. Cf. George E. Mendenhall, "The Census Lists of Numbers 1 and 26," *Journal of Biblical Literature,* LXXVII (March, 1958), 52–66.

		Asher DAN Naphtali		
		Merarites		
Manasseh EPHRAIM Benjamin	Gershonites	TABERNACLE AND COURT	Moses Aaron and Sons	Issachar JUDAH Zebulun
		Kohathites		
		Simeon REUBEN Gad		

Problems peculiar to an encampment of so populous a nation required special regulations (5:1–31). From the hygienic and ceremonial viewpoint, precautionary measures were necessary for lepers, other diseased persons, and those who cared for the deceased. Theft required an offering and restitution. Marital unfaithfulness was subject to severe punishment after an unusual test, which involved a miracle, had revealed the guilty party. With no subsequent reference to such a procedure it is reasonable to regard this as a temporary method used only during the wilderness journey.

The Nazarite vow may have been a common practice which required regulation (6:1–21). By taking this vow a person voluntarily consecrated himself for unusual service to God. Three in number were the obligations of a Nazarite: to deny himself the use of grapevine products, even grape juice and raisins; to let the hair of his head grow as a public sign that he had taken a vow; and to abstain from contact with any dead body. A severe penalty was imposed when such a vow was broken, even when it happened unintentionally. As a voluntary commitment for a stated time, this vow would be terminated only by a public ceremony at the conclusion of the prescribed period.

One of the most impressive occasions during Israel's encampment at Mount Sinai was the beginning of the second year. At that time the tabernacle with all its furnishings was erected and dedicated (Ex. 40:1–33). Additional information about this climactic event, when the tabernacle became the center of Israel's religious life, is recorded in Num. 6:22–9:14. Moses, who officiated at the initiation of tabernacle worship, conveyed to priests and people further directions from the Lord regarding their religious service (cf. 6:22; 7:89; 8:5).

The priests received a formula for blessing the congregation (Num.

6:22–27). This well-known prayer assured the Israelites not only of God's care and protection but also of prosperity and well-being.

When the tabernacle had been fully dedicated the tribal leaders presented their offerings. Anticipating the practical problems of transporting the tabernacle, six covered wagons and twelve oxen were provided for this purpose. These were assigned to the Levites in charge. For the dedication of the altar each leader brought elaborate sacrifices which were offered on twelve successive days. So significant were these gifts and offerings that each day's offerings are listed (Num. 7:10–88). Aaron was also instructed to light the lamps in the tabernacle (8:1–4).

The Levites were publicly presented and dedicated for their service in assisting the priests (8:5–26). Whereas Moses alone had officiated when Aaron and his sons were sanctified for priestly service, he was assisted by Aaron in the installation rites and ceremonies for the Levites.

The Passover, marking the first anniversary of the departure from Egypt, was observed during the first month of the second year (9:1–14). The report on this festive celebration is brief, but special emphasis is given to the requirement that everyone participate, even the strangers[3] in the camp. A special provision was made for those who were prevented from participation because of defilement, so that they could observe the Passover the second month. Since the Israelites did not break up camp until the twentieth day, everyone was able to enter into the celebration of the first Passover following the Exodus.

Before Israel broke camp and left Mount Sinai, adequate provision was made for guidance on the journey to Canaan (9:15–10:10). With the dedication of the tabernacle God's presence was visibly portrayed in the pillar of cloud and fire which could be seen both day and night. The same divine manifestation had provided protection and guidance when the people were led out of Egypt (Ex. 13:21–22; 14:19–20). When Israel encamped the cloud hovered over the holy of holies. En route the cloud led the way.

The counterpart to divine guidance was efficient human organization. The signal conveyed by the cloud was interpreted and executed by men responsible for leadership. Moses was ordered to provide two silver trumpets. The blowing of one trumpet summoned the tribal leaders to the tabernacle. The sound of both called for a public assembly of all the people. One long continuous peal from both trumpets ("sound an alarm") was the signal for the various camps to be in readiness to advance in a prearranged order. Thus the proper co-ordination of the human and the divine made it possible

[3] A stranger, in contrast to a temporary resident known as a foreigner, was a man who left his own people and sought permanent residence among another group of people (Ex. 12:19; 20:10; Deut. 5:14; 10:18; 14:29; 23:8). Cf. Ludwig Kohler, *A Dictionary of the Hebrew Old Testament in English and German* (Grand Rapids: Eerdmans, 1951), Vol. I, p. 192.

for such a large nation to proceed in an orderly manner through the wilderness.

Wilderness Wanderings

After having encamped at Mount Sinai for almost a year the Israelites proceeded northward toward the promised land. Nearly four decades later they arrived on the eastern banks of the Jordan River. Comparatively brief is the narration of their journey (Num. 10:11–22:1). It may conveniently be considered under the following subdivisions:

I. From Mount Sinai to Kadesh	Numbers	10:11–12:16
Order of procedure		10:11–35
Murmurings and judgments		11:1–12:16
II. The Kadesh crisis		13:1–14:45
The spies and their reports		13:1–33
Rebellion and judgment		14:1–45
III. The years of wandering		15:1–19:22
Laws—future and present		15:1–41
The great rebellion		16:1–50
Vindication of appointed leaders		17:1–19:22
IV. From Kadesh to the Plains of Moab		20:1–22:1
Death of Miriam		20:1
Sins of Moses and Aaron		20:2–13
Edom refuses Israel passage		20:14–21
Death of Aaron		20:22–29
Israel avenges defeat by Canaanites		21:1–3
The brazen serpent		21:4–9
March around Moab		21:10–20
Defeat of Sihon and Og		21:21–35
Arrival on the Plains of Moab		22:1

After eleven days Israel reached Kadesh in the wilderness of Paran (Deut. 1:2). Marching as an organized unit, the camp of Judah led the way, followed by the Gershonites and Merarites, who had charge of transporting the tabernacle. Next in order came the camp of Reuben. Succeeding them came the Kohathites, who carried the ark and other tabernacle furniture. Completing the procession were the camps of Ephraim and Dan. In addition to divine guidance Moses requested the aid of Hobab,[4] whose familiarity with the desert qualified him to furnish scouting service for Israel's

[4] The Hebrew word "hothen," which is usually rendered as father-in-law can also be applied to brother-in-law. This may have been applicable only after Jethro (Reuel) died and Hobab became the family leader. Cf. MacRae, *op. cit.*, p. 175.

forward march. Apparently he agreed to accompany them, since his descendants later resided in Canaan (Judg. 1:16; 4:11).

En route the Israelites complained and rebelled. Pressed and perplexed, Moses appealed to God in prayer. In response he was instructed to select seventy elders whom God endued to share his responsibilities. In addition God sent a great wind to bring an abundant supply of quails to the Israelites.[5] The intemperate and indulgent people ate them uncooked, so that the gratification of their lust became a plague which caused the death of many. Appropriately this place was named Kibroth-hattaavah, meaning "graves of lust."

Dissatisfaction and jealousy spread to the leaders. Even Aaron and Miriam questioned their brother's position of leadership.[6] Moses was vindicated when Miriam was afflicted with leprosy. Aaron repented immediately, never again to challenge his brother's authority, and through Moses' intercessory prayer Miriam was restored.

From the wilderness of Paran Moses sent twelve spies into the land of Canaan. When they returned Israel was encamped at Kadesh, approximately forty miles south and somewhat west of Beersheba. The men unanimously reported both the excellency of the land and the potential strength and ferocity of the inhabitants. But in the prospects for conquest they were not agreed. Ten declared that occupation was impossible and stirred up public sentiment for an immediate return to Egypt. Two—Joshua[7] and Caleb—confidently asserted that with divine aid conquest was possible. The people—unwilling to believe that the God who had recently delivered them from Egypt would also enable them to conquer and occupy the promised land—became an insolent mob, which threatened to stone Joshua and Caleb. In desperation they even considered selecting a new leader.

God in judgment contemplated annihilation of rebellious Israel. When Moses became aware of this he made intercession and obtained pardon for his people. Nevertheless, the ten faithless spies died in a plague and all the people aged twenty and older, excepting Joshua and Caleb, were denied entrance into Canaan. Stirred by the death of the ten spies and the verdict of a prolonged period of wilderness wanderings, they confessed their sin. That their repentance was not genuine is apparent in their rebellious attempt to

[5] These quails, a type of partridge, migrate twice a year and at times are caught in great abundance on the Mediterranean coasts or islands.

[6] This opposition was veiled in their disapproval of his marriage. It is unlikely that the complaint was against Zipporah, to whom Moses had been married more than forty years earlier. Probably Zipporah died—her death is not reported in the Bible—and Moses had married an Ethiopian woman.

[7] In listing the spies notation is made of "Joshua," former name "Hoshea." Cf. Num. 13:8, 16; Deut. 32:44. Joshua was already distinguished as a military leader (Ex. 17) and servant of Moses (Num. 11:28).

enter Palestine immediately. In this they were defeated by the Amalekites and Canaanites.

While the Israelites marked time in the wilderness (15:1–20:13), an entire generation died. The laws in Num. 15, perhaps given soon after this punitive verdict had been announced, show the contrast between judgment for willful sin and mercy for the repentant individual who has sinned in ignorance. In addition, the instructions for sacrifice in Canaan provide a hope for the younger generation in their anticipation of actually living in the land promised to them.

The great rebellion led by Korah, Dathan, and Abiram represents two mutinous groups, mutually strengthened through their co-operative effort (Num. 16:1–50).[8] The ecclesiastical leadership of the Aaronic family, to whom the priesthood was restricted, was challenged by Korah and supporting Levites. The political authority of Moses was called into question by Dathan and Abiram, who aspired to his position by virtue of being descendants of Reuben, the oldest son of Jacob.

In divine judgment both Moses and Aaron were vindicated. The earth opened to swallow up Dathan and Abiram together with their families. Korah vanished with them.[9] Before this rebellion completely subsided more than 14,000 people had perished in the camp of Israel.

After the death of the insurrectionists Israel received a miraculous sign precluding any further desire to question the authority of their leaders (17:1–11). Among twelve rods, each representing a tribe, the rod of Levi produced buds, blossoms, and almonds. In addition to confirming Moses and Aaron in their divine appointments, the inscription of Aaron's name on this rod specifically designated him as the priest of Israel. Preservation of this rod in the tabernacle served as permanent evidence of God's will.

To alleviate the fears of the people in approaching the tabernacle, the responsibilities of the priests and Levites were reaffirmed and clearly delineated (17:12–18:32). The priesthood was restricted to Aaron and his family. The Levites were designated as servants of the priests. Provision for their livelihood was made through the tithe given by the people. The Levites in turn gave a tenth of their income to the priests. For this reason the Levites were not to be included in the allotment of land when the Israelites settled in Canaan.

The pollution resulting from the plague and the burial of so many people at one time necessitated a special ceremony for the purification of the

[8] For a detailed analysis see MacRae, *op. cit.*, pp. 182–183.

[9] The difference in the attitudes of the two groups may account for the fact that Korah's family did not perish with him. His descendants occupy an honored place in later times. Samuel ranks perhaps next to Moses as a great prophet. Heman, a grandson of Samuel, was an outstanding singer during David's reign. A number of psalms are designated as "for the sons of Korah."

camp (19:1–22). Eleazar, a son of Aaron, officiated. This ritual, which impressively reminded the Israelites of the nature of death (5:1–4) and provided hygienic protection, was ordained as a permanent statute.

Experiences of the Israelites as they journeyed via Ezion-geber and Elath to the Plains of Moab are summarized in Num. 20:1–22:1. Prior to their departure from Kadesh Miriam died. When the people contended with Moses because of water shortage, he was instructed to command a rock to supply water. Irate and impatient, Moses smote the rock and water gushed forth in abundance. But for his disobedience he was denied entrance into Canaan.

From Kadesh Moses sent messengers to the king of Edom requesting permission to march through their land on the King's Highway. Not only was this request denied but the Edomite army was sent to guard the border. This unfriendly attitude was frequently denounced by the prophets.[10]

Before Israel left the Edomite border Aaron died on top of Mount Hor. Eleazar was vested in his father's garments and appointed high priest in Israel. Before proceeding Israel was attacked by a Canaanite king, but God granted victory. This place was named Hormah.

Realizing that they were moving southward around Edom the people became impatient and complained against God as well as Moses. Divine punishment came in a scourge of serpents, causing many Israelites to die.[11] Penitent, the people turned to Moses, who provided relief through the erection of a bronze serpent. Anyone bitten by a serpent was healed by a look at the serpent of brass. Jesus used this incident as a symbol of his death on the cross, applying the same principle—anyone who turned to him would not perish but have eternal life (John 3:14–16).

Israel moved southward by way of Elath and Ezion-geber, circumventing Edom as well as Moab and proceeding north to the Arnon valley. The three accounts as given in Numbers (21 and 33) and Deuteronomy (2) refer to various places not identifiable today. Israel was forbidden to fight against the Moabites and the Ammonites, the descendants of Lot. However, when the two Amorite rulers—Sihon, king of Heshbon, and Og, king of Bashan—refused Israel passage and responded with an army, the Israelites defeated them and occupied their land north of the valley of Arnon. Here on the Plains of Moab, recently taken by the Amorites, the Israelites established their camp.

Instructions for Entering Canaan

While encamped northeast of the Dead Sea, the nation of Israel re-

[10] Cf. Is. 34:1–17; Jer. 49:7–22; Ezek. 25:12–14; 35:1–15.

[11] For modern occurrences of similar scourges see T. E. Lawrence, *The Seven Pillars of Wisdom*, pp. 269–270.

ceived final instructions for the conquest and occupation of the promised land. The providential care of Israel in the shadows of Moab and the careful preparation of the people on the eve of their entrance into Canaan are recorded in Num. 22–36. The various aspects of this provision may be observed in the following outline:

I. Preservation of God's chosen people	22:2–25:18
Balak's design to curse Israel	22:2–40
Balaam's blessings	22:41–24:24
Seduction and judgment	24:25–25:18
II. Preparation for conquest	26:1–33:49
The new generation	26:1–65
Inheritance problems	27:1–11
A new leader	27:12–23
Sacrifices and vows	28:1–30:16
Vengeance on the Midianites	31:1–54
Transjordan apportioned	32:1–42
Review of Israel's journey	33:1–49
III. Anticipation of occupation	33:50–36:13
The land to be conquered	33:50–34:15
Leaders appointed for allotting the land	34:16–29
Levitical and refuge cities	35:1–34
Inheritance regulations	36:1–13

The subtle designs of the Moabites on God's chosen nation were more formidable than open warfare (22:2–25:18). Overcome with fear when the Amorites were defeated, Balak, the Moabite king, devised plans for the destruction of Israel. In co-operation with the elders of Midian he engaged the prophet Balaam from Mesopotamia to curse the people encamped across the Arnon River.

Balaam refused the first invitation, being explicitly warned not to go and not to curse Israel. The fees for divination, however, were so enticing that he yielded to Balak's repeated appeal. On this mission, which was contrary to God's clearly revealed will, Balaam had the shocking experience of being audibly rebuked by his donkey. The prophet was thus impressively reminded that he was going to Moab to speak only God's message.[12]

Balaam faithfully declared God's message four times. On three different mountains Balak and his princes prepared offerings to provide an atmosphere for cursing, but each time the prophet spoke words of blessing. Keenly dis-

[12] MacRae, *op. cit.*, p. 188, suggests that Balak provided a feast to celebrate Balaam's coming, Num. 22:40. The Hebrew word "Zabah" translated "offered" in AV and "sacrificed" in ASV and RSV is better rendered "killed," as in Deut. 12:15, 21; I Sam. 28:24; II Chron. 18:2, and Ezek. 34:3, or "slew," as in I Kings 1:9, 19, 25; 19:21; and II Kings 23:20.

appointed, the Moabite king rebuked him and ordered him to cease. Although Balak dismissed him without a reward, Balaam uttered a fourth prophecy before he left. In this he distinctly delineated Israel's future victories over Moab, Edom, and Amalek.[13]

Balak was more successful in his next scheme against Israel. Instead of returning to his Mesopotamian home, Balaam remained with the Midianites and offered evil counsel to Balak (31:16). The Moabites and Midianites followed his advice and seduced many Israelites into immorality and idolatry. Through the worship of Baal-peor with immoral rites, the participants incurred divine wrath. In order to save a greater number of people from judgment, the guilty Israelite leaders were immediately hanged. Phinehas, a son of Eleazar, displayed great zeal in counteracting those who precipitated this plague in which thousands died. Subsequently the descendants of Phinehas served as priests in Israel. The command to punish the Midianites for their demoralizing influence upon Israel was executed under the leadership of Moses (31:1-54). Not least among the fatalities of notable leaders was Balaam, the son of Beor.

After this crisis Moses made preparation to condition his people for the conquest of Canaan. The census taken under the supervision of Eleazar was in part a military appraisal of Israel's manpower (26:1-65). The total count was actually somewhat lower than the count taken nearly forty years earlier. Joshua was appointed and publicly consecrated as the new leader (27:12-23). The solution given to the inheritance problem raised by the daughters of Zelophehad (27:1-11) indicated God's will that the promised land be kept in small holdings and passed on to the heirs. Additional instructions are also given concerning regular offerings, festivals, and the keeping of vows after settlement in the land of promise (28:1-30:16).

Seeing that the land east of the Jordan was excellent grazing territory, the tribes of Reuben and Gad appealed to Moses for permission to settle there permanently. Reluctantly he granted their request. To make sure that the conquest of Canaan would not be jeopardized by lack of co-operation, however, he exacted a pledge of their support. This verbal commitment was publicly repeated two times. The land of Gilead was then alloted to Reuben, Gad, and half of the Manasseh tribe (32:1-42).

Moses also prepared a written report on Israel's journey through the wilderness (Num. 33:2). Because of his training and experience it seems reasonable to assume that he kept accurate records of this eventful trek from Egypt to Canaan for the consideration of posterity (33:1-49).

Looking forward Moses anticipated the needs of the Israelites when they would enter Canaan (33:50-36:13). He admonished them to destroy

[13] Agag in 24:7 perhaps was a general name for an Amalekite king similar to Pharaoh for the Egyptian ruler.

the idolatrous inhabitants and possess their land. In addition to Joshua and Eleazar ten tribal leaders were assigned the responsibility of dividing the land to the remaining nine and a half tribes. None of the princes, listed in Num. 1, nor any of their sons are in this new group. In lieu of land, forty-eight cities located throughout Canaan are designated for the Levites. Cities of refuge, designed to prevent the starting of blood feuds, are described by Moses. Before his death he set aside three cities east of the Jordan for this purpose (Deut. 4:41-43).[14] In the final chapter of Numbers Moses deals with the problem of inheritance, limiting women who inherit land to marriage with members of their own tribe.

Retrospect and Prospect

Moses was aware of the fact that his ministry was nearly completed. Although not permitted to enter the promised land, he coveted God's blessing for the Israelites who anticipated the privilege of conquest and possession. As a faithful leader he appeals to this new generation—none of whom were over sixty years of age, excepting Joshua and Caleb. The words of Moses, constituting the book of Deuteronomy, may be considered under the following outline:

I. Appeal to learn from the past	1:1-4:43
Introduction and historical context	1:1-5
Failure to trust God—thirty-eight years of wandering	1:6-2:23
Conquest and allotment	2:24-3:29
God's unique revelation to Israel	4:1-40
Cities of refuge	4:41-43
II. Appeal to love God	4:44-11:33
The law with Moses as mediator	4:44-5:33
The Israel—God relationship	6:1-11:32
Wholehearted love Godward	6:1-9
God will provide the land	6:10-7:26
Lessons from the wilderness experience	8:1-10:10
Exclusive wholehearted love	10:11-11:32
III. Appeal to live as God's people	12:1-26:15
Holiness in worship—love for fellowmen	12:1-16:17
Jurisdiction, covenant obligations, and kingship	16:18-17:20
Priests and prophets vs religion of the Canaanites	18:1-22
Legal procedures	19:1-21

[14] Num. 35:9–34 is the fullest description for the cities of refuge; supplementary information is given in Deut. 19:1–13. Joshua designated three cities west of the Jordan for this purpose (Josh. 20:1–9).

War, murder, and family affairs	20:1-21:23
Miscellaneous laws	22:1-25:19
IV. Renewal of the covenant	27:1-29:1
V. A choice of life or death	29:2-30:20
VI. Continuity of the covenant—Moses to Joshua	31:1-34:12

The book of Deuteronomy represents a renewal of the covenant between God and Israel, which had been established at Mount Sinai (identified as Mount Horeb in Exodus 3:1, 17:6, and 33:6; and all references in Deuteronomy except 33:2).[15] The source of this was in God, whose acts of loving kindness in the exodus experience were initiated by His love for Israel. The essence of the covenant lies in the relationship between God and Israel with the operative principle being love. It is only as man or the individual Israelite responded to the love initiated by God to man that the relationship became operative.

Against the background of the failure of the previous generation that died in the wilderness, Moses appeals to the Israelites to love God—love Him exclusively, wholeheartedly, without reservation, "with all your heart, with all your soul, with all your strength" (6:5). Love was not a matter of legalistic obedience to the ten commandments or the law as a whole. Love was a living relationship involving a loving commitment and wholehearted devotion to God.

God's love had been extended to the Israelites beginning with Abraham, Isaac, and Jacob (4:37), and displayed in Israel's liberation from Egyptian bondage. This God—"I am the Lord your God who brought you out of Egypt"—the Israelites were to love exclusively—"you shall have no other gods beside me" (5:6-7).

Although Moses repeats the ten commandments, his focal point throughout this appeal is the first commandment, which involves exclusive love and devotion Godward. Moses does not express a legalistic concern about details of sacrifice, feasts, and seasons, or the priesthood and tabernacle as delineated in Exodus, Leviticus, and Numbers. Love for God is to be expressed in the total pattern of living, 10:12-13. Obedience issues out of love for God. Reverence issues out of respect for God. That Moses is emphasizing a spiritual relationship is apparent in his admonition to "circumcise your hearts . . . do not be stiffnecked" (10:16).

[15] Increasingly, studies in Deuteronomy give recognition to the overall literary structure of the book as a form of ancient Near Eastern vassal treaties. Considering Deuteronomy as a literary account of the renewal of the covenant with the essential parts of standard treaty patterns, Meredith Kline in *The Structure of Biblical Authority* offers the following outline: Preamble 1:1-5; Historical Prologue 1:6-4:49; Stipulations 5-26; Curses and Blessings or Covenant Ratification 27-30; Succession Arrangements or Covenant Continuity 31-34. For further discussion of Old Testament studies on Deuteronomy as a fourteenth/thirteenth century B.C. literary composition and a reasonable delineation of Mosaic authorship of the Pentateuch, see R. K. Harrison, *Introduction to the Old Testament,* pp. 1-662. Cf. also P. C. Craigie, *The Book of Deuteronomy,* pp. 17-86.

No area of living was beyond this relationship established in this covenant. The variety of legislation delineated in Deuteronomy 12–26 is a mixture of religious, ceremonial, criminal, and civil laws providing guidance for the Israelites in living as God's holy people in their contemporary culture. All of life was under God's dominion. The claim that they had a love relationship with God was to be evident in their pattern of behavior as provided in these specific stipulations.

Unique in Israelite history is the appeal Moses makes to his audience on the plains of Moab as he leads them in their renewal of the covenant. Their decision—choosing life and good or death and evil (30:15–20)—is ultimately a matter of basic importance. Providing a written copy of the law deposited with the priests for public reading every seven years, Moses turns the leadership over to Joshua. The covenant ceremony is concluded with the song of Moses, chapter 32. Anticipating the conquest and occupation of the promised land by the Israelites, Moses encourages them with his final blessing (chapter 33). Before his death he is privileged to view the promised land from Mount Nebo.

SELECTED READING

CRAIGIE, PETER C. *The Book of Deuteronomy.* Grand Rapids: Wm. B. Eerdmans Publishing Co., 1976.

DEERE, JOHN S. Deuteronomy. *Bible Knowledge Commentary.* Wheaton: Scripture Press, 1985.

KITCHEN, K. A. *Ancient Orient and Old Testament.* Chicago: Inter-Varsity Press, 1966.

KLINE, M. G. *Treaty of the Great King.* Grand Rapids: Wm. B. Eerdmans Publishing Co., 1963.

MAYES, A. D. H. Deuteronomy. *New Century Bible Commentary.* Grand Rapids: W. B. Eerdmans Publishing Co., 1981.

SCHULTZ, S. J. *Deuteronomy—Gospel of Love.* Chicago: Moody Press, 1973.

———. *The Gospel of Moses.* Chicago: Moody Press, 1979.

———. *The Prophets Speak.* New York: Harper & Row, 1968.

THOMPSON, J. A. *Deuteronomy.* Downers Grove: Inter-Varsity Press, 1974.

WENHAM, GORDON J. *Numbers: An Introduction and Commentary.* Downers Grove: Inter-Varsity Press, 1981.

Chart III ESTABLISHMENT OF ISRAEL IN CANAAN

Egypt*		Canaan		Other Nations	
1417	Amen-hotep III	1406	*Joshua* as leader Conquest Division Last days		Hittite advance from the north neutralized Egyptian influence
		1376	*Elders* of Israel		
1379	Amen-hotep IV Akh-en-Aton	1366	Oppression by Mesopotamians	1366	Cushan-Rishathaim in Mesopotamia
1361	Tut-ankh-Amon	1358	Othniel—deliverance and rest forty years	1358	
1348	Harmhab				
		1318	Oppression by Moab		Eglon, king of Moab
1318	Seti I—punitive expeditions into Palestine	1301	*Ehud*—deliverance and peace for eighty years		
1304–1237	Ramses II			1286	Battle of Kadesh
				1280	Hittite-Egyptian non-aggression pact
	Mer-ne-Ptah and others	1221	Oppression by Canaanites	1221	Canaanite Kingdom (Hazor)—King Jabin
1200–	Ramses III–XI	1201	*Deborah* and *Barak*—deliverance and 40-year peace		
		1161	Oppression by Midianites	1161	Midianites oppress Israel; occupy valley of Jezreel
		1154	Gideon—deliverance and 40-year peace	1128	Ammonite advance and oppression east of Jordan
		1114	Abimelech—king for three years		
		1111–1105	Jephthah—6-year rule ending oppression	1105	Philistine oppression
				1100	Tiglath-pileser I in Assyria
1085	21st Dynasty		Samson's judgeship about twenty years during this period		
		1066	(?) Eli		
		1046	(?) Samuel		
	22nd Dynasty	1026	(?) Saul		
		1011	David	1000	Ashur-rabi II in Assyria
		971	Solomon	969–936	Hiram in Phoenicia
945	Shishak				
		931	Division of the Kingdom		

* For the revised dates on Egyptian rulers see the article on "Chronology" prepared by the late William Christopher Hayes for the revised *Cambridge Ancient History,* I, Chapter VI. This was published by the Syndies of the Cambridge University Press in 1964 as a Synopsis of Volume I, Chapter VI. Cf. also the article by M. B. Rowton "The Material from Western Asia and the Chronology of the Nineteenth Dynasty" in *Journal of Near Eastern Studies,* Vol. 25, No. 4, 1966, pp. 240–258.

Chapter VI

Occupation of Canaan

The long-awaited day had arrived. With the death of Moses Joshua was commissioned to lead the nation of Israel in the conquest of Palestine. Centuries had passed since the patriarchs had been promised that their descendants would inherit the land of Canaan. In the meantime each successive generation of the Palestinian populace had been influenced by various peoples from the Fertile Crescent. Motivated by economic and military interests, they traversed Canaan from time to time.

Memoirs of Canaan

In the heyday of military success the powerful Twelfth Dynasty (2000–1780 B.C.) spasmodically extended Egyptian control through Palestine as far north as the Euphrates. In the subsequent decades Egypt not only declined in power but was occupied by the powerful Hyksos, who ruled from Avaris in the Delta. Shortly before 1550 B.C. the rule of the Hyksos intruders was terminated in the land of the Nile.

The Hittite kingdom had its beginning in Asia Minor as early as the nineteenth century B.C. Referred to as the "children of Heth" in the Old Testament, the Hittites are frequently mentioned as occupants of Canaan. By 1600 their power had so increased in Asia Minor that they extended their domain into Syria and even destroyed Babylon on the Euphrates by 1550 B.C. Within the following century the expansion of Hittite rule was halted by two rising kingdoms.

About the time that the Hyksos people were invading Egypt and Babylonia was flourishing under the First Dynasty best exemplified by Hammurapi, the new kingdom of Mitanni emerged in the highlands of Media. These Indo-Iranian people were composed of two groups: the common class, known as Hurrians, and the nobility, or ruling class, called Aryans. Coming from the territory east of Haran these Mitanni people continually extended their kingdom westward so that by 1500 B.C. they reached the Mediterranean Sea. The chief sport of the Aryan people was horse racing. Treatises written on the subject of raising and training horses were discovered early in the present century at Boghazköy, where they had been preserved by the Hittites who conquered the Mitanni people. By 1500 B.C., the Mitanni power halted the advance of the Hittites for about a century.

The Egyptians frequently marched their armies through Canaan to challenge Mitanni might. Thut-mose III made seventeen or eighteen campaigns into the regions of Syria and beyond. During the first attempts toward Asiatic conquest a Syrian confederacy, supported by the king of Kadesh (located on the Orontes River), withstood the Egyptian advance. Very likely the land of Syria—a land with prosperous cities, fertile plains, rich mineral wealth and other natural resources, and vital trade routes linking the flourishing Nile and Euphrates valleys—had been under Mitanni sway. After the defeat of the Syrians at Megiddo, Egyptian control expanded into Syria. For a short while the Mitanni seemed to bolster Kadesh as a buffer state, but eventually Thut-mose III marched his armies across the Euphrates and temporarily ended Mitanni dominion in Syria. When Thut-mose died, virtually all of Syria was under Egyptian rule.

Friction continued between Egyptian and Mitanni might during the reigns of Amen-hotep II (1450–1425) and Thut-mose IV (1425–1417) so that Syria vacillated in its allegiance. Although Saushshatar, king of Mitanni, extended his power eastward as far as Ashur and on beyond the Tigris River, his son Artatama seems to have been subjected to pressure from the Hittite power. This threat may have caused Artatama I to make a peaceful agreement with Thut-mose IV. Under the terms of this policy Mitannian princesses were married to Pharaohs during three successive reigns. At this time Damascus was under Egyptian administration. The Amarna letters (*ca.* 1400 B.C.) reflect the conditions in Syria indicating that diplomatic and fraternal relationships existed between the royal families of Mitanni and Egypt.

Hittite power soon increased and challenged this Mitanni-Egyptian control of the Fertile Crescent. Under King Shuppiluliume (*ca.* 1380–1346) the Hittites crossed the Euphrates as far as Washshukkanni, reducing Mitanni to a buffer state between the Hittite kingdom and the rising Assyrian empire in the Tigris Valley. This, of course, eliminated Mitanni as a political factor in Palestine. Although the Mitanni kingdom was completely absorbed by the Assyrians (*ca.* 1250 B.C.), the Hurrians, known as Horites in the Old Testament, were in Canaan when the Israelites entered. Possibly the Hivites were also of Mitanni origin.

With the elimination of the Mitanni threat the Hittites looked southward. For about a century the Hittites, from their capital at Boghazköy, and the Egyptians vied for control of the vacillating frontier of Syria. During this period Kadesh became the center of a revived Amorite kingdom. Very likely it adopted a policy of expediency in maintaining friendship with the strongest power.

When Ramses II (1304–1237 B.C.) came to the throne the Egyptians renewed their efforts to eliminate the Hittites from northern Palestine in order to recover their Asiatic possessions. Mutwatallis, the Hittite king, was firmly entrenched in the city of Kadesh and supported by armies from Syrian cities as well as Carchemish, Ugarit, and other towns in this area. Ramses extended his boundary up to Beirut at the expense of the Phoenicians and then marched up the Orontes to Kadesh, confronting an enemy that engaged the Egyptians in warfare for almost two decades. This battle of Kadesh in 1286 B.C. was far from decisive for the Egyptians. After numerous other conquests of cities in Canaan and Syria, Ramses II and Hattusil, the Hittite king, concluded a treaty in 1280 B.C.—an outstanding nonaggression pact in history. Copies of this famous agreement have been found in Babylonia, Boghazköy, and Egypt. Although no actual boundaries are mentioned in the treaty, very likely the Amorite state formed the neutralizing influence between the Egyptians and the Hittites.

In the days of Merneptah invaders from the north known as Aryans destroyed the Hittite empire and weakened the Amorites, destroying Kadesh and other strongholds. Although the Hittite kingdom disintegrated, the Hittites are frequently mentioned in the Old Testament. Ramses III repulsed these invaders from the north in a great battle by land and sea and once more unified Palestine under Egyptian control. After Ramses III Egyptian power declined, allowing for the infiltration of the Arameans into the area of Syria, which became a powerful nation about two centuries later.

The people of Canaan were not organized into strong political units. Geographical factors as well as the pressure of surrounding nations from the Fertile Crescent, who used Canaan as a buffer territory, account for the fact that the Canaanites never formed a strong united empire. Numerous city-states controlled as much local territory as possible, with the city well fortified to resist possible enemy attack. When armies marched through Canaan, these cities often averted attack by the payment of tribute. However, when people came in to occupy the land, as Israel did under Joshua, these city-states formed leagues and united in opposing the invader. This is well illustrated in the Book of Joshua.

The location of Palestine in the Fertile Crescent and the geographical configuration of the land itself often affected its cultural and political developments. Upon the alluvial plain of the Tigris and Euphrates as well as in the Nile Valley numerous petty city-kingdoms and small principalities or districts were more than once united into one great nation. This was not so easily accomplished in Syria-Palestine, since the topography was nonconducive to amalgamation. As a result Canaan was in a weaker condition, since none of the city-kingdoms were equal in strength to the invading forces that came from the stronger kingdoms along the Nile or the Euphrates. At the same time Canaan was the coveted prize of these stronger nations. Being located between the two great centers of civilization, Canaan with its fertile valleys was frequently subject to invasion by the stronger powers. Kinglets not strong enough to withstand the invading force might find it expedient momentarily to humble themselves by paying tribute to such a kingdom as Egypt. Often, however, when the invader withdrew the "gifts" were discontinued. Although these city-kingdoms were easily conquered, it was difficult for the victors to retain them as permanent possessions.

The religion of Canaan was polytheistic.[1] El was considered the chief among the Canaanitic deities. Likened to a bull in a herd of cows, the people referred to him as "father bull" and regarded him as creator. Asherah was the wife of El. In the days of Elijah, Jezebel sponsored four hundred prophets of Asherah (I Kings 18:19). King Manasseh placed her image in the temple (II Kings 21:7). Chief among the seventy gods and goddesses that were considered offspring of El and Asherah was Hadad, more commonly known as Baal, meaning "Lord." As reigning king of the gods he controlled heaven and earth. As god of rain and storm he was responsible for vegetation and fertility. Anath, the goddess who loved war, was his sister as well as his spouse. In the ninth century Ashtoreth, or Astarte, goddess of the evening star, was worshiped as his wife. Mot, the god of death, was the chief enemy of Baal. Yomm, the god of the sea, was defeated by Baal. These and many other gods introduce the catalogue of the Canaanitic pantheon.

Since the gods of the Canaanites had no moral character, it is not surprising that the morality of the people was extremely low. The brutality and immorality in the stories about these gods is far worse than anything found in the Near East. Since this was reflected in the Canaanitic society, the Canaanites in Joshua's day practiced child sacrifice, sacred prostitution, and snake worship in their rites and ceremonies associated with religion. Naturally their civilization degenerated under this demoralizing influence.

The Scriptures attest this sordid condition by numerous prohibitions given as warnings to the Israelites.[2] This degrading religious influence was already apparent in the days of Abraham (Gen. 15:16; 19:5). Centuries later Moses solemnly charged his people to destroy the Canaanites—not only

[1] For further information see G. E. Wright, *Biblical Archaeology,* pp. 98–119.

[2] Until 1930 the only secular source concerning this religious condition of the Canaanites was Philo of Byblus, a Phoenician scholar who wrote a history of the Phoenicians and Canaanites. Cf. Merrill F. Unger, *Archeology and the Old Testament,* pp. 167 ff.

to punish them for their iniquity but to prevent the contamination of God's chosen people (Lev. 18:24–28; 20–23; Deut. 12:31; 20:17–18).

Era of Conquest

Experience and training had prepared Joshua for the challenging assignment of conquering Canaan. At Rephidim he led the Israelite army in defeating Amalek (Ex. 17:8–16). As a spy he gained firsthand knowledge of the existing conditions in Palestine (Num. 13–14).

Under Moses' tutelage Joshua was trained for leadership and prepared for directing the conquest and occupation of the promised land.

As was the case in the account of the wilderness sojourn, the record of Joshua's activity is incomplete. No mention is made of the conquest of the Shechem area between Mount Ebal and Mount Gerizim, but it was here that Joshua assembled all Israel to listen to the reading of the law of Moses (Josh. 8:30–35). Very likely many other local areas were conquered and occupied, although not mentioned in Joshua. During the lifetime of Joshua the land of Canaan was possessed by the Israelites but by no means were all the inhabitants driven out. Thus, the Book of Joshua must be considered as only a partial account of Joshua's enterprise. It lends itself to the following subdivisions:

I. Entrance into Canaan	1:1–4:24
Joshua assumes leadership	1:1–18
Two spies sent to Jericho	2:1–24
Passage over Jordan	3:1–17
Memorials	4:1–24
II. Defeat of opposing forces	5:1–12:24
Preparation for conquest	5:1–15
Central campaign—Jericho and Ai	6:1–8:35
Southern campaign—Amorite league	9:1–10:43
Northern campaign—Canaanite league	11:1–15
Tabulation of the conquest	11:16–12:24
III. Allotment of Canaan	13:1–24:33
Plan for division	13:1–14:15
Tribal allotment	15:1–19:51
Refuge and Levite cities	20:1–21:45
Farewell and death of Joshua	22:1–24:33

The length of time allotted to the conquest and division of Canaan is not stated. Assuming that Joshua was Caleb's age, the events recorded in the Book of Joshua occurred in a period of twenty-five to thirty years.[3]

[3] Joshua spent 40 years in the wilderness (Josh. 5:6). He died at the age of 110 (24:29). Caleb was 40 years old when Moses sent Joshua and Caleb as spies (14:7–10).

Entrance into Canaan

As Joshua assumed leadership of Israel he was assured of the full support of the armed forces of the Reubenites, Gadites, and the tribe of Manasseh, who had settled east of the Jordan in the inheritance allotted to them before Moses' death. It seems quite reasonable to assume that the pledge of support in Josh. 1:16–18 is the response of the whole nation of Israel as Joshua issued the orders for preparation to pass over Jordan. Two spies were then dispatched to Jericho to view the land. From Rahab, who harbored these spies, it was learned that the inhabitants of Canaan were conscious of Israel's God, who had supernaturally intervened for Israel. After a narrow escape the two men returned, assuring Joshua and Israel that the Lord had paved the way to a victorious conquest (Josh. 2:1–24).

As a visible confirmation of the promise that God would be with Joshua as he had been with Moses, and the additional assurance of victory in Palestine, God provided a miraculous passage through Jordan. This constituted a reasonable basis for every Israelite to exercise a faith in God (Josh. 3:7–13). With the priests who carried the ark leading the way and standing in the midst of the Jordan, the Israelites passed through on dry ground.

How the waters were stopped to make this passage possible is not stated in the record. Certain facts stated are, however, significant for consideration. The place of crossing is identified as "over against Jericho," which would be approximately five miles north of the Dead Sea. The waters were cut off or stopped at Adam, which today is identified with ed Damieh, located 20 miles from the Dead Sea or about 15 miles from where Israel actually crossed.[4] The Jordan follows a course of 200 miles in the 60-mile distance between the Sea of Galilee and the Dead Sea, descending 600 feet. At Adam limestone cliffs overhang the banks of the stream. As recently as 1927 part of a cliff 150 feet high fell into the Jordan, blocking the water for twenty-one and a half hours. Whether or not God caused this to occur when Israel passed over the river bed is not stated. But, since God employed natural means to accomplish his will on other occasions (Ex. 14:21), the possibility exists that an earthquake might have been the means of causing an obstruction at that time.

Provision was also made that Israel should not forget this great event. Two memorials were erected for this purpose. Under the supervision of Joshua twelve stones were piled up to mark the place where the priests stood with the ark of the covenant in the midst of the Jordan while the people of Israel marched across the river, Josh. 4:9. At Gilgal a second memorial cairn was erected, Josh. 4:3, 8, and 20. Twelve men representing the tribes of Israel carried twelve stones to Gilgal for this memorial which reminded

[4] Cf. J. Garstang, *Joshua Judges* (London: Constable, 1931), pp. 136–137.

coming generations of the miraculous provision that had been made for the Israelites in crossing the Jordan River. In this way God's mighty acts were to be remembered among the Israelites for years to come.

The Conquest

Encamped at Gilgal, Israel was realistically prepared for living in Canaan as God's chosen nation. For forty years, while the unbelieving generation died in the wilderness, circumcision as a sign of the covenant relationship (Gen. 17:1–27) had not been observed. Through this rite the new generation was painfully reminded of the covenant and of the promise God had made to bring them into the land "flowing with milk and honey." Entrance into the land was also marked by the Passover observance and cessation of the provision of manna. The redeemed people would henceforth eat of the fruits of the land.

Joshua himself was prepared for conquest through an experience similar to that which Moses had when God called him (Ex. 3). By a theophany God imparted to Joshua the consciousness that the conquest of the land was not dependent solely upon him but that he was divinely commissioned and empowered. Even though he was in charge of Israel, Joshua was but a servant and subject to the commander of the army of the Lord (Josh. 5:13–15).

The conquest of Jericho was a sample victory.[5] Israel did not attack the city according to regular military strategy but simply followed the instructions of the Lord. Once a day for six days the Israelites marched around the city. On the seventh day when they marched around it seven times the walls of the city fell and they could enter and take possession. But the Israelites were not allowed to appropriate any of the spoils for themselves. The things that were not destroyed—metallic objects—were placed in the treasury of the Lord. Except for Rahab and her father's household, the inhabitants of Jericho were wiped out.

The miraculous conquest of Jericho was a convincing demonstration to the Israelites that their enemies could be overwhelmed. Ai was the next objective for conquest. Following the advice of his reconnaissance party Joshua sent an army of three thousand men, which suffered a severe defeat. Prayerful investigation by Joshua and the elders revealed the fact that Achan had sinned in the conquest of Jericho by appropriating for himself an attractive garment of Mesopotamian origin plus some silver and gold. For this deliberate act in defiance of the command to devote all the spoils to the Lord, Achan and his family were stoned in the valley of Achor.

Assured of success, Joshua renewed his plans to conquer Ai. Contrary to their previous procedure, the Israelites were to seize the livestock and other movable property. The enemy forces were lured into the open so that

[5] For discussion of the date of Jericho's fall see chap. III in this volume.

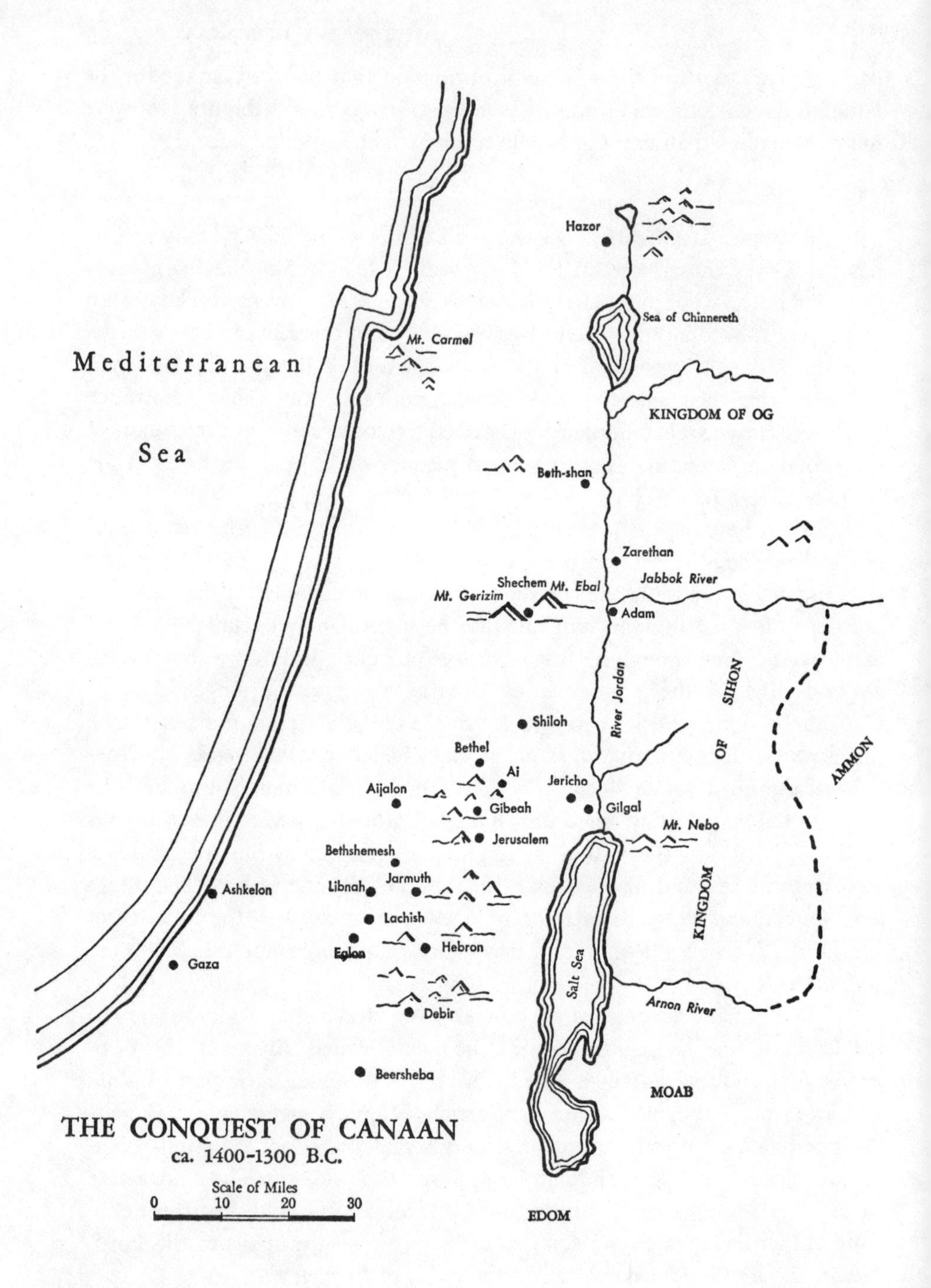

Hazor
Sea of Chinnereth
Mt. Carmel
Mediterranean
Sea
KINGDOM OF OG
Beth-shan
Zarethan
Jabbok River
Shechem
Mt. Ebal
Mt. Gerizim
Adam
River Jordan
KINGDOM OF SIHON
AMMON
Shiloh
Bethel
Ai
Aijalon
Jericho
Gibeah
Gilgal
Mt. Nebo
Jerusalem
Bethshemesh
Ashkelon
Libnah
Jarmuth
Lachish
Hebron
Eglon
Gaza
Salt Sea
Arnon River
Debir
Beersheba
MOAB
THE CONQUEST OF CANAAN
ca. 1400-1300 B.C.
Scale of Miles
0
10
20
30
EDOM

the thirty thousand men who had been stationed beyond the city by night were able to attack Ai from the rear and set it afire. The defenders were annihilated, their king was hanged, and the site was reduced to rubble.

Wright identifies et Tell, located one and a half miles southeast of Bethel, as the location of Ai. Excavations at this site indicate that et Tell flourished as a Canaanite fortress *ca.* 3300–2400 B.C. Subsequently it was destroyed and lay in ruins until about 1000 B.C. Bethel, however, was a flourishing city during this time and, according to Albright who excavated there in 1934, was destroyed during the thirteenth century. Since nothing is stated in the Book of Joshua about its destruction, Wright suggests three possible explanations: (1) the story of Ai is a later invention to account for the ruins; (2) the people of Bethel used Ai as a military outpost; (3) Albright's theory that the story of the conquest of Bethel was later transferred to Ai. Wright supports the last theory, assuming the late date of exodus and conquest.[6]

Recently, David Livingston has proposed an unnamed tel located 1½ miles from Bireh as the site of Ai, based on his suggestion that Bireh rather than Baitin be identified with Bethel. Since neither Bireh nor the unnamed tel have been excavated, these identifications are theoretical. After examining the above mentioned theories of identification, Bimson concludes that Ai continues to remain an anomaly.[7]

Although nothing is definitely stated about the conquest of Bethel, this city, which figures so prominently in Old Testament times from the days of Abraham's entrance into Canaan, is mentioned in Josh. 8:9, 12, and 17. A reasonable inference is that the Bethelites were involved in this battle of Ai. No claim is made for its destruction, but the king of Bethel is listed as having been killed (Josh. 12:16). The spies sent to Ai convey the impression that Ai was not very large (Josh. 7:3). Later, when Israel makes its second attack, the people of Ai as well as the inhabitants of Bethel vacate their cities to pursue the enemy (Josh. 8: 17). It is probable that only Ai was destroyed at this time and Bethel was occupied without destruction. The thirteenth-century conflagration may be identified with the account given in Judg. 1:22–26, subsequent to the time of Joshua.

Following this great victory, the Israelites erected an altar on Mount Ebal in order to present their offerings to the Lord, according to the command of Moses. Here Joshua made a copy of the law of Moses. With Israel divided so that one half of the people stood in front of Mount Ebal and the other half in front of Mount Gerizim facing the ark, the law of Moses was read to the people (Josh. 8:30–35). Thus the Israelites were solemnly reminded of their responsibilities as they were on the verge of occupying the

[6] Wright, *op cit.*, pp. 80–81.
[7] John J. Bimson, *Redating the Exodus and Conquest,* (Sheffield, 1978) pp. 215–225.

promised land, lest they be turned aside from the course upon which God had set them.

When the news of the conquest of Jericho and Ai spread throughout Canaan, the people in various localities organized resistance to Israel's occupation (Josh. 9:1–2). The inhabitants of Gibeon, a city located eight miles north of Jerusalem, shrewdly devised a plan of deception. Feigning to be from a far country by evidence of their worn-out clothing and spoiled food, they came to the Israelite camp at Gilgal and expressed their fear of Israel's God, offering to be servants if Joshua would enter into a covenant with them. Because they failed to seek divine guidance Israel's leaders fell for the fiction and a peace treaty was negotiated with the Gibeonites. After three days it was discovered that Gibeon and its three dependent villages were nearby. Although the Israelites murmured against their leaders, the treaty was not violated. Instead, the Gibeonites were held responsible for supplying wood and water for the Israelite camp.

Gibeon was one of the great cities of Palestine. When it capitulated to Israel, the king of Jerusalem was greatly alarmed. In response to his appeal other Amorite kings from Hebron, Jarmuth, Lachish, and Eglon formed a coalition with him to attack the city of Gibeon. Having made an alliance with Israel, the beleaguered city immediately dispatched messengers to appeal for aid from that quarter. By an all-night march from Gilgal, Joshua unexpectedly appeared at Gibeon, where he defeated and routed the enemy through the Beth-horon pass (also known as the valley of Ajalon) as far as Azekah and Makkedah.

Supernatural aid in this battle resulted in a smashing victory for the Israelites. Besides the element of surprise and panic in the enemy camp, hailstones accounted for more casualties among the Amorites than did the fighting soldiers of Israel (Josh. 10:11). Furthermore, a long day was afforded the Israelites in pursuing the enemy. The ambiguity of the language concerning this long day of Joshua has given rise to various interpretations. Was this language poetical? Did Joshua ask for more sunshine or for relief from the heat of the day?[8] If this is poetical language, then this is merely an appeal by Joshua for help and strength.[9] As a result the Israelites were so invigorated that a day's work was accomplished in half a day. Accepted as a prolongation of light this was a miracle in which the sun or the moon and earth were stopped.[10] If the sun and moon retained their regular courses, it may have been a miracle of refraction or a supernaturally given mirage, extending the

[8] For a summary of various views see Bernard Ramm, *The Christian View of Science and Scripture* (Grand Rapids: Eerdmans, 1955), pp. 156–161.

[9] For a representative discussion see the article entitled "Sun" in Davis, *Dictionary of the Bible* (4th rev. ed.; Grand Rapids: Baker Book House, 1954), pp. 748–749.

[10] Cf. R. A. Torrey, *Difficulties in the Bible* (1907), p. 53; Josephus, *Antiquities of the Jews,* v. 1:17, and Ecclus. 46:4.

light of day so that sun and moon seemed to be out of their regular courses. This gave Israel more time to pursue the enemy.[11] Joshua's appeal for divine aid may have been a request for relief from the burning heat of the sun, commanding the sun to be silent or dumb, i.e., keep from shining. In response God sent a hailstorm which brought both relief from solar heat and destruction to the enemy. The soldiers, being refreshed, made a day's march in half a day from Gibeon to Makkedah, a distance of thirty miles,[12] and it seemed to them like a whole day when the day was only half over. Although the Joshua account does not give us the details of how this happened, it is apparent that God intervened in behalf of Israel and the Amorite league was utterly defeated.

At Makkedah the five kings of the Amorite league were trapped in a cave and were subsequently dispatched by Joshua. With the conquest of Makkedah and Libnah, the latter being located in the entrance to the vale of Elah where David later smote Goliath, the kings of these two cities likewise were killed. Joshua then assaulted the well-fortified city of Lachish (modern Tell ed-Duweir) and on the second day of siege overthrew this stronghold. When the king of Gezer attempted to relieve Lachish he also perished with his force; however, no claim is made for the conquest of Gezer. Next Israel moved on in victory to take Eglon, which is presently identified with modern Tell el-Hesi. From there the troops struck eastward into the hill country and beset Hebron, which was not easily defended. Then moving southwest they stormed and took Debir, or Kirjath-sepher. Although the strong city-states of Gezer and Jerusalem were not conquered, they were isolated by this campaign so that the whole southern area, from Gibeon to Kadesh-barnea and Gaza, was under the control of Israel when Joshua led his battle-hardened warriors back to the camp at Gilgal.

The conquest and occupation of northern Canaan is very briefly described. The opposition was organized and led by Jabin, king of Hazor, who had at his command a great force of chariotry. A great battle took place near the waters of Merom with the result that the Canaanite coalition was utterly defeated by Joshua. The horses and chariots were destroyed and the city of Hazor was burned to the ground. There is no mention of the destruction of other cities in Galilee.

Hazor, identified as Tell el-Qedah, is strategically located about fifteen

[11] Cf. A. Rendle Short, *Modern Discovery and the Bible* (London: Intervarsity Fellowship of Evangelical Unions, 1943), p. 117, and Lowell Butler, *"Mirages are Light Benders," Journal of the American Scientific Affiliation,* December, 1951.

[12] Cf. D. Maunder, "The Battle of Beth-Horon," *The International Standard Bible Encyclopedia,* I, 446–449. Cf. also Robert Dick Wilson, "What does the 'the sun stood still' mean?" *Moody Monthly,* 21:67 (October, 1920), interprets the words translated "stand still" to mean "darken" on the basis of Babylonian astronomy. Hugh J. Blair, "Joshua," in *The New Bible Commentary,* p. 231, suggests that Joshua made this request in the morning so that the hailstorm prolonged the darkness.

miles north of the Sea of Galilee and about five miles west of the Jordan River. In 1926–28 John Garstang directed an archaeological excavation of this site. More recently, major excavations of Hazor were conducted by Dr. Yigael Yadin, 1955–58.[13] The acropolis itself consisting of twenty-five acres reaching a height of one hundred and thirty feet apparently was founded in the third millennium B.C. A lower area to the north consisting of one hundred and fifty acres was occupied during the second millennium B.C., perhaps having a population as high as 40,000. In Egyptian and Babylonian records Hazor is frequently mentioned, indicating its strategic importance. The lower city apparently was built during the second half of the eighteenth century or the Hyksos era. After Joshua destroyed this powerful center Canaanite power at Hazor must have been re-established sufficiently to suppress Israel until it was crushed once more (Jud. 4:2), after which Hazor was incorporated by the tribe of Naphtali.

In summary form Josh. 11:16–12:24 accounts for Israel's conquest of the whole land of Canaan. The territory covered by the occupation forces extended from Kadesh-barnea, or the extremities of the Negeb, as far north as the valley of Lebanon, below Mount Hermon. On the east side of the Jordan rift the area which previously had been conquered under Moses extended from Mount Hermon in the north to the valley of the Arnon, east of the Dead Sea.

Thirty-one kings are listed as having been defeated by Joshua. With so many city-states, each having its own king, in such a small country, it was possible for Joshua and the Israelites to defeat these local rulers in small federations. Even though the kings were defeated, not all the cities were actually captured or occupied. Through this conquest Joshua subdued the inhabitants to the extent that during the subsequent period of peace the Israelites were able to settle in the promised land.

Allotment of Canaan

Although the leading kings had been defeated and a period of peace prevailed, there still remained many unoccupied areas in the land (13:1–7). Joshua was divinely commissioned to allot the conquered territory to the nine and a half tribes. Reuben, Gad, and half of Manasseh had received their allotments east of the Jordan under Moses and Eleazar (Josh. 13:8–33; Num. 32).

During the period of conquest the camp of Israel was located at Gilgal, a little to the northeast of Jericho, near the Jordan. Under the supervision of Joshua and Eleazar allotment was made to some of the tribes while still

[13] Cf. Yigael Yadin, "Excavations at Hazor, 1955–58," in *The Biblical Archaeologist Reader* II (Garden City, N.J.: 1964), pp. 191–224.

encamped here. Caleb, who had been a man of unusual faith forty-five years prior to this time, when the twelve spies were sent into Canaan (Num. 13–14), now received special consideration by being awarded the city of Hebron for his inheritance (14:6–15). The tribe of Judah appropriated the area between the Dead Sea and the Mediterranean Sea which included the city of Bethlehem. Ephraim and half of Manasseh were given most of the area west of the Jordan between the Sea of Galilee and the Dead Sea (Josh. 16:1–17:18).

Shiloh was established as the religious center for Israel (Josh. 18:1). It was here that the remaining tribes were challenged to possess their assigned territories. While Simeon was given the land south of Judah, the tribes of Benjamin and Dan received their allotment immediately to the north of Judah. North of Manasseh, beginning with the Megiddo valley and Mount Carmel, Issachar, Zebulun, Asher, and Naphtali were given their possession.

Cities of refuge were designated throughout the land (20:1–9). West of the Jordan these cities were Kedesh in Naphtali, Shechem in Ephraim, and Hebron in Judah. East of the Jordan, in each of the tribal areas, were the following: Bezer in Reuben, Ramoth in Gilead within the boundaries of Gad, and Golan in Bashan in the area of Manasseh. To these cities anyone could flee for safety from blood revenge in case of manslaughter.

The tribe of Levi received no territorial allotment, for they were responsible for the religious services throughout the nation. The various tribes were charged with the obligation of assigning cities to the Levites. Grazing land around each of the forty-eight cities was likewise provided, so that the Levites could pasture their flocks and herds.

With a commendation for their faithful service and an admonition to remain true to God, Joshua dismissed the Transjordanian tribes who had served with the rest of the nation under him in the conquest of the territory west of the Jordan. Upon their return to Transjordan they erected an altar—an action which alarmed the Israelites who had settled in Canaan proper. Phinehas, the son of the high priest, was sent from Shiloh to appraise the situation. His investigation assured him that the altar in the land of Gilead served the purpose of maintaining proper worship of God.

How long Joshua lived after his military campaigns is not stated in the Bible. An inference based on Josh. 14:6–12 is that the conquest of Canaan was accomplished in a period of about seven years. Joshua may have died shortly after this or he may have lived on some twenty or thirty years at the maximum. Before he died, at the age of 110, he assembled Israel at Shechem and sternly admonished them to fear the Lord. He reminded them that God had called Abraham from serving idols and had verified the covenant made with the patriarchs by bringing Israel into the promised land. A public covenant was made by which the leaders assured Joshua that they would serve

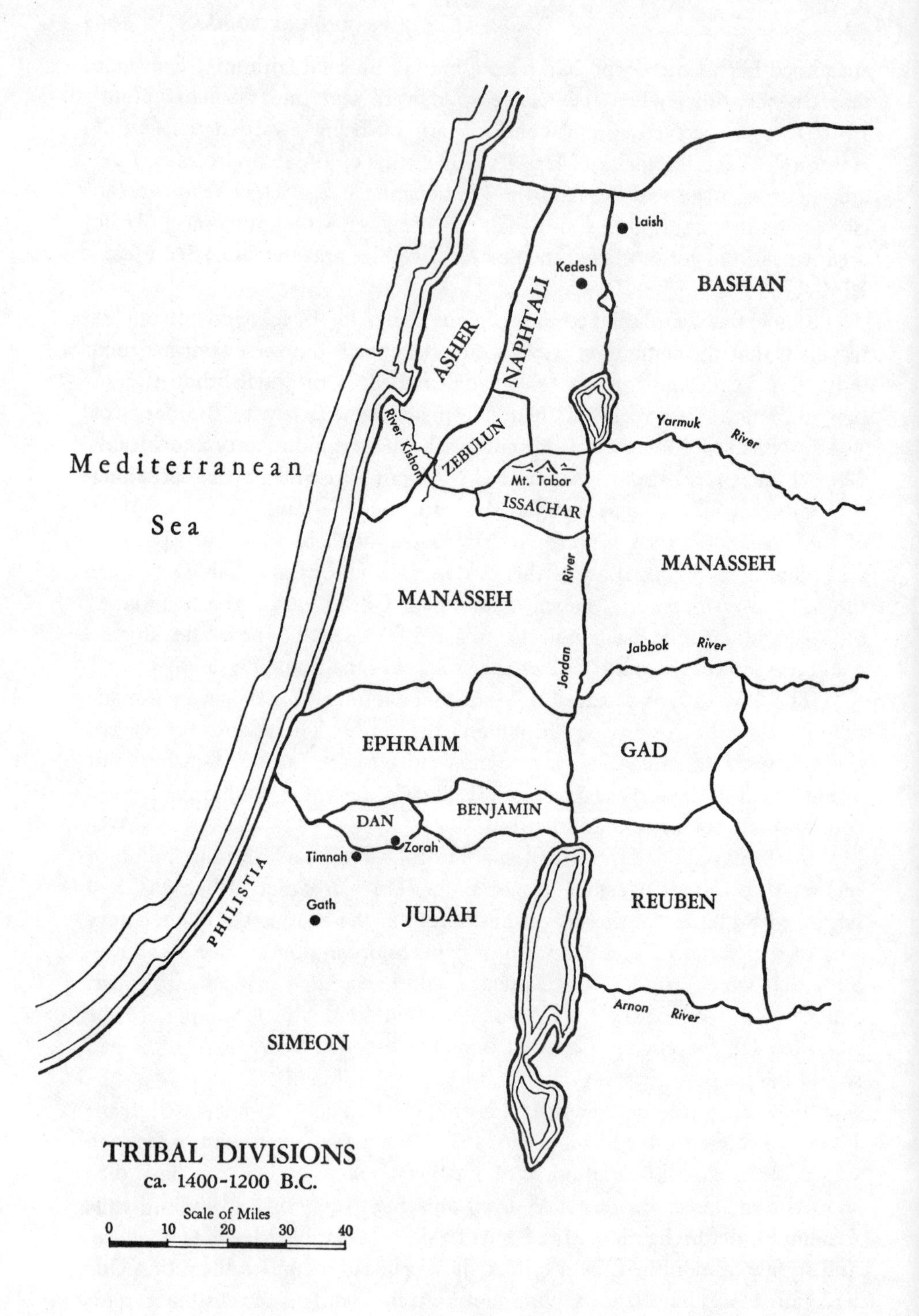

Laish
Kedesh
BASHAN
ASHER
NAPHTALI
River Kishon
ZEBULUN
Yarmuk River
Mediterranean
Sea
Mt. Tabor
ISSACHAR
MANASSEH
River
MANASSEH
Jabbok River
Jordan
EPHRAIM
GAD
BENJAMIN
DAN
Zorah
Timnah
PHILISTIA
Gath
JUDAH
REUBEN
Arnon River
SIMEON
TRIBAL DIVISIONS
ca. 1400-1200 B.C.
Scale of Miles
0
10
20
30
40

the Lord. After the death of Joshua Israel fulfilled this promise only until the passing of the older generation.

When Judges Ruled

The events recorded in the Book of Judges are closely related to the developments in Joshua's day. Since the Canaanites had not been fully dislodged, and the occupation by Israel was not complete, similar conditions continued into the period of the judges. Consequently warfare continued as local areas or cities were reoccupied in the course of time. References such as Judg. 1:1, 2:6–10, and 20:26–28 seem to indicate that the events in Joshua and Judges are closely related chronologically or are even synchronous.

The chronology for this period is difficult to ascertain. The fact that forty to fifty different methods have been suggested to account for the era of the judges is indicative of the problems. The years as allotted to each judge in the biblical account are as follows:

	years	
Mesopotamian oppression	8	3:8
Othniel—deliverance and rest	40	3:11
Moab oppression	18	3:14
Ehud—deliverance and rest	80	3:30
Canaanite oppression—Jabin	20	4:3
Deborah and Barak—deliverance and rest	40	5:31
Midianite oppression	7	6:1
Gideon—deliverance and rest	40	8:28
Abimelech—puppet king	3	9:22
Tola—period of judgeship	23	10:2
Jair—period of judgeship	22	10:3
Ammonite oppression	18	10:8
Jephthah—deliverance and rest	6	12:7
Ibzan—judgeship	7	12:9
Elon—judgeship	19	12:11
Abdon—judgeship	8	12:14
Philistine oppression	40	13:1
Samson—exploits and judgeship	20	15:20
Total	410 years	

Undoubtedly it is such a tabulation as this that Paul has in mind when he divides the period from Joshua to Samuel, including forty years for Eli's judgeship (Acts 13:20). Even with the acceptance of the early date of the occupation of Canaan under Joshua (*ca.* 1400 B.C.), it is impossible to allow for a chronological sequence for these years, since David was fully established on the throne of Israel by 1000 B.C. In I Kings 6:1 a period of 480 years is allowed from the time of the Exodus to the fourth year of Solomon's reign. Even by allowing a minimum of 20 years each for Eli, Samuel, and Saul, 40 years for David, 4 years for Solomon, 40 years for the wilderness wanderings, and a minimum of 10 years for Joshua and the elders, a total of 154 years would have to be added to 410, making a grand tabulation of 566 years. The obvious conclusion is that the periods in Judges do not all fall into a chronological sequence.

Garstang accounts for this era by regarding Shamgar, Tola, Jair, Ibzan, Elon, and Abdon as local judges whose years are synchronous with those of other periods mentioned.[14] By omitting these from the chronological tabulation the total number of years between the Exodus and the fourth year of Solomon's reign approximates the 480-year figure. In Judg. 11:26, three hundred years is given as the time that elapsed between the defeat of the Ammonites under Moses and the days of Jephthah. By subtracting the years for Joshua and the elders and adding twenty years for Samson, the time allotted to the judges from Othniel to Samson would approximate three centuries (*ca.* 1360–1060 B.C.).

The late date for the conquest under Joshua (1250–1225 B.C.) limits the period allotted to the judges, including the days of Eli, Samuel, and Saul, to two centuries or less. With this computation I Kings 6:1 and Judg. 11:26 are regarded as late insertions and not reliable historically. Although Garstang regards the reference in Kings as an insertion, he dates it early and accepts it as reliable. This shorter chronology would necessitate further synchronization of periods of oppression and rests during the days of the judges.

Obviously any chronological scheme proposed for this era of the judges is but a suggested solution. Scriptural data are insufficient to establish an absolute chronology. It seems quite certain that the authors of Joshua and Judges did not intend to give an account that would neatly fit into a complete chronology for the period. Faithfulness to the traditions of I Kings 6:1 and Judg. 11:26 demands the longer chronology.

Israel had no political capital in the days of the judges. Shiloh, which was established as the religious center in the days of Joshua (Josh. 18:1), continued as such into the days of Eli (I Sam. 1:3). Since Israel had no king (Judg. 17:6; 18:1; 19:1 and 21:25), there was no central place where a judge would officiate. These judges rose to places of leadership as the local or national situation might demand. The influence and recognition of many of them was undoubtedly limited to their local community or tribe. Some of them were military leaders who delivered the Israelites from the oppressing enemy, while others were acknowledged as magistrates to whom the people looked for legal and political decisions. With neither central government nor

[14] J. Garstang, *op. cit.*, pp. 51–66.

capital, the Israelite tribes were ruled spasmodically without immediate succession when a given judge died. With some of the judges restricted to local areas, it is also reasonable to assume that several judgeships overlapped.

For the biblical portrayal of the conditions in this era as given in Judges and Ruth, consider the following analysis:

I. Prevailing conditions	1:1–3:6
Unoccupied areas	1:1–2:5
Religious-political cycles	2:6–3:6
II. Oppressing nations and deliverers	3:7–16:31
Mesopotamia—Othniel	3:7–11
Moab—Ehud	3:12–30
Philistia—Shamgar	3:31
Canaan (Hazor)—Deborah and Barak	4:1–5:31
Midian—Gideon (Jerubbaal)	6:1–8:35
Abimelech, Tola, and Jair	9:1–10:5
Ammon—Jephthah	10:6–12:7
Ibzan, Elon, and Abdon	12:8–15
Philistia—Samson	13:1–16:31
III. Cultural conditions in the days of the judges	17:1–Ruth 4:22
Micah and his idolatry	17:1–13
Migration of the Danites	18:1–31
Crime and civil war	19:1–21:25
The story of Ruth	Ruth 1:1–4:22

The quotation "Every man did that which was right in his own eyes" (21:25) clearly describes the prevailing conditions throughout the entire period of the judges.

The opening verse of Judges suggests that the book is concerned with developments which took place after the death of Joshua. The account in Judg. 2:6–10 may support the idea that some of these events refer in part to the conquest of certain cities under Joshua. The conquest of Hebron in Judg. 1:10–15 may parallel the account in Josh. 15:14–19. Other statements reflect the changes that occurred over a long period of time. Jerusalem was not conquered in the days of Joshua (15:63). According to Judg. 1:8, the city was burned by the people of Judah, but in verse 21 it is clearly stated that the Benjaminites did not dislodge the Jebusites from Jerusalem. The city was not actually occupied by the Israelites until the days of David. The Judahite victory must have been only temporary.

Although Joshua had defeated the main forces of opposition as he led Israel into Canaan and divided the land to the various tribes, many locales remained in the hands of the Canaanites and other inhabitants. In his final word to the Israelites Joshua warned the people not to mix or intermarry with the local inhabitants who remained but admonished them to drive out these idolatrous people and occupy their land. Further attempts were made to dislodge these people, but the record clearly indicates that the Israelites were only partially obedient.

While some areas were conquered, certain strongly fortified cities such as Taanach and Megiddo remained in the possession of the Canaanites. When Israel was strong enough she would subject these people to forced labor and taxation, but she failed in her commission to drive them out of the land. Consequently, the Amorites, Canaanites, and others remained in the land that Israel had been given for complete possession and occupation. It would seem quite natural that when Israel was weak these people even repossessed cities and villages that Israel had once conquered (cf. Judg. 1:34).

Partial occupation of the land left Israel with continual difficulties. The cycle of developments recurred again and again. Through fraternization with the inhabitants the Israelites participated in Baal worship as they forsook the worship of God. The peoples particularly mentioned who caused Israel to turn from God are the Canaanites, Hittites, Amorites, Perizzites, Hivites, and Jebusites. During this period of apostasy intermarriage led to further neglect of service and devotion to God. In the course of a generation the populace of Israel became so idolatrous that God's blessings promised through Moses and Joshua were withdrawn. By worshiping Baal the Israelites were breaking the first commandment of the Decalogue.

Judgment came in the form of oppression. Neither Egypt nor Mesopotamia was powerful enough to dominate the Fertile Crescent during this era. Egyptian influence in Palestine had diminished during the reign of Tut-ankh-Amon (*ca.* 1360 B.C.). Assyria was rising in power (*ca.* 1250) but did not yet threaten interference in Canaan. This allowed peoples from the immediate areas as well as city-states to encroach upon Israel's possession of Canaan. Those listed as political opponents for this era are the Mesopotamians, Moabites, Philistines, Canaanites, Midianites, and Ammonites. These invaders took advantage of the Israelites by taking their property and crops. When the situation became unbearable, they became desperate enough to turn to God.

Repentance was the next part of the cycle. As the Israelites lost their independence and served the oppressors they recognized that they were suffering the consequences of disobeying God. When they became conscious of their sin they penitently turned to God. Their appeal was not in vain.

Deliverance came through champions whom God raised up to challenge the oppressors. Military leaders who led the Israelites in attacking the enemy nations were Othniel, Ehud, Shamgar, Deborah and Barak, Gideon, Jephthah, and Samson. Specially endued with divine enablement, these leaders repulsed the foes and Israel again enjoyed a period of rest.

These religious-political cycles recurred frequently in the days of the judges. Sin, sorrow, supplication, and salvation were the usual order. Each generation apparently had enough people who became conscious of the possibility of securing God's favor and blessing that idolatry was renounced and adherence to God's precepts restored.

Judges and Oppressing Nations

Oppression for an eight-year period by an invading force from upper Mesopotamia introduces the first cycle. Garstang suggests that Cushan-Rishataim was a Hittite king who had annexed northern Mesopotamia, also known as Mitanni, and extended his power down into the land of Israel.[15] Othniel, from the tribe of Judah, took the initiative in championing the cause of Israel as the Spirit of the Lord came upon him. A forty-year period of rest followed.

Moab was the next nation to invade Israel. Supported by the Ammonites and Amalekites, the Moabites gained a foothold in Israelite territory and exacted tribute. Ehud, from the tribe of Benjamin, was raised up as the deliverer to terminate the eighteen years of Moabite domination. Having paid the tribute Ehud gained a private audience with Eglon, the king of Moab. By using his sword with his left hand, Ehud caught Eglon off guard and killed him; then he made good his escape before the mischief was discovered. The Moabites were demoralized, while the Israelites were emboldened to support Ehud in an all-out offensive against the enemy. Approximately 10,000 Moabites lost their lives in the encounter, which gave Israel an overwhelming victory. With the expulsion of Moab, Israel had rest for a period of eighty years. During this era Ramses II, who ruled in Egypt (*ca.* 1290–1224 B.C.), and Merneptah his son (*ca.* 1224–1214), maintained a balance of power with the Hittites by controlling Palestine as far as southern Syria. The only mention of Israel in Egyptian inscriptions comes from Merneptah's boast that Israel was laid waste.[16] On a whole, peaceful conditions prevailed for some time.

Only one verse is allotted to the career of Shamgar. Nothing is indicated about an oppression, nor are any details given concerning Shamgar's origin or background. A logical inference seems to be that the Philistines were penetrating into the territory of Israel and that Shamgar rose to resist them, killing 600 in his valiant effort.

Harassment by the Canaanites followed for a period of twenty years as Egyptian influence in Palestine declined under Merneptah and other weak rulers near the end of the thirteenth century. While Jabin, king of the Ca-

[15] *Ibid.*, p. 62. Or could this have been an Aramean group?
[16] Steindorff and Seele, *When Egypt Ruled the East*, p. 252.

naanites, ruled at Hazor, located north of the Sea of Galilee, Sisera, the commander of Jabin's army, harried the Israelites from Harosheth-ha-goiim, located near the Kishon River at the northwest entrance into the plain of Esdraelon.

During the days of this Canaanite oppression Deborah gained recognition as a prophetess in the land of Ephraim near Ramah and Bethel. Sending for Barak she not only admonished him to lead in battle but personally joined him at Kedesh in Naphtali. There Barak assembled a fighting force and proceeded southward to Mount Tabor, located at the northeastern tip of the Esdraelon triangular plain. However, since Sisera had the advantage of 900 chariots in his fighting force, Barak was afraid to assume the responsibility of fighting the Canaanites with his 10,000 swordsmen. Even though Deborah assured him of victory as the Canaanite forces were decoyed to the Kishon, Barak would not venture out without her joint leadership.

The Canaanite forces were surprisingly routed. Careful examination of the account seems to indicate that when the chariots of the enemy were in the valley of Kishon a sudden heavy rainfall reduced the advantage of the Canaanites. Chariotry had to be abandoned when it bogged down in the mud (5:4, 20, 21; 4:15).[17] With the Canaanite forces defeated and Sisera killed by Jael, the Israelites secured relief which was to endure for forty years. The victory was celebrated in a song expressing praise for divine aid (Judg. 5).

Israel's reversion to idolatry was followed by incursions from the Syrian Desert by hostile camel-riding nomads, known as Midianites, Amalekites, and Sons of the East, who came to seize the crops and livestock of the Israelites. Seven years of this depredation became exceedingly trying, so much so that Israelites had to seek safety in caves and mountain strongholds.

At a village called Ophrah, Gideon was busily and secretly engaged in threshing grain for his father when the angel of the Lord commissioned him to deliver his people. Although Ophrah cannot be definitely identified, it was probably located near the valley of Jezreel in central Palestine where the Midianite pressure was the greatest. Gideon's first assignment was to tear down the altar of Baal on his father's estate. Although the townspeople were quite alarmed at this, Gideon's father, Joash, did not defend idolatry. For this memorable and bold deed Gideon was named Jerubbaal, meaning, "Let Baal contend (against him)."

When the enemy forces were encamped in the valley of Jezreel, Gideon assembled an army. By the use of a fleece twice-exposed he ascertained that God had indeed called him to deliver Israel (Judg. 6:36–40). When Gideon announced to his army of 32,000 gathered from Manasseh, Asher, Zebulun,

[17] Garstang, *op. cit.*, pp. 298–299, points out that during World War I cavalry movements were endangered in this same area by a 15-minute rain.

and Naphthali that any who were fearful should go home he saw 22,000 men leave the ranks. As a result of the next test he lost another 9,700 men. With an alert company of only 300 men he prepared for battle against the nomadic hordes.

On the slopes of Mount Moreh, toward the eastern end of the Megiddo plain, lay encamped the great host of Midianites with their camels. Gideon, dividing his band of 300 men into three companies, made a surprise attack by night. In the beginning of the middle watch (after 10 P.M.), when the enemy was in deep sleep, Gideon's men blew the trumpets, smashed their jars, and shouted the battle cry, "The sword of the Lord and of Gideon." The Midianites fled in confusion across the Jordan. By faith in God Gideon thus put the foe to flight and delivered the Israelites from oppression (cf. Heb. 11:32).

In the pursuit of the Midianites the lawless condition in the days of the judges is again reflected (Judg. 8). After pacifying the jealous Ephraimites, who had not shared in the great victory, Gideon routed the Midianites in Transjordan, taking a sizable loot of golden earrings, camel collars, crescents, pendants, as well as purple garments worn by Midianite kings. As a result the people offered Gideon hereditary kingship. Gideon's refusal reflects his attitude of resistance against the trend toward monarchism. However, Gideon did make a golden ephod from the spoils taken from the enemy. Whether this was an idol or a simple memorial of his victory or a counterattraction to the ephod worn by the high priest (Ex. 27:6–14) is not certain. In any case, the object became a snare to Gideon and his family, as well as to the Israelites, by paving the way to idolatry. Although Gideon had gained security for Israel from the invaders for forty years through his military feat, his influence in religion was negated. Soon after his death the people openly turned to worship of Baal, forgetting that God had granted them deliverance.

Abimelech, a son of Gideon's concubine, asserted himself as king at Shechem for a period of three years after the death of Gideon. He gained the adherence of the Shechemites by treacherously slaying all of the seventy sons of Gideon except Jotham. The latter, addressing the men of Shechem from Mount Gerizim by means of a parable, compares Abimelech to a bramble that was invited to reign over the trees. He invoked God's curse upon Shechem for their mistreatment of Gideon's family.

Revolt soon broke out under Gaal, who incited the Shechemites to rebel. In the course of the civil strife that followed Abimelech was finally killed by a millstone which a woman dropped on his head when he approached a fortified tower within the city. This ended all attempts to establish kingship in Israel in the days of the judges.

Little is known about Tola and Jair. Since no great feats concerning them are mentioned, their responsibilities were merely judicial. Tola from the tribe of Issachar, held forth at Shamir, located somewhere in the hill country of Ephraim. A 23-year rule is assigned to him.

Jair judged in the Gileadite country east of Jordan for twenty-two years. The fact that he had a family of thirty sons indicates not only an ostentatious polygamy but also his rank and position of wealth in the culture of that day.

Apostasy again prevailed as Israel turned to Baal and other pagan deities. This time oppression came from two directions: the Philistines pressed in from the southwest and the Ammonites invaded from the east. Deliverance in the Transjordan area came under the leadership of Jephthah.

Because he was the son of a harlot Jephthah was ostracized from his home community early in life. He became a brigand chief or marauder captain in Tob, which probably was located northeast of Gilead. When the Gileadites looked for a leader Jephthah was invited back. Before he accepted this assignment a solemn compact was made whereby the Gileadite elders recognized him as leader.

When Jephthah appealed to the Ammonites they responded with force. Before going out to battle he made a vow which he was obligated to fulfill if he returned victoriously. Empowered by the Spirit of the Lord Jephthah gained a great victory so that the Israelites were delivered from the Ammonites who had oppressed them for eighteen years. When Ephraim protested that they had not been asked to share in the battle against the Ammonites, he successfully met their military threat with his army.

Did Jephthah actually sacrifice his daughter to fulfill his vow? In this dilemma he certainly could not have pleased God by offering a human sacrifice, which nowhere in Scripture had divine approval. In fact, this was one of the gross sins for which the Canaanites were to be exterminated. On the other hand, how could he please God by not keeping his vow? Although vows in Israel were voluntary, once a person made a vow he was under obligation to fulfill it (Num. 6:1–21). The clear implication in Judg. 11 is that Jephthah fulfilled his vow (v. 39). His manner of doing it has been subject to various interpretations.

That Israelite leaders did not conform to pure religion in the days of the judges is apparent in the biblical record.[18] Jephthah, who had a half-Canaanite background, may have conformed to prevailing heathen customs in actually sacrificing his daughter.[19] Since mountains were viewed as sym-

[18] Gideon made a golden ephod which led the Israelites into idolatry. Samson's life was by no means an example of pure religion.

[19] This view was held by Jewish and Christian interpreters until the twelfth century. For a full discussion see the International Critical Commentary on *Judges* by George Foote Moore (New York: Scribner's, 1895), pp. 301–305. Cf. also F. F. Bruce "Judges," in *The New Bible Commentary,* p. 250. Cf. also *Modern Science and the Christian Faith* (Wheaton: Van Kampen, 1948), pp. 134–135.

bols of fertility by the Canaanites, his daughter went to the mountains to mourn her virginity in order to ward off any possible cessation of the land's fertility.[20] Periodically during each year Israelite maidens would spend four days re-enacting the mourning of the sacrificed girl.[21]

If Jephthah's familiarity with the law made him conscious of God's displeasure in human sacrifice he may have dedicated his daughter to tabernacle service.[22] By so doing he would have fulfilled his vow and conformed to the essential idea of complete consecration signified in the burnt offering. Since this daughter was his only child, Jephthah forfeited the hopes of posterity.[23] In this way he may have met the obligations of his vow without human sacrifice—a vow which perhaps had been hastily made while under pressure.

Although the manner in which Jephthah fulfilled his vow is not delineated in the biblical narrative, he met the challenge of delivering his people from oppression and is listed as a hero of faith (Heb. 11:32).

Ibzan judged Israel for seven years. Whether Bethlehem, the place of his activity and burial, is the well-known city in Judah or a village in Zebulon is not certain. The mention of thirty sons and thirty daughters indicates his position of wealth and influence.

Elon has ten years allotted to him as judge. Ajalon, in the land of Zebulon, was his home and place of service to his people.

Abdon, the next judge listed, lived in Ephraim. Being in a position to furnish seventy members of his family with asses, Abdon must have been a man of great wealth and influence in his country. He judged Israel for eight years.

Israel was oppressed simultaneously by the Ammonites and the Philistines (Judg. 10:6). While Jephthah defeated the former, Samson is the hero who resisted and challenged the power of the latter. Since Samson never fully released Israel from Philistine domination, it is difficult to date the 40-year period mentioned in Judg. 13:1. Twenty years are allotted to the period of Samson's leadership (Judg. 15:20).

Samson was a great hero endowed with supernatural strength and re-

[20] For discussion of fertility rites see J. D. Frazer, *The Golden Bough* (London: Macmillan & Co., 1890).

[21] Dr. Dwight W. Young suggests in supporting this view that the problematic word "Tana" is probably an Aramaism meaning "to repeat, re-enact" and is related to the Hebrew word "Shana."

[22] For this view see C. F. Keil, commentary on *Judges*, pp. 388–395. David Kimchi (12th century) and other rabbis took this viewpoint, comparing Jephthah's act to Abraham's experience where human sacrifice was not actually executed.

[23] Jephthah's familiarity with Israel's history as recorded in Numbers is apparent in Num. 11:12–28. Human sacrifice was forbidden, Lev. 20:2. To be childless or left without heirs was considered a calamity in Israel. Hannah (I Sam. 1) dedicated her son to tabernacle service. For incidental references to women in such service see Ex. 38:8 and I Sam. 2:22.

membered primarily for his military exploits. That he was a Nazarite was announced to his Danite parents before his birth. Manoah and his wife were instructed through divine revelation that their son would begin the deliverance of Israel from Philistine oppression. Throughout the account numerous references are made to the fact that the Spirit of the Lord was upon him (13:25; 14:5, 19; 15:14). His activities were limited to the maritime plain and hill country of Judah, where he endeavored to stem the Philistine occupation of Israelite territory.

Numerous stories, which may be but a sample of all that Samson did, are recorded in the Book of Judges. On his way to Timnah he ripped a lion apart with his bare hands. When he was obliged to furnish thirty festal garments to the Philistines, who dishonestly obtained the answer to the riddle he posed at his wedding at Timnah, he killed thirty of their own people at Ashkelon. On another occasion he released three hundred foxes with burning firebrands to destroy Philistine crops. In response to their reprisal, Samson slaughtered many Philistines near Etam. When the men of Judah delivered him bound into the hands of the enemy, his bonds were loosed as the Spirit of the Lord came upon him. Singlehanded he slew a thousand men with the jawbone of an ass. At Gaza he removed the gates by night and carried them nearly forty miles east to a hill near Hebron.

Samson's entanglement with Delilah, whose sympathies were with the Philistines, brought about his downfall. Three times he successfully repulsed the Philistines when the woman betrayed him into their hands. However, when he revealed the secret of his power to her and his hair was cut, Samson lost his strength. The Philistines gouged out his eyes and forced him to grind at the mill as a slave. But God restored his strength for his final feat, and he pulled down the pillars of the temple of Dagon, killing more Philistines than he had killed during his previous encounters.

In spite of his weakness, Samson gained renown among the heroes of faith (Heb. 11:32). Endowed with such great strength he undoubtedly could have done much more but, ensnared by sin, he failed in his mission to deliver Israel. At best he restrained the Philistines temporarily so that Israel was not displaced from the promised land.

Religious, Political, and Social Conditions

The closing chapters of Judges and the Book of Ruth describe the conditions that existed in the days of heroic leaders such as Deborah, Gideon, and Samson. Without cross references to the activities of any of the particular judges named in the preceding chapters, it is difficult to date these developments specifically. Rabbis associate the story of Micah and the Danite migration with the age of Othniel, but because of the lack of historical detail it is impossible to be certain of the reliability of this and similar rabbinical traditions. The most that can be done is to limit these events to the days "when the judges ruled" and there was "no king in Israel" (Ruth 1:1 and Judg. 21:25).

Micah and his shrine are an example of the religious apostasy that prevailed in the days of the judges. When Micah, an Ephraimite, restored 1,160 stolen shekels to his mother, she gave 200 shekels to a silversmith, who made a graven image, carved out of wood and overlaid with silver, as well as a molten image made entirely of silver. With these idolatrous symbols Micah set up a shrine to which he added an ephod and teraphim and made one of his sons a priest. When a Levite from Bethlehem chanced to stop at this chapel on Mount Ephraim, Micah made an agreement to hire him as his official priest in the hope that the Lord would prosper his enterprise.

Five Danites sent as a reconnaissance party to locate more land for their tribe stopped at Micah's shrine to ask advice of this Levite. After being assured of success, they went on their way and found favorable conditions for the conquest of more territory at Laish, a city located in the vicinity of the headwaters of the Jordan. As a result, six hundred Danites migrated north. On the way they convinced the Levite that it was better for him to serve as priest for a tribe rather than for an individual. When Micah and his neighbors objected, the Danites, being stronger, simply took the Levite and the gods of Micah north to Laish, thereafter called Dan. Here Jonathan, who undoubtedly is the Levite, set up a shrine for the Danites as a substitute for Shiloh. If no omission occurs in the genealogy (18:30) of this Jonathan, it is quite likely that the migration took place in the early days of the judges.

The sex crime at Gibeah and the developments that followed led to civil war in Israel. A Levite from the hill country of Ephraim and his concubine, on returning from a visit to the woman's parents in Bethlehem, stopped at Gibeah for the night. They had passed Jebus, hoping to receive better hospitality in Gibeah, which was a Benjaminite city. During the night the men of Gibeah demanded and then seized the Levite's concubine. In the morning she was found dead at the door. He took the corpse to his home and cut it into twelve pieces, which he sent throughout the land. All Israel, from Dan to Beersheba, was so shocked at this atrocity that they gathered at Mizpah. Here, before a gathering of 400,000 men, the Levite told of his mistreatment by the Benjaminites.

When the tribe of Benjamin refused to surrender the men of Gibeah who had committed this crime, civil war developed. The Benjaminites mustered a fighting force of 26,000 men, including a slinger division of 700. The rest of Israel then met at Bethel, where the ark of the Lord was located, to receive battle briefing from Phinehas the high priest. Twice the Israelite forces were defeated in their attack on Gibeah. The third time, however, they conquered and burned the city, killing all the Benjaminites except 600 who fled and found refuge in the rock of Rimmon. The destruction and devastation of Benjamin was quite extensive, so that the tribe was utterly disgraced. After four months a reconciliation was effected with the remaining 600 men. Provision was then made for the restoration and marriage of these men so that the Benjaminites could be reinstated in the nation of Israel.

The story of Ruth provides a glimpse into a more peaceful era in the days when judges ruled.[24] This narrative accounts for the migration of an Israelite family—Elimelech, Naomi, and their two sons—to Moab when there was famine in Judah. Here the two sons married two Moabite women, Ruth and Orpah. After the death of her husband and both of her sons, Naomi returned to Bethlehem accompanied by Ruth. In the course of time Ruth was married to Boaz and subsequently figured in the Davidic lineage of the royal family in Israel.

SELECTED READING

ARMERDING, CARL E. "Judges" in *The New Layman's Bible Commentary.* Grand Rapids: Zondervan Publishing House, 1979.

BOLING, ROBERT G. *Judges: Introduction, Translation and Commentary.* The Anchor Bible. Garden City: Doubleday, 1970.

BLAIKIE, WILLIAM G. *The Book of Joshua.* The Expositor's Bible. New York: Hodder & Stoughton, n.d. Reprint. Minneapolis: Klock & Klock Christian Publishers, 1978.

CAMPBELL, DONALD K. "Joshua" in *Bible Knowledge Commentary.* Wheaton: Scripture Press, 1985.

ENNS, PAUL. *Joshua, Judges, Ruth.* Bible Study Commentary Series. Grand Rapids: Zondervan Publishing House, 1982.

HAMLIN, E. JOHN. "Joshua: Inheriting the Land" in *International Theological Commentary.* Grand Rapids: Wm. B. Eerdmans Publishing Co., 1983.

LEWIS, A. *Judges–Ruth.* Chicago: Moody Press, 1979.

LINDSEY, F. DUANE. "Judges" in *Bible Knowledge Commentary.* Wheaton: Scripture Press, 1985.

MORRIS, LEON. *Judges and Ruth.* Downers Grove: Inter-Varsity Press, 1968.

REED, JOHN W. "Ruth" in *Bible Knowledge Commentary.* Wheaton: Scripture Press, 1985.

SCHAEFFER, FRANCIS. *Joshua and the Flow of History.* Downers Grove: Inter-Varsity Press, 1975.

WOUDSTRA, MARTIN H. "The Book of Joshua" in *The New International Commentary on the Old Testament.* Grand Rapids: Wm. B. Eerdmans Publishing Co., 1981.

---

[24] Josephus, *Antiquities* v. 9:1, dated the story of Ruth in the days of Eli. The reference to Salmon, the father of Boaz, as the husband of Rahab points to an earlier date. Since Boaz was the great-grandfather of David, the genealogy in Matthew allows for gaps.

Chapter VII

Times of Transition

In the eleventh and tenth centuries Israel established and maintained the most powerful monarchy in its entire history. Neither before nor after did the nation have such extensive boundaries and command so much international respect. Such expansion was possible largely because no interference could come from the extremities of the Fertile Crescent during this era.

Neighboring Nations

Egypt had declined to a very weakened position. Ramses III (*ca.* 1198–1167), the twentieth-dynasty Pharaoh who had been strong enough to repulse outside invaders, died at the hand of an assassin. Under Ramses IV–XII (*ca.* 1167–1085), the power of Egyptian kings gradually succumbed to the politically aggressive priestly family.[1] By 1085 B.C. Heri-Hor, the high priest, began to rule Egypt from Karnak in Thebes while petty princes controlled Tanis. Egypt's loss of prestige is reflected by the disrespectful treatment afforded Wen-Amun[2] in his journeys to Byblos as an Egyptian envoy (*ca.* 1080 B.C.). Not until the fourth year of Rehoboam (*ca.* 927 B.C.) was Egypt in a position to invade Palestine (I Kings 14:25–26).

The Assyrians under Tiglath-pileser I (*ca.* 1113–1074 B.C.) extended their influence westward into Syria and Phoenicia. Before long, however, the Assyrians themselves felt the effects of invasion from the West.[3] During the reign of Ashur-rabi II (*ca.* 1012–975), Assyrian settlements along the Euphrates were displaced by migrating Aramean tribes. Only after 875 B.C.

[1] According to the Papyrus Harris, approximately 15 per cent of the agricultural land was under the control of the priests while 2 per cent of the population served as slaves.

[2] For the journey of Wen-Amon to Phoenicia see Pritchard, *Ancient Near Eastern Texts,* pp. 25–29.

[3] Merrill F. Unger, *Israel and the Aramaeans of Damascus,* pp. 38–46.

did Assyria regain control of the upper Euphrates Valley to challenge the western powers in Palestine.

The archenemy that seriously threatened Israel's rise to power was Philistia. Repulsed in their attempt to penetrate Egypt, the Philistines settled in large numbers on the maritime plain in Palestine shortly after 1200 B.C.[4] Five cities became Philistine strongholds: Ashkelon, Ashdod, Ekron, Gaza, and Gath (I Sam. 6:17). Over each of these independent cities ruled a "lord" who supervised the cultivation of the adjoining land. Although they were actively competing with the Phoenicians for the lucrative sea trade, as reported by Wen-Amun, the Philistines threatened to overrun Israel in the days of Samson, Eli, Samuel, and Saul. Independent in themselves, the five city rulers united on occasion for political and military purposes.

The real explanation of Philistine superiority over Israel is found in the fact that the Philistines held the secrets of smelting iron. The Hittites in Asia Minor had been iron founders before 1200 B.C., but the Philistines became the first to use this process in Palestine. By guarding this monopoly carefully they held Israel at their mercy. This is clearly reflected in I Sam. 13:19–22: "Now there was no smith found throughout all the land of Israel." Not only were the Israelites without smiths to make swords and spears, but they were even dependent upon the Philistines to sharpen their farming implements. With these overwhelming odds against her, Israel was on the verge of being subjected to hopeless slavery by the Philistines.

Although Saul offered some resistance to the advancing enemy, it was not until the time of David that the power of the Philistines was broken. By the occupation of Edom David learned the secrets of using iron and gained access to the natural resources in the Sinaitic peninsula. He thus was able to unite firmly the nation of Israel and to establish military supremacy, which never again was seriously challenged by the Philistines.

From the north the main threat to Israel's expansion came from Aram.[5] As early as patriarchal times Arameans had settled in the Khabur district in upper Mesopotamia, known as Aram-Naharaim. The area under their control may well have extended westward to Aleppo and southward to Kadesh on the Orontes. How extensively they had settled the Damascus area and southward during the days of the judges is not certain.

The most powerful Aramean state was Zobah, located north of Damascus. Hadadezer, ruler of Zobah, extended his domain to the Euphrates (II Sam. 8:3–9) and possibly even wrested some Assyrian colonies from Ashur-rabi II, king of Assyria (*ca.* 1012–975 B.C.). Hittite dynasties in

[4] James H. Breasted, *A History of Egypt* (New York, 1912), p. 512.

[5] The common name for "Aramea" in the Old Testament is "Syria." For a more detailed analysis see Unger, *op. cit.*, pp. 38–55.

Hamath and Carchemish were gradually replaced by the Aramaeans as they expanded northward. Other Aramean states situated southeastward of Damascus were Maacah, Geshur, and Tob. East of Jordan and south of Mount Hermon lay Maacah, with Geshur directly to the south.[6] Since his mother came from this area, Absalom fled to Geshur for safety after he slew Amnon.[7] Tob (Judg. 3:11) was southeast of the Sea of Galilee but north of Gilead.[8] These states under Hadadezer's leadership represented a formidable block to Israel's expansion in the days of David.

The Phoenicians or Canaanites occupied the Mediterranean seacoast to the north. While the Arameans were forming a strong kingdom beyond the Lebanon range, the Phoenicians concentrated on maritime interests. By the time of David the cities of Tyre and Sidon had established a strong state including the immediate coastal territory. By trade and treaty they extended their influence commercially throughout the Mediterranean world. Hiram, king of Tyre, and David, king of Israel, found it mutually beneficial to maintain an attitude of friendship without military friction.

The Edomites, who inhabited the mountainous area south of the Dead Sea, were governed by kings before Israel's rise to monarchy (Gen. 36: 31–39). Although Saul fought with the Edomites (I Sam. 14:47), it was David who actually subdued them. The statement that they became the servants of David, who stationed garrisons throughout their land, has far-reaching import (II Sam. 8:14). From Edom's mines David gained natural resources such as copper and iron, which Israel sorely needed to break the Philistine monopoly in the production of armament.

The Amalekites, also descendants of Esau (Gen. 36:12), held territory west of Edom toward the Egyptian frontier. Saul attempted to destroy the Amalekites (I Sam. 15) but failed to effect a thorough purge. Later the Amalekites raided Ziklag, a city occupied by David when he was a fugitive in Philistine territory, but subsequently they are hardly mentioned

The Moabites, located east of the Dead Sea, were defeated by Saul (I Sam. 14:47) and conquered by David. For about two centuries they remained subservient to Israel as a tributary nation.

The Ammonites occupied the fringe territory on Israel's eastern border. Saul defeated them at Jabesh-gilead when he established himself as king (I Sam. 11:1–11). When the Ammonites defied David's overtures of friendship by an alliance with the Arameans he not only vanquished them (II Sam. 10) but also conquered Rabbath Ammon, their capital city (II Sam. 12:27). Never again did they challenge Israelite superiority during the kingdom period.

[6] Cf. Deut. 3:14; Josh. 12:5 and 13:11.
[7] Cf. II Sam. 3:3; 13:37.
[8] Cf. II Sam. 10:8–10.

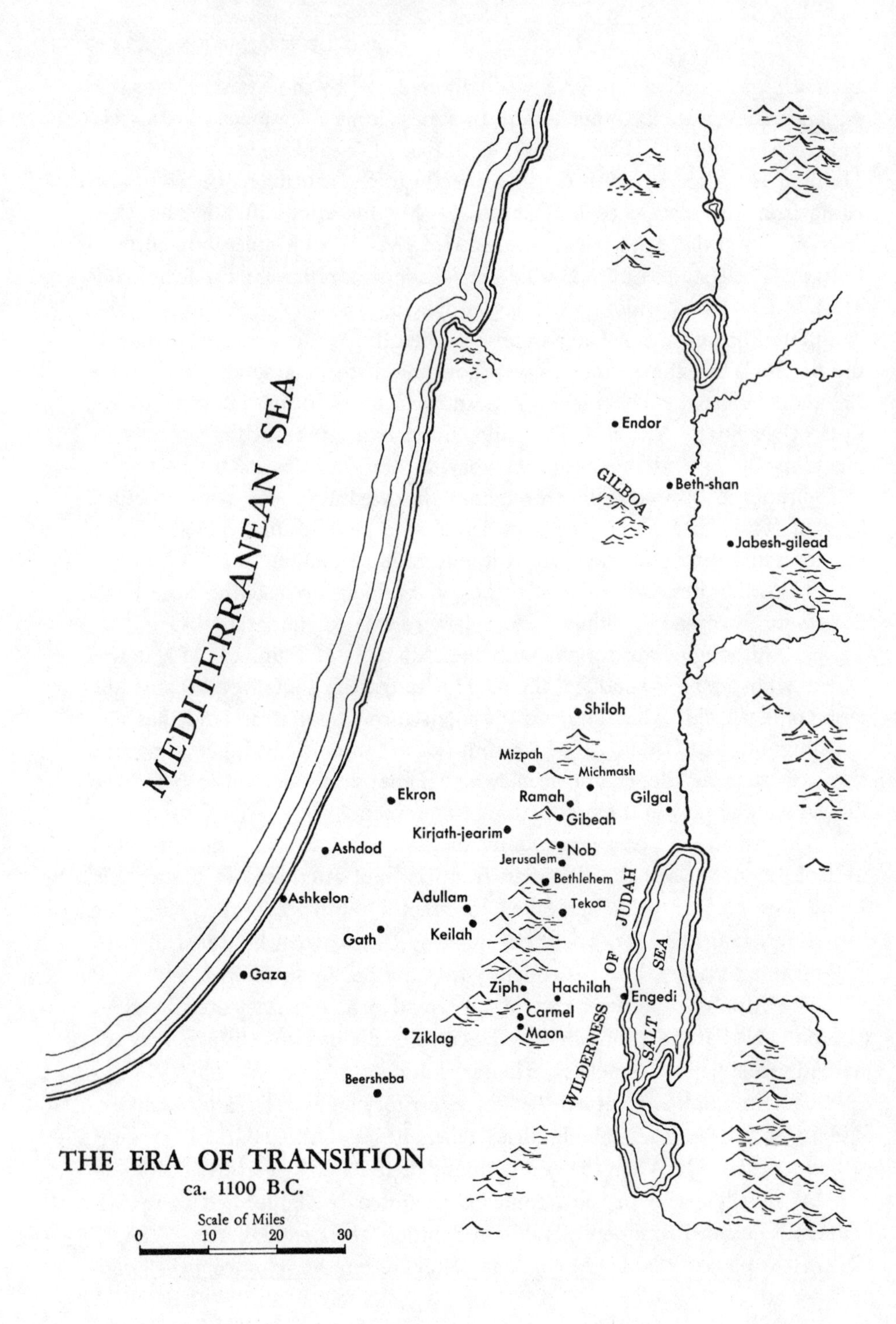

THE ERA OF TRANSITION
ca. 1100 B.C.

Under the Leadership of Eli and Samuel

The times of Eli and Samuel mark the era of transition from the spasmodic and intermittent leadership of judges to the rise of an Israelite monarchy. The two men are not mentioned in the Book of Judges, but are given consideration in the opening chapters of I Samuel (1:1–8:22) as an introduction to the narrative about Israel's first king. These chapters may be subdivided as follows:

I. Eli as priest and judge	1:1–4:22
Birth of Samuel	1:1–2:11
Tabernacle service	2:12–26
Two warnings to Eli	2:27–3:21
Judgment on Eli	4:1–22
II. Samuel as prophet, priest, and judge	5:1–8:22
The ark restored to Israel	5:1–7:2
Revival and victory	7:3–14
Summary of Samuel's ministry	7:15–8:3
Request for a king	8:4–22
III. Leadership transferred to Saul	9:1–12:25
Samuel anoints Saul privately	9:1–10:16
Saul chosen by Israel	10:17–27
Victory over the Ammonites	11:1–11
Saul's public inauguration	11:12–12:25

The story of Eli serves as a background for the ministry of Samuel. As high priest Eli was in charge of worship and sacrifice in the tabernacle at Shiloh. It was to him that the Israelites looked for guidance and leadership in religious and civil affairs.

The religion of Israel was at an all-time low in the days of Eli. He failed to teach his own sons to revere God; "they knew not the Lord" (I Sam. 2:12). Under his jurisdiction they assumed priestly responsibilities, taking advantage of the people as they came to sacrifice and worship. Not only did they rob God in demanding the priestly portion before sacrifice was made, but they conducted themselves in such a manner that the people abhorred bringing their sacrifices to Shiloh. They also profaned the sanctuary with the baseness and debauchery common in Canaanite religion. As one would expect, they refused to heed their father's scathing denunciation of this behavior. It is not surprising that Israel continued to degenerate into increasingly corrupt religious practices.

Into this abhorrent atmosphere Samuel was brought in his childhood days and entrusted to Eli's care. Dedicated to God and encouraged by a godly mother, Samuel grew up in the environment of the tabernacle impervious to the godless influence of Eli's sons.

An unnamed prophet rebuked Eli because he honored his sons more than he honored God (I Sam. 2:27 ff.). His laxity had provoked God's judgment; therefore his sons would lose their lives and a faithful priest would minister in their stead. Reiteration of this decree came to Samuel when God spoke to him during the nighttime (I Sam. 3:1–18).

Swiftly and suddenly these prophetic words received fulfillment. When the frightened Israelites saw that they were losing an encounter with the Philistines they prevailed upon Eli's sons to bring the ark of the covenant, Israel's most sacred object, onto the battlefield. Religion had reached such a low ebb that the people believed that the ark, which represented the very presence of God, would save them from defeat. But they could not force God to serve them. Their defeat was crushing. The enemy captured the ark, slaying the sons of Eli. Small wonder that when Eli heard the shocking news that the ark was in the hands of the Philistines he collapsed and died!

This was a fateful day for Israel. Although the Bible says nothing about the destruction of Shiloh, other evidence vouches that at this time the Philistines reduced to ruins the central shrine which had held the tribes together. Four centuries later Jeremiah warned the inhabitants of Jerusalem not to put their confidence in the Temple (Jer. 7:12–24; 26:6–9). As the Israelites had trusted in the ark for safety, so Jeremiah's generation assumed that Jerusalem as God's dwelling place just could not fall into the hands of the Gentile nations. Jeremiah suggested that they look at the ruins of Shiloh and profit by that historic example. Archaeological excavations point to the razing of Shiloh in the eleventh century. Its destruction at this time accounts for the fact that shortly thereafter the priests officiated at Nob (I Sam. 21:1). It is also noteworthy in this connection that Israel at no time attempted to return the ark to Shiloh.

The Philistine victory effectively demoralized the Israelites. When Eli's daughter-in-law gave birth to a son she fittingly named him "Ichabod" because she sensed keenly that God's blessing had been withdrawn from Israel (I Sam. 4:19–22). The child's name means "Where is the glory?" and at the same time may demonstrate that Canaanite religion had already permeated Israelite thinking, for to a devotee of Baal it would have been an allusion to the death of the fertility god.[9]

Samuel's place in the history of Israel is unique. Being the last of the judges he exercised civil jurisdiction throughout the land of Israel. Moreover,

[9] C. H. Gordon, *Ugaritic Manual* (Rome: Pontificium Institutum Biblicum, 1955), p. 236.

he gained recognition as the greatest prophet in Israel since Mosaic times He also officiated as the leading priest, though he was not of the lineage of Aaron, to whom the responsibilities of high priesthood belonged.

The Bible has preserved comparatively little about the actual ministry of this great leader. When Eli died and the threat of Philistine oppression became more pronounced, the Israelites naturally turned to Samuel for leadership. After he escaped the despoiling of the shrine at Shiloh, Samuel made his home in Ramah, where he erected an altar. There is no indication, however, that this became the religious or civil center of the nation. The tabernacle, which according to Psalm 78:60 had been abandoned by God, is not mentioned in connection with Samuel. Israel regained the ark from the Philistines (I Sam. 5:1–7:2) but kept it at Kirjath-jearim in the private home of Abinadab until the days of David. Apparently it was not in public use during this time. Samuel, nonetheless, performed priestly duties by sacrificing at Mizpah, Ramah, Gilgal, Bethlehem, and wherever he saw the need throughout the land.[10] He continued to fulfill this function even after he turned the affairs of state over to Saul.

In the course of time Samuel gathered about himself a prophetic band over whom he must have wielded considerable influence (I Sam. 19:18–24). It is quite likely that Nathan, Gad, and other prophets active in David's time received their impetus from Samuel.

To execute his judicial responsibilities Samuel annually went to Bethel, Gilgal, and Mizpah (I Sam. 7:15–17). One may infer that in the earlier years, before he delegated responsibilities to his sons Joel and Abiah (I Sam. 8:1–5), he included such distant points as Beersheba in his circuit through the nation.

It is to Samuel's credit that he prevailed upon Israel to purge Canaanite cultic worship from her ranks (I Sam. 7:3 ff.). At Mizpah the people repentantly gathered for prayer, fasting, and sacrifice. Word of the convocation leaked out to the Philistines, who thereupon took advantage of the situation to launch an assault. In the midst of the fray a severe thunderstorm struck fear into the hearts of the Philistine mercenaries, producing confusion and causing them to flee. Evidently the peals of thunder took on portentous meaning to the Philistines, for not again did they attempt to engage the Israelites in battle while Samuel was in command of the tribes.

Eventually the tribal leaders felt that they should bolster their resistance to Philistine aggression and, accordingly, clamored for a king. As an excuse for the establishment of a monarchy they pointed out that Samuel was now an old man and his sons were morally unfit to take his place. Samuel astutely rejected their proposal, eloquently imploring them "not to impose upon

[10] Cf. I Sam. 7:5–9; 7:17; 13:8; 16:2.

themselves a Canaanite institution alien to their own way of life."[11] When in spite of this they persisted in their demand, Samuel acquiesced but only after divine intervention (I Sam. 8).

When Samuel reluctantly consented to the innovation of kingship he had no idea whom God would choose. One day while officiating at a sacrifice he was met by a Benjaminite who came to consult him concerning the location of his father's straying asses. Forewarned of his coming, Samuel realized that Saul was God's choice to be Israel's first king. Not only did Samuel entertain Saul as the guest of honor at the sacrificial feast but privately anointed him as "captain over his inheritance," thereby indicating that kingship was a sacred trust. While returning to Gibeah Saul witnessed the fulfillment of Samuel's predictive words in confirmation of his being chosen for this responsibility. At a subsequent convocation at Mizpah Saul was publicly chosen and enthusiastically supported by the majority in the popular acclaim "Long live the king" (I Sam. 10:17–24). Since Israel had no capital, he returned to his native city of Gibeah in Benjamin.

The Ammonite threat to Jabesh-gilead provides opportunity for Saul to assert his leadership.[12] In response to his national appeal the people rally to his support, resulting in an overwhelming victory over the Ammonites. Assembling all Israel at Gilgal, Samuel publicly endorses Saul as king. He reminds them that God has granted their request. On the basis of Israel's history he assures them of national prosperity, provided the king as well as the citizens obey the Mosaic law. This message of Samuel was divinely confirmed to the Israelites in a sudden rain—a phenomenon during wheat harvest.[13] The people were profoundly impressed and appealed to Samuel for his continued intercession. Although the Israelites had turned to a king for leadership, the words of assurance from Samuel—the prophet who had stemmed the tide of apostasy and initiated an effective prophetic movement in his teaching ministry—made them conscious of his sincere interest in their welfare: "God forbid that I should sin against the Lord in ceasing to pray for you."

Israel's First King

Saul enjoyed the enthusiastic support of his people after an initial victory over the Ammonites at Jabesh-gilead. True, not all viewed his accession

[11] I. Mendelsohn, "Samuel's Denunciation of Kingship in the Light of the Akkadian Documents from Ugarit," BASOR 143 (October, 1956), p. 22.

[12] The brutal humiliation of having one eye struck out as a punishment has been attested in Ugarit as a curse. Cf. Gordon, *The World of the Old Testament* (Garden City: Doubleday, 1958), p. 158.

[13] Normally Palestine has virtually no rain from April to October. To have rain during the wheat harvest, about May 15 to June 15, was considered a miracle.

with unfeigned satisfaction, but these diehards could not withstand his overwhelming popularity (I Sam. 10:27; 11:12, 13). And yet through deliberate disobedience Saul soon ruined his opportunities for success. Because of suspicion and hatred his efforts were so misdirected and national strength so dissipated that his reign ended in utter failure.

The biblical account of Saul's reign as given in I Sam. 13:1–31:13 may be conveniently subdivided as follows:

I. National victories and personal failures	13:1–15:35
Saul fails to wait for Samuel	13:1–15a
Philistines defeated at Michmash	13:15b–14:46
Surrounding nations subdued	14:47–52
Disobedience in an Amalekite victory	15:1–35
II. Saul the king and David the fugitive	16:1–26:25
David's rise to national fame	16:1–17:58
Saul seeks to ensnare David	18:1–19:24
Friendship of David and Jonathan	20:1–42
David's flight and its consequences	21:1–22:23
Saul's pursuit of David	23:1–26:25
III. The Philistine-Israelite conflict	27:1–31:13
Philistines afford David refuge	27:1–28:2
Saul seeks help in Endor	28:3–25
David recovers his possessions	29:1–30:31
Death of Saul	31:1–13

Saul was a warrior who led his nation in numerous military victories. At the strategic location on a hill three miles north of Jerusalem Saul fortified Gibeah[14] to counteract the Philistine military superiority. By capitalizing on the successful attack by his son Jonathan, Saul routed the Philistines in the battle of Michmash (I Sam. 13–14). Among other nations defeated by Saul (I Sam. 14:47–48) were the Amalekites (I Sam. 15:1–9).

The initial success of Israel's first king did not obscure his personal weaknesses. The king of Israel had a unique position among contemporary rulers in that he was responsible for acknowledging the prophet who represented God. In this respect Saul failed twice. Impatiently awaiting Samuel's arrival at Gilgal, Saul officiated at the sacrifice himself (I Sam. 13:8). In his victory over the Amalekites he yielded to the pressure of the people instead of executing Samuel's instructions. The prophet solemnly warned him that God is not pleased with sacrifices which are substituted for obedience. With this stinging rebuke Samuel left King Saul to his own devices. Through his disobedience Saul had forfeited the kingdom.

[14] Saul may have suffered severe defeat at first and then rebuilt Gibeah as a strong palace-fort. Cf. Wright, *Biblical Archaeology,* pp. 121–123.

The anointing of David by Samuel in a private ceremony was unknown to Saul.[15] With the slaying of Goliath David emerges into the national limelight. When sent by his father to take supplies to his brothers who served in the Israelite army encamped against the Philistines he heard the blasphemous threats of Goliath. David reasoned that God, who had aided him in killing bears and lions, would also enable him to kill this enemy who defied the armies of Israel. When the Philistines realized that Goliath, the giant of Gath, had been slain, they fled before Israel. National recognition of the hero David was expressed subsequently in the popular saying, "Saul hath slain his thousands, and David his ten thousands."

On previous occasions David had performed as a musician in the king's court to calm Saul's troubled spirit. So serious was the king's mental disorder that he even attempted to kill the youthful musician. After this heroic feat Saul not only took cognizance of David—possibly to reward his family with tax exemption—but also attached him permanently to the royal court.

Left to his own resources Saul became suspicious and extremely jealous of David. By numerous subtle schemes Saul tried to remove this young national hero. Exposed to the javelin thrusts of Saul or the dangers of battle, David successfully escaped every maneuver designed for his doom. Even when Saul personally went to Naioth, where David had taken refuge with Samuel, he was influenced by the spirit of the prophets to the extent that he was unable to harm or seize David.[16]

Being attached to the royal court proved advantageous to David in several respects. In military exploits he distinguished himself by leading Israelite army units in successful attacks against the Philistines. In his personal relations with Jonathan he shared in one of the noblest friendships noted in Old Testament times. Through his intimate association with the king's son David was enabled to appraise the dastardly designs of Saul more minutely and thus secure himself against unnecessary danger. When David and Jonathan realized that the time had come for David to flee they sealed their friendship with a covenant (I Sam. 20:11–23).

David fled to the Philistines for safety. Denied refuge by Achish, king of Gath, he went to Adullam where four hundred fellow tribesmen gathered about him. Having the care of such a large group, he in time made arrangements for some of his people to reside in Moabite country. Among the advisers associated with him was the prophet Gad.

When Saul heard that Abimelech, the priest at Nob, had furnished supplies to David en route to Philistia, he ordered his execution along with

[15] I Sam. 16–18 is not necessarily in chronological order. For further study see E. J. Young, *Introduction to the Old Testament* (Grand Rapids: Eerdmans, 1949), p. 179, and *New Bible Commentary*, p. 271–272.

[16] For discussion of Saul among the prophets see *New Bible Commentary*, p. 298.

eighty-five other priests. Abiathar, the son of Abimelech, escaped and joined David's fugitive band.

Before long Saul gave vent to his malicious feelings toward David by open pursuit. Several times David was seriously endangered. After relieving the city of Keilah from Philistine attacks he resided there until he was dislodged by Saul. Escaping to Ziph, three miles south of Hebron, he was betrayed by the Ziphites and surrounded by Saul's army. A timely Philistine raid prevented Saul from closing in on David this time. Subsequently in another expedition to Engedi (I Sam. 24) and finally at Hachilah Saul was frustrated in his efforts to kill him.

Several times David had the personal opportunity to slay the king of Israel. Each time he refused, acknowledging that Saul was the Lord's anointed. Although Saul was deeply moved and temporarily admitted his aberration, he soon resumed open hostility.

While David and his company were in the wilderness of Paran they rendered service to the residents of that area by protecting their property from marauding bands of robbers.[17] Nabal, a sheepmaster in Maon who was shearing his sheep near the village of Carmel, ignored David's appeal for "protection money." To cover up his own covetousness in refusing to share his wealth Nabal implied that David had run away from his master. Sensing that the situation was serious, Abigail, the wife of Nabal, judiciously averted revenge by her personal appeal to David with elaborate gifts. When Nabal recovered from his intoxication and learned how narrowly he had escaped revenge at the hands of David he was so shocked that he died ten days later. Subsequently Abigail became the wife of David.

David feared that some day Saul might overtake him unawares. To secure himself and his company of over six hundred men plus women and children he was granted permission by Achish to reside in the Philistine town of Ziklag. Here he remained for approximately the last year and a half of Saul's reign. Near the end of this period David accompanied the Philistines to Aphek to fight against Israel. He was denied participation. He returned to Ziklag in time to recover his possessions lost in an Amalekite raid.

The Israelite armies encamped on Mount Gilboa to fight the Philistines. More than the fear of the enemy, whom he had defeated on previous occasions, troubled the king of Israel at this time. Samuel, long ago ignored by Saul, was not available for interview. Saul turned to God but there was no answer for him by dream, by Urim, or by prophet. He was panic-stricken. In desperation he turned to spiritualistic mediums which he himself had banned in the past.[18] Locating the woman at Endor, who had a familiar

[17] Cf. Cyrus Gordon, *The World of the Old Testament,* p. 163.

[18] Occultism as practiced by the surrounding polytheistic nations was contrary to the Mosaic law. Cf. Lev. 19:31; 20:6, 27; Deut. 18:10–11. For further discussion see

spirit, Saul asked for Samuel. Whatever power this woman possessed, it is apparent in the record (I Sam. 28:3–25) that the intervention of supernatural power in bringing up the prophet Samuel in spirit form was beyond her control. Saul was reminded once more by Samuel that through his own disobedience he had forfeited the kingdom. In his message to Saul the prophet predicted the death of the king and his three sons, as well as the defeat of Israel.

Heavy in heart and with the thought of these tragic developments awaiting him, Saul returned to camp that dismal night. In the course of the battle in the Jezreel plain the Israelite forces were routed, retreating to Mount Gilboa. During the pursuit the Philistines took the lives of the king's three sons. Saul himself was wounded by enemy archers. To avoid ruthless treatment at the hands of the enemy he fell on his sword, thus ending his own life. The Philistines won a decisive victory, gaining indisputable control of the fertile valley from the coast to the Jordan River. They also occupied many cities from which the Israelites were forced to flee. The bodies of Saul and his sons were mutilated and hung on the Philistine fortress at Beth-shan, but the citizens of Jabesh-gilead rescued them for burial. Later, David provided for a transfer of the remains to Saul's family lot at Zela in the tribe of Benjamin (II Sam. 21:11).

Tragic indeed was the termination of Saul's reign as the first king of Israel.[19] Although God-chosen and anointed by the praying prophet Samuel, he failed to realize that obedience was essential in the sacred and unique trust afforded him by God—to be "captain over his inheritance."

SELECTED READING

Ackroyd, Peter R. *The First Book of Samuel.* Cambridge: Cambridge University Press, 1971.

Baldwin, Joyce G. *1 and 2 Samuel.* Donners Grove: Inter-Varsity Press, 1988.

Laney, J. Carl. *First and Second Samuel.* Chicago: Moody Press, 1982.

Merrill, Eugene H. "I and II Samuel" in *Bible Knowledge Commentary.* Wheaton: Scripture Press, 1985.

Vos, Howard F. *1, 2 Samuel.* Grand Rapids: Zondervan Publishing House, 1983.

Wood, Leon. *Israel's United Monarchy.* Grand Rapids: Baker Book House, 1975.

Merrill F. Unger, *Biblical Demonology: A Study of the Spiritual Forces Behind the Present World Unrest* (Wheaton, Ill., 1952), pp. 148–152.

[19] Although the terminal date for Saul's reign is approximately 1011 B.C., the specific dates for Eli, Samuel, and the beginning of Saul's reign are uncertain.

Chapter VIII

Union of Israel under David and Solomon

The golden age of David and Solomon was never duplicated in Old Testament times. Territorial expansion and religious ideals, as envisioned by Moses, were realized to a greater degree than ever before or after in Israel's history. In subsequent centuries the prophetic hopes for the restoration of Israel's fortunes repeatedly referred to the Davidic kingdom as ideal.

Davidic Union and Expansion

David's political endeavors were marked with success. In less than a decade after Saul's death all Israel rallied to the support of David, who had begun his reign with only the small kingdom of Judah. Through military success and friendly overtures he soon controlled the territory from the river of Egypt and the gulf of Aqaba to the Phoenician coast and the land of Hamath. The international respect and recognition which David gained for Israel went unchallenged by foreign powers until the closing years of Solomon's reign.

The new king also distinguished himself as a religious leader. Although denied the privilege of building the Temple, he made elaborate provisions for its erection under his son Solomon. Through David's leadership the priests and Levites were extensively organized for effective participation in the religious activities of the entire nation.[1]

[1] Undoubtedly many of the cities allotted to the Levites or designated as cities of refuge under Moses and Joshua were not used as such until the time of David, when the heathen occupants were dislodged. Cf. Merrill F. Unger, *Archeology and the Old Testament*, pp. 210–211, and W. F. Albright, *Archaeology and the Religion of Israel*, p. 123.

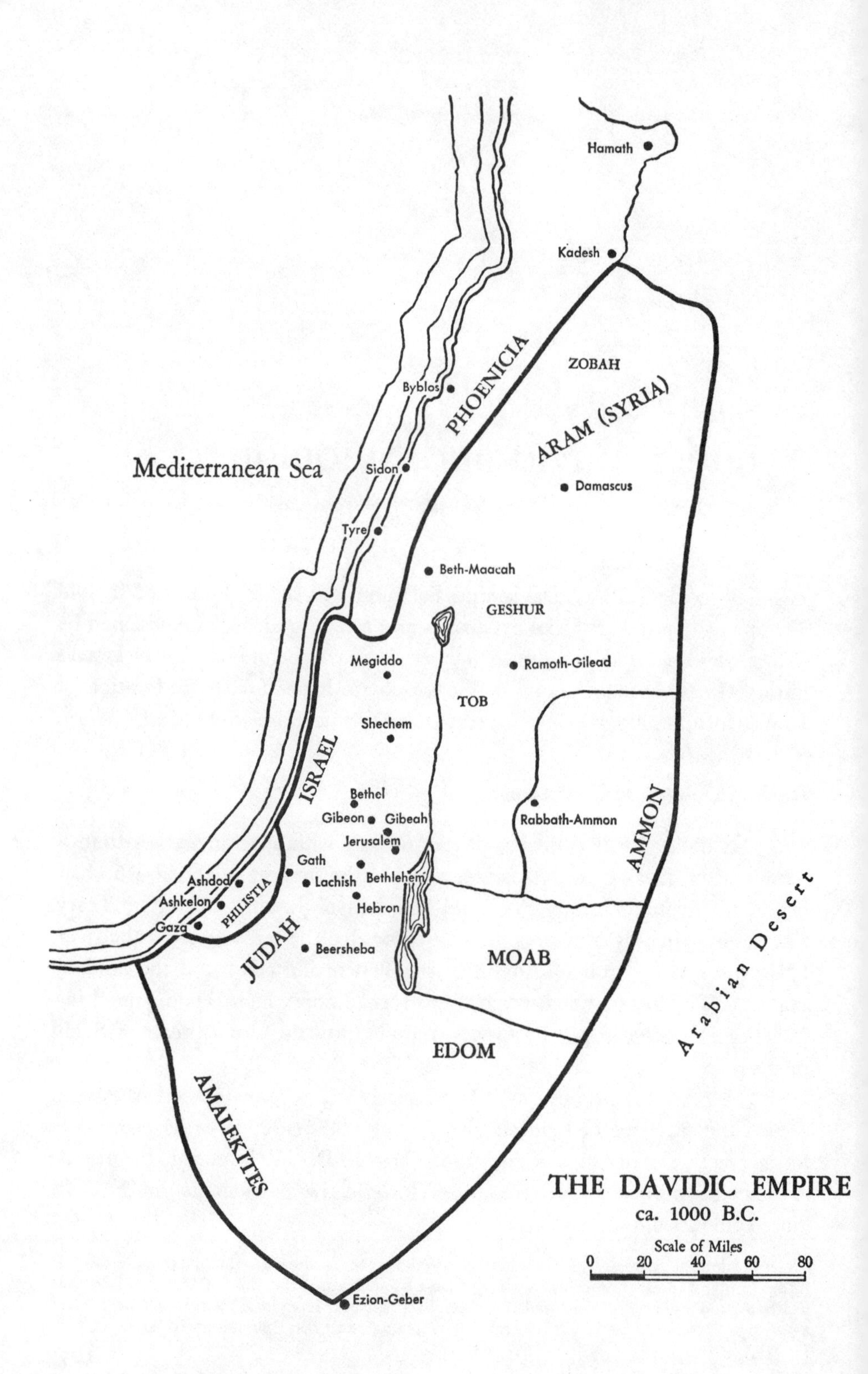
Hamath
Kadesh
ZOBAH
PHOENICIA
ARAM (SYRIA)
Byblos
Mediterranean Sea
Sidon
Damascus
Tyre
Beth-Maacah
GESHUR
Megiddo
Ramoth-Gilead
TOB
Shechem
ISRAEL
Bethel
Gibeon
Gibeah
Rabbath-Ammon
Jerusalem
AMMON
Gath
Ashdod
Lachish
Bethlehem
Ashkelon
PHILISTIA
Hebron
Gaza
JUDAH
Beersheba
MOAB
Arabian Desert
EDOM
AMALEKITES
THE DAVIDIC EMPIRE
ca. 1000 B.C.
Scale of Miles
0 20 40 60 80
Ezion-Geber

The Book of II Samuel depicts the reign of David in great detail. A lengthy section (11–20) provides the exclusive account of sin, crime, and rebellion in the royal family. The transfer of the kingdom to Solomon and the death of David are reported in the opening chapters of I Kings. The Book of I Chronicles, also an account of the Davidic period, represents an independent unit, focusing attention upon David as the first ruler in a continuing dynasty. By way of introduction to the establishment of the Davidic throne, the Chronicler traces the genealogical background of the twelve tribes over whom David ruled. Saul is but briefly mentioned, after which David is introduced as king of all Israel. The organization of Israel politically as well as religiously is more elaborately given and the supremacy of David over the surrounding nations receives a greater emphasis. Before concluding with the death of David, the last eight chapters in this book give an extensive description of his preparation for the building of the Temple. Consequently I Chronicles is a valuable complement to the record in II Samuel.

The outline of David's reign as given in this chapter represents a suggested chronological arrangement of the events as recorded in II Samuel and I Chronicles:

The King of Judah

	II Sam.	I Chron.
Genealogical background		1:1–9:44
David laments Saul's death	1:1–27	10:1–14
Disintegration of Saul's dynasty	2:1–4:12	

Born in turbulent times, David was subjected to a rugged period of training in preparation for the kingship of Israel. He was requisitioned by the king for military service after slaying Goliath and gained invaluable experience in military exploits against the Philistines. After he was forced to leave the court he led a fugitive band and ingratiated himself with the landholders and sheepmasters in southern Israel by providing protective service. At the same time he negotiated successful diplomatic relations with the Philistines and Moabites while he was regarded as an outlaw of Israel.

David was in Philistine country when Saul's army was decisively defeated on Mount Gilboa. Shortly after David had rescued his wives and recovered the spoil which had been seized by Amalekite raiders a messenger reported to him the fateful events that had taken place in Israel. Overcome by grief, David gave immortal tribute to Saul and Jonathan in one of the greatest elegies in the Old Testament. Not only had Israel lost her king, but David keenly felt the loss of his most intimate friend, Jonathan. When the newsbearer, an Amalekite, anticipated a reward by claiming credit for Saul's death, David ordered his execution for having touched the Lord's anointed.

After ascertaining God's approval David returned to the land of Israel.

At Hebron the leaders of his own tribe (Judah) anointed and acknowledged him as their king. He was well known to the clans of this area, having protected the landholders and shared with them the spoils obtained in raiding their enemies (I Sam. 30:26–31). As king of Judah David sent a message of commendation to the men of Jabesh for giving King Saul a respectable burial. No doubt this friendly and gracious gesture also had political implications in that David was bidding for their support.

Israel was in serious trouble when Saul's reign ended. The capital at Gibeah either experienced destruction or gradually fell into ruins.[2] Eventually Abner, the head of the Israelite army, was able to restore enough order to have Ishbosheth (Ishbaal) anointed as king. The enthronement took place in Gilead, for the Philistines had control over the land west of the Jordan.[3] Since the son of Saul reigned over the northern tribes only two years (II Sam. 2:10) during the seven and a half years in which David ruled in Hebron, it appears that the Philistine problem delayed the accession of the new king for about five years.

Thus the people of Judah pledged their allegiance to David, while the rest of the Israelites remained loyal to the dynasty of Saul under the leadership of Abner and Ishbosheth. As a result civil war prevailed. After being severely rebuked by Ishbosheth, Abner appealed to David and offered him the support of all Israel. In accordance with David's request Michal, the daughter of Saul, was restored to him as wife. This was accomplished under the supervision of Abner with Ishbosheth's consent. Thereby it was publicly conveyed to Israel that David held no animosity toward Saul's dynasty. Abner himself went to Hebron where he promised David the allegiance of his people. After this alliance had been completed Abner was killed by Joab in order to avenge the death of his brother Asahel, whom Abner had slain in civil strife. The death of Abner left Israel without strong leadership. Before long Ishbosheth was murdered by two men from the tribe of Benjamin. When the murderers appeared before David they were immediately executed. He disapproved of their slaying a righteous person. Without malice or vengeance David gained the recognition of all Israel while the dynasty of Saul was eliminated from political leadership.

Jerusalem—the National Capital

	II Sam.	I Chron.
The conquest of Jerusalem	5:1–9	11:1–9
David's military strength	23:8–39	11:10–12:40
Recognition by Philistia and Phoenicia	5:10–25	14:1–17

[2] G. E. Wright, *Biblical Archaeology,* pp. 122–123.
[3] E. Mould, *Essentials of Bible History* (rev. ed.; New York, 1951), p. 188, attributes this choice of capital to Philistine occupation.

Jerusalem—center of religion	6:1-23	13:1-14
		15:1-16:43
An eternal throne	7:1-29	17:1-27

There is no indication that the Philistines interfered with David's ascendancy as king in Hebron. It is possible that they simply regarded him as a vassel as long as the rest of Israel, being torn by civil warfare, offered no unified resistance.[4]

But they became alarmed when David gained the acceptance of the whole nation. A Philistine attack (II Sam. 5:17-25 and I Chron. 14:8-17) very likely took place before the conquest and occupation of Zion. Twice David defeated them, thus preventing their interference in the unification of Israel under the new king. No doubt the Philistine threat itself had a unifying effect on Israel.

In looking for a central location for the capital of a united Israel David turned to Jerusalem. This was a strategic location and less vulnerable to attack. As a Canaanite fortress occupied by Jebusites it had successfully resisted conquest and occupation by the Israelites. In Egyptian records as early as 1900 B.C. this city had been referred to as Jerusalem. When David challenged his men to conquer the city and expel the Jebusites, Joab accepted and was rewarded with appointment as chief of the military staff in Israel. With the occupation of the fortress by David it became known as the "city of David" (I Chron. 11:17).

In the Davidic period Jerusalem occupied the brow of a hill directly south of the temple area at an approximate elevation of 2,500 feet above sea level.[5] The site is known more particularly as Ophel. Along the east side was the Kidron valley, joining to the south with the valley of Hinnom, which extended to the west. Separating it from a western elevation, which in modern times is called Mount Zion, was the Tyropoeon valley. According to Josephus, there was a valley on the north end separating Ophel from the site used for the Temple. Apparently this Ophel-Zion area was of a higher elevation than the temple site at the time of Davidic conquest. In the second century B.C., however, the Maccabees leveled the hill, dumping the debris of the Davidic city into the valley below. As a result, archaeologists have been unable to link confidently any artifacts with David's reign.

Successfully established as king over the twelve tribes of Israel, David reorganized the government. During his days as an outlaw he had a following of hundreds of men. These were well organized under his command at Ziklag, and later at Hebron (I Chron. 11:10-12:22). These men had so distinguished themselves in military exploits that they were appointed princes and

[4] B. W. Anderson, *Understanding the Old Testament* (Englewood Cliffs, N.J., 1957), p. 134.

[5] G. E. Wright, *op. cit.*, p. 126.

leaders. When all Israel rallied to David's support, the organization was enlarged to include the whole nation, with Jerusalem as the center (I Chron. 12:23-40). By contracting with the Phoenicians a magnifical palace was built for David the king (II Sam. 5:11-12).

At the same time Jerusalem became the religious center for the whole nation (I Chron. 13:1-17:27 and II Sam. 6:1-7:29). When David attempted to move the ark of the covenant from the home of Abinadab at Kirjath-jearim by means of a cart instead of having it borne by the priests (Num. 4) Uzzah was suddenly slain. Instead of taking the ark to Jerusalem David stored it at the home of Obed-edom in Gibeah. When he sensed that the Lord was blessing this home David immediately transferred it to Jerusalem to be housed in a tent or a tabernacle. Proper worship was now restored to Israel on a national scale.[6]

With the renewed interest in Israel's religion David became desirous of building a more permanent house of worship. When he shared this plan with Nathan, the prophet, it met with immediate approval. The next night, however, God commissioned Nathan to inform the king that the building of the Temple should be postponed until David's son was established on the throne. This was divine assurance for David that his son would succeed him and that he would not be subjected to such a calamitous fate as befell King Saul. The magnitude of this promise to David, however, extends far beyond the time and scope of Solomon's kingdom. The seed of David included more than Solomon, since the commitment clearly stated that the Davidic throne was to be established forever. Even if iniquity and sin prevailed in David's posterity, God would temporarily judge and punish but would not forfeit his promise nor withdraw his mercy indefinitely.

No earthly kingdom or dynasty has ever had eternal duration—such as the heaven and the earth. Neither did the earthly throne of David—without linking his lineage with Jesus, who is specifically identified in the New Testament as the son of David. This assurance, given to David through the prophet Nathan, constitutes another link in the series of Messianic promises given in Old Testament times. God was gradually unfolding the initial commitment that ultimate victory would come through the seed of the woman (Gen. 3:15). A fuller revelation of the Messiah and his eternal kingdom is given by the prophets in subsequent centuries.

Why was David denied the privilege of building the Temple? In the closing years of his reign he came to the realization that he had been commissioned as a military statesman to establish the kingdom of Israel (I Chron. 28:3; 22:8). Whereas David's reign was characterized by warfare, Solomon enjoyed a period of peace. Perhaps peace prevailed at the time

[6] Jerusalem was not the exclusive center of worship. The Mosaic tabernacle and altar of sacrifice remained at Gibeon (II Chron. 1:3).

David expressed his intentions to build a temple, but there is no way to ascertain in Scripture how the subsequently reported wars are related chronologically to this message by Nathan. Possibly not until the end of his reign did David come to realize that the days of Solomon would be a more opportune time for building a temple.

Prosperity and Supremacy

	II Sam.	I Chron.
List of nations conquered	8:1-13	18:1-13
David shares responsibility and blessing	8:15-9:13	18:14-17
The famine	21:1-14	
Defeat of Ammonites, Syrians,	10:1-18	
and Philistines	21:15-22	19:1-20:8
Song of deliverance (Ps. 18)	22:1-51	

The expansion of the Davidic rule from the tribal area of Judah to a vast empire stretching its domain from the river of Egypt to regions of the Euphrates receives scant attention in the Bible. And yet this record is of basic importance historically, since Israel was the leading nation in the Fertile Crescent at the beginning of the tenth century B.C. Fortunately archaeological excavations have yielded complementary information.

David was immediately challenged by the Philistines when he was recognized as king of all Israel (II Sam. 5:17-25). He defeated them twice, but over a period of time it is quite likely that there were frequent battles before he reduced them to a tributary and subservient state. The capture of one of their chief cities, Gath, and the slaying of the Philistine giants (II Sam. 8:1 and 21:15-22) are very likely sample encounters in this crucial period when Israel gained the upper hand.

Beth-shan was conquered during this period.[7] At Debir and Beth-shemesh casemated walls suggested that David built a line of defense against the Philistines.[8] The observations that the Philistines had the monopoly on iron in the days of Samuel (I Sam. 3:19-20) and that David freely used it near the end of his reign (I Chron. 22:3) suggest that a long chapter could have been written on the economic revolution in Israel. The period of outlawry and Philistine residence not only provided David with preparation in military leadership but undoubtedly gave him firsthand acquaintance with the formula and methods used by the Philistines in the production of arms. Perhaps many of the plans for military and economic expansion were made

[7] G. E. Wright, *op. cit.*, p. 124.
[8] W. F. Albright, *The Biblical Period* (Pittsburgh, 1950), pp. 24–25.

while David was at Hebron but were actually executed after Jerusalem was made the capital. The Philistines had reason to be alarmed when war-torn and defeated Israel was unified under David.

The conquest and occupation of Edom was strategically important. It gave David a valuable source of natural resources. The Arabah desert which extends southward from the Dead Sea to the gulf of Aqaba, was rich in iron and copper needed to break the Philistine monopoly. To make sure that this supply would not be endangered the Israelites established garrisons throughout Edom (II Sam. 8:14).

Apparently Israel had little interference from Moab and the Amalekites at this time. They are listed among the nations that were subservient, sending silver and gold to David.

To the northeast the rise of Davidic might in expanding the state of Israel was challenged by the Ammonite and Aramean tribes. The former had settled from Carchemish on the Euphrates to the eastern borders of Palestine. They were already regarded as enemies in the days of Saul (I Sam. 14:47). When David was an outlaw at least one of these Aramean states must have been friendly toward him, since Talmai, the king of Geshur, had given him his daughter Maacah as wife (II Sam. 3:3). Now that David had defeated the Philistines and concluded a treaty with the Phoenicians, the Arameans feared the rise of Israelite power. Expansion of Israel endangered their wealth and challenged their control of fertile plains and extensive trade. After shamefully mistreating David's goodwill messengers, the Ammonites immediately involved the Arameans in the opposition of Israel, but their combined forces were scattered by David's troops.

Later the city of Rabbath in Ammon was captured by the Israelites (I Chron. 20:1). The Aramean forces then organized under Hadadezer,[9] who employed or gathered forces from as far north as Aram-Naharaim or Mesopotamia (I Chron. 19:6). This time Israelite forces advanced up to Helam, defeating this strong coalition. This spelled doom for the Aramean-Ammonite alliance.

Subsequent to this, David attacked Hadadezer once more when the Syrians[10] were reaching out to the Euphrates to claim territory under Assyrian control (II Sam. 8:3). Damascus, which was so closely allied with Hadadezer (I Chron. 18:3–8), came under the control of David, thus adding another victory for the Israelites. Their garrisons occupied the city, placing it under heavy tribute, and Hadadezer conceded large quantities of gold and bronze to David. The domination of the Aramean states up to Hamath, on the Orontes, added greatly to the resources enriching Israel. Not until the

[9] M. F. Unger, *Israel and the Aramaeans,* pp. 38–55.

[10] G. E. Wright, *op. cit.,* p. 124. Chronologically this event follows the attack David made on the Ammonite-Syrian alliance in II Sam. 10:1–14.

closing years of David's reign was the Israelite administration of Damascus challenged.

In these days of national expansion the provisions made for Mephibosheth illustrate the magnanimous attitude of David toward his predecessor's descendants (II Sam. 9:1–13). When David learned of the misfortune that had befallen Jonathan's son, Mephibosheth, he allotted him a pension from the royal treasury. The invalid was given a home in Jerusalem and placed under care of the servant Ziba.

Mephibosheth received special consideration in a subsequent crisis (II Sam. 21:1–14), when famine occurred in the land of Israel. God revealed to David that this famine was a judgment for Saul's terrible crime of attempting to exterminate the Gibeonites with whom Joshua had made a covenant (Josh. 9:3 ff.). Realizing that this could only be expiated (Num. 35:31 ff.), David allowed the Gibeonites to execute seven of Saul's descendants. Mephibosheth, however, was spared. When David was informed of the mourning of Rizpah, a concubine of Saul, he provided for the proper burial of the bones of these seven victims in the family sepulcher in Benjamin. The remains of Saul and Jonathan were also transferred to this place. With this the famine came to an end.

As king of the Israelite empire David did not fail to acknowledge God as the one who granted Israel military victories and material prosperity. In a psalm of thanksgiving (II Sam. 22:1–51) David expresses his praise to the omnipotent One for deliverance from his enemies in Israel as well as from the heathen nations. This psalm is also recorded in chapter 18 of Psalms. It represents but a sample of many that he composed on various occasions during his checkered career as a shepherd boy, a servant at the royal court, an outlaw of Israel, and finally as the architect and builder of Israel's largest empire.[11]

Sin in the Royal Family

	II Sam.
David's crime and repentance	11:1–12:31
Amnon's crime and results	13:1–36
Absalom's defeat in rebellion	13:37–18:33
David recovers the throne	19:1–20:26

Character imperfections in a member of the royal family are not minimized in the Hebrew Scriptures. A king of Israel who indulged in sin could not expect to escape the judgments of God. At the same time David, as a

[11] The variations in these two chapters are similar to the synoptic problem in the Gospels. C. F. Keil, *The Books of Samuel,* suggests that these two chapters came from a common source.

truly penitent sinner, acknowledged his iniquity and thus qualified as a man who pleased God (I Sam. 13:14).

David practiced polygamy (II Sam. 3:2–5; 11:27). Although this is definitely forbidden in the fuller revelation of the New Testament, it was tolerated in Old Testament times because of the hardness of Israel's heart. It was also freely practiced by surrounding nations. A harem at the court was the accepted thing. Although warned about the multiplicity of wives in the Mosaic law (Deut. 17:17), David acquired many. Some of these marriages undoubtedly had political implications, such as his marriage to Michal, the daughter of Saul, and to Maacah, the daughter of Talmai, king of Geshur. Like others, David had to suffer the consequences as the crimes of incest, murder, and rebellion unfolded in his family life.

David's sin of adultery and murder constituted a perfect crime from the human standpoint. It was at a time of military success and empire expansion. The Philistines had already been defeated and the Aramean-Ammonite coalition had been broken the previous year. While David remained in Jerusalem, the Israelite armies under the command of Joab were sent to conquer the Ammonite city of Rabbah. Being enticed by Bathsheba, David committed adultery. He knew that she was the wife of Uriah, the Hittite, a loyal mercenary in the army of Israel. The king recalled Uriah from the front line but then sent him back to Joab with a letter arranging for him to be killed in battle by the enemy. When reports came to Jerusalem that Uriah had fallen in an Ammonite battle, David married Bathsheba. Perhaps the facts of David's heinous crime were concealed, since a front-line casualty was a common occurrence. Even if this was known to Joab, who was he to challenge or reprove the king?

Although David was responsible to no one in his kingdom, he failed to realize that this "perfect crime" was known to God. For a despot in a heathen nation adultery and murder might have passed unchallenged; but this could not be so in Israel, where a king held his position as a sacred trust. When Nathan depicted David's crime in the dramatic story of the rich man who took advantage of his poor servant David became enraged that such injustice might prevail under his jurisdiction. Nathan boldly declared that David was the man guilty of murder and adultery. Fortunately for Nathan, the king repented. David's spiritual crises found lofty expression in poetry (Pss. 32 and 51). He was granted forgiveness but grave, indeed, were the domestic consequences (II Sam. 12:11).

Immorality and murder within the family soon involved David in civil strife and rebellion. David's lack of discipline and self-restraint set a poor example for his sons. Amnon's immoral behavior with his half sister resulted in his assassination by Absalom, another son of David. Naturally Absalom incurred the disfavor of his father. As a result he found it expedient to leave

Jerusalem, taking refuge with Talmai, his grandfther in Geshur. Here he remained for three years.

In the meantime Joab was seeking to effect a reconciliation between David and Absalom. By employing a woman from Tekoah (II Sam. 14) Joab secured authorization from the king to bring Absalom to Jerusalem, with the understanding that he could not appear at the royal court. After two years Absalom finally received permission to come into the king's presence. Having regained the favor of his father, he secured for himself a royal guard of fifty men with horses and chariots. For four years[12] handsome Absalom was exceedingly active in public relations at the gates of Jerusalem, winning the favor and approval of the Israelites. Pretending to fulfill a vow, he secured leave from the king to go down to Hebron.

The rebellion Absalom staged at Hebron was a complete surprise to David. Spies had been sent throughout the land to proclaim that Absalom would be made king at the sound of the trumpet blast. Very likely many of the people who had been duly impressed by Absalom concluded that he, as David's son, was now taking over the kingdom. At any rate, many people supported Absalom, including David's counselor Ahithophel. The rebel forces, led by Absalom, marched into Jerusalem and David, who was unprepared to resist, fled to Mahanaim beyond the Jordan. Hushai, a devoted friend and counselor, followed David's advice and remained in Jerusalem to counteract the counsel of Ahithophel. The latter, who may have planned the whole rebellion and pledged his support to Absalom from the beginning, advised Absalom to let him pursue David immediately, before any opposition could be organized. But Absalom asked for the opinion of Hushai, who persuaded him to postpone the pursuit, thus gaining valuable time needed by David for organizing his forces. Having turned traitor and realizing that David would be restored, Ahithophel hanged himself.

David was a brilliant militarist. He prepared his forces for battle and soon put Absalom's armies to flight. Joab, contrary to the orders of David, killed Absalom while pursuing the enemy. David, having lost his sense of priority, mourned the death of his son instead of celebrating the victory. This turn of events caused Joab to rebuke the king for neglecting the welfare of the Israelites who had given him loyal support.

With Absalom removed, the people again turned to David for leadership. The tribe of Judah, who had supported the rebel son of David, was the last group to welcome him back after he made a hasty concession by substituting Amasa for Joab.

When David returned to the capital another rebellion developed out of the prevailing confusion. Sheba, a Benjaminite, capitalizing on the fact

[12] The Syriac Vulgate and others adopt "four" instead of "forty." Absalom was born at Hebron. David's total reign was 40 years.

that Judah had brought David back to Jerusalem, stirred up opposition to him. Amasa was commissioned to suppress this rebellion. In subsequent developments Joab killed Amasa and then led the pursuit of Sheba, who was beheaded on the Syrian frontier by the people of Abel-beth-maacah. Joab blew the trumpet, returned to Jerusalem, and continued to serve as commander of the army under David.

Through nearly a decade of David's reign the solemn words spoken by Nathan were realistically fulfilled. Beginning with Amnon's immorality and continuing to the suppression of Sheba's rebellion, evil had fermented in David's own house.

Retrospect and Prospect

	II Sam.	I Chron.
Sin in numbering the people	24:1–25	21:1–27
Solomon charged to build the Temple		21:28–22:19
Duties of Levites		23:1–26:28
Civil officers		26:29–27:34
Charge to officials and people		28:1–29:22
Last words of David	23:1–7	
Death of David		29:22–30

A favorite project of David's during the last years of his life was making preparations for building the Temple. Elaborate plans and detailed arrangements were carefully made in the acquisition of building materials. The kingdom was well organized for efficient use of local and foreign labor. David even outlined the details for religious worship in the proposed structure.

The military and civil organization of the kingdom developed gradually throughout David's reign as the empire expanded. The basic pattern of organization utilized by David may have been similar to Egyptian practice.[13] The recorder or chronicler was in charge of the archives and, as such, had the very important position of being public relations man between the king and his officers. The scribe or secretary was responsible for domestic and foreign correspondence, and accordingly had a hand in matters of diplomacy. In a later period of David's reign (II Sam. 20:23–25) an additional officer is listed as being in charge of forced labor. Very likely other high officials were added as the government responsibilities multiplied. Matters of judgment apparently were handled by the king himself (II Sam. 14:4–17; 15:1–6).

The commander in chief of military forces was Joab. Outstanding in ability and leadership, he was not only responsible for military victories but exerted considerable influence upon David himself. A unit of foreign troops

[13] W. F. Albright, *Archaeology and the Religion of Israel*, p. 120. For a more elaborate treatment see Wright, *op. cit.*, pp. 124–125.

or mercenaries, composed of Cherethites and Pelethites under the command of Benaiah, may have been David's personal army. The king also had a confidential counselor. Ahithophel had served in this capacity until he supported Absalom in his rebellion. The mighty men who had attached themselves to David before he became king were now known as a council or legion of honor (I Chron. 11:10–47; II Sam. 23:8–39). When David organized his kingdom with Jerusalem as the capital there were thirty men in this group. In time more were added to the ranks of men who distinguished themselves by heroic deeds. From this select group of heroes twelve men were chosen to be in charge of the national army, consisting of twelve units (I Chron. 27:1–24). Throughout the realm David appointed supervisors over his farms, orchards, and livestock (I Chron. 27:25–31).

The military census of Israel and the punitive consequences for the king and his people are closely related to David's elaborate plans for the building of the Temple. The reason for divine punishment upon David, as well as the whole nation, is not explicitly stated. The king ordered the census taken. Joab objected but was overruled (II Sam. 24). In less than ten months he completed the numbering of Israel with the exception of the tribes of Levi and Benjamin. The military strength of Israel was approximately one and a half million,[14] which would suggest a total population of about five or six million.[15]

David was keenly conscious of the fact that he had sinned in taking this census. Since both accounts precede this incident with a list of military heroes, the census may have been motivated by pride and a reliance on military strength for Israel's national achievements.[16] At the same time, David's carnal state of mind in imposing this census was viewed as a judgment on Israel (II Sam. 24:1; and I Chron. 21:1). Perhaps Israel was punished for the rebellions under Absalom and Sheba during David's reign.

David, penitent for this sin, was informed through Gad, the prophet, that he could choose one of the following punishments: a three-year famine, a three-month period of military reverses, or a three-day pestilence. David resigned himself and his nation to God's mercy by choosing the last of the three. The pestilence lasted only one day, but 70,000 people died throughout

[14] This figure represents the people qualified for military service, since the actual army is listed as 288,000 in I Chron. 27:1–15. Note the variation: II Sam. 24:9 lists 800,000 men for Israel and 500,000 men for Judah. I Chron. 21:5 lists 300,000 more for Israel and 30,000 less for Judah. Since these items were not listed in the official records of the king, I Chron. 27:24, both sources give approximate round numbers with the exact reason for the variation not given in either account. See Keil, *op. cit.,* in commentary on II Sam. 24.

[15] Albright suggests that the total population of Israel under Solomon was only about 750,000 people. He regards the census accounts in Num. 1 and 26 as recensions of the Davidic census. See *Biblical Period,* pp. 59–60 (fn. 75). A. Edersheim regards a population for Israel of five or six million as not excessive. See *Bible History of the Old Testament* (Grand Rapids: reprint 1949), Vol. II, p. 40.

[16] See Keil, *op. cit.,* in comments on II Sam. 24.

Israel. In the meantime David and the elders, clothed in sackcloth, recognized the angel of the Lord standing by the threshing floor, just north of Jerusalem on Mount Moriah. Recognizing that this was the destroying angel, David offered intercessory prayer for his people. Through instructions given by Gad, David purchased this threshing floor from Ornan, the Jebusite. As he offered a sacrifice before God David was conscious of divine response when the pestilence ceased, terminating the judgment upon his people. The destroying angel disappeared and Jerusalem was saved.

David was so impressed that he determined to make the threshing floor the location of the altar of burnt offering. Here the Temple was to be erected. It may well have been here that Abraham, approximately a millennium earlier, had been willing to offer his son Isaac and likewise had had a divine revelation and approval.

Although Mount Moriah was outside the city of Zion (Jerusalem) in David's time, Solomon included it in the capital city. David had previously brought the ark to Jerusalem and housed it in a tent. The altar of burnt offering and the tabernacle built under the supervision of Moses were located in Gibeon, a high place five or six miles northwest of Jerusalem. Since David had been denied the privilege of actually building the Temple, it is quite likely that no specific plans had been developed previously as to the location and erection of the central sanctuary. Through the theophany on the threshing floor David concluded that this was the place where the house of God should be built.

David reflected on the fact that he had been a man of war and bloodshed. Perhaps now he realized that had he attempted to build the Temple it would have been disrupted by the foreign and civil wars that erupted so frequently during his reign. The seven and a half years at Hebron had been a period of preparation. During the next decade Jerusalem was established as the national capital, while the nation was unified in the conquest of the surrounding nations. Very likely Solomon was born during this time. It must have been toward the end of the second decade of David's reign that Absalom murdered Amnon, since Absalom was born while David was at Hebron. The domestic troubles ending in the rebellion by Absalom lasted about ten years and would probably coincide with the third decade of David's reign. When David had successfully established the military supremacy of Israel and organized the nation it seemed timely to concentrate on preparations for building the Temple.

With Mount Moriah as the location, David envisioned the house of God being built under the supervision of Solomon, his son. He took a census of the foreigners in the land and immediately organized them for working with stone, metal, and timber. Earlier in his reign David had made arrangements with the people of Tyre and Sidon to build his palace in Jerusalem (II Sam. 5:11). Cedars for the building project were furnished by Hiram, king of Tyre. Solomon was charged with the responsibility of obeying the law as it had been given through Moses. As king of Israel he was accountable to God and, if obedient, would enjoy God's blessing.

In a public assembly David charged the princes and priesthood to recognize Solomon as his successor. He then proceeded to outline carefully the temple services. The 38,000 Levites were organized into units and assigned to the regular ministry of the Temple. Smaller units were given responsibilities as gatekeepers, while musicians' guilds had charge of the vocal and instrumental music. Other Levites were assigned as treasurers to care for the lavish gifts dedicated by Israelite princes throughout the nation (I Chron. 26:20 ff.). These donations were essential for the execution of the carefully made plans for the Temple (I Chron. 28:11–29:9). The stage was now set for the glorious reign of Solomon.

The last words of David (II Sam. 23:1–7) reveal the greatness of Israel's most honored hero. Another song (II Sam. 22), expressing his thanksgiving and praise for a lifetime replete with great victories and deliverances, may have been composed in the closing year of his life and closely associated with this poem. Here he speaks prophetically about the eternal endurance of his kingdom. God had spoken to him, affirming an everlasting covenant. This testimony by David would have made a fitting epitaph for his tomb.

The Golden Era of Solomon

Peace and prosperity characterize the reign of Solomon. David had established the kingdom—now Solomon was to reap the benefits of his father's labors.

The account of this era is briefly given in I Kings 1:1–11:43 and II Chronicles 1:1–9:31. The focal point in both books is the building and dedication of the Temple, which receives much more consideration than any other aspect of Solomon's reign. Other building projects, trade and commerce, industrial progress, and the wise administration of the kingdom are but briefly mentioned. Many of these activities, barely mentioned in the biblical record, have been illuminated through archaeological excavations during the past three decades. Except for the building of the Temple, which is assigned to the first decade of his reign, and the building of his palace, which was completed thirteen years later, there is little information that could be used as a basis for a chronological analysis of Solomon's reign. Consequently the treatment below will be topical, bringing together data from the two accounts, which are interwoven in the following outline:

	I Kings	II Chron.
I. Solomon established as king		
Solomon emerges as sole ruler	1:1–2:46	
Prayer for wisdom at Gibeon	3:1–15	1:1–13
Wisdom in administration	3:16–4:34	
Trade and prosperity		1:14–17
II. The building program		
The Temple in Jerusalem	5:1–7:51	2:1–5:1
(Solomon's palace—I Kings 7:1–8)		
Dedication of the Temple	8:1–9:9	5:2–8:16
Settlement with Hiram of Tyre	9:10–25	
III. International relations		
Naval ventures at Ezion-geber	9:26–28	8:17–18
The Queen of Sheba	10:1–13	9:1–12
Revenue and trade	10:14–29	9:13–31
IV. Apostasy and death		
Foreign wives and idolatry	11:1–8	
Judgment and adversaries	11:9–43	

Establishment of the Throne

Solomon's accession to his father's throne was not without opposition. As long as Solomon had not been publicly crowned Adonijah fostered ambitions to succeed David. In a sense he was justified. Amnon and Absalom had been killed. Chileab, the third oldest son of David, apparently had died, since he is not mentioned, and Adonijah was next in line. On the other hand, David's inherent weakness in domestic problems was evident in the lack of discipline in his family (I Kings 1:6). Evidently Adonijah had not been taught to respect the divinely revealed fact that Solomon was to be heir to the Davidic throne (II Sam. 7:12; I Kings 1:17). Following in the pattern of Absalom, his brother, Adonijah appropriated an escort of fifty men complete with horses and chariots, enlisted the support of Joab, invited Abiathar the priest at Jerusalem, and proceeded to have himself anointed as king. This event took place in the royal gardens at En-rogel south of Jerusalem. Conspicuously absent in this gathering of government officials and the royal family were Nathan the prophet, Benaiah the commander of David's personal army, Zadok the officiating priest at Gilbeah, and Solomon with his mother, Bathsheba.

When the news of this festal gathering reached the palace Nathan and Bathsheba immediately appealed to David. As a result Solomon rode on King David's mule to Gihon, escorted by Benaiah and the royal army. Here, on the eastern slope of Mount Ophel, Zadok anointed Solomon and thus publicly declared him king of Israel. The people of Jerusalem joined in public acclaim: "Long live King Solomon!" When the noise of this coronation resounded through the Kidron valley, Adonijah and his supporters were greatly disturbed. Celebration ceased immediately, the people dispersed, and Adonijah sought safety at the horns of the altar in the tabernacle in Jerusalem. Only after Solomon assured him of his life, subject to good behavior, did Adonijah leave this sacred asylum.

At a subsequent gathering Solomon was officially crowned and recognized (I Chron. 28:1 ff.).[17] With officials and statesmen from the whole nation present, David delivered a charge to the people outlining their responsibilities to Solomon, the king of God's choice.

In a private charge to Solomon (I Kings 2:1–12) David reminded his son of his responsibility to obey the law of Moses.[18] In his dying words he impressed upon Solomon the fact that innocent blood had been shed by Joab in the killing of Abner and Amasa, of Shimei's disrespectful treatment of David in his flight from Jerusalem, and of the hospitality afforded him by Barzillai, the Gileadite, in the days of Absalom's rebellion.

After David's death Solomon strengthened his claim to the throne by eliminating every possible conspirator. Adonijah's request to marry Abishag, the Shunamite maiden,[19] was interpreted by Solomon as treason. Adonijah was executed. Abiathar was removed from the place of honor he had held under David and was banished to Anathoth. Since he was of the lineage of Eli (I Sam. 14:3–4), Abiathar's deposition marked the fulfillment of the solemn words spoken to Eli by an unnamed prophet who came to Shiloh (I Sam. 2:27–37). Although Joab had been guilty of treasonable conduct in his support of Adonijah, he was primarily executed for the crimes committed during David's reign. Shimei, who was on parole, failed to abide by the restrictions placed on him and likewise suffered the death penalty.

Solomon assumed the leadership of Israel at an early age. Certainly he was less than thirty, perhaps about twenty years of age. Sensing his need for divine wisdom he assembled the Israelites at Gideon, where the tabernacle and the bronze altar were located, and made a great sacrifice. Through a dream he received divine assurance that his request for wisdom would be granted. In addition to a discerning mind God would also endow him with riches, honor, and long life, conditioned by his obedience (I Kings 3:14).

Solomon's sagacity became a source of wonderment. The decision rendered by the king when two women were contending for one living child (I Kings 3:16–28) undoubtedly represents but a sample of the cases demonstrating his wisdom. As this and other reports circulated throughout the

[17] Edersheim, *op. cit.*, Vol. II, p. 55.

[18] For the interpretation that the law of Moses was written after the days of Solomon see Anderson, *op. cit.*, pp. 288–324.

[19] The nurse who provided physical therapy for David just before his death. This had no sexual implications. Cf. Gordon, *The World of the Old Testament*, p. 180.

nation the Israelites recognized that the king's prayer for widsom had been answered.

Organization of the Kingdom

Comparatively little information is given about the organization of Solomon's vast empire. Apparently it was simple in its beginning but undoubtedly became more complex with the passing years of increasing responsibility. The king himself constituted the final court of appeals, as is exemplified in the contention of the two women. In I Kings 4:1-6 appointments are listed for the following offices: three priests, two scribes or secretaries, one recorder or chancellor, one supervisor of officials, one priestly courtier, one palace supervisor, one officer in charge of forced labor, and one commander of the army. This represents but a slight expansion of the offices instituted by David.

For taxation purposes the nation was divided into twelve districts (I Kings 4:7-19). The officer in charge of each district had to supply provisions for the central government one month of each year. During the other eleven months he would collect and store the provisions in the warehouses within his district. One day's supply for the king and his court of army and building personnel consisted of over 300 bushels of flour, almost 700 bushels of meal, 10 fattened cattle, 20 pasture-fed cattle, and 100 sheep, plus other animals and fowl (I Kings 4:22-23). This required extensive organization within each district.

Solomon maintained a large armed force (I Kings 4:24-28). In addition to the organization of the army as established by David, Solomon also used a fighting force of 1,400 chariots and 12,000 horsemen whom he stationed in Jerusalem and the chariot cities throughout the nation (II Chron. 1:14-17). This added to the burden of taxation by requiring a regular supply of barley and hay. Efficient organization and wise administration was essential in maintaining a state of prosperity and progress.

Construction of the Temple

Most important in the vast and extensive building program of Solomon was the Temple. While other building projects are merely mentioned, approximately 50 per cent of the biblical account of Solomon's reign is given to the building and dedication of this focal center in the religion of Israel. It marked the fulfillment of the sincere desire David expressed in the early part of his reign in Jerusalem—to establish a central place of worship.

The treaty arrangements which David had made with Hiram, king of Tyre, were continued by Solomon. As "king of the Sidonians" Hiram ruled over Tyre and Sidon, which constituted a political unit from the twelfth to the seventh centuries B.C. Hiram was a wealthy and powerful ruler with extensive commercial contacts throughout the Mediterranean world. Since

Israel had a strong army and the Phoenicians had a powerful navy, it was mutually beneficial to maintain friendly relations. As the Phoenicians were advanced in architecture and workmanship of costly building materials, which they controlled in their commerce, it was particularly wise for Solomon to foster the favor of Hiram. Architects and technicians from Phoenicia were sent to Jerusalem. Chief of these was Hiram (Huramabi), whose father was from Tyre and whose mother was an Israelitess from the tribe of Dan (II Chron. 2:14). For skilled help and the delivery of the Lebanon timber Solomon made payment in grain, oil, and wine.

Labor for the construction of the Temple was carefully organized. Thirty thousand Israelites were drafted to prepare the cedars of Lebanon for the Temple. Under Adoniram, who was in charge of this levy, only 10,000 men worked each month, returning to their homes for two months. From the aliens living in Israel a total of 150,000 men were used as burden bearers (70,000) and stone cutters (80,000) plus 3,600 foremen (II Chron. 2:17-18). In II Chron. 8:10 a group of 250 foremen are mentioned who were Israelites. On the basis of I Kings 5:16 and 9:23 there were 3,300 foremen over whom were 550 chief officers. Apparently 250 of these were Israelites. Both accounts have a total of 3,850 men who supervised this force of 150,000 workers.

No archaeological remains of the Solomonic Temple are known to modern excavators. In recent excavations a sanctuary has been identified in Arad, a city located about 18½ miles east-northeast of Beersheba, which is dated by Yohanan Aharoni in the time of Solomon.[20] The mountain peak, Moriah, located to the north of Jerusalem and occupied by David, was leveled sufficiently for Solomon's Temple. It is difficult to appraise the size of the area of that time, since this building was destroyed in 586 B.C. by the Babylonian king. After being rebuilt in 520 B.C., the Temple was again demolished in A.D. 70. Since the seventh century A.D. the Mohammedan mosque, the Dome of the Rock, has been standing on this site which is regarded as the most sacred spot in world history. Today this temple area covers 35 to 40 acres, indicating that the top of Mount Moriah is considerably larger now than it was in the days of Solomon.

The Temple was twice as large as the Mosaic tabernacle in its basic floor area. As a permanent structure it was much more elaborate and spacious, with appropriate additions and a much larger surrounding court. The Temple proper faced east, with a porch or entry 15 feet deep extending across the front. A double door 15 feet wide inlaid with gold and decorated with flowers, palm trees, and cherubim opened into the holy place. This room, 30 feet wide, 45 feet high, and extending 60 feet in length, had cy-

[20] *Encyclopedia of Archaeological Excavations in the Holy Land,* vol. I, pp. 74-89.

press-wood floors and was paneled in cedar around and above. Inlaid gold leaf with carved cherubim figures adorned the walls. Natural lighting was provided through windows on each side near the top. Along each side in this room were five golden tables for the shewbread and five seven-branched candlesticks made of pure gold. At the far end was the altar of incense made of cedar wood and inlaid with gold.

Beyond the altar were two folding doors which led into the holy of holies, or most holy place. This room also was 30 feet wide but only 30 feet deep and 30 feet high. Even when these doors were open a veil of blue, purple, and crimson fabrics and fine linen obscured the view of this most sacred area. Within was the ark, which was considered the most sacred object. On each side stood a huge cherubim with a 15-foot wingspread, so that the four wings extended across the entire room.

Three tiers of chambers were attached to the outside walls of the Temple on the north and south sides as well as the west end. These chambers undoubtedly were used by officials and as storage space. On each side of the entry to the Temple stood a huge pillar, one named Boaz and the other Jachin. According to I Kings 7:15 ff., they were 24 feet high, 18 feet in circumference, made of bronze, and adorned with pomegranates.[21] On top of each was a capital made of molten bronze 7½ feet high.

Extending eastward in front of the Temple were two open courts (II Chron. 4:9). The first area, the court of the priests, was 150 feet wide and 300 feet long. Here stood the huge altar of burnt offering facing the Temple. Made of bronze with a base 30 feet square and 15 feet high, this altar was about four times as large as the one used in Mosaic times. The molten or bronze sea, standing southeast of the entrance, was equally impressive in this court. Shaped as a bowl, it was 7½ feet high, 15 feet in diameter, with a 45-foot perimeter. It was cast in bronze three inches thick and rested on 12 oxen, three facing in each direction. A reasonable estimate of the weight of this gigantic laver is approximately 25 tons. According to I Kings 7:46, this bronze sea, the huge pillars, and the expensive vessels made for the Temple were all cast in the clay beds of the Jordan valley.

In addition to this huge laver, which provided water for the priests and Levites in their temple service, there were furnished ten smaller lavers of brass, five on each side of the Temple (I Kings 7:38; II Chron. 4:6). These were six feet high and rested on wheels so that they could be taken where, in the course of the sacrifice, they were most needed for the washing of the various parts of the animal.

[21] The same figure, 24 feet or 18 cubits, is given as the height of this pillar in II Kings 25:17 and Jer. 52:21. In II Chron. 3:15 the height is given as 35 cubits. Keil, *op. cit.,* suggests that this is due to the confusion of two letters in the transmission of the Hebrew text.

Also in the court of the priests stood the bronze platform (II Chron. 6:13). It was here that King Solomon stood during the dedication ceremonies.

Eastward steps led down from the court of the priests to the outer court or great court (II Chron. 4:9). By analogy with measurements of the Mosaic tabernacle this area was 300 feet broad and 600 feet long. This large court was surrounded by a solid stone wall through which four massive gates, overlaid with bronze, regulated entrance into the area of the Temple (I Chron. 26:13–16). According to Ezekiel 11:1, the eastern gate served as the main entrance. Large colonnades and chambers in this area provided storage space for the priests and Levites so that they could properly fulfill their respective duties.

The matter of contemporary influence in the building of the Temple has been reconsidered in recent decades. The biblical accounts have been carefully examined in the light of archaeological remains regarding temples and religions in contemporary civilizations in Egypt, Mesopotamia, and Phoenicia. Although Edersheim[22] wrote (1880) that the plan and design of Solomon's Temple were strictly Jewish, it is the general consensus of archaeologists today that the art and architecture were basically Phoenician. It is clearly indicated in Scripture that David employed architects and technicians from Hiram, king of Tyre. While Israel furnished the labor, the Phoenicians supplied the artisans and supervisors for the actual construction. Since the excavation of the Syrian Tell Tainat (ancient Hattina) in 1936 by the University of Chicago, it has been apparent that the type of art and architecture of the Jerusalem Temple was common to Phoenicia in the tenth century B.C. Therefore, it seems reasonable to credit the Phoenician artisans and architects with the final plans of the Temple, since David and Solomon employed them for this particular service.[23] With the limited information available it would be difficult to mark a clear line of distinction between the plans presented by the kings of Israel and the contribution made by the Phoenicians in the building of the Temple.

Dedication of the Temple

Since the Temple was completed in the eighth month of the eleventh year (I Kings 6:37–38), it is quite likely that the dedication ceremonies were held in the seventh month of the twelfth year and not a month before it was completed. This would have allowed time for elaborate planning for this great historic event (I Kings 8:1–9; II Chron. 5:2–7:22). For this occasion all Israel was represented by elders and leaders.

[22] See *ibid.*, p. 72.

[23] See Wright, *op. cit.*, pp. 136–145, and Unger, *Archeology and the Old Testament*, pp. 228–234.

The Feast of Tabernacles, which not only reminded the Israelites that they once were pilgrims in the wilderness but also was an occasion for thanksgiving after the time of harvest, began on the fifteenth day of the seventh month. Edersheim[24] concludes that the dedication ceremonies took place during the week preceding the Feast of Tabernacles. The entire celebration lasted two weeks (II Chron. 7:4–10) and involved all Israel through representatives from Hamath to the borders of Egypt. Keil, in his comment on I Kings 8:63, suggests that there were 100,000 fathers and 20,000 elders present. This would account for the thousands of animals that were brought for the unprecedented occasion.[25]

Solomon was the key person in the dedication ceremonies. His position as king in Israel was unique. Under the covenant all Israelites were God's servants (Lev. 25:42, 55; Jer. 30:10, and other passages) and viewed as a kingdom of priests unto God (Ex. 19:6). Throughout the dedicatory services Solomon takes the position of a servant of God, representing the nation chosen by God to be his people. This relationship with God was common to the prophet, priest, and layman, as well as the king, in true recognition of the dignity of man. In this capacity Solomon offered prayer, delivered the dedicatory address, and officiated at the offering of sacrifices.

In the religious history of Israel the dedication of the Temple was the most significant event since the people left Sinai. The sudden transformation from slavery in Egypt to an independent nation in the wilderness was a momentous demonstration of God's power in behalf of his nation. At that time the tabernacle was erected to aid them in their recognition and service of God. Now the Temple was erected under Solomon. This constituted the confirmation of the establishment of the Davidic throne in Israel. As the presence of God was visibly manifested in the pillar of cloud over the tabernacle, so the glory of God hovered over the Temple and signified God's blessing and benediction. This divinely confirmed the establishment of the kingdom as anticipated by Moses (Deut. 17:14–20).

Extensive Building Projects

The palace of Solomon (House of the Forest of Lebanon) is but briefly mentioned (I Kings 7:1–12; II Chron. 8:1). It was completed in thirteen years, making a twenty-year building period for temple and palace. Most likely it was located on the southern slope of Mount Moriah between the Temple and Zion, the city of David. This palace was complex and elaborate, containing government offices, living quarters for the daughter of Pharaoh, as well as Solomon's own private residence, and covered an area of 150 by

[24] Edersheim, *op. cit.*, p. 88.
[24] Keil, op. cit., commentary on passage.

75 by 45 feet. Included in this great building program was the extension of the walls of Zion (Jerusalem) northward so as to enclose both palace and temple within the walls of the capital city of Israel.[26]

Solomon's powerful standing army also required much building activity throughout the kingdom. The construction of store cities for administrative purposes and the defense system were closely integrated. An impressive list of cities, which is suggestive of Solomon's extensive building program, is given in I Kings 9:15–22 and II Chron. 8:1–11. Gezer, which had been a Canaanite stronghold, was captured by Pharaoh of Egypt and used as a fort by Solomon after he received it as a dowry. Excavations at the 13-acre site of Megiddo indicate that Solomon had adequate accommodations here for 450 horses and 150 chariots. This fortress guarded the important Megiddo or Esdraelon valley through which ran the most important highway between Egypt and Syria. From the military and commercial standpoint this road was vital to Israel. Hazor likewise has been excavated, first under Garstang and more recently under Israeli supervision. Other cities mentioned are Beth-horon, Baalath, Tamar, Hamath-zobah, and Tadmor. Besides these, other cities functioned as headquarters or capitals of the administrative districts (I Kings 4:7–19). Archaeological findings at Beth-shemesh and Lachish indicate that buildings with large rooms were provided in these cities for storing supplies.[27] Undoubtedly lengthy descriptions could have been written about the building program of Solomon, concerning which the biblical account is merely suggestive.

Trade, Commerce, and Revenue

Ezion-geber and Elath are briefly noted in I Kings 9:26–28 and II Chron. 8:17–18 as the seaport of Solomon on the gulf of Aqaba. Tell el-Kheleifeh at the northern end of this gulf is the only site known presently to show the occupational history of Elath, Ezion-geber. If this Tell does not specifically identify the site of these cities, then it is quite likely that this may have been a suburb of Ezion-geber and Elath. Tell el-Kheleifeh, as a fortified industrial maritime, storage, and caravansary center for these cities, may have ranked equal in importance with other fortified district and chariot cities such as Hazor, Megiddo, and Gezer.[28]

Copper and iron mines were numerous throughout the Wadi Arabah. David had already established fortifications throughout the land of Edom when he established his kingdom (II Sam. 8:14). Numerous smelting centers in the Wadi Arabah may have supplied Tell el-Kheleifeh with iron and copper ore for further refinement and the production of molds for trading

[26] Millo, I Kings 9:15, 24, was a citadel or supporting terrace in the wall.

[27] For discussion of Solomonic and Omride storerooms and/or stables at Megiddo, see *Encyclopedia of Archaeological Excavations in the Holy Land* III (Jerusalem, 1977) pp. 830-56.

purposes. In the Jordan valley (I Kings 7:45–46), and down through the Wadi Arabah, Solomon must have realized the truth of the statement in Deut. 8:9 that the promised land had natural resources in copper.

By developing and controlling the metal industry of Palestine Solomon was in a position to trade. The Phoenicians, under Hiram, had contact with metal refineries in distant points on the Mediterranean, such as Spain, and so were in a position not only to build refineries for Solomon but also to aid in commerce. Israeli ships took iron and copper as far as southwest Arabia (modern Yemen) and the African coast of Ethiopia.[29] In exchange they brought gold, silver, ivory, and monkeys to Israel. These extensive naval expeditions bringing gold from Ophir lasted "three years" (II Chron. 9:21), or one full year plus parts of two years. They netted Solomon excessive wealth so that he was rated as the richest of all kings (II Chron. 9:20–22; I Kings 10:11–22).

The Israelites obtained horses and chariotry from Hittite rulers in Cilicia and its neighbor, Egypt.[30] The middlemen in the horse and chariot trade between Asia Minor and Israel were the Arameans (I Kings 10:25–29; II Chron. 1:14–17). Although David hamstrung or lamed all the horses he captured, with the exception of one hundred (II Sam. 8:4), it is obvious that Solomon accumulated a considerable force. This was important for protection as well as control of all the commerce that crossed Israel's territory. Solomon's income was also increased by the vast camel caravans engaged in spice trade from southern Arabia up to Syria and Phoenicia, as well as Egypt.

King Solomon gained such international respect and recognition that his wealth was greatly increased by gifts from far and near. In answer to his initial request he had been divinely endowed with wisdom so that people from other lands came to hear his proverbs, his songs, and his speeches on various subjects (I Kings 4:29–34). If the account of the visit by the Queen of Sheba is but a sample of what happened frequently during Solomon's reign, then one can see that gold became plentiful in Israel's capital.[31] The fact that the queen traveled over 1,200 miles by camel may also have been motivated by commercial interests. The naval expeditions from Ezion-geber may have stimulated negotiations for favorable trade agreements. Her mission was quite successful (I Kings 10:13). Although Solomon, in addition to granting her requests, returned to her all that she had brought, it is doubtful that he did the same for all the kings and governors of Arabia who

[28] Cf. Nelson Glueck, "Ezion-geber," in *Biblical Archaeologist* XXVIII (1965), 69–87.

[29] The word "Tarshish" may mean "refinery." See Albright, *Archaeology and the Religion of Israel,* p. 136. Since the Phoenicians controlled Mediterranean commerce, Solomon's naval enterprises were limited to the Red Sea. His ships of "Tarshish" meant that the point of origin was the "refinery" at Ezion-geber. See Unger, *op. cit.,* p. 225.

[30] This refers to a province near Cilicia, which may have received its name as a military outpost for Thut-mose III.

[31] Mould, *op. cit.,* p. 199.

brought gifts to him (II Chron. 9:12–14). While it is difficult to ascertain the value of the wealth described here, there is no doubt that Solomon represented the epitome in wealth and wisdom of all the kings who had ruled in Jerusalem.

Apostasy and Its Consequences

The final chapter of Solomon's reign is tragic (I Kings 11). Why the king of Israel, who reached the zenith of success in wisdom, wealth, fame, and international acclaim under divine blessing, should terminate his 40-year reign under omens of failure is most perplexing! Consequently some have regarded the record as unreliable and contradictory and have sought other explanations.[32] The truth of the matter is that Solomon, who played the leading role at the dedication of the Temple, departed from wholehearted devotion to God—an experience parallel to that of Israel in the wilderness after the building of the tabernacle. Solomon broke the very first commandment by his inclusive policy of allowing idol worship at Jerusalem.

Intermarriage between the royal families was a common practice in the Near East. At the beginning of his reign Solomon made an alliance with Pharaoh by accepting the latter's daughter in marriage. Although he brought her to Jerusalem, there is no indication that she was permitted to bring her idolatry along (I Kings 3:1).[33] At the height of his success Solomon took wives from the Moabites, Ammonites, Edomites, Sidonians, and Hittites. Besides that, he acquired a harem of 700 wives and princesses, plus 300 concubines. Whether this was motivated by diplomatic and political expediency to ensure peace and safety or by an attempt to surpass sovereigns of other nations whose luxury was expressed in a large harem is not indicated. Nevertheless, it was contrary to the expressed commands of God (Deut. 17:17). Solomon permitted the multiplicity of wives to be his ruination by allowing his heart to be turned away from God.[34]

Solomon not only tolerated idolatry, but he himself gave recognition to Ashtoreth, the fertility goddess of the Phoenicians, who was known as Astarte among the Greeks and Ishtar among the Babylonians. For the worship of Milcom or Molech, the god of the Ammonites, and for Chemosh, the god of the Moabites, Solomon erected a high place on a mountain east of Jerusalem. These were not removed for three and a half centuries, but remained as an abomination in the proximity of the Temple until the days of Josiah (II Kings 23:13). He also built altars to other foreign gods not mentioned by name (I Kings 11:8).

[32] See Keil, *op. cit.*, at reference.

[33] This marriage may have been related to later developments. Jeroboam found refuge in Egypt. Soon after Solomon's death the king of Egypt took treasures from Jerusalem.

[34] Foreign trade may have had a bearing on this development. Providing places for these foreigners to worship may have promoted their interest in coming to Jerusalem.

Idolatry, which was a violation of the opening words of the Decalogue (Ex. 20), could not be tolerated. God's rebuff (I Kings 11:9–13) was probably delivered to Solomon through the prophet Ahijah, who appears later in the chapter. Because of his disobedience, the kingdom of Israel was to be divided. The dynasty of David would continue to rule over part of the kingdom for the sake of David, with whom God had made a covenant, and because of Jerusalem, which God had chosen. God would not break his covenantal promise, even though Solomon had forfeited his blessings and favor, so temporary judgment was in the offing. Also, for David's sake, the kingdom would not be disrupted during Solomon's lifetime but adversaries would arise to threaten peace and safety before the termination of his reign.

Hadad, the Edomite, was one leader who opposed Solomon. In the conquest of Edom by Joab, Hadad, who was of the royal family, had been rescued by servants and taken to Egypt as a child. Here he married the sister of the Egyptian queen and enjoyed the favor and privileges of the royal court. After the death of Joab and David, he returned to Edom and in time became sufficiently established so that he constituted a threat to Solomon in his closing years (I Kings 11:14–23). Solomon's position as "copper king" was at stake, as well as the lucrative Arabian trade and commerce on the Red Sea.

Rezon[35] of Damascus posed perhaps an even greater threat (I Kings 11:23–25). The formation of an independent Aramaean or Syrian kingdom constituted a serious political threat involving commercial consequences. Although David had conquered Hamath when the power of Hadadezer was broken, Solomon found it necessary to suppress a rebellion there and build store cities (II Chron. 8:3–4). He even controlled Tiphsah on the Euphrates (I Kings 4:24), which was extremely important for dominating the trade routes. In the course of Solomon's reign Rezon was able to establish himself in Damascus, where he became the embodiment of continual danger to the peace and prosperity of Israel in the closing years of Solomon's reign.

As matters turned out, one of Solomon's own men—Jeroboam, son of Nebat—proved to be the real disruptive factor in Israel. Being a very capable man, he had been placed in charge of the forced labor unit which repaired the walls of Jerusalem and built Millo. He used this opportunity to his own political advantage and gained a following. One day Ahijah, the prophet, met him and tore his new mantle into twelve pieces, giving him ten. Through this symbolic act he informed Jeroboam that Solomon's kingdom would be divided, leaving but two tribes to the Davidic dynasty, while ten would constitute his kingdom. On condition of his wholehearted obedience Jeroboam was assured that his kingdom would be as permanently established as that of David.

[35] Unger, *Israel and the Aramaeans*, pp. 51–55.

Apparently Jeroboam was not willing to await for developments; it is implied that he openly indicated his opposition to the king. At any rate, Solomon suspected an insurrection and sought to kill Jeroboam. Consequently Jeroboam fled to Egypt, where he found an asylum with Shishak until the death of Solomon.

Even though the kingdom was sustained and not divided until after his death, Solomon was subjected to the anguish of rebellion at home and secession in various parts of his realm. As a result of his personal failure to obey and serve God wholeheartedly the general welfare and peaceful prosperity of the kingdom were endangered.

SELECTED READING

ACKROYD, P. R. *The Second Book of Samuel.* Cambridge: Cambridge University Press, 1977.

CARLSON, R. A. *David, The Chosen King: A Tradition-Historical Approach to the Second Book of Samuel.* Stockholm: Almquist and Wiksell, 1964.

CRAIGIE, P. C. *The Problem of War in the Old Testament.* Grand Rapids: Wm. B. Eerdmans Publishing Co., 1978.

DAVIS, JOHN, and J. C. WHITCOMB, JR. *A History of Israel From Conquest to Exile.* Grand Rapids: Baker Book House, 1979.

LEWIS, JACK. *Historical Background of Bible History.* Grand Rapids: Baker Book House, 1971.

MERRILL, EUGENE. *A Historical Survey of the Old Testament.* Nutley: Craig Press, 1966.

———. "I & II Chronicles" in *Bible Knowledge Commentary.* Wheaton: Scripture Press, 1985.

MYERS, J. M. *I and II Chronicles.* The Anchor Bible. Garden City: Doubleday, 1965.

NOTH, MARTIN. *The History of Israel.* 2nd ed. London: A & C Black, 1965.

OSWALT, J. N. "Chronology of the Old Testament" in *The International Standard Bible Encyclopedia,* 1:673–685. Grand Rapids: Wm. B. Eerdmans Publishing Co., 1979.

WALTON, JOHN W. *Chronological Charts of the Old Testament.* Grand Rapids: Zondervan Publishing House, 1977.

WILLIAMSON, H. G. M. "I and II Chronicles" in *The New Century Bible Commentary.* Grand Rapids: Wm. B. Eerdmans Publishing Co., 1982.

WISEMAN, D.J. (ed.) *Peoples of Old Testament Times.* Oxford: Clarendon, 1973.

Chart IV KINGS AND PROPHETS—DIVIDED KINGDOM, 931–586

Date	Northern K.	Prophets	Southern K.	Assyria	Syria
931	*Jeroboam Dyn.*	Ahijah	Rehoboam		Rezon
	Jeroboam	Shemaiah			
		Iddo	Abijah		
	Nadab		Asa		
909	*Baasha Dyn.*	Azariah			
	Baasha	Hanani			
		Jehu			
	Elah				
	(Zimri)				
885	*Omri Dynasty*				
	Omri (Tibni)	Elijah	Jehoshaphat	Ashurnarsipal	Benhadad
	Ahab	Micaiah			
		Eliezer			
	Ahaziah	Elisha	Jehoram		
	Joram	Jehoiada	Ahaziah		
				Shalmaneser III	
841	*Jehu Dynasty*		Athaliah		Hazael
	Jehu	Zechariah	Joash		
	Jehoahaz		Amaziah		Benhadad
	Jehoash	Jonah	Azariah		
	Jeroboam II	Hosea			
		Amos			
	Zechariah				
752	*Last Kings*		Jotham		
	Shallum				
	Menahem	Isaiah		Tiglath-pileser III	
	Pekahiah	Oded	Ahaz		Rezin
	Pekah			Shalmaneser V	
	Hoshea			Sargon II	
722	*Fall of Samaria*	Micah	Hezekiah	Sennacherib	
			Manasseh	Esarhaddon	
				Ashurbanipal	
			Amon		
640		Jeremiah	Josiah	*Babylon*	
		Huldah		Nabopolassar	
			Jehoahaz		
			Jehoiakim	Nebuchadnezzar	
			Jehoiachin		
		(Ezekiel)	Zedekiah		
		(Daniel)			
586			*Fall of Jerusalem*		

Chapter IX

The Divided Kingdom

The two kingdoms arising after Solomon's death are commonly differentiated by the appellations "Northern" and "Southern." The latter designates the smaller state ruled by the Davidic dynasty from its capital at Jerusalem until 586 B.C. It consisted of the tribes of Judah and Benjamin, who supported Rehoboam with an army when the rest of the tribes seceded in rebellion against the oppressive measures of Solomon and his son (I Kings 12:21). The "Northern Kingdom" designates the seceding tribes, who made Jeroboam their king. This kingdom endured until 722 B.C., with its capital successively at Shechem, Tirzah, and Samaria.

The common biblical designations for these two kingdoms are "Israel" and "Judah." The former usually is restricted in its use to the Northern Kingdom, while the latter refers to the Southern Kingdom. Originally the name "Israel" was given to Jacob (Gen. 32:22–32). During his lifetime it was already applied to his sons (Gen. 44:7), and ever since then any descendant of Jacob has been properly referred to as an "Israelite." From patriarchal times to the occupation of Canaan "Israel" specified the whole Hebrew nation. This designation prevailed throughout the monarchy of David and Solomon, even though there was a divided rule in the early part of David's reign.

The tribe of Judah, which was strategically located and exceptionally strong, came into prominence during the time of Saul (cf. I Sam. 11:8, etc.). After the division in 931 B.C. the name "Judah" identified the Southern Kingdom, which continued its allegiance to the Davidic dynasty. Unless otherwise indicated, the names "Israel" and "Judah" in this volume represent the Northern and Southern Kingdoms respectively.[1]

[1] "Israel" is also used in the Bible as a term for identifying the faithful remnant or the people of God. Consequently its usage in the Scripture should be interpreted in context.

Another appellation for the Northern Kingdom is "Ephraim." Although this name originally was given to one of the sons of Joseph (Gen. 41:52), it specifically designated the leading tribe of secession. Being located to the north of Benjamin and Judah, "Ephraim" represented the opposition to Judah and often included the whole Northern Kingdom (cf. Isaiah and Hosea).

Chronology

This is the first period in Old Testament history when any dates can be fixed with virtual certainty. Secular history, uncovered through archaeological research, provides an eponym list which accounts for every year in Assyrian history from 891 to 648 B.C.[2] Ptolemy, an outstanding scholar living about A.D. 70–161, composed a canon listing the Babylonian and Persian rulers from the time of Nabonassar, 747 B.C., to Darius III, 332 B.C.[3] Beyond that he lists the Greek rulers, Alexander and Philip, the Ptolemaic rulers of Egypt, and the Roman rulers down to A.D. 161. As an astronomer, geographer, historian, and chronologist Ptolemy gives vital information. Most valuable to modern historians is the astronomical material that has made it possible to check the accuracy of his data at numerous points so that "the canon of Ptolemy may be used as a historical guide with the fullest confidence."[4]

Two significant facts furnish the link between Assyrian history and the biblical account of the Hebrew kings during the divided kingdom period. Assyrian inscriptions indicate that Ahab, king of Israel, participated in the battle of Karkar (853 B.C.) against Shalmaneser III, and that Jehu, another king of Israel, paid tribute to the same Assyrian king in 841 B.C. By equating the biblical data concerning the Hebrew kings Ahaziah and Joram to this twelve-year period of Assyrian history Thiele has suggested a clue to the proper interpretation of chronology.[5] With these two dates definitely established in the synchronism between Assyrian and Hebrew history, he proposes a scheme of absolute chronology for the period from the disruption of the kingdom to the fall of Jerusalem. This serves as a practical key to the interpretation of the numerous chronological references in the accounts of Kings and Chronicles.

[2] For a complete list see E. R. Thiele, *The Mysterious Numbers of the Hebrew Kings* (University of Chicago Press, 1951), pp. 287–292. Also see D. D. Luckenbill, *Ancient Records of Assyria and Babylonia II* (University of Chicago Press, 1927), pp. 430 ff.

[3] See Thiele, *op. cit.*, p. 293.

[4] *Ibid.*, p. 47.

[5] See *ibid.*, pp. 53–54. By allowing for the reigns of Ahaziah and Joram during this period it seems necessary to regard 853 as the last year of Ahab and 841 as the accession year of Jehu.

Allowing for a variable factor of one year, the terminal dates for Israel (the fall of Samaria) and for Judah (the fall of Jerusalem) are fixed respectively as 722 and 586 B.C. The same can be said for the battle of Karkar in 853 B.C. The date for the beginning of the two kingdoms is subject to more variation.

A simple addition of all the years allotted to the Hebrew kings totals almost four centuries. On the basis of this tabulation many scholars, such as Hales, Oppert, Graetz, Ussher, and Mahler, have dated the disruption of the Solomonic kingdom within the period of 990–953 B.C. The most publicized date is that given by Ussher, adopted by Edersheim, and incorporated in the margin of many Bibles during the past century. Recent archaeological discoveries related to contemporary history of the Near East have illuminated many biblical passages necessitating a reinterpretation of biblical data.

The divided kingdom period is equated to about three and a half centuries. On the basis of Assyrian chronology and contemporary Near Eastern history Olmstead, Kittel, Albright, and others date the beginning of this period within the years of 937–922 B.C. The most widely popularized date in current Old Testament literature is 922 B.C.[6]

The most thorough study of the chronology for the period of the Divided Kingdom is published in the book by E. R. Thiele, *The Mysterious Numbers of the Hebrew Kings*. By a detailed analysis of both statistical data in the biblical account and contemporary history he concluded that 931 B.C. is the most reasonable date for the beginning of this period. Whereas a number of chronologies have been constructed on the assumption that numerous errors exist in the present text of Kings and Chronicles, Thiele begins with the assumption that the present text is reliable. With this approach the number of chronological references that remain problematical in the light of our present understanding of the period is far less than the textual problems that evolve as a result of the a priori assumption that the Hebrew text is in error.[7] Although unsolved problems remain in Thiele's chronology, it seems to be the most reasonable and complete interpretation of the scriptural data and contemporary historical facts presently known to us. Should the date 959 B.C. for the beginning of Solomon's Temple be confirmed as correct, it might call for a reinterpretation of part of this chronology. At present this date is accepted with a high degree of probability.[8] Throughout this analysis of the divided kingdom period Thiele's chronology is adopted as standard. Any deviation from it is indicated.

Some of the basic factors which have a bearing on an analysis of the

[6] See W. F. Albright, "The Chronology of the Divided Monarchy of Israel," *Bulletin of the American Schools of Oriental Research,* No. 100 (December, 1945), pp. 16–22.

[7] See Thiele's discussion of this in Chap. XI on "Modern Chronological Systems." Note particularly his analysis of Albright's chronology, pp. 244–252.

[8] See Wright, *Biblical Archaeology,* p. 146.

chronological data for this period deserve brief consideration.[9] In Judah the accession-year system of counting was used from the beginning to the time of Jehoram (*ca.* 850 B.C.), who adopted the nonaccession-year system which had been used in Israel from the days of Jeroboam I.[10] During the reigns of Jehoash and Amaziah (*ca.* 800 B.C.) both kingdoms changed to the accession-year system.[11]

The matter of coregency must be considered in establishing a chronology for this period. Sometimes the years during which a father and son ruled together were credited to both kings in reckoning the length of their reigns.

Important Dates

A certain number of dates are significant for a proper understanding of any historical period. The three most significant events for this era of the divided kingdom are the following:

931—The Division of the Kingdom
722—The Fall of Samaria
586—The Fall of Jerusalem

Without resorting to tabular lists of rulers for these kingdoms, with dates for each king, it is appropriate to suggest a chronological index for these centuries. The development in the Northern Kingdom lends itself to a simple chronological scheme as follows:

931—Dynasty of Jeroboam I
909—Dynasty of Baasha
885—Dynasty of Omri
841—Dynasty of Jehu
752—Last Kings
722—Fall of Samaria

All the kings, the prophets, and important events can be approximately dated by using this chronological framework.[12]

The contemporary events in the Southern Kingdom may be conveniently related to this frame of reference. By placing the four outstanding kings of Judah in their proper sequence and adding one date it becomes a

[9] For a fuller treatment read Chap. II, "Fundamental Principles of Hebrew Chronology," by Thiele, *op. cit.*, pp. 14–41.

[10] In the nonaccession-year system a king's initial year—whether one or twelve months—is counted as one year.

[11] The nonaccession method was common to Egypt. Thiele attributes this change to Assyrian influence, p. 41.

[12] The historical developments during the divided kingdom era are vitally important for a proper understanding of the Old Testament prophetical books. In addition many other prophets had an active part in Israel's history.

simple matter to develop a working chronology in simplified form. Approximate dates become readily apparent on the basis of the following outline:

931—Dynasty of Jeroboam I	Rehoboam
909—Dynasty of Baasha	
885—Dynasty of Omri	Jehoshaphat
841—Dynasty of Jehu	
752—Last Kings	Uzziah
722—Fall of Samaria	
	Hezekiah
640—	Josiah
586—	Fall of Jerusalem

By using these suggested dates as a working scheme the matter of chronological data in the biblical account can be reduced to a minimum. Although the individual dates for each king are given subsequently, they are not necessary for an understanding of the general development. For survey purposes the above dates are sufficient, while the individual dates become significant in a detailed study.

Biblical Account

The primary literary source for the divided kingdom era is I Kings 11:1 to II Kings 25:30 and II Chronicles 10:1–36:23. Supplementary material may be found in Isaiah, Jeremiah, and other prophets reflecting contemporary culture.

The only source presenting a continuous historical account of the Northern Kingdom is I Kings 12:1–II Kings 17:41. Integrated in this record are contemporaneous events in the Southern Kingdom. With the Northern Kingdom terminating in 722 B.C., the author of Kings continues the running account of the Southern Kingdom in II Kings 18:1–25:30 to the fall of Jerusalem in 586 B.C. A parallel record for the Southern Kingdom from 931 to 586 B.C. is given in II Chronicles 10:1–36:23, where the author concludes with a closing reference to the release from captivity under Cyrus (538 B.C.). The account in Chronicles supplements the Northern Kingdom history recorded in the Books of Kings only where it has a direct bearing on the developments in the Southern Kingdom.

Since each kingdom has a list of approximately twenty rulers, a simple analysis is essential in order to avoid confusion. The memorization of two lists of kings often precludes a careful analysis of this period as background essential in the study of the prophetic messages in the Old Testament. Since a number of families ruled in the Northern Kingdom in contrast to one dynasty in Judah, a simple outline based on leading dynasties in Israel is suggested. This may be used as a convenient frame of reference for the association of other names and events. Note the following:

Israel	Outline of Kings	Judah
Dynasty of Jeroboam	I Kings 12–15	Rehoboam
		Abijah
Dynasty of Baasha	I Kings 15–16	Asa
Dynasty of Omri	I Kings 16–22	Jehoshaphat
	II Kings 1–9	Joram
		Ahaziah
Dynasty of Jehu	II Kings 10–15	Athaliah
		Joash
		Amaziah
		Uzziah
Last Kings	II Kings 15–17	Jotham
		Ahaz
	II Kings 18–25	Hezekiah to Zedekiah

Since Israel ceased to exist as an independent government the last part of Kings is devoted to an account of the Southern Kingdom. Israel was reduced to an Assyrian province.

For a detailed outline of the biblical account for the divided kingdom period as given in Kings and Chronicles see the following:

Israel	Judah
Jeroboam I Kings 12:25–14:20	Rehoboam I Kings 12:1–24 II Chron. 10:1–12:16 Abijam (Abijah) I Kings 15:1–8 II Chron. 13:1–22
Nadab I Kings 15:25–31	Asa I Kings 15:9–24 II Chron. 14:1–16:14
Baasha I Kings 15:32–16:7	
Elah I Kings 16:8–14	
Zimri I Kings 16:15–20	
Omri I Kings 16:21–28	

Ahab
I Kings 16:29–22:40

Ahaziah
I Kings 22:51–53
II Kings 1:1–18
Joram (Jehoram)
II Kings 1:19–8:15

II Kings 9:1–37
Jehu
II Kings 10:1–36

Jehoahaz
II Kings 13:1–9

Jehoash (Joash)
II Kings 13:10–24

Jeroboam II
II Kings 14:23–29

Zechariah
II Kings 15:8–12
Shallum
II Kings 15:13–15
Menahem
II Kings 15:16–22
Pekahiah
II Kings 15:23–26
Pekah
II Kings 15:27–31

Hoshea
II Kings 17:1–41

Jehoshaphat
I Kings 22:41–50
II Chron. 17:1–20:37

Jehoram (Joram)
II Kings 8:16–24
II Chron. 21:1–20
Ahaziah
II Kings 8:25–29
II Chron. 22:1–9
Athaliah
II Kings 11:1–21
II Chron. 22:10–23:21
Joash (Jehoash)
II Kings 12:1–21
II Chron. 24:1–27
Amaziah
II Kings 14:1–22
II Chron. 25:1–28
Uzziah (Azariah)
II Kings 15:1–7
II Chron. 26:1–23

Jotham
II Kings 15:32–38
II Chron. 27:1–9
Ahaz
II Kings 16:1–20
II Chron. 28:1–27

Hezekiah
  II Kings 18:1–20:21
  II Chron. 29:1–32:33
Manasseh
  II Kings 21:1–18
  II Chron. 33:1–20
Amon
  II Kings 21:19–26
  II Chron. 33:21–25
Josiah
  II Kings 22:1–23:30
  II Chron. 34:1–35:27
Jehoahaz (Shallum)
  II Kings 23:31–34
  II Chron. 36:1–4
Jehoiakim (Eliakim)
  II Kings 23:35–24:7
  II Chron. 36:5–8
Jehoiachin (Jeconiah)
  II Kings 24:8–17
  II Chron. 36:9–10
Zedekiah (Mattaniah)
  II Kings 24:18–25:7
  II Chron. 36:11–21
The Exile and return
  II Kings 25:8–30
  II Chron. 36:22–23

Concurrent Events

International relations are vitally significant during these centuries when the Solomonic empire divided into two kingdoms—which finally succumbed to foreign powers. Being strategically located in the Fertile Crescent between Egypt and Mesopotamia, they could not escape the pressure of various nations which rose to great power during this period. Consequently for a proper understanding of the biblical history these nations warrant consideration.

The Kingdom of Aram (Syria)[13]

The kingdom of Aramea, with Damascus as its capital, is better known as Syria. For about two centuries it enjoyed power and prosperity at the ex-

[13] For a history of Aram see M. F. Unger, *Israel and the Aramaeans of Damascus.*

pense of Israel. When David expanded his kingdom he defeated Hadadezer, ruler of Zobah, and established amity with Toi, king of Hamath. Solomon extended the frontier of his kingdom over a hundred miles beyond Damascus and Zobah, conquering Hamath on the Orontes and establishing store cities in that area. During the latter part of his reign, Rezon, who had been a young military officer under Hadadezer at Zobah prior to his defeat by David, seized Damascus and laid the foundation for the rise of the Aramean or Syrian kingdom. Rebellion under Rehoboam provided this opportunity. For the next two centuries Syria became a contender for power in the Syro-Palestinian area.

War between Judah and the Northern Kingdom, with Asa and Baasha as respective rulers, afforded Syria, under Benhadad, the opportunity to emerge as the strongest nation in Canaan near the end of the ninth century B.C. When Baasha began to fortify the border city of Ramah, only five miles north of Jerusalem, Asa sent temple treasures up to Benhadad as a bribe, making an alliance with him against the Northern Kingdom. Although this accomplished Asa's immediate purpose and relieved him of the military pressure from Baasha, it in reality gave Syria the upper hand so that both Israelite kingdoms were in time threatened by invasion from the north. By taking possession of some of the northern territory in Israel, Benhadad was able to control the caravan routes to Phoenicia, which brought immense wealth to Damascus—strengthening the kingdom of Syria.

The supremacy of Syria as a military and commercial power was tempered by the Northern Kingdom when the dynasty of Omri began to rule in 885 B.C. Omri broke Syria's commercial monopoly with Phoenicia by establishing friendly relations with Ethbaal, king of Sidon. This resulted in the marriage of Jezebel and Ahab. The rising power of Assyria on the east served as another check on Syria in the days of Ahab. During the years that Ashurnasirpal, king of Assyria, was content to bypass Syria to the north in extending his contact to the Mediterranean, Ahab and Benhadad frequently opposed each other. In the course of time Ahab gained the balance of power. In 853 B.C., however, Ahab and Benhadad united their forces in the famous battle at Karkar in the Orontes valley, north of Hamath.[14] Although Shalmaneser III claimed a great victory, it is doubtful whether it was decisive, since he did not advance to Hamath nor Damascus until several years later. Immediately after this, Syro-Ephraimitic hostility continued, Ahab being killed in battle. As Assyria renewed her attacks on Syria, Benhadad may not have had the support of Joram. When Benhadad died, about 843 B.C., Syria

[14] The King of Syria identified as Benhadad in the biblical records from *ca.* 900-843 B.C may refer to two different rulers by the same name. If so, it is likely that the second Benhadad began to rule about 860 B.C. For the viewpoint that 57 years should be ascribed to one king, see M. F. Unger, *Archaeology and the Old Testament,* pp. 240-41.

was hard pressed by the Assyrian invaders as well as the lack of support from the Northern Kingdom.

Hazael, the next ruler, usurped the throne and became one of the most powerful kings—extending Syria's domain into Palestine. Although Jehu, the new king in Israel, submitted to Shalmaneser III by paying him taxes (841 B.C.), Hazael withstood the invasion of this Assyrian king singlehanded. In a few years Hazael was able to enlarge his kingdom when the Assyrians withdrew. Extensive territory was annexed from the Northern Kingdom at Jehu's expense. After 814 B.C. Jehoahaz, king of Israel, was so weak that Hazael's armies passed through his territory and took possession of the Philistine plain, destroying Gath and exacting tribute from the king of Judah at Jerusalem.

Benhadad (*ca.* 801 B.C.) failed to maintain the kingdom established by his father Hazael. During the last few years of his reign, Adadnirari III of Assyria subdued Damascus sufficiently to exact a heavy tribute. Besides this, Benhadad faced hostile opposition from Syrian states to the north. This left Damascus in such a weakened condition that when the Assyrian pressure continued Joash reclaimed for Israel much of the territory taken by Hazael. In the days of Jeroboam II (793–753) Syria even lost Damascus and the "approaches to Hamath," restoring the northern boundary held by David and Solomon (II Sam. 8:5–11).

Damascus once more had an opportunity to assert herself when the powerful Jeroboam died in 753 B.C. Rezin (*ca.* 750–732 B.C.), the last of the Aramean kings at Damascus, regained Syrian independence. With the accession of Tiglath-pileser III to the Assyrian throne (745 B.C.) both Syria and Israel were subject to invasion and heavy tribute. While Tiglath-pileser (Pul) was fighting in Armenia (737–735 B.C.), Rezin and Pekah organized an alliance to avoid the payment of tribute. Although Edom and Philistia joined Syria and Israel in this anti-Assyrian alliance, Ahaz, king of Judah, sent tribute to Pul, pledging his allegiance. In response to this invitation Pul made a campaign against Philistia, establishing contact with Ahaz, and by 732 had conquered Damascus. Samaria was saved at this time when Pekah was replaced by Hoshea, who willingly paid tribute as a puppet king. With the death of Rezin and the fall of Damascus the kingdom of Syria came to its end, never to rise again.

The Great Assyrian Empire

In the northeast corner of the Fertile Crescent, stretching some 350 miles along the Tigris River at an approximate width of 200 miles, is the land known as Assyria. The name probably comes from the national god, Ashur, after whom one of its leading cities was named. The importance of

Assyria during the divided kingdom period is immediately apparent in the fact that at the height of its power it absorbed the kingdoms of Syria, Israel, Judah, and even Egypt as far as Thebes. For approximately two and a half centuries it exerted a tremendous influence upon the developments in the land of Canaan and therefore frequently appears in the biblical record.

Although some scholars trace the beginnings of Assyria to the early part of the third millennium, little is known prior to the nineteenth century, when aggressive trading settlements from this area extended their commercial interests into Asia Minor. In the days of Shamshi-Adad I (*ca.* 1748–1716) Assyria enjoyed a period of prosperity with Ashur as its leading city. For several centuries thereafter Assyria was overshadowed by the Hittite kingdom in Asia Minor and the Mitanni kingdom which dominated the upper Tigris-Euphrates area.

Assyrian history proper had its beginnings about 1100 B.C. with the reign of Tiglath-pileser I (*ca.* 1114–1076 B.C.). According to his annals, he extended the power of his nation westward to the Mediterranean Sea, overpowering the small and weaker nations in that area. However, during the next two centuries Assyrian power recedes into the background while Israel, under David and Solomon, rises to a dominant power in the Fertile Crescent.

Beginning with the ninth century Assyria emerges as a rising power. Assyrian eponym lists from about 892 B.C. to 648 B.C. make it possible to correlate and integrate the history of Assyria with the developments in Israel as recorded in the biblical account. Ashurnasirpal II (883–859 B.C.) established Calah as his capital. After developing a strong military power he began pushing westward, terrorizing the opposing nations with his ruthlessness and cruelty, crossing the Euphrates, and establishing commercial contacts on the Mediterranean. Frequent contacts with the Syrians to the south brought on an important battle at Karkar on the Orontes River in 853 B.C. in the days of his son Shalmaneser III (858–824 B.C.). In the coalition headed by Benhadad of Damascus, Ahab, king of Israel, furnished 2,000 chariots and 10,000 soldiers, constituting the largest unit in this group. Although the Assyrian king claimed the victory, it is doubtful whether it was decisive, since Shalmaneser III avoided contact with the Syrians for several years after this. In 848 and again in 845 B.C. Benhadad resisted two more Assyrian invasions, but no mention is made of any Israelite forces aiding the Syrians at this time. Jehu, who usurped the throne in Samaria (841 B.C.), made subservient overtures to Shalmaneser III by sending him tribute. This left Hazael, the new king in Damascus, with the problem of resisting Assyrian aggression. Although Shalmaneser harassed Syria for a few years in the days of Hazael, he found it expedient to turn his attention to the conquest of areas in the north after 837 B.C., giving Canaan relief from Assyrian pressure for several decades.

For nearly a century Assyrian power fades into the background. Shamshi-Adad V (823–811 B.C.) was kept busy suppressing revolts in various parts of the kingdom. Adadnirari III (810–783) attacked Damascus before the turn of the century, enabling the Israelites to get relief from oppression by Syria. Shalmaneser IV (782–773), Ashurdan III (772–755), and Ashurnirari (754–745) successfully maintained Assyria as a powerful nation but were not strong enough to enlarge it as did the following ruler.

Tilgath-pileser III (745–727 B.C.) was an outstanding warrior who led his nation in further conquests. In Babylon, where he was recognized as king, he was known as Pulu. I Kings 15:19 refers to him as Pul. In the conquest of additional territory westward he adopted the policy of dividing the area into subject provinces for more secure control. Although this practice may have been used formerly, he was effective in notoriously terrorizing the nations by exchanging large groups of people in a conquered city with captives from a distant area. This definitely checked the possibility of rebellion. It also served as a leveling process linguistically so that the Aramaic language displaced others in the large kingdom area. At the beginning of his reign Pul exacted tribute from Menahem, king of Israel, and Rezin, king of Damascus. Since Judah was the strongest nation in Canaan at this time, it is possible that Azariah may have organized a coalition of forces to oppose the Assyrians. It seems that his successors, Jotham and Ahaz, resisted pressure from Israel and Syria to join them as well as Philistia and Edom in opposing Pul. Instead Ahaz issued friendly overtures to Pul, in response to which the Assyrian forces advanced as far as Philistia in 733 B.C., possessing territory at the expense of these opposing nations. After a terrible siege the great city of Damascus fell, Rezin was killed, and the Syrian kingdom capitulated. Samaria averted conquest by replacing Pekah with Hoshea.

Shalmaneser V (727–722 B.C.) carried on his father's policies. In the days of Hoshea the Israelites were anxious to terminate their subservience to Assyria. Shalmaneser responded with an invasion of the country and for three years besieged Samaria. In 722 B.C. Sargon II, who served as a general in the army, usurped the throne and founded a new dynasty in Assyria. In the records he claims that he captured Samaria, although some believe that Shalmaneser V really took the city and Sargon claimed the credit. Ruling from 721–705 B.C., he used Ashur, Calah, and Nineveh as capitals, but finally built the great city of Khorsabad for which he is best remembered. His campaign against Ashdod in 711 may be the one mentioned in Is. 20:1. Sargon's reign was abruptly terminated by his death in battle.

Sennacherib (704–681 B.C.) made the city of Nineveh famous as his great capital by building a wall some 40 to 50 feet high around a 2½-mile length along the Tigris River. In his annals he lists the conquest of Sidon,

Joppa, forty-six walled cities in Judah, and his assault on Jerusalem in the days of Hezekiah. In 681 he was killed by two of his sons.

Although Sennacherib had been stopped at the borders of Egypt, his son Esarhaddon (681–668 B.C.) advanced into Egypt and defeated Taharka. His interest in Babylonia is evidenced by his rebuilding of the city of Babylon, possibly because his wife was of the Babylonian nobility. Sennacherib appointed Samassumukin as Babylonian ruler, but the latter rebelled, after a sixteen-year rule, against his brother Ashurbanipal and perished in the burning of Babylon (648 B.C.).[15] During Esarhaddon's reign Manasseh, king of Judah, was taken captive to Babylon (II Chron. 33:10–13). Death came to Esarhaddon as he was marching his armies to Egypt.

During the reign of Ashurbanipal (668–*ca.* 630 B.C.), the Assyrian Empire reached its zenith in wealth and prestige. In Egypt he marched his armies some five hundred miles up the Nile River to capture Thebes in 663 B.C. Civil war (652 B.C.) with his brother, who was in charge of Babylon, resulted in the capture of that city in 648. Although he was cruel and ruthless as a military general, Ashurbanipal is best remembered for his keen interest in religious, scientific, and literary works. Sending scribes all over Assyria and Babylonia to copy records of creation, floods, ancient history and the like, he amassed much material in the great royal library of Nineveh.

In less than three decades after Ashurbanipal's death the Assyrian kingdom, which had exerted such tremendous influence throughout the Fertile Crescent, faded away—never to rise again. The three succeeding rulers were unable to cope with the rising kingdoms of Media[16] and Babylonia. Nineveh fell in 612 B.C. With the battles of Haran (609) and Carchemish (605) the last vestige of Assyrian opposition disappeared. Expanding westward, the Babylonian kingdom[17] absorbed the Southern Kingdom and destroyed Jerusalem in 586 B.C.

SELECTED READING

ALBRIGHT, W. F. *The Biblical Period from Abraham to Ezra.* New York: Harper & Row, 1963.

AVI-YONAH, MICHAEL (ed.) *A History of the Holy Land.* Toronto: The Macmillan Company, 1969.

BRIGHT, JOHN. *A History of Israel.* 3rd ed. Philadelphia: Westminster Press, 1981.

[15] D.J. Wiseman, *Chronicles of Chaldaean Kings (626–556* B.C.) *in the British Museum* (London, 1956), p. 5.

[16] Cyaxares established the Median Kingdom in 633 and later sealed an alliance with Babylon by the marriage of Amytis, his paternal granddaughter, to Nebuchadnezzar the son of Nabopolassar.

[17] For a survey of Babylonian expansion see Chap. XV in this volume.

Davis, John J., and John C. Whitcomb, Jr. *A History of Israel.* Grand Rapids: Baker Book House, 1980.

Gray, John. *I & II Kings.* 2nd ed. Philadelphia: Westminster Press, 1970.

Hasel, G. F. "Books of Chronicles" in *The International Standard Bible Encyclopedia,* 1:667–673. Grand Rapids: Wm. B. Eerdmans Publishing Co., 1979.

Hayes, John H., and J. Maxwell Miller (eds.) *Israelite and Judean History.* Philadelphia: Westminster Press, 1977.

Herrmann, Siegfried. *A History of Israel in Old Testament Times.* Philadelphia: Fortress Press, 1975.

Kitchen, K. A. *The Third Intermediate Period in Egypt (1100–650).* Warminster: Aris and Phillips Ltd., 1973.

Merrill, Eugene H. *An Historical Survey of the Old Testament.* Nutley: Craig, 1969.

———. "I and II Chronicles" in *Bible Knowledge Commentary.* Wheaton: Scripture Press, 1985.

Noth, Martin. *The History of Israel.* New York: Harper & Row, 1960.

Patterson, Richard D., and Hermann J. Austel. "I and II Kings" in *Expositor's Bible Commentary,* 4:1–300. Grand Rapids: Zondervan Publishing House, 1988.

Payne, David F. *The Kingdoms of the Lord.* Grand Rapids: Wm. B. Eerdmans Publishing Co., 1981.

Payne, J. Barton. "I and II Chronicles" in *Expositor's Bible Commentary* 4:301–562. Grand Rapids: Zondervan Publishing House, 1988.

Pfeiffer, Charles F. *Old Testament History.* Grand Rapids: Baker Book House, 1973.

Thiele, E. R. *A Chronology of the Hebrew Kings.* Grand Rapids: Zondervan Publishing House, 1977.

———. *The Mysterious Numbers of the Hebrew Kings.* Chicago: University of Chicago Press, 1951; rev. ed., Grand Rapids: Wm. B. Eerdmans Publishing Co., 1965.

Unger, Merrill. *Israel and the Aramaeans of Damascus.* London: James Clarke & Co., Ltd., 1965.

Wood, Leon J. *Israel's United Monarchy.* Grand Rapids: Baker Book House, 1979.

———. *A Survey of Israel's History.* Rev. ed. Grand Rapids: Zondervan Publishing House, 1979.

———. *The Prophets of Israel.* Grand Rapids: Baker Book House, 1979.

Chapter X

The Northern Secession

The union of Israel established by David terminated with Solomon's death. Foremost among the resultant division was the Northern Kingdom—located between Judah and Syria. In less than a century (931–841 B.C.) three dynasties had risen and fallen in this new kingdom.

The Royal Family of Jeroboam

Jeroboam I distinguished himself as an administrator under Solomon while supervising the construction of the wall of Jerusalem known as Millo (I Kings 11:26–29). When the prophet Ahijah dramatically imparted a divine message by ripping his mantle into twelve pieces he gave ten to Jeroboam signifying that he was to rule over ten tribes of Israel. Unlike David, who was also king-elect long before he ascended to the throne, Jeroboam showed signs of rebellion and incurred the disfavor of Solomon. Consequently he fled to Egypt, where he found refuge until after Solomon's death.

When Rehoboam the son of Solomon called for a national assembly at Shechem, Jeroboam was invited back to champion the cause of the elders who requested a reduction in taxes. Ignoring this, Rehoboam faced a rebellion and fled to Jerusalem. While Judah and Benjamin rallied to his support the seceding tribes made Jeroboam king. Civil war and bloodshed were averted when Rehoboam heeded the warning of the prophet Shemaiah to restrain his forces. This gave Jeroboam opportunity to establish himself as king of Israel.

Civil war prevailed during the 22-year reign of Jeroboam, although Scripture does not indicate the extent of this war. Undoubtedly Rehoboam's aggressiveness was tempered by the threat of Egyptian invasion, but II

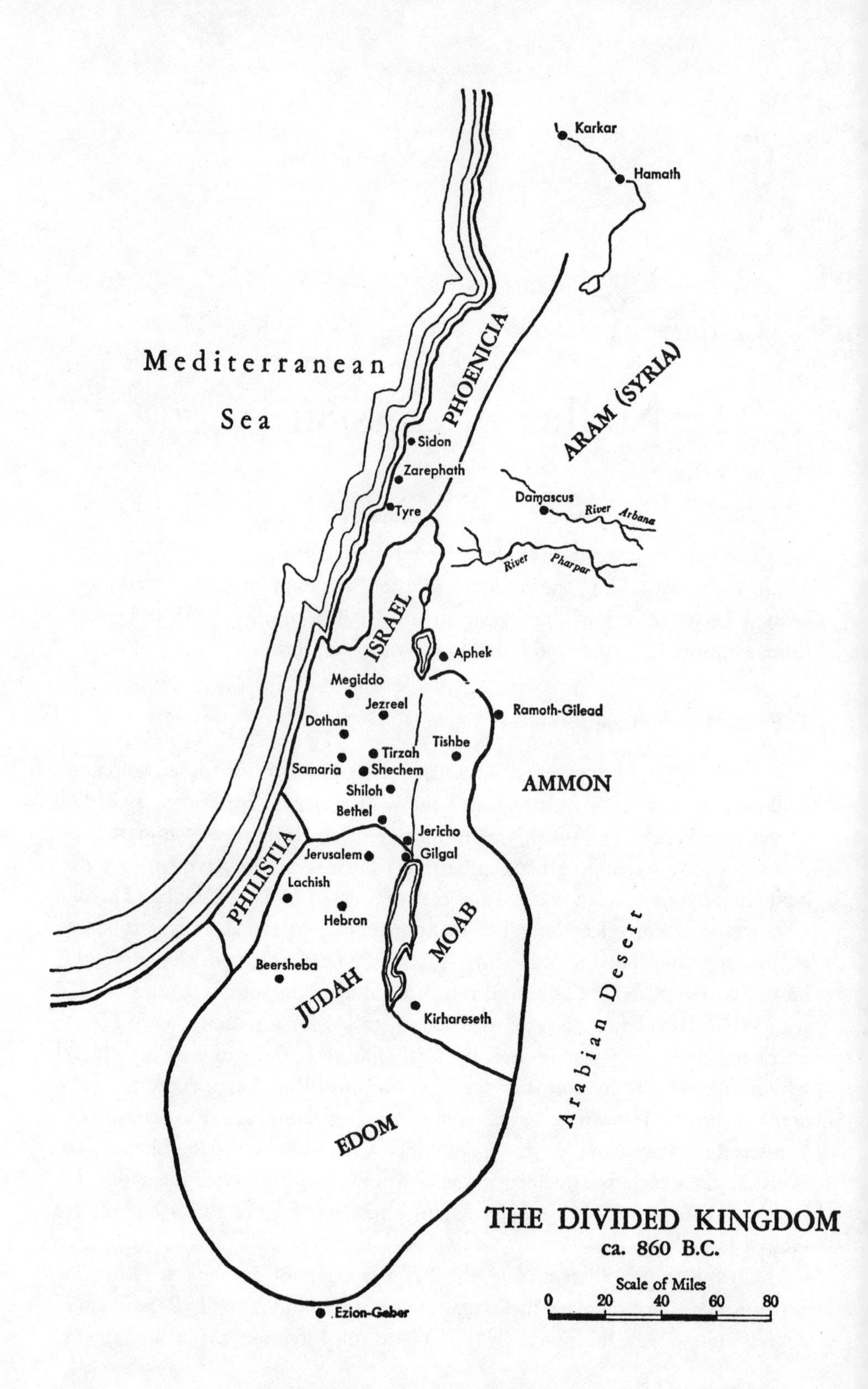
Karkar
Hamath
Mediterranean
Sea
PHOENICIA
ARAM (SYRIA)
Sidon
Zarephath
Tyre
Damascus
River Arbana
River Pharpar
ISRAEL
Aphek
Megiddo
Jezreel
Dothan
Ramoth-Gilead
Tishbe
Tirzah
Samaria
Shechem
AMMON
Shiloh
Bethel
Jericho
PHILISTIA
Jerusalem
Gilgal
Lachish
Hebron
MOAB
Beersheba
JUDAH
Arabian Desert
Kirhareseth
EDOM
THE DIVIDED KINGDOM
ca. 860 B.C.
Scale of Miles
0
20
40
60
80
Ezion-Geber

Chron. 12:15 reports continual warfare. Even towns in the Northern Kingdom were raided by Shishak.[1] After Rehoboam's death, Jeroboam attacked Judah, whose new king, Abijam, had repulsed Israel to the extent of taking control of Bethel and other Israelite cities (II Chron. 13:13–20). This may have have had some effect upon Jeroboam's choice of a capital. At first Shechem was fortified as the capital city. Whether or not the fortification of Penuel, east of Jordan, had the same implication is not certain.[2] Jeroboam resided in the beautiful city of Tirzah, which was used as the capital under the next dynasty (I Kings 14:17).[3] Apparently Jeroboam found it expedient to retain the organizational pattern of the kingdom as it had prevailed in Solomonic times.

Jeroboam took the initiative in religious matters. Naturally he did not wish his people to attend the sacred festivities at Jerusalem, lest they turn their allegiance to Rehoboam. By erecting golden calves at Dan and Bethel he instituted idolatry in Israel (II Chron. 11:13–15). He appointed priests freely, ignoring Mosaic restrictions and allowing the Israelites to offer sacrifices at various high places throughout the land. As chief priest he not only officiated at the altar but also changed a feast day from the seventh to the eighth month (I Kings 12:25–13:34).

Jeroboam's aggressiveness in religion was tempered when he was warned by an unnamed prophet from Judah. This man of God boldly warned the king as he stood and burned incense at the altar in Bethel. The king immediately ordered his arrest. The prophet's message, however, received divine confirmation in the rending of the altar and the inability of the king to withdraw the hand he had pointed toward the faithful man of God. Suddenly the king's defiant command changed into a plea for intercession. Jeroboam's hand was restored as the prophet prayed. The king wanted to reward the prophet but the latter would not even accept hospitality. The man of God was under divine orders to leave immediately.

The sequel to the faithful ministry of this man of God is noteworthy. Being deceived by an old prophet from Bethel, the prophet from Judah accepted his hospitality and so precipitated divine judgment. On his way home he was killed by a lion and brought back to Bethel for burial. Perhaps the tomb of this prophet served as a reminder to succeeding generations that obedience to God was essential. Certainly it should have had significance for Jeroboam.

[1] Albright, *Biblical Period,* p. 30.

[2] E. Mould, *Essentials of Bible History,* p. 223, suggests that Jeroboam changed his capital to Penuel as a result of military pressure from Judah.

[3] Modern Tell el-Farah, seven miles northeast of Shechem on the road leading to Beth-shan, is thought to be Tirzah. Identification is not certain. Excavations by Father R. de Vaux in 1947 favor this. See Wright, *Biblical Archaeology,* p. 151. Cf. Josh. 12:24 and Song of Songs 6:4.

Another warning came to Jeroboam through the prophet Ahijah. When his son, Abijah, became seriously ill, Jeroboam sent his wife to consult this aged prophet at Shiloh. Although she was disguised, the blind prophet recognized her immediately. She was sent back to Tirzah with the sobering message that the child would not recover. Furthermore, the prophet warned her that failure to keep God's commandments would precipitate divine judgment—extermination of Jeroboam's dynasty and captivity for the Israelites. Before she reached home the child died.

In spite of all the prophetic warnings Jeroboam continued in idolatry. Civil strife undoubtedly so weakened Israel that Jeroboam even lost the city of Bethel to Judah in the days of Abijah, the son of Rehoboam.

Within a few short years the ominous warning of the prophet was fulfilled. Nadab, Jeroboam's son, reigned less than two years. While besieging the Philistine city of Gibbethon he was assassinated by Baasha.

Baasha's Dynasty

Baasha, of the tribe of Isaachar, established himself as king over Israel at Tirzah. Although chronic war with Judah prevailed throughout his reign, a notable crisis occurred when he attempted to fortify Ramah. Apparently many Israelites deserted to Judah in the year 896–895 B.C. (II Chron. 15:9).[4] To counteract this, Baasha advanced his frontier to Ramah, five miles north of Jerusalem. By occupying this important city he could control the main roads from the north, converging at Ramah and leading to Jerusalem. In return for this aggressive act, Asa, king of Judah, scored a diplomatic victory by renewing an alliance with Benhadad I of Damascus. As a result, Benhadad nullified his alliance with Israel and invaded the northern territory of Baasha, taking control of such cities as Kedesh, Hazor, Merom, and Zephath. He also acquired the rich fertile acreage west of Lake Galilee as well as the plains west of Mount Hermon. This also gave Syria control of lucrative caravan trade routes to Accho, on the Phoenician coast. In the face of this pressure from the north, Baasha abandoned the fortification of Ramah, thus alleviating the threat to Jerusalem.

In the days of Baasha the prophet Jehu, son of Hanani, was actively proclaiming the Lord's message. He admonished Baasha to serve God who had exalted him to the kingship. Unfortunately Baasha ignored the prophet's advice and continued in the sinful ways of Jeroboam.

Elah succeeded his father, Baasha, and reigned less than two (886–885). Being found drunk in the home of his chief steward, Elah was

[4] E. R. Thiele, *The Mysterious Numbers of the Hebrew Kings,* pp. 57–60. Cf. M. Unger, *Israel and the Aramaeans of Damascus,* p. 59, who follows Albright and dates this about 879 B.C.

assassinated by Zimri, who was in command of half the royal chariots. In a few short days the word of Jehu was fulfilled as Zimri killed all the relatives and friends of the family of Baasha and Elah.

Zimri's reign as king of Israel was hastily established and abruptly terminated—all within seven days. Undoubtedly he had failed to clear his plans with Omri, who was in charge of the Israelite troops encamped against Gibbethon. It is obvious that Zimri did not have Omri's support, since the latter marched his troops against Tirzah. In desperation Zimri secluded himself in the royal palace while it was being reduced to ashes. Since he had had only a seven-day reign, Zimri hardly deserves mention as a ruling dynasty.

The Omride Rulers

Omri was the founder of the most notorious dynasty in the Northern Kingdom. Although the scriptural account of his twelve-year reign is confined to eight verses (I Kings 16:21-28), Omri established the international prestige of the Northern Kingdom.

While commanding the army under Elah (perhaps also under Baasha), Omri gained valuable military experience. With military support he took over the kingdom within seven days after Elah's assassination. Apparently he was opposed by Tibni, who died six years later and left Omri sole ruler of Israel.

Samaria was the new site for his capital. Under his orders it was established as the best fortified city in all Israel. Strategically located seven miles northwest of Shechem on the road leading to Phoenicia, Galilee, and Esdraelon, Samaria was secured as the impregnable capital of Israel for over a century and a half until it was conquered by the Assyrians in 722 B.C.

Excavations at Samaria were started in 1908 by two great American archaeologists, George A. Reisner and Clarence S. Fisher, who supervised the Harvard expedition which was continued by others in subsequent years.[5] Apparently Omri and Ahab constructed a strong wall around the palace and courtyard. With another wall on a lower terrace and an additional wall at the bottom of the hill, the city was well secured against invaders. The masonry and workmanship in these walls was so superior that its equal has not been found anywhere else in Palestine. Ivories used as inlays found in these ruins date back to the times of the Omride dynasty, indicating importation and trade with Phoenicia and Damascus.

Omri successfully established a favorable foreign policy. According to the Moabite stone, which was discovered in 1868 at the capital, Dibon, by Clermont-Ganneau and is presently located in the Louvre Museum in Paris,

[5] See Wright, *op. cit.*, pp. 151–155, and J. P. Free, *Archaeology and Bible History*, pp. 181–183.

it was Omri who subjected the Moabites to Israel.[6] By collecting tribute and controlling trade Israel gained great wealth. Omri established friendly relations with Phoenicia which were sealed in the marriage of Ahab, his son, and Jezebel, the daughter of Ethbaal, king of the Sidonians (I Kings 16:31).[7] This was vitally significant for Israel's commercial expansion and undoubtedly initiated a policy of religious syncretism which blossomed in the days of Ahab and Jezebel. The latter seems to be implied in I Kings 16:25 where Omri is charged with more evil than all the kings before him.

Syro-Israelitic relations in the days of Omri are somewhat ambiguous (I Kings 20:34). It seems unlikely that Omri, who was so shrewd and successful as militarist and diplomat, would have conceded cities to Syria and granted trading rights in his capital city. During the days of Baasha the Syrians, under Benhadad, gained control of the wealthy caravan routes westward to Accho, but undoubtedly Omri challenged this monopoly by his treaty with Phoenicia and the building of Samaria with its strong fortifications. By interpreting the word "father" as "predecessor" in the above text and applying the word "Samaria" to the Northern Kingdom, the concessions Israel made to Syria have reference to the days of Jeroboam.[8] Without conclusive evidence to the contrary it seems reasonable to conclude that Israel was not invaded by Syria and was not tributary to Benhadad in the days of Omri. It is possible that Omri may have had some contact with Assyria which certainly would have tempered the Syrian attitude toward Israel.

Although civil war had prevailed between Israel and Judah in the days of Baasha, there is no indication in Scripture that this continued under Omri. Very likely warfare was replaced by friendly overtures toward the Southern Kingdom, which culminated in intermarriage between the royal families of Israel and Judah.

When Omri died in 874 B.C. the city of Samaria became a lasting monument to his rule. Even though he had established the kingdom of Israel, his sinfulness had exceeded that of all his predecessors.

Ahab (874–853) was the outstanding king of the Omride dynasty. Heir of a kingdom that had favorable policies regarding surrounding nations, Ahab successfully expanded the political and commercial interests of Israel during his 22-year reign.

Being married to Jezebel from Sidon, Ahab fostered favorable relations with the Phoenicians. Increasing commerce between these two countries represented a serious threat to the lucrative trading interest of Syria. And it may well be that Benhadad countered this Phoenician-Israelite affinity with

[6] See J. B. Pritchard, ed., *Ancient Near Eastern Texts,* pp. 320–321.

[7] If Ahaziah, the son of Athaliah the daughter of Ahab and Jezebel, was 22 in 842 B.C., then the Ahab-Jezebel marriage took place during the reign of Omri. See Unger's discussion, *op. cit.,* p. 63.

[8] *Ibid.,* pp. 61–64.

a diplomatic move that resulted either in royal intermarriage or in religious devotion to the Tyrian god, Melcarth.[9] As long as this competition with Syria did not break out into open warfare Ahab shrewdly took advantage of the opportunity to secure the welfare of his nation.

Throughout Israel Ahab built and fortified many cities including Jericho (I Kings 16:34; 22:39). Beyond that he exacted a heavy tribute in livestock from Moab (II Kings 3:4), which gave him a favorable balance of trade with Phoenicia and Syria. With Judah he ensured a policy of friendship by the marriage of his daughter, Athaliah, to Jehoram, son of Jehoshaphat (*ca.* 865 B.C.).[10] The support of Judah strengthened Israel against Syria. By maintaining peace and developing a lucrative trade Ahab was able to continue the building program in Samaria. The wealth he lavished on himself is indicated in I Kings 22:39, where reference is made to an "ivory house." The ivory discovered by archaeologists in the ruins of Samaria may well be from Ahab's time.

While Omri may have introduced Baal, the god of Tyre, into Israel, Ahab promoted worship of this idol. In his great capital city of Samaria he built a temple to Baal (I Kings 16:30–33). Hundreds of prophets were brought into Israel to make Baalism the religion of Ahab's people. In view of this, Ahab earned the reputation of being the most sinful of all kings who had ruled Israel.

Elijah was God's messenger in this era of rank apostasy. Without any information concerning his call or background, he emerged suddenly from Gilead and announced a drought[11] in Israel which would be terminated only by his word. For three and a half years (James 5:17) Elijah was in seclusion. As long as the water supply lasted at the brook Cherith Elijah was fed by ravens. The rest of this period he was cared for by a widow in Zarephath[12] whose provisions were miraculously multiplied daily. Another great miracle performed here was the restoration of the widow's son.

While there was famine in Israel drastic repercussions occurred. Unable to locate Elijah, Jezebel killed some of the prophets of the Lord but Obadiah, a servant of Ahab, protected one hundred by hiding them in caves and providing for their welfare. Throughout Israel and in the surrounding countries there was an intensive search for Elijah, but he could not be found. Then the prophet returned to Israel and asked Obadiah to summon Ahab.

[9] See *ibid.*, p. 65.

[10] Note that Albright considers Athaliah the sister rather than the daughter of Jezebel. See Unger's discussion, *op. cit.*, p. 63, f. 2. However, Thiele's chronology allows sufficient time for Athaliah to be the daughter of Ahab and Jezebel.

[11] For the attestation of this drought in Phoenician history see Gordon, *The World of the Old Testament*, p. 198.

[12] It is interesting to note that God did not need to remove Elijah far from the point of danger: Zarephath was located between Tyre and Sidon, which were frequently visited by Jezebel.

When the king charged Elijah with troubling Israel the prophet boldly reprimanded Ahab and his family for neglecting the commandments of the Lord and worshiping Baal. With Elijah giving the orders, Ahab summoned the 450 prophets of Baal and the 400 prophets of Asherah who were sustained by Jezebel. Because famine prevailed throughout the nation there was decisive action. With all Israel and the prophets gathered before him at Mount Carmel, Elijah courageously confronted the people with the fact that they could not serve God and Baal at the same time. The prophets of Baal were challenged to prevail upon their god to ignite the prepared offering. From morning until late afternoon they performed their vain rituals while Elijah ridiculed their futile efforts. Elijah then repaired the altar of the Lord, prepared the sacrifice, drenched it with water and called upon God for divine confirmation. The offering was consumed, and all Israel acknowledged God. Immediately the false prophets were executed at the brook Kishon. After Elijah had prevailed in prayer on the mountaintop he warned Ahab that the long-awaited rain would soon begin. Hurriedly Ahab made the fifteen-mile chariot trip to Jezreel, but Elijah preceded him.

Ahab gave Jezebel a firsthand report of events at Mount Carmel. Immediately she threatened Elijah. Fortunately he was given 24-hour notice. Although he had fearlessly defied the hundreds of false prophets the day before, he now headed for the nearest border in an effort to leave Israel. Going south he left his servant at Beersheba and continued a day's journey farther, where he relaxed under a juniper (broom) tree and prayed that he might die. Refreshments were provided by an angelic messenger and the discouraged prophet was instructed to continue down to Mount Horeb. Here he had a divine revelation, was assured that there were 7,000 in Israel who had not accepted Baalism, and was given a threefold commission: to anoint Hazael as king of Syria, Jehu as king over Israel, and call Elisha as his own successor. When Elijah returned to Israel he imparted God's call to Elisha by the transfer of his mantle. Elisha then became his coworker.

By effective diplomacy and favorable treaties Ahab was able to maintain peaceful relations with surrounding countries until the latter part of his reign. The motivation behind Syria's attack on the rising Israelite kingdom is not stated (I Kings 20:1–43). Perhaps the Syrian king took advantage of Israel after the country had suffered from a famine.[13] It may also be possible that the Assyrian threat motivated Benhadad to aggressive action at this time.[14] Supported by thirty-two vassal kings, the Syrians besieged Samaria. Advised by a prophet, Ahab employed his district governors to muster a force of 7,000 for a surprise attack. With the support of the regular troops the

[13] Cf. E. Meyer, *Geschichte des Altertums,* II, 2 (1931), 332.

[14] See E. Kraeling, *Aram and Israel,* Columbia University Oriental Studies, Vol. 13 (1918), p. 51.

Israelites routed the Syrians, who incurred great losses in men, horses, and chariots. Benhadad barely escaped with his life.

The Syrians returned to fight Israel again the following spring—in accordance with the prophet's warning to Ahab. By brilliant strategy Ahab once more defeated Benhadad. Although vastly outnumbered, Ahab encamped on the hills, struck with sudden fury, and gained a decisive victory in the capture of Aphek, three miles east of the Sea of Galilee.[15] Benhadad was captured but Ahab released him and even allowed him to state his own peace terms, whereby some cities were restored to Israel and trading rights were granted to the victors in Damascus. This generous and gracious treatment of Israel's worst enemy was part of Ahab's foreign policy of establishing friendly alliances with surrounding nations. Ahab may have anticipated Assyrian aggression, so that the treaty of Aphek represented his plan to retain Syria as a friendly buffer state.

Ahab failed to acknowledge God in this significant military victory (I Kings 20:26–43). En route to Samaria a prophet dramatically reminded him that an ordinary soldier forfeits his life for disobedience. How much more so the king of Israel who had not fulfilled his commission when God granted him victory. The prophet's ominous warning spoiled Ahab's victory celebration.

The final encounter between Elijah and Ahab took place in Naboth's vineyard (I Kings 21:1–29). Frustrated in his attempt to purchase this vineyard, Ahab's disappointment was readily apparent to his wife Jezebel. Ruthless Jezebel had no respect for Israelite law and gave no heed to Naboth's conscientious refusal to sell his inherited possession—not even to a king. Accused by false witnesses, Naboth was condemned by the elders and stoned. Ahab had little opportunity to enjoy his coveted possession as he was soon met by Elijah. Boldly this spokesman for God indicted Ahab for shedding innocent blood. For this gross injustice the Omride dynasty was doomed to destruction. Even though Ahab repented, this judgment was tempered only by postponement until after his death.

Although not mentioned in Scripture, the battle of Karkar (853 B.C.) was significant enough to warrant detailed consideration in Assyrian annals, occurring during the three-year truce between Syria and Israel (I Kings 22:1). The Assyrians under Ashurnasirpal II (883–859 B.C.) had established contacts with the Mediterranean but avoided any aggression toward Syria and Israel. Shalmaneser III (859–824 B.C.), however, encountered opposition. After taking numerous cities north of Karkar the Assyrians were halted in their advance by a strong coalition which Shalmaneser listed in his monolith inscription as follows: Hadadezer (Benhadad) of Damascus

[15] For location of Aphek see F. M. Abel, *Geographie de la Palestine* (Paris, 1938), Vol. II, p. 246.

had 1,200 chariots, 1,200 cavalrymen, and 20,000 infantry; King Irhuleni of Hameth contributed 700 chariots, 700 cavalrymen, and 10,000 infantry; Ahab the Israelite furnished 2,000 chariots and 10,000 infantry.[16] Although Ahab is not credited with any cavalry, he is remembered for making the greatest contribution in chariotry used in Israel since Davidic times. Shalmaneser boasts of a great victory. How decisive it was is questionable, since the Assyrians did not advance to Hamath nor resume their attack during the next five or six years.

With the immediate danger of an Assyrian invasion averted, the three-year truce between Israel and Syria was ended when Ahab attempted to recover Ramoth-gilead (I Kings 22:1–40). Thiele suggests that the battle of Karkar took place in July or early August so that this Syro-Israelite battle occurred later the same year before Ahab had disbanded his troops.[17] Affinity between the royal families of Israel and Judah involved Jehoshaphat in this attempt to oust the Syrians from Ramoth-gilead. For three years Benhadad's failure to restore this city, in accordance with the Aphek pact, had undoubtedly been overlooked by Ahab as they faced the common Assyrian threat.

Jehoshaphat supported Ahab in this venture but was genuinely concerned about divine guidance. Ahab's 400 prophets unanimously assured the kings of victory with Zedekiah even using a pair of iron horns to demonstrate how Ahab would gore the Syrians. But King Jehoshaphat had an uneasy conscience. Although Micaiah sarcastically encouraged the kings to venture out against Syria, he asserted sincerely that Ahab would be killed in this battle. As a result, Micaiah was imprisoned with royal orders for his release if Ahab returned in peace.

Knowing this, Ahab disguised himself while Israel and Judah launched their attack on Ramoth-gilead. Recognizing Ahab's ability as a successful leader of Israel, the king of Syria gave orders to kill him. When the Syrians pursued the royal chariot and recognized its occupant to be Jehoshaphat they relented. Unknown to the Syrians a stray arrow pierced Ahab, fatally wounding him. Not only was Israel without a shepherd, as Micaiah had predicted, but the words of Elijah the prophet were literally fulfilled in the death of Ahab (I Kings 21:19).

Ahab was succeeded by Ahaziah, who reigned approximately one year (853–852 B.C.). Two things are to be remembered about his foreign affairs. Not only was Ahaziah unsuccessful in reclaiming Moab for the Omride dynasty (II Kings 3:5) but his joint naval expedition with Jehoshaphat at the gulf of Aqaba also ended in failure (II Chron. 20:35). When Ahaziah proposed another venture Jehoshaphat, having been rebuked for this alliance by the prophet Eliezer, refused to co-operate (I Kings 22:47–49).

[16] Pritchard, *op. cit.*, pp. 276–281.
[17] See Thiele, *op. cit.*, pp. 62–63.

Upon the occasion of a serious fall he ignored the prophet Elijah and sent messengers to Baalzebub at Ekron.[18] Elijah intercepted these messengers with the solemn warning that Ahaziah would not recover. After several attempts to capture Elijah had been repulsed the prophet was taken directly to the king. As with Ahab his father, Elijah personally warned Ahaziah that God's judgment awaited him because he had recognized heathen gods and ignored the God of Israel. This may have been Elijah's last appearance before a king (*ca.* 852 B.C.),[19] since no mention is made of any association with Joram, king of Israel.

Elijah and Elisha had co-operated in establishing schools for prophets. When Elisha realized that their joint ministry was nearing conclusion he asked that he might have a double share of the spirit that had rested upon Elijah. Fiery horses and chariot separated the two companions and Elijah was taken into heaven by a whirlwind. When Elisha saw his master disappear he picked up Elijah's mantle and recrossed the Jordan with the consciousness that his request had been granted. At Jericho the people fully acknowledged Elisha as God's prophet. In response to their request he miraculously sweetened their bitter water. Going on to Bethel he was jeered and ridiculed by a group of boys, who were then devoured by bears in divine judgment. From there Elisha went to Mount Carmel and on to Samaria, having been publicly established as the prophet of the Lord in Israel.

Joram, another son of Ahab and Jezebel, became king of Israel after the death of Ahaziah in 852 B.C. During the twelve years of this last Omride king in Israel Elisha was frequently associated with Joram. Consequently the account allotted to this period (II Kings 3:1–9:26) is largely devoted to the helpful ministry of this great prophet.

The rebellion of Moab was one of the first problems facing Joram when he became king of Israel. Enlisting the support of Jehoshaphat, Joram led the united armies of Israel and Judah in a seven-day march around the southern end of the Dead Sea, where Edom joined the alliance. Although Israel controlled the Moabite land north of the Arnon River, Joram planned his attack from the south. While encamped in the desert area along the Moabite-Edomite border the allied armies were confronted with a water shortage. When Elisha was located he assured the three kings of a miraculous water supply because of Jehoshaphat's presence. The next morning the Moabites attacked but were repulsed. Retreating from the advancing invaders the king of Moab took refuge in Kirhareseth (modern Kerak), which was built

[18] Under this name the sun-god Baal was acknowledged as the god who produced and controlled flies.

[19] The letter that Elijah wrote to Jehoram, king of Judah, II Chron. 21:12–15, would possibly favor a later date. This is the only written message credited to Elijah.

on an elevation of 3,720 feet above the Mediterranean. In desperation Mesha offered his eldest son as a burnt offering to the Moabite God, Chemosh. Terrified, the allied invaders left Moab without resubjugating it to Israel.

Elisha had a very effective ministry throughout Israel. One day a widow, whose husband had been one of the prophets, appealed to Elisha to help rescue her sons from a creditor who was about to take them into slavery. Through the miraculous multiplication of oil she was able to raise enough money to pay her debt (II Kings 4:1-7).

While traveling with his servant, Gehazi, Elisha enjoyed the hospitality of a wealthy hostess in Shunem, a few miles north of Jezreel. For this deed of kindness Elisha assured her that in due time she would have a son. The promised child was born the next spring. When this son died from sunstroke the Shunammite mother went to Elisha's home on Mount Carmel and appealed for help. Her son was restored to life (II Kings 4:8-37). Some time later, when a famine was pending, Elisha advised this Shunammite woman to move to a more prosperous community. After a seven-year sojourn in Philistine country she returned and was aided by Gehazi in recovering her possessions (II Kings 8:1-6).

When the prophets at Gilgal were confronted with a famine Elisha provided an antidote for the poisonous plant they were preparing to eat. He also multiplied twenty barley loaves and a few ears of corn so that one hundred men were fed, with food to spare (II Kings 4:38-44).

The story of Naaman (II Kings 5:1-27) involves Elisha with the political leaders of Syria as well as Israel. Through a captive Israelite maid in his home Naaman, the leprous captain of the Syrian army, heard about the healing ministry of the prophet Elisha. Carrying letters written by Benhadad, Naaman arrived in Samaria and requested Joram to cure him of his leprosy. Terrified, Joram tore his clothes because he feared the Syrian king was looking for trouble. Elisha saved the day by appropriately reminding Joram of the prophet in Israel.

Appearing at the home of Elisha, Naaman was given simple instructions to wash in the Jordan seven times. After finally yielding to the persuasion of his servants to obey the prophet's simple command, he was healed. He returned to offer Elisha a reward, which the prophet declined. With a commitment to worship the Lord who had healed him through Elisha, the Syrian captain left for Damascus. The sad corollary to the healing of Naaman is the fact that Gehazi, Elisha's servant, was smitten with leprosy as punishment for his attempt to appropriate the reward which Elisha had declined.

When Elisha visited one of the schools of the prophets some of the seminary students were proposing to erect another building because their accommodations were too small. Accompanied by Elisha, they went to the Jordan to cut down trees for this project. When one of them lost his axhead in the water, Elisha performed a miracle by causing it to float (II Kings 6:1-7).[20]

Warfare between Israel and Syria was carried on intermittently during the reign of Joram (II Kings 6:8-17:20). When Benhadad realized that his military movements into Israel were countered by Joram he suspected that some Syrian had turned traitor. Such was not the case; it was Elisha, in his prophetic ministry, who had advised the king of Israel. Therefore the Syrians were sent to capture Elisha. When the prophet's servant saw the mighty army of Syria surrounding Dothan he was fearful until Elisha reminded him of the fiery chariots and horses round about them. In response to Elisha's prayer the Syrian host was blinded so that the prophet was able to lead them from Dothan to Samaria. In the presence of the Israelite king the blindness was removed. Joram was instructed to provide a feast for them, then dismiss them.

Later Benhadad encamped his army around Samaria, subjecting the city to famine. When the food shortage became so desperate that mothers were eating their own children, Elisha announced that there would be an abundance of food within twenty-four hours. In the meantime four lepers in the vicinity of Samaria decided to take a chance on going into the Syrian camp. They were desperate and at the point of starvation. As they entered the Syrian quarters they found that the invaders had left everything in the camp when they fled for their lives. Through supernatural manifestation the Syrians had been terrified when they heard the sound of chariots, horses, and a great army. When the lepers shared the good news of abundant provisions with the Samaritans, the gates were opened and the people of Samaria had plenty of food, according to the words of Elisha. The captain who had refused to believe Elisha saw the supply but never enjoyed the plentiful provisions—he was trampled to death at the gate of Samaria.

Elisha's ministry was known not only throughout Israel but in Syria as well as in Judah and Edom. Through the healing of Naaman and the peculiar encounter of the Syrian armies with this prophet, Elisha was recognized as the "man of God" even in Damascus, the Syrian capital. Toward the end of Joram's reign (*ca.* 843 or 842 B.C.) Elisha made a visit to Damascus (II kings 8:7-15). When Benhadad heard of this he sent his servant, Hazael, to Elisha. With gifts impressively distributed on a caravan of forty camels, according to Oriental custom, Hazael made inquiry of the prophet whether or not Benhadad, king of Syria, would recover from his illness. Elisha dramatically portrayed to Hazael the devastation and suffering awaiting his fellow Israelites. Then the prophet fulfilled part of the commission given to

[20] Edersheim calls attention to the fact that the Hebrew word used for "float" is used in only two other places, Deut. 11:4 and Lam. 3:54, in the Old Testament. See *Bible History,* Vol. VI, p. 161.

Elijah at Mount Horeb (I Kings 19:15) by informing Hazael that he would be the next king of Syria. When Hazael returned to Benhadad he delivered Elisha's message, and smothered the ailing king with a wet blanket the following day. Hazael then seized the Syrian throne in Damascus.[21]

With the change of kings on the Syrian throne, Joram made an attempt to recover Ramoth-gilead during the last year of his reign (II Kings 8:28–29). In this effort he was supported by his nephew, Ahaziah, who had been ruling in Jerusalem about one year (II Chron. 22:5). Although Joram captured this strategic fortress, he was wounded in the battle. While he was recuperating at Jezreel, Ahaziah, king of Judah, went to visit him. Jehu was left in charge of the Israelite army stationed at Ramoth-gilead, east of the Jordan.

Elisha comes into focus again on the national scene as he performs the other unfulfilled mission given to Elijah at Mount Horeb (I Kings 19:15–16). This time Elisha did not go himself but sent one of his followers to Ramoth-gilead to anoint Jehu king of Israel (II Kings 9:1 ff.). Jehu was charged with the responsibility of avenging the blood of the prophets and servants of the Lord. The family of Ahab and Jezebel was to be exterminated as the dynasties of Jeroboam and Baasha had been before Omri.

With the blowing of the trumpet Jehu was proclaimed king. In a quick assault on Jezreel, Joram was fatally wounded and thrown on the plot of ground Ahab had taken at the expense of Naboth's blood. Here was fulfilled the word of Elijah (I Kings 21). Ahaziah attempted to flee but was also mortally wounded. He escaped to Megiddo, where he died and was taken to Jerusalem for burial. Although Jezebel made an appeal to Jehu, she was ruthlessly thrown out of a window to her death. Her body was eaten by dogs. Judgment thus came upon the dynasty of Omri, literally fulfilling the words of the prophet Elijah.

[21] For confirmation of this succession in Syria in secular sources see Unger, *op. cit.*, p. 75.

Chapter XI

The Southern Loyalists

The disruption of the Solomonic kingdom left the Davidic dynasty with a small segment of its former empire. With Jerusalem as its capital the royal line of David maintained an uninterrupted succession, ruling the small kingdom of Judah for nearly a century. Only six kings reigned during these nine decades (931–841 B.C.).

Rehoboam's Kingdom

Gathering at Shechem in 931 B.C. the Israelites under the leadership of Jeroboam appealed to Rehoboam, heir to Solomon's throne, to reduce the taxes. Three days they waited for the verdict. While the elders advised Rehoboam to lighten the tax load, the younger men suggested that their taxes should be increased. When Rehoboam announced that he would follow the policy of the latter he faced an open rebellion. Escaping to Jerusalem he called for militia to suppress the uprising but only the men of Judah and Benjamin responded to the call. Upon Shemaiah's advice Rehoboam did not suppress the rebellion.

Although Rehoboam's taxation policy was the immediate cause for the disruption of the kingdom, a number of other developments are noteworthy. Jealousy had existed for some time between the tribes of Judah and Ephraim (cf. Judg. 8:1–3; 12:1–6; II Sam. 2:9; 19:42–43). Although David had united all Israel into one great kingdom, the heavy contribution in taxes and labor made by the other tribes to Jerusalem precipitated rebellion. The death of Solomon provided opportunity for these other tribes to rebel against Judah.

Egypt may have had a vital part in the disruption of the Solomonic kingdom. There Jeroboam found refuge during the latter days of Solomon.

Hadad, the Edomite, found asylum in Egypt during his early years but returned to Edom even during the time of Solomon (I Kings 11:14-22). Although no details are given, it may well be that Egypt supported Jeroboam in rebelling against the Davidic dynasty.[1]

Another factor which contributed to the division of the kingdom is explicitly mentioned in the biblical account—Solomon's apostasy and idolatry (I Kings 11:9-13). For David's sake judgment was postponed until the death of Solomon. Rehoboam had to suffer the consequences.

As the actual division of the kingdom became a reality the priests and Levites from various parts of the nation came into the Southern Kingdom. Jeroboam substituted idolatry for the true religion of Israel. He dismissed those who had been in religious service, so that many abandoned their property and settled in Judah. This promoted real religious fervor throughout the Southern Kingdom during the first three years of Rehoboam's reign (II Chron. 11:13-17).

During the early years of his kingship Rehoboam was very active in building and fortifying many cities throughout Judah and Benjamin. In each he placed commanders—establishing and strengthening his kingdom. These cities were also used for the distribution of his family, since Rehoboam followed the example of his father and practiced polygamy.

Rehoboam began his reign with sincere religious devotion. When the kingdom was well established he and his people apostatized (II Chron. 12:1). As a result Shishak, king of Egypt, invaded Judah in the fifth year of Rehoboam's reign and took many of the fortified cities, even coming into Jerusalem. When Shemaiah announced that this was a judgment of God upon them, the king and princes humbled themselves. In response, the prophet assured them that the Egyptian invasion would be tempered and Judah would not be destroyed. According to the Karnak List, Shishak the Egyptian, supported by barbarians from Libya and Ethiopia, subdued some 150 places in Edom, Philistia, Judah, and even Israel, including Megiddo.[2] Besides his devastation of Judah, Shishak raided Jerusalem, appropriating some of the temple treasures. The splendid display of glittering golden shields gave way to shields of bronze in the days of Rehoboam.

In spite of his initial religious fervor Rehoboam succumbed to idolatry. Iddo, the prophet who wrote a history of Rehoboam's reign, may have been God's messenger to advise the king. In addition to increased idolatry and invasions by Egypt, intermittent warfare between the North and the South made the days of Rehoboam times of turmoil. The Southern Kingdom declined rapidly under his leadership.

[1] W. F. Albright, *The Biblical Period,* pp. 29–31.
[2] *Ibid.,* p. 30.

Abijah Continues Idolatry

During his three-year reign Abijah (913-910 B.C.) merely carried on the policies of his shortsighted father (I Kings 15:1-8; II Chron. 13:1-22). He activated the chronic warfare between Israel and Judah by aggressively challenging Jeroboam within Ephraimite territory. An encircling movement brought the troops of Israel into an advantageous position, but in the conflict that followed Abijah's outnumbered forces routed the Israelites. By taking Bethel, Ephron, and Jeshanah with their surrounding villages Abijah weakened the Northern Kingdom.

Abijah continued in the tradition of religious inclusivism begun by Solomon and promoted by Rehoboam. He did not abolish the service of God in the Temple but simultaneously condoned the worship of foreign gods. The extent of this is more fully reflected in the reforms of his successor. Thus idolatry became stronger and more widespread throughout the kingdom of Judah in the days of Abijah. This idolatrous policy would have resulted in the removal of the royal family from Jerusalem had it not been for the covenantal promise made to David (I Kings 15:4-5).

Asa Initiates Reform

Asa ruled in Jerusalem for forty-one years (910-869 B.C.). Peaceful conditions prevailed for at least the first ten years of his long reign. Chronological considerations imply that he was very young when Abijah died. Perhaps this had some bearing on the fact that Maacah continued as queen mother during the first fourteen or fifteen years of Asa's reign. In spite of her influence he adopted a program of reform in which foreign altars and high places were removed and pillars and asherim were broken down. The people were admonished to keep the Mosaic law and commandments. Politically this time of peace was used advantageously by the young king to fortify the cities of Judah and strengthen his army.

In the fourteenth year of his reign (897-896 B.C.) Judah was attacked from the south by a strong army of Ethiopians. It may be that Zerah, their leader, did this under pressure from Osorkon I, successor to Shishak on the throne of Egypt.[3] With divine aid Asa and his army repulsed the invaders, pursued them as far as Gerar, and returned to Jerusalem with abundant spoils of war such as cattle, sheep, and camels.

Admonished by the prophet Azariah after this great victory, Asa courageously activated his reform throughout his kingdom by removing idols

[3] *Ibid.*, p. 32.

in various cities. In the third month of the fifteenth year he assembled his own people as well as many from the Northern Kingdom who had deserted to him when they recognized that God was with him. Abundant sacrifices were made in these festivities after the reparation of the altar of the Lord. Encouraged by the prophet and the king, the people entered into a covenant to serve God wholeheartedly. Undoubtedly it was with this public support that Asa removed Maacah as queen mother. The image of Asherah, the Canaanite goddess of fertility, was crushed and burned in the valley of Kidron. Owing to popular support these religious festivities were greater than any held in Jerusalem since the dedication of Solomon's Temple.

Such religious celebrations in Judah undoubtedly disturbed Baasha. Israel had been defeated by Abijah shortly before Asa become king. Since then it had been further weakened by revolution when the dynasty of Jeroboam was ousted. Contemporarily Asa established his kingdom during a peaceful era. The defection of his people to Jerusalem in the fifteenth year of Asa (896–895 B.C.) prompted Baasha to fortify Ramah (II Chron. 16:1).[4] Since the leading roads from the Northern Kingdom converged at Ramah, five miles north of Jerusalem, Asa considered Baasha's aggressive act of strategic importance. By sending Benhadad, the Syrian king, a gift of silver and gold taken from the Temple Asa countered the Israelite aggression. Benhhadad then seized territory and cities in Northern Israel. When Baasha withdrew from Ramah, Asa utilized the stones and timbers collected there for the building of Geba and Mizpah.

Although Asa's alliance with Benhadad appeared to be successful, Hanani, the prophet, severely rebuked the king for his ungodly affiliation. He boldly reminded Asa that he had trusted God in successfully opposing the Libyans and Ethiopians under Zerah. When faced with this problem he had ignored God. Consequently he would be subjected to wars hereafter. Upon hearing this Asa became so angry that he imprisoned Hanani. Others likewise suffered because of his antagonism.

Nothing is recorded about the wars or activities during the rest of Asa's long reign. Two years prior to his death he was stricken with a fatal disease. Even in this period of suffering he failed to seek the Lord. Although Asa was a godly and righteous leader during the first fifteen years of his reign, there is no indication in the biblical record that he ever recovered from his attitude of defiance of the prophet's word. Apparently the rest of his 41-year reign was not characterized by the positive righteous activity that marked his beginning. His imprisonment of Hanani, the prophet, seems to imply that he had no fear of the Lord or his messenger (II Chron. 17:3).

[4] Cf. Thiele's discussion in *The Mysterious Numbers of the Hebrew Kings,* pp. 57–60. The thirty-sixth year dates from the beginning of the Southern Kingdom.

Jehoshaphat—A Pious Administrator

The 25-year reign of Jehoshaphat (872–848 B.C.) was one of the most encouraging and hopeful eras in the religious history of Judah. In the early years of his reign Jehoshaphat revived the policies of religious reform which had been so effective in the first part of Asa's kingship. Since Jehoshaphat was thirty-five years old when he began to rule, he very likely had during his childhood come under the influence of Judah's great religious leaders. His program was well organized. Five princes who were accompanied by nine principal Levites and two priests were sent throughout Judah to teach the law. Besides this, the high places and the asherim were removed so that the people would not be diverted to them. Instead of seeking Baal, as the people probably had done during the last two decades of Asa's reign, this king and his people turned to God.

This revived interest in God had a wholesome effect upon surrounding nations as well as upon Judah. As Jehoshaphat fortified his cities, the Philistines and Arabs did not declare war on Judah but acknowledged the superiority of the Southern Kingdom by bringing presents and tribute to the king. This providential favor and support encouraged him in the building of store cities and fortresses throughout his land and he stationed military units in them. In addition he had five army commanders in Jerusalem who were directly responsible to him (II Chron. 17:1–19). Consequently under Jehoshaphat the Southern Kingdom prospered religiously and politically.

Friendly relations existed between Israel and Judah. The marriage alliance between the Davidic and Omride dynasties very likely was made in the first decade of Jehoshaphat's reign (*ca.* 865 B.C.), since Ahaziah the son of this union was twenty-two years of age when he ascended the throne of Judah in 841 B.C. (II Kings 8:26).[5] This bond with the ruling dynasty of the Northern Kingdom insured Jehoshaphat against attack and invasion from the north.

Apparently more than a decade of Jehoshaphat's reign passes without notice between the first two verses of II Chron. 18. The year was 853 B.C. After the battle of Karkar in which Ahab had participated in the Syrian alliance to stem the advancing strength of the Assyrians, Ahab entertained Jehoshaphat most sumptuously in Samaria. As Ahab contemplated the recovery of Ramoth-gilead which Benhadad the Syrian king had not returned to him in accordance with the treaty of Aphek, he invited Jehoshaphat to join him in battle. The king of Judah responded favorably but insisted on securing the services and advice of a true prophet. Micaiah predicted that

[5] Note that II Chron. 22:2 gives his age as 42, but in the light of II Chron. 21:20 and II Kings 8:17 the number 42 is a transcriptional error.

Ahab would be killed in battle. Knowing this, Ahab disguised himself. While he was fatally wounded by a stray arrow, Jehoshaphat narrowly escaped, returning in peace to Jerusalem.

Boldly Jehu confronted Jehoshaphat with the word of the Lord. His fraternization with Israel's royal family was displeasing to God. Judgment was sure to follow. For Jehu this was a most courageous act since his father, Hanani, had been imprisoned by Asa for rebuking the king. In concluding his message Jehu complimented Jehoshaphat for removing the asherim and seeking after God.

In contrast to his father Asa, Jehoshaphat responded favorably to this rebuke. He went personally throughout Judah from Beersheba to Ephraim to encourage the people to turn to God. He implemented this reform by appointing judges in all the fortified cities and admonishing them to judge righteously in the fear of God rather than show partiality or accept bribes. Disputed cases could be appealed to Jerusalem, where Levites, priests, and heads of leading families were charged with rendering just decisions.[6] Amariah, the chief priest, was ultimately responsible for all religious cases. Civil and criminal matters rested finally with Zebadiah, the governor of the house of Judah.

Shortly after this Jehoshaphat was confronted with a terrifying invasion from the southeast. A messenger reported that a great multitude of Ammonites and Moabites was coming up against Judah from the land of Edom, south of the Dead Sea. If this was the punishment intimated in Jehu's prediction of the pending wrath of God, then Jehoshaphat had wisely prepared his people.[7] When he proclaimed a fast, the people from all the cities of Judah responded immediately. In the new court of the Temple the king himself led in prayer, acknowledging that God had given them the promised land, manifested his presence in the Temple dedicated in the days of Solomon, and promised them deliverance if they humbly appealed to him. In the simple words "neither know we what to do: but our eyes are upon thee" Jehoshaphat expressed his faith in God when he concluded his prayer (II Chron. 20:12). Through Jahaziel, a Levite of the sons of Asaph, the assembly received the divine assurance that even without fighting they should yet see a great victory. In response Jehoshaphat and his people bowed down and worshiped God as the Levites audibly praised the Lord.

The next morning the king led his people to the wilderness of Tekoa and admonished them to exercise faith in God and the prophets. Chanting praises to God, the people marched toward the enemy. The enemy forces were thrown into confusion and massacred each other. The people of Judah

[6] For the historical background of this see Ex. 18:21–22; Deut. 1:13–17; 16:18–20.
[7] Edersheim interprets this as the judgment announced by Jehu. See *Bible History*, Vol. VI, p. 78.

spent three whole days collecting the spoils of war. On the fourth day Jehoshaphat assembled his people in the valley of Berachah for a thanksgiving service—recognizing that God had given them the victory.[8] In a triumphant march the king led them back to Jerusalem. The fear of God fell on nations round about as they heard of this miraculous victory. Jehoshaphat again enjoyed peace and quietness.

With a new king, Ahaziah, on the Omride throne in Israel, Jehoshaphat once more entered into close affinity with this wicked family. In a united effort they attempted to launch ships at Ezion-geber for commercial purposes. In accordance with the prediction of the prophet Eliezer the ships were wrecked (II Chron. 20:35–37). When Ahaziah proposed another venture Jehoshaphat declined (II Kings 22:47–49).

Before the end of his reign Jehoshaphat again entered into an alliance with a king of Israel. This time it was Joram, another son of Ahab. When Ahab died, Moab ceased paying tribute to Israel. Apparently Ahaziah, in his short reign, did nothing about this. When Joram became king he invited Jehoshaphat to join forces with him in a march through Edom to subdue Moab (II Kings 3:1–27).[9] Jehoshaphat was once more made conscious of the fact that he was in an alliance with ungodly kings when the prophet Elisha saved the three armies from destruction.

Jehoshaphat died in 848 B.C. In sharp contrast to the Omride dynasty, he led his people in fighting idolatry. For his intimate association with the godless and wicked kings of Israel, however, he was severely rebuked by various prophets. This policy of intermarriage did not seriously affect his nation as long as he lived but it almost eliminated the Davidic dynasty from Judah less than a decade after his death. The fruition of his inclusivist policy largely nullified the lifetime efforts of godly Jehoshaphat.

Jehoram Reverts to Idolatry

Jehoram, the son of Jehoshaphat, ruled over Judah for eight years (848–841 B.C.). Although he was coregent with his father, he did not assume much responsibility until after Jehoshaphat's death. In the scriptural account (II Chron. 21:1–20; II Kings 8:16–24) some dates are given on the basis of his accession in 853, while others refer to 848 B.C. when he assumed full control of the kingdom.[10]

[8] Since the partition of Palestine Dr. Lambie has erected the Berachah Hospital in this same valley.

[9] For further discussion see Chapter X.

[10] Note that Thiele's discussion of this clarifies such apparent contradictions as II Kings 1:17 and 8:16. See *Mysterious Numbers of the Hebrew Kings,* pp. 61–65. Jehoram was perhaps made coregent before Jehoshaphat joined Ahab in battle against Syria in 853 B.C.

The death of Jehoshaphat brought rapid changes in Judah. The peaceful rule that had prevailed under Jehoshaphat was soon replaced by bloodshed and gross idolatry. As soon as Jehoram was secure on the throne he murdered his six brothers, whom Jehoshaphat had assigned to various fortified cities. Some of the princes suffered the same fate. The fact that he espoused the sinful ways of Ahab and Jezebel can reasonably be attributed to the influence of his wife, Athaliah. He restored high places and idolatry which his father had removed. Changes also were effected in other matters. According to Thiele, Jehoram at this time even adopted for Judah the nonaccession-year system of numbering used in the Northern Kingdom.[11]

Elijah, the prophet, severely reproached Jehoram in writing (II Chron. 21:11–15). Through this Jehoram was warned of impending judgment for his crime in killing his brothers and leading Judah into the sinful ways of the Northern Kingdom. The gloomy future held a plague for Judah and an incurable disease for the king himself.

Edom revolted against Jehoram. Although he and his army were surrounded by the Edomites, Jehoram fought his way out and escaped, and Edom gained independence. The Philistines and Arabs who had acknowledged Jehoshaphat by paying him tribute not only revolted but also advanced into Jerusalem, even raiding the king's house. They carried away with them vast treasures and took captive the family of Jehoram with the exception of Athaliah and one son, Jehoahaz or Ahaziah.

Two years before his death Jehoram was stricken with a fatal disease. After a period of terrible suffering he died in 841. The tragic and shocking effects of his short reign are reflected in the fact that no one regretted his death. He was not even accorded the usual honor of being buried in the tombs of the kings.

Ahaziah Promotes Baalism

Ahaziah had the shortest reign during this period, being king of Judah less than a year (841 B.C.).[12] Whereas Jehoram had murdered all his brothers when he became king, the sons of Jehoram were all killed by the Arabs with the exception of Ahaziah. Consequently the people of Judah had no choice but to crown Ahaziah king. Under the personal counsel of his mother the wickedness of Ahab and Jezebel found full expression when Ahaziah became king of Judah. Under her domination and the influence of

[11] Thiele, *op. cit.,* p. 62. This system was used in Israel, whereas Judah used the accession-year system.

[12] Note that he is also called "Jehoahaz" in II Chron. 21:17 and "Azariah" in II Chron. 22:6.

his uncle, Joram, who ruled in Samaria, Ahaziah had little choice. The pattern had already been set by his father.

Following his uncle's advice, the new king joined the Israelites in battle against Syria. Since Hazael had just replaced Benhadad as king of Damascus, Joram decided that this was the opportune time to recover Ramoth-gilead from the Syrians. In the ensuing conflict Joram was wounded. Ahaziah was with Joram in Jezreel, the summer palace of the Omride dynasty, when the revolution erupted in Israel. As Jehu marched on Jezreel, Joram was mortally wounded while Ahaziah took refuge in Samaria. In further pursuit he was fatally wounded and died in Megiddo. As a mark of respect for Jehoshaphat, this grandson, Ahaziah, was given a royal burial in Jerusalem.

With no qualified heir available to take over the kingdom of Judah, Athaliah seized the throne in Jerusalem. To secure her position she began the execution of the royal family (II Chron. 22:10–12). What Jezebel, her mother, had done to the prophets in Israel Athaliah did to the Davidic family in Judah. Through the marriage alliance arranged by Jehoshaphat with wicked Ahab, this granddaughter of Ethbaal, king of Tyre, had become the wife of the heir to the Davidic throne. Undoubtedly she did not assert herself as long as Jehoshaphat lived. What she did in Judah after his death is tragically apparent in the developments that unfolded in the days of her husband, Jehoram, and her son, Ahaziah. A six-year reign of terror followed (841–835 B.C.).

Chapter XII

Revolution, Recovery, and Ruin

The Jehu line occupied the throne for almost a century, longer than any other dynasty in the Northern Kingdom (841–753 B.C.). When Jehu was enthroned through a revolution, Israel was weakened and reduced to its smallest geographical area yielding land to aggressive neighbors. Under the fourth king of this family the Northern Kingdom reached its peak in international prestige. This ephemeral prosperity faded into oblivion in less than three decades under the advancing Assyrian power.

The Dynasty of Jehu

A bloody revolution took place in Israel when Jehu, an army captain, dislodged the Omride dynasty. In his occupation of Jezreel he disposed of Joram, the Israelite king, Ahaziah, the king of Judah, and Jezebel—the one responsible for making Baalism such an effective part of Israel's religion.

Marching to Samaria, Jehu slew seventy sons of Ahab's family and directed the execution of all the Baal zealots who had been inveigled into mass celebrations in the temple erected by Ahab. Since religion and politics had been so intimately fused in the Omride dynasty the ruthless destruction of Baalism was a matter of expediency for Jehu.

Jehu was troubled on every hand. By exterminating the Omride dynasty he forfeited the favor of Judah and Phoenicia, whose royal families were closely allied with Jezebel. Nor did he join the new Syrian king, Hazael, in opposing the Assyrian westward advance.

On the famous Black Obelisk discovered by Layard in 1846 Shalmaneser III reports that he received tribute from Jehu. After five unsuccessful attacks on Damascus, the Assyrian king marched his armies to the Mediterranean coast north of Beirut and collected tribute from Tyre and Sidon as well as from the king of Israel.[1] By this conciliatory move Jehu warded off an Assyrian invasion of Israel but incurred the antagonism of Hazael by placating Shalmaneser III. During the early years of this period (841–837 B.C.) Hazael resisted Assyrian aggression singlehandedly. While some of the cities to the north were conquered, Damascus successfully withstood the crisis. The Assyrians did not renew their attacks for almost two decades. This allowed Hazael to direct his well-seasoned military might southward in a renewal of the war with Israel. At Jehu's expense the Syrians occupied the land of Gilead and Bashan, east of the Jordan (II Kings 10:32–33). Having come to the throne of Israel by means of a bloody insurrection Jehu apparently never unified his nation sufficiently to withstand Hazael's might. It is doubtful whether Hazael reduced Jehu to Syrian vassalage, but for the rest of Jehu's days Israel was harassed and troubled by this aggressive Syrian king.

Although Jehu did away with Baalism he did not conform to the law of God. Idolatry still prevailed from Dan to Bethel—therefore the divine warning that his sons would reign after him only to the fourth generation.

Jehoahaz

Jehoahaz, the son of Jehu, had the same Syrian king to reckon with throughout his reign (814–798 B.C.). Hazael took advantage of the new ruler in Israel by extending the Syrian domain into the hill country of Ephraim. Israel's army was reduced to 50 horsemen, 10 chariots, and 10,000 footmen. In Ahab's day Israel had furnished 2,000 chariots in the battle of Karkar. Hazael even advanced beyond Israel to capture Gath and threatened the conquest of Jerusalem during the reign of Jehoahaz (II Kings 12:17).

Syria's gradual absorption of Israel weakened the Northern Kingdom to such an extent that Jehoahaz was ineffective in resisting other invaders. Surrounding nations such as the Edomites, Ammonites, Philistines, and Tyrians took advantage of Israel's plight. This is reflected by Amos (1:6–15) and Isaiah (9:12).

Under the pressure of foreign oppression Jehoahaz turned to God—and Israel was not completely overrun by the Syrians. In spite of this relief he did not depart from Jeroboam's idolatry nor did he destroy the asherim in Samaria (II Kings 13:1–9).

Jehoash

Jehoash, the third king in the Jehu dynasty, ruled Israel for sixteen years (798–782 B.C.). With the death of Hazael, shortly before the turn of

[1] The portrait of this transaction may still be seen on the cliff at the mouth of the Dog River near Beirut, Lebanon. Cf. G. E. Wright, *Biblical Archaeology*, pp. 156–157.

the century, it was possible to begin the restoration of Israel's fortunes under the leadership of Jehoash.

Elisha, the prophet, was still living when Jehoash ascended the throne. The silence of the Scriptures warrants the conclusion that neither Jehu nor Jehoahaz had much to do with Elisha. When the prophet was near death, Jehoash went down to see him. Weeping in his presence, the king expressed concern for the safety of Israel. On his deathbed Elisha dramatically instructed the king to shoot his arrow, assuring him that this signified Israelite victory over Syria. The final miracle associated with Elisha occurred after his death. A dead man thrown into Elisha's tomb during a Moabite raid was restored to life.

With the change of kings in Syria Jehoash was able to build up a stronger fighting force. Benhadad II was definitely placed in a defensive position as Jehoash regained much of the territory occupied by the Syrians under Hazael. The retrievement of the area east of Jordan may not have been accomplished until the time of his successor, but this was a period of preparation in which Israel began to rise in power and prestige.

During the reign of Jehoash, Amaziah, king of Judah, hired an Israelite army to aid in subjugating the Edomites (II Chron. 25:6); however, upon the advice of a prophet he dismissed them before going to battle. As they returned to Israel they plundered the cities en route from Beth-horon to Samaria, killing 3,000 people (II Chron. 25:13). Returning in triumph from an Edomite victory, Amaziah challenged Jehoash to battle. The latter responded with a warning about the fate of the thistle that made a request of the cedar of Lebanon. Evidently Amaziah did not get the point. In the ensuing military encounter Jehoash not only defeated Amaziah but invaded Judah, broke down part of the wall of Jerusalem, plundered the palace and Temple, and took some hostages back to Samaria. On the basis of synchronizing the chronology of this period Thiele has concluded that this battle took place in 791–790 B.C.[2]

Although Jehoash was disturbed over the loss of Elisha he was not sincerely interested in serving God but continued his idolatrous ways. His short reign marked the turning point in the fortunes of Israel as Elisha had predicted.

Jeroboam II

Jeroboam, the fourth ruler in the Jehu dynasty, was the outstanding king in the Northern Kingdom. He reigned for forty-one years (793–753 B.C.) including twelve years of coregency with his father. By the time he assumed full control of the kingdom (781 B.C.) he was in a position to take complete advantage of the opportunities for expansion.

[2] Thiele, *The Mysterious Numbers of the Hebrew Kings*, pp. 68–72.

Like Omri, the strongest king before him, the historiography of Jeroboam II is very brief in Scripture (II Kings 14:23–29). The vast political and commerical expansion under this powerful king is summarized in the prophecy of Jonah, the son of Amittai, who may have been the prophet by that name sent on a mission to Nineveh (Jonah 1:1). Jonah predicted that Jeroboam would restore Israel from the Dead Sea to the borders of Hamath.

Secular sources confirm biblical references that Benhadad II was not able to retain the kingdom established by his father, Hazael.[3] Two attacks on Syria by Adadnirari III (805–802) and Shalmaneser IV (773) weakened her considerably at the expense of Assyria. Besides that, Zakir of Hamath formed a coalition that defeated Benhadad II and asserted independence from Syria during this priod. This gave Jeroboam opportunity to recover the territory east of the Jordan which the Syrians had controlled for about a century. After 773 B.C. the Assyrian kings were so occupied with local and national problems that they did not make advances toward Palestine until after the time of Jeroboam. Consequently the Israelite kingdom enjoyed peaceful prosperity unequaled since the days of Solomon and David.

Samaria, which had been founded by Omri, was now refortified by Jeroboam. The wall was widened against the day of invasion to as much as thirty-three feet in some strategic places. The fortifications were so well built that about a half century later the Assyrians spent three years conquering the city.

Amos and Hosea, whose books appear in the lists of Minor Prophets, reflect the prosperity of this period. The military and commercial success of Jeroboam brought an abundance of wealth to Israel. With this luxury came a moral decline and religious indifference which these prophets boldly challenged. Jeroboam II had done evil in the sight of the Lord and caused Israel to sin as the first king of Israel had done.

Zechariah

When Jeroboam II died in 753 B.C. he was succeeded by his son, Zechariah, whose reign lasted only six months. He was murdered by Shallum (II Kings 15:8–12). This abruptly ended the rule of the Jehu dynasty.

The Last Kings

The people who heard Amos and Hosea little realized how soon the threatened judgment would come upon Israel. In a period of only three decades (752–722 B.C.) the powerful Northern Kingdom ceased to exist as an independent nation. Under the expanding empire of Assyria it capitulated—never to rise again as an Israelite kingdom.

[3] See Unger, *Israel and the Arameans of Damascus*, pp. 83–95.

Shallum (752 B.C.)

Shallum had the shortest reign in the Northern Kingdom excepting Zimri's seven-day rule. After killing Zechariah and seizing the throne he ruled for only one month. He was assassinated.

Menahem (752–741 B.C.)

Menahem had better prospects. He was able to establish himself so successfully that he remained on the throne for approximately a decade. Little is known about his domestic policies except that he continued in the idolatrous pattern of Jeroboam I.

Menahem's most serious problem was Assyrian aggression. In 745 B.C. Tiglath-pileser III, or Pul, began to rule in Assyria as one of the most powerful kings of that nation.[4] He terrorized the nations by introducing the policy of taking conquered people to distant lands. Leading citizens, executives, and political officials were replaced by foreigners in order to prevent any further rebellion after conquest. In the years 743–738 Tiglath-pileser III waged a northwestern campaign which involved the nations of Palestine. Archaeological evidence favors the theory that Uzziah, king of Judah, led the forces of Western Asia against the powerful Assyrian advance.[5] In the Assyrian chronicle Menahem is cited as being re-enthroned on the condition that he pay tribute.[6] Although the exact time for this payment cannot be conclusively established, Thiele advances evidence that favors the early part of this northwestern campaign as coinciding with the closing year of Menahem's reign.[7] Pacified by this concession Pul returned to Assyria and Menahem died in peace, with his son assuming the leadership of the Northern Kingdom.

Pekahiah (741–739 B.C.)

Pekahiah followed the policies of his father. In continuing the collection of taxes as a vassal of Assyria Pekahiah must have encountered opposition from his own people. Very likely Pekah championed a movement for revolt against Assyria and was responsible for the assassination of Pekahiah.

Pekah (739–731 B.C.)

Pekah's reign of eight years marked a period of both national and international crises. Although Syria, with its capital of Damascus, may have been subjugated to Israel in the days of Jeroboam II, it asserted itself under

[4] Cf. I Chron. 5:26. See Thiele's discussion of this, *op. cit.,* pp. 76–77. Apparently "Pul" was the name taken by "Tiglath-pileser" when he took the Babylonian throne.

[5] See Wright, *op. cit.,* p. 161.

[6] Cf. D. Winton Thomas, *Documents from Old Testament Times* (New York: Nelson & Sons, 1958), pp. 53–58.

[7] Thiele, *op. cit.,* pp. 75–98.

the leadership of a new king, Rezin, during this period of Israel's decline. Facing a common foe in the Assyrians, Pekah was strengthened in his anti-Assyrian policy by collaboration with Rezin. While the Assyrians were primarily occupied with a campaign in Urartu (737–735 B.C.), these two kings endeavored to build a solid western alliance to resist Assyrian invasion.

In Judah the current pro-Assyrian party apparently was successful (735 B.C.) in bringing Ahaz into active control of the kingdom even though Jotham was still living. Consequently he resisted overtures from Israel and Syria to co-operate with them against Assyria. In 734 Tiglath-pileser III invaded Philistia. Ahaz may have appealed to the Assyrians to relieve him from Philistine pressure (II Chron. 28:16–21) or perhaps he was already a tributary of Tiglath-pileser. Unger suggests that it was during this Philistine invasion that the Assyrians captured cities in the Northern Kingdom (II Kings 15:29).[8]

Syro-Israelite pressure on Judah terminated in actual fighting known as the Syro-Ephraimitic War (II Kings 16:5–9; II Chron. 28:5–15; Is. 7:1–8:8). Syrian armies marched down to Elath to recover that seaport of Judah for the Edomites who undoubtedly supported the coalition against Assyria. Although Jerusalem was besieged and captives from Judah were brought to Samaria and Damascus, the Southern Kingdom was not subjugated or coerced into this anti-Assyrian alliance.

Two important developments affected the withdrawal of the invading forces from Judah. When the captives were brought to Samaria a prophet, Oded by name, declared this to be divine judgment upon Judah and warned the Israelites of God's impending wrath. Owing to pressure from the princes and an Israelite assembly the captives were released by the army officials.

The other important fact was that Ahaz refused to yield to the Syro-Ephraimitic demands but appealed directly to Tiglath-pileser for help. The Assyrian king had undoubtedly formulated his plans for subduing the Westland. This invitation immediately stimulated him to action—Damascus becoming the focal point of attack in the campaigns of 733 and 732 B.C. Tiglath-pileser boasts of taking 591 towns in this Syrian area followed by the capitulation of Damascus in 732. Syria was rendered impotent to interfere with the westward advance of Assyria. For the next century Damascus and its provinces—which for two hundred years had constituted the influential kingdom of Syria—were subject to Assyrian control.

The fall of Damascus had subsequent repercussions in Samaria. Pekah, who had come to power as the champion of an anti-Assyrian policy, now lost face. With Syria prostrate before Assyrian might, Israel's chances of survival were hopeless. Pekah became the victim of a conspiracy led by Hoshea, the

[8] Unger, *op. cit.*, p. 100.

next king. Undoubtedly it was the removal of Pekah that saved Samaria from conquest at this time.

Hoshea (731–722 B.C.)

As Hoshea became king of the Northern Kingdom in 731 B.C. he had little choice in his initial policy. He was a vassal of Tiglath-pileser, who boasted of placing him on the throne in Samaria.

Hoshea's domain was largely confined to the hill country of Ephraim. Galilee and the territory east of Jordan had been under Assyrian control since the campaign of 734. Tiglath-pileser III may have conquered Megiddo during this series of western advances and used it as the administrative capital for his Galilean provinces.[9]

In 727 B.C. Tiglath-pileser III, the great king of Assyria, died. Hoping that Shalmaneser V would not be able to maintain control of his extensive territory, Hoshea depended on the support of Egypt as he discontinued his tributary payments to Assyria. Such, however, was not the case. Shalmaneser V marched his armies into Israel and besieged the strongly fortified city of Samaria in 725 B.C. For three years Hoshea was able to withstand the onslaught of the powerful Assyrian army but he finally surrendered in 722 B.C.[10]

This terminated the Northern Kingdom. Under the Assyrian policy of deportation, Israelites were taken into the regions of Persia. According to Assyrian annals, Sargon, Shalmaneser's successor, claimed nearly 28,000 victims.[11] In return, colonists from Babylonia were settled in Samaria—the Northern Kingdom was reduced to the status of an Assyrian province.

For two centuries the Israelites had followed the pattern set by Jeroboam I, founder of the Northern Kingdom. Even with the change of dynasties, Israel never divorced herself from the idolatry that was diametrically opposed to the law of God as prescribed in the Decalogue. Throughout this period faithful prophets proclaimed God's message, warning the kings as well as the people of impending judgment. For their gross idolatry and failure to serve God the Israelites were subjected to captivity at the hands of the Assyrian rulers.

[9] See Wright, *op. cit.*, p. 161.

[10] Although Sargon II takes credit for the conquest of Samaria, Shalmaneser V was still king of Assyria. It is possible that Sargon was general of the army and thus was in charge of the siege. For the most adequate discussion of this date see Thiele, *op. cit.*, pp. 121–128.

[11] Thomas, *op. cit.*, pp. 58–63.

Chapter XIII

Judah Survives Assyrian Imperialism

The ninety-year rule of the Davidic dynasty in Jerusalem was abruptly terminated with the accession of Athaliah in 841 B.C. The fruition of the inclusivist policy of godless alliances as practiced by Jehoshaphat brought the wicked daughter of Ahab and Jezebel to the throne in Judah less than a decade after the death of Jehoshaphat. In accordance with the divine promise made to David, the royal line was restored after an interlude of seven years.

During this period, when eight kings of the Davidic dynasty ruled over Judah, the most significant religious era was the reign of Hezekiah. Contemporary with him was the great prophet Isaiah, who provides supplementary information. The historical account for these two centuries is recorded in II Kings 11:1–21:26 and II Chron. 22:10–33:25.

Athaliah—A Reign of Terror

With the burial of her son Ahaziah Athaliah seized the throne in the Southern Kingdom in 841 B.C. To ensure her position as ruler she ordered the execution of everyone of royal descent and thus initiated a reign of terror. Apparently no heirs to the throne escaped her except Joash, the infant son of Ahaziah. During Athaliah's seven-year reign Jehosheba, a sister of Ahaziah, hid the royal heir in the Temple.

A drastic change in religious climate followed the death of Jehoshaphat. Being a Baal zealot like her mother Jezebel, Athaliah promoted this idolatrous practice in Jerusalem and throughout Judah. The dedicated objects in the Temple were appropriated for the worship of Baal. Mattan served Baal as high priest in Jerusalem. Undoubtedly the bloodshed and persecution of Baalism in the Northern Kingdom under Jehu made Athaliah all the more ardent in establishing the fertility cult in Judah at this time.

Jehoiada, a priest who had witnessed the religious revivals under Asa and Jehoshaphat, was instrumental in restoring the royal line. At the opportune time he secured the support of the palace guards and Joash was crowned king in the court of the Temple. When Athaliah heard the shouts of acclamation she attempted to enter, but was arrested and executed in the palace.

Joash—Reform and Relapse

Joash was but a lad of seven when he began his long reign (835–796 B.C.). Since Jehoiada instigated the coronation of Joash, the state policies were formulated and directed by him as long as he lived.

With the execution of Athaliah the Baal worship also was destroyed. The altars of Baal were broken down and Mattan the priest was killed. Jehoiada initiated a covenant in which the people promised to serve God. As long as he lived general interest prevailed in true worship, although some of the high places remained in use.

The Temple and its services had been greatly neglected during the reign of terror. Joash, in accordance with the advice of Jehoiada, supported the restoration of regular burnt offerings. As the Temple was to be officially used again, it became obvious that repairs were needed. For this purpose the priests were instructed to collect funds throughout the nation, but they were unsuccessful in their efforts. In the twenty-third year of Joash's reign (*ca.* 812 B.C.) a new method of collecting was adopted. A box was placed in the court at the right side of the altar. In response to a public proclamation, the people gave enthusiastically at first just as they had when Moses called for gifts to build the tabernacle. Craftsmen set about repairing and refurbishing the precincts. From the remaining silver and gold they fashioned appropriate furnishings. The liberality of the people for this purpose did not diminish the regular contributions to the priests. Popular support of the true religion reached a new peak under Jehoiada's influence, with restoration of the Temple.

Within a short time judgment came upon Judah. After the death of Jehoiada apostasy swept in as the princes of Judah persuaded Joash to revert to idols and the asherim service. Although prophets faithfully warned the people, the latter ignored the admonitions. When Zechariah, the son of Jehoiada, warned the people that they would not prosper if they continued to disobey the commandments of the Lord, he was stoned in the court of the Temple. Joash did not even remember the kindness of Jehoiada by saving the life of Zechariah.

Hazael had already extended his Syro-Palestinian kingdom southward at the expense of the Northern Kingdom. After the conquest of Gath on the Philistine plain he set his face toward Jerusalem, only thirty miles inland (II Kings 12:17–18). To avoid an invasion by this militant king, Joash stripped the Temple of the treasures that had been dedicated since the time of Jehoshaphat and sent them to Hazael along with the gold from the palace treasury. Because of this sign of subservience Jerusalem was spared the humiliating experience of siege and conquest. Presumably it was the failure to pay tribute that impelled the Aramean king to send a contingent of troops against Jerusalem some time later (II Chron. 24:23–24).[1] Since the "king of Damascus" is not identified by name, it is highly probable that Benhadad II had already replaced Hazael on the Syrian throne. This time the Syrian army entered Jerusalem.[2] After killing some of the princes and leaving Joash in a wounded condition they returned to Damascus with the spoils. The palace servants took advantage of the situation to avenge the blood of Zechariah by assassinating their king. Joash was buried in the city of David, but not in the tombs of the kings.

Whereas Asa had defeated a large enemy force with his small army because he placed his trust in God, Joash was overcome by a small enemy unit. This was clearly a judgment of God. After Jehoiada's death Joash permitted apostasy to permeate Judah and even tolerated the shedding of innocent blood.

Amaziah—Victory and Defeat

With the abrupt termination of the reign of Joash, Amaziah was immediately crowned king of Judah. Although he reigned a total of twenty-nine years (796–767 B.C.) he was sole ruler for only a short period. After 791 B.C. Uzziah, his son, began to reign as coregent on the Davidic throne.

Both Judah and Israel had suffered seriously under the aggressive power of Hazael, king of Syria. His death at the turn of the century marked the turning point in the fortunes of the Hebrew kingdoms. Jehoash, who ascended the throne in Samaria in 798 B.C., developed a strong army which in time challenged Syrian might. Amaziah adopted a similar policy for Judah which enabled his nation to recuperate from invasion and royal bloodshed.

One of Amaziah's first aggressive acts was to recover Edom. Joram had defeated the Edomites but had failed to subject them to Judah. Although

[1] While E. L. Curtis, *International Critical Commentary,* "in loc.," interprets this passage as a different version of the event mentioned in the previous passage, Unger, *Israel and the Aramaeans of Damascus,* pp. 79–80, advocates two different events in sequence.

[2] The date of Hazael's death and Benhadad II's accession is not definitely known beyond the suggestion of approximately 800 B.C.

Amaziah had an army of 300,000 men, he hired an additional 100,000 soldiers from Jehoash, king of Israel. A man of God came to warn him that if he used these Israelite soldiers Judah would be defeated in battle. Consequently Amaziah dismissed the contingents from the Northern Kingdom, even though he had paid for their services. With his own army he defeated the Edomites and captured Seir, the capital. Returning to Jerusalem Amaziah introduced the Edomite gods to his people and worshiped them. His idolatry did not go unchallenged, however; for a prophet announced that Amaziah would suffer defeat for his folly in failing to acknowledge God (II Chron. 25:1–16).

Amaziah, with a victory over Edom to his credit, was so confident of his military might that he challenged Jehoash to a battle. The Israelite troops, who had been dismissed without military service, were so provoked that they plundered the cities of Judah from Beth-horon to Samaria (II Chron. 25:10, 13). This may have had a bearing on the deliberate decision by Amaziah to break the peace which had existed between Israel and Judah for almost a century. Jehoash bluntly accused Amaziah of being too arrogant and warned him that the thistle, which made a presumptuous request of the cedar of Lebanon, was trampled down by a wild beast. Amaziah paid no heed and persisted in matching his army against that of the Northern Kingdom. In the battle at Beth-shemesh Judah was utterly defeated. The victors broke down part of the wall of Jerusalem, plundered the city, and took Amaziah captive (II Kings 14:11–14). With royal hostages and much spoil Jehoash returned jubilantly to Samaria. How disastrous this defeat was for Amaziah is not fully stated in the Scriptures. The act of breaching the wall meant total subjugation in the language of the ancient world.[3]

Thiele dates Israel's invasion of Jerusalem in 791–790 B.C.[4] This coincides with the time when sixteen-year-old Uzziah began to reign. With the capture of Amaziah, who had made such a blunder in his foolhardy challenge to Israel, the leaders of Judah made Uzziah coregent. The fact that Amaziah lived fifteen years after the death of Jehoash (II Kings 14:17) suggests that possibly the king of Judah was held prisoner as long as Jehoash lived. In 782–781 he was released and restored to the throne of Judah while Uzziah continued as coregent. At this time Jeroboam II, who had already been coregent with his father since 793, assumed full command of the expanding Northern Kingdom. The release of Amaziah may have been part of his goodwill policy toward Judah as he directed his effort toward regaining the territory which had been lost to Syria.

The close association of Israel and Judah in the days of Jehoash and

[3] See Max Vogelstein, *Jeroboam II, The Rise and Fall of His Empire* (Cincinnati, 1945), p. 9.

[4] Thiele, *The Mysterious Numbers of the Hebrew Kings*, pp. 68–72.

Amaziah most likely accounted for the change in the system of dating. The nonaccession-year system had been used in Israel since the time of Jeroboam I and in Judah since Jehoram's reign. Now both kingdoms adopted the accession-year system. If Judah was subservient to Israel, it logically follows that both adopted the system of reckoning that became common in Western Asia under the growing influence of Assyria.[5]

Although at the beginning of his reign Amaziah had bright hopes for retrieving the fortunes of Judah, his prospects for success were shattered with his capture by Jehoash. When he was restored to the Davidic throne in Jerusalem in either 790 or 781, he must have been quite ineffective in leading his nation back to a position of supremacy. Throughout the rest of his reign Judah was overshadowed by Israelite expansion. Amaziah finally fled to Lachish, where he became the victim of pursuing assassins.

Uzziah or Azariah—Prosperity

Outstanding in Judah's history is the reign of Uzziah (791–740 B.C.). Even though rather crucial events occurred during his 52-year rule, the biblical account is relatively brief (II Chron. 26:1–23; II Kings 14:21–22; 15:1–7). Noteworthy is the fact that during this long period Uzziah was sole ruler for only seventeen years. So effective was he in lifting Judah from vassalage to a strong national power that he is recognized as the most able sovereign the Southern Kingdom had known since Solomon.[6]

The order of events during this part of the eighth century can be seen by the following timetable:

798	Jehoash begins reign in Israel
797–96	Amaziah succeeds Joash in Judah
793–92	Jeroboam II made coruler with Jehoash
791–90	Uzziah begins coregency with Amaziah (Judah defeated—Amaziah taken captive)
782–81	Jehoash died—Jeroboam II becomes sole ruler (Amaziah probably released at this time)
768–67	Amaziah assassinated—Uzziah assumes sole rulership
753	Jeroboam's reign ends—Zechariah rules six months
752	Shallum (one-month rule) is replaced by Menahem
750	Uzziah smitten with leprosy—Jotham made coruler
742–41	Pekahiah becomes king of Israel
740–39	Uzziah's reign ends

When Uzziah was suddenly elevated to the kingship the national hopes

[5] *Ibid.*, p. 41.
[6] Mould, *Essentials of Bible History*, p. 243.

of Judah had sunk to the lowest point since the division of the Solomonic kingdom. The defeat at the hands of Israel was nothing less than a calamity. It is doubtful that Uzziah was able to do much more than retain a semblance of organized government during the days of Jehoash. He may have rebuilt the walls of Jerusalem; but if Amaziah remained in prison during the rest of Jehoash's reign, it would have been futile for Judah to assert its military strength at this time. Even though Amaziah gained his freedom in 782 B.C. when Jehoash died, it is doubtful that he had the respect of his people when the whole nation was suffering the consequences of his disastrous policy. Very likely Uzziah continued to wield considerable influence in the affairs of state, since Amaziah finally fled to Lachish.

The silence of Scripture concerning the relationship between Israel and Judah in the days of Jeroboam II and Uzziah seems to warrant the conclusion that friendliness and co-operation prevailed. Judah's vassalage to Israel must have terminated, at the latest, with Amaziah's death or perhaps with his release fifteen years earlier. Besides restoring the walls of Jerusalem Uzziah improved the fortifications surrounding the capital city. The army was well organized and equipped with superlative weapons.

Military preparedness led to expansion. To the southwest the walls of Gath were razed. Jabneh and Ashdod also capitulated to Judah as Uzziah pushed onward to defeat the Philistines and Arabs. Whereas Amaziah had subjugated Edom, Uzziah was now able to extend Judah's borders as far south as Elath on the gulf of Aqaba. The recent discovery of a seal of Jotham, Uzziah's son, attests Judean activity at Elath during this period.[7] Eastward Judah imposed its power over the Ammonites, who paid tribute to Uzziah. This may well have been tempered by Jeroboam's expansion east of Jordan. On the other hand, the domestic troubles in Israel after Jeroboam's death could have allowed Uzziah a freer hand in the Transjordan area.[8]

Economically Judah fared well under Uzziah. The king was vitally interested in agriculture and animal husbandry. Large herds in desert areas necessitated the digging of wells and the erection of towers for protection. Vinedressers expanded their production. If Uzziah promoted these interests early in his long reign, it must have had a favorable effect upon the economic status of the whole nation.

Territorial expansion placed Judah in control of important commercial cities and highways leading into Arabia, Egypt, and other countries. At Elath on the Red Sea the copper and iron mining industries, which flourished under David and Solomon, were reclaimed for the Southern Kingdom. Although Judah lagged behind the Northern Kingdom in its military and economic expansion, it enjoyed a steady growth under Uzziah's leadership

[7] Albright, *The Biblical Period*, p. 39.
[8] *Ibid.*, pp. 39–40.

and continued its prosperity even when Israel began to decline after Jeroboam's death. Judah's growth and influence during this period were second only to those experienced in the days of David and Solomon.[9]

Uzziah's prosperity was directly related to his dependence upon God (II Chron. 26:5, 7). Zechariah, a prophet otherwise unknown, effectively instructed the king who, until about 750 B.C. had a wholesome and humble attitude toward God. At the height of his success, however, Uzziah assumed that he could enter the Temple and burn incense. With the support of eighty priests the high priest, whose name was also Azariah, confronted Uzziah with the fact that this was the prerogative of those consecrated for the purpose (Ex. 30:7 and Num. 18:1–7). In anger the king defied the priests. As a result of divine judgment Uzziah became leprous. For the rest of his reign he was ostracized from the palace and denied the ordinary social privileges. He could not even enter the Temple. Jotham was made coruler and assumed the royal responsibilities for the remainder of his father's life.

The ominous threat of Assyrian aggression also dampened the national hopes of Judah during the last decade of Uzziah's long and successful reign. If he had cherished hopes of restoring the whole Solomonic empire to Judah after the death of Jeroboam II, Uzziah saw them shattered by the rising Assyrian power. In 745 B.C. Tiglath-pileser III began to carve out his empire. In his initial attack he subdued Babylon. Then he turned westward to defeat Sarduris III, king of Urartu. During this northwestern campaign (743–738 B.C.) he encountered opposition when he moved into Syria. In his annals he mentions fighting at Arpad against Azariah, king of Judah.[10] This battle is dated by Thiele in the beginning of this northwestern campaign, preferably in 743. Although Tiglath-pileser crushed the opposition led by Azariah (Uzziah), he made no claim to having collected tribute from Judah. Since Menahem had paid an enormous sum to avoid a punitive invasion by the ferocious Assyrians, Tiglath-pileser did not advance his armies southward to Judah at this time. Uzziah was able, therefore, to maintain an anti-Assyrian policy with pro-Assyrian Israel as a buffer state to the north.

Jotham—Anti-Assyrian Policy

Jotham was closely associated with his father from 750 to 740 B.C. Since Uzziah was such a strong and forceful ruler, Jotham had a secondary position as regent of Judah. When he assumed full control in 740–39, he continued the policies of his father.

[9] Anderson, *Understanding the Old Testament,* p. 254.

[10] For a fuller discussion see Thiele, *op. cit.,* pp. 75–98. Although A. T. Olmstead, *History of Assyria,* p. 186, suggests that this refers to a nation in Syria, the biblical identification is supported by Haydn, Luckenbill, C. R. Hall, Albright, and most recently noted by Wright, *Biblical Archaeology,* p. 161.

The domestic enterprises of Jotham provided for the erection of citadels and towers to encourage farming throughout Judah. Cities were built in strategic places. At Jerusalem he promoted religious interest by building an upper gate at the Temple, but he did not interfere with the high places where the people worshiped idols.

The Ammonites in all likelihood had rebelled against Judah at Uzziah's death. Jotham subsequently smothered the revolt and exacted tribute. The fact that payment is noted for the second and third year of Jotham (II Chron. 27:5) may imply that the problems with Assyria became so momentous that Judah was unable to insist upon the levy.[11]

With an ominous Assyrian invasion pending, Jotham faced trouble in maintaining his anti-Assyrian policy. When the Assyrian armies became active in the regions of Mount Nal and Urartu in 736–735, a pro-Assyrian party in Jerusalem elevated Ahaz to the Davidic throne as coregent with Jotham. Assyrian records confirm 735 as the date for the accession of Ahaz.

Jotham died in 732 B.C. His total reign was reckoned at twenty years, but he had reigned alone for only three or four years. As coruler with his father he had very little opportunity to assert himself. Later the Assyrian threat precipitated the crisis which placed him in retirement while Ahaz championed friendship with the capital on the Tigris.

Ahaz—Pro-Assyrian Administration

The twenty-year reign of Ahaz (II Chron. 28:1–27; II Kings 16:1–20) was beset with difficulties. The Assyrian kings were advancing in their quest to control the Fertile Crescent and Ahaz was continually subjected to international pressure.

The Northern Kingdom had already subscribed to Pekah's policy of resistance. At the age of twenty Ahaz was confronted with the perplexing problem of maintaining peace with Syria and Israel. In 734 Tiglath-pileser III marched his armies into Philistia. It is quite possible that Ahaz may have appealed to the Assyrian king when the Philistines extensively raided the outlying districts of Judah. His alignment with Tiglath-pileser soon brought Ahaz into serious straits. Later that year, after the Assyrian invaders had retreated, Pekah and Rezin declared war on Judah.

At the time of this distressing crisis Isaiah had been active in the prophetic ministry about six years. With a message from God he confronted Ahaz with the solution to his problem. Faith in God was the key to victory over Israel and Syria. Pekah and Rezin intended to place a puppet ruler on the Davidic throne in Jerusalem, but God would nullify the Syro-Ephraimitic scheme in

[11] See Thiele, *op. cit.*, p. 117.

The remaining walls of the Palace Library in which collapsed shelves with thousands of cuneiform tablets were found. (*Photo courtesy of J. Ramsay Homa*)

Cuneiform tablets and other finds, including a four-inch-long sphinx carved out of steatite and covered in gold, excavated in and adjoining the Palace Library, Tel Mardikh, in 1976. (*Photo courtesy of J. Ramsay Homa*)

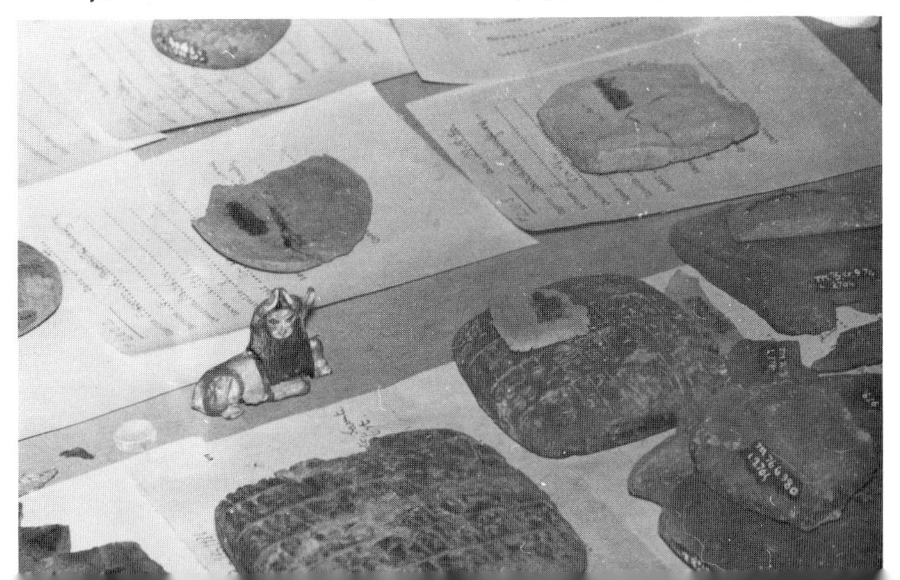

Jerusalem, lower center (city of David, II S 8), was the Jebusite fortress conquered by David (cf. K. Kenyon, *Jerusalem: Excavating 3000 Years of History*, p. 27) with Gihon Spring in the Kidron Valley. The Mosque area was the site of Solomon's temple. (*Photo courtesy of Dr. Richard Cleave, Pictoral Archive [Near Eastern History] Est.*)

Archaeologists uncovering the buried city of Tell Dothan. The walls, rooms, and buildings are of Elisha's day, 850–800 B.C. (II Kings 6). (*Photo courtesy of Dothan II*)

Ceramic vessels, bronze bowls, and tools buried with human remains in a Dothan family tomb of the Late Bronze Age (1400–1200 B.C.). (*Photo courtesy of Dothan II*)

Administrative building where Dothanites presented tax payments of olives, wheat, and other commodities during the Israelite Monarchy (9–8th centuries B.C.). (*Photo courtesy of Dothan II*)

Ring flask from a Dothan tomb. (*Photo courtesy of Dothan II*)

Infant jar burial associated with Iron II (900–700 B.C.) occupation at Tell Dothan. Burial included bronze anklet and ceramic jar for food. (*Photo courtesy of Dothan II*)

response to faith (Is. 7:1 ff.). The stubbornly wicked Ahaz ignored Isaiah. In defiance, he sought a way out of his difficulty by making a desperate appeal to Tiglath-pileser III.

When the armies of Syria and Israel invaded Judah they besieged but could not take Jerusalem, which had so recently been refortified by Uzziah. Nevertheless, Judah incurred great losses as thousands were killed and others were taken captive to Samaria and Damascus. But fortunately there were some in the Northern Kingdom who had not repudiated God. When a prophet reproached the clan leaders, they responded by effecting the release of their Judean captives.

Though hard pressed, Ahaz survived the Syro-Ephraimitic attack. His entreaty to Tiglath-pileser brought immediate results. In two successive campaigns (733 and 732) the Assyrians overran Syria and Israel. In Samaria Pekah was replaced by Hoshea, who pledged his loyalty to the Assyrian king.

Ahaz met Tiglath-pileser in Damascus and assured him of Judah's vassalage. So impressed was Ahaz that he ordered Urijah, the priest, to duplicate the Damascus altar in the Temple at Jerusalem. Upon his return the king himself took the lead in advancing pagan worship and thus brought condemnation upon his own head.

Throughout his reign Ahaz maintained a pro-Assyrian policy. As rulers changed in Assyria and the Northern Kingdom came to an end with Hoshea's rebellion, Ahaz successfully guided his nation through the international crises. Even though Judah had forfeited its freedom and paid heavy tribute to Assyria, economic prosperity as it had been established under the sound policies of Uzziah prevailed. Wealth was less concentrated than in the Northern Kingdom, where it had exclusively benefited the aristocracy. As long as devastating armies did not disturb the status quo Judah could afford to pay a considerable levy to Assyria.

Even with the great prophet Isaiah as a contemporary, Ahaz promoted the most obnoxious idolatrous practices. In accordance with heathen customs he had his son walk through fire. He not only took many treasures out of the Temple to meet the demands of the Assyrian king, but also introduced foreign cults into the very place where God alone was to be worshiped. Little wonder that Judah incurred God's wrath.

Hezekiah[12]—A Righteous King

Hezekiah began his reign in 716 B.C. His 29-year leadership marks an

[12] By adopting 716–715 B.C. as the date for the beginning of Hezekiah's reign biblical chronology synchronizes with the chronology of Syria, Assyria, Babylon, and Egypt. Thiele discusses the problems related to this most difficult period, *op. cit.*, pp. 99–152. II Kings 17:1 and 18:1, 9, and 10 represent an adjusted synchronism. Although this may not be the final solution, it seems to be the most satisfactory.

outstanding religious era in the history of Judah. Although beleaguered by the Assyrians, Hezekiah survived the crucial attack on Jerusalem in 701. During the last decade of his reign, Manasseh was associated with Hezekiah as co-regent. In addition to the account in II Kings 18–20 and II Chron. 29–32, pertinent information about Hezekiah's life is recorded in Is. 36–39.

In a drastic reaction to the deliberate idolatry of his father, Hezekiah began his reign with the most extensive reform in the history of the Southern Kingdom. As a young man of twenty-five he had witnessed the gradual disintegration of the Northern Kingdom and the Assyrian conquest of Samaria, only about forty miles north of Jerusalem. With the keen realization that Israel's captivity was the consequence of a broken covenant and disobedience to God (II Kings 18:9–12), Hezekiah placed his confidence in the God of Israel. During the early years of his reign he led an effective reform, not only in Judah but also in parts of Israel. Since Judah already was a vassal of Assyria, Hezekiah acknowledged the suzerainty of Sargon II (721–705 B.C.). Although Assyrian troops were dispatched to Ashdod in 711 B.C., the king of Judah had no serious interference from Assyria.

Hezekiah immediately reopened the Temple. Levites were called in to repair and cleanse the place of worship. That which had been used for idols was removed to the brook Kidron, while the vessels that had been desecrated by Ahaz were sanctified. In sixteen days the Temple was ready for worship.

Hezekiah and the officials of Jerusalem initiated the sacrifices in the Temple. Musical groups with their harps, cymbals, and lyres participated, as had been the custom in the time of David. Liturgical singing accompanied the presentation of the burnt offering. Singers praised God in the words of David and Asaph as the people worshiped.

In an attempt to heal the breach that had separated Israel and Judah since Solomon's death, the king sent letters throughout the land inviting all to come to Jerusalem for the Passover. Although some ignored Hezekiah's appeal, many responded from Asher, Manasseh, Ephraim and Issachar, as well as Judah, to celebrate the festival. In counsel with those who initiated the worship in the Temple, Hezekiah announced the celebration of the Passover one month later than prescribed so as to allow time for adequate preparation. Otherwise the observance was carried out in accordance with the law of Moses. The postponement was likely a conciliatory measure to gain the participation of the northern tribes who had been following the observance date instituted by Jeroboam I (I Kings 12:32). When some priests came without proper sanctification, Hezekiah prayed for their cleansing. A large congregation assembled in Jerusalem to participate in the reformation. Altars throughout the capital were removed to the Kidron valley for destruction. Led by the priests and Levites, the people offered sacrifices, sang jubilantly,

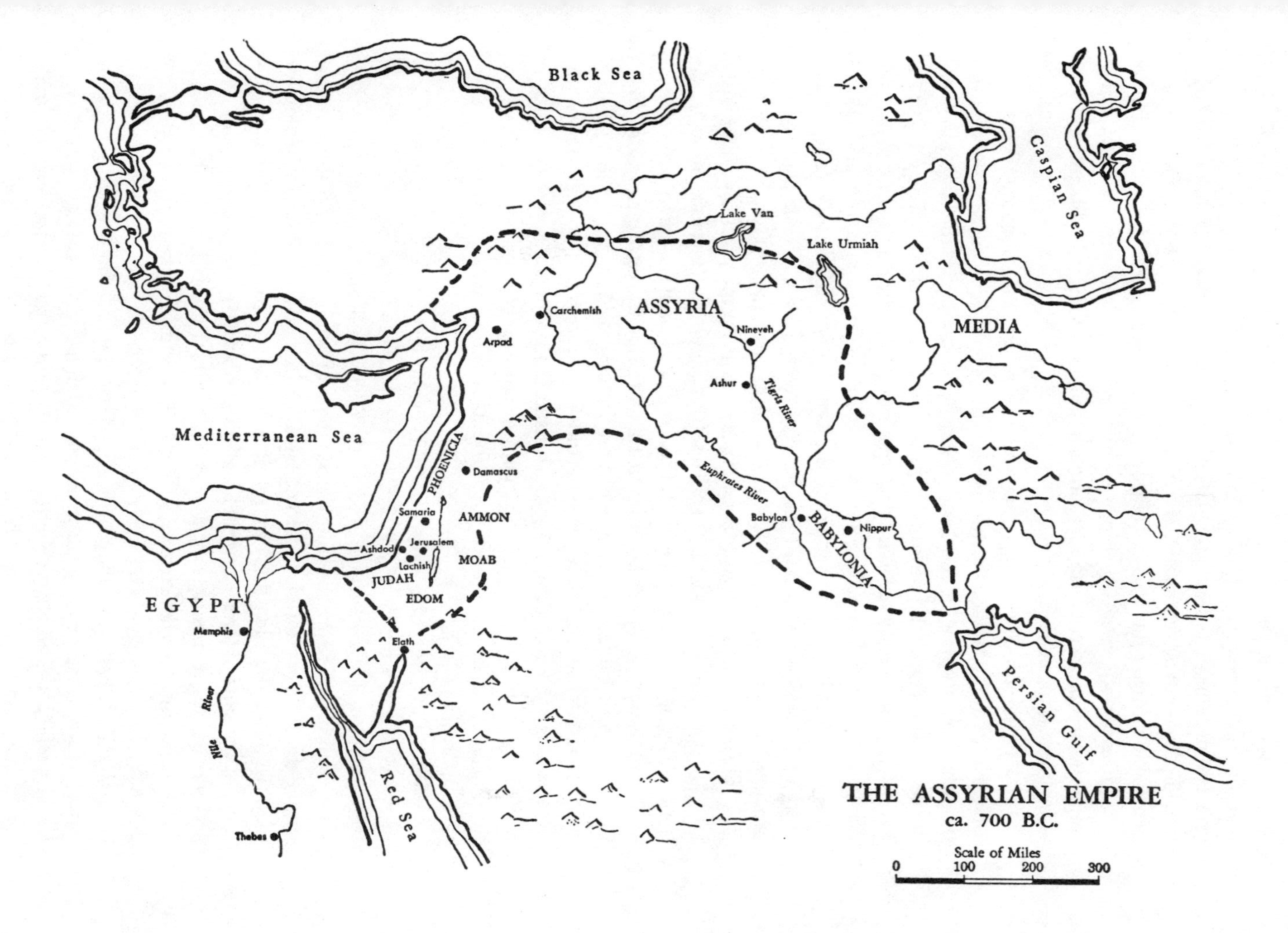

THE ASSYRIAN EMPIRE
ca. 700 B.C.

and rejoiced before the Lord. At no time since the dedication of the Temple had Jerusalem seen such a joyful celebration.

From Jerusalem the reformation extended throughout Judah, Benjamin, Ephraim, and Manasseh. Hezekiah had even destroyed the bronze serpent which Moses had made (Num. 21:4-9) because the people were now using it as an object of worship. Inspired by the king's example and leadership, the people went out to demolish pillars, asherim, high places, and altars throughout the land.

In Jerusalem Hezekiah organized the priests and Levites for regular services. The tithe was reinstituted for the support of those who devoted themselves to the law of the Lord. Plans were made for the regular observances of the feasts and seasons as prescribed in the written law (II Chron. 31:2 ff.). The people responded so generously to Hezekiah that their contributions were sufficient to allot support to all the Levites and priests who had responsibilities in the service of the Lord. The reformation under Hezekiah was decidedly successful as he endeavored to conform the religious practice of his people to the law and commandments of God.

Throughout this record of religious reform no mention is made of Isaiah. Neither does the noted prophet refer to Hezekiah's reformation in his book. Although Ahaz had defied Isaiah, it is reasonable to assume that Hezekiah and Isaiah co-operated fully in this attempt to restore the worship of God. The only biblical reference to Sargon, king of Assyria (Is. 20:1), shows Isaiah's activity at this time. Furthermore, the conquest of Ashdod by the Assyrians is the occasion for Isaiah to issue the prophetic warning that it is futile for Judah to depend upon Egypt for deliverance. Fortunately Hezekiah did not become involved with the Ashdod rebellion and thus prevented attack upon Jerusalem.

With the death of Sargon II (705) revolutions broke out in many parts of the Assyrian Empire. By 702 Merodach-baladan was quelled, removed from the Babylonian throne, and replaced by Bel-ibni, a native Chaldean who probably was a member of the same royal family. In Egypt nationalism surged forward under the energetic leadership of Shabako, an Ethiopian king, who had founded the Twenty-fifth Dynasty *ca.* 710 B.C. With other nations in the Fertile Crescent rebelling against him, Sennacherib, son of Sargon, turned his armies westward. After subduing Phoenicia and other coastal resistance, the Assyrian armies successfully occupied the Philistine area in 701 B.C.

Hezekiah had anticipated the Assyrian attack. Following his great religious reformation he concentrated on a defense program in counsel with leading officials of his government. Fortifications around Jerusalem were reinforced. Craftsmen produced shields and weapons, while combat commanders organized the fighting forces. To assure Jerusalem of an adequate water supply during a prolonged siege, Hezekiah constructed a tunnel connecting the Siloam pool with the spring of Gihon. Through 1,777 feet of solid rock the Judean engineers channeled fresh water into the pool of Siloam, also constructed during this time. Ever since its discovery in 1880, when the inscription on its wall was deciphered, the Siloam tunnel has been an attraction for tourists.[13] The Siloam pool being south of Jerusalem, the city wall was extended to enclose this vital source of water. When it became apparent that the Assyrian armies were advancing toward Jerusalem other springs of water were cut off so that the enemy could not use them.

Although Hezekiah did all in his power to prepare for the Assyrian attack, he did not depend wholly upon human resources. Earlier, when the people assembled at the city square, Hezekiah had encouraged them as he boldly expressed his confidence in God, "With him is an arm of flesh; but with us is the Lord our God to help us, and to fight our battles" (II Chron. 32:8).

Sennacherib's threat became a reality in 701 B.C (II Kings 18-20; II Chron. 32; Isa. 36-39). Although Shabako, king of Nubia (716-702 B.C), avoided confrontation with Assyria, Shebitko (702-690) ventured an aggressive encounter against Sennacherib. Kitchen suggests that Tirhakah (age twenty or twenty-one) may have been army commander in 701 and the reference to him as king appropriate, since he became king in 690 B.C.[14]

The Assyrians entered Palestine from the north taking Sidon, Joppa, and other cities en route. During the siege and conquest of Ekron Sennacherib defeated the Egyptians at Eltekeh. Hezekiah not only was forced to release Padi, the king of Ekron whom he had taken captive, but also paid a heavy tribute stripping the Temple of its silver and gold (II Kings 18:14).

Most likely it was during this period of Assyrian pressure *ca.* 701 B.C. that Hezekiah became severely ill. Although Isaiah warned the king to prepare for death, God intervened. Twofold was the divine promise to the king of Judah—a fifteen year extension of his life and deliverance of Jerusalem from the Assyrian threat (Isa. 38:4-6).

[13] For this inscription see Pritchard, *Ancient Near Eastern Texts,* p. 321.

[14] For a detailed delineation of this two campaign interpretation see Stanley M. Horton, *Isaiah's Greatest Years* (unpublished thesis, Central Baptist Seminary, Kansas City, Kansas), May 1959.

Cf. K. A. Kitchen, *The Third Intermediate Period in Egypt (1100–650),* pp. 158-61, 383-87 (Warminster: Aris and Philips Ltd., 1973). The possibility of a subsequent threat by Sennacherib—perhaps after he destroyed Babylon in 689 B.C.—may be reflected in Isa. 37:9 ff., where the reaction of Hezekiah stands in contrast to his attitude of defeat and hopelessness in chapter 37:1 ff., when he "tore his clothes and put on sackcloth" and summoned Isaiah. When he received the letter, 37:14, Hezekiah spread it before the Lord and confidently expressed his faith in God for deliverance. This attitude could reflect his experience in a previous deliverance and the period of peace and prosperity during the extended years of his life.

In the meantime Sennacherib was besieging Lachish. Perhaps it was with the knowledge that Hezekiah put his trust in God for deliverance that the Assyrian king sent his officers to the Fuller's Field highway near the Jerusalem wall to incite the people to surrender. Sennacherib even claimed that he was God-commissioned in demanding their capitulation and cited an impressive list of conquests where other nations had not been delivered by their gods. Isaiah, however, assured the king and his people of safety.

While besieging Libnah Sennacherib heard rumors of a Babylonian revolt. The Assyrians departed immediately. Even though he had conquered forty-six walled cities belonging to Hezekiah he makes no such claim for Jerusalem. He boasted of some 200,000 Judean captives and reported that Hezekiah was shut up in Jerusalem like a caged bird.

The acclaim and recognition of surrounding nations was expressed in abundant gifts to the Judean king (II Chron. 32:23). Merodach-baladan, the powerful Babylonian leader who was still stirring up rebellions, extended his congratulations to Hezekiah on his recovery—perhaps a recognition of the king's successful recovery from the economic hardships of Assyrian occupation (II Chron. 32:31) as well as his personal restoration to health.[15] The Babylonian embassy very likely was duly impressed with the display of wealth in Jerusalem. Hezekiah's triumph, however, was tempered by the subsequent warning of Isaiah that succeeding generations would be subjected to Babylonian captivity. Nevertheless this outstanding deliverance may have given the religious reformation a new impetus while peace and prosperity prevailed during the extended reign of Hezekiah.

Knowing that he had but fifteen years before the termination of his reign, it would seem natural for Hezekiah to associate his son Manasseh with him on the throne at the earliest possible opportunity. In 696–695 Manasseh became a "son of the law" at the age of twelve and at the same time began his coregency.[16]

In the Tigris-Euphrates area the Assyrian king suppressed rebellions and in 689 B.C. destroyed the city of Babylon. Proceeding successfully into Arabia Sennacherib heard of the advance of Tirhakah. Since Egypt may have been the real objective of the Assyrian campaign in 701 B.C. it may well be that Sennacherib hoped to ward off Judean interference by dispatching letters to Hezekiah with an ultimatum of surrender. Whereas the Assyrian officers had threatened the people this directive was addressed to Hezekiah personally. This time the king went to the Temple to pray. Through Isaiah he was assured that the Assyrian king would return by the way he came. Just where the army was encamped when it incurred the loss of 185,000 troops is not

[15] Thiele, *op. cit.*, p. 156.
[16] *Ibid.*, pp. 155–156.

indicated in the scriptural records but apparently it never reached Jerusalem. Hezekiah's reign continued in peace.

Unlike a number of his ancestors, Hezekiah was buried in honor. With sincere devotion to the task he had led his people in the greatest reformation in Judah's history. Since the Northern Kingdom had ceased to maintain an independent government, this religious reform extended into that territory. Except for the Assyrian threat, Hezekiah had enjoyed a peaceful reign.

Manasseh—Idolatry and Reform

Manasseh is credited with the longest reign in the history of Judah (II Kings 21:1–17; II Chron. 33:1–20); including the decade of coregency with Hezekiah he was king for fifty-five years (696–642 B.C.). But his rule was the antithesis of his father's. From the pinnacle of religious fervor the Southern Kingdom catapulted into its darkest era of idolatry under the leadership of Manasseh. In character and practice he resembled his grandfather, Ahaz, although the latter had died before the birth of Manasseh. Very likely Manasseh did not begin the reversal of his father's policies until after the latter's death.

By rebuilding the high places, erecting altars to Baal, and constructing asherim Manasseh plunged Judah into gross idolatry such as Ahab and Jezebel had promoted in the Northern Kingdom. Through religious rites and ceremonies, star and planetary worship was instituted. Even the Ammonite deity Moloch was acknowledged by the Hebrew king in the sacrifice of children in the Hinnom valley, outside Jerusalem. Human sacrifice was one of the most abominable rites of Canaanitic paganism and was associated by the Psalmist with demon worship (Ps. 106:36–37). Astrology, divination, and occultism were officially sanctioned as common practices. In open defiance of God, altars for worshiping the host of heaven were placed in the courts of the Temple, while graven images of Asherah, the wife of Baal, were placed in the Temple itself. In addition, Manasseh shed much innocent blood. It seems reasonable to infer that many voices of protest to such gross idolatry were silenced in death (II Kings 21:16). Since the last mention of the great prophet Isaiah is associated with Hezekiah in the historical record, it is likely that tradition is correct in attributing the martyrdom of Isaiah to the wicked king Manasseh. The moral and religious conditions in Judah were worse than those of the nations which had been exterminated or expelled from Canaan. Manasseh thus represented the low point of wickedness in the long list of Davidic kings. The judgments predicted by Isaiah were sure to come.

The historical accounts do not indicate the extent to which Manasseh was influenced by Assyria in his idolatrous policies. Assyria reached the pinnacle of wealth and prestige under Esarhaddon and Ashurbanipal. Without question, Manasseh curried the political favor of Assyria in subservient vassalage while Esarhaddon (681–669 B.C.) extended his control down into Egypt. In contrast to Sennacherib, Esarhaddon adopted a conciliatory policy and rebuilt Babylon. In 678 he subjugated Tyre, even though the populace escaped to the nearby island fortress. Memphis was occupied in 673 and a few years later Tirhaka, the last king of the Twenty-fifth Dynasty, was captured. In his list of twenty-two kings from the Hittite country, Esarhaddon mentions Manasseh, king of Judah, among those who made a compulsory visit to Nineveh in 678 B.C. Although Babylon had been rebuilt by that time, it is not at all certain that he also was taken there by Esarhaddon.[17]

With the destruction of Thebes in 663 B.C., Ashurbanipal extended Assyrian control five hundred miles along the Nile into Upper Egypt. A bloody civil war shook the Assyrian Empire (652) in the rebellion of Shamash-shum-ukin, who was a brother of Ashurbanipal and vassal king of Babylon. By the time this insurrection climaxed in the conquest of Babylon in 648, rebellions had erupted in Syria and Palestine. Judah may have participated by joining Edom and Moab, who are named in the Assyrian inscriptions.[18] Moab's autonomy was terminated at this time and Judah's king, Manasseh, was taken captive to Babylon but subsequently released (II Chron. 33: 10–13).

Though we have no definite chronological information for dating the exact time of Manasseh's captivity and release, the biblical account favors the last decade of his reign. If he was captured in 648 and even returned to Jerusalem as vassal king in the same year, he had relatively little time left to undo the religious practices he had fostered for so many years. However, he repented in captivity and now acknowledged God. In a reformation beginning in Jerusalem he exemplified the fear of God and commanded the people of Judah to serve the Lord God of Israel. It is doubtful that his reform was very effective, since those who had served under Hezekiah in true worship had previously been removed or executed.

Amon—Apostasy

Amon succeeded his father, Manasseh, as king of Judah in 642. Without hesitation he reverted to the idolatrous practices that had been initiated and promoted by Manasseh during the major part of his kingship. The early training of Amon had made a decidedly greater impact upon him than the belated period of reformation.

In 640 B.C. slaves in the palace slew Amon. Although his reign was

[17] See Unger, *Archeology and the Old Testament,* pp. 280–281. He identifies this captivity with II Chron. 33:11.

[18] See Albright, *op. cit.,* p. 44.

brief, the godless example set forth during these two years provided opportunity for Judah to revert to a terrible state of apostasy.

During the course of the past two centuries the fortunes of the Southern Kingdom had risen and fallen. The reigns of Athaliah, Ahaz, and Manasseh had witnessed unrestrained idolatry. Religious reform began with Joash, gathered momentum under Uzziah, and reached an unprecedented level under Hezekiah. Politically Judah reached its lowest point in the days of Amaziah when Jehoash, from the Northern Kingdom, invaded Jerusalem. Throughout these two centuries the prosperity and autonomous rule of Judah were overshadowed by the expanding interests of Assyrian kings.

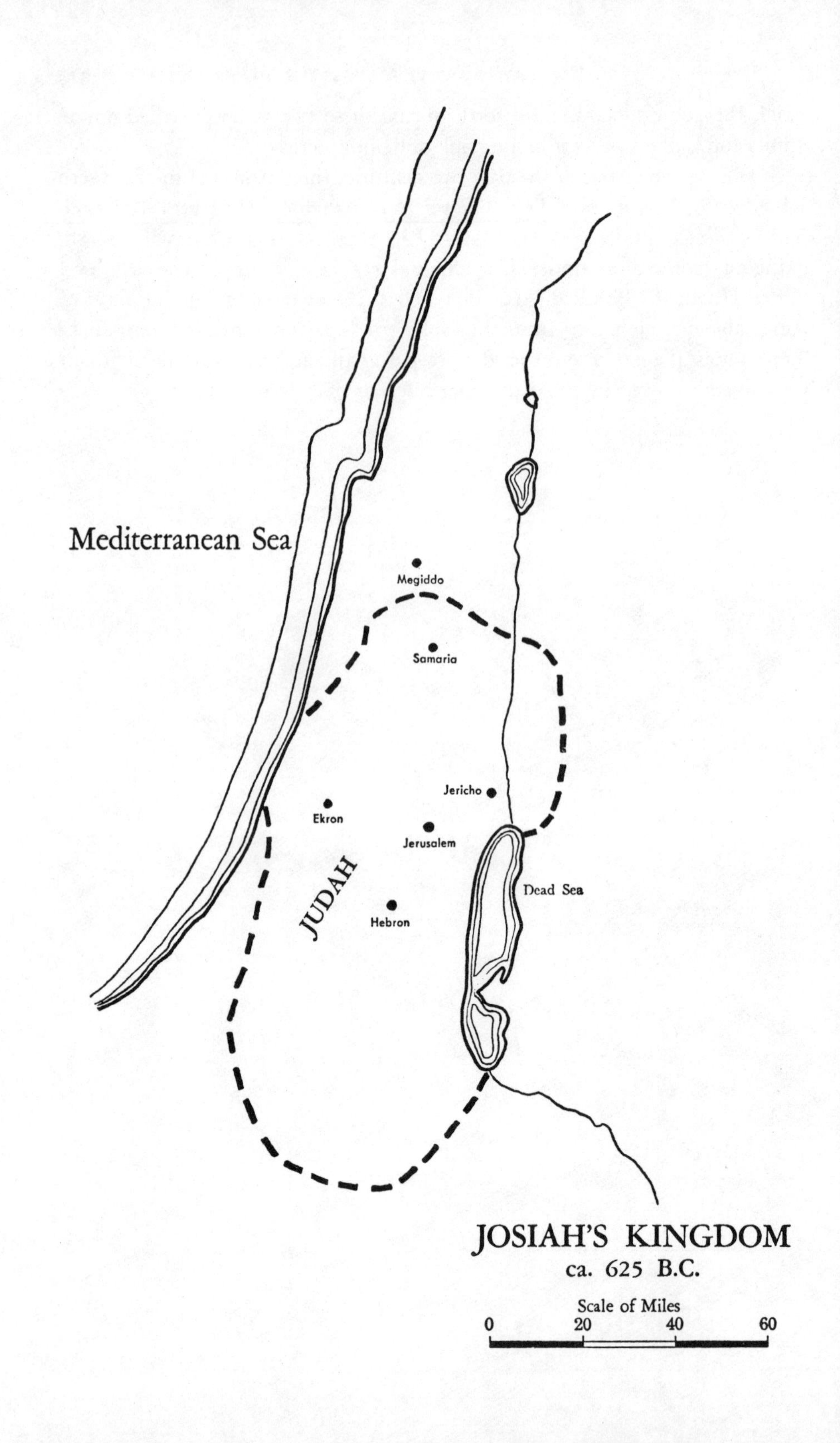
Mediterranean Sea
Megiddo
Samaria
Jericho
Ekron
Jerusalem
JUDAH
Hebron
Dead Sea
JOSIAH'S KINGDOM
ca. 625 B.C.
Scale of Miles
0
20
40
60

Chapter XIV

Fading Hopes of Davidic Kings

For over a century Judah had survived the successful expansion of the Assyrian Empire. Ever since Ahaz had forfeited Judah's freedom in a treaty with Tiglath-pileser III this little kingdom weathered crisis after crisis as a vassal to five more Assyrian rulers. Treaties, diplomatic maneuvers, resistance, and supernatural intervention had a vital bearing on the continuous existence of a semiautonomous government when both wicked and righteous kings occupied the Davidic throne. Now that Assyria was relaxing her clutch on Judah nationalistic hopes rose once more during the three decades of Josiah's reign. The abrupt termination of his leadership marked the beginning of the end for the Southern Kingdom. Before twenty-five years had passed these hopes began to fade under the rising power of the Babylonian Empire. In 586 B.C. the ruins of Jerusalem were a realistic reminder of Isaiah's prediction that the Davidic dynasty would succumb to Babylonia.

Josian Era of Optimism

At the early age of eight Josiah was suddenly crowned king—succeeding his father, Amon. After a reign of thirty-one years (640–609 B.C.) he was killed in battle at Megiddo. The activities of Josiah (summarized in II Kings 22:1–23:30 and II Chron. 34:1–35:27) are primarily limited to his religious reformations.

The declining influence of Assyria in the closing years of Ashurbanipal, who died about 630 B.C., afforded Judah the opportunity to extend its influence over the territory to the north. It is likely that the political leaders anticipated the possibility of including the northern tribes and even the Solomonic kingdom boundaries in the Southern Kingdom. With the fall of the Assyrian city of Ashur to the Medes in 614, and the destruction of Nineveh in 612 by the allied forces of Media and Babylonia, Judah's prospects were even more favorable. During this period of political unrest and rebellion in the East Judah gained complete freedom from Assyrian vassalage, which naturally gave rise to nationalism.

With idolatry permeating the kingdom, the religious prospects for the boy-king were anything but hopeful. It is doubtful whether the reformation of Manasseh had penetrated into the ranks of the people, especially if his captivity and penitent return occurred during the last decade of his reign. Amon was decidedly wicked. His two-year reign provided enough time for the people to revert to idolatrous policies in the administration of the kingdom. Most likely these continued when his eight-year-old son was suddenly elevated to the throne. In this course of rank apostasy Judah could expect nothing less than judgment, according to the warnings of Isaiah and other prophets.

As Josiah grew to manhood he reacted to the sinful conditions of his time. At the age of sixteen he was earnestly taking God into account rather than conforming to idolatrous practices. In four years his devotion to God had crystallized to the point that he began a religious reformation (628 B.C.). In the eighteenth year of his reign (622 B.C.), while the Temple was being repaired, the book of the law was recovered. Prompted by the reading of this "book of the Lord given by Moses" and warned of impending judgment by Huldah, the prophetess, Josiah and his people observed the Passover in a manner unprecedented in the history of Judah. Although the scriptural account is silent about specific religious activities during the remaining thirteen years of his reign, Josiah continued his godly leadership with the assurance that peace would prevail during the rest of his life (II Chron. 34:28).

The reformation began in 628 and reached its climax with the Passover observance in 622 B.C. Since neither Kings nor Chronicles provide a detailed chronological order of events, it may well be that the summary accounts of each book apply to this whole period.[1] By this time it was politically safe for Josiah to remove any religious practices that were associated with Judah's vassalage to Assyria.

Drastic measures were needed to rid the land of idolatry. After a twelve-year appraisal of the conditions, Josiah boldly asserted his kingly authority and abolished pagan practices throughout Judah as well as among the northern tribes. Altars of Baal were broken down, asherim were destroyed, and vessels dedicated to idol worship were removed. In the Temple, where women wove hangings for Asherah, chambers of cult prostitution were renovated. Horses, which were dedicated to the sun, were removed from the entrance and the chariots were destroyed by fire. The horrible practice of child sacrifice was abruptly abolished. The altars erected by Manasseh in the court of the

[1] See C. F. Keil in his commentary on II Chron. 34.

Temple were crushed and the pieces scattered in the Kidron valley. Even some of the high places erected by Solomon must have been in current use, since Josiah razed them and desecrated them with dead men's bones.

Priests dedicated to idol worship were removed from office; they had been serving by royal appointment of former kings. By their deposition the burning of incense to Baal, to the sun, moon, and stars ceased. Even though Josiah deposed them from priestly service he made material provision for them from temple revenues.

At Bethel the altar which had been erected by Jeroboam I also was destroyed by Josiah. For over three hundred years this had been the public high place for idolatrous practice introduced by the first ruler of the Northern Kingdom. This altar was pulverized and the asherah which probably had replaced the golden calf was burned.[2] When the bones from the adjoining cemetery were collected for public defilement of this high place, Josiah noticed the monument to the prophet of Judah who had so boldly denounced Jeroboam (I Kings 13). Being informed that the man of God was buried here, Josiah ordered that the tomb should not be opened.

Throughout the cities of Samaria (the Northern Kingdom) reformation was the order of the day. High places were removed and priests were arrested for their idolatrous ministry.

The constructive aspect of this reformation came to fruition in the reparation of the Temple in Jerusalem. With contributions from Judah and the tribes north the Levites were charged with the supervision of this timely project. Since the time of Joash (two centuries earlier) the Temple had been subject to long periods of neglect—especially under Manasseh. When Hilkiah, the high priest, began to gather funds for distribution to the workmen he found the book of the law. Hilkiah handed it to Shaphan, secretary to the king. He examined it and immediately read it to Josiah. The king was terribly disturbed when he realized that the people of Judah had not observed the law. Immediately Hilkiah and the government officials were ordered to secure someone who could give them advice. Huldah, the prophetess residing in Jerusalem, had a timely message for them, clear and simple: The curses and judgments for idolatry were inevitable. Jerusalem would not be spared the wrath of God. Josiah, however, would be spared the anguish of Jerusalem's destruction since he had penitently responded to the book of the law.

Under the king's leadership the elders of Judah, priests, and Levites and the populace of Jerusalem assembled for public reading of the newly found book. In a solemn covenant King Josiah, supported by the people, promised that he would devote himself wholly to obedience to the law.

[2] Note the fulfillment of the prediction by the unnamed prophet from Judah, I Kings 13:1–3.

Immediately plans were expedited for the observance of the Passover. Priests were appointed and temple service was reinstated. Careful attention was given to the pattern of organization for the Levites, as ordained by David and Solomon. In the Passover ritual great care was exercised to conform to that which was "written in the book of Moses" (II Chron. 35:13). In its conformity to the law and extensive participation this Passover observance surpassed all similar festivities since the days of Samuel (II Chron. 35:18).[3]

The content of the book of the law found in the Temple is not specifically indicated. Numerous references in the biblical account associate its origin with Moses. On the basis of that simple fact the book of the law may have included all of the Pentateuch or contained only a copy of Deuteronomy.[4] Those who regard the Pentateuch as a composite literary production, reaching its final form in the fifth century B.C., limit the book of the law to the bulk of Deuteronomy or less.[5] Since the reformation had already been in progress for six years when the book was recovered, Josiah had previous knowledge concerning the true religion. When the book was read before him he was terrified because of Judah's failure to obey the law. Nothing in the biblical record indicates that this book was published at this time or even ratified by the people. It was considered as authoritative, and Josiah feared the consequences of disobedience. Having been given by Moses, the book of the law had been the rule of religious practice ever since then. Joshua, the judges, and the kings, together with the whole nation, had been under obligation to conform to its requirements in obedience. What alarmed Josiah when he asked for prophetic advice was the fact that "our fathers have not kept the word of the Lord" (II Chron. 34:21). Ignorance of the law was no excuse even though the book of the law had been lost for some time.

Gross idolatry had prevailed for over half a century before Josiah began to rule. In fact, Manasseh and Amon had persecuted those who advocated conformity to true religion. Since Manasseh had even shed innocent blood, it is reasonable to charge him with the destruction of all copies of the law in circulation in Judah. In the absence of written copies, Josiah very likely associated himself with priests and elders who had sufficient knowledge of the law to give him oral instruction. From this came the firm conviction, during the first twelve years of his reign, that a national reform was necessary. When the book of the law was actually read before him he vividly realized that curses and judgment were due an idolatrous people. Knowing all too

[3] See Keil in commentary on II Kings 23:20 and Edersheim, *The Bible History,* Vol. VI, p. 190.

[4] See John D. Davis, *A Dictionary of the Bible* (4th rev. ed., 1954), in his article "Josiah."

[5] For an elaborate discussion see G. E. Wright, *Interpreter's Bible,* Vol. II, pp. 311–330. Also B. W. Anderson, *Understanding the Old Testament,* pp. 288–324.

well the wicked practices common to his fathers, he still was shocked that destruction might come in his day.

Had the book of the law actually been lost? Very likely there were those during Manasseh's reign who had enough interest to preserve some copies of the law. Since every copy was handwritten, relatively few were in circulation. After the voices of Isaiah and others had been silenced the righteous people decreased rapidly under persecution. If Joash, the royal heir, could be hidden from wicked Athaliah for six years, it is reasonable to conclude that a book of the law could have been hidden from wicked Manasseh for half a century.

Another possibility concerning the preservation of this book of the law is the suggestion based on archaeology.[6] Since valuable records and documents were placed in cornerstones of important buildings in ancient as well as in modern times, this book of the law may have been preserved in the cornerstone of the Temple.[7] Here Josiah's repairmen found it. Before David's death he charged Solomon, as king of Israel, to conform to all that is "written in the law of Moses" (I Kings 2:3). In the building of the Temple it would have been appropriate to place the whole Pentateuch, or at least the laws of Moses, in the cornerstone. Perhaps this was the providential provision for safekeeping of the Pentateuch for over three centuries when Judah, at times, was subjected to rulers who defied God's covenant with Israel. Taken out of the Temple in the reformation days of Josiah, it became the "living word" once more in a generation that took the book of the law with them into Babylonian captivity.

Whether the reformation under Josiah represented a genuine revival among the common people is doubtful. Since it was initiated and executed under royal orders, the opposition was restrained as long as Josiah lived.[8] Immediately after his death the people reverted to idolatry under Jehoiakim.

Jeremiah was called to the prophetic ministry in the thirteenth year of Josiah, 627 B.C. Since Josiah had already begun his reform, it is reasonable to conclude that prophet and king worked hand in hand.[9] Jeremiah's preaching (chapters 2–4) reflects the strained relationship between God and Israel. Like a faithless wife who breaks her marriage vows Israel had forsaken God. Jeremiah realistically warned them that Jerusalem could expect the same fate that had befallen Samaria a century earlier. How much of Jeremiah 1–20 is related to Josian times is difficult to ascertain. Although it may seem strange that the prophetic word came from Huldah instead of Jeremiah

[6] See Dr. J. P. Free, *Archaeology and Bible History,* pp. 215–216.

[7] Cf. Deut. 31:25–26. Moses made provision for its safekeeping with the ark. In a permanent building like the Temple the cornerstone would have been the logical place.

[8] See Edersheim, *op. cit.*, p. 181.

[9] The ministry of Jeremiah during Josiah's reign is not recorded in Kings and Chronicles. His experiences during Jehoiakim's reign suggest that the revival was not genuine.

when the book of the law was read, the urgency for an immediate solution to the king's problem may have involved Huldah, who resided in Jerusalem. Jeremiah lived in Anathoth—three miles northeast of the city.

As the news of the fall of Ashur (614) and the destruction of Nineveh (612) was circulated in Jerusalem, Josiah undoubtedly turned his attention to international affairs. In a state of military preparedness he made his fatal mistake. In 609 the Assyrians were fighting a losing battle with their government in exile at Haran. Necho, king of Egypt, marched his armies through Palestine to aid the Assyrians. Since Josiah had little concern for the preservation of the Assyrians, he rushed his armies up to Megiddo in an effort to stop the Egyptians.[10] Josiah was fatally wounded when his armies were routed. Suddenly the national and religious hopes of Judah vanished as the 39-year-old king was entombed in the city of David. After eighteen years of intimate association with Josiah, the great prophet is singled out by name in the concluding paragraph—"and Jeremiah lamented for Josiah."

Babylonian Supremacy

The people of Judah enthroned Jehoahaz in Jerusalem (II Chron. 36:1–4). And the new king had to suffer the consequences of Josiah's meddling in Egyptian affairs. He ruled only three months, in the year 609 B.C. (II Kings 23:31–34).

Having defeated Judah at Megiddo, the Egyptians marched north to Carchemish, temporarily halting the westward advance of the Babylonians. Pharaoh Necho established his headquarters at Riblah (II Kings 23:31–34). Jehoahaz was deposed as king of Judah and taken prisoner to Egypt via Riblah. There Jehoahaz, also known as Shallum, died as predicted by the prophet Jeremiah (22:11–12).

Jehoiakim (609–598 B.C.)

Jehoiakim, another son of Josiah, began his reign as the choice of Necho. Not only did the Egyptian Pharaoh change his name from Eliakim to Jehoiakim, he also exacted a heavy tribute from Judah (II Kings 23:35). For eleven years he continued as king of Judah. Until the Babylonians dislodged the Egyptians from Carchemish (605 B.C.) Jehoiakim remained subject to Necho.

Jeremiah faced severe opposition while Jehoiakim reigned. Standing in the Temple court Jeremiah predicted Babylonian captivity for the inhabitants

[10] Note the translation of II Kings 23:29, which in the light of archaeology preferably reads: ". . . the king of Egypt went *to* the king of Assyria." See C. J. Gadd, *The Fall of Nineveh* (London, 1923), p. 41. Also Merrill F. Unger, *Archeology and the Old Testament,* p. 282.

of Jerusalem. When the people heard that the Temple would be destroyed[11] they appealed to the political leaders to kill Jeremiah (Jer. 26); however, some of the elders rallied to his defense, citing Micah's experience a century earlier. That prophet also had announced the doom of Jerusalem, but Hezekiah had not harmed him. Although Uriah, a contemporary prophet, was martyred by Jehoiakim for preaching the same message, Jeremiah's life was spared. Ahikam, a prominent political figure, supported Jeremiah in this time of danger.

During the fourth year of Jehoiakim's reign Jeremiah's scroll was read before the king. As Jehoiakim listened to the message of judgment he cut the scroll in pieces and threw them into the fire. In contrast to Josiah—who repented and turned to God—Jehoiakim defiantly ignored the warnings (Jer. 36:1–32).

Jeremiah impressively demonstrated the portentous message before the people—he announced that he was under divine orders to hide his new linen waistcloth on the rocky banks of the Euphrates. When it was spoiled he brought it back for public exhibition, warning them that the pride of Judah would be marred in a similar manner (Jer. 13:1–11).

On another occasion Jeremiah led the priests and elders to the valley of Hinnom, where human sacrifices were offered. Breaking a potter's vessel before this crowd Jeremiah courageously warned that Jerusalem would be broken into fragments by God. So extensive would be the destruction that even this accursed valley would be used as a burial ground. No wonder that the priest Pashur seized Jeremiah and confined him to the stocks for one night (Jer. 19:1–20:18). Although discouraged, Jeremiah was reminded of the lesson learned in the potter's house—that God would have to expose Judah to captivity in order to mold the desired vessel.

The fourth year of Jehoiakim (605) was a crucial time in Jerusalem. In the decisive battle at Carchemish in early summer the Egyptians were routed by the Babylonians. By August Nebuchadnezzar had advanced far enough into southern Palestine to claim treasures and hostages in Jerusalem—Daniel and his friends being the most noteworthy among the Judean captives (Dan. 1:1). Although Jehoiakim retained his throne, the return of the Babylonians into Syria in 604, to Ashkelon in 603, and a clash with Necho on the borders of Egypt in 601 frustrated any attempts to terminate Babylonian vassalage. Since this Egyptian encounter was indecisive—with both armies retreating after heavy losses—Jehoiakim may have taken this opportunity to withhold tribute.[12] Although Nebuchadnezzar did not send his con-

[11] This may not have been the first time Jeremiah delivered such an ominous message (Jer. 7–10)—as long as Josiah lived the prophet had nothing to fear.

[12] D. J. Wiseman, *Chronicles of Chaldaean Kings (626–556* B.C.) *in the British Museum,* pp. 26–28.

quering army to Jerusalem for several years, he incited raids on Judah by marauding Chaldean bands supported by Moabites, Ammonites, and Syrians. In the course of this warfare Jehoiakim's reign was abruptly terminated by death, leaving a precarious anti-Babylonian policy to his young son, Jehoiachin.

The way in which Jehoiakim met death is not reported in Kings or Chronicles. The burning of Jeremiah's scroll precipitated divine judgment upon Jehoiakim—his body would be exposed to the heat by day and the frost by night, indicating that he would not have a royal burial (Jer. 36:27–32). On another occasion Jeremiah predicted that Jehoiakim would have the burial of an ass—his body would be cast out beyond the gates of Jerusalem (Jer. 22:18–19). Since neither of the historical accounts reports the circumstances of Jehoiakim's death, nor even mentions his burial, the conclusion that this defiant king was killed in battle seems warranted. In wartime it was impossible to provide an honorable burial.

Jehoiachin, also known as Coniah or Jeconiah, lasted only three months as king in Jerusalem. In 597 the Babylonian armies surrounded the city. Realizing that it was futile to resist, Jehoiachin surrendered to Nebuchadnezzar. This time the Babylonian king was not merely taking a few prisoners and asking for the verbal assurance of tribute and allegiance. The Babylonians stripped the Temple and the royal treasuries. Jehoiachin and his queen mother were taken prisoner. Accompanying them into Babylonian captivity were palace officials, executives, artisans, and all leaders of the community. Not least among these thousands was Ezekiel. Mattaniah, whose name Nebuchadnezzar changed to Zedekiah, was left in charge of the people who remained in Jerusalem.

Zedekiah (597–586 B.C.)

Zedekiah was the youngest son of Josiah. Since Jehoiachin was considered the rightful heir to the Davidic throne, Zedekiah was regarded as a puppet king—subject to the Babylonian sovereign. After a decade of weak and vacillating policies, Zedekiah forfeited the national government of Judah. Jerusalem was destroyed in 586.

Jeremiah continued his faithful ministry through anxious years of warfare, famine, and destruction. Having been left with the lower-class people in Jerusalem, Jeremiah had an appropriate message for his audience based on a vision of two baskets of figs (Jer. 24). The good figs represented the captives who had been taken away. The bad figs, which could not be eaten, were the people remaining in Jerusalem. Captivity awaited them in due time. They should not pride themselves on having escaped.

Jeremiah wrote letters to the exiles in Babylon encouraging them to adjust themselves to exilic conditions. They could not expect to return to Judah for seventy years (Jer. 25:11–12; 29:10).

Zedekiah was under constant pressure to join the Egyptians in a rebellion against Babylon. When Psammetichus II succeeded Necho (594) Edom, Moab, Ammon, and Phoenicia joined Egypt in an anti-Babylonian coalition, creating a crisis in Judah. With a wooden yoke around his neck Jeremiah dramatically announced that Nebuchadnezzar was God's servant to whom the nations should willingly submit. Zedekiah was assured that submission to the Babylonian king would avert the destruction of Jerusalem (Jer. 27).[13]

The opposition to Jeremiah mounted as false prophets advised a rebellion. They even confused the captives by telling them that the temple treasures would soon be returned. Contrary to the advice of Jeremiah, they assured the exiles of speedy restoration of their homeland. One day Hananiah took Jeremiah's yoke bars, broke them, publicly claiming that in like manner the Babylonian yoke would be broken within two years. Stunned, Jeremiah went on his way. He soon returned with a God-given message. New yoke bars—not of wood but of iron—would place the nations in Nebuchadnezzar's clutches, from which there would be no escape. As for Hananiah, Jeremiah announced that he would die before the end of the year—and so it happened. The funeral of Hananiah was public confirmation that Jeremiah was truly God's messenger.

Although Zedekiah survived the first crisis, he yielded to the aggressive plans for rebellion in 588 when the new Pharaoh of Egypt organized an expedition into Asia. With Ammon and Judah rebelling, Nebuchadnezzar swiftly established himself at Riblah, in Syria. Immediately his army besieged Jerusalem. Although Zedekiah would not surrender, as Jeremiah advised, he tried his best to find a favorable solution. He announced the release of slaves, which, in time of famine, was advantageous to the owners as they would not have to allot them rations. When the siege of Jerusalem was suddenly lifted as the Babylonian forces turned toward Egypt, the owners immediately reclaimed their slaves (Jer. 37). Jeremiah now warned that the Babylonians would soon renew their siege.

One day while on his way to Anathoth Jeremiah was arrested, beaten, and imprisoned on the charge that he was pro-Babylonian. Zedekiah called for him. In a secret interview Zedekiah once more was given the advice that he should not listen to those who favored resistance to Nebuchadnezzar. At his own request Jeremiah was not returned to prison but placed in the court of the guard. When the palace officials objected, Zedekiah yielded to their demand to kill Jeremiah. As a result, the princes lowered the faithful prophet

[13] Note that the reading "Jehoiakim" in verse 1 is regarded as a transcriptional or scribal error. Verses 3 and 12 confirm the reading "Zedekiah."

into a cistern, hoping that he would perish in the mire. God's promise to deliver Jeremiah was fulfilled when an Ethiopian eunuch restored him to the court of the guard. Soon the Babylonian army renewed the siege of Jerusalem. Undoubtedly many of the citizens accepted the fact that capitulation to Nebuchadnezzar was inevitable. For such a time as this Jeremiah had a new message. Given the option to purchase a field in the city of Anathoth, Jeremiah, even though imprisoned, immediately purchased the property and took especial care to execute the sale legally. This represented the restoration of the exiles to the promised land (Jer. 32).

In a final secret interview Zedekiah once more listened to Jeremiah's pleading voice. Obedience and surrender were preferable even at this late date. Resistance could only bring disaster. Fearing the leaders who were determined to hold out to the bitter end Zedekiah failed to yield.

In the summer of 586 the Babylonians entered the city of Jerusalem through a breach in the wall. Zedekiah attempted to escape but was captured at Jericho and taken to Riblah. After the execution of his sons Zedekiah, the last king of Judah, was blinded and taken in chains to Babylon. The great Solomonic Temple, which had been the pride and glory of Israel for almost four centuries, was reduced to ashes and the city of Jerusalem lay in ruins.

Chapter XV

The Jews Among the Nations

Since Davidic times Jerusalem had embodied the national hopes of Israel. The Temple represented the focal point of religious devotion, while the Davidic throne on Mount Zion provided, at least for the kingdom of Judah, political optimism for national survival. Although Jerusalem had been reduced from its prominent position of international respect and prestige in the glory of the Solomonic era to the state of vassalage in the heyday of Assyrian success, it still stood as the capital of Judah when Nineveh was destroyed in 612 B.C. For over four centuries it had continued as the seat of government for the Davidic throne as Damascus, Samaria, and Nineveh, with their respective governments, rose and fell.

Jerusalem was destroyed in 586 B.C. The Temple was reduced to ashes and the Jews were taken captive. The territory known as the kingdom of Judah was absorbed by the Edomites on the south and the Babylonian province of Samaria on the north. Demolished and desolate, Jerusalem became a byword among the nations.

As long as the government in Jerusalem remained intact, annals were kept. The Books of Kings and Chronicles represent the continuous history of Davidic rule in Jerusalem. With the termination of a nationally organized existence it is unlikely that official chronicles were kept; at least none are now available. Consequently little is known about the general welfare of the people scattered throughout Babylonia. Limited references in scriptural and extrabiblical sources afford some information concerning the fortunes of the Jews in exile.

The new home of the Jews was Babylonia. The Neo-Babylonian kingdom that replaced Assyrian control in the west was responsible for the fall of Jerusalem. The Jews remained in exile as long as Babylonian rulers maintained international supremacy. When Babylon was conquered by the Medo-

Chart V Exilic Times

	JUDAH	BABYLON	MEDO-PERSIA	EGYPT
639	Josiah			
626		Nabopolassar		
609	Jehoahaz Jehoiakim			Necho
605		Nebuchadnezzar		
597	Jehoiachin Zedekiah			Psammetichus
594				
588				Apries
586	Jerusalem destroyed			
568				Amasis
562		Awel-Marduk		
560		Neriglissar		
559			Cyrus	
556		Nabonidus (Belshazzar)		
539	Edict—return of the Jews	Fall of Babylon		
530			Cambyses	
522	Zerubbabel Haggai, Zechariah		Darius	
515	Temple completed			
485			Xerxes	
479			(Esther)	
464			Artaxerxes I	
457	Ezra			
444	Nehemiah			
423			Darius II	
404			Artaxerxes II	

Persians in 539 B.C. the Jews were granted the privilege of re-establishing their national home in Palestine. Although some of them returned to rebuild the Temple and rehabilitate Jerusalem, the Jewish state never regained completely independent status but remained a province of the Persian Empire. Many Jews remained in exile, never to return to their native land.

Babylonia—626–539 B.C.

Under Assyrian domination Babylonia had constituted a very important province. Although frequent attempts were made by Babylonian rulers to declare their independence they did not succeed until after the death of Ashurbanipal about 633 B.C.[1] Samassumukin became governor of Babylon in accordance with a treaty made by Esarhaddon.[2] After a sixteen-year rule Samassumukin rebelled against his brother, Ashurbanipal, and perished in the siege and burning of Babylon (648 B.C.). The successor appointed by Ashurbanipal was Kandalanu whose rule most likely terminated in an unsuccessful insurrection (627 B.C.). Rebellion continued in Babylon under the uncertainty of Assyrian rule after Ashurbanipal's death.[3] Nabopolassar emerged as the political leader who continued to champion the cause of Babylonian independence.

Nabopolassar—626–605 B.C.[4]

Nabopolassar's opposition to Assyrian forces marching to Nippur, sixty miles southeast of Babylon, precipitated an Assyrian assault. Babylon's successful resistance to this attack resulted in the recognition of Nabopolassar as king of Babylon on November 22–23, 626 B.C.[5] By 622 he apparently was strong enough to conquer Nippur, which was strategically important for the control of traffic on the Tigris and Euphrates rivers.[6]

In 616 B.C. Nabopolassar routed the Assyrians northward along the Euphrates as far as Haran, returning with lucrative plunder before the As-

[1] D. J. Wiseman, *Chronicles of Chaldaean Kings (626–556* B.C.) *in the British Museum* (London: Trustees of the British Museum, 1956). Wiseman dates the accession of Sinsariskun to the Assyrian throne in 629 B.C. Note his discussion of this problem on pp. 90–93.

[2] *Ibid.*, p. 5, refers to the Nimrud treaty tablet (nd. 4327) found in 1955.

[3] See Sidney Smith, *Babylonian Historical Texts* (London, 1924), p. 24. This is based on the Babylonian Chronicle B.M. 86379 first published by L. W. King in 1907.

[4] Primary sources for Nabopolassar are the British Museum tablets nos. 25127 (626–623 B.C.), 21901 (616–609), 22047 (608–606), published by the Trustees of the British Museum by D. J. Wiseman in 1956 under the title *Chronicles of Chaldaean Kings* (626–556 B.C.). Tablet B.M. 21901 had been published by C. J. Gadd, *The Fall of Nineveh* (London, 1923).

[5] See Wiseman, *op. cit.*, p. 7.

[6] *Ibid.*, p. 11.

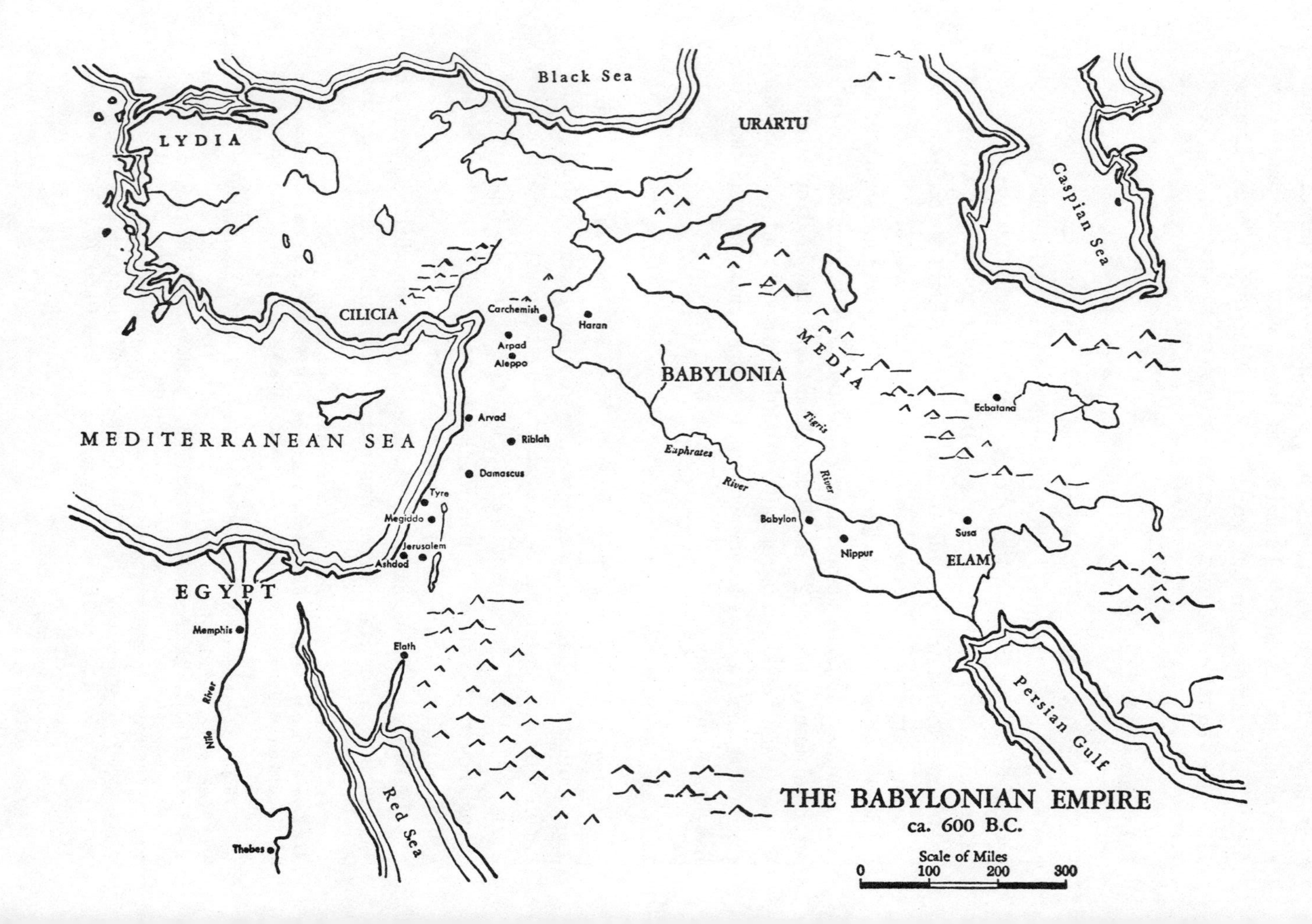

THE BABYLONIAN EMPIRE
ca. 600 B.C.

syrian army could launch a counterattack.[7] This caused Assyria to ally itself with Egypt, which had been freed from Assyrian domination by Psammetichus I in 654 B.C.[8]

After repeated raids on Assyria the city of Ashur fell to the Medes under Cyaxares in 614 B.C. The result of the Babylonian efforts to aid the Medes in this conquest was a Medo-Babylonian alliance confirmed by marriage.[9] In 612 B.C. the Medes and Babylonians converged on Nineveh, razing the great Assyrian capital and dividing the spoils.[10] It may well be that Sinsariskun, the Assyrian king, perished in the destruction of Nineveh.

The Assyrians who managed to escape retreated westward to Haran. For several years the Babylonians made raids and conquests at various points along the Euphrates but avoided any direct conflict with Ashuruballit, the Assyrian king at Haran. In 609 B.C., with the support of Umman-manda forces, Nabopolassar marched toward Haran. The Assyrians, who by this time had been joined by Egyptian forces, abandoned Haran and retreated to the western banks of the Euphrates. Consequently Nabopolassar occupied Haran without a struggle, leaving a garrison there when he returned to Babylon. The Babylonian army came back to Haran when Ashuruballit attempted to recapture the city. This time Ashuruballit apparently escaped with his Assyrian forces northward to Urartu, since Nabopolassar directed his campaign into that area; and there is no further mention of Assyrians or Ashuruballit in the chronicles.[11]

After directing his expeditions northeastward for a few years Nabopolassar renewed his efforts to cope with the Egyptian troops along the upper Euphrates. Late in 607, and continuing in the next year, the Babylonians engaged the Egyptians in several encounters and returned home early in the year 605. This was the last time Nabopolassar led his army in battle.

Nebuchadnezzar[12]*—605–562* B.C.

In the spring of 605 B.C. Nabopolassar sent Nebuchadnezzar, the crown prince, and the Babylonian army to deal with the Egyptian threat on the

[7] The tablets or chronicles for the years 622–617 are missing but apparently Nabopolassar continued with success.

[8] Wiseman, *op. cit.,* p. 12.

[9] The marriage of Nabopolassar's son, Nebuchadnezzar, and Amytis, daughter of the son of Cyaxares. Cf. C. J. Gadd, *The Fall of Nineveh,* pp. 10–11.

[10] Who were the Umman-manda mentioned in this campaign as allied with Babylon? Some scholars equate them with the Medes, while others identify them as the Scythians. Although Wiseman, *op. cit.,* pp. 15–16, favors the former, note his discussion listing historical sources for both views.

[11] *Ibid.,* p. 19.

[12] The Babylonian Chronicles for the first ten years of Nebuchadnezzar's reign are published in the volume by Wiseman, *op. cit.,* under B.M. 21946 (605–595 B.C.), pp. 66 ff.

upper Euphrates.[13] With determination he marched directly to Carchemish, which the Egyptians had held since 609 when Necho came up to aid the Assyrian forces. The Egyptians were decisively defeated at Carchemish in early summer. In pursuit of their enemies the Babylonians fought another battle at Hamath. By August Nebuchadnezzar had control of Syria and Palestine, the Egyptians retreating to their own land. Wiseman correctly observes that this had a decided effect upon Judah.[14] Although Nebuchadnezzar may have established himself at Riblah, which later became his headquarters, he undoubtedly sent his army far enough south to expel the Egyptians from Palestine. Jehoiakim, who had been a vassal of Necho, now became subject to Nebuchadnezzar. Treasures from the Jerusalem Temple and token hostages, including Daniel, were seized and taken to Babylon (Dan. 1:1).

On August 15–16, 605 B.C., Nabopolassar died.[15] The crown prince immediately rushed to Babylon. On the day of his arrival, September 6–7, Nebuchadnezzar was crowned king of Babylon. Having secured the throne, he returned to his army in the west to ensure the Babylonian position and the collection of tribute. The next year (604) he marched his army into Syria once more. This time he required the kings from various cities to appear before him with tribute. Along with the rulers of Damascus, Tyre, and Sidon, Jehoiakim of Jerusalem acquiesced, remaining subject to the Babylonians for three years (II Kings 24:1).[16] Ashkelon resisted the Babylonians unrealistically hoping that Egypt would come to its aid.[17] Nebuchadnezzar left this city in ruins when he returned to Babylon in February, 603.

During the next few years Nebuchadnezzar's control of Syria and Palestine was not seriously challenged. In 601 the Babylonian army once more displayed its might by marching about victoriously in Syria and aiding the local governors in the collection of tribute. Later that year Nebuchadnezzar took personal command of the army and marched into Egypt.[18] Necho II marshaled his forces to resist the Babylonian aggression. The Babylonian chronicle frankly states that both sides suffered heavy losses in the ensuing

[13] Wiseman suggests that Nabopolassar remained at home for political reasons or, as Berosus implies, he could not endure battle fatigue because of age or health.

[14] Wiseman, *op. cit.*, p. 26.

[15] *Ibid.*, p. 26.

[16] *Ibid.*, p. 28.

[17] *Ibid.*, p. 28, identifies the Saqqara papyrus, no. 86984 (Cairo Museum), an Aramaic letter which appeals to Pharaoh for help, with this siege of Ashkelon. See note 5 on the same page for varied opinions.

[18] *Ibid.*, p. 30, suggests that the reference by Josephus, *Antiquities of the Jews* X. 6 (87), applies here prior to this battle. In the fourth year of Nebuchadnezzar and the eighth year of Jehoiakim the latter again resumed his tribute payments to the former in response to a threat of war. Although Necho had retreated to Egypt after the decisive battle of Carchemish, he was strong enough to influence Jehoiakim to withhold tribute from Nebuchadnezzar. The king of Babylon undoubtedly ensured the support of Jehoiakim before he advanced to fight Egypt.

conflict.[19] It is likely that this setback accounts for the retreat of Nebuchadnezzar and his concentration during the following year on amassing horses and chariots to re-equip his army. This also may have deterred the Babylonian monarch from invading Egypt for many years to come.[20] In 599 the Babylonians returned to Syria to extend their control of the western Syrian Desert areas and to fortify Riblah and Hamath as strong bases for aggression against Egypt.[21]

In December of 598 B.C. Nebuchadnezzar once more marched his armies westward. Although the chronicle account is brief, it definitely identifies Jerusalem as the objective.[22] Apparently Jehoiakim had withheld tribute from Nebuchadnezzar in dependence upon Egypt, even though Jeremiah had constantly warned him against such a policy. According to Josephus, Jehoiakim was surprised when the Babylonian march was directed against him instead of Egypt.[23] After a short siege Jerusalem surrendered to the Babylonians on March 15–16, 597 B.C.[24] Since Jehoiakim had died on December 6–7, 598, his son Jehoiachin was the king of Judah who actually yielded.[25] With other members of the royal family and some ten thousand leading citizens of Jerusalem, Jehoiachin was taken captive to Babylon. In addition, vast treasures from Judah were confiscated for Babylonia. Zedekiah, an uncle of Jehoiachin, was appointed puppet king in Jerusalem.

For the years 596–594 B.C. the Babylonian Chronicles report that Nebuchadnezzar continued his control in the west, encountered some opposition in the east, and suppressed a rebellion in Babylon. The last lines in the extant chronicles state that in December, 594 B.C., Nebuchadnezzar mustered his troops and marched into Syria and Palestine.[26] For the remaining thirty-three years of Nebuchadnezzar's reign no official records, such as these chronicles, are available.

Nebuchadnezzar's activities in Judah in the following decade are well attested in biblical records in Kings, Chronicles, and Jeremiah. As a result of Zedekiah's rebellion the siege of Jerusalem began in January, 588. Although the siege was temporarily lifted as the Babylonians directed their efforts toward Egypt, the kingdom of Judah finally capitulated. Zedekiah tried to escape but was captured at Jericho and taken to Riblah, where his sons were killed while he looked on. After being blinded he was taken to Baby-

[19] British Museum tablet 21946, lines 4–5. See Wiseman, *op. cit.*, p. 71.

[20] The only invasion of Egypt by Nebuchadnezzar known in secular sources occurred in 568–67 B.C. See Wiseman, *op. cit.*, p. 30.

[21] *Ibid.*, p. 32.

[22] B.M. 21946, Wiseman, *op. cit.*, pp. 66–74 and 32–33.

[23] Josephus, *Antiquities of the Jews* X. 6 (88–89).

[24] Wiseman, *op. cit.*, p. 72, B.M. 21946, line 12. This was the second day of Adar.

[25] Wiseman, *op. cit.*, pp. 33–35. He suggests that Jehoiakim may have been killed in a previous Babylonian approach to Jerusalem, since he died before the main forces left Babylon in December, 598.

[26] B.M. 21946. Wiseman, *op. cit.*, pp. 74–75.

lonia, where he died. On August 15, 586 B.C., the final destruction of Jerusalem in Old Testament times began.[27] Denuded of its population by exile, the capital of Judah was abandoned in ruins. Thus ended the Davidic government of Judah in the days of Nebuchadnezzar.

Another British Museum tablet, which appears to be a religious text and not a part of the Babylonian Chronicles series, reports a campaign of Nebuchadnezzar in his thirty-seventh year (568–567 B.C.) against the Pharaoh Amasis.[28] It appears that Apries, the king of Egypt, had been defeated by Nebuchadnezzar in 572 and replaced on the throne by Amasis. When the latter rebelled in 568–567 Nebuchadnezzar marched his army into Egypt.

The extensive building program of Nebuchadnezzar is well known from the king's own inscriptions.[29] Having inherited a firmly established kingdom, Nebuchadnezzar during his long reign devoted intensive efforts toward construction projects in Babylonia. The beauty and majesty of the royal city of Babylon was unsurpassed in ancient times. Nebuchadnezzar's arrogant boast that he built this great city by his might and for his glory is recognized as historically accurate (Dan. 4:30).[30]

Babylon was defensively fortified by a moat and a double wall. Throughout the city a vast system of streets and canals was built to facilitate transportation. Along the broad processional street and in the palace were lions, bulls, and dragons made of colored enamel bricks. The noted Ishtar gate marked the impressive entrance into this street. Bricks used in ordinary construction bore the imprint of Nebuchadnezzar's own name. Some twenty temples in Babylon and Borsippa are credited to this famous king.[31] The outstanding undertaking in the temple area was the reconstruction of the ziggurat. The hanging gardens, built by Nebuchadnezzar to please his Median queen, were regarded by the Greeks as one of the seven wonders of the world.

The study of some three hundred cuneiform texts found in a vaulted building near the Ishtar gate has resulted in the identification of Jews in the land of exile during the reign of Nebuchadnezzar.[32] On these tablets, dated *ca.* 595–570 B.C., are listed the rations assigned to captives from Egypt, Philistia, Phoenicia, Asia Minor, Persia, and Judah. Most significant is the mention of Jehoiachin with his five sons or princes. It is clear from these

[27] E. R. Thiele, *The Mysterious Numbers of the Hebrew Kings,* p. 165.

[28] These British Museum tablets nos. 33041 and 33053 were first published by T. G. Pinches in 1878. They are reproduced by Wiseman in *op. cit.* on plates XX–XXI. Note his discussion and bibliography on p. 94.

[29] Beginning in 1899 the Deutsch Orientgesellschaft under the direction of Robert Koldewey thoroughly excavated the city of Babylon. See Koldewey, *Das wieder erstehende Babylon* (4th ed.; Leipzig, 1925).

[30] Jack Finegan, *Light from the Ancient Past* (Princeton, 1959), p. 224.

[31] R. Koldewey, *Das Ishtar-Tor in Babylon* (1918).

[32] Ernst F. Weidner in *Mélanges Syriens à Monsieur René Dussaud* II (1939), pp. 923–927. The reference, p. 935, to prisoners from Pirindi and Hume held in Babylon may indicate that Nebuchadnezzar had conquered Cilicia between 595 and 570 B.C.

documents that the Babylonians as well as the Jews recognized Jehoiachin as heir to the Jewish throne.

The glory of the Babylonian kingdom began to fade with the death of Nebuchadnezzar in 562 B.C. His marked success had enlarged the small kingdom of Babylon to span the Near East from Susa to the Mediterranean, from the Persian Gulf to the upper Tigris, and from the Taurus Mountains down to the first cataract in Egypt. As an adventurous builder he made the city of Babylon the mightiest fortress in the world, adorned with unsurpassed splendor and beauty. The power and genius that characterized his 43-year reign were never equaled by any of his successors.

Awel-Marduk—562–560 B.C.

Awel-Marduk, also known as Evil-Merodach, ruled for only two years over the empire he inherited from his father. Although Josephus[33] appraises him as a harsh ruler, the Scriptures indicate his generosity toward Jehoiachin.[34] This former king of Judah who had been taken into exile in 597 B.C. was now released at the age of fifty-five. Awel-Marduk's reign was abruptly terminated when he was murdered by Neriglissar, who was enthroned August 13, 560 B.C.[35]

Neriglissar—560–556 B.C.

Neriglissar came to the throne either by dint of his leading a revolution supported by the priests and the army or as heir to the throne by virtue of his marriage to Nebuchadnezzar's daughter.[36] It is highly probable that Neriglissar is correctly identified with Nergal-sharezer,[37] the "Rab-mag" or chief officer who released Jeremiah in 586 after the conquest of Jerusalem (Jer. 39:3, 13). Popularly known as Neriglissar, he is mentioned in contracts at Babylon and Opis as the son of a wealthy landowner.[38] According to another text which has been dated in the reign of Nebuchadnezzar, Neriglissar was appointed to control the business affairs of the sun-god temple at Sippar.[39] If Neriglissar is the individual mentioned by that name on contracts as early as 595 B.C., then he must have been at least middle-aged or older when he seized the Babylonian throne.

Until recently Neriglissar was primarily known for his activities in restoring the Esagila temple of Marduk at Babylon and the Ezida temple of

[33] See *Against Apion* i. 20 (147).

[34] Cf. Jer. 52:31–34 and II Kings 25:27–30.

[35] Richard A. Parker and Waldo H. Dubberstein, *Babylonian Chronology, 626* B.C.–A.D. *45* (1942), p. 10.

[36] Cf. L. W. King, *History of Babylon* (London: Chatto & Windus, 1919), p. 280.

[37] See the article "Nergal-sharezar," p. 485 in *Harper's Bible Dictionary* (New York: Harper & Brothers, 1952).

[38] British Museum tablets nos. 33117, 30414, and 33142 published by Strassmaier as nos. 369, 411, and 419.

[39] According to another text, B.M. 55920. See Wiseman, *op. cit.*, p. 39.

Nebo at Borsippa. In addition, he rebuilt the chapel of destiny (focal point of the New Year festival at Babylon), repaired an old palace, and built canals as any king was expected to do. A new chronicle tablet recently published portrays Neriglissar as very aggressive and vigorous in maintaining control throughout the empire.[40]

In the third year of Neriglissar's reign Appuasu, king of Pirindu in West Cilicia, advanced across the coastal plain into East Cilicia to raid and plunder Hume. Neriglissar immediately moved his armies to repulse the invader and pursued him as far as Ura, beyond the Lamos River. Appuasu escaped but his army was dispersed. Instead of advancing to Lydda Neriglissar marched to the coast to conquer the rocky island of Pitusu, with a garrison of 6,000 men, displaying his ability in the use of land and sea forces. He returned to Babylon as victor in February-March, 556 B.C.

Cilicia had formerly been controlled by Assyrian kings but regained independence after the death of Ashurbanipal, *ca.* 631 B.C. Although there are no Babylonian chronicles available concerning Nebuchadnezzar's reign after his tenth year (594 B.C.), it has been suggested that he conquered Cilicia between 595–570.[41] In the list of prisoners held in Babylonian captivity during this period appear references to exiles from Pirindu and Hume.[42]

After Neriglissar died in 556 B.C. his young son, Labashi-Marduk, ruled but a few months. Among the courtiers who deposed and killed the young king was Nabonidus, who seized the throne.

Nabonidus—556–539 B.C.

When Nabonidus began to rule he claimed that he was the rightful successor to the Babylonian throne.[43] Marduk was also duly recognized at the New Year's festival on March 31, 555 B.C. with Nabonidus not only participating as king, but also providing elaborate gifts for the Esagila temple.[44]

The religious interests of the new king were not rooted in Babylon but in Haran, where his parents devotedly worshiped the moon-god Sin. Since the destruction of the Sin temple at Haran in 610 B.C., which was carefully attributed to the Medes, this cult had not been restored. Nabonidus conveniently made a treaty with Cyrus, who rebelled against the Medes, so that the Babylonian ruler was able to restore the cult of Sin in Haran. He concentrated on this religious interest with such devotion that for several years he suspended the New Year celebrations at Babylon, failing to appear in the

[40] See Wiseman's discussion and map, *op. cit.*, pp. 39 ff.

[41] *Ibid.*, p. 39.

[42] E. F. Weidner, *"Jojachin, König von Juda in babylonischen Keilschriften," Mélanges Syriens*, II (1938), 935.

[43] S. Langdon, *Die neubabylonischen Königsinchriften* (1912), Nabonid No. 8.

[44] A. T. Olmstead, *History of the Persian Empire* (University of Chicago Press, 1948), p. 35.

procession of Marduk.[45] This annual cultic ritual had always brought a lucrative return in trade and commerce for the businessmen of Babylon. Thus the suspension of the festival for several years offended not only the priests but also the commercial leaders in this great city. The result was that by 548 B.C. Nabonidus was forced to delegate his authority to Belshazzar and retire to the city of Tema in Arabia. Here Nabonidus manifested an interest in the caravan trade as well as in the promotion of the moon-god cult.[46]

Although Nabonidus disregarded the city of Babylon, he attempted to maintain the empire. In 554 he sent armies into Hume and the Amanus Mountains and on south through Syria; by the end of 553 he had killed the king of Edom. From there he advanced to Tema, where he built a palace. Sometime later Belshazzar was given control in Babylon, since the chronicle for each year from 549 to 545 B.C. begins with the statement that the king was in Tema.[47]

In the meantime Cyrus had advanced against Media. By 550 he had gained the upper hand and conquered Ecbatana and laid claim to the Median rule over Assyria and beyond in the Fertile Crescent. Three years later he marched his army through the Cilician gates into Cappadocia, where he encountered Croesus of Lydia in an indecisive battle. Although the balance of power had been sufficiently disturbed when Cyrus overpowered the Medes that Nabonidus of Babylon, Amasis of Egypt, and Croesus had formed an alliance, neither of the latter's allies was there to help.[48] Croesus retreated to Sardis hoping that by the next spring he would have received sufficient support to overthrow his enemy. Even though winter was setting in, Cyrus advanced west to Sardis in a surprise move and captured Croesus in the fall of 547 B.C. With his westernmost foe defeated Cyrus returned to Persia.

Undoubtedly these developments seriously disturbed Nabonidus and he returned to Babylon. By 546 B.C. the annual New Year festival had not been held for a number of years due to the king's absence; misrule and graft prevailed, and the people were subjected to economic hardships.[49] In subsequent years, as Cyrus was extending his empire into Iranian territory, cities such as Susa, under Gobryas' leadership, rebelled against the Babylonian alliance

[45] According to the Nabonidus-Chronicle, the king was in Tema during the seventh to eleventh years, so the festival could not be observed. This Chronicle was first published by T. G. Pinches, *Transactions of the Biblical Society of Archaeology,* VII (London, 1882), 139 ff., by Sidney Smith, *Babylonian Historical Texts, Relating to the Downfall of Babylon* (London, 1924), pp. 110 ff., and by A. Leo Oppenheim in *Ancient Near Eastern Texts,* ed. by P. Pritchard (Princeton, 1950), pp. 305 ff.

[46] Caravan traffic is mentioned in Job 6:19 and Is. 21:4. Note also the reference to Tema in Gen. 25:15.

[47] R. P. Dougherty, *Nabonidus and Belshazzar* (London: H. Milford, Oxford University Press, 1929), pp. 114 ff.

[48] A. T. Olmstead, *History of the Persian Empire* (Chicago, 1948), pp. 34 ff.

[49] Dougherty, *Records from Erech, Time of Nabonidus* (Yale Oriental Series Babylonian Texts, Vol. 6, 1930, Yale University Press), No. 154.

with Cyrus. In desperation Nabonidus rescued some of the gods in these cities and brought them to Babylon.

On New Year's Day in April, 539, Nabonidus made an attempt to celebrate the festival properly.[50] Although many gods from surrounding cities were brought in, the priests of Marduk and Nebo did not enthusiastically rally to the king's support. By October 11, 539, the city of Sippar feared Cyrus so much that it surrendered without a battle. Two days later Gobryas took Babylon with the troops of Cyrus. While Belshazzar was slain, Nabonidus may have escaped but was subsequently captured and apparently received favorable treatment after his release. Before the end of October Cyrus himself entered Babylon as victor and conqueror.[51]

Persia—539–400 B.C.

At the beginning of the first millennium B.C. successive waves of Aryan tribes invaded and established themselves upon the Iranian plateau.[52] Two groups eventually emerged as historically important: the Medes and the Persians.

Under the dynamic leadership of Cyaxares, Media asserted herself as a threat to Assyrian supremacy during the last half of the seventh century. In 612 B.C. the combined forces of Media and Babylon destroyed Nineveh. Nebuchadnezzar's marriage to the granddaughter of Cyaxares sealed this alliance so that a delicate balance of power prevailed throughout the period of Babylonian expansion and supremacy.

Cyrus the Great—559–530 B.C.

Persia became a first-rate international power under Cyrus the Great.[53] He came to the throne in 559 as a vassal of Media, having under his control only Persia and some Elamite territory known as Anshan. For him there were kingdoms to conquer. Astyages (585–550) exercised a weak rule over the Median empire. Babylonia was still very powerful under Neriglissar but began to show signs of weakness as Nabonidus neglected affairs of state to devote his time to the restoration of moon worship at Haran. Lydia in the

[50] See Nabonidus-Chronicle, reference cited.

[51] For chronology see Parker and Dubberstein, *op. cit.*, p. 11.

[52] Ernst Herzfeld, *Archaeological History of Iran* (1935), p. 8. See also R. Ghirshman, *Iran from the Earliest Times to the Islamic Conquest,* tr. from the French (Baltimore: Harmondsworth, Penguin books, 1954).

[53] Persia was the first real world empire. Unlike preceding empires, Persia included many diverse races—several Semitic groups, Medes, Armenians, Greeks, Egyptians, Indians, and Persians themselves. Factors that enabled the Persians to hold this diversity in a semblance of unity for over 200 years are: (1) effective organization, (2) a strong army, (3) Persian tolerance, (4) an excellent road system.

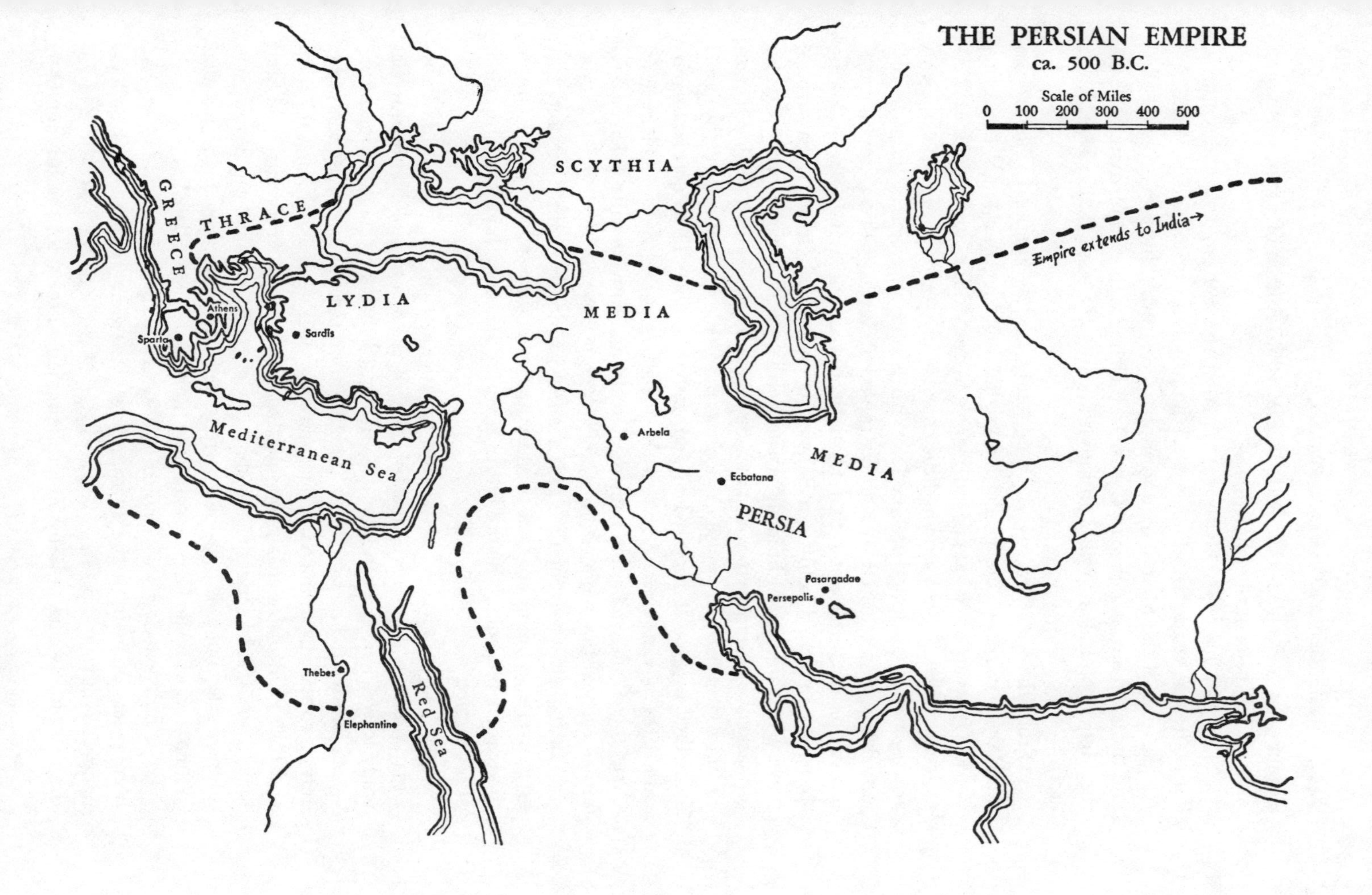
THE PERSIAN EMPIRE
ca. 500 B.C.
Scale of Miles
0 100 200 300 400 500
SCYTHIA
GREECE
THRACE
LYDIA
Athens
Sparta
Sardis
MEDIA
Empire extends to India→
Mediterranean Sea
Arbela
MEDIA
Ecbatana
PERSIA
Pasargadae
Persepolis
Thebes
Elephantine
Red Sea

distant west had allied itself with Media, while Amasis of Egypt was nominally under the control of Babylon.

Early in his reign Cyrus consolidated the Persian tribes about him. Thereafter he made an alliance with Babylonia against Media. When Astyages, ruler of the Medes, tried to suppress the revolt, his own army rebelled and turned their king over to Cyrus. In their resultant subjugation to Persia the Medes continued to play an important role (cf. Esth. 1:19; Dan. 5:28, etc.).

From the west Croesus, the notoriously wealthy king of Lydia, crossed the Halys River to challenge Persian might. Bypassing Babylon in the spring of 547 Cyrus advanced along the Tigris and crossed the Euphrates into Cappadocia. When Croesus declined the conciliatory overtures of Cyrus, the two armies met in an indecisive battle. With winter approaching Croesus dismissed his army and retreated to his capital at Sardis with a minimum protective force. Anticipating that Cyrus would attack him in the following spring, he requested help from Babylonia, Egypt, and Greece. In a surprise move Cyrus proceeded immediately to Sardis. Croesus had superior cavalry but lacked the infantry to withstand the attack. Cyrus astutely deployed camels in front of his own troops. As soon as the Lydian horses caught the camel scent they became terror-stricken and unmanageable. The Persians thereby gained the advantage and routed the foe. By securing Sardis and Miletus, Cyrus solved his encounter with the Greeks on the western frontier and returned eastward to conquer other lands.[54]

In the east Cyrus marched his armies victoriously to the Oxus and Jaxartes rivers, claiming Sogdian territory and extending Persian sovereignty to the borders of India.[55] Before returning to Persia he had doubled the extent of his empire.

Next Cyrus directed his interest toward the rich, fertile plains in Babylonia, where a population dissatisfied with the reforms of Nabonidus was ready to welcome the conqueror. Cyrus sensed that the time was ripe for invasion and wasted no time in leading his troops through the mountain passes and on to the alluvium. As various outlying cities such as Ur, Larsa, Erech, and Kish yielded to Persian conquest, Nabonidus rescued the local gods and took them for safekeeping to the great city of Babylon, which supposedly was impregnable. But the Babylonians retreated before the advancing invader. Within a short while Cyrus established himself as king of Babylon.

In Babylon Cyrus was hailed as a great liberator. The gods which had been taken there from the surrounding cities were restored to their local temples. Not only did Cyrus acknowledge Marduk as the god who had enthroned him as king in Babylon but he remained there for several months to

[54] Olmstead, *op. cit.*, p. 41. Cf. also Herodotus i. 71 ff.
[55] Olmstead, *op. cit.*, pp. 46–49.

celebrate the New Year festival.[56] This was politically expedient to assure him of popular support as he assumed control of the vast Babylonian Empire extending west through Syria and Palestine to the borders of Egypt.

The Assyrians and Babylonians were notorious for their policy of taking conquered peoples to a foreign land. The reversal of this policy distinguished Cyrus as the welcomed deliverer. He encouraged uprooted peoples to return to their homelands and restore the gods to their temples.[57] The Jews, whose capital city and temple still lay in ruins, were among those who benefited from Cyrus' benevolence.

In 530 Cyrus led his army to the northern frontier. While invading the land beyond the Araxes River west of the Caspian Sea he was fatally wounded in battle. Cambyses had his father's body taken back to Pasargadae, the capital of Persia, for proper burial.

The tomb which Cyrus had constructed for himself still stands on a platform at an elevation of 17 feet with six steps leading down to a rectangular pavement 44 by 48 feet.[58] Here Cyrus was placed in a sarcophagus of gold resting on a couch with feet of wrought gold. Elaborate apparel, expensive jewelry, a Persian sword, Babylonian tapestries, and other luxuries were carefully entombed in the resting place of the great empire builder. Surrounding the pavement was a canal beyond which were beautiful gardens. Guards with royal provisions kept vigil near the tomb. Each month they sacrificed a horse to this distinguished hero. Two centuries later when Alexander the Great discovered that vandals had raided the tomb he ordered the restoration of the body as well as all the treasures.[59] Today the empty tomb bears witness to the greatness of Cyrus, who won for the Persians their empire but eventually was begrudged the resting place he had so elaborately prepared.

Cambyses—530–522 B.C.

When Cyrus left Babylon in 538 B.C. he appointed his son Cambyses to represent the Persian king in the royal processions on New Year's Day. By duly recognizing Marduk, Nebo, and Bel and by retaining the officers and palace dignitaries of Babylon, Cambyses became well established in Babylonia with headquarters at Sippar.

[56] Pritchard, *op. cit.*, pp. 315–316.

[57] Cyrus cylinder in *ibid.*, pp. 315–316. Apparently Astyages of Media, Croesus of Lydia, and Nabonidus of Babylonia were well treated by Cyrus. According to Robert William Rogers, *History of Ancient Persia* (New York, 1929), p. 49, Croesus was assigned to Barene in Media, where he was allotted a royal income in a semiregal state with a guard of 5,000 cavalry and an infantry of 10,000 men.

[58] See *ibid.*, p. 69, for a bibliography on the tomb of Cyrus. The best discussion, according to Rogers, is in *Persia, Past and Present* by A. V. Williams Jackson, pp. 278–293.

[59] Arrian, *Anabasis* 6. 29, as translated by E. I. Robson in *Loeb Classical Library* (1929–33), II, 197.

With the sudden death of Cyrus in 530 Cambyses asserted himself as king of Persia. After he secured recognition from the many provinces his father had brought under Persian control Cambyses turned his attention to the conquest of Egypt, which still lay beyond the bounds of the empire.

Amasis had for years anticipated the imperialistic dreams of Persia. In 547 he may have had an alliance with Croesus. He also developed friendships and sought coalitions with the Greeks.

On his way to Egypt Cambyses encamped at Gaza, where he acquired camels from the Nabataeans[60] for the 55-mile march through the desert. Two men who turned traitor to Amasis threw in their lot with the Persian conqueror. Phanes, a Greek mercenary chief, deserted the Pharaoh and supplied Cambyses with important military intelligence. Polycrates of Samos broke his alliance with Amasis to aid Cambyses with Greek troops and ships.

Upon his arrival in the Nile Delta Cambyses learned that the elderly Amasis had died. The new Pharaoh, Psamtik III, son of Amasis, sallied forth with Greek mercenaries and Egyptian soldiers to attack the intruding force. In the battle of Pelusium (525 B.C.) the Egyptians were decisively defeated by the Persians. Although Psamtik tried to secure himself in the city of Memphis, he was unable to escape his pursuers. Cambyses accorded the captive king favorable treatment but later Psamtik attempted rebellion and was executed. The victorious invader appropriated the titles of Egyptian kingship and had himself depicted on monuments as Pharaoh.

For the next few years Cambyses cultivated friendship with the Greeks in order to promote the lucrative trade they brought to Egypt. This move extended Persian domination over the more advanced and wealthiest half of the Greek world.[61] Cambyses also tried to expand his domain west to Carthage and south to Nubia and Ethiopia by military force but in these attempts he failed.

Leaving Egypt under Aryandes as satrap, Cambyses started his return to Persia. Near Mount Carmel news reached him that a usurper, Gaumata by name, had seized the Persian throne. The claim of Gaumata to be Smerdis, another son of Cyrus whom Cambyses had previously executed,[62] perturbed Cambyses so greatly that he committed suicide. For eight months Gaumata held the reins of government. The end of his short-lived reign precipitated revolts by various provinces.

Darius I—522–486 B.C.

Darius I, also known as Darius the Great, saved the Persian Empire in this time of crisis. Having served in the army under Cyrus he became spear-

[60] According to Olmstead, *op. cit.*, p. 88, this is the first mention of the Nabataeans. See Herodotus iii. 4 ff.

[61] Olmstead, *op. cit.*, p. 88.

[62] Rogers, *op. cit.*, p. 71.

bearer for Cambyses in Egypt. When the latter's reign was abruptly terminated en route from Egypt to Persia, Darius rushed eastward. He executed Gaumata in September, 522 B.C., and seized the throne. Three months later rebellious Babylon came under his control.[63] After two years of hard fighting he dissipated all opposition in Armenia and Media.

Darius returned to Egypt as king in 519–518.[64] What contact he had en route with the Jewish settlement at Jerusalem is not known. At the beginning of his reign he granted permission to resume the building of the Temple (Ezra 6:1 and Hag. 1:1). Since it was completed in 515 B.C. it seems reasonable to assume that the Persian advance through Palestine did not affect the state of affairs at Jerusalem.[65] In Egypt Darius occupied Memphis without much opposition and reinstated Aryandes as satrap.

In 513 Darius personally marched his armies westward across the Bosporus and the Danube to meet the Scythians coming down from the steppes of Russia.[66] This venture proved unsuccessful but he returned to add Thrace to his empire and spent the next year in Sardis. This initiated a series of engagements with the Greeks. The Persian control of Greek colonies developed into a conflict that ultimately proved disastrous for the Persians. The westward advance of the Persians was abruptly halted in a crucial defeat at Marathon in 490 B.C.

Darius had achieved success in suppressing rebellions but he was a genius in administration. He demonstrated this by organizing his vast empire into twenty satrapies.[67] To strengthen the empire internally he promulgated laws in the name of Ahuramazda, the Zoroastrian god symbolized by the winged disk. Darius entitled his book of laws *The Ordinance of Good Regulations.* His statutes exhibit dependence upon earlier Mesopotamian codifications, especially that of Hammurapi.[68] For distribution to his people the laws were written in Aramaic on parchment. Within a century Plato recognized Darius as the great lawgiver of the Persians.

An exceptional flair for architecture prompted Darius to undertake outstanding building projects in the capital cities and elsewhere. Ecbatana, which had been the Median capital in former days, now became a favorite royal summer home, while Susa served as a choice winter residence.

Persepolis, twenty-five miles southwest of Pasargadae, was developed as

[63] For dates see Parker and Dubberstein, *op. cit.,* p. 13.

[64] Cf. R. A. Parker, "Darius and His Egyptian Campaign," *American Journal of Semitic Language and Literatures,* LVIII (1941), 373 ff.

[65] Olmstsead, *op. cit.,* p. 142, uses the argument from silence to assume that Zerubbabel rebelled and was executed since he is not subsequently mentioned in any record. Albright, *The Biblical Period,* p. 50, asserts that since nothing is known about Zerubbabel's death there is no reason to suppose that he was disloyal to Darius.

[66] See Rogers, *op. cit.,* p. 118.

[67] For discussion see *Cambridge Ancient History, IV,* 194 ff.

[68] For a comparison of the laws of Darius and the code of Hammurapi see Olmstead, *op. cit.,* pp. 119–134.

the most important city of the Persian Empire. Darius prepared an elaborately carved rock tomb for himself in a cliff near Persepolis. In the far distant land of Egypt he promoted the construction of a canal between the Red Sea and the Nile River.[69]

Susa, sixty miles northward of the mouth of the Tigris, was centrally located for administrative purposes. The plain between the Choaspes and Ulai rivers Darius made into a productive fruitland by means of an efficient canal system. The elaborate royal palace begun by Darius and beautified by his successors was the greatest Persian monument in this city. According to an inscription by Darius, this palace was adorned with cedar from Lebanon, ivory from India, and silver from Egypt.[70] Today little remains of this structure beyond a mere outline of the courts and pavements. Because of excessive summer heat Susa was not an ideal location for a permanent capital.

Persepolis, the first city of the Persian Empire, was the most impressive capital. The palace of Darius, the Tachara, was begun by him but enlarged and completed by succeeding rulers. Columns of this tremendous structure still bear testimony to Persian construction and art.[71] Persepolis was strategically fortified with a triple defense. On the crest of the "Mountain of Mercy," on which this great capital was built, was a row of walls and towers. Beyond it was the vast plain presently known as Marv Dasht.

Most notable among Persian inscriptions is the rock-hewn memorial near Behistun. The large relief representing Darius' victory over the rebels is supplemented by three cuneiform inscriptions in Old Persian, Akkadian or Babylonian, and Elamite. Since the victory panel was carved on the face of a cliff 500 feet above the plain, with only a narrow ledge below it, the inscription remained unread for more than two millennia. In 1835 Sir Henry C. Rawlinson copied and deciphered this record—securing for modern scholars the key for deciphering the Babylonian language and increasing the understanding of the Persian.[72] An Aramaic copy of this inscription among the papyri discovered at Elephantine in Egypt indicates that it was widely circulated throughout the Persian Empire.

Xerxes I—486–465 B.C.

Xerxes was heir-elect to the Persian throne when Darius died in 486 B.C. For twelve years he had served as a viceroy at Babylon under the rule

[69] See R. G. Kent in *Journal of Near Eastern Studies,* pp. 415–421.

[70] Cf. J. M. Unvala, *A Survey of Persian Art,* Vol. I, p. 339.

[71] Persepolis was excavated by the Oriental Institute of the University of Chicago in 1931–34 and 1935–39. For a report on the first expedition see Ernst Herzfeld, *op. cit.,* and for the latter see Erich F. Schmidt, *The Treasury of Persepolis and Other Discoveries in the Homeland of the Achaemenians* in the *Oriental Institute Communications,* 21 (1939), 14 ff.

[72] See H. C. Rawlinson, *The Persian Cuneiform Inscription at Behistun* (1846). More recently George Cameron made new photographs. See *Journal of Near Eastern Studies,* 2 (1943), 115 ff.

of his father. When he took over the empire there were incomplete building projects, religious reforms, and rebellions in various parts of the domain awaiting his attention.

Among the rebellious cities which received severe punishment under Xerxes was Babylon. Here in 482 B.C. the fortifications erected by Nebuchadnezzar were destroyed, the Esagila temple was razed, and the 800-pound solid gold statue of Marduk was carried away and melted for bullion. Babylon lost its identification by being incorporated with Assyria.[73]

Although vitally interested in continuing the building program at Persepolis, Xerxes yielded to insistent counselors and reluctantly directed his energies toward the expansion of the northwestern frontier. At the head of his enormous Persian army he advanced toward Greece with the support of his navy composed of Phoenician, Greek, and Egyptian units. The army suffered reverses at Thermopylae, the fleet was defeated at Salamis, and finally the Persians were decisively routed at Plataea and the cape Mycale. In 479 Xerxes retreated to Persia, relinquishing the conquest of Greece.

At home Xerxes resumed his building program. In Persepolis he completed the Apadana where thirteen of the seventy-two pillars upholding the roof of this spacious audience hall still stand. In sculpture Xerxes displayed Persian art at its best. This was magnificently displayed by adorning the stairway of the Apadana with sculptured figures of Susian and Persian guards.

Although Xerxes was inferior as a military leader and will always be remembered for his defeat in Greece, he overshadowed his predecessors as a builder. It was to his credit that Persepolis became the outstanding city of the Persian kings, excelling in sculpture and architecture.

In 465 B.C. Xerxes was assassinated by Artabanus, the head of the palace guard. He was buried in the rock-hewn tomb which he had excavated next to that of Darius the Great.

Artaxerxes I—464–425 B.C.

With the support of the assassin Artabanus, Artaxerxes Longimanus seized the throne of his father. After disposing of other aspirants to the throne he successfully suppressed rebellions in Egypt (460 B.C.) and a revolt in Syria (448). The Athenians negotiated a treaty with him by which both parties agreed to maintain the *status quo*. During his reign Ezra and Nehemiah journeyed to Jerusalem with the king's approval to aid the Jews.

The dynasty fell into decline under the succeeding kings, Darius II (423–404) and Artaxerxes II (404–359). Artaxerxes III (359–338) effected a resurgence of unity and strength, but the end was soon to come. During the rule of Darius III, Alexander the Great with superior military

[73] See Olmstead, *op. cit.*, pp. 236–237.

tactics broke the power of the Persian army (331) and incorporated the Near East into his realm.

Exilic Conditions and Prophetic Hopes

The last two centuries of Old Testament times represent an era of exilic conditions for the greater part of Israel. During the conquest by Nebuchadnezzar many Israelite captives were taken to Babylon. After the destruction of Jerusalem other Jews migrated to Egypt. Although some of the exiles returned from Babylonia after 539 B.C. to re-establish a Jewish state at Jerusalem, they never regained the position of independence and international recognition Israel had once had under the Davidic rule.

The transition from a national state to Babylonian exile was gradual for the people of Judah. At least four times during the days of Nebuchadnezzar were captives from Jerusalem taken to Babylon.

According to Berosus, the Babylonian king Nabopolassar sent his son Nebuchadnezzar in 605 B.C. to suppress rebellion in the west.[74] During this campaign the latter received news of his father's death. Leaving the captives from Judah, Phoenicia, and Syria with his army, Nebuchadnezzar rushed back to establish himself on the throne of Babylon. Biblical evidence (Dan. 1:1) dates this in the third year of Jehoiakim, who continued as the ruler in Jerusalem for eight more years after this crisis.[75] The extent of this captivity is not indicated but Daniel and his friends were among the royal family and nobility taken into exile at this time. From these captive Israelites young men were taken into the court for training in the king's service. Some of the experiences of Daniel and his associates at the court of Babylon are well known from the accounts in Dan. 1–5.

The second Babylonian invasion of Judah occurred in 597 B.C. This was most crucial for the Southern Kingdom. By withholding tribute from Babylonia Jehoiakim invoked calamity. Since Nebuchadnezzar was busy elsewhere, he incited the surrounding states to raid Jerusalem. Apparently Jehoiakim was killed during one of these raids, leaving the Davidic throne to his eighteen-year-old son Jehoiachin. The latter's reign of three months was abruptly terminated when he surrendered to the Babylonian armies (II Kings 24:10–17). Babylonian sources confirm that this invasion took place in March, 597 B.C.[76] The Lachish letters likewise indicate a Judean invasion at

[74] Josephus *Against Apion* i. 132–139; *Antiquities* x. 219–223. More recently confirmed in British Museum tablet no. 21946. See Wiseman, *op. cit.*, p. 26. Cf. also D. Winton Thomas, *Documents from Old Testament Times*, pp. 78–79.

[75] Scholars who date the Book of Daniel in the second century B.C. do not regard Daniel as a historical character nor do they accept this reference as historically reliable. Cf. Anderson, *Understanding the Old Testament*, pp. 515–530. Also *Interpreter's Bible*, VI, "Daniel," pp. 355 ff.

[76] Wiseman, *op. cit.*, p. 33.

this time.[77] Not only was the king taken captive but with him went thousands of leading figures in Jerusalem such as craftsmen, smiths, chief officials, princes, and men of war. Zedekiah, an uncle of Jehoiachin, was left to rule the poorer class of people that remained in the land.

King Jehoiachin's captivity did not prevent the citizens of Judah as well as the exiles from regarding him as their legitimate king. Stamped jar handles excavated at ancient Debir and Beth-shemesh in 1928–1930 indicate that people held property in the name of Jehoiachin even during the reign of Zedekiah.[78] Cuneiform texts discovered in Babylon refer to Jehoiachin as the king of Judah.[79] When Jerusalem was later destroyed the sons of Jehoiachin had rations assigned to them under royal supervision, yet the sons of Zedekiah were all slaughtered. Though Jerusalem retained a semblance of government for another eleven years, the captivity of 597 had a devastating effect upon the land of Judah.

In 586 the land bore the brunt of yet another invasion, with even more drastic and dire results. Jerusalem with its temple was destroyed. Judah existed no more as a national state. With Jerusalem in ruins, the capital was abandoned by the people who remained in the land. Under the leadership of Gedaliah, who had been appointed governor of Judah by Nebuchadnezzar, the remnant gravitated to Mizpah (II Kings 24:2; Jer. 40:14). Within a few months Gedaliah was assassinated by Ishmael and the discouraged remnant migrated to Egypt. Along the dusty road with them trudged Jeremiah the prophet.

A fourth deportation is mentioned in Jeremiah 52:30. Josephus[80] reports that more Jews were taken captive to Babylon in 582 B.C. when Nebuchadnezzar subjugated Egypt.

According to Berosus, the Jewish colonies were assigned suitable settlements throughout Babylonia as prescribed by Nebuchadnezzar. The river Chebar, near which Ezekiel had his first vision and prophetic call (Ezek. 1:1), has been identified as the Nar Kabari canal near Babylon.[81] Tel-abib (Ezek. 3:15), another center of captivity, presumably was in this same vicinity.

Nebuchadnezzar devoted his interest to beautifying the city of Babylon to such an extent that the Greeks recognized it as one of the wonders of the ancient world. There is no reason to doubt that Jewish captives were assigned

[77] See C. F. Whitley, *The Exilic Age* (London: Westminster Press, 1957), p. 61.

[78] W. F. Albright, "The Seal of Eliakim and the Latest Pre-Exilic History of Judah," *Journal of Biblical Literature*, 51 (1932).

[79] E. F. Weidner, "Jejachin-König von Juda in babylonischen Keilschriftexten," *Mélanges Syriens offerts à Monsieur René Dussaud,* II (1939), 923–935. Cf. also D. Winton Thomas, *op. cit.,* pp. 84–86.

[80] *Antiquities* x. 9, 7.

[81] H. V. Hilprecht, *Explorations of Bible Lands* (Edinburgh, 1903), p. 412.

to labor at the great capital.[82] The Weidner texts mention Jewish names along with those of skilled workmen from other states who were used by Nebuchadnezzar in a successful endeavor to make his capital more impressive than any Assyrian city had ever been.[83] In this way the Babylonian king made wise use of the craftsmen, artisans, and skilled workmen captured in Jerusalem.

The environs of Babylon may at first have been the center of Jewish settlements, but the captives spread throughout the empire as more freedom was granted to them under the Babylonians and, later, under the Persians. Excavations at Nippur yielded tablets containing names common to the Ezra-Nehemiah record, indicating that a Jewish colony existed there in exilic times.[84] Nippur, sixty miles southeast of Babylon, continued as a Jewish community until its destruction around A.D. 900.[85] Other places noted as Jewish settlements are Tel-melah and Tel-harsa (Neh. 7:61), Ahava and Casiphia (Ezra 8:15, 17). In addition to these Josephus mentions Neerda and Nisibis somewhere along the Euphrates (*Antiquities* 18:9).

Longing for their homeland pervaded the exiles. This was especially true as long as the government of Jerusalem remained intact. False prophets fostered a spirit of revolt in Babylon, with the result that two rebels lost their lives at the hands of Nebuchadnezzar's henchmen (Jer. 29). Shortly after the captivity in 597 Hananiah predicted that within two years the Jews would break the Babylonian yoke (Jer. 28). Ezekiel in his day also encountered inciters of insurgency (Ezek. 13). Jeremiah, who was well known to the captives because of his long ministry at Jerusalem, wrote letters advising them to settle down in Babylon, build houses, plant vineyards, and plan on a 70-year period of captivity (Jer. 29).

When the hopes of immediate return vanished in the fall and destruction of Jerusalem in 586, the exiled Judeans resigned themselves to the long captivity which Jeremiah had predicted. Such Babylonian names as Immer and Cherub (Neh. 7:61) suggested to Albright that the Jews assumed a pastoral and agricultural life in the fertile plain along the Euphrates.[86] The Jews also became involved in mercantile enterprises throughout the empire. Records from the fifth century indicate that they had become very active in the business and commerce centered at Nippur.[87]

Linguistically the average Jew faced a new problem. Even before the

[82] Whitley, *op. cit.*, pp. 61 ff.

[83] Pritchard, *op. cit.* (2nd ed.; Princeton, 1955), p. 308.

[84] H. V. Hilprecht and A. T. Clay, *Babylonian Expedition of the University of Pennsylvania,* Series A, Vols. 9–10 (1898, 1904).

[85] Whitley, *op. cit.*, p. 70. Cf. James A. Montgomery, *Aramaic Incantation Texts from Nippur* (Philahelphia, 1913).

[86] "The Seal of Jehoiakim," *Journal of Bible Literature,* 51 (1932), 100.

[87] A. T. Clay, *Business Documents of Murashu Sons of Nippur,* University of Pennsylvania Publications of the Babylonian Section, Vol. 2, No. I (1912), 1–54.

time of Sennacherib the Aramean tribes had infiltrated Babylonia and eventually became the predominant element in the population so that Aramaic came into common use.[88] As early as the seventh century it was the language of international diplomacy of the Assyrians (II Kings 18:17–27).[89] Although this transition to a new language created a linguistic problem for most of the Jews, it is quite likely that some may have been conversant with Aramaic—in fact some perhaps had studied Aramaic in Jerusalem. In addition the Israelites from the Northern Kingdom, who already were in Babylonia, undoubtedly were affluent in Hebrew as well as Aramaic.

Although references are limited, the available evidence reveals that the captives were accorded favorable treatment. Jeremiah addressed his correspondence to "the elders of the captivity" (Jer. 29:2). Ezekiel met with the "elders of the house of Judah" (8:1), indicating that they were at liberty to organize for religious purposes. On other occasions the "elders of Israel" came to see Ezekiel (14:1 and 20:1).[90] Ezekiel apparently had freedom to carry on a wide ministry among the captives. He was married and lived in his own home and freely discussed religious matters with the elders as they met with him or came to his home. Through symbolic acts in public Ezekiel discussed the political fortunes and doom of the Southern Kingdom until Jerusalem was destroyed in 586. After that he continued to encourage his people with the hopes and prospects of a restored Davidic kingdom.

The experience of Daniel and his colleagues likewise portrays the favorable treatment accorded the captives from Judah. From the first captives taken in 605 B.C. youths were selected from the nobility and royal family of Judah for education and training in the Babylonian court (Dan. 1:1–7). Through the opportunity to interpret Nebuchadnezzar's dream Daniel was catapulted into the chief position among the wise men of Babylon. At his request his three friends also were assigned important positions in the province of Babylon. Throughout the long reign of Nebuchadnezzar Daniel and his friends gained more and more recognition through the crises recorded in the Book of Daniel. It is reasonable to assume that other captives likewise were entrusted with responsible positions at the Babylonian court. Daniel was made next-in-command during the co-rulership of Belshazzar and Naboni-

[88] Conclusive evidence that Aramaic replaced Akkadian as the international diplomatic language is apparent in an Aramaic letter discovered in Saqqara, Egypt, in 1942 and published in 1948, in which a Palestinian king appealed to Egypt for help. See John Bright, "A New Letter in Aramaic written to a Pharaoh in Egypt," *Biblical Archeologist* XII, no. 2 (May, 1949), 46 ff.

[89] R. A. Bowman, "Arameans, Aramaic, and the Bible," *Journal of Near Eastern Studies*, 7 (1948), 71–73.

[90] Oesterly suggests that Israelites who had been residing in Babylon for over a century were recognized as nationals with all the privileges of citizenship. Oesterly and Robinson, *Hebrew Religion* (2nd ed., 1937), pp. 283–284.

dus.[91] After the fall of Babylon in 539 B.C. Daniel continued his distinctive government service under Darius the Mede and Cyrus the Persian.

The treatment accorded Jehoiachin and his sons likewise speaks of the beneficent care provided for some Jewish captives.[92] Jehoiachin had his own attendants with adequate provisions allotted for his whole family, even though he was not officially released from prison until 562, at Nebuchadnezzar's death (II Kings 25:27–30). The listing of other men from Judah on these tablets indicates that bounteous provisions were not limited to the royal family.

The fortunes of Esther at the Persian court of Xerxes I typify the treatment accorded the Jews by their overlords. Nehemiah is another who served at the royal court. Through his personal contact with Artaxerxes he had opportunity to advance the welfare of those who had returned to rebuild Jerusalem.

Whitley justifiably calls in question the descriptions of some writers who depict the lot of the Jews in Babylonian captivity as one of suffering and slavery.[93] Ewald based his conclusions on selected parts of Isaiah, the Psalms, and Lamentations in asserting that conditions became increasingly worse for the captive Jews.[94] Historical evidence seems to be lacking to support the idea that the Jewish captives were mistreated physically or suppressed in their civic and religious activities during the days of Babylonian supremacy.[95] The limited evidence extant from biblical and archaeological sources supports the assertion of George Adam Smith that the condition of the Jews was honorable and without excessive suffering.[96]

The exiles from Jerusalem who were conscious of the reasons for the captivity must have experienced a deep sense of humiliation and anguish of soul. For forty years Jeremiah had faithfully warned his fellow citizens of pending judgment—Jerusalem would be so devastated that every passer-by would be horrified at the sight (Jer. 19:8). In spite of the warnings they had confidence that God would not permit his temple to be destroyed. As custodians of the law these people did not believe God would let them go into captivity. Now, in comparing the Solomonic glory and international fame of Israel with the ruins of Jerusalem, many gave vent to their shame and sorrow. The Book of Lamentations vividly deplores the fact that Jerusalem had become an international spectacle. Daniel acknowledged in his prayer that his people had become a reproach and a byword among the nations (Dan.

[91] Dougherty, *Nabonidus and Belshazzar,* pp. 105–200.
[92] Pritchard, *op. cit.,* p. 308.
[93] Whitley, *op. cit.,* p. 79.
[94] Ewald, *History of the Jews,* Vol. 5, p. 7.
[95] Whitley doubts that the evidence presented by J. M. Wilkie in his article, "Nabonidus and the Later Jewish Exiles," in the *Journal of Theological Studies,* April, 1951, pp. 33–34, justifies the case for a religious persecution under Nabonidus.
[96] G. A. Smith, *Book of Isaiah XL–LXVI* (new ed., 1927), p. 59.

9:16). Such suffering was more burdensome to the captives who were concerned about Israel's future than any physical hardship they had to endure in the land of their exile.

Both Jeremiah and Ezekiel foretold that God would restore the Jews to their own land. Another source of comfort and hope for the exiles was the message of Isaiah. In his writings he had predicted the Babylonian exile (Is. 39:6). He also assured them of their return under Cyrus (Is. 44:28). Beginning with chapter 40 he elaborated on this encouraging message which he had already declared in the earlier chapters. God was omnipotent. All nations were under his control. God used the nations and their kings to bring judgment upon Israel and in like manner could use them to restore the fortunes of his people. The appearance of Cyrus as leader of Persia must have raised the restoration hopes of the exiles who exercised faith in the predictive message of the prophets.

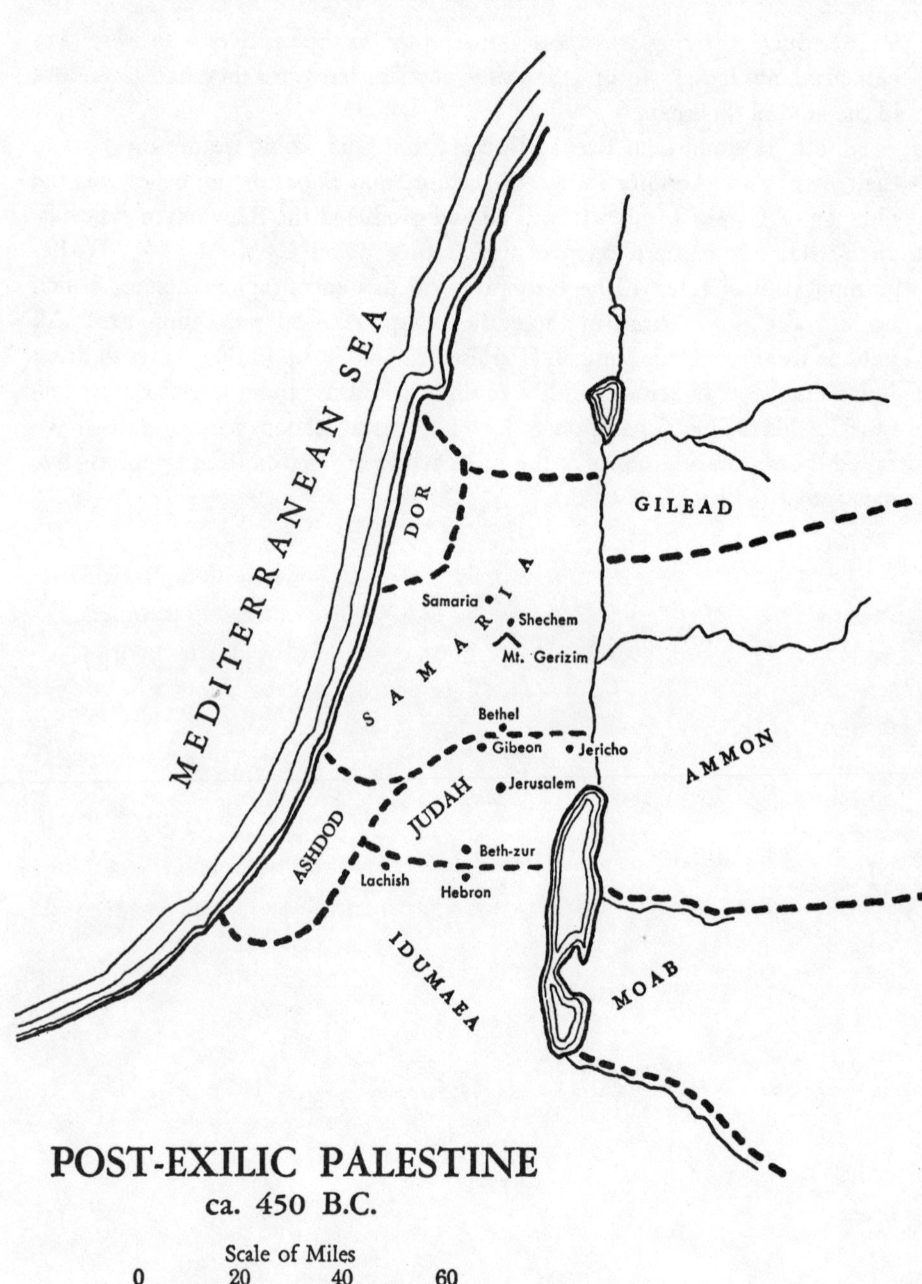

POST-EXILIC PALESTINE
ca. 450 B.C.

Chapter XVI

The Good Hand of God

With the international crisis in 539 B.C., whereby Persia gained supremacy over Babylon, came the opportunity for the Jews to re-establish themselves in Jerusalem. But by this time many of the exiles were so comfortably situated by the waters of Babylon that they ignored the decree permitting their return to Palestine. Consequently the land of exile continued to be the home of Jews for generations to come.

Biblical sources deal primarily with the exiles who returned to their homeland. The memoirs of Ezra and Nehemiah, though brief and selective, present the essential facts concerning the welfare of the restored Jewish state in Jerusalem. Esther, the only Old Testament book devoted exclusively to the fortunes of Jews who did not return, also belongs to this period. In order to maintain a historical sequence the present study treats the story of Esther along with Ezra-Nehemiah. Chronologically this material falls into four periods: (1) Jerusalem re-established, Ezra 1–6 (*ca.* 539–515 B.C.); (2) Esther the Queen, Esth. 1–10 (*ca.* 483); (3) Ezra the Reformer, Ezra 7–10 (*ca.* 457); (4) Nehemiah the Governor, Neh. 1–13 (*ca.* 444).

Jerusalem Re-established

Facing opposition and hardships in Judea, Jews who had returned were not at once able to complete the building of the Temple. Approximately twenty-three years elapsed before they attained their primary objective. The account as given in Ezra 1:1–6:22 may conveniently be subdivided as follows:

I. Return from Babylon to Jerusalem	1:1–2:70
The edict by Cyrus	1:1–4

The preparation	1:5–11
The list of emigrants	2:1–70
II. Settlement at Jerusalem	3:1–4:24
The altar erected—worship instituted	3:1–3
Feast of Tabernacles observed	3:4–7
Temple foundation laid	3:8–13
Cessation of building	4:1–24
(Opposition in later times)	4:6–23
III. The new Temple	5:1–6:22
Leaders stirred to action	5:1–2
Appeal to Darius	5:3–17
The royal decree	6:1–12
Temple completed	6:13–15
Temple dedicated	6:16–18
Feasts instituted	6:19–22

Return from Babylon

When Cyrus entered the city of Babylon in 539 he claimed that he had been sent by Marduk, the chief of Babylonian gods, who was looking for a righteous prince.[1] Consequently the occupation of Babylon occurred without a battle or the destruction of the city. Immediately Cyrus announced a policy which was the exact reversal of the ruthless practice of displacing conquered peoples. Beginning with Tiglath-pileser III (745 B.C.) the Assyrian kings had terrorized subjugated nations by removing them to distant lands. Subsequently the Babylonians had followed the Assyrian example. Cyrus, on the other hand, publicly proclaimed that displaced people could return to their homelands and worship their gods in their own sanctuaries.[2]

Two copies of Cyrus' proclamation for the Jews are preserved in the Book of Ezra. The first account (1:2–4) is in Hebrew while the second (6:3–5) is given in Aramaic. A recent study indicates that the latter represents a "dikrona," an official Aramaic term denoting an oral decree by a ruler.[3] This was not intended for publication but served as a memorandum for the proper official to initiate legal action. Ezra 6:2 indicates that the Aramaic copy was located in the government files in Ecbatana, the summer residence of Cyrus in 538 B.C.

The Hebrew document was prepared for publication to the exiled Is-

[1] Parker and Dubberstein, *Babylonian Chronology 626 B.C.–A.D. 45*, p. 11. Robert W. Rogers, *Cuneiform Parallels to the Old Testament* (New York, 1912), p. 381.

[2] For a copy of this general proclamation see Pritchard, *Ancient Near Eastern Texts*, p. 316.

[3] Elias J. Bickerman, "The Edict of Cyrus in Ezra 1," *JBL*, LXV (1946), 249–275. Cf. E. Meyer, *Entstehung des Judenthums* (Halle: Niemeyer, 1896), pp. 8 ff.

raelites. In Jewish communities throughout the empire it was verbally announced in the Hebrew language. Adapting it to their religion, the Persian king claimed that he was commissioned by the Lord God of heaven to build a temple at Jerusalem. Accordingly he was allowing the Jews to return to the land of Judah. He encouraged those who remained to support the emigrants with offerings of gold, silver, beasts, and other supplies for the reestablishment of the Jerusalem Temple. Even as Cyrus had acknowledged Marduk when he entered Babylon, so here he gave recognition to the God of the Jews. Although this may have been only a matter of political expediency on his part, he nevertheless fulfilled Isaiah's prediction that after their exile God would use Cyrus to bring the Jews back to their own land (Is. 45:1–4).

In response to this proclamation thousands of exiles prepared to return. Cyrus ordered his treasurer to restore to the Jews the vessels that Nebuchadnezzar had taken from Jerusalem.[4] These vessels were entrusted to Sheshbazzar, a prince of Judah, who was responsible for transporting them.[5] Unique among the nations, the Jews had no statue of their God to be restored, although this provision was included in the general decree made by Cyrus.[6] The ark of the covenant, which was the most sacred object Israel possessed, had undoubtedly been lost in the destruction of Jerusalem. With the approval and official support of the king of Persia the exiles successfully made the long, hazardous trek to Jerusalem intent on rebuilding the Temple that had been in ruins for approximately fifty years. Although the exact date of this return is not given, it most likely occurred in 538 B.C. or possibly the following year.

According to the record in Ezra 2, approximately 50,000 exiles returned to Jerusalem.[7] Of the eleven leaders named, Zerubbabel and Joshua (Jeshua) appear to have been the most active in guiding the people in their attempt to restore order out of the chaotic conditions. The former, being the grandson of Jehoiachin, represented the house of David in political leadership. The latter served as the high priest officiating in religious matters.

[4] For a discussion of the textual problems that exist regarding the number of vessels restored, Ezra 1: 9–11, see *Commentary* by C. F. Keil at reference.

[5] Sheshbazzar is identified by Wright, *Biblical Archaeology,* p. 202, as "Shenassar" mentioned in I Chron. 3:18 as a son of Jehoiachin. Keil in *Commentary* on Ezra 1:8 suggests that Sheshbazzar is the Chaldean name for Zerubbabel. *Harper's Bible Dictionary* equates these two names by suggesting that the former is a cryptogram for the latter. In Ezra 5:14 Sheshbazzar is identified as the governor and in 5:16 is credited with laying the foundation of the Temple.

[6] Note the boast by Cyrus that he restored foreign gods to their sanctuaries. J. B. Pritchard, *op. cit.,* pp. 315–316.

[7] Albright, *The Biblical Period,* p. 62, note 122, interprets this figure to represent the total population in Judah at the time of Nehemiah in 444 B.C. Ezra 2 represents this as the total number that returned from Babylonian captivity. Nehemiah found this list when he returned, Neh. 7:5.

Settlement at Jerusalem

By the seventh month of the year of their return the people were sufficiently settled in the environs of Jerusalem to gather en masse to build the altar of the God of Israel and re-establish the burnt offerings as prescribed by Moses (Ex. 29:38 ff.). On the fifteenth day of this month they observed the Feast of Booths or Tabernacles according to the written requirements (Lev. 23:34 ff.). With these impressive festivities worship was restored at Jerusalem so that the new moon and other appointed feasts followed in due season. Upon the restoration of worship the people provided money and produce for the masons and carpenters who negotiated with the Phoenicians for building materials in accordance with the permission granted by Cyrus.

Construction of the Temple began in the second month of the next year under the supervision of Zerubbabel and Joshua. Levites twenty years of age and older served as overseers. The foundation of the Temple was laid during an appropriate ceremony with the priests robed in vestments serving as trumpeteers. According to directions given by David, king of Israel, the sons of Asaph offered praises accompanied by cymbals. Apparently there was antiphonal singing in which one choir sang "Praise the Lord for he is good," while the other responded with "And his mercy endureth forever."[8] Thereupon the assembled multitude joined in triumphant praise. But not all shouted for joy; older people who could still remember the glory and beauty of Solomon's Temple wept bitterly and unashamedly.

When the officials of Samaria learned of the reconstruction in Jerusalem they attempted to interfere, for they apparently regarded Judah as part of their province. Claiming that they had worshiped the same God ever since the time that Esarhaddon (681–668 B.C.) had placed them in Palestine, they requested Zerubbabel and other leaders to let them participate in the building of the Temple. When their request was denied they became openly hostile and adopted a policy of frustrating and discouraging the struggling colony. They successfully hindered work on the Temple throughout the rest of the reign of Cyrus and the reign of Cambyses, even until the second year of the reign of Darius (520 B.C.).

Inserted in the Ezra narrative at this point is the report of subsequent opposition. Ezra 4:6–23 is the account of enemy interference during the days of Ahasuerus or Xerxes (485–465) and the reign of Artaxerxes (464–424). The foreigners, settled in the cities of Samaria, appealed to Artaxerxes to investigate the historical records concerning the rebellions and seditions that had taken place at Jerusalem in times past. As a result a royal decree empowered Samaritan leaders to stop the Jews in their effort to rebuild the city

[8] Although Keil, in *Commentary* on Ezra 3:11, maintains that the text does not require this interpretation, he quotes Clericus and others who favored it.

of Jerusalem. Since Nehemiah came to Jerusalem in 444 B.C., authorized by Artaxerxes to rebuild the walls, it is likely that this decree favoring the Samaritans was issued in the early years of his reign, presumably prior to the coming of Ezra in 457 B.C.[9]

The New Temple

In the second year of Darius (520 B.C.) the Jews resumed work on the Temple. Haggai, with God's message for the occasion, stirred up the people and leaders by reminding them that they had become so absorbed in building their own houses that they had neglected the place of worship.[10] In less than a month's time Zerubbabel and Joshua led the people in a renewed effort to rebuild the Temple (Hag. 1:1–15). Shortly thereafter the prophet Zechariah collaborated with Haggai in stimulating the building program (Zech. 1:1).

Resumption of building activities in Jerusalem immediately caught the attention of Tattenai, the satrap of Syria, and his colleagues who represented the interests of Persia in this area. Although they came to Jerusalem to make a thorough investigation, they deferred action while awaiting the verdict of Darius. In a letter addressed to the Persian king they reported their findings concerning the past and present developments regarding the erection of the Temple. They were primarily concerned with the Jewish claim that Cyrus had granted permission to build the Temple.

Following this lead Darius ordered a search in the archives at Babylonia and Ecbatana, capital of Media. In the latter a dikrona was found noting in Aramaic the edict of Cyrus. Besides verifying this decree Darius issued strict orders forbidding Tattenai and his associates to interfere. In addition, he commanded that royal revenue from the province of Syria should be allotted to the Jews for their building program. He also instructed them to provide an adequate supply of daily sacrifices so that the priests at Jerusalem might intercede for the welfare of the Persian king. Consequently Tattenai's inquiry, which was intended to be injurious, providentially resulted in providing not only the political support of Darius but also the material aid from the immediate district officials for the project.

The Temple was completed in five years, 520–515 B.C. Although erected

[9] For a thorough discussion regarding the date of this opposition see publication by H. H. Rowley entitled "Nehemiah's Mission and Its Background" appearing in the *Bulletin of the John Rylands Library,* 37, No. 2 (March, 1955), 528–561. He dates this opposition shortly before Nehemiah's return in 444 and Ezra's return subsequent to the coming of Nehemiah.

[10] Albright regards Haggai and Zechariah as opportunists who took advantage of the rebellions throughout the Persian Empire following the accession of Darius Hystaspes in 522. Two months prior to Haggai's initial message a man named Nebuchadnezzar led a Babylonian rebellion, which still appeared successful when Haggai delivered his fourth message two months later. *The Biblical Period* (Pittsburgh, 1950), pp. 49–50.

on the same site it could not have equaled in beauty or workmanship the structure built by Solomon after David's elaborate preparation with his unequaled resources. On the basis of I Macc. 1:21 and 4:49–51 it is apparent that the furnishings were inferior. In the holy place were the altar of incense, the table of shewbread, and a seven-branched candelabrum (Solomon in his day had lavishly provided ten candelabra). The ark of the covenant was missing in the most holy place. Josephus indicates that each year on the Day of Atonement the high priest placed his censer on the slab of stone that marked the former position of the ark.[11]

Parrot in his studies on the Temple concludes that the plans of Solomon's sanctuary were most probably followed by Zerubbabel.[12] Sparse references in Ezra and the Maccabean books can at best serve only as suggestions. According to Ezra 5:8 and 6:3–4, large stones with timber joists were used in construction of the walls. The measurements given are incomplete in the present text. A recent interpretation of a decree by Antiochus III of Syria (223–187 B.C.) indicates the existence of an inner and an outer court.[13] Everyone was admitted to the latter court but only Jews who had conformed to the Levitical purity laws were allowed to enter the inner court.[14] Rooms were also provided in the courts for the storage of various offerings as well as vessels used in the Temple. One of these rooms was appropriated by the Ammonite Tobiah for a short period during Nehemiah's time (Neh. 13:4–9).

The dedication ceremonies for this temple must have been impressive.[15] Elaborate offerings consisted of 100 bulls, 200 rams, 400 lambs, and a sin offering of 12 he-goats representing the twelve tribes of Israel. The last offering signified that this worship represented the entire nation with whom the covenant was made. With this dedication service the priests and Levites initiated their regular services in the sanctuary as prescribed for them in the law of Moses.

The next month the Jews observed the Passover. With proper purification ceremonies the priests and Levites were prepared to officiate at the celebration of this historic observance. The priests thus were qualified to sprinkle the blood while the Levites killed the lambs for the whole congregation. Al-

[11] *Jewish Wars,* v. 5, 5.

[12] André Parrot, *The Temple of Jerusalem,* trans. by B. E. Hooke from the French (London: SMC Press, 1957), pp. 68–75.

[13] See *ibid.,* p. 73, where he refers to the study by E. Bickerman, "Une proclamation seleucide relative au Temple de Jerusalem," in *Syria,* XXV (1946–48), 67–85.

[14] Note also the vague references to temple courts in I Mac. 4:38, 48; 7:33; 9:54; II Macc. 6:4.

[15] The Temple was completed on the third day of the month of Adar, which begins in the middle of February. This was the last month of the Hebrew religious year. The first month of the year was Nisan, which begins with the middle of March. The 14th day of this month was the date for the Passover. Formerly this month was known as Abib, Ex. 13:3.

though originally the head of each family killed the Passover lamb (Ex. 12:6), the Levites had been assigned this duty on a community basis from the days of Josiah (II Chron. 30:17) when many of the laity were not qualified to do so. In this way the Levites also lightened the strenuous duties of the priests as they offered the sacrifices and sprinkled the blood (II Chron. 35:11–14).

Israelites who were still living in Palestine joined the returned exiles in this joyous celebration. By separating themselves from the heathen practices to which they had succumbed, these Israelites renewed their allegiance to God as they worshiped in the Temple.

The dedication of the Temple and the observance of the Passover in the spring of 515 B.C. marked a historic crisis in Jerusalem. The hopes of the exiles had been realized in re-establishing the Temple as their place of worship. At the same time they were reminded by the Passover of Israel's redemption from Egyptian bondage. In addition they enjoyed the reality of restoration from Babylonian exile.

The Story of Esther

The biblical record is almost completely silent concerning the Jewish state at Jerusalem from the time of the completion of the Temple in the sixth year of Darius (515 B.C.) to the reign of Artaxerxes I beginning in 464 B.C. The story of Esther constitutes the main biblical source for this period. Historically it is identified with the reign of Ahasuerus, or Xerxes (485–465 B.C.) and is restricted to the welfare of the exiles who did not return to Jerusalem.[16]

Although the name of God is not mentioned in the Book of Esther, divine providence and supernatural care are apparent throughout. Fasting is recognized as a religious practice. The feast of Purim commemorating the deliverance of the Jews finds a reasonable explanation when the events in Esther are recognized as the historical background. The reference to this feast in II Macc. 15:36 as the day of Mordecai indicates that it was observed in the second century B.C. In the days of Josephus Purim was celebrated for a whole week (*Antiquities* xi. 6:13).

The Book of Esther may be outlined as follows:

I. Jews at the Persian court	1:1–2:23
Vashti removed by Ahasuerus	1:1–22
Esther chosen as queen	2:1–18
Mordecai saves the king's life	2:19–23

[16] For a brief treatment of the story of Esther as "historical fiction" see the article entitled "Esther" in *Harper's Bible Dictionary*, p. 174. Ira M. Price, *The Dramatic Story of Old Testament History* (New York: Fleming H. Revell Company, 1929), pp. 385–388, recognizes its historicity.

II. The threat to the Jewish people	3:1–5:14
Haman's plot to destroy the Jews	3:1–15
The Jews fear annihilation	4:1–3
Mordecai alerts Esther	4:4–17
Esther risks her life	5:1–14
III. The triumph of the Jews	6:1–10:3
Mordecai receives royal honor	6:1–11
Esther intercedes—Haman hanged	6:12–7:10
Mordecai promoted	8:1–17
Revenge by the Jews	9:1–15
The feast of Purim	9:16–32
Mordecai continues in high honor	10:1–3

Shushan (or Susa), the capital of Persia, is the geographical point of interest in the Book of Esther. Since the days of Cyrus it had shared the distinction of being a royal city like Babylon and Ecbatana. The magnificent palace of Xerxes occupied two and a half acres of the acropolis of this great Elamite city. Chronologically the events of Esther are dated in the third to twelfth years of Xerxes (*ca.* 483–471 B.C.).

Jews at the Persian Court

From his vast empire extending from India to Ethiopia Xerxes assembled the governors and officials to Susa for a six months' period during the third year of his reign. In a climactic seven-day celebration he entertained them in drinking and banqueting while Queen Vashti was hostess at a banquet for the women. On the seventh day Xerxes, while intoxicated, demanded the appearance of Vashti to display her crown and beauty before his festive audience of government dignitaries. She ignored the orders of the king, refusing to hazard her royal prestige. Xerxes was furious! He conferred with his wise men, who advised him to dismiss the queen. The king acted upon this advice and banished Vashti from the royal court. Women throughout the empire were advised to honor their husbands lest they follow the example of Vashti.

When Xerxes realized that Vashti had been permanently ostracized by his royal edict, he arranged for the selection of a new queen. Maidens were chosen throughout the Persian Empire and brought to the court of the king at Susa. Among them was Esther, a Jewish orphan who had been adopted by her cousin Mordecai. In due time, when the virgins appeared before the king, Esther, who had concealed her racial identity, was favored above all others and crowned queen of Persia. In the seventh year of Xerxes' reign she received public acknowledgment at a royal banquet before the princes.[17]

[17] The interval between Vashti's dismissal in the third year and Esther's recognition

The king displayed his pleasure over the recognition of Esther as queen by announcing tax reductions and liberally distributing gifts.

Prior to Esther's elevation Mordecai expressed his deep concern over the welfare of his cousin by lingering near the royal court. Likewise he maintained his close contact with Esther after she became queen. Thus it happened that Mordecai, while loitering at the palace gate, learned that two guards were conspiring to kill the king. Through Esther the plot was reported to proper authorities and the culprits were hanged. In the official chronicle Mordecai was credited with saving the king's life.

Threat to the Jewish People

Haman, an influential member of Xerxes' court, was advanced in rank above all his associates. In conformity with the king's command he was duly honored by everyone except Mordecai, who as a Jew refused to do obeisance.[18] Although Haman was incensed he did not dare to single Mordecai out for punishment. However, Haman knew that Mordecai was a Jew and therefore developed plans for the execution of all the Jewish people. He diplomatically appealed to the king for the execution of the Jews. Not only did he cast suspicion on them as being dangerous to the empire but he assured the king of enormous financial gain through the confiscation of their property. The king promptly granted the request and gave Haman the signet ring to seal the order. Consequently on the thirteenth day of Nisan (the first month) an edict was issued for the annihilation of the Jews throughout the Persian Empire. Haman designated the thirteenth of Adar (the twelfth month) as the date of execution.[19]

Wherever this decree was made public the Jews responded with fasting and mourning. When Mordecai himself appeared at the palace gate in sackcloth and ashes, Esther dispatched a new suit of clothes to him. He refused the offer and alerted Esther concerning the plight of the Jews. When Esther spoke of the personal danger that was involved in approaching the king without an invitation, Mordecai suggested that she had been entrusted with the position of queen for just such an opportunity as this. Thereupon Esther resolved to risk her life for her people and requested that they give themselves to fasting for three days.

---

as queen in the seventh year is explained by the fact that Xerxes was engaged in fighting the Greeks. In 480 B.C. his navy was defeated at Salamis. The next year his army met reverses at Plataea.

[18] See Keil, *Commentary* on Esth. 3:3–4. As a devout Jew Mordecai did not conform. According to II Sam. 14:4, 18:28, and other passages, Israelites customarily acknowledge kings by bowing. In Persia such an act may have involved an acknowledgment of the ruler as divine. Spartans, according to Herodotus, refused to honor Xerxes in this fashion.

[19] The explanation in Esth. 3:7 equates casting Pur with casting the lot. For the archaeological significance of the Pur or "die" found at Susa by M. Dieulafoy see Ira M. Price, *The Monuments and the Old Testament* (Philadelphia, 1925), p. 408.

On the third day Esther made her appeal to the king. She invited the king and Haman to dinner. On this occasion she did not make known her real concern but simply requested that the king and Haman return for another dinner engagement the next day. On his way home Haman was again infuriated when Mordecai refused to bow before him. To his wife and a group of friends he boastfully reported all the royal honors accorded him but indicated that all the joys of promotion were dissipated by the attitude of Mordecai. Upon their advice to have Mordecai hanged Haman immediately ordered the erection of gallows for the execution.

Triumph of the Jews

That same night Xerxes could not fall asleep. His sleeplessness may have evoked a feeling that something had been left undone. At any rate he had the royal chronicles read to him. Immediately after he learned to his surprise that Mordecai had never been rewarded for exposing the plot of the palace guards, Haman arrived at the court hoping to secure the king's approval for the execution of Mordecai. The king immediately asked Haman what should be done for a man whom the king wished to honor. Haman, fully confident that he himself would be the recipient, recommended that such a one should be arrayed in royal robes, escorted by a noble prince through the open square of the city on the king's horse, and proclaimed by a high official as the king's choice for special recognition and honor. Shocked indeed was Haman when the king ordered him to escort Mordecai in the manner he had suggested.

Matters were fast coming to a head. At her second banquet Esther hesitated no longer. Courageously in the presence of Haman she implored the king to save her and her people from annihilation. When the king inquired who might have such designs on Esther's people, she forthrightly identified Haman as the culprit. In a rage the king stormed out of the room. Realizing the seriousness of the situation Haman pleaded for his life before the queen. When the king returned he found Haman prostrate on the couch where Esther was seated. Mistaking Haman's intentions Xerxes ordered his execution. Ironically Haman was hanged on the gallows he had prepared for Mordecai.

After Haman's dishonorable decease Mordecai became an influential member of Xerxes' court. The former command to slay the Jews was effectively annulled, of course. Moreover, with the king's approval Mordecai issued a new edict stating that the Jews should avenge themselves of any enemies who might attack them. The Jews were so jubilant at this announcement that many began to fear the consequences. Not a few took up the outward forms of the Jewish religion in order to avoid violence.[20]

The crucial date was the thirteenth of Adar, which Haman had desig-

[20] Dissimulation is still practiced in Iran. Cf. C. H. Gordon, *The World of the Old Testament,* pp. 283–284.

nated for the annihilation of the Jews and the confiscation of their property. In the fighting that broke out thousands of non-Jews were slain. Peace was quickly restored, however, and the Jews instituted an annual celebration to commemorate their deliverance. Purim was the name for this holiday because Haman had determined this date by casting the lot, or Pur.[21]

Ezra the Reformer

Fifty-eight years pass in silence between Ezra 6 and 7. Little is known about events in Jerusalem from the dedication of the Temple (515 B.C.) to the return of Ezra (457 B.C.) in the seventh year of Artaxerxes, king of Persia.[22]

A brief record of Ezra's activities in Jerusalem and the return of the exiles under his leadership is given in Ezra 7:1–10:44. For an analysis of this passage note the following:

I. Return of Ezra	7:1–8:36
Preparation	7:1–10
Decree of Artaxerxes	7:11–28
Organization for return	8:1–30
Journey and arrival	8:31–36
II. Reformation in Jerusalem	9:1–10:44
Problem of mixed marriages	9:1–5
Ezra's prayer	9:6–15
Public assembly	10:1–15
Punishment of the guilty	10:16–44

Chronologically the data given in these chapters do not necessarily cover more than one year. The following seems to be the order of events:

[21] Since its beginning Purim has been one of the most popular observances. After fasting on the 13th day of Adar the Jews would meet in the synagogue in the evening as the 14th day began for the public reading of the Book of Esther. At the mention of Haman they would respond in unison, "Let his name be blotted out." The next morning they would reassemble for the exchange of gifts. See Davis, *Dictionary of the Bible* (4th rev. ed.; Grand Rapids, 1954), p. 639.

[22] Currently there is considerable disagreement about the date of Ezra. Van Hoonacker in the *Journal of Biblical Literature* (1921), pp. 104–124, equated the "seventh year of Artaxerxes" with the year 398 B.C. in the reign of Artaxerxes II. Albright followed this view in *From Stone Age to Christianity* (1940), p. 248. In his second edition (1946, p. 366) he dated Ezra in the 37th year of Artaxerxes, or about 428 B.C. Cf. also *The Biblical Period* (1950), p. 53 and note 133. For an exhaustive survey of the history of this problem and an excellent bibliography see H. H. Rowley, "The Chronological Order of Ezra and Nehemiah," in *The Servant of the Lord and Other Essays on the Old Testament* (London: Lutterworth Press, 1952), pp. 131–159. Although he favors a later date for Ezra, he admits that the majority of scholars still date Ezra before Nehemiah, p. 132.

Nisan (first month)

1–3 encampment by the river Ahava

4–11 preparation for the journey

12 beginning of journey to Jerusalem

Ab (fifth month)

1st day of this month they arrive in Jerusalem

Kislev (ninth month)

public assembly called in Jerusalem after Ezra is informed about mixed marriages

Tabeth (tenth month)

beginning of examination of guilty parties and ending of the 1st day of Nisan

Return of Ezra

Among the exiles in Babylonia Ezra, a pious Levite of the Aaronic family, devoted himself to the study of Torah. His interest in mastering the law of Moses found expression in a teaching ministry to his people. Always eager to return to Palestine Ezra appealed to Artaxerxes for approval of his return movement. To encourage exiles to return to Jerusalem under Ezra's leadership, the Persian king issued a significant decree (Ezra 7:11–26), commissioning Ezra to appoint magistrates and judges in the Jewish province. In addition, Ezra was empowered to confiscate property and imprison or execute anyone who did not conform.

Artaxerxes made most generous financial provisions for Ezra's mission. Generous royal contributions, freewill offerings contributed by the exiles, and vessels for sacred use were given to Ezra for the Jerusalem Temple. Artaxerxes had such confidence in Ezra that he gave him a blank check on the royal treasury for anything he deemed necessary for temple service. Provincial rulers beyond the Euphrates were ordered to supply Ezra with food and money lest the royal family incur the wrath of Israel's God. Furthermore, all those engaged in temple service at Jerusalem—singers, servants, doorkeepers, and priests—were exempt from taxation.

Acknowledging God's favor and encouraged by the wholehearted support of Artaxerxes, Ezra assembled the leading men of Israel on the banks of the river Ahava on the first day of Nisan.[23] When Ezra noticed that the Levites were conspicuously absent, he appointed a delegation to appeal to Iddo at Casiphia.[24] In response 40 Levites and 220 temple servants joined the migration party. Before the Jerusalem-bound company of approximately

[23] Ahava was either a river or a canal in Babylonia, undoubtedly near the Euphrates, which has never been specifically identified in modern times.

[24] Casiphia very likely was a center of Jewish exiles, possibly in the vicinity of Babylon but not identifiable at present.

1,800 men and their families Ezra candidly confessed that he was ashamed to ask the king for police protection. In fasting and prayer they appealed to God for divine protection as they began the long and treacherous trek of nearly a thousand miles to Jerusalem.

The journey began on the twelfth day of Nisan. Three and a half months later, on the first day of Ab, they arrived in Jerusalem. After the priests and Levites checked the treasures and vessels from Babylon into the Temple the returning exiles offered elaborate offerings in the court. In due time satraps and governors throughout Syria and Palestine assured Ezra of their aid and support for the Jewish state.

Reformation in Jerusalem

A local committee of officials reported to Ezra that Israelites were guilty of intermarriage with heathen inhabitants. Even religious and civil leaders were among the participants. Ezra not only tore his garments to signify his deep grief but pulled his hair to express his moral indignation and wrath. Shocked and stunned he sat in the Temple court while people who feared the consequences gathered around him. At the time of the evening sacrifice he rose from his fasting and with torn garments knelt in prayer, audibly confessing Israel's sin.

A great crowd joined Ezra as he prayed and wept publicly. Shecaniah, speaking for the people, suggested that there was hope for them in a new covenant and assured Ezra of full support in removing these social evils. Immediately Ezra exacted an oath of conformity from the leaders.

Withdrawing to the chamber of Johanan for the night,[25] Ezra continued in fasting, prayer, and mourning over the sinfulness of his people. By proclamation throughout the land the people were urged, under the threat of excommunication and the forfeiture of their property, to assemble in Jerusalem in three days. On the twentieth day of the month of Kislev they met in the open square before the Temple.

Ezra addressed the trembling congregation and impressed upon them the seriousness of their offense. When they expressed their willingness to conform he agreed to let the officials represent them so that the congregation could be dismissed, since it was the rainy season. Assisted by a select group of men and aided by representatives from various parts of the Jewish state Ezra conducted a three-month examination of the guilty parties.

An impressive list of priests, Levites, and laity, totaling 114, was guilty

[25] Keil in his *Commentary* on Ezra 10:6 concurs with Ewald that nothing further is known about Johanan the son of Eliashib since both of these names were quite common. This chamber may have been named after Eliashib mentioned in I Chron. 24:12. Those who date Ezra in a later period identify this reference with Eliashib, who served as priest in 432 when Nehemiah returned the second time to Jerusalem, and Johanan, who succeeded his father as priest. See Albright, *The Biblical Period,* p. 64, note 133.

of intermarriage. Among the eighteen guilty priests were close relatives of Joshua, the high priest, who had returned with Zerubbabel. In fact a comparison of Ezra 10:18–22 with 2:36–39 indicates that none of the orders of returning priests were free of intermarriage. Sacrificing a ram for a guilt offering the guilty parties made a solemn pledge to annul their marriages.

Nehemiah the Governor

The historicity of Nehemiah has never been questioned by any competent scholar.[26] Emerging as one of the most colorful figures in the postexilic era he served his people effectively from the year 444 B.C. He forfeited his position at the Persian court to serve his own nation in the rebuilding of Jerusalem. His physical handicap as a eunuch became an asset in devoted service and distinguished leadership during the years that he was active governor of the Jewish state.[27]

Ezra had been in Jerusalem thirteen years when Nehemiah arrived. While the former was a learned scribe and teacher, the latter demonstrated strong aggressive leadership in civic and political affairs. The successful rebuilding of the walls in spite of enemy opposition[28] provided security for the returned exiles so that they could devote themselves, under Ezra's leadership, to the religious responsibilities as prescribed in the law. In this way the governorship of Nehemiah provided the most favorable conditions for the enlarged ministry of Ezra.

The chronological data given in Nehemiah allots twelve years to Nehemiah's first term as governor, beginning in the twentieth year of Artaxerxes (444 B.C.). In the twelfth year of this term (Neh. 13:6) Nehemiah returned to Persia (432). How soon he returned to Jerusalem or how long he continued as governor is not indicated.

The events related in Neh. 1–12 could all have occurred during the first year of his leadership.[29] On the first day of the first month, Nisan (444 B.C.), Nehemiah was granted his request to go to Jerusalem (Neh. 2:1). Being a man of decisive action he undoubtedly left shortly after this. The reparation of the walls was completed in Elul, the sixth month (Neh. 6:15). Since this project was begun a few days after his arrival and completed in

[26] Albright, *The Biblical Period,* p. 51.

[27] R. Kittel, *Geschichte des Volkis Israel,* Vol. III, pt. 2, pp. 614 f.

[28] In 408 B.C. the Jews from Elephantine appealed to Bagoas as Persian governor of Judah. When he began or who preceded him is not known. See Cowley, *Aramaic Papyri,* p. 108, or Pritchard, *Ancient Near Eastern Texts,* pp. 491–492.

[29] Albright outlines the chronology for Nehemiah briefly as follows: Hanani's visit in December, 445; Nehemiah's arrival in Jerusalem, 440; reparation of walls begun in 439 and finished in 437. Cf. *The Biblical Period,* pp. 51–52, notes 126 and 127. Albright follows Mowinckel, *Statholderen Nehemia* (Kristiania, 1916), in preferring the chronological data of Josephus to those given in the Hebrew text.

fifty-two days, the time allowed for his preparation and journey is about four months. During the seventh month (Tishri) Nehemiah fully co-operated with Ezra in the religious observances (Neh. 7–10), continued his registration and very likely dedicated the walls in the period immediately following (Neh. 11–12). Except for a few statements that summarize the policies of Nehemiah, the reader is left with the impression that all these developments occurred within the first year after his return.

The Book of Nehemiah lends itself to the following subdivisions:

I. Commissioned by Artaxerxes	1:1–2:8
Report from Jerusalem	1:1–3
Nehemiah's prayer	1:4–11
Favor with the king	2:1–8
II. The Jerusalem mission	2:9–6:19
Successful journey	2:9–10
Inspection and appraisal	2:11–16
Opposition—Sanballat and Tobiah	2:17–20
Organized for building and defense	3:1–32
Success in building and defense	4:1–23
Economic policy	5:1–19
Completion of the walls	6:1–19
III. Reformation under Ezra	7:1–10:39
Nehemiah plans registration	7:1–73
Reading of the law of Moses	8:1–12
The Feast of Tabernacles	8:13–18
Worship service	9:1–5
The prayer	9:6–38
Covenant to keep the law	10:1–39
IV. Nehemiah's program and policies	11:1–13:31
Register of the Jewish state	11:1–12:26
Dedication of the wall	12:27–43
Temple assignments	12:44–47
Reading of the law	13:1–3
Tobiah expelled	13:4–9
Levite support reinstated	13:10–14
Sabbath commerce restricted	13:15–22
Mixed marriages	13:23–29
Summary	13:30–31

Commissioned by Artaxerxes

Among the thousands of Jewish exiles who had not returned to Judah was Nehemiah. In his quest for success he had been especially fortunate in rising to high rank among the Persian court officials, being cupbearer to Artaxerxes Longimanus. Living in the treasure city of Susa about a hundred miles northeast of the Persian Gulf he was comfortably situated in Persia's capital. When the report came to him that the walls of Jerusalem were still in ruins Nehemiah was grief-stricken. For days he mourned as he fasted, wept, and prayed for his people in Jerusalem.

The prayer recorded in Neh. 1:5–11 represents the essence of Nehemiah's intercession during this period of mourning. It reflects his familiarity with Israel's history, the covenant at Mount Sinai, the law given to Moses, which had been broken by Israel, and the promise of restoration for repentant exiles. Nehemiah acknowledged the God of the covenant as the God of heaven—appealing to him to be merciful to Israel. In conclusion he asked that God might grant him favor with the king of Persia, his master.

After three months of prayerful concern Nehemiah was faced with a golden opportunity. As he was waiting on Artaxerxes the king noticed that he was extremely sad. To his master's inquiry Nehemiah in fear and trembling expressed his grief over the chaotic condition of Jerusalem. When Artaxerxes graciously asked him to state his desires Nehemiah quickly uttered a silent prayer and boldly requested that the king send him to rebuild Jerusalem, the city of his fathers' sepulchers. The king of Persia not only duly authorized Nehemiah to go on this mission but issued letters on his behalf sending orders to the governors beyond the Euphrates to supply him with building materials for the walls and gates of the city as well as his own private home.

The Jerusalem Mission

Nehemiah's arrival at Jerusalem complete with army officers and cavalry alarmed the surrounding governors. Accompanied by a small committee, Nehemiah promptly made a nocturnal tour of the city inspecting the condition of the walls. He then gathered the people and confronted them with the proposal to rebuild the walls. Enthusiastically they rallied to his support. As an efficient organizer Nehemiah assigned the people to various gates and sections of the walls of Jerusalem (3:1–32).

Such sudden and intensive activity aroused opposition from surrounding provinces. Influential leaders, such as Sanballat the Horonite, Tobiah the Ammonite, and Geshem the Arab, charged the Jews with rebellion as soon as the work began.[30] When they realized that the reparation project

[30] Sanballat is mentioned in the *Aramaic Papyri* written by the Jews at Elephantine who appealed to the sons of Sanballat for aid in 407 B.C. This makes Sanballat a contemporary of Nehemiah. See Cowley, *op. cit.* The name Tobiah, cut in a rock in Aramaic script near Amman, Jordan, dates back to about 400 B.C. This may actually refer to Tobiah the enemy of Nehemiah. Cf. Albright, *Archaeology of Palestine and the Bible,* pp. 171, 222.

was progressing rapidly they were enraged to the point of organizing resistance. Consequently Sanballat and Tobiah, supported by the Arabs, the Ammonites, and the Ashdodites, made plans to attack Jerusalem.

By this time the wall was completed to half its height. Nehemiah not only prayed but assigned guards day and night. Along the lowest parts of the wall guard duty was allotted to various families. Upon the realization that the enemies were frustrated in their scheme by this efficient and effective guard system the Jews resumed their building efforts. One half of the people continued the repairs with sword in readiness while the other half remained on active guard duty. Furthermore, at the sound of the trumpet, everyone was under orders to rush immediately to the point of danger to resist enemy attack. None of the laborers were allowed to leave Jerusalem. They worked from dawn to dark and remained on guard during the night.

This intensive effort to complete the reparation was especially difficult for the poorer classes of people. Economically they found it hard to pay taxes, interest, and support their families while helping to rebuild the walls. Some even faced the prospects of enslaving their children in lieu of their mounting debts. Immediately Nehemiah called a public assembly and exacted a promise from the offenders to return to the needy people that which had been taken. Interest payments were canceled. As administrator Nehemiah himself set the example. He did not collect from the people his gubernatorial allowance in food and money during the twelve years of his first term as his predecessors had done. In addition, 150 Jews and officials who frequented Jerusalem were guests at Nehemiah's table without charge. Neither had he nor his servants acquired mortgages on land by the loan of money and corn as they helped the needy. In this way Nehemiah effectively solved the economic crisis during the crucial days of reparation.

When the enemies of the Jews heard that the walls were nearing completion in spite of their opposition they devised plans to ensnare Nehemiah. Four times Sanballat and Geshem invited him to meet them in one of the villages in the vale of Ono. Suspecting that they had evil intentions Nehemiah declined the invitation, giving the reasonable excuse that he was too busy. The fifth overture was an open letter from Sanballat charging Nehemiah with plans for rebellion and personal ambition to be king. With the warning that this would be reported to the king of Persia, Sanballat urged Nehemiah to join them in a meeting to discuss the matter. Nehemiah boldly replied to this threat by accusing Sanballat of using his imagination. At the same time he uttered a prayer that God might strengthen him in his responsibility.

The next scheme was to bring reproach on Nehemiah before his own people. Cunningly Sanballat and Tobiah employed a false prophet, Shemaiah, to intimidate and mislead the Jewish governor. When Nehemiah had occasion to call on Shemaiah, who had confined himself to his residence, the false prophet suggested that they take refuge in the Temple.[31] He warned Nehemiah about the plot to kill him. Emphatically Nehemiah said "No!" In the first place he would not flee. Furthermore he would not go into the Temple.[32] Undoubtedly Nehemiah foresaw that such an act would expose him to severe criticism from his own people and perhaps the judgment of God for entering the Temple, since he was not a priest. He fully realized that Shemaiah was a false prophet who had been hired by Sanballat and Tobiah. In prayer Nehemiah expressed his desire that God would not only remember these two enemies of his but also the prophetess Nodiah and other false prophets who tried to intimidate him.

Added to all these problems was the fact that Tobiah and his son Johanan were related to prominent families in Judah. Tobiah's father-in-law, Shecaniah, was the son of Arah, who returned with Zerubbabel (Ezra 2:5). Johanan's father-in-law, Meshullam, was an active participant in rebuilding the walls (Neh. 3:4, 30). Even the high priest Eliashib was allied to Tobiah, although his relationship is not stated. Consequently there was frequent correspondence between Tobiah and these families in Judah. This effective channel of communication made it most difficult for Nehemiah, for his actions and announced plans were constantly reported to Tobiah. Even though Tobiah's relatives gave complimentary reports about his good deeds, Nehemiah knew that Tobiah had nothing but evil intentions toward the people of Jerusalem.

In spite of all this opposition the wall of Jerusalem was completed in fifty-two days.[33] The enemies lost face and surrounding nations were duly impressed, realizing anew that God had favored Nehemiah. The successful termination of Nehemiah's reparation project in the face of enemy opposition established the respect and prestige of the Jewish state among the provinces west of the Euphrates.

[31] "And he was shut up"—Keil, *Commentary* on Neh. 6:10, suggests that Shemaiah confined himself to his home, called for Nehemiah to impress upon him that he himself was in so great a danger that he could not leave home. Hence his advice that they both take refuge in the Temple.

[32] The question Nehemiah asks in 6:11 is ambiguous. Would he actually save his life by going into the Temple or would he be punished by death, according to Num. 18:7? See Keil, *Commentary* on Neh. 6:11.

[33] Josephus, *Antiquities* xi. 5:7 allots two years and four months for the reparation of the walls. Keil, *Commentary* on Neh. 6:15, gives the following reasons in favor of the Hebrew text's allowing only fifty-two days:

1. the urgency to complete the task immediately.
2. the intensive zeal and the large number of builders from Tekoa, Jericho, Gibeon, Mizpah, etc.
3. such a concentrated effort in work and guard duty could hardly have continued for two years.
4. the walls were repaired where needed—large parts of the wall and the gate of Ephraim had not been destroyed.

Albright and others follow Josephus instead of the Hebrew. See Albright, *Biblical Period,* p. 52.

Reformation under Ezra

With Jerusalem securely enclosed Nehemiah turned his attention to other problems. A guard system essential in preventing enemy attack was entrusted to Hanani, the brother of Nehemiah, and Hananiah, who already had charge of the citadel adjoining the Temple area to the north. In addition to the gatekeepers who were responsible for the court Nehemiah recruited singers and Levites, assigning them to the gates and walls of the entire city.

Civilians living within Jerusalem were charged with guard duty during the night at respective parts of the walls near their own homes. Even though ninety years had passed since the city had been resettled, there were areas so sparsely populated that the defense was inadequate. Faced with this problem Nehemiah called for the leaders to register all the people in the province in order to recruit some for settlement in Jerusalem. While contemplating the execution of this plan he found the genealogical register of the people who had returned from the exile in the days of Zerubbabel. With the exception of minor variations, which may be due to clerical or transcriptional errors, this register in Neh. 7:6–73 is identical with the list recorded in Ezra 2:3–67.

Before Nehemiah had opportunity to execute his plans the people began to gather for the religious activities of the seventh month, Tishri, during which the Feast of Trumpets, the Day of Atonement, and the Feast of Tabernacles were observed (Lev. 23:23–43).[34] Nehemiah fully supported the people in their religious devotion—his name appears first on the list of those who signed the covenant (Neh. 10:1). Undoubtedly his administrative program gave precedence to the religious activities during this month and were resumed with renewed effort in the subsequent period. Nehemiah, who was not a priest, recedes into the background during the religious activities, being mentioned only twice in Neh. 8–10.

Ezra, the priest and scribe, emerges as the outstanding religious leader. Coming about thirteen years earlier as a renowned teacher of the law he undoubtedly was well known to all people throughout the province. Although not recorded in Ezra or Nehemiah, it is most reasonable to assume that Ezra had in previous years assembled the people for the observance of the feasts and seasons. This year the people had reason to make it the greatest celebration ever. Behind the closed walls of Jerusalem they could gather in peace and safety without the fear of enemy attack. Undoubtedly the morale of the people must have been strengthened through Nehemiah's successful leadership.

The Feast of Trumpets distinguished the first day of the seventh month

[34] There is no reasonable basis for assuming that Nehemiah gives us a complete account of all the activities. Very likely the Day of Atonement was observed on the 10th of Tishri. The Feast of Trumpets and the Feast of Tabernacles were of special interest that year.

from all other new moons. As the people assembled this year in the Water Gate Square, due south of the Temple court, they unanimously requested Ezra to read the law of Moses. Standing on a wooden platform he read the law to the standing congregation from dawn to midday. To aid the people in their understanding the Levites expounded the law intermittently as Ezra read. When the reading moved the people to tears, Nehemiah, supported by Ezra and the teaching Levites, admonished them to rejoice and make this a festive occasion by sharing the prepared food in common fellowship.

On the second day the family representatives, the priests, and the Levites met with Ezra for careful study of the law. When they realized that God had revealed through Moses that the Israelites were to dwell in booths for observance of the Feast of Tabernacles (Lev. 23:39-43) they instructed the people by public proclamation. With enthusiasm the people went out into the hills and brought in olive, myrtle, and palm branches in abundance, erecting booths everywhere—on the roofs of houses, in private and public courts, and in public squares. So widespread was the participation that this proved to be the outstanding observance of the Feast of Tabernacles since the days of Joshua, who had led Israel in the conquest of Canaan.[35]

The law was publicly read each day during the seven days of this feast (Tishri 15:21). On the eighth day there was a holy convocation and prescribed sacrifices were offered.

After a one-day intermission the people reassembled for prayer and fasting. Ezra and assisting Levites conducted the public services, leading the people in the reading of the law, confession of sin, and the offering of thanks to God. In a long and significant prayer (9:6-37) God's justice and mercy are duly acknowledged.[36]

In a written covenant, signed by Nehemiah and other representatives of the congregation, the people bound themselves by an oath to keep the law of God which had been given by Moses. Two laws were singled out for emphasis: intermarriage with the heathen and the keeping of the Sabbath. The latter not only precluded commercialism on the Sabbath but included the observance of the other feast days and the promise to fallow the ground every seventh year.

The implications of this commitment were realistic and practical. Each individual was obliged to pay annually one third of a shekel for the support of the Temple ministry[37]—this ensured the constant provision of shewbread,

[35] Keil, *Commentary* on Neh. 8:17, suggests that this may simply mean that never before had the whole congregation participated so fully or that the making of booths had never been so enthusiastically demonstrated in previous celebrations. Cf. I Kings 8:65 and Ezra 3:4.

[36] The Hebrew text in Neh. 9:6 does not identify the individual who offered this prayer. The LXX is specific in naming Ezra, which has reasonable confirmation from the context.

[37] The value of one shekel is approximately 65 cents. According to Ex. 30:13, each

the daily and special feast day offerings. Wood for the offerings was requisitioned by lot. The people acknowledged their obligation to give the tithe, the first-fruits, the first born, and other contributions prescribed by the law. While the first-born and the first-fruits were to be brought to the priests at the Temple, the tithe could be collected by the Levites throughout the province and brought by them to the chambers in the Temple. In this way the people made a public commitment not to neglect the house of God.

Nehemiah's Program and Policies

Nehemiah resumed the execution of his plan for increasing the population of Jerusalem, thus ensuring civil defense. He was confident that this was in divine order (Neh. 7:5). Undoubtedly he brought the registration up to date by using the genealogical register from the time of Zerubbabel. By casting lots one tenth of the population was drafted to change their residence to the city of Jerusalem. In this way the sparsely settled areas within the city were sufficiently occupied to provide adequate defense.

The register of those who lived in Jerusalem and surrounding towns (Neh. 11:3-36) represents the population as it was during the days of Ezra and Nehemiah. The residents of Jerusalem are listed under heads of families while the inhabitants throughout the province are merely noted by villages. The register of priests and Levites (Neh. 12:1-26) in part dates back to the time of Zerubbabel and extends to the time of Nehemiah.[38]

The dedication of the walls of Jerusalem involved the entire province. Civil and religious leaders and all other participants were organized into two processions. Headed by Ezra and Nehemiah one proceeded to the right and the other to the left as they marched on the walls of Jerusalem. When the two companies met at the Temple a great service of thanksgiving was conducted with music furnished by an orchestra and choirs. Abundant sacrifices were presented as an expression of joy and thanksgiving. Even women and children shared the joys of this festive occasion as they participated in the feasting that accompanied these offerings. So extensive and joyous was the celebration that the triumphant noise was heard afar.

As an efficient administrator Nehemiah organized the priests and Levites to take care of the tithes and other contributions made by the people (Neh. 12:44 ff.). From various provincial towns these gifts were properly channeled to Jerusalem through responsible Levites so that the priests and Levites could effectively perform their duties.[39] The singers and gatekeepers

---

man twenty years old and up was required to pay half a shekel annually. Keil, *Commentary* on Neh. 10:33, suggests that this was reduced because of the poverty of the returned exiles.

[38] For a comparison and discussion of this list of priests with the list of those who signed the covenant, Neh. 10:3–9, and those who returned from Babylon, Ezra 2:36–39 and Neh. 7:39–42, see Keil, *Commentary* on Neh. 12:1–26.

[39] These events in Neh. 12:44–13:3 may have occurred soon after the dedication and

also received their regular support so that they could serve as prescribed by David and Solomon (II Chron. 8:14). As the people rejoiced in the ministry of the priests and Levites they willingly supported the Temple ministration.

The reading of the book of Moses made them conscious of the fact that the Ammonites and Moabites should not be welcomed into the Jewish assembly.[40] Proper steps were taken to conform to the law.

During his twelfth year as governor of Judah (*ca.* 432 B.C.) Nehemiah made a trip back to Persia. The length of his stay is not indicated but after some time Artaxerxes again granted him leave to return to Jerusalem.

During the time of Nehemiah's absence religious laxity prevailed. Eliashib the high priest had granted Tobiah the Ammonite a chamber in the Temple court. Allowances had not been provided for the Levites and Temple singers. And since the people had neglected to bring in the daily offerings from which the tithe and the first-fruits were allotted to the Levites, the latter went out into the country to make a living.

Nehemiah was indignant when he discovered that the chamber formerly used for storing Levitical provisions had been occupied by Tobiah the Ammonite. Immediately he threw out the furniture, ordered the chambers renovated, restored the vessels, and replaced the meal offerings and the frankincense.

Next the officials were called into account. Boldly Nehemiah charged them with neglect of the Temple by failing to collect the tithe. Men whom he considered trustworthy were then appointed treasurers over the storehouses. The Levites once more received their allotments. Nehemiah again expressed a prayer that God might remember his good deeds toward the Temple and its staff.

Sabbath observance was next on Nehemiah's reform list. Not only did the Jews work and sell on the Sabbath but they also permitted Tyrians residing in Jerusalem to promote business on this day. He warned the nobles of Judah that this was the sin that had precipitated Judah's captivity and the destruction of Jerusalem. In consequence Nehemiah ordered the gates of Jerusalem closed on the Sabbath. He assigned his own servants as guards to stop commercial traffic. A personal warning from Nehemiah even terminated the arrival on the Sabbath of merchants who then awaited the opening of the gates at the end of this holy day. For this he also requested remembrance by God.

Mixed marriages were the last major problem dealt with by Nehemiah. Some of the Jews had intermarried with women from Ashdod, Moab, and

---

the covenant or in the following years. They are representative of the conditions and customs that prevailed during the days of Nehemiah.

[40] The particular passages dealing with this problem are Num. 22:2 ff. and Deut. 23:4–6.

Ammon. Since the children spoke the language of their respective mothers, it is quite probable that these people lived at the extremities of the Jewish state. From these men who had intermarried Nehemiah exacted an oath to desist from such connections and reminded them that even Solomon had been led into sin through foreign wives.

With the grandson of Eliashib the high priest Nehemiah took drastic action. He had married the daughter of Sanballat, governor of Samaria, who had caused Nehemiah no end of trouble during the first year when the Jews repaired the walls of Jerusalem. Nehemiah immediately expelled him from Judah.[41]

With a brief summary of the religious reforms and provisions for proper temple service Nehemiah concludes the account of his activities. Earnestly zealous for the cause of God he utters a final prayer: "Remember me, O my God, for good."

SELECTED READING

ACKROYD, PETER R. *Exile and Restoration.* Philadelphia: Westminster Press, 1968.

———. *Israel Under Babylon and Persia.* London: Oxford University Press, 1970.

———. *Chronicles, Ezra, Nehemiah.* London: SMC, 1973.

BALDWIN, JOYCE G. "Esther" in *The New Bible Commentary: Revised.* D. Guthrie (ed.). Grand Rapids: Wm. B. Eerdmans Publishing Co., 1970.

———. *Esther.* Downers Grove: Inter-Varsity Press, 1984.

BROCKINGTON, L. H. *Ezra, Nehemiah and Esther.* London: Nelson, 1969.

CLINES, D. J. A. *Ezra, Nehemiah, Esther.* Grand Rapids: Wm. B. Eerdmans Publishing Co., 1984.

COGGINS, R. J. *The Books of Ezra and Nehemiah.* New York: Cambridge University Press, 1976.

CONTENAU, G. *Everyday Life in Babylon and Assyria.* London: Edward Arnold, Publishers, Ltd., 1954.

CUNDALL, A. E. "Ezra-Nehemiah" in *The New Bible Commentary: Revised.* D. Guthrie (ed.). Grand Rapids: Wm. B. Eerdmans Publishing Co., 1970.

FENSHAM, F. CHARLES. *The Books of Ezra and Nehemiah.* Grand Rapids: Wm. B. Eerdmans Publishing Co., 1982.

GADD, C. J. *The Fall of Nineveh.* London: The British Museum, 1923.

GETZ, GENE A. "Nehemiah" in *Bible Knowledge Commentary.* Wheaton: Scripture Press, 1985.

[41] The expulsion of Sanballat's son-in-law from Jerusalem may have been the beginning of the rival worship established in Samaria. Since he was the grandson of Eliashib, the high priest in Judah, he may have been instrumental in promoting the building of a temple on Mount Gerizim. Although Josephus, *Antiquities of the Jews* viii. 3, places this a century later, it is quite probable that these developments date back to Nehemiah.

GIRSHMAN, R. *Iran.* Baltimore: Penguin Books, Inc., 1954.

HERZFELD, E. *Archaeological History of Iran.* London: Oxford University Press, 1935.

HOOKE, S. H. *Babylonian and Assyrian Religion.* London: Hutchinson's University Library, 1953.

HUEY, F. B., JR. "Esther" in *Expositor's Bible Commentary,* 4:773–840. Grand Rapids: Zondervan Publishing House, 1988.

KIDNER, DEREK. *Ezra and Nehemiah.* Downers Grove: Inter-Varsity Press, 1979.

MACQUEEN, J. G. *Babylon.* New York: Frederick A. Praeger, 1965.

MARGUERON, JEAN-CLAUDE. *Mesopotamia.* Cleveland: World Publishing Co., 1965.

MARTIN, JOHN A. "Ezra, Esther" in *Bible Knowledge Commentary.* Wheaton: Scripture Press, 1985.

MYERS, J. M. *Ezra-Nehemiah.* The Anchor Bible. Garden City: Doubleday, 1965.

NORTH, R. *Guide to Biblical Iran.* Rome: Pontifical Biblical Inst., 1956.

NOTH, M. *The History of Israel.* New York: Harper & Row, 1958.

OLMSTEAD, A. *The History of the Persian Empire.* Chicago: University of Chicago Press, 1948.

PALLIS, S. A. *The Antiquity of Iraq.* Copenhagen: Munksgaard, 1956.

PARKER, R. A., and W. H. DUBBERSTEIN. *Babylonian Chronology 626 B.C.–A.D. 45.* Chicago: University of Chicago Press, 1942.

ROGERS, R. *A History of Ancient Persia.* New York: Scribner's, 1929.

ROUX, GEORGES. *Ancient Iraq.* Pelican Book, A828, 1966.

SAGGS, H. *Everyday Life in Babylonia and Assyria.* New York: G. P. Putnam's Sons, 1965.

———. *The Greatness That Was Babylon.* London: Sidgwick, 1962.

TURNBULL, R. G. *The Book of Nehemiah.* Grand Rapids: Baker Book House, 1968.

WHITCOMB, JOHN C. *Esther: Triumph of God's Sovereignty.* Chicago: Moody Press, 1979.

WHITLEY, C. *The Exilic Age.* London: Westminster Press, 1957.

WILLIAMSON, H. G. M. *Ezra, Nehemiah.* Waco: Word Books, 1985.

WISEMAN, D. J. *Chronicles of Chaldaean Kings (626–566 B.C.) in the British Museum.* London: British Museum, 1956.

WISEMAN, D. J., and E. YAMAUCHI. *Archaeology and the Bible.* Grand Rapids: Zondervan Publishing House, 1979.

WRIGHT, J. S. *The Building of the Second Temple.* London: The Tyndale Press, 1958.

———. *The Date of Ezra's Coming to Jerusalem.* London: The Tyndale Press, 1946.

YAMAUCHI, EDWIN. *Greece and Babylon.* Grand Rapids: Baker Book House, 1967.

———. "Ezra–Nehemiah" in *Expositor's Bible Commentary.* Vol. 4:563–571. Grand Rapids: Zondervan Publishing House, 1988.

Chapter XVII

Interpretation of Life

Five literary units commonly known as poetical books are: Job, Psalms, Proverbs, Ecclesiastes, and the Song of Songs. None of these could properly be classified as historical or prophetical books. As part of the Old Testament canon they provide additional insight into the life of the Israelites.[1]

The poetical books cannot be dated with certainty. Allusions to historical data are so limited in this literature that the time of composition is relatively insignificant. Nor is the authorship of primary importance. Kings, prophets, philosophers, poets, common people—all are represented among the contributors, many of whom are anonymous.

Reflected in this literature are the problems, experiences, beliefs, philosophies, and attitudes of the Israelites. Such a wide variety of interests are expressed that these writings have well-nigh a universal appeal. The frequent use by the common people throughout the world and the voluminous literature written since Old Testament times indicate that the poetical books deal with problems and truths familiar to all mankind. Notwithstanding the differences in time, culture, and civilization, the basic ideas expressed by the Israelite writers in their interpretation of life are still vitally important to man everywhere.

Job—The Problem of Suffering

Human suffering is the age-old problem discussed in the Book of Job. This question has continued to be one of man's unsolved problems. Nor does the Book of Job provide a final solution. However, significant truths are projected in this extended discussion.

[1] For a more comprehensive analysis of wisdom and Songs of Israel, see C. Hassell Bullock, *An Introduction to the Poetic Books of the Old Testament* (Chicago: Moody Press, 1988).

Regarded as a unit the Book of Job in its present form may be appropriately designated as an epic-drama. Although the main part of the composition is poetical and in the form of a debate, the framework is prose. In the latter the narrative provides the basis for the whole discussion. Neither the date for its historical background nor the time of composition of this book can be ascertained with assurance and the author remains anonymous.

The Book of Job has been recognized as one of the greatest poetic productions of all times. Among the Hebrew writers the author of this book displays the most extensive vocabulary—he is at times referred to as the Shakespeare of Old Testament times. Exhibited in this book are vast resources of knowledge, a superb style of forceful expression, profundity of thought, excellent command of language, noble ideals, a high standard of ethics, and a genuine love for nature. The religious and philosophical ideas have claimed the consideration of the greatest theologians and philosophers down to the present day.

Not only have a multiplicity of interpretations—too numerous for consideration in this volume—been suggested for the Book of Job, but the text itself has suffered considerably from extensive emendations, conjectures, fantastic corrections, and reconstructions.[2] Numerous have been the rearrangements and the speculations concerning its origin.

The beginning reader should consider this book as a unit.[3] Varied interpretations and numerous theories of origin merit investigation by the advanced student, but the simple truth conveyed by this book as a unit is a significant facet of Old Testament revelation. To guide the reader in his understanding of the message this book may be subdivided as follows:

I. Introduction or historical setting	1:1–3:26
II. The dialogue with his three friends	4:1–31:40
A. Cycle one	4:1–14:22
Eliphaz	4:1–5:27
Job	6:1–7:21
Bildad	8:1–22
Job	9:1–10:22
Zophar	11:1–20
Job	12:1–14:22

[2] E. J. Kissane, *The Book of Job* (New York, 1946), p. xli, points out that the indulgence of critics like H. Torczyner, *Das Buch Hiob* (Wien, 1920), who considers Job merely a collection of fragments, conveys a false impression of the state of the Hebrew text of Job. Poetry of the highest order, extensive vocabulary, large proportion of *hapax legomena,* subtle and obscure arguments, repetition of the same opinions in different words—all these led to errors of transcription and translation as the scribes did not fully understand the language.

[3] See Aage Bentzen, *Introduction to the Old Testament,* Vol. II, pp. 174–179, who regards the prose and most of the poetic sections as a unit.

B. Cycle two		15:1–21:34
Eliphaz	15:1–35	
Job	16:1–17:16	
Bildad	18:1–21	
Job	19:1–29	
Zophar	20:1–29	
Job	21:1–34	
C. Cycle three		22:1–31:40
Eliphaz	22:1–30	
Job	23:1–24:25	
Bildad	25:1–6	
Job	26:1–31:40	

III. The speeches of Elihu	32:1–37:24
IV. The speeches of the Almighty	38:1–41:34
V. The conclusion	42:1–17

Job's homeland was the land of Uz.[4] Although specific chronological correlations are lacking, the times in which Job lived seem to fit best into the patriarchal era.[5] The misfortunes of this just man provide the setting for the dialogue that constitutes the major part of the book.

Vividly the man Job is portrayed in three different situations: in times of unprecedented prosperity, extreme poverty, and immeasurable personal suffering. The faith of Job reaches beyond the mundane to an eternal hope. Even though the latter is not clearly delineated, Job does not utterly despair during his crucial time of suffering.

Job is described as a God-fearing individual whose equal was nowhere to be found in the human race (1:1, 8; 2:3; 42:7–8). The high standard of ethics by which he lived was beyond the realization of most men (29–31). Even after his friends had scrutinized his whole pattern of behavior, Job's moral conduct remained beyond reproach.

To begin with, Job was the wealthiest man in the East. Material possessions, however, did not obscure his devotion to God. In times of feasting he continually made sacrifices for the welfare of his family (1:1–5). The use of his wealth in aiding the needy is reflected throughout the rest of the book.

Suddenly Job is reduced to extreme poverty. In four catastrophic developments he loses all his material possessions. Two of these misfortunes

[4] Probably northwest Arabia or Edom. See *Harper's Bible Dictionary,* p. 792, for discussion.

[5] Reasons given for this correlation: (1) family conditions; (2) no reference to the law or religious conditions of later times; (3) no reference to the teaching of the prophets; (4) the simplicity of life is similar to that of the patriarchs. Cf. S. C. Yoder, *Poetry of the Old Testament* (Scottdale, Pa.: Herald Press, 1948), p. 83.

apparently come from natural sources—attacks by the Sabeans and Chaldeans. The other two—a consuming fire, and a great wind—were beyond man's control. Job not only was bankrupt materially but lost all his children.

Job was dumfounded—he tore his clothes and shaved his head. Then he turned to God in worship. Recognizing that all he owned had come to him from God, he also acknowledged that in the providence of God he had lost everything. For this he blessed God, charging him with no wrong.

Afflicted with terrible boils (2:7–8) Job seated himself on an ash heap and desperately sought relief by scraping himself with a potsherd. At this point his wife advised him to curse God and die. Once again this righteous man rose above circumstances and acknowledged God as the controller of the fortunes of life.

Three friends—Eliphaz, Bildad, and Zophar—came to call on Job with the avowed purpose of comforting him. They hardly recognized him in his state of suffering. So stunned were these three that they sat in silence for seven days. Job finally broke the stillness by cursing the day of his birth—nonexistence would be better than to endure such suffering. In anguish of soul and physical torment he pondered the enigma of his existence in the question: why was I ever born?[6]

The underlying problem in the entire discussion was the fact that neither Job nor his friends knew the reason for these apparent misfortunes. Unknown to them were the developments behind the scenes. Satan appeared before God to challenge Job's devotion and faith. He made the accusation that Job simply served God for material reward and was granted permission to strip the richest man in the East of all earthly possessions but was not permitted to harm Job himself. When Job's resultant philosophy of life did not bear out Satan's wager, God granted the accuser liberty to afflict Job but with the specific restriction to spare his life. Even though Job had cursed the day of his birth he never cursed God. Fully conscious of his suffering and having no explanation, Job raised the question "why?" as he delved into the mystery of his peculiar lot in life.

Reluctantly his friends tried to comfort him who had instructed and helped others in days past (4:1 ff.). Eliphaz cautiously pointed out that no mortal man with limited wisdom could appear perfectly righteous before an omnipotent God. Failing to recognize Job's genuine devotion to God Eliphaz assumed that he was suffering for his sin (4–5).

In reply Job portrayed the intensity of his misery which even his friends did not understand. To him it seemed as though God had abandoned him to continuous suffering. In vain he longed for a crisis in which he could find either relief in death or pardon for his sin (6–7).

[6] Note that Jeremiah also cursed the day of his birth, Jer. 20.

Bildad immediately retorted that God would not pervert justice. Appealing to tradition and asserting that God would not reject a blameless man, Bildad implied that Job was suffering justly for his own sin (8).

"How can a man be just before God?" was Job's next question. No one was God's equal—God is omnipotent and does as he wills without giving account to anyone. With no umpire or daysman to intervene or explain the cause of his suffering, Job appealed directly to the Almighty. Loathing life in such an unbearable state, Job hoped for relief in death (9–10).

Zophar boldly rebuked Job for raising such questions. God could reveal his sin but divine wisdom and power were beyond man's understanding. He advised Job to repent and implied his guilt by concluding that the only hope for the wicked was in death (11).

Job courageously asserts that God, in his wisdom and sovereignty, controls the lives of man and nations, as well as of beasts (12:1–25). Job advises his friends to be silent and resolves to make his appeal to God, with whom his only hope for vindication rests (13:1–27). Experiencing no relief from bodily pain, Job in despair appeals to God to hide him in the grave, assuming or hoping there would be a resurrection (13:28–14:22).[7]

Eliphaz, asserting that Job was too arrogant, insists that tradition has the answer: Suffering is the result of sin. In delineating the full pay for sinners, Eliphaz makes sure that all the things that have happened to Job were included (15:1–35, NIV).

Job reminds his friends that they are miserable comforters. Feeling abandoned by God and anticipating that he would die before his vindication, Job expresses the hope that "'my witness is in heaven; my advocate is on high. My intercessor is my friend.'" His spirit is broken. In despair he has no hope for the present but death (16:1–17:16, NIV).

Bildad has little to add. Once more he reaffirms to Job the certainty that the wicked will, in this life, receive payment in full. Death is their punishment, without a surviving memory. No mention is made of retribution after death (18:1–21).

Forsaken by his friends, alienated from his family, abhorred by his wife, and ignored by his servants, Job portrays his lonely plight of suffering under the hand of God. Appealing directly to God, Job expects his vindication to come after his death. Reflecting his personal relationship with God, he boldly asserts, "I know that my Redeemer lives. . . . I will see God" (19:25–26, NIV). Job's anticipation of an umpire (9:33) and a "witness in heaven" (16:19) as a mediator now crystallizes in the hope that God is "my Redeemer" (*goel*, cf. Num. 35:12–28; Ex. 6:6; Isa. 43:1).[8]

[7] Cf. Elmer B. Smick, "Job," in *Expositor's Bible Commentary* (Grand Rapids: Zondervan, 1988), 4:923.

[8] Ibid., 4:941–944.

In a masterly literary style Zophar asserts that the joys of the wicked are but for a moment. Their punishment begins in this life and continues after death (20:1–29).

In this speech (21:1–34) Job challenges his friends to examine the experience of wicked people throughout the world who prospered, enjoyed life to the full, were given an honorable burial, and were respected for their success. The simplistic view of his friends was wrong and lacked confirmation by observers who have a broad knowledge of people and their affairs.

In this third cycle Eliphaz, not answering Job's shocking statements, agrees with his friends that Job is very wicked (22:1–30). He accuses him of believing that God in his remoteness is not aware of Job's tyrannical treatment of the oppressed (vv. 6–20). In an extensive appeal surpassing that of any prophet, Eliphaz advises Job to turn to God in repentance.

Job is confident that God would agree with his claim to be an upright man, and he searches for an encounter with God for his own vindication (23:1–7). Not understanding the mystery of God's ways with him nor having an immediate sense of God's presence or answers to his questions, Job expresses his commitment to God. He is confident that in testing he would "'come forth as gold,'" affirming his faith in the uniqueness and sovereignty of God (23:1–17, NIV). As to the wicked who continue to prosper, Job complains that God has not demonstrated his justice by punishing them openly for their evil deeds against the innocent (24:1–24). Knowing that he did not deserve his suffering, Job wonders about the age-old principle of divine retribution. He concludes with the challenge for anyone to prove him a liar.

Bildad then asserts that God is too pure to be accessible to the individual, who "'is but a maggot,'" to claim righteousness before God (25:1–6, NIV). Repeatedly, Job expresses his determination to be vindicated as blameless in God's tribunal (10:1–7; 13:3, 13–19; 16:18–21; 19:23–27; 23:2–7). Bildad considers this impossible because of the majesty and power of God.

This angers Job. He is aware of his friends' agreement that he is a reprobate sinner—not a righteous or blameless person temporarily suffering for his sin. Continuing with the theme of God's power, he asserts that that has nothing to do with the possibility of man's reconciliation with God. Humbly, Job asserts the marvelous, majestic, and mysterious power of an omnipotent God before whom the individual—not as a worm—stands with unanswered questions (26:1–14).

In this closing disclosure (27:1–23) Job speaks directly to his friends, asserting his righteousness and integrity. Dramatically, he portrays God's just punishment and wrath that awaits the wicked.

With no speaker identified, this poem (28:1–28) speaks to the inability of one's efforts to penetrate secrets that belong only to God. Neither Job nor his counselors have found a wisdom solution to the mystery of his suffering.

Elaborating on the elusiveness of wisdom, the speaker concludes that only God knows the way to wisdom. Fear him; that is wisdom.

In a concluding monologue (29:1–31:40) Job, delineating his ethical standards, rests his case with the desire that God will hear him. After recalling his former happiness, honor, and wealth, he laments his loss of dignity and his friendship with God. Job attests his loyalty to God as his sovereign Lord and then calls down curses on his own head if his claim is false. In this final protestation of his innocence he calls for vindication before God that he is blameless (1:8; 2:3)—a perspective he maintains throughout the dialogue (cf. 27:5).

Having listened to the dialogue, Elihu is angered and enters the debate with great enthusiasm (32:1–37:24). Elihu limits his attack to Job's statements in the dialogue and reflects a more balanced theology than that of the counselors who falsely accused Job of a wicked life. In charging Job with acting inconsistently and seeking vindication, Elihu assures him that God as a merciful teacher has a redemptive purpose in Job's suffering that is disciplinary and not simply judgmental. Seeing himself as a teacher of wisdom, Elihu does not completely condemn Job but wants him to be cleared. Elihu recognizes God's mercy and grace (33:23–30), unlike the counselors, who emphasized God's justice. Elihu rightly asserts, with a human perspective of Job's spiritual condition, that suffering may instruct and correct, but he does not solve the mystery of Job's suffering.

In a multitude of words neither Job nor his friends have solved the mystery of suffering, the problem of retribution, or the disciplinary designs in Job's particular lot in life. Neither do the speeches of the Almighty present a reasoned argument to afford a detailed logical or theological explanation of the mystery of Job's suffering (38:1–41:34).

In his first speech (38:1–40:2) God confronts Job with a portrayal of the majesty and wonders of the physical universe and the marvels of the animal kingdom. Overwhelmed with such mysteries and paradoxes for which he had no answers, Job comes to understand that God knows what he is doing in the universe. Through this theophany Job becomes awe-struck by God's presence; God has not abandoned him. Given no answers as to his suffering, Job by faith accepts God as his creator, sustainer, and friend. He is so moved by this experience that his concern to be vindicated is obscured by his answer, "'I am unworthy—how can I reply to you?'" (40:4, NIV).

In his second speech (40:6–41:34) God tells about his power and ability to crush the wicked, showing Job that God is Lord also of the moral order and rebuking Job for questioning God's justice (40:8). To correct Job's misunderstanding of God's attitude toward wickedness, God portrays in graphic descriptions the powers of evil, using mythological terminology. Though these two awesome creatures, Behemoth and Leviathan, are used symbolically, their features are drawn from animals like the hippopotamus and the crocodile. God, who has power over these creatures before whom humanity is impotent, is also supreme in the realm of justice as "'king over all that are proud'" (41:34, NIV). This encounter of seeing and hearing God convinces Job that God is Lord of the moral order as well as Lord of creation. Contritely Job confesses that he has spoken without understanding (42:1-6).[9]

What Job does not know is that Satan has been proved wrong in his accusations against him (1:1-2:10). God has not reversed his judgment about Job. God rebukes Job for speaking "'words without knowledge'" (38:2, NIV) and for questioning God's justice (40:8) but not for earlier sins. For falsely accusing Job that he was suffering for his sin, the three friends are instructed to bring sacrifices and to ask Job to pray for them (42:7-9). God identifies Job as "'my servant'" (42:8, NIV) and restores his fortunes in double measure, assuring him through this testing that God is his friend.

Psalms—Hymnology of Israel

For more than two millennia the Book of Psalms has been the most popular collection of writings in the Old Testament canon. The Psalms were used in worship services by the Israelites beginning with Davidic times. The Christian Church has incorporated the Psalms in liturgy and ritual throughout the centuries. Throughout all times the Book of Psalms has merited more personal interest and greater usage in public worship than any other book in the Old Testament, reaching beyond geographical and racial limitations.[10]

The popularity of the Psalms rests in the fact that they reflect the common experiences of the human race. Composed by numerous authors, the various Psalms express the emotions, personal feelings, attitudes, gratitude, and interests of the average individual. Universally people have identified their lot in life with that of the Psalmists.

Approximately two-thirds of the 150 Psalms are assigned to various authors by title.[11] The remainder are anonymous. In identifying authorship

[9] Ibid., 4:1055-1056.

[10] On the basis of Hebrew and Greek texts and other sources the liturgical use of the following Psalms has been suggested: 30—Feast of Dedication; 7—Purim; 29—Pentecost; 83 or 135—Passover; 137—commemoration of the destruction of the Temple; 29—last days of the Feast of Tabernacles; and the following were sung during the daily burnt offering: 24—Sunday; 38—Monday; 82—Tuesday; 94—Wednesday; 81—Thursday; 93—Friday; 38 and 92—Sabbath. Cf. R. H. Pfeiffer, *The Books of the Old Testament* (New York: Harper & Brothers, 1957), pp. 195-196.

[11] The present division of Psalms does not appear on the earliest Hebrew manuscripts still in existence. The total number varies in different arrangements. The Jerusalem Talmud has a total of 147. The LXX combines Pss. 9 and 10, and also 114 and 115, but divides 116 and 147 into two each, and adds one apocryphal Psalm, making a total of 150.

seventy-three are ascribed to David, twelve to Asaph, ten to the sons of Korah, two to Solomon, one to Moses, and one each to the Ezrahites Heman and Ethan.[12] The titles may also provide information concerning the occasion of the composition of the Psalm and musical instructions for proper use in worship.[13]

How and when the Psalms were collected has been subject to much speculation. Since David had such a genuine interest in establishing worship and began the liturgical use of some of them, it is reasonable to associate the early collections with him as king of Israel (I Chron. 15–16). Singing of songs in the house of the Lord also was introduced by David (I Chron. 6:31). In all likelihood Solomon, Jehoshaphat, Hezekiah, Josiah, and others contributed toward the arrangement and extended use of the Psalms in subsequent centuries. Ezra, in the postexilic era, may have been the final editor of the book.

With few exceptions each Psalm is a single unit, unrelated to the preceding or succeeding ones. Consequently this lengthy book having 150 chapters is very difficult to outline. A fivefold division preserved in the Hebrew text and most ancient versions is as follows: I (Pss. 1–41), II (42–72), III (73–89), IV (90–106), V (107–150). Each of these units ends with a doxology. In the last division the final Psalm serves as the concluding doxology. Although numerous suggestions have been offered for this arrangement, questions still remain concerning the history or purpose of these divisions.

Subject matter seems to provide the best basis for a systematic study of the Psalms. Various types may be classified in certain groups since they represent a similarity of experience as the background and have a common theme. Inasmuch as the entire Psalter cannot be given consideration in this brief treatment, the following classification, with examples for each category, may be used as suggestive for further study:

I. Prayers of the righteous—17, 20, 25, 28, 40, 42, 55, etc.
II. Penitential Psalms—6, 32, 38, 51, 102, etc.
III. Psalms of Praise—65, 95–100, 111–118, 146–150
IV. Pilgrim Psalms—120–134
V. Historical Psalms—78, 105, 106, etc.
VI. Messianic Psalms—22, 110, etc.
VII. Alphabetic Psalms—25, 34, 111–112, 119, etc.

[12] The Hebrew phrase "ledhavidh" may sometimes mean "belonging to David" but the contents of such Psalms as 3, 18, 34, 51–54, 56–57, 59–60, and others establish the fact of Davidic authorship. Consequently many others may have been written by him. Cf. E. J. Young, *Introduction to the Old Testament* (Grand Rapids: Eerdmans, 1949), pp. 87-300. Cf. also the unpublished thesis by Elaine Nordstrom, "A Chronological Arrangement of the Psalms of David," Wheaton College Library, Wheaton, Ill.

[13] The fact that some of the terms used in the titles of the Psalms were not understood by the translators of the LXX favors their antiquity.

Man's need for deliverance is universal. This was expressed in many Psalms in which the righteous voiced their appeal to God for divine aid. Pressed by anxiety, care, immediate danger, a feeling of vindication, or the need for a revival the longing soul humbly turned to God.

Most intensively expressed are the inner longings of the penitent individuals. With a few exceptions these Psalms are ascribed to David. Freely he uttered his feelings in sincere confession of sin. Most exemplary is Ps. 51 for which historical background is provided in the title as well as in II Sam. 12:1–13. Fully conscious of his terrible guilt, which was expressed with a threefold emphasis—sin, iniquity, and transgression—David in no wise sought to evade personal accountability. Overwhelmed and utterly humbled he turned to God in faith, realizing that a broken and contrite spirit is acceptable to God. The sacrifices and services of a penitent individual delight the God of mercy. Ps. 32, related to the same experience, indicates the divine guidance and praise that become a reality in the life of one who has penitently confessed his sin.

Psalms of praise are more numerous. These expressions of exultation and gratitude often came as a natural sequence to a great deliverance. Praise to God frequently came from individuals as they viewed his creative works in nature (Pss. 8, 19, etc.). Thanksgiving for harvest (65), joy in adoration (95–100), festive celebrations (111–118), and the "Great Hallels" (146–150) became important parts of the Psalmody of Israel.

The pilgrim Psalms (120–134) are labeled "Songs of Ascents" or "Songs of Degrees" in our English Bibles. The historical background for this designation is unknown. Various theories have been advanced and it is now generally assumed that these Psalms were associated with the annual pilgrimages of the Israelites to Zion for the three great festivals.[14] This distinctive group has been recognized as a miniature Psalter, since their content represents a wide variety of emotions and experiences.

In the historical Psalms the Psalmists reflected on God's dealings with Israel in days past. Israel had a history of varied experiences which furnished a rich background inspiring their poets and song writers. Throughout these Psalms there are numerous references to the miraculous deliverances and divine favors afforded Israel in times past.

Messianic Psalms prophetically indicated some aspect of the Messiah as he was revealed in the New Testament. Outstanding in this classification is Ps. 22, which has several references that parallel the passion of Jesus—portrayed in the four Gospels. Although this group reflects the emotional experiences of the authors, their expressions, under divine inspiration, had prophetic import. Interrelated to the life and message of Jesus, this element

[14] Cf. Leslie S. M'Caw, "The Psalms," in *The New Bible Commentary*, p. 498.

in the Psalms is vitally significant as interpreted in the New Testament. Vaguely expressed in Psalms of worship, the Messianic references became more apparent as they were fulfilled in Jesus, the Messiah.[15]

Another group of Psalms may be classified by the use of acrostic arrangements. Most familiar in this category is Ps. 119. For each series of eight verses a successive letter of the Hebrew alphabet is used. In other Psalms only a single line may be allotted to each letter. Naturally the use of this device cannot be effectively transmitted to the English versions.

With this analysis before him the beginning reader will recognize that the Book of Psalms is as diverse as a church hymnal. Extended classification of the Psalms necessarily increases duplication in the various categories. May this consideration be but a beginning for further study of each individual Psalm.

Proverbs—An Anthology of Israel

The Book of Proverbs is a superb anthology of wise sayings. Provocative in thought, a proverb points up a simple, self-evident truth, representing commonsense wisdom expressed in short, crisp form. In the course of time a proverb—*mashal* in the Hebrew, meaning *likeness* or *comparison*—not only became an effective tool of instruction but gained extensive use as a type of didactic discourse.

In this book Solomon is credited as the author of chapters 1–24 (cf. 1:1; 10:1). Several centuries after these chapters were written, "more proverbs of Solomon"—chapters 25–29—were added by "the men of Hezekiah king of Judah." The date and identity of Agur and Lemuel, to whom chapters 30 and 31 are attributed respectively, are unknown to this day.

The association of wisdom with Solomon is well attested in Kings and Chronicles. The historical account of this great king portrays him as the embodiment of wisdom in the glory of Israel's most prosperous period. In humble dependence upon God, he began his reign with a prayer for wisdom. In his love for God, in his concern to render righteous judgment, and in his wise administration of domestic and foreign affairs, Solomon represented the essence of practical wisdom (I Kings 3:3–28; 4:29–30; 5:12). Surpassing all the wise men of his day, he gained such international fame that foreign rulers, most notably the Queen of Sheba, came to express their admiration and to seek his wisdom (II Chron. 9:1–24).

Versatile in literary efforts, Solomon gave discourses on subjects of common interest, such as plant and animal life. The parts of the Book of

[15] Cf. the Messianic references in the following Psalms: 2:7—Heb. 1:5 and Acts 13:33; 16:9-10—Acts 2:31-32; 40:6-7—Heb. 10:9; 41:9—John 13:18; 45:6—Heb. 1:8; 68:18—Eph. 4:8; 110:1—Matt. 22:43-46; 110:4—Heb. 7:17; 118:22—Matt. 21:42.

Proverbs ascribed to him are but a sample of his words of wisdom; he has been credited with the composition of 3,000 proverbs and 1,005 songs.

Texts from wisdom literature were used in Egyptian and Mesopotamian centers over a thousand years before Solomon's time. In official schools this literature was used as instructional material—often addressed to "my son" from a "father"—to train courtiers and administrative advisers in the royal courts.

No doubt, Solomon was familiar with contemporary wisdom literature, some dating back to the third millennium B.C. The Book of Proverbs, in its profoundly religious tone and keen concern for social and moral conduct, compares more favorably with Deuteronomy than with ancient Egyptian literature.

The fundamental nature of the wisdom exemplified in Proverbs is theological: "The fear of the Lord is the beginning of knowledge . . . " (1:7, NIV; cf. 3:5–7; 9:10; Job 28:28). This reverence for God is basic to an understanding of its message and interpretation. Basic to all of life is the God-man relationship. Out of this vertical kinship issues every aspect of interrelationships on the horizontal level, reflecting the two great commandments emphasized by Moses (Deut. 6:5; Lev. 19:18) and Jesus (Mark 12:28–34). Proverbs is an extended commentary on the laws of love, which constitute the essence of the Old Testament (Matt. 22:34–40). While Proverbs is silent on salvation-history, worship, and Israel's covenant relationship, its references to God and his creation in chapters 1–9 provide the basis for the discernment and display of the order that holds all of life together, as delineated in this entire book.

The theological assumptions in Proverbs are more important than the immediate context of a given verse, since "as a general rule each proverb ostensibly stands on its own merits and its meaning is independent of the preceding and succeeding sayings."[16] An underlying principle is that the natural and social-moral orders are fundamentally related. The nature of the proverbs is such that they should not be interpreted as prophecy or as promises about certain effects and results. Rather, they are best viewed as theological and pragmatic principles. That a child instructed in God-fearing ways will persist in that way (cf. 22:6) is stated here as a principle of education and commitment and not as a specific promise. The prosperity of the righteous (3:2; 10:3) and the suffering of the wicked (10:27; 13:25), recognized as a general principle, is normally true, but should be viewed from a long-range perspective (cf. Ps. 73 and Job 1–2).

Consider the following outline for an analysis of Proverbs:

[16] Cf. Bullock, op. cit., p. 162.

I.	Purpose and theme	1:1–1:7
II.	Wisdom versus folly	1:8–9:18
	A. Wisdom's protection from evil	1:8–2:22
	B. The challenge to seek wisdom and avoid folly	3:1–4:27
	C. The perils of adultery	5:1–7:27
	D. The appeal of wisdom and the lure of folly	8:1–9:18
III.	Ethical maxims	10:1–22:16
	A. Antithetical statements—the right and the wrong	10:1–15:33
	B. Parallelisms—to fear God is true wisdom	15:16–22:16
IV.	Thirty sayings of the wise	22:17–24:22
V.	Solomon's proverbs collected by Hezekiah's men	25:1–29:27
VI.	The words of Agur and Lemuel	30:1–31:9
VII.	An acrostic poem: A Wife of Noble Character	31:10–31

Reverence and respect for God as the beginning of knowledge and wisdom is the keynote to the Book of Proverbs (1:7). Personal acknowledgment of God is the foundation for righteous living. A recognition of God, exemplified in daily life, is the true application of wisdom. As in Deuteronomy (30:15–20), so in Proverbs (3:1 ff.; 8:36; 12:28) is it a matter of life and death.

A discussion of wisdom and folly is embodied in 1:8–9:18. The discussion is set forth in a teacher-pupil or father-son relationship, with the listener frequently addressed as "my son." From the school of experience come words of instruction to the youth venturing out on the untried ways of life. Wisdom is personified. It speaks with irrefutable logic. It pleads with youth to consider all the advantages that wisdom offers and warns young people against the ways of folly, realistically pointing out the dangers of sexual crimes, bad company, and other deadly temptations. In a final appeal wisdom spreads an enticing banquet table. Folly leads to ruin and death, but the votaries of wisdom are assured of God's favor.

This next section, 10:1–22:16, consists largely of short aphorisms. Contrasts expressed in extended delineations in the previous chapters are stated here in one-verse units, which at times are grouped in clusters on a given subject. The structure is largely antithetical in chapters 10–15 and synonymous or synthetic in 16–22.[17] Various aspects of the behavior patterns of the wise and of the foolish are brought into focus. Wealth, integrity, law observance, speech, honesty, arrogance, punishment, reward, politics, bribery, statesmanship, society, family life, reputation, character—almost every phase of life is portrayed in proper perspective. Repeatedly, Israel's trust in God as Sovereign and accountability to him are reflected in these proverbs.

The next section, 22:17–24:34, consists of connected clusters of proverbs that are longer than the couplets in the preceding chapters. Its mood

[17] Ibid., pp. 159–161.

also changes from sayings in the indicative to admonitions in the jussive or imperative. The dangers of oppression, etiquette at a royal table, the folly of teaching a fool or following wayward women or becoming drunk with wine, the fear of God, and the benefits of wisdom receive consideration in this teacher-pupil discourse.

The thirty sayings (22:20) in this section have been compared with the Egyptian "Wisdom of Amen-em-ope" which has thirty units and dates from 1000 B.C. or earlier.[18] Similarities between these two documents have been widely acknowledged, but the dependence of one on the other has not been established with certainty.

Proverbs collected by the men of Hezekiah are grouped together in 25–29. The fall of the Northern Kingdom and the advancing threat of the Assyrian armies, as well as the religious revival during Hezekiah's reign, may have stimulated literary activities in the royal court in Jerusalem. Not beyond reason is the possibility that Isaiah and Micah were in this group of men. These proverbs provide advice for kings and subjects, with special attention given to the behavior patterns of fools. In the opportunity that life offers, the fool exhibits folly, while the wise person demonstrates the ways of wisdom.

The last two chapters are independent units. Agur, an unknown author, speaks of human limitations and the need for God's word as guidance. He raises rhetorical questions (characteristic of ancient forms of literature), speaking in duads and foursomes of various problems in life, and concluding with practical advice.

Lemuel is brief in offering his advice to kings (31:1–9). An alphabetical poem to a wife of noble character reminds the reader of the keynote of this book in the words, "A woman who fears the Lord is to be praised" (31:30, NIV; cf. 1:7).

Ecclesiastes—Investigation of Life

An investigation and examination of the basic questions of life is delineated in the Book of Ecclesiastes. Generally classified as wisdom literature, it belongs to a genre of philosophical discourse unique in the ancient Near

[18] The attempt to match these units with thirty separate sayings in 22:17–24:22 have not been uniformly accepted. Whereas E. J. Young, in *An Introduction to the Old Testament*, rev. ed. (Grand Rapids: Eerdmans, 1960), p. 314, contends that Amenemope borrowed from Solomon, R. N. Whybry, *The Book of Proverbs* (Cambridge: Cambridge U., 1972), p. 132, asserts that "it is almost certain that it was the Israelite author who knew and made use of the Egyptian work." More recently, John Ruffle, in "The Teaching of Amenemope and Its Connection with the Book of Proverbs," *Tyndale Bulletin* 28 (1977): 37, has seriously brought into question this assertion. For further discussion cf. Bullock, op. cit., pp. 163–164, and K. A. Kitchen, "Egypt" in *The New Bible Dictionary* (London: Inter-Varsity Fellowship, 1962), pp. 347–348.

East. Seven times the author identifies himself as *Qoheleth*, or the one who gathers people together to hear him.

The author's examination of life is in the context of the Old Testament revelation.[19] Recognizing life as God's gift, the author believed in God's providence and sovereignty. A basic element in his faith was a reverence and respect for God, to whom man is accountable at life's end. This divine imperative—to fear God and keep his commandments—is the essence of the God-man relationship as revealed through Moses. The author's emphasis on the enjoyment of life in this context was well recognized by the Jews as they read Ecclesiastes publicly in their joyous celebration of the Feast of Tabernacles.

Could Solomon have written this unique treatise?[20] Since the syntax, orthography, and lexicography of Ecclesiastes have affinity with early Canaanite and Phoenician characteristics going back into the tenth century B.C., the possibility exists that Solomon was the author. However, the date cannot be determined linguistically, since Ecclesiastes is a unique genre that does not fit into any known period of the history of the Hebrew language.[21] Consequently, could it have been written later as an impersonation used as a literary form by the author seeking "to recapture a certain spirit represented by a historical person and to speak through his spirit?"[22]

Consider Solomon's life-style and fitness as portrayed in I Kings 1–11 and the experience and perspective of the author of Ecclesiastes (1:16; 2:4–10; 7:20, 28; 12:9). Solomon was endowed with great wealth (I Kings 7:1–8) and unrivaled wisdom (3:12; 4:29–34). He had a large retinue of servants (9:17–19), he was engaged in extensive building operations (10:14–29), and he was known for his literary activities (4:32–34).[23]

Although Solomon reached the zenith of success in wisdom, wealth, fame, and international acclaim, he incurred the anger of God (I Kings 11:9). His wholehearted devotion to God was broken by his inclusive policy of allowing idol worship at Jerusalem, where he had dedicated the Temple. Aware of the adversaries that threatened him, Solomon may have come to

[19] Cf. 3:14 with Deut. 4:2 and 12:1; 4:13 with I Sam. 15:22; 5:4–6 with Deut. 23:22–25; 7:20 with I Kings 8:46; 12:7 with Gen. 3:19.

[20] Robert Gordis, in *Koheleth—The Man and His World* (New York: Block Publishing Co., 1955), p. 121, states that "the view that Solomon is the author has been universally abandoned today."

[21] Gleason Archer, *Survey of Old Testament Introduction* (Chicago: Moody Press, 1974), pp. 466–467.

[22] C. Hassell Bullock, in *An Introduction to the Old Testament Poetic Books* (Chicago: Moody Press, 1988), pp. 183–191, states that the author "assumed the personality of Solomon as a literary device to convey his ideas."

[23] For discussion of correlation of the allusions made throughout the books of Ecclesiastes and I Kings 1–11 see C. D. Ginsburg, *The Song of Songs and Coheleth* (New York: KTAV, 1970), p. 244.

an attitude of repentance and humility as he reflected on the divine promise to his father David (II Sam. 7:14–15).[24] After this apostasy he may have written the Book of Ecclesiastes, expressing his true reverence for God and applying his knowledge of God's revelation to a God-fearing perspective for living. Ecclesiastes may have been written with an appeal to a wider audience—perhaps to neighboring nations that had influenced him in his apostasy—in order to set forth a proper perspective of life.[25]

The four-fold division of this book, which recognizes the conclusion as the focal point in each section, is worthy of consideration:[26]

I. Life as God's gift to enjoy	1:1–2:26
Life's cyclical nature	1:1–11
Experience in wisdom, pleasure, and wealth	1:12–2:11
Life's purpose	2:12–23
Conclusion	2:24–26
II. God's plan and providence governing life	3:1–5:20
God's set time for everything in life	3:1–15
Questions of inequity and death in God's plan	3:16–4:16
A reverence for God in one's vows and riches	5:1–17
Conclusion	5:18–20
III. Questions about divine providence	6:1–8:15
The limitations of prosperity	6:1–7:15
Character evaluation	7:16–29
The responsibility of righteous government	8:1–14
Conclusion	8:15
IV. Living with unsolved mysteries	8:16–12:14
The enjoyment of life with limited wisdom	8:16–9:9
Diligence in work	9:10–11:6
A reverence for God while enjoying life	11:7–12:8
Conclusion	12:9–14

In examining all the activities in life about him, the author observes that within nature or labor there is no residuum or ultimate profit for humanity. It is not found in nature with its endless cycles (1:4–11). In his own search for human wisdom and philosophy, pleasure and wealth, the author comes to realize that death overtakes the wise person and the fool

[24] Noteworthy is the reference in II Chronicles 11:16–17 that those who were seeking the Lord were "walking in the ways of David and Solomon." This very likely refers to Solomon after he had returned to a God-fearing manner of life. Both David and Solomon had reason to repent and to experience divine mercy.

[25] Walter Kaiser, Jr., in *Ecclesiastes* (Chicago: Moody Press, 1979), pp. 25–42, delineates the view that Solomon wrote Ecclesiastes.

[26] Ibid., pp. 20–24.

(1:1–2:23). He concludes that there is nothing inherently good in people. The ability to enjoy and obtain satisfaction in the things about us in life—even in eating and drinking—can come to us only as we accept life as God's gift (2:24–26).

The author further observes that the term of life for humanity as well as for the plant world is set in the scope of God's plan. Abiding values, however, can be found only in accepting life as a gift from God, to whom humanity is accountable (3:1–15). The author is disappointed as he observes injustice, death, oppression, envy and greed, and political isolation and instability. These obstacles negate the thesis that God is omnipotent and has a plan in operation that involves every person and every event (4:1–16). None of these obstacles should be allowed to interfere with one's relationship with God. One should keep one's vows and "stand in awe of God" (5:7, NIV). Retribution awaits the self-seeking (5:1–17). Enjoyment in life comes in the recognition that the capacity to enjoy is a gift of God (5:18–20).

Attainments in this world, such as prosperity, may be disappointing and are not necessarily good when properly evaluated. No one knows the real advantage of things accumulated, and no one knows the future. Prosperity without the ability to enjoy it is futile (6:1–12). Adversity such as grief and pain may be more beneficial than the festivities of an apparently prosperous man. Good and ill fortune come from God. A human verdict based on observation is limited (7:1–15). Even though in the beginning "God made mankind upright" (7:29, NIV), men and women, as finite creatures, have fallen from original goodness (7:16–29). God's purpose in human government, which is to be respected, is righteous administration. In spite of inequities in this life, the God-fearing as well as the wicked are under God's control. Ultimately, the former will fare better than the latter. Therefore, enjoy life (8:1–15).

In spite of the mysteries and uncertainties, one should work and enjoy life; no one knows when this opportunity will be terminated in death. Apply wisdom, which is better than folly, in enjoying God's gift of life (8:16–9:18). Temperance in all things should regulate the enjoyment of life. A little folly may bring much sorrow and deprive one of numerous benefits (10:1–11:6). Enjoy life to the full, with the awareness that the final reckoning is with God (11:7–10).

In a beautiful but sobering allegory of old age, the author warns youth to remember their creator in the early years of life. The potential for serving God will diminish as bodily organs and mental faculties deteriorate (12:1–7). Succinctly stated, the author's final admonition is "Fear God and keep his commandments" (12:8–14).

Song of Solomon

The Song of Solomon is a love poem that by title is associated with Solomon, Israel's literary king. It is impossible to ascertain whether this book was written by him, dedicated to him, edited or published by him. Very likely this book was composed in the Solomonic era.[27]

Poetical in form, the Song of Solomon expresses the warm emotions of human love in a series of monologues, dialogues, and soliloquies, which are better treated as components of a single unit than as a collection of songs. Throughout this Song the dignity and purity of human love are portrayed in a series of poems in which the desires, fears, feelings, concerns, and hopes of two young lovers are explicitly expressed. The characters are presented in a quasi-dramatic action in a variety of scenes—the royal court of Jerusalem, a garden, a countryside or pastoral surrounding—fitting the settings of different parts of the poem.[28]

This Song, like the Book of Esther, does not mention the name of God and lacks the basic theological and cultic words in the Hebrew Old Testament. While recognizing that love has its origin in God (cf. 8:6), this Song "is more concerned with the value of 'mere' human emotion and simply takes for granted the whole theological structure of the Old Testament people and God's love for them."[29] Furthermore, this Song is one of four Old Testament books not quoted in the New Testament—nor do any New Testament writers suggest that it has a Christological interpretation or application.[30]

Unlike allegorical writing, this Song mentions real places, such as Engedi (1:14), Sharon (2:1), Lebanon (3:9), Tirzah (6:4), Damascus (7:4), Jerusalem (8:4), and others. Though not identified by name, real people—

[27] Cf. G. Lloyd Carr, *The Song of Solomon*, p. 18, and C. Hassell Bullock, *An Introduction to the Old Testament Poetical Books*, p. 222.

[28] Was Solomon involved in the action of this Song? Although Solomon's name appears several times in the text, three references (1:5 and 8:11–12) "can be understood best as general or generic statements that have no precise reference to Solomon as a real person involved in the action of the poem. The king, with all his wealth and splendor, is introduced here only as a symbol of the class of society for which the desire is the same as possession." In the context of the wedding song (3:6–11, where Solomon is mentioned three times) "the identification of Solomon with the lover is not made in the text itself." Cf. G. Lloyd Carr, op. cit., pp. 19–21, 48. For the position that there are three characters in this book—the maiden, King Solomon, and the shepherd as the maiden's true love—see C. H. Bullock, op. cit., pp. 224 ff.

[29] Ibid., pp. 43–44.

[30] Allegory and typology are two approaches used frequently in interpreting the Song of Solomon. The allegorical method, which "is originally a pagan Greek method of interpretation" dating back to Philo and Origen, ignores the grammatical-historical meaning of the text. Typology recognizes the historicity or factualness of the Old Testament account, which allegory denies, "but then finds in that account a clear, parallel link with some event or teaching in the New Testament which the Old Testament foreshadowed." Cf. ibid., pp. 21 ff.

the lover and his beloved, the watchman, the shepherd, the city-girls—participate in the "various episodes that set up a situation and then resolve it (e.g., 3:1–5)" without revealing any progressive story line. "The overall impression is one of the ebb and flow of the relationship and a kind of cyclic repetition of themes and ideas."[31]

The "natural" interpretation recognizes this Song as a passion-filled love poem in which a lover and his beloved celebrate openly the sensual purity of marital love.[32] As such, it may be considered a dramatic commentary on what Moses taught about marriage, and an expansion of the first recorded love song in history (Gen. 2:23). In the creation story the fulfillment of the creative act is unity, support, and an openness before each other and before God, in which the dignity and purity of human love are celebrated. For the ancient Hebrew, sexuality was confined to an established marital relationship and considered as one of the facts of life to be enjoyed. Throughout this book the theme of total dedication and commitment, as well as of permanent obligation, is regarded as central to that relationship (cf. reference to a wedding in 3:6–11).[33]

The content of this Song—a celebration of the love that the shepherd-lover shares with his beloved—lends itself to the following outline:

I.	Mutual appeal in a love dialogue	1:1–2:7
II.	Mutual admiration and separation	2:8–3:5
III.	Wedding song, admiration, and consummation	3:6–5:1
IV.	Mutual response and love renewal	5:2–8:4
V.	Affirmation, commitment, and communion	8:5–14

Although the literal interpretation speaks of human love, the providential inclusion of this book in the Jewish canon undoubtedly has a spiritual significance. The rabbis interpreted its application as a picture of God's love for the Jews in the exodus experience, as they read the Song of Songs at the Passover festival. For the Jews the marital love represented God's love for Israel as indicated by Isaiah (50:1; 54:4–5), Jeremiah (3:1–20), Ezekiel (16 and 23), and Hosea (1–3). In the New Testament this God-Israel relationship is illustrated by Christ and the church (Matt. 9:15; John 3:29; II Cor. 11:2; Eph. 5:23–32; Rev. 19:7; 21:2, 9; 22:17).

[31] Cf. ibid., p. 23.

[32] For a discussion advocating a "natural" interpretation, see M. G. Kline, "The Song of Songs," *Christianity Today*, Vol. III, No. 15, April 27, 1959, pp. 22 ff. G. L. Carr, op. cit., p. 34, uses both "natural" and "literal," preferring the former, which allows for figures of speech.

[33] Cf. Marvin R. Wilson, *Our Father Abraham* (Grand Rapids: Eerdmans Publishing Company, 1989), p. 200. Cf. also Carr, op. cit., pp. 34–36.

SELECTED READING

ALDEN, ROBERT L. *Proverbs: A Commentary on an Ancient Book of Timeless Advice.* Grand Rapids: Baker Book House, 1983.

ALLEN, LESLIE C. "Psalms 101–150" in *Word Biblical Commentary.* Vol. 21. Waco: Word Books, 1983.

ANDERSON, F. I. *Job: An Introduction and Commentary.* Downers Grove: Inter-Varsity Press, 1976.

ARCHER, GLEASON L., JR. *The Book of Job: God's Answer to the Problems of Undeserved Suffering.* Grand Rapids: Baker Book House, 1982.

BULLOCK, C. HASSELL. *An Introduction to the Poetic Books of the Old Testament.* Chicago: Moody Press, 1988.

CARR, G. LLOYD. *The Song of Solomon.* Downers Grove: Inter-Varsity Press, 1984.

CRAIGIE, PETER C. "Psalms 1–50" in *Word Biblical Commentary.* Vol. 19. Waco: Word Books, 1983.

ELLISON, H. L. *From Tragedy to Triumph: The Message of the Book of Job.* Grand Rapids: Wm. B. Eerdmans Publishing Co., 1958.

HARRIS, R. LAIRD. "Proverbs" in *The Wycliffe Bible Commentary.* Chicago: Moody Press, 1962.

KAISER, WALTER C., JR. *Ecclesiastes: Total Life.* Chicago: Moody Press, 1979.

SMICK, ELMER B. "Job" in *Expositor's Bible Commentary.* Grand Rapids: Zondervan Publishing House, 1988.

Chapter XVIII

Isaiah and His Message

To understand the message of this book it is necessary to be familiar with the historical setting of the prophet and the people to whom he delivered his message. Many of the allusions, references, and warnings can be misunderstood unless the political developments in Judah as related to the surrounding nations are carefully considered.

With the Prophet in Jerusalem

Little is known about Isaiah's lineage, birth, youth, or education beyond the fact that he was the son of Amoz. Apparently he was born and reared in Jerusalem. Since his call to the prophetic ministry is definitely dated in the year that Uzziah died (740 B.C.), it is reasonable to date his birth 765–760 B.C.

Isaiah was born in days of prosperity. Judah was regaining her military and economic strength under the competent leadership of Uzziah. Previously the foolish policies of Amaziah had subjected Judah to invasion and oppression by Israel and possibly the reproach of Amaziah's imprisonment. The latter event may have brought about the recognition of Uzziah as coruler as early as 792–91 B.C. With the change of kings in Israel Amaziah was restored to the throne (782–81), only to be assassinated (768 B.C.). This gave Uzziah sole control of Judah and the opportunity to assert his effective leadership.

Ominous developments soon cast lengthening shadows across Judah's future hopes. In Samaria Jeroboam's death in 753 was followed by revolution and bloodshed until Menahem seized the throne. In Judah Uzziah was smitten with leprosy as a divine judgment for assuming priestly duties. Although Jotham was made coruler at this time (*ca.* 750 B.C.), Uzziah continued in active leadership. Economic prosperity prevailed as Judah extended its boundary southward, including Elath on the gulf of Aqaba. To the east the Ammonites were tributary to Judah.

Most portentous was the rise of Tiglath-pileser III, or Pul, to the Assyrian throne in 745 B.C. The subsequent conquest of Babylon by the Assyrians precipitated a unified preparation of Palestinian rulers for Assyrian aggression. In 743–738 this expectation became a reality as the Assyrian army advanced westward in several campaigns. The Assyrian king reports in his annals that he defeated a Palestinian force under the leadership of Azariah or Uzziah of Judah. Thiele dates this in the first year of this period.[1] Menahem, the king of Israel, also made a heavy payment of tribute to the king of Assyria (II Kings 15:19).

Under the pending threat of Assyrian aggression rapid changes occurred in Israel and these undoubtedly had their repercussions in Judah. When Menahem died he was succeeded by his son Pekahiah, who was murdered by Pekah after a two-year rule. The latter seized the throne in Samaria in 740–39 and began an aggressive anti-Assyrian policy. The death of Uzziah, the outstanding king of Judah since the days of David and Solomon, occurred the same year.

During this year of tension at home and abroad the young man Isaiah received his prophetic call. It is likely that he had observed international developments with keen interest when Judah's hope for national survival faded before the advancing armies of Assyria. What Isaiah's religious attitude was at this time is not indicated. He may have been familiar with Amos and Hosea, who were active in the Northern Kingdom. As a youth he might have come in contact with Zechariah, the prophet who had such a favorable influence upon Uzziah. In this crucial year he was called to be a spokesman for God—to deliver God's message to a generation facing unprecedented historical developments.

While Pekah firmly resisted the Assyrians a pro-Assyrian party was gaining power in Judah. Apparently this movement was responsible for elevating Ahaz to the throne in 736–35 B.C. when the Assyrian armies were active in Nal and Urartu. Ahaz may have precipitated the Assyrian invasion of Philistia in 734. At least after their retreat Pekah of Samaria and Rezin of Damascus issued an ultimatum to Ahaz to join them in opposing Assyria. At this point Isaiah became involved. He was specifically commissioned to advise the king to rely on God (Is. 7:1 ff.). Ignoring the prophet's advice Ahaz made a treaty with Tiglath-pileser III. Although Judah was invaded by the Syro-Ephraimitic armies and lost Edom as a tributary, Ahaz survived with the advance of the Assyrian army. Successive Assyrian campaigns resulted

[1] For a defense of this date see Thiele, *The Mysterious Numbers of the Hebrew Kings*, pp. 75–98

in the conquest and capitulation of Syria in 732 B.C. Simultaneously Pekah was executed and replaced by Hoshea, who assured the Assyrian king of Israel's tribute. Ahaz met Tiglath-pileser at Damascus and sealed his alliance by introducing Assyrian cult worship in the Temple at Jerusalem.

Isaiah's activity during the rest of the reign of Ahaz is obscure. He must have shared the keen interest and anxiety of the citizens of Judah concerning the struggles at Samaria—about forty miles north of Jerusalem. When Shalmaneser succeeded Tiglath-pileser on the Assyrian throne Hoshea terminated his subservience. Following a three-year siege by the Assyrians Hoshea was killed and Samaria conquered by the invader in 722. Apparently Ahaz was able to maintain favorable diplomatic relations with Assyria, thus preventing the invasion of Judah at this time. There is no indication that Ahaz ever acknowledged Isaiah as a true prophet.

A new day dawned for Isaiah with Hezekiah's accession (716–15 B.C.). Ahaz had defied the prophet by supporting idolatrous worship in the Temple, but Hezekiah pursued a radically different course of action. Enthusiastically he introduced reforms, repaired and cleansed the Temple, and issued invitations to Israelites from Beersheba to Dan to join in the religious activities at Jerusalem. While Isaiah does not mention these reforms in his book, the national celebration of the Passover and the conformity to the law of Moses must have encouraged him concerning Judah's future.

Present-day knowledge of Judo-Assyrian relations during the reign of Sargon II (722–705 B.C.) is quite limited. In the biblical record Sargon is mentioned only once (Is. 20:1). It is known that Ashdod was conquered by the Assyrians in 711 B.C. Isaiah faithfully warned his people that they should not look to Egypt for support even though Shabako, the Ethiopian, had successfully established the Twenty-fifth Dynasty the previous year. For three years Isaiah walked about barefoot and clad as a slave, explaining his action as symbolic of the fate of Egypt and Ethiopia. How foolish his people were to seek Egyptian aid in rebelling against Assyria! Apparently Hezekiah maintained favorable relations with Assyria during this period by paying tribute. According to a fragmentary prism, Sargon boasts of receiving "gifts" from Judah.[2] Accordingly, Jerusalem was safe from attack at this time.

In the meantime Hezekiah was building up his defenses. The Siloam tunnel was constructed so that Jerusalem would be assured of an adequate

[2] For a translation of this Assyrian record see Pritchard, *Ancient Near Eastern Texts*, p. 287. This revolt probably began in 713 when Azuri, the king of Ashdod, tried to shed Assyrian domination. Sargon deposed him and appointed Ahimiti. Rejecting Sargon's appointee the people chose Jamani as king. The latter led a revolt with Judah, Edom, and Moab as allies and the promise of support from Egypt. When the Assyrian army approached, the rebellion collapsed; Jamani fled to Egypt, but later was surrendered to Sargon. By paying tribute the allies averted serious consequences. Ashdod became Assyria's capital in the occupation of this area.

water supply in case of an extended siege. Long before this, in the days of Ahaz, Isaiah had boldly declared that Assyria would extend its conquest and control into the kingdom of Judah.

In the crucial developments that followed Sennacherib's rise to power in Assyria (705 B.C.) Isaiah had vital and timely advice for Hezekiah. Nationalism emerged in rebellions throughout the Assyrian Empire. Not the least in Sennacherib's success in suppressing these uprisings was the replacement of Merodach-baladan by Bel-ibni on the Babylonian throne in 702. The next year the Assyrians directed their advance westward. Through miraculous intervention Hezekiah survived.[3]

How long Isaiah lived is not known from existing records. Beyond his association with Hezekiah about 700 B.C. little evidence is available concerning his latter years. With no scriptural evidence to the contrary it is reasonable to concur with the suggestions indicating that Isaiah continued his ministry into the reign of Manasseh. If the record of Sennacherib's death is acknowledged as Isaian in origin, then the prophet still lived in 680 B.C. to indicate what finally happened to the Assyrian king who spoke so disparagingly of the God in whom Hezekiah had placed his trust. Tradition credits Manasseh with the martyrdom of Isaiah—the prophet was sawn in two when he was discovered hiding in a hollow tree trunk. From the standpoint of longevity it is valid to project Isaiah's ministry into the days of Manasseh. That Isaiah was in his twenties when he received his prophetic call in 740 B.C. is a logical assumption. His age at the time of his death after 680 B.C. would not necessarily have taken him beyond his eighties.

The Writings of Isaiah

Did Isaiah write the book that bears his name? No competent scholar doubts the historicity of Isaiah nor the fact that part of the book was written by him. Some limit the contribution of Isaiah himself to selected portions from 1 to 32, while others credit him with all sixty-six chapters.

The most popular analysis of this book is the tripart division. Although there is lack of unanimity among scholars as to details, the following analysis represents a general agreement among those who do not support the unity of Isaiah.[4]

The First Isaiah consists of 1–39. Within this division only limited selections from 1–11, 13–23, and 28–32 are actually ascribed to the eighth-century prophet. The greater part of this section has its origin in subsequent

[3] See Chap. XIII.

[4] For representative examples see Anderson, *Understanding the Old Testament,* pp. 256 ff. and 399 ff., the article entitled "Isaiah" in *Harper's Bible Dictionary,* p. 284, and *Interpreter's Bible,* Vol. V, pp. 149 ff.

periods. The Second Isaiah, or Deutero-Isaiah, 40–55, is attributed to an anonymous author who lived after 580 B.C. This writer lived among the captives in Babylonia and reflected exilic conditions in his writings.[5] In spite of the fact that numerous scholars acclaim him as one of the more outstanding Old Testament prophets, neither his real name nor any facts attest his existence. The Third Isaiah, or Trito-Isaiah, 56–66, is attributed to a writer who depicts conditions in Judah during the fifth century; scholars date this author prior to the return of Nehemiah in 444 B.C.[6] Most of those who support this analysis do not limit the Book of Isaiah to three authors. Numerous writers, most of whom lived subsequent to the exile, as late as the second century B.C., made fragmentary contributions.

The view that Isaiah wrote the whole book bearing his name dates back to at least the second century B.C. Although modern writers[7] may claim that there is "universal agreement among scholars" for a diversity of authorship, the unity of Isaiah has been ably defended. The popularity of the modern theory has tended to eclipse the arguments of those who have been convinced that Isaiah, the eighth-century prophet, was responsible for the entire book.

In defending the unity of Isaiah a writer has pointed out that the modern theory cannot be regarded as quite satisfactory as long as it does not explain the tradition of its Isaian origin.[8] Jewish statements in the second century B.C. attribute the entire book to Isaiah. The recently discovered Dead Sea Scrolls, dating back to the same period, verify the fact that the entire book was considered a unit at that time.[9]

Analysis of His Book

The Book of Isaiah is one of the most comprehensive of all Old Testament books. In the Hebrew text Isaiah ranks fifth in length after Jeremiah, Psalms, Genesis, and Ezekiel. In the New Testament Isaiah is quoted by name twenty times, which exceeds the total number of references to all other writing prophets in New Testament books.

Various themes can be traced throughout the book. The attributes and characteristics of God, the remnant, the Messiah, the Messianic kingdom, hopes of restoration, God's use of foreign nations, and many other ideas recur frequently in the messages of the prophet.

The following outline surveys the content of Isaiah:

[5] Anderson, *op. cit.*, p. 395.

[6] See *Harper's Bible Dictionary* under the article "Isaiah."

[7] Anderson, *op. cit.*, p. 399.

[8] E. J. Kissane, *The Book of Isaiah,* Vol. II, p. lviii. See also R. K. Harrison's excellent discussion in *Introduction to the Old Testament* (Grand Rapids, 1969), pp. 764–800.

[9] Cf. R. K. Harrison, *op. cit.*, pp. 786 ff.

I.	The message and the messenger	1:1–6:13
II.	The kingdom prospects—contemporary and future	7:1–12:6
III.	Panorama of nations	13:1–23:18
IV.	Israel in a world setting	24:1–27:13
V.	True and false hopes in Zion	28:1–35:10
VI.	Jerusalem's judgment delayed	36:1–39:8
VII.	The promise of divine deliverance	40:1–56:8
VIII.	God's universal kingdom established	56:9–66:24

With this outline as a guide the Book of Isaiah can be analyzed more fully by considering each division separately.

I. The message and the messenger—1:1–6:13

Introduction	1:1
Sinful nation condemned	1:2–31
Promise of absolute peace	2:1–5
The vanity of trusting idols	2:6–3:26
Salvation for a remnant	4:1–6
The parable of a vineyard	5:1–30
The call to service	6:1–13

This passage may well be considered an introduction. Nearly all the major themes developed later are initially mentioned here. Careful reading and analysis of these introductory chapters provides a basis for better understanding of the remainder of the book.

Did Isaiah receive his call to prophetic service after he delivered the messages in 1–5?[10] Why does he record his call in 6 instead of 1 as is the case in Jeremiah and Ezekiel? Perhaps he wished to portray the extreme sinfulness of his generation and thus provide the reader with a better understanding of Isaiah's reluctance in accepting the responsibility placed upon him in this prophetic ministry.

Isaiah 1 portrays the extremely sinful and moral conditions. Israel has forsaken God and is worse than an ox which at least has enough sense to return to his owner's crib for fodder. The people are worse than Sodom and Gomorrah in their religious formality. The sacrifices which they faithfully bring, in conformity to the law, are displeasing as long as social injustice prevails. Sacrifice and prayer are an abomination to God if not offered in a spirit of contrition, humility, and obedience. Condemnation rests upon the

[10] The Vulgate translates Isaiah's response in 6:5 as "quia tacui" or "for I have been silent." This follows the rabbinical view that Isaiah had been deprived of his office for not rebuking Uzziah in assuming priestly duties, and now was recalled to service. Kissane correctly points out that this view was based on the confusion of two Hebrew words "damah" (to perish) and "damem" (to be silent). See Kissane, *op. cit.*, Vol. I at verse reference.

sinful people of Judah. Zion, which represents capitol hill, is to be "redeemed by justice," signifying that judgment will come upon all the sinful (Is. 1:27–31). The only hope expressed in this opening chapter is given to the obedient (vss. 18–21).

In direct contrast to this doom of Jerusalem Isaiah holds forth the brightest hope of restoration. With no uncertainty he announces that in the future Zion will be destroyed and plowed as a field but in a subsequent period will be restored as the governing center of all nations.[11] Peace and righteousness will go forth from Zion to all peoples. Universal peace shall prevail when Zion will have been re-established as the central government of all nations.

By admonishing his people to turn to God in obedience (2:5), Isaiah brings their attention back to contemporary problems. As long as they are trusting in idols and living in sin this hope does not apply to them. Judgment awaits them but salvation is promised to those who put their trust in God (2:6–4:1). Through the process of purification and judgment the remnant will enjoy God's protection and blessing. They shall share in the glory of the restored Zion (4:2–6).

Isaiah vividly illustrates his message in 5. The parable of the vineyard has been labeled as one of the most perfect of its kind in the Bible.[12] Israel is God's vineyard. After exhausting all possibilities of making it productive the owner decides to destroy his vineyard. Consequently the woes and judgments pronounced upon Judah are just and reasonable, since God has exercised his love and mercy without realizing the fruits of righteous living in his chosen people.

To this sinful generation Isaiah is called to be a spokesman for God. No wonder he is fearful and trembles when he becomes conscious of the glory of a holy God whose justice requires judgment on sin. Assured of cleansing and the forgiveness of his sin Isaiah in willing obedience agrees to be God's messenger. He is not assured of city-wide response to his ministry. The fact that he is to warn the people until cities are waste and without inhabitants should have suggested to him that relatively few would heed his warning; however, he is not to despair. He is given a ray of hope—when the forest is destroyed a stump will remain, signifying a remnant in the destruction of Judah.

The call of Isaiah represents a fitting climax to this introductory section. Although most of this passage emphasizes the contemporary sinfulness of the people and the judgment awaiting them, the call of a prophet indicates God's concern for his people. In the ministry of Isaiah God's mercy is expressed to Judah before the judgment is executed.

[11] See Mic. 4:1–4, which is parallel to this passage in Isaiah. Note the context in Micah.

[12] See Kissane, *op. cit.*, in commentary on chapter 5.

II. The kingdom prospects—contemporary and future—7:1–12:6

Immediate deliverance from Rezin and Pekah	7:1–16
Pending Assyrian invasion	7:17–8:8
Promise of complete deliverance	8:9–9:7
Judgment of Ephraim, Syria, and Assyria	9:8–10:34
Conditions of peace and blessing	11:1–12:6

The crisis which raised the question of kingdom prospects was the Syro-Ephraimitic war in 734. Following the Assyrian invasion of Philistia early that year Pekah and Rezin formed an alliance to halt the Assyrians. When Ahaz refused to join them Israel and Syria declared war on Judah.

At the precise moment when Ahaz and his people are terrified by the prospects of an invasion, Isaiah comes with a message from God. Ahaz is inspecting his water supply outside Jerusalem in preparation for the pending attack and possible siege. Isaiah's simple advice in this crucial moment is that Ahaz should take no action—the two kings whom he fears are but two smoldering sticks or stumps soon to be extinguished.[13] Assyria is the real threat to Judah (5:26). Consequently Isaiah warns Ahaz to trust in God for deliverance.[14]

Assyria becomes the focal point of Isaiah's message as he discusses the prospects of the kingdom of Judah. The consequences of Ahaz' alliance with Pul will be worse than anything that had happened in Judah since the death of Solomon and the division of the kingdom. Like a man whose hair is completely shorn from head to toe by a razor, so Judah will be shorn by Assyria (7:20). In 8 Assyria is likened to a river rushing through Palestine and absorbing Judah to the neck. It is noteworthy that Isaiah does not predict the termination of Judah's national existence—a fate which will surely come to Israel and Syria.

The advance and success of Assyria as a godless nation undoubtedly poses serious problems for the people in Judah. Will God permit his chosen nation to be absorbed by a heathen power? Isaiah clearly indicates that God hires the razor and causes the waters of Assyrian might to sweep through Judah. Since the people ignore the prophet and turn to familiar spirits (Is. 8:19), a practice which was forbidden in the law (Deut. 18:14–22), God must chastise his own.

Assyria is a rod in the hand of God (Is. 10:5). Will Assyrian might be so great that Jerusalem will be destroyed? Will Jerusalem meet the same fate

[13] Is. 7:8, Kissane, commentary on reference, follows Procksch Grotius, Michaelis and Guthe in reading "six or five years" instead of "sixty-five" and interprets this as a general time reference for the disintegration of the Northern Kingdom which rebelled against Assyria and capitulated in 722. Allis, *The Unity of Isaiah,* pp. 11–12, points out that 65 years after this prediction Esarhaddon died, in 669 B.C. During his reign he repopulated Samaria with foreigners, II Kings 17:24.

[14] Cf. II Chron. 28 and II Kings 16:5 ff.

before the advancing armies of Assyria as Calno, Carchemish, Hamath, Arpad, Damascus, and Samaria? The prophet clearly presents the basic truth of an omnipotent God who uses Assyria as a rod or staff in his hand. After he has accomplished his purpose in bringing judgment upon his people in Mount Zion and Jerusalem, God will deal with Assyria. Even as an ax or a saw is wielded by the artisan, so Assyria is subject to God and his control. The rod cannot use its owner and neither will Assyria use God. Isaiah boldly assures the people of Zion (10:24) that they should not fear Assyria's invasion. God's judgment on Jerusalem will be accomplished. Assyria will shake its fist at Jerusalem but God will halt the king in his plans to destroy the city. The assurance that this heathen nation is under God's control provides the basis of comfort and hope for those who place their trust in the Lord of hosts.

The prospects of the future kingdom offer the counterpart to the temporary discouragement in Isaiah's time. His generation faces dark days. With a godless king on the Davidic throne and Assyrian cult worship prevailing in Jerusalem the godly remnant must have been disheartened as they anticipated the pending Assyrian invasion. With assurance of deliverance from this enemy Isaiah offers renewed hope for the future.

The hopes for the future kingdom previously mentioned (2:1–5) are clarified in this passage. Here they are interwoven with contemporary problems. In contrast to godless rulers Isaiah unfolds the prospects of a godly king on the Davidic throne. In contrast to the temporal kingdom of Judah he elaborates on the promise of a universal and everlasting kingdom.

The righteous ruler is introduced in 7:14 as Immanuel, meaning "God with us."[15] Certainly wicked Ahaz, who refused to ask for a sign, does not understand the full significance of this promise, the fulfillment of which is not dated. Undoubtedly this simple promise is vague and ambiguous for those who hear Isaiah give it in a time of national crisis—they may easily have confused it with the birth of Isaiah's son, named Maher-shalal-hashbaz. Although Immanuel's land (8:5–10) is to be overrun by the Assyrians and presently delivered, the promise of a greater future deliverance is assured in 9:1–7. This will be accomplished in the birth of a son who is identified as "Mighty God," who will establish a government and peace without end. In 11 his Davidic origin is indicated but his characteristics reach beyond the human. He is divine in the exercise of righteous judgment through his omniscience and omnipotence.

The kingdom will be universal. The knowledge of the Lord shall prevail throughout the world. The wicked are destroyed by spoken word of the righteous ruler as absolute rightousness prevails among mankind. Even the

[15] For representative discussions of this text identifying it with the Messiah see Burnes and Kissane in commentary at reference. Cf. also Allis, *op. cit.*, p. 12, and E. J. Young, *Studies in Isaiah* (London: Tyndale Press, 1954), pp. 143–198.

animal world will be affected in the establishment of this kingdom. Zion will no more be the object of attack and conquest but will be the center of universal rule and peace as already indicated in 2. Chapter 12 expresses the praise and gratitude of the citizens of the future kingdom. God—not man—has established Zion as the abode of the Holy One of Israel.

III. Panorama of nations—13:1–23:18

Doom of Babylon and its ruler	13:1–14:27
Philistia's fall—no hope for recovery	14:28–32
Moab punished for pride	15:1–16:14
Fate of Syria and Israel	17:1–18:7
Egypt will acknowledge the Lord of Hosts	19:1–25
Ashdod and allies defeated by Assyria	20:1–6
Fall of Babylon	21:1–10
The distress of Edom	21:11–12
The fate of Arabia	21:13–17
Judah's pending destruction	22:1–14
Judgment of Shebna the steward	22:15–25
Tyre judged and restored	23:1–18

The panoramic view of the nations is vitally related to the kingdom prospects in the preceding chapters. During the last century and a half of the national existence of Judah, from Isaiah's time to the fall of Jerusalem, kings and kingdoms rose and fell. To the people of Judah and Jerusalem, who had the consciousness that they were God's chosen people through whom Zion would ultimately be re-established, these prophecies involving other nations were vitally significant.

Several basic themes are apparent in the messages concerning the nations. Although introduced in the preceding twelve chapters, they are more fully developed and interrelated in this passage. Assyria, which was Judah's number one problem in Isaian and subsequent periods, receives little consideration in this passage. Attention is focused upon other prominent nations.

The sovereignty and supremacy of God is basic throughout this entire passage. The title "Lord of hosts" occurs at least 23 times in these eleven chapters. Isaiah acknowledged God as such when he saw the "king the Lord of hosts" at the time of his call to the prophetic ministry (6:5).[16] In the Lord of hosts, who used Assyria as a rod for judgment, rested the assurance of the establishment of the everlasting kingdom (9:7).

The purposes and plans of this Lord of hosts are frequently expressed throughout the messages concerning the nations. Judgment from God does

[16] In four of the references the title appears as "Lord God of hosts." When David challenged Goliath he went in the "name of the Lord of hosts, the God of the armies of Israel," I Sam. 17:45.

not fall upon the nations by accident but according to a divine plan. Pride and arrogance are punished as God is ignored—regardless of its occurrence in heathen nations, Israel, Judah, or even in an individual such as Shebna the steward (22:15–25). No haughty individual or nation can escape.

The most graphic example is in the opening chapters of this passage (13:1–14:27). Babylon with its king is singled out for judgment. Although the heyday of Babylonian power was still in the future, Isaiah predicted in the days of Hezekiah (39) that Babylon would be responsible for the captivity of Judah. For the people who survived the destruction of Jerusalem under the Babylonians these chapters must have had special significance. Judgment awaited this kingdom which was temporarily used in the plan of God to purge Judah of her sin. By that time the people had already witnessed the fall of Assyria and this passage assured them that Babylon would likewise be judged.

Although Babylon is specifically mentioned, the king of Babylon is not identified. Commentaries differ widely in relating this to various kingdoms and numerous kings of Babylon or Assyria. The basic principle, however, is that any nation or individual exalting himself above God will sooner or later be dethroned by the Lord of hosts. The difficulties of relating the details of this passage to Babylon historically and the lack of agreement in identifying this king in history may suggest that much more is involved than a temporary world power and its ruler. This arrogant king may represent the evil forces which have opposed God—apparent in the human race ever since the fall of man (Gen. 3). This evil power will involve individuals and nations in opposition to the Omnipotent One until the final judgment when God deposes once for all. The destruction of the evil nation represented by Babylon is likened to the fate of Sodom and Gomorrah, which have never been repopulated. The deposition of the tyrant or evil one, represented by the king of Babylon, indicates that all those associated with him will be destroyed, thus removing all opposition. The finality of the destruction is significant.

By contrast, the theme of Israel's restoration and kingdom hopes recurs throughout this passage. The assurance that Israel would have a world-wide kingdom with Zion as its capital, introduced in 2, was a major theme in 7–12, where special emphasis was focused upon the righteous ruler. In these chapters the theme of Israel's ultimate hopes is not forgotten. It is the Lord of hosts who decreed Babylon's fall (21:10). Israel is still God's heritage (19:25) even though she is temporarily judged. Not only will the nation of Israel be restored (14:1–2) but aliens will be afforded a refuge there. Zion was founded by the Lord (14:32) and will be the recipient of gifts (18:7). While other nations and kings are judged, a righteous ruler will be established on the Davidic throne (16:5). Such were the unparalleled promises of restoration repeatedly given to Israel for comfort and hope in periods when the Israelites were subjected to the judgments of God.

IV. Israel in a world setting—24:1–27:13

The destruction of Jerusalem	24:1–13a
The righteous remnant and the wicked report to the Lord of hosts in Zion	24:13b–23
Song of praise by the redeemed	25:1–26:6
Prayer of the remnant in tribulation	26:7–19
Assurance of deliverance and return to Mount Zion	26:20–27:13

In these chapters the remnant becomes the focal point of interest. Throughout the periods of judgment a righteous remnant is assured of survival and restoration is promised—it may once more enjoy the blessings of God under the righteous ruler on Mount Zion.

Isaiah's messages were often related to a contemporary development. Jerusalem's doom had been clearly announced in his opening chapter and repeatedly emphasized in subsequent messages. In 24:1–13a Isaiah portrays the ruin awaiting the beloved city of Judah. Jerusalem will be desolate and her gates reduced to ruins. This became a vivid reality in 586 B.C.

The remnant, however, is gathered from distant coastlands and the ends of the earth (24:13b ff.), while the wicked are punished by the Lord of hosts. The wonders of the sky involving the sun and moon are associated here, as well as in other passages, with this great judgment as the Lord reigns in Zion.[17] The context of this passage seems to indicate a world-wide scope. The disposal of those who oppose God and the establishment of the remnant in Zion, in a universal kingdom without end, can hardly be limited to a local or even a national situation.

Most appropriate is the song of the redeemed that follows in 25:1–26:6. They respond with thanksgiving and praise as they rejoice in their salvation and enjoy the blessings of the Lord. Reproach, suffering, and shame will disappear as God wipes away all tears and eliminates death.

The prayer in 26:7–19 expresses the earnest desire of the people in times of great tribulation and suffering before they are regathered. Israel voices a hope while writhing in anguish and awaiting deliverance. Under the rule of the wicked as victims of prevailing unrighteousness they express their faith and hope in God, appealing to him for divine intervention.

Deliverance is promised in the reply (26:20–27:13). Israel, God's vineyard, will once more be fruitful. Purged from their sin the people will be gathered one by one as a remnant to worship the Lord in Jerusalem.

[17] Cf. Is. 13:10, 34:4, Joel 2:10–11, Matt. 24:29–30, Acts 2:19–20, and numerous other passages.

V. True and false hopes in Zion—28:1–35:10

God's plan prevails	28:1–29:24
Futility of an alliance with Egypt	30:1–31:9
Blessings for those who trust in God	32:1–33:24
Nations judged—Israel restored to Zion	34:1–35:10

Foreign alliances are a constant problem in Jerusalem during the days of Isaiah's ministry. By political intrigue and diplomacy the leaders of Judah hope to ensure their survival as a nation by aligning themselves with the victors. Ahaz replaces his father Jotham on the Davidic throne when the pro-Assyrian party gains control in Judah in 735. He defies the warnings of Isaiah and makes an alliance with Tiglath-pileser in the early years of his reign. Hezekiah, the next king, joins in an alliance with Edom, Moab, and Ashdod in resisting Assyria. This coalition anticipates support from Egypt, but Ashdod falls in 711 while the other nations offer tribute to the Assyrians to avert invasion.

Isaiah constantly warns against the folly of relying on foreign nations. He labels these alliances a "covenant with death." By contrast his advice is that they should place their faith in God, the true King of Israel. Whether it is Ahaz, the godless king, or Hezekiah, the godly ruler, who responds with friendly overtures to the Babylonian embassy, the prophet Isaiah constantly rebukes the leaders of Judah for depending upon other nations instead of looking to God for deliverance.

None of the chapters in this section is specifially dated. Since the alliance with Egypt receives such prominent consideration in 30–31, this entire passage may be dated in the days of Hezekiah when Judah had hopes of freeing herself from Assyrian domination.[18] In the early years of Sennacherib this interest in Egyptian aid undoubtedly posed a serious problem in Jerusalem.

Do 28–29 reflect the same historical background? Does the "covenant with death" in 28:15 refer to an alliance with Egypt in the days of Hezekiah or could it possibly refer to the alliance Ahaz made with Tiglath-pileser in 734 B.C.? The latter view merits some consideration. Ahaz, instead of placing his faith in God, ignores Isaiah by making an alliance with the Assyrians. The passing of the crisis of the Syro-Ephraimitic war and the apparently successful venture of a Judo-Assyrian union in 732, when Ahaz personally meets Tiglath-pileser in Damascus, may have been the occasion for excessive celebration in Jerusalem. Ahaz and his godless associates, who are supported by priests and prophets in the introduction of Assyrian cult worship into Jerusalem, probably are Isaiah's audience to whom he directs the stern words of warning and rebuke recorded in 28–29. Ahaz and his supporters undoubt-

[18] See Kissane, *op. cit.,* in discussion of chapters 28–29.

edly concluded that the overwhelming scourge (28:15) of Assyrian invasion would not affect Judah because she had made a treaty with this powerful nation.

Whether the opening chapters of this passage reflect an alliance with Assyria or with Egypt the warning is clear that such schemes will end in failure. Where Egypt is specifically identified (30:2), the warning explicitly states that dependence upon Egyptian help is not in the plan of God. Humiliation and shame will be their lot. In 31:1–3 a vivid contrast is made between the Egyptians, with their horses and chariots, and the Lord, whom Judah should consult. When the Lord stretches out his hand against them both Egypt and those whom she would help will perish. Assyria likewise will be terror-stricken (30:31) and overthrown (31:8–9). This will not be accomplished by man's efforts or man's sword but by the decree of the Lord from Zion. The fierce Assyrians will be destroyed and become the victims of treachery (33:1). Ultimately the wrath and vengeance of God will be executed upon all the nations of the world (34:1 ff.). Consequently confidence and trust in any nation through an alliance can never serve as an adequate substitute for a simple faith in God.

The antithesis to this warning against political alliances is the admonition to trust in God. The provision is made in Zion and the promises related to its establishment so that those who exercise faith need not be anxious (28:16).[19] God's plan for Zion as unfolded in these chapters affords a reasonable basis for the faith of the remnant who are willing to place their faith in God.

Two simple illustrations suggest that God had an eternal purpose in his dealings with his people (28:23–29). A farmer does not plow his field repeatedly without purpose. He plows in order to sow, so that in due time he may reap a crop. Neither is grain threshed or beaten endlessly. The purpose of threshing is to separate the grain from the stalk. God's purpose is not to destroy Israel but to send judgment for the purification of his people, separating the righteous remnant from the wicked. Jerusalem, named Ariel, will be subjected to judgment, but the Lord of hosts will intervene and provide sudden deliverance (29:1–8).

Even though Israel has only a formal religion, honoring God with lip service rather than from their hearts (29:9–24), God will bring about a transformation. As a potter God will accomplish his purpose. Israel will once more be blessed—prospering and multiplying, regaining prestige among the nations. Although they are a rebellious people (30:8–14) they are assured of restoration through faith in God (30:15–26).

[19] "To hasten" is the usual meaning of this verb. The Greek reads "shall not be ashamed," and so is quoted in Rom. 9:33. A noun from the same root used in Job 20:2 means "anxiety." See Kissane, *op. cit.,* at reference.

Righteousness will prevail under the righteous king in Zion (32:1–8). This future hope offers no excuse for complacency. The people of Jerusalem are warned that judgment and destruction will precede these blessings until the Spirit is manifested from on high (32:9–20). The prayer of the suffering and afflicted (33:2–9) will not go unheeded. Sinners will be judged, while the righteous remnant shall enjoy the blessings of the Lord (33:10–24).

Climactic is the gathering of all nations for a world judgment and the restoration of Zion (34–35). Previously it was indicated that God would sift the nations in a sieve of destruction (30:27–28). Even the host of heaven will respond when this judgment is executed. Edom, which represented an advanced civilization from the thirteenth to the sixth century B.C.[20] and was extremely wealthy in Isaian times,[21] is introduced after all the nations of the world are summoned for judgment. Zion and Edom respectively represent the geographical location for God's blessings and judgments. Since the day of vengeance is a time of recompense for the cause of Zion, this judgment could hardly be restricted to Edom. Many other nations were and have been guilty of offending Zion.

The glory of Zion as portrayed in 35 affords a hopeful contrast to the horrible judgments of God upon the sinful nations. The remnant returns to the promised land, which has been transformed from a wilderness into a land of plenty. God has redeemed his righteous ones from the clutches of the oppressors and is bringing them back to Zion to enjoy everlasting bliss. Zion will triumph over all nations.

VI. Jerusalem's judgment delayed—36:1–39:8

Miraculous deliverance from Assyria	36:1–37:38
Hezekiah's recovery and psalm of praise	38:1–22
Prediction of Babylon captivity	39:1–8

These chapters[22] have sometimes been labeled the "Book of Hezekiah." The king of Judah is confronted with the ultimatum of surrendering Jerusalem to the Assyrians. Orally as well as by letter Sennacherib tries to disconcert Hezekiah and his people—harassing them about relying on Egypt or trusting in God for deliverance. Sarcastically the Assyrian king even offers Hezekiah two thousand horses if he will furnish riders for them. By listing a series of conquered cities whose gods had not aided them Sennacherib claims that he is sent by God and that prayer for the remnant of Judah is ridiculous.

[20] See Nelson Glueck, *The Other Side of the Jordan* (New Haven, Conn., 1940), pp. 145 ff.

[21] See Pritchard, *op. cit.*, pp. 291–292.

[22] Although Kissane, *op. cit.*, Vol. I, p. 395, maintains the unity of Isaiah, he suggests that chapters 35–39 were originally compiled by the author of Kings. He quotes J. Knabenbauer, *Commentarius in Isaiam Prophetam*, ed. F. Zorrell, 1922, and N. Schlogl, *Das Buch des Propheten Jesaia* (Wien, 1915), as scholars who support the Isaian origin of these chapters on Hezekiah which were later incorporated in II Kings.

Hezekiah resorts to prayer, literally spreading the letter out before him as he appeals to God for deliverance.[23]

Isaiah boldly announces the safety of Jerusalem. Even though the presence of the Assyrians had prevented the sowing of crops for the coming harvest, the invaders will be expelled in time to reap what grew of itself.

Hezekiah's serious illness apparently occurs during this period of international pressure. When Isaiah warns him to prepare for death Hezekiah prays earnestly, receiving the assurance through Isaiah that his life will be extended for fifteen years. Deliverance from the Assyrian threat comes simultaneously. The confirmatory sign is the miraculous return of the shadow on the sun dial which Ahaz had probably obtained from Assyria through his personal contacts with Tiglath-pileser.[24] In gratitude for this personal deliverance and restoration to health, Hezekiah responds with a psalm of praise. Congratulations on his recovery are extended to him by a Babylonian embassy sent by Merodach-baladan. Hezekiah's cordial reception of the Babylonians is the occasion for a significant prediction. Isaiah's inquiry implies that Hezekiah had deviated from his simple trust in God and possibly had hopes that the Babylonians would aid Judah in shedding Assyrian supremacy. In simple but stern words the prophet warns Hezekiah that the treasures will be taken to Babylon and that his sons will serve as eunuchs in the Babylonian palace. Even in the heyday of Assyrian power Isaiah predicts Babylonian captivity for Judah, seventy-five years before the days of Babylonian supremacy. Although the international situation (*ca.* 700 B.C.) might have warranted a forecast of Judah's capitulation to Assyrian might, Isaiah specifically predicted Judah's exile to Babylon. Its fulfillment was not dated beyond the statement that it would occur subsequent to the reign of Hezekiah.

VII. The promise of divine deliverance—40:1–56:8

Comfort through faith in God	40:1–31
Israel as God's chosen servant	41:1–29
The ideal versus the sinful servant	42:1–25
Israel restored from Babylonian captivity	43:1–45:25
Babylon with her idols demoted	46:1–47:15
God's appeal to sinful Israel	48:1–50:11
Israel alerted in hope	51:1–52:12
Deliverance through a suffering servant	52:13–53:12
Salvation for Israel and foreigners	54:1–56:8

The promise of divine deliverance in 40–56 is not necessarily related to any particular incident in Hezekiah's time. The perspective of this passage is

[23] For a probable chronological sequence of events recorded here see pp. 213–215.
[24] See Kissane, *op. cit.*, at reference, Is. 38:7–8.

Israel's exile in Babylon.[25] In the later years of his ministry Isaiah may well have been concerned with the needs of the people who would be taken into exile when Jerusalem would be left in ruins and Judah's national existence terminated by the Babylonians. The ascendance of wicked Manasseh to the Davidic throne undoubtedly dims the immediate prospects of the righteous remnant. Surely with Isaiah they anticipate the imminence of Judah's doom as they witness the shedding of innocent blood in Jerusalem.

For Isaiah the coming exile is certain. That Babylon is the destination of their final exile is equally certain since he specifically indicates this in his message to Hezekiah (39). Exilic conditions are well known to Isaiah and his people at Jerusalem. The Assyrians had not only taken people from Samaria into exile in 722 but in the conquest of cities in Judah by Sennacherib in 701 undoubtedly many of Isaiah's acquaintances were taken captive. Letters and reports from these exiles graphically portrayed prevailing conditions among them.

With historical facts and the predictions of 1–39 as a background Isaiah has a most appropriate message of hope and comfort for those who anticipate Babylonian exile. Many details become significant as some predictions become history in the subsequent periods. At all times, however, this is a message of comfort, assurance, and hope for those who place their trust in God.

Various themes are interwoven throughout this magnificent passage. With deliverance as the basic theme not only are assurance and hope given but the provision for the accomplishment of these promises is vividly portrayed. In scope and magnitude as well as literary excellence this great message is unsurpassed. Doubtless it was a source of comfort and blessing to the immediate audience of Isaiah as well as to those who went into Babylonian exile.

Deliverance and restoration are developed in three aspects: Israel's return from captivity under Cyrus, deliverance from sin, and the ultimate establishment of righteousness when Israel and foreigners will enjoy God's blessings forever. The scope of fulfillment covers a long period of time. Initial fulfillment comes in part with the return from captivity under Zerubbabel, Ezra, and Nehemiah; atonement for sin was historically unfolded in New Testament times; the establishment of the universal kingdom is still pending.

The guarantee of this great deliverance rested in a God who could

[25] See D. Moritz Drechsler, *Der Prophet Jesaja, Ubersetz und Erklärt*, Zweiter Theil, Zweit Hälfte (ed. by Franz Delitzsch and August Hahn). Since Drechsler had not completed his work on Isaiah the commentary on chapters 40–66 is largely the work of Hahn. In an appendix to this commentary Delitzsch develops the viewpoint that Isaiah 40–66 does not reflect the days of Hezekiah even though it is written by Isaiah but is written from the standpoint of Babylonian exile. E. J. Young, *op. cit.*, p. 20, regards this appendix by Delitzsch as an "especially valuable feature" of Drechsler's commentary.

accomplish all things. As captives looking for help, the people did not need a message of condemnation. Those who were subjected to the reality of the exile were conscious of their sinful past for which they were suffering in accordance with Isaiah's warnings. To inspire faith and assure comfort Isaiah emphasizes the attributes and characteristics of God.

The opening chapter introduces this promise of deliverance in magnificent style. While suffering in exile Israel is assured of comfort and pardon for her iniquity in preparation for the revelation of God's glory which will be revealed before all mankind as God establishes his rule in Zion. Omnipotent, eternal, and infinite in wisdom God created all things, directs and controls all the nations, and has perfect knowledge and understanding of Israel in her suffering. Those who wait on God shall prosper. Faith in this Omnipotent One, who cannot be compared to idols, brings comfort and hope.

This graphic portrayal of God's infinite resources is a most appropriate prelude to the majestic development of the theme of deliverance. Frequent references to God throughout subsequent chapters are based on the realization that he has no limitations in the fulfillment of the promises made to his people. Throughout the entire passage the plans and purposes of God are interwoven with the assurance of deliverance. The words of comfort have a sure foundation. The Lord God of Israel is unique, incomparably great, and transcends all the works of his hands. Frequently a contrast between God and the heathen idols is vividly pictured. Trusting in a god made by man (46:5–13) becomes ironically ridiculous in contrast to faith in the unique God of Israel, the Lord of hosts.[26]

The servant theme is fascinating and intriguingly interesting. Twenty times the word "servant" occurs—introduced in 41:8 and finally mentioned in 53:11. The identity of the servant may be ambiguous in some instances. In a number of usages the servant is identified in the context. For an introductory consideration of this passage note that the servant may refer to Israel or to the ideal servant who has a significant role in the promised deliverance.

The initial use of the word "servant" is specifically identified with Israel (41:8–9). God chose Israel when he called Abraham and he assures his people that they will be restored and exalted as a nation above all nations. However, Israel as God's servant is blind, deaf, and disobedient (42:19). This was already indicated to Isaiah in his call so that judgment was announced upon sinful Judah (1–6). Since God created and chose this nation he will not abandon her (44:1–2, 21). Deliverance from exile is assured.

[26] The name "Jehovah" or "Lord" occurs 421 times in Isaiah—228 times in 1–39 and 193 times in 40–66. For discussion see R. D. Wilson, "The Names of God in the Old Testament," *Princeton Theological Review,* XVIII, 461 f. The title "Lord of hosts" occurs 40 times in 1–39. While this title is mentioned only six times in this passage, the "Lord of hosts" is clearly identified as the God of Israel who cared for them.

Jerusalem will be restored in the days of Cyrus. Israel will be brought back from Babylonian captivity (48:20).

Early in this passage the ideal servant is introduced as an individual through whom God will bring justice to the nations (42:1–4). This servant, also chosen by God, will be endowed with God's spirit so that he will not fail to accomplish the purpose of establishing justice in the earth and extending His law to distant lands (Is. 2:1–5 and 11:1–16). In contrast to the nation that was chosen but failed, this ideal servant will fulfill God's purpose.

Israel in her failure is in need of salvation. Atonement must be provided for Israel's sin, which God promises to blot out (44:22). To achieve this the ideal servant (49:1–6) has been chosen—not only to bring salvation to Israel but to be a light to the Gentiles. Ultimately this servant will have all nations prostrate before him (49:7 and 9:2–7). Before that can be accomplished, however, a sacrifice for sin must be provided. This servant who is to be exalted (52:13) must first make atonement for sin through suffering and death. Thus the ideal servant is identified with the suffering servant.

The suffering servant is most dramatically portrayed in 52:13–53:12. Basically significant is the fact that this servant is righteous and innocent. In contrast to Israel, who suffered for her sin in double measure (40:2), this servant suffers solely for the sins of others. Through vicarious suffering atonement is provided.

The climactic use of the word "servant" in 53:11 provides for the imputation of righteousness to those whose iniquities and sins are pardoned through vicarious sacrifice. This servant does not waver nor falter in the purpose for which he was chosen. Redemption is provided in his death.

The immediate concern of the Babylonian exiles was the prospect of return to Jerusalem. This was promised for the time of Cyrus, whom God designates as a shepherd. Whereas God used Assyria as a rod in his hand to bring judgment (7–12), the ruler Cyrus will be used to bring the captives back to Jerusalem. A greater restoration is promised through the servant in the ultimate exaltation of Zion above all nations (49:1–26). This had already been frequently mentioned in preceding chapters. The outstanding and significant deliverance, however, is the provision for atonement for sin, made possible only through the death of the suffering servant.

This salvation is so unique and distinct that Israel is alerted, in magnificent language, to take note of the suffering and death of the ideal servant. Thrice Israel is admonished to listen in preparation for the coming deliverance (51:1–8). As God chose Abraham and multiplied him to become a great nation, so Zion will be comforted in universal blessings and everlasting triumph. In the three following strains Israel is called to rouse from sleep (51:9–52:6). Messengers are alerted to proclaim peace and publish good tidings in anticipation of the Lord's return to Zion (52:7–12). But the message of hope presented in the following passage is not the deliverance from exile but the provision for the deliverance from sin through the suffering servant (52:13–53:12).

When the servant returns to Zion in triumph nations and kings will be amazed and astonished that the exalted servant is the one whom they did not recognize in his suffering. As a root out of dry ground he has prospered. Despised and rejected this man of sorrows was laden with iniquity and led as a lamb to the slaughter. Deprived of justice and judgment he was condemned to death by his own generation. But God accepted this servant in his death as a sacrifice for sin, through whom many obtained righteousness. For bearing the sins of many this servant is assured of a heritage and a spoil with the great and strong.

Out of a fruitless and barren nation God will bring forth a prosperous people (54:1–17). Israel was temporarily judged and forsaken. As God prospered the ravager in bringing destruction and judgment, so he assures prosperity to his people who are identified as his servants. They shall not be put to shame nor defeated but will possess the nations and be established in righteousness.

The message of pardon and hope is issued to one and all in 55:1–56:8. Response to this gracious invitation brings life and blessing. As the wicked forsakes his way and the unrighteous man his thoughts he may enjoy the mercy of the Lord and obtain pardon from God since atonement was provided in the death of the suffering servant. Salvation is offered to the one who turns to God by abandoning his sinful ways. The universal aspect is apparent in the fact that foreigners and eunuchs will conform to the ways of the Lord. Strange nations and people from afar will associate themselves with the Lord. The Temple will be the house of prayer for all peoples. The travail of soul by the righteous suffering servant will be satisfied in fruition—many individuals from all nations shall become the righteous servants of the Lord.

VIII. God's universal kingdom established—56:9–66:24

Self-righteous living versus God's standard	56:9–59:21
The redeemer brings blessings to Zion	60:1–63:6
God discerns the genuine	63:7–65:16
The new heaven and the new earth	65:17–66:24

Having developed the theme of deliverance so adequately, Isaiah reverts to the contemporary conditions of his people. The glory of Zion in its ultimate state has significance only as the individual has the assurance of participation—hence the comparison between the righteous and the unrighteous.

In the opening chapters a sharp distinction is drawn (56:9–59:21) between religious practice as Isaiah observed it and God's requirements. The cleavage between the standards of God and those of man are so obvious that this passage represents an appeal to the individual to depart from current practice and conform to the requirements of true religion.

Idolatry and oppression of the poor prevail among the laity as well as the leaders, who are labeled as blind watchmen (56:9–57:13). Simultaneously they pray and fast expecting God to favor them with righteous judgments (58:1–5). Sin and iniquity in the form of social injustice, oppression, deeds of violence, and bloodshed continue in open practice (59:1–8). God is displeased with such doings—judgment and condemnation await the guilty (cf. also chaps. 1–5).

By contrast God delights in the individual who is contrite and humble in heart (57:15). Genuine fasting pleasing to God involves practice of the social gospel: loose the bands of wickedness, feed the hungry, and relieve the oppressed (58:6 ff. Cf. also chap. 1). These people are assured of answered prayer (58:9), guidance, and abundant blessings (vs. 11). Those who replace pleasure and business on God's holy day with a genuine and sincere delight in God are assured of his promised favor (vss. 13–14). Ritualistic practice and conformity do not meet God's requirements for true religion.

Since national sins and iniquities separated man from God (59:1–15a), he assures the righteous people of divine intervention and deliverance by sending a redeemer to Zion. When he finds no one in the human race who can adequately intervene he sends the redeemer clothed in garments of vengeance, wearing the breastplate of righteousness and the helmet of salvation. This One will vindicate the righteous (59:15b–21).

The glorious prospects of Zion are once more portrayed with the coming of the redeemer to establish Israel as the center and delight of all nations (60:1–22). This capital will be known as the city of the Lord and the Zion of the Holy One of Israel. The glory of God will be displayed so universally that the sun and the moon will be needed no more. This kingdom will continue forever, as previously indicated in Isaiah 9:2–7 and other related passages. This glorious prospect is presented as a future hope. The date of fulfillment is not given beyond the simple concluding promise that God will bring it in his own time.

In preparation for the coming glory to be revealed God sends his messenger to Zion—anointed by the Spirit of the Lord (61:1–11). This messenger comes with good tidings to proclaim the time of God's favor when the brokenhearted may be healed, captives may be released, mourners may be comforted, and despondency may be turned into praise. God's people shall be known as priests of the Lord while others acknowledge the divine blessing upon their ministry. Righteousness and praise shall sprout forth before all nations.

The vindication and restoration of Zion follows in natural order (62:1–63:6). Zion, which has been forsaken and desolate, will become God's delight as he rejoices in his people as a bridegroom rejoices over his bride. Watchmen are encouraged to appeal to God day and night until Jerusalem is established as the praise of the nations.

Once more the lines of demarcation are clearly drawn in the succeeding chapters (63:7–65:16) between the recipients of God's blessings and the offenders subjected to God's curse. The initial passage (63:7–64:12) represents an appeal to God for help. On the basis of God's favor to Israel in the past the prayer expresses a demand for divine intervention. God is blamed for causing the people to err and hardening their hearts (63:17), delivering them into the power of iniquity (64:7), and making them what they are (64:8). God's answer to their prayer (65:1–7) reflects his attitude toward the self-righteous who ignored him during the time that he was available. They had spurned his appeals and failed to turn to him in the day of mercy—their self-righteous appeal comes too late.

The day of judgment is upon them (65:8–16). Those who did not answer God's call nor listened when he spoke are doomed—they ignored God's mercy which preceded judgment. By contrast God's servants, mentioned seven times in these nine verses, are the recipients of his everlasting blessings.

Finally Isaiah describes the ultimate blessings for the righteous in Zion in terms of the new heaven and the new earth (65:17–66:24). Jerusalem again is the focal point from which blessings extend universally. Peaceful conditions prevail even among the animals. Even though heaven is God's throne and the earth his footstool, he takes delight in individuals who are humble and contrite in spirit. Even though they have been subjected to scorn and ridicule they will triumph in the establishment of Zion, while offenders will be subjected to condemnation. As the enemies are judged it will be apparent that God's hand is upon his servants. The redeemed from all nations share in the blessings of Zion while those who rebelled are subjected to endless punishment (66:24).

SELECTED READING

Allis, O. T. *The Unity of Isaiah.* Philadelphia: Presbyterian and Reformed Publishing Co., 1950.

Beecher, Willis A. *The Prophets and the Promise.* New York: Thomas Y. Crowell Co., 1905.

Childs, B. S. *Isaiah and the Assyrian Crisis.* London: SCM Press, 1967.

FREEMAN, H. E. *An Introduction to the Old Testament Prophets.* Chicago: Moody Press, 1968.

GOTTWALD, N. *All the Kingdoms of the Earth.* New York: Harper & Row, 1964.

GROGAN, GEOFFREY W. "Isaiah" in *Expositor's Bible Commentary.* Grand Rapids: Zondervan Publishing House, 1986.

HINDSON, E. E. *Isaiah's Immanuel.* Philadelphia: Presbyterian and Reformed Publishing Co., 1978.

KISSANE, ED. J. *The Book of Isaiah.* Vol. I, Dublin: Browne and Nolan, 1941; Vol. II, The Richview Press, 1943.

LEUPOLD, H. D. *Expositions of Isaiah (1–39).* Grand Rapids: Baker Book House, 1968.

MACRAE, A. A. *The Gospel of Isaiah.* Chicago: Moody Press, 1977.

———. "Some Principles in Interpretation of Isaiah as Illustrated by chapter 24" in *New Perspectives on the Old Testament.* J. B. Payne (ed.). Waco: Word Books, 1970.

MARTIN, ALFRED, and MARTIN, JOHN A. *Isaiah: The Glory of the Messiah.* Chicago: Moody Press, 1983.

MARTIN, JOHN A. "Isaiah" in *Bible Knowledge Commentary.* Wheaton: Scripture Press, 1985.

OSWALT, JOHN N. "Isaiah 1–39" in *The New International Commentary.* Grand Rapids: Wm. B. Eerdmans Publishing Co., 1986.

RAMM, B. *Special Revelation and the Word of God.* Grand Rapids: Wm. B. Eerdmans Publishing Co., 1961.

SCHULTZ, S. J. "Old Testament Prophets in Today's World" in *Interpreting the Word of God.* S. J. Schultz and M. A. Inch (eds.). Chicago: Moody Press, 1976.

———. "Hermeneutical Principles for Interpreting Prophecy" in *Literature and Meaning of Scripture.* M. Inch and H. Bullock (eds.). Grand Rapids: Baker Book House, 1981.

———. *The Prophets Speak.* New York: Harper & Row, 1968.

WALVOORD, J. *The Nations in Prophecy.* Grand Rapids: Zondervan Publishing House, 1967.

WOOD, LEON J. *The Prophets of Israel.* Grand Rapids: Baker Book House, 1979.

YOUNG, E. J. *The Book of Isaiah, I, II, III.* Grand Rapids: Wm. B. Eerdmans Publishing Co., I (1966), II (1968), III (1969).

———. *My Servants the Prophets.* Grand Rapids: Wm. B. Eerdmans Publishing Co., 1952.

———. *Who Wrote Isaiah?* Grand Rapids: Wm. B. Eerdmans Publishing Co., 1958.

Chart VI TIMES OF ISAIAH

782–81—Amaziah probably released from prison when Jeroboam II assumes sole rule in Israel after the death of Jehoash
768—Uzziah assumes sole rule in Judah—death of Amaziah
760—approximate date for Isaiah's birth
753—Jeroboam's reign ends in Israel
750—Uzziah stricken with leprosy
745—Tiglath-pileser III begins rule in Assyria
743—Assyrians defeat Sarduris III king of Urartu
Uzziah and allies defeated by Assyrians in battle of Arpad
740—Jotham assumes sole rule—death of Uzziah
736–35—Assyrian armies in Nal and Urartu
Pekah begins rule in Israel
735—Ahaz made king by pro-Assyrian party in Judah
734—Assyrian armies invade Philistia
Syro-Ephraimitic war after retreat of Assyrians
733—Assyrian invasion of Syria
732—Damascus conquered by Assyrians, ending Syrian rule
Pekah replaced by Hoshea in Samaria
727—Shalmaneser V begins rule in Assyria
722—fall of Samaria
accession of Sargon II to the Assyrian throne
716–15—Hezekiah begins reign in Judah
religious reform—Temple cleansed
711—Assyrian troops in Ashdod
709–8—birth of Manasseh
705—Sennacherib begins rule in Assyria
702—Bel-ibni replaces Merodach-baladan on Babylonian throne
702–1—Hezekiah's sickness—threat by Sennacherib—Isaiah assures safety
Babylonian embassy from Merodach-baladan in exile visit Jerusalem
697–6—Manasseh made coregent
688—Sennacherib's second threat to Hezekiah
687–6—Hezekiah dies—Manasseh begins sole rule
680—Isaiah may have been martyred by Manasseh

Chapter XIX

Jeremiah—A Man of Fortitude

To live with Jeremiah is to understand his people, his message, and his problems. He has much to say to his own generation as he passionately warns them of impending doom. But compared to Isaiah he devotes relatively little space to future hopes of restoration. Judgment is imminent in his time, especially after Josiah's death. He concentrates on current problems in an effort to turn his generation Godward. A man with a vital message during the last forty years of Judah's national existence as a kingdom, Jeremiah relates more of his personal experiences than does any other prophet in Old Testament times.

A Forty-Year Ministry[1]

About the time that Manasseh announced the birth of the crown prince, Josiah, the birth of Jeremiah in Anathoth surely received little notice.[2] Being reared in this village only three miles northeast of the capital, Jeremiah became conversant with the currents that swept through Jerusalem.

Josiah became king at the age of eight when Amon was killed (640 B.C.). Eight years later it became evident that the sixteen-year-old king was concerned about obeying God. After four more years Josiah took positive measures to purge his nation of idolatry. Shrines and altars of foreign gods were destroyed in Jerusalem and other cities from Simeon in the south to

[1] See Chap. XIV for a survey of the political developments during Jeremiah's lifetime.

[2] S. L. Caiger, *Lives of the Prophets* (London, 1949), p. 174, suggests that Jeremiah was twelve years old in 640 B.C., dating his birth in 652 and making him four years older than Josiah. E. A. Leslie, *Jeremiah,* p. 22, and J. Skinner, *Prophecy and Religion,* p. 24, suggest Jeremiah was under twenty years at the time of his call. This would date his birth after 648 B.C.

Naphtali in the north. During his teens Jeremiah must have heard frequent discussions in his priestly home about the religious devotion of the new king.

During the period of this nation-wide reform Jeremiah was called to the prophetic ministry, around 627 B.C. Where he was or how he received the call is not recorded in chapter 1. By contrast to the majestic vision of Isaiah or the elaborate revelation of Ezekiel, the call of Jeremiah is unique in its simplicity. Nevertheless, he was definitely conscious of a divine call to be a prophet. In two simple visions this call was confirmed. The almond rod signified the certainty of the fulfillment of the prophetic word while the boiling caldron indicated the nature of his message. As he became conscious of the fact that he would encounter much opposition he also received the divine assurance that God would fortify and enable him to withstand the attacks and would deliver him in time of trouble.

Little is indicated in the scriptural records concerning Jeremiah's activities during the first eighteen years of his ministry (627–609). Whether or not he participated publicly in the Josian reforms—beginning in 628 and culminating in the observance of the Passover in 622—is not recorded by the contemporary historians nor by the prophet himself. When the "book of the law" was discovered in the Temple it was Huldah the prophetess and not Jeremiah who explained its contents to the king. However, the simple statement that Jeremiah mourned the death of Josiah in 609 (II Chron. 35:25) and the common religious interest of both prophet and king warrant the conclusion that he actively supported Josiah's reformation.

How many of Jeremiah's messages recorded in his book reflect Josian times is difficult to determine. The charge that Israel was apostate (2:6) is generally dated in the early years of his ministry.[3] Even though the national revival may not have permeated the masses, it is likely that open opposition to Jeremiah was at a minimum during Josiah's reign.

Although the national problem of Assyrian interference had subsided, so that Judah enjoyed considerable independence under Josiah, the international developments in the Tigris-Euphrates area were observed in Jerusalem with intense interest. Undoubtedly any fear that the Babylonian rise to power in the east would have serious implications for Jerusalem was tempered by the optimism of Josiah's reformation. The news of the fall of Nineveh in 612 very likely was welcomed in Judah as assurance of no more Assyrian interference. Fear of the revival of Assyrian power prompted Josiah to block the Egyptians at Megiddo (609 B.C.), preventing them from aiding the Assyrians who were retreating before the Babylonian advance.

[3] For a chronological arrangement of the book of Jeremiah see Elmer A. Leslie, *Jeremiah* (New York: Abingdon Press, 1954). In his arrangement he assumes (p. 113) that Jeremiah was silent from 621–609 B.C.

The sudden death of Josiah was crucial for Judah as well as for Jeremiah personally. While the prophet mourned the loss of this godly king, his nation was thrust into a whirl of international conflicts. Jehoahaz reigned but three months before Necho, of Egypt, took him captive and placed Jehoiakim on the Davidic throne in Jerusalem. Not only did this sudden turn of events leave Jeremiah without godly political support but almost abandoned him to the wiles of apostate leaders who enjoyed Jehoiakim's favor.

The years 609–586 were the most hectic—unparalleled in Old Testament times. Politically the sun was setting on Judah's national existence as international conflicts brought shadows of extinction that ultimately left Jerusalem in ruins. In religious matters most of the old evils eliminated by Josiah returned under Jehoahaz. Canaanitic, Egyptian, and Assyrian idols were openly replaced after Josiah's funeral.[4] Jeremiah fearlessly and persistently warned his people of coming disaster. Since he ministered to an apostate nation with godless leadership he was subjected to persecution by his own people. A martyr's death undoubtedly would have been a relief compared to the constant suffering and anguish that Jeremiah endured as he continued his ministry among a people whose national life was in the process of disintegration. Instead of obeying God's message as delivered by the prophet they persecuted the messenger.

Crisis after crisis brought Judah nearer destruction as Jeremiah's warnings continued to be ignored. The year 605 B.C. marked the beginning of Babylonian captivity for some of the citizens of Jerusalem while Jehoiakim pledged his allegiance to the invading Babylonians.[5] In the Egyptian-Babylonian struggle during the remainder of his reign Jehoiakim made the fatal mistake of rebelling against Nebuchadnezzar, precipitating the crisis of 598–597. Not only did death abruptly end Jehoiakim's reign but his son Jehoiachin and approximately ten thousand leading citizens of Jerusalem were taken into exile. This left the city with only a semblance of national existence while the remaining poorer classes controlled the government under their puppet king Zedekiah.

The religious and political struggle continued for another decade as Judah's national hopes faded. At times Zedekiah was concerned about Jeremiah's advice but more frequently he yielded to the pressure of the pro-Egyptian party in Jerusalem which favored rebellion against Nebuchadnezzar. Consequently Jeremiah suffered with his people as they endured the final siege of Jerusalem. With his own eyes the faithful prophet saw the fulfillment of the predictions that prophets before him had so frequently voiced. After forty years of patient warning Jeremiah witnessed the horrible result:

[4] Cf. Caiger, *op. cit.*, p. 194.
[5] D. J. Wiseman, *Chronicles of Chaldaean Kings*, p. 26.

Jerusalem was reduced to a smoldering heap of ruins and the Temple was razed.

Jeremiah faced more opposition and encountered more enemies than any other Old Testament prophet. Follow him as he suffers for the message he proclaims. When breaking the potter's vessel before the public assembly of the priests and elders in the valley of Hinnom he is arrested in the Temple court. Pashur, the priest, beats him and puts him in the stocks for the night (19–20). On another occasion he proclaims in the court of the Temple that the sanctuary will be destroyed. The priests and prophets rise against him en masse and demand his execution. While Ahikam and other princes come to Jeremiah's defense, saving his life, Jehoiakim sheds the blood of Uriah, another prophet who proclaimed the same message (26).

Personal encounter with a false prophet comes in the person of Hananiah (28). Jeremiah is publicly portraying Babylonian captivity by wearing wooden yoke bars. Hananiah snatches them from him, breaks them, and denies the message. After a brief seclusion Jeremiah once again appears as God's spokesman. In accordance with his prediction, Hananiah dies before the end of the year.

Other false prophets are active in Jerusalem as well as among the captives in Babylon opposing Jeremiah and his message (29). Among these are Ahab and Zedekiah, who stir up the exiles to counteract Jeremiah's advice that they should settle down and adjust to a seventy-year period of captivity. Shemaiah, one of the captives, even wrote to Jerusalem to incite Zephaniah and his fellow priests to rebuke and imprison Jeremiah. Other passages reflect opposition from various unnamed prophets.

Even the people of Jeremiah's home town rose against him. This is reflected in the brief references in 11:21–23. The citizens of Anathoth threatened to kill him if he did not stop prophesying in the name of the Lord.

Not least among his enemies were the civil rulers. Well remembered among Jeremiah's experiences is his encounter with Jehoiakim. One day Jeremiah sent his scribe Baruch to the Temple to read publicly the Lord's message of judgment with the admonition to repent. Being alarmed, some of the political leaders reported this to Jehoiakim but advised Jeremiah and Baruch to hide. When the scroll was read before Jehoiakim he blatantly defied the warning and burned the scroll in the brazier, vainly ordering the arrest of the prophet and his scribe.

Jeremiah suffered the consequences of a vacillating policy under Zedekiah's weak rule. This became especially crucial for the prophet during the final years of Zedekiah's reign. When the Babylonian siege was temporarily lifted Jeremiah was arrested on his way out of Jerusalem, charged with pro-Babylonian sympathy, beaten and imprisoned. When the siege was resumed

Zedekiah sought the prophet's advice. In response to Jeremiah's rebuke and appeal the king transferred him to the court of the guard. Under pressure Zedekiah again abandoned Jeremiah to the mercy of his political associates, who threw the prophet into a cistern where he was left to sink into the mire. Ebed-melech, an Ethiopian eunuch, rescued Jeremiah and restored him to the court of the guard, where Zedekiah had one more interview with him before the fall of Jerusalem.

Even after the destruction of Jerusalem Jeremiah is often frustrated in attempting to help his people (42:1–43:7). When the homeless and discouraged leaders finally appeal to him to ascertain the Lord's will for them, he waits on God for guidance. But when he informs them that they should remain in Palestine in order to enjoy God's blessing, the people deliberately disobey and migrate to Egypt, taking the aged prophet with them.

Jeremiah had relatively few friends during the days of Jehoiakim and Zedekiah. Most loyal and devoted was Baruch who served as the prophet's secretary. He recorded Jeremiah's messages, read them in the Temple court (36:6), served as business manager when Jeremiah was in prison (32: 9–14), and finally accompanied his master to Egypt.

Among the community leaders who saved Jeremiah from execution at the demands of the priests and prophets (26:16–24) were the princes led by Ahikam. During the Babylonian siege, when Jeremiah was abandoned to die in the pit, Ebed-melech proved to be a friend in need. Zedekiah responded with enough personal interest to assure the prophet safety in the court of the guard during the remainder of the siege of Jerusalem.

Through times of opposition and sufferings Jeremiah experienced a deep inner conflict. Penetrating grief pierced his soul as he realized that his calloused people were indifferent to the warnings and would be subjected to God's terrible judgments. This was the cause of his weeping day and night—not the personal suffering he had to endure (9:1). Consequently the ascription of "weeping prophet" to Jeremiah denotes strength and courage and willingness to face the bitter realities of coming judgment with his people.

Throughout his ministry Jeremiah could not escape the God-given conviction that he was God's messenger. True to human experience he sank to the depths of despondency in times of persecution, cursing the day in which he was born (20). When remaining silent to avoid the consequences the word of God became a burning fire within which compelled him to continue in the prophetic ministry. Continually he experienced the divine sustenance promised to him in chapter 1. Often threatened and on the brink of death in the pressures of life Jeremiah was providentially sustained as a living witness for God in the fading years of Judah's national life.

How long Jeremiah lived after his forty-year ministry in Jerusalem is not known. At Tahpanhes, the modern Tel Defenneh in the eastern Nile Delta, Jeremiah dramatically portrayed his last dated message (43–44).[6] Very likely Jeremiah died in Egypt.

The Book of Jeremiah

Divisions of the Book of Jeremiah for outline purposes are less apparent than in many other prophetic books. For a brief survey of its contents note the following units:

I.	The prophet and his people	1:1–18:23
II.	The prophet and the leaders	19:1–29:32
III.	The promise of restoration	30:1–33:26
IV.	Disintegration of the kingdom	34:1–39:18
V.	The migration to Egypt	40:1–45:5
VI.	Prophecies concerning nations and cities	46:1–51:64
VII.	Appendix or conclusion	52:1–34

The modern reader of Jeremiah may be disturbed by the fact that dated events and messages are not in chronological order. Beyond that many passages are not dated at all. Consequently it is difficult to arrange with absolute certainty the content of this book in a chronological scheme.[7]

Chapter 1 recording Jeremiah's call is dated in the thirteenth year of Josiah (627 B.C.). Chapters 2–6 are generally recognized as Jeremiah's message to his people during the early years of his ministry (cf. 3:6). How much of 7–20 is related to the reign of Josiah or Jehoiakim may be difficult to determine. Passages specifically dated in Jehoiakim's reign are 25–26, 35–36, and 45–46. Events occurring during Zedekiah's reign are recorded in 21, 24, 27–29, 32–34, and 37–39. Chapters 40–44 reflect the developments subsequent to the fall of Jerusalem in 586 B.C. while others are too difficult to date.

I. The prophet and his people—1:1–18:23

Introduction	1:1–3
Call to service	1:4–19
Apostate condition of Israel	2:1–6:30
Faith in temples and idols condemned	7:1–10:25
The covenant without obedience is futile	11:1–12:17
Two signs of captivity	13:1–27

[6] Sir Flinders Petrie excavated and verified this site in 1883–1884. See G. A. Barton, *Archaeology and the Bible*, p. 28.

[7] Commentary by Leslie, *op. cit.*, represents the most recent attempt to arrange the Book of Jeremiah chronologically. Note also Caiger, *op. cit.*, p. 222, and Davis, *Dictionary of the Bible* under "Jeremiah."

Intercessory prayer is useless	14:1–15:21
The sign of imminent captivity	16:1–21
Faith in man denounced	17:1–27
A lesson in the potter's house	18:1–23

In his ministry Jeremiah was associated with the last five kings of Judah. When he was called to the prophetic ministry he was approximately the same age as 21-year-old Josiah who had ruled the kingdom since he was eight.

Responding to a divine call Jeremiah became aware of the fact that God had a plan and purpose for him even before the time of his birth. He was God-commissioned and divinely fortified against fear and opposition. He was also God-equipped—the message was not his own; he was only the human agency through whom God conveyed his warning to the people.

Two visions supplement his call. The almond tree is the first to show signs of life in Palestine with the coming of spring. As certain as the budding of the almond tree in January is the assurance that God's word will be performed. The boiling caldron indicates the nature of his message—judgment will break forth in the north.

In his call Jeremiah is clearly informed that he will face opposition. The essence of his message is God's judgment upon apostate Israel. Consequently he can expect opposition from kings, princes, priests, and laity. With this sober warning comes the assurance of God's enabling.

Israel's apostate condition is appalling (2–6). The Israelites are guilty of forsaking God, the fountain of living waters and the source of all their blessings. As a substitute they have chosen foreign gods which Jeremiah compares to broken cisterns that can hold no water. To worship heathen gods is comparable to adultery in the marriage relationship. As a faithless wife leaves her husband, so Israel has forsaken God. The historic example of God's judgment on Israel in 722 B.C. should be sufficient warning. As a lion roaring from his thicket God is arousing nations to bring judgment on Judah. Israel has spurned God's mercy. The time of God's wrath has come and the evil that is breaking forth on Judah is the fruit of her own devices (6:19).

Jeremiah's audiences are skeptical about the coming judgment (7–10).[8] They ignore his bold announcements that the Temple is to be destroyed, complacently believing that God has chosen this sanctuary as his dwelling place—confident that God will not allow heathen rulers to destroy the place which was filled with his glory in the days of Solomon (II Chron. 5–7). Jeremiah points to the ruins north of Jerusalem as evidence that the taber-

[8] Leslie, *op. cit.*, p. 114, and Anderson, *Understanding the Old Testament*, p. 331, identify chapters 7 and 26 as the same incident. T. Laetsch, *Jeremiah* (St. Louis, 1952), pp. 93 f., dates chapter 7 in the days of Josiah. Note his analysis of the reasons advanced for the late date. He concludes that chapter 7 fits into the Josian reforms.

nacle did not save Shiloh from destruction in days past.[9] Neither will the Temple insure Jerusalem against the day of judgment.

Obedience is the key to a right relationship with God. By their social evils and idolatry the people have made the Temple a den of robbers even though they continue their prescribed sacrifices. Formal religion and ritual cannot serve as a substitute for obedience to God.

Jeremiah is grief-stricken as he sees the indifference of his people. He wants to pray for his nation but God forbids intercession (7:16). In the cities of Judah and in the streets of Jerusalem they are worshiping other gods.[10] It is too late for him to intercede in their behalf. In the meantime the people find comfort in the fact that they are custodians of the law (8:8) and hope that this will save them from the predicted doom. But the prophet is reminded that God's terrible judgment is certain.

Crushed in his own soul Jeremiah realizes that the harvest is past, the summer is ended, and his people are not saved. Plaintively he asks whether there is no balm in Gilead to heal his people. Were it possible he would weep day and night for them. Even though judgment is coming on the nation, God gives assurance that the individual who glories not in his might, riches, or wisdom but in the fact that he knows and understands the Lord in his delightful practice of kindness, justice, and righteousness in the earth is conforming to God's advice. God as king of the nations is to be feared (10).

Again Jeremiah is commissioned to announce God's curse upon the disobedient (11). Obedience was the key to their covenant relationship with God from the beginning of their nationhood (Ex. 19:5). The covenant itself is ineffective and useless without obedience. With idols and altars as numerous as the cities of Judah and the streets of Jerusalem the people are due for judgment. Jeremiah is again forbidden to pray for them (11:14). Threatened and warned by his own people in Anathoth he is utterly discouraged as he sees the prosperity of the wicked. He utters a prayer of complaint to God (12:1–4). In answer God challenges him to surmount greater difficulties and assures him that God's consuming anger is about to be released and exhibited throughout the land.

Two symbols portray God's impending judgment on Judah (13:1–14):

Jeremiah appears in public with a new linen waistcloth. At God's command he takes it to the Euphrates to hide it in the cleft of a rock.[11] At a

[9] Although the scriptural account is silent, scholars generally recognize the probability that Shiloh was destroyed in the days of Eli and Samuel. See W. F. Albright, *Archaeology and the Religion of Israel,* p. 104. Cf. Jer. 7:12–14 and 26:6–9.

[10] For a discussion of idolatry during Manasseh's time which Josiah tried to eliminate but returned after his death see W. L. Reed, *The Asherah in the Old Testament* (Ft. Worth, Texas: Texas Christian University Press, 1949). Also commentaries by Laetsch and by Leslie at Scripture references.

[11] P. Volz, *Jeremias,* p. 149, interprets this as a parable. H. Schmidt, *Die Grossen Propheten* (2nd ed.), pp. 219–220, suggests a local identification, while W. Rudolph,

subsequent time he recovers this garment which, in the Orient, is considered to be a man's most intimate and prized ornament. It is marred beyond use. In like manner God is planning to expose his chosen people to judgment at the hands of the nations.

Containers, either earthen jars or skins of animals, filled with wine also are symbolic. The kings, prophets, priests, and citizens will be so filled with wine and drunkenness that wisdom will fade into stupefaction and helplessness in time of crisis. The obvious result will be the ruination of the kingdom.[12]

As the prophet sees the pending doom approaching he realizes that his people are disobedient and indifferent (13:15–27). He envisions his sorrow, expressed in bitter weeping and tears, when his people will go into captivity. He is reminded that the people will be suffering for their own sins. They have forgotten God. As a leopard is unable to change his spots, so Israel cannot change her wicked ways.

A severe drought brings suffering to his people as well as to the animals (14:1 ff.). Jeremiah is deeply moved. Again he intercedes for Judah, confessing their sins. Once more God reminds him not to intercede since neither fasting nor offerings will avert the coming judgment. Jeremiah then appeals to God to spare the people because the false prophets are responsible for misleading them. When he raises the plaintive question about Judah's utter rejection, hoping that God will respond to his plea, he receives the most sobering reply: even if Moses and Samuel should intercede for Judah God will not relent. God is sending the sword to slay, the dogs to tear, the birds and the beasts to devour Judah for her sins because the people have rejected him and spurned his blessings. Despondent and overcome with sorrow Jeremiah once more takes comfort in God's word, being assured of divine restoration and fortitude to prevail against all opposition.

Time is seldom indicated in prophetic messages. The imminence of the judgment on Judah, however, is rather clearly revealed (16:1 ff.). Jeremiah is forbidden to marry. Should he marry and have children he would expose his family to the terrible conditions of invasion, siege, famine, conquest, and captivity. Judah's doom is near and certain. God has withdrawn his peace because they have forsaken him, served and worshiped idols, and refused to

---

Jeremias (Tübingen, 1947), at reference interprets this as a vision. Others including Peake, *Jeremiah* II, p. 193, Leslie, *op. cit.*, p. 86, and Laetsch, *op. cit.*, pp. 136–137, consider this as an actual experience in which the prophet twice went to the Euphrates near Carchemish. Caiger, *op. cit.*, pp. 192–193, considers Jeremiah as a man of means who had real estate and cash as resources and may even have visited the court of Nabopolassar in Babylon.

[12] Although Leslie, *op. cit.*, p. 228, dates this near the end of Zedekiah's reign, the attitude of the people in ignoring it might be more appropriate in Josiah's time since it seemed more ridiculous to think of a drunken ruler in the days of Josiah than in subsequent years.

obey his law. In consequence God is sending hunters and fishers to seek out all who are guilty so that Judah will know his power and might. Her sin is inscribed with a diamond point and publicly visible on the horns of the altar so that there is no chance to escape God's fierce anger. Once more the way of blessing and the way of curse are clearly outlined (17:5 ff.).

In the potter's house Jeremiah learns the lesson that Israel as well as other nations are as clay in the hands of the potter (18). As the potter can discard, remold, or finish a marred vessel, so God can do with Israel. The application is pertinent—God is bringing judgment for disobedience. Incensed by this warning the prophet's audience plots to get rid of the messenger.

II. The prophet and the leaders—19:1–29:32

The priests and elders—Jeremiah imprisoned	19:1–20:18
Zedekiah confers with Jeremiah	21:1–14
Captivity for kings and false prophets	22:1–24:10
Cup of wrath for all nations	25:1–38
Ahikam saves Jeremiah from martyrdom	26:1–24
False prophets in Jerusalem and Babylon	27:1–29:32

In a dramatic demonstration before an assembly of elders and priests in the valley of Hinnom Jeremiah boldly asserts that Jerusalem will be destroyed (19:1 ff.).[13] By breaking a potter's vessel he portrays the fate of Judah. In consequence Pashur, the priest, beats Jeremiah and confines him to the stocks near the upper Benjamin gate for the night. In a serious but normal reaction Jeremiah curses the day on which he was born (20) but ultimately resolves his conflict, realizing that God's word cannot be confined.

The occasion for the exchange of messages between Zedekiah and Jeremiah (21) is the siege of Jerusalem, which began on January 15, 588 B.C.[14] With the Babylonian army surrounding the city the king is concerned about the prospects for deliverance. He is familiar with his nation's history and knows that in times past God had miraculously defeated the invading armies (cf. Is. 37–38). In response to Zedekiah's arrogant request Jeremiah specifically predicts Judah's capitulation. God is fighting against her and will cause the enemy to come into the city and burn it with fire. Only by surrender can Zedekiah save his life.

In a general message, perhaps during the reign of Jehoiakim, the prophet Jeremiah denounces the wicked rulers who are responsible for injustice and

[13] This incident is best dated in the days of Jehoiakim. It is doubtful that any priest would have imprisoned Jeremiah in the days of Josiah. See commentaries by Laetsch and by Leslie at references.

[14] Although at least 17 years separate the events in chapters 20 and 21, Leslie suggests that the account in 21 relieves the harsh treatment Jeremiah received in 20. See also Rudolph, *op. cit.*, p. 116.

oppression (22). Specifically he predicts that Jehoahaz will not return from Egyptian captivity but will die there. Jehoiakim (22:13–23), precipitating God's curse in judgment by his evil ways, will have the burial of an ass with no one lamenting his death. His son Coniah (Jehoiachin) will be taken into captivity. By contrast (23) Israel is assured of regathering in the future so that the people may enjoy security and righteousness under a Davidic ruler who will be known by the name "the Lord is our righteousness." Consequently the contemporary priests and prophets are vociferously denounced as false shepherds who lead the people astray.

After Jehoiachin and some leading citizens of Judah have been taken into Babylonian captivity, in 597 B.C., Jeremiah has a timely message for the people who remain (24). Apparently they pride themselves on the fact that they escaped captivity and consider themselves favored by God. In a vision Jeremiah sees two baskets of figs. The good figs represent the exiles and will return. The people who remain in Jerusalem will be discarded like bad figs. God has rejected his people and will make them a byword and a curse wherever they are scattered.

In the crucial fourth year of Jehoiakim's reign (605 B.C.) Jeremiah again steps forth with an appropriate word from the Lord (25).[15] He pointedly reminds them that for twenty-three years they have ignored his warnings. In consequence, for their disobedience God is bringing his servant Nebuchadnezzar to Palestine and will subject them to a seventy-year captivity. With the wine cup of wrath as a figure Jeremiah declares to them that judgment will begin with Jerusalem, extend to numerous nations round about, and finally be visited on Babylon itself.

Near the beginning of Jehoiakim's reign Jeremiah addresses the people coming to worship at the Temple (26), warning them that Jerusalem will be reduced to ruins.[16] He cites the historic example of Shiloh's destruction—the ruins of which can still be seen north of Jerusalem. Incited by the priests and prophets the people react violently. They seize Jeremiah. After the princes hear the death charge they listen to the prophet's appeal. He reminds them that they will shed innocent blood by his execution, since God has sent him. As the leaders realize that Hezekiah in days past had not killed Micah for predicting Jerusalem's destruction, they reason that Jeremiah likewise does not deserve death. Although Ahikam and the princes save the life of Jeremiah, the godless king, Jehoiakim, is responsible for the arrest and martyrdom of Uriah who proclaimed the same message.

One of the most impressive prophetic acts of Jeremiah occurred in the

[15] Cf. Chap. XV.

[16] If Jeremiah delivered this message in the days of Josiah (chapter 7) and repeated it during Jehoiakim's reign (chapter 26) the mob reaction is due to the change in religious climate and the attitudes of the two kings.

year 594 B.C. (27). Although Zedekiah was a vassal of Nebuchadnezzar, there was constant agitation for revolt. Emissaries from Edom, Moab, Ammon, Tyre, and Sidon assemble in Jerusalem to join Egypt and Judah in a conspiracy against Babylon. Before these representatives Jeremiah appears wearing yoke bars and announces that God has given all these lands into the hands of Nebuchadnezzar. Therefore it is wise to submit to the Babylonians. For Zedekiah there is a special word of warning not to listen to the false prophets. Jeremiah also warns the priests and people that the remaining temple vessels and furnishings will be carried away by the conquerors. The foreign delegates are alerted not to be misled by their false prophets. Submission to Nebuchadnezzar is in divine order. Rebellion will bring destruction and exile.

Shortly after this the false prophet Hananiah boldly opposes Jeremiah. Coming from Gibeon, Hananiah announces in the Temple that within two years Nebuchadnezzar will return the vessels and the exiles taken to Babylon in 597. Before all the people he seizes the wooden yoke bars that Jeremiah is wearing and breaks them in pieces to demonstrate what the people will do to the Babylonian yoke. Jeremiah temporarily goes into seclusion but later returns with a new message from God. Hananiah has broken wooden bars but God is replacing them with iron bars of servitude upon the neck of all these nations. Hananiah is warned that for his false prophecy he will die before the end of the year. In the seventh month of that same year the funeral of Hananiah undoubtedly was a public confirmation of the veracity of Jeremiah's message.

Even leaders among the exiles cause Jeremiah no end of trouble. His concern for the captives in Babylon is expressed in a letter sent with Elasah and Gemariah.[17] These prominent citizens of Jerusalem are sent by Zedekiah to Nebuchadnezzar undoubtedly assuring him of Judah's loyalty even while rebellion is being plotted in Jerusalem. In his letter Jeremiah warns the exiles not to believe the false prophets who predict a speedy return. He reminds them that the captivity will last seventy years. He even predicts that Zedekiah and Ahab, two of the false prophets, will be arrested and executed by Nebuchadnezzar.

Jeremiah's letter initiates further correspondence (29:24–32). Shemaiah, one of the ringleaders in Babylon who is plotting an early return to Jerusalem, writes to Zephaniah the priest, the overseer in the Temple. He reprimands Zephaniah for not rebuking Jeremiah and advises him to confine the prophet to stocks for writing to the exiles. When Jeremiah hears this

[17] See Leslie, *op. cit.*, p. 209. Elasah was the son of Shaphan, Josiah's secretary of state. Elasah's brother Gemariah was in charge of the chamber in the upper temple court where Baruch read the message of Jeremiah publicly, 36:10. The other representative sent by Zedekiah was Gemariah the son of Hilkiah, the priest in Josiah's reign.

letter read he denounces Shemaiah and indicates that none of his descendants will share in the restoration blessings.

III. The promise of restoration—30:1–33:26

The remnant restored—a new covenant	30:1–31:40
Jeremiah's real estate purchase	32:1–44
Fulfillment of the Davidic covenant	33:1–26

Jeremiah specifically assures Israel of restoration. The exiles will be brought back to their own land to serve God under a ruler designated as "David their king" (30:9). When God destroys all nations, Israel will be restored after a period of chastisement. God, who scatters Israel, will bring back to Zion both Judah and Israel in a new covenant (31:31). In this new relationship the law will be inscribed on their hearts and they shall all know God with the assurance of sins forgiven. As certain as the luminaries exist in their fixed orders, so certain is the promise of restoration for God's nation, Israel.

The future hopes of restoration are most realistically impressed upon Jeremiah (32) during the Babylonian siege of Jerusalem in 587 B.C. While confined to the court of the guard he is divinely instructed to purchase a piece of property in Anathoth from his cousin Hanamel. When the latter appears with the offer, Jeremiah promptly buys the field. With meticulous care the money is weighed, the purchase deed is drawn up in duplicate, signed, and sealed by witnesses. Baruch then is instructed to place the original and the copy in pottery jars for safekeeping.[18]

To the witnesses and observers this transaction must have seemed utterly ridiculous. Who could be so foolish as to purchase property when the city was about to be destroyed? Most surprising was the fact that Jeremiah, who for forty years had predicted the capitulation of Judah's national government, now should acquire title to a piece of land. This prophetic act had great significance; it conveyed God's simple promise that in this land houses and lands should again be bought. Jeremiah's investment simply represented the future prosperity of Judah.

After completing this transaction Jeremiah prays (32:16–25). Sword, famine, and pestilence are a stark reality as the futile resistance against the Babylonian siege continues. Jeremiah himself is perplexed about this purchase he has made at a time when Israel's God of mercy is abandoning the nation to destruction and captivity. The faithful prophet is reminded that Jerusalem roused God's wrath and anger by idolatry and disobedience (32:

[18] For a detailed description of the custom of writing duplicate deeds in the fourth century B.C. according to the Elephantine papyri see Volz, *op. cit.*, and E. Sellin's *Kommentar zum Alten Testament*, pp. 306 f. Also quoted in Laetsch, *op. cit.*, p. 261.

26–35). Nevertheless, God who scatters them will bring them back and restore their fortune (32:36–44).

While national ruin is fast approaching Jeremiah receives an elaboration of the promise of restoration. With an admonition to call upon God, the creator, the people through Jeremiah are challenged to expect things unknown. In this land which is now in the jaws of destruction a righteous branch will spring forth from David so that righteousness and justice will again prevail. Davidic rule and Levitical service will be re-established. Jerusalem and Judah will once more be God's delight. This covenant is as certain as the fixed periods of day and night. As the great judgment which Jeremiah had announced almost forty years previously is about to culminate in the destruction of Jerusalem, promises and blessings for the future are vividly impressed upon the faithful prophet.

IV. Disintegration of the kingdom—34:1–39:18

Unfaithful leaders contrasted with Rechabites	34:1–22
Warning to laity and leaders	35:1–36:32
The fall of Jerusalem	37:1–39:18

The darkest years of Judah's national existence are briefly summarized in these chapters. The destruction of Jerusalem is the greatest of all judgments in the Old Testament history of Israel. The events recorded in 35–36, dating back to the reign of Jehoiakim, suggest a reasonable basis for the judgment which became a reality in the days of Zedekiah.

King Zedekiah has frequently been warned of coming judgment. Now that the Babylonian armies are actually besieging Jerusalem (588) Zedekiah is specifically told that Judah's capital city will be burned with fire. The only hope for him personally is to surrender to Nebuchadnezzar (34). Refusing to conform in obedience to Jeremiah's advice Zedekiah apparently works out a substitute compromise. In accordance with a covenant between the king and his people all the Hebrew slaves are released in Jerusalem.[19] The motivation for this dramatic act is not indicated. Perhaps the slaves had become a liability during the siege so that by their release they would have to sustain themselves or possibly they would fight better as free men. In all likelihood not many were motivated by a sincere religious desire to conform to the law since they revoked their covenant as soon as the siege was temporarily lifted while the Babylonians pursued the Egyptians (37:5). In no uncertain terms Jeremiah announces God's dreadful judgment on Zedekiah and all the men who broke the terms of their covenant (34:17–22). The Babylonians will return to burn the city of Jerusalem.

In 35–36 historic incidents from the time of Jehoiakim are recorded, clearly indicating that such an attitude of religious indifference had long pre-

[19] Cf. Ex. 21:2–11 and Deut. 15:12–18.

vailed in Judah. On one occasion Jeremiah led some Rechabites, who had taken refuge in Jerusalem as the Babylonians occupied Palestine, into the Temple.[20] He offered them wine but they refused in obedience to the command of their forefather Jonadab who lived in the days of Jehu, king of Israel. For 250 years they had been faithful to a man-made rule not to drink wine, not to plant vineyards, not to build houses but to dwell in tents. If the Rechabites were willing to conform to a human judgment, how much more should the people of Judah obey God who had repeatedly sent his prophets to warn them against serving idols. In contrast to the curse that God was sending upon Jerusalem the Rechabites would be blessed.

Jehoiakim, the son of godly Josiah, is not only disobedient but defiant toward Jeremiah and his message. In the fourth year of his reign Jeremiah instructs Baruch to record the messages he had given previously. The next year as the people assemble in Jerusalem to observe a fast Baruch publicly reads Jeremiah's message in the Temple court, warning the people to turn from their evil ways. Some of the princes are frightened and report to the king, who orders the scroll to be brought before him. While Jeremiah and Baruch hide, the scroll is read before Jehoiakim, who cuts it up and burns it in the brazier. Although the king orders their arrest they are nowhere to be found. At God's command the prophet once more dictates his message to his scribe. This time a special judgment is pronounced upon Jehoiakim for burning the scroll (36:27–31). Conditions will be such at the time of his death that he will not have a royal burial but his body will be exposed to the heat by day and the frost by night.

Some of the developments during the siege of Jerusalem are recorded in 37–39. For the sake of clarity the order of events may be tabulated as follows[21]:

Siege begins on January 15, 588	39:1; 52:4
Warning to Zedekiah	34:1–7
Zedekiah's inquiry—Jeremiah's reply	21:1–14
Covenant to release slaves	34:8–10
Siege temporarily lifted	37:5
Slaves reclaimed—Jeremiah's rebuke	34:11–22
Jeremiah arrested, beaten, and imprisoned	37:11–16
Siege resumed	
Zedekiah's inquiry—Jeremiah transferred	37:17–21
Jeremiah's real estate purchase	32:1–33:26

[20] The Rechabites, named after Rechab whose son Jonadab was active in aiding Jehu in the expulsion of Baal worship in the Northern Kingdom in 841 B.C. They traced their origin back to Hemath, a Kenite in the days of Moses. Cf. I Chron. 2:55; Num. 10:29–32; Judg. 1:16; 4:11, 17; I Sam. 15:6; 27:10; 30:29.

[21] For dating events during this period see Thiele, *The Mysterious Numbers of the Hebrew Kings,* pp. 153–166.

Jeremiah thrown into cistern		38:1–6
Ebed-melech rescues Jeremiah		38:7–13
Zedekiah's last interview with Jeremiah		38:14–28
Jerusalem conquered, July 19, 586		39:1–18
Jerusalem destroyed, August 15, 586	II Kings	25:8–10

During this 2½-year siege Jeremiah constantly advises the king that surrender to the Babylonians would be best for him. Throughout this period Zedekiah seems to be frustrated as he turns to Jeremiah for advice or yields to the pressure of the pro-Egyptian party by continuing resistance to the Babylonians. In vain he hopes for better news from Jeremiah. Finally the Babylonians break into Jerusalem. Zedekiah escapes as far as Jericho but is captured and brought before Nebuchadnezzar at Riblah. After being forced to witness the slaughter of his own sons and numerous nobles Zedekiah is blinded and led captive to the land of exile. So are fulfilled the apparently contradictory prophecies that Zedekiah should not see the land to which he would be taken as a captive.[22]

V. The migration to Egypt—40:1–45:5

Settlement at Mizpah under Gedaliah	40:1–12
Bloodshed and disruption	40:13–41:18
En route to Egypt	42:1–43:7
Jeremiah's messages in Egypt	43:8–44:30
The promise to Baruch	45:1–5

Jeremiah receives the most cordial treatment at the hands of the conquering Babylonians. Although manacled and taken to Ramah he is released by Nebuzar-adan the captain of Nebuchadnezzar's army. Given the choice Jeremiah chooses to stay with the remnant in Palestine even though he was assured favorable treatment if he went to Babylon.

With Jerusalem in smoldering ruins the remnant that remained in Palestine settles at Mizpah, probably the present site of Nebi Samwil. Located about ten miles north of Jerusalem, the city of Mizpah becomes the capital of the Babylonian province of Judah under the rule of Gedaliah, governor under Nebuchadnezzar. Scattered throughout the land are numerous guerrilla troops dispersed by the invading Babylonians. At first they rally to Gedaliah's support but a few weeks later Ishmael, one of these captains, is used by Baalis, chieftain of the Bedouin Ammonites, in a plot to kill Gedaliah. In a few days Ishmael brutally kills seventy out of eighty pilgrims en route to Jerusalem from the north and forces the Mizpah citizens to march victims southward, hoping to take them to Ammon across the Jordan. En route they

[22] Cf. Ezek. 12:13; 17:16; Jer. 32:4–5; 34:3–5.

are rescued at Gibeon by Johanan and taken to Chimham, a caravansary near Bethlehem, while Ishmael escapes.

Sudden changes find this remnant homeless and utterly discouraged. In a few months they had not only seen Jerusalem reduced to ruins but had been dislodged from their new settlement at Mizpah. In desperate need of guidance they now turn to Jeremiah.

Although they intend to go to Egypt in fear of the Babylonians, the people prevail upon Jeremiah to inquire of the Lord concerning their future. After a ten-day period, which tests their patience, Jeremiah has an answer. They are to remain in Palestine (42:10). Migration to Egypt would mean war, famine, and death. In deliberate disobedience and charging Jeremiah with not giving the full message of God, Johanan and his associates lead the remnant down to Egypt (43:1–7). With the people moving en masse Jeremiah and his scribe Baruch very likely had no choice but to go with them.

While at Tahpanhes in Egypt Jeremiah warns his people by a symbolic message that God would also send his servant Nebuchadnezzar into Egypt to execute judgment (43:8–13). In the next chapter Jeremiah outlines the recent developments in a final message. Jerusalem is in ruins because the Israelites have ignored God's warnings through the prophets. The evil that has come upon them is just and righteous in view of their disobedience. Israel has become a curse and a taunt among all nations because she has provoked God to anger. Now the people are apostate and so defiant that Jeremiah's words fail to move them to repentance. They boldly tell him that they will not obey and claim that evil has come upon them because they ceased to worship the queen of heaven. Jeremiah's concluding words clearly indicate that God's judgment awaits them and when it comes they will realize that God is fulfilling his word.

Although 45 reports an event which occurred some two decades earlier, at this point it has a singular significance in the Book of Jeremiah. Shortly after the first captivity in 605 B.C. Baruch was instructed to write down Jeremiah's message. Evidently Baruch laments and becomes despondent as he anticipates the terrible condemnation and judgment awaiting Judah. Personally he sees nothing ahead except gloom, poverty, famine, war, and desolation. Baruch is admonished not to seek great things but to realize that life itself is God's gift. God assures him that his life will be spared as a prize of war. Now after the destruction of Jerusalem Baruch is still with Jeremiah, indicating that God has fulfilled his promise.

VI. Prophecies concerning nations and cities—46:1–51:64

Egypt	46:1–28
Philistia	47:1–7
Moab	48:1–47

Ammon	49:1-6
Edom	49:7-22
Damascus	49:23-27
Kedar and Hazor	49:28-33
Elam	49:34-39
Babylon	50:1-51:64

The fourth year of Jehoiakim was a turning point in Judah's political history. In the decisive battle of Carchemish the Babylonians routed the Egyptians so that subsequently the advancing armies of Nebuchadnezzar occupied Palestine. With international problems developing into serious consequences for Judah, the prophet Jeremiah delivers a number of appropriate messages dated in Jehoiakim's fourth year. Significant among them are the prophecies concerning the nations.[23]

Not only does Egypt suffer defeat at Carchemish but ultimately Nebuchadnezzar will advance some five hundred miles up the Nile to punish Amon of Thebes (46). By contrast Israel will be comforted. Philistia will be ruined by invasion from the north (47). Moab's national life will be destroyed suddenly and her glory turned to shame. Because of her pride she cannot escape destruction but is assured return from captivity in the end (48). Ammon will be subjected to judgment, possessed by Israel, and scattered without the promise of restoration (49:1-6). Edom also is doomed. Suddenly she will be reduced from her exalted position so that passers-by will hiss at her (49:7-22). Damascus, Kedar, Hazor, and Elam likewise await judgment (49:23-39).

Babylon comes in for the most extensive consideration in the prophecies against the nations (50:1-51:64). This greatest and most powerful of all nations during the last two decades of Judah's national life will be humbled for her pride. The Lord of hosts will summon the Medes against her. Before the omnipotent God and great creator the mighty nation of Babylon with her idols faces destruction. With these words of denunciation Jeremiah sends Seraiah, a brother of Baruch, to Babylon (51:59-64). After reading this message of judgment at Babylon Seraiah ties the scroll to a rock and throws it into the Euphrates. In a similar manner Babylon's doom is to sink and never to rise again.

VII. Appendix or conclusion—52:1-34

Conquest and plunder of Jerusalem	52:1-23
Condemnation of officials	52:24-27
Deportations	52:28-34

[23] Leslie, *op. cit.*, p. 161, suggests that the superscription in 46:1 dates the entire section 46:3–49:33 in the year 605.

This brief summary of the reign of Zedekiah, the fall of Jerusalem, and the deportations fittingly concludes the Book of Jeremiah. After forty years of preaching Jeremiah witnesses the fulfillment of the message that he had faithfully proclaimed. Zedekiah and his associates suffer the consequences of their disobedience. The vessels and furnishings of the Temple and its court are enumerated in vss. 17-23 as being taken to Babylon before the Temple is destroyed, in accordance with the predictions of Jeremiah. Jehoiachin, who surrendered, was given generous provisions and finally released at the end of Nebuchadnezzar's reign.

Lamentations

The theme of the Book of Lamentations is the destruction and desolation that came to Jerusalem in 586 B.C. God is acknowledged as righteous in punishing his chosen nation for its disobedience. Since God is faithful, there is hope in the confession of sin and an implicit faith in him.

Descriptive of the content of this book are the Hebrew word "Qinoth" or "dirges" in the Talmud, the Greek word "Threnoi" or "elegies" in the Septuagint, and "Threni" or "lamentations" in the Latin versions. The Jews read this book on the ninth of Ab in commemoration of the destruction of Jerusalem. Ancient rabbis who attributed this book to Jeremiah grouped it with the Kethubim, or five scrolls, that were read at various public observances.

In arrangement the first four chapters are alphabetic acrostics. Each chapter has 22 verses or a multiple thereof. The 22 letters of the Hebrew alphabet are used successively to begin each verse in 1 and 2. Chapters 3 and 4 allot three and two verses respectively to each Hebrew letter. Although 5 has 22 verses it does not represent an alphabetic acrostic. This alphabetic scheme, also used in numerous Psalms, escapes the reader of the versions.

The Book of Lamentations was attributed to Jeremiah up to the past few centuries.[24] The Talmud, the Septuagint, ancient church fathers, and church leaders to the eighteenth century considered the prophet to be the author. Since then numerous suggestions ascribe Lamentations to various unknown and unidentified authors during the sixth and third centuries B.C.[25]

The most reasonable and natural interpretation suggests that this book expresses the feelings and reactions of an eyewitness. Among those known from that period Jeremiah seems to be the best qualified. For four decades he had predicted the destruction of Jerusalem. Bypassing the city on his way

[24] In 1712 Herman von der Hardt in a publication at Helmstaedt ascribed the five chapters of Lamentations to Daniel, Shadrach, Meshach, Abednego, and Jehoiachin. See Laetsch, *op. cit.*, p. 375.

[25] For representative discussions of non-Jeremian authorship of Lamentations see R. H. Pfeiffer, *Introduction to the Old Testament*, pp. 722–723.

to Egypt he must have taken one last look at the ruins of his beloved city which for over four centuries had represented the glory and pride of his nation, Israel. Who could have had a more appropriate background for writing Lamentations than the prophet Jeremiah?

The Book of Lamentations may be subdivided as follows:

I. Jerusalem past and present	1:1–22
Desolate conditions	1:1–6
Past memories	1:7–11
God-sent sorrow	1:12–17
God's righteousness acknowledged	1:18–22
II. God's dealings with Zion	2:1–22
God's wrath exhibited	2:1–10
Search for comfort	2:11–22
III. Suffering analyzed	3:1–66
The reality of suffering	3:1–18
God's faithfulness to the contrite	3:19–30
God is author of good and evil	3:31–39
The only hope is in God	3:40–66
IV. Sin is the basis of suffering	4:1–22
The lot of enduring suffering	4:1–12
The charge of shedding innocent blood	4:13–22
V. The prayer of the suffering	5:1–22
Confession of sin	5:1–18
The final appeal	5:19–22

Realistically the author sees Jerusalem in ruins. Once she was a princess but now is reduced to a vassal. In contrast to her past glory she is now in a state of suffering and distress. Those who pass by cannot conceive of her sorrow. There is no one to comfort her.

God's wrath is exhibited in Zion (2). The Lord has terminated the law and all religious observances, has removed the priests, prophets, and kings, and has caused the enemy to raze her palaces and sanctuary. Exposed to the hissing and derision of surrounding enemies the victims plaintively search for comfort.

Suffering is a bitter reality. Jeremiah himself may have experienced such treatment at the hands of his own people as is described in 3:1–18. Jerusalem's glory is gone—there is no hope for her apart from divine intervention. For those who seek God—the contrite—suffering is tempered by the everlasting mercies of the Almighty. As the author of good as well as evil God brings judgment on the wicked (vss. 19–39). By confession of sin and faith in him there is hope that he will avenge them (vss. 40–66).

Zion's fate seems to be worse than that of Sodom. Sudden destruction appears to be preferable to continual suffering for sin. Led by false prophets and priests Jerusalem has shed the innocent blood of the righteous. Consequently she is subjected to her present fate while awaiting brighter prospects (4:22).

The concluding chapter expresses a prayer for God's mercy. The author vividly pictures the plight of God's people as exiles in foreign lands. Can the Lord have forgotten his people? Zion is in ruins and Israel seems to be abandoned. Out of a broken heart, crushed and overwhelmed with sorrow, the author makes his plaintive appeal to the God who reigns forever, imploring him to restore his own. In confession of sin and an implicit faith in God rests the final appeal for restoration.

SELECTED READING

Bright, John. *Jeremiah.* The Anchor Bible. Garden City: Doubleday, 1966.

Dyer, Charles H. "Jeremiah and Lamentations" in *Bible Knowledge Commentary.* Wheaton: Scripture Press, 1985.

Ellison, H. L. "Lamentations" in *Expositor's Bible Commentary.* Grand Rapids: Zondervan Publishing House, 1986.

Feinberg, C. L. "Jeremiah" in *Expositor's Bible Commentary.* Grand Rapids: Zondervan Publishing House, 1986.

Gottwald, N. K. *Studies in the Book of Lamentations.* Naperville: Alec R. Allenson, 1962.

Harrison, R. K. *Jeremiah and Lamentations: An Introduction and Commentary.* Downers Grove: Inter-Varsity Press, 1973.

Jensen, I. L. *Jeremiah: Prophet of Judgment.* Chicago: Moody Press, 1966.

Kaiser, Walter C., Jr. *A Bible Approach to Personal Suffering.* Chicago: Moody Press, 1982.

Laetsch, Theodore. *Jeremiah.* St. Louis: Concordia Publishing House, 1965.

Leslie, Elmer. *Jeremiah.* Nashville: Abingdon Press, 1954.

Schaeffer, Francis. *Death in the City.* Downers Grove: Inter-Varsity Press, 1965.

Streane, A. W. *Jeremiah and Lamentations.* Cambridge: University Press, 1881.

Swindoll, Charles R. *The Lamentations of Jeremiah.* Bible Study Guide. Fullerton: Insight for Living, 1977.

Thompson, J. A. *The Book of Jeremiah.* Grand Rapids: Wm. B. Eerdmans Publishing Co., 1980.

Chart VII TIMES OF JEREMIAH

650—birth of Jeremiah—approximate date
648—birth of Josiah
641—accession of Amon to Davidic throne
640—accession of Josiah
632—Josiah begins search after God—II Chron. 34:3
628—Josiah begins reforms
627—Jeremiah's call to the prophetic ministry
626—Nabopolassar's accession to the Babylonian throne
622—book of the law found in the Temple—Passover observed
612—fall of Nineveh
610—Haran captured by Babylonians
609—Josiah killed—Jehoahaz reigns for three months
Assyro-Egyptian army abandons siege of Haran and retreats to Carchemish
Jehoiakim replaces Jehoahaz in Judah
605—early in year Egyptians from Carchemish defeat Babylonians at Quramati
Babylonians decisively defeat the Egyptians at Carchemish
first captivity of Judah—Jehoiakim pledges allegiance to Babylon
Nebuchadnezzar's accession to the Babylonian throne
601—inconclusive battle between Babylonians and Egyptians
598—Jehoiakim dies—siege of Jerusalem
597—Jehoiachin taken captive after three-month reign
second captivity—Zedekiah becomes king
588—siege of Jerusalem begins January 15
accession of Hophra to Egyptian throne
586—July 19, Babylonians enter Jerusalem
August 15, Temple burned
Gedaliah killed—migration to Egypt

Chapter XX

Ezekiel—The Watchman of Israel

Ezekiel is deeply involved in the problems of his generation. Beginning his ministry as a prophet on the eve of Judah's capitulation six years before the destruction of Jerusalem, he cannot escape the implications of national disaster. He is keenly conscious of the seriousness of the situation as his nation nears the crisis of God's terrible judgment. His message is specific, pertinent, and concentrated on the issues confronting his fellow exiles. When Jerusalem's destruction has become history, he turns his attention to the future hopes of Israel as a nation.

A Prophet among the Exiles

At the time of Ezekiel's birth (622/21 B.C.)[1] Jerusalem was astir with the greatest celebration of the Passover in centuries as Josiah's kingdom was temporarily responding to nation-wide reforms. Not only did optimistic hopes prevail religiously but the fading influence of Assyrian domination in Palestine gave rise to brighter prospects politically. Ashurbanipal, whose reign as Assyrian ruler ended about 630 B.C., had not been succeeded by kings powerful enough to resist aggressive Median and Babylonian advances. The news of Nineveh's fall in 612 undoubtedly relieved Judah of fears that Assyrian armies would ever again threaten her independence.

With religious activities flourishing in the Temple under royal support, Ezekiel, a member of a priestly family, must have enjoyed pleasant associations with the devout people of Judah. His home may have been located on the eastern wall of Jerusalem, so that the outer courts were his playground

[1] For a recent study on the date of Ezekiel see Carl Gordon Howie, *The Date and Composition of Ezekiel,* Journal of Biblical Literature Monograph Series, Vol. IV (Philadelphia, 1950). According to Chap. II, "The Date of the Prophecy," pp. 27–46, he dates Ezekiel's ministry 593 (1:2) to 571 (29:17) B.C. on the basis of fact and tradition.

and the adjoining precincts of the Temple constituted classrooms for his formal training and education.[2] These early years under the shadow of Solomon's Temple acquainted him with every detail of this magnificent edifice as well as the rituals of daily ministration. In addition Ezekiel may have assisted his father and other priests during his boyhood years. Consequently when he was taken to Babylon he had vivid memories of the Temple and its place in the life of his people.

Although Ezekiel as a boy of nine may not have been impressed with the news of Nineveh's fall, the developments that followed could not possibly have failed to make an indelible impression upon him in his formative years. After the sudden departure of Josiah and his army for Megiddo to block the Egyptian advance northward to aid the retreating Assyrians, Josiah is killed (609 B.C.). Every citizen in Jerusalem must have been shocked to see the rapid changes. The funeral of Josiah, the coronation of Jehoahaz, the captivity of Jehoahaz, and the coronation of Jehoiakim as an Egyptian vassal on the Davidic throne—all occurred in the matter of three months' time. More disturbing to the whole kingdom must have been the news of the decisive battle at Carchemish in 605, as the Babylonians took advantage of this victory to pursue the retreating Egyptians, under Necho, down to the borders of Egypt. Perhaps Ezekiel as a youth of sixteen or seventeen considered himself fortunate to escape being included with Daniel and others who were taken as hostages to Babylon in 605 B.C.

Even though he never mentions or refers to Jeremiah, it is unlikely that Ezekiel was unaware of the message of this prophet who was so well known in Jerusalem. Surely Ezekiel had witnessed the mob reaction to Jeremiah's temple sermon (Jer. 26) when the princes refused to allow the execution of Jeremiah by the people and their religious leaders. Perhaps he was puzzled by the fact that Jehoiakim could shed the blood of Uriah the prophet and boldly burn the scroll of Jeremiah without being subjected to immediate judgment.

When Ezekiel was in his early twenties the citizens of Jerusalem were troubled by Jehoiakim's foreign policy. In 605 when the Egyptians retreated to their own borders Jehoiakim became a vassal of Nebuchadnezzar as token hostages were taken into exile.[3] The following year Jehoiakim and other kings acknowledged Nebuchadnezzar as sovereign while the Babylonian armies marched unopposed throughout Syro-Palestine. After three years of subservience Jehoiakim rebelled and Nebuchadnezzar returned to Palestine in 601.[4] Apparently Jehoiakim solved his problem by diplomacy and contin-

[2] See Stephen L. Caiger, *Lives of the Prophets,* p. 223.

[3] For a discussion of these developments see D. J. Wiseman, *Chronicles of the Chaldaean Kings,* pp. 23–32, and his translation of tablet B.M. 21946, pp. 67–74. Cf. also Dan. 1:1.

[4] Cf. II Kings 24:1.

ued as ruler on the Davidic throne while the Babylonians and the Egyptians engaged in an indecisive battle. Vacillating in his loyalty Jehoiakim finally precipitated serious trouble. Perhaps he had hopes that Egypt would save him when he rebelled once more. Before the main force of the Babylonian army arrived, however, Jehoiakim's death brought Jehoiachin to the throne. When the Babylonians besieged Jerusalem the city was spared destruction by Jehoiachin's surrender. Approximately ten thousand of the leading citizens of Judah accompanied their young king into the land of exile.

This time Ezekiel was not on the sidelines merely to observe what happened to others. Exile became part of his personal experience. At the age of twenty-five he was suddenly transferred from Jerusalem and the Temple, which was his center of interest as a priest, to the camp for exiles by the waters of Babylon. Although the Temple was not destroyed, many of the sacred vessels were desecrated by the ruthless invaders who took them as spoils of war for use in their heathen temples.[5]

In this new environment Ezekiel and his fellow captives settled in Tel-abib on the banks of the river Chebar not far from Babylon. The exiles were given tracts of land and apparently lived under favorable conditions. Religious and civil organizations were permitted so that the elders were able to make themselves quite comfortable and in the course of time to develop commercial interests. Thus the exiles had considerable freedom and opportunities to establish a respectable standard of living.[6]

Seemingly the worst aspect of their captivity is the fact that they cannot return to Palestine. Even though this is a political impossibility as they see Nebuchadnezzar increase his power and dominion, they are optimistic. False prophets among the exiles assure them of an early return to their native land.[7] Reports from Jerusalem, where Hananiah predicts that the Babylonian yoke will be broken in two years (Jer. 28:1 ff.) encourage the exiles to hope for a speedy return. When Jeremiah advises by letter that they should settle down and prepare for a seventy-year period of exile, the false prophets become more active (Jer. 29). Shemaiah writes back to Jerusalem charging Jeremiah with the responsibility for their captivity, and demands that he be confined to the stocks. In a public letter to the exiles Jeremiah in turn identifies Shemaiah as a false prophet. Apparently the activity of the false prophets becomes so serious that two of their leaders are executed.

In the fourth year of his reign (594 B.C.) Zedekiah himself makes a trip to Babylonia. Whether or not the exiles are allowed to crowd into Babylon to see Zedekiah drive past in his chariot, it is doubtful that, beyond the initial

[5] Cf. Dan. 5:1–4.

[6] See C. F. Whitley, *The Exilic Age* (London, 1957). Also see preceding chapters on Ezra, Nehemiah, and Esther in this volume.

[7] Cf. Jer. 29:21 and Ezek. 13:3, 16.

excitement, the appearance of Zedekiah in person to pay tribute raised the hopes for a speedy return. Most likely it dampened their prospects for release, and should have sobered their thinking concerning the predictions of Jeremiah, that Jerusalem would be destroyed during his lifetime.

The next year Ezekiel receives a call to the prophetic ministry. To what extent he has shared the false hopes of his fellow exiles is not indicated. He is commissioned to be a watchman for his associates in captivity. His message is essentially the same as that which Jeremiah had consistently proclaimed, namely, the destruction of Jerusalem. In opposition to the false prophets and to a people who were hoping for an immediate return to Jerusalem, Ezekiel is called to warn the people that their beloved city will be destroyed. They will not return to their native land in the near future.

In his presentation Ezekiel is a master of allegory. Symbolism, dramatized personal experiences, and visions are more intimately entwined in his life and teaching than in that of any other prophet in Old Testament times. From the time of his call in 593 until the news of Jerusalem's destruction is reported, Ezekiel directs his efforts toward convincing his people that Jerusalem is awaiting God's judgment. In view of the sinful and idolatrous condition prevailing in the land of Judah, it is reasonable to expect Jerusalem's fall. In his public ministry as well as in his response to inquiry by the delegation of elders he boldly asserts that Jerusalem cannot possibly escape the coming day of retribution.

After the fall of Jerusalem Ezekiel turns his attention to hopes for the future. Restoration prospects constitute the theme of his new message. With the destruction of Jerusalem and the Temple a reality, the exiles perhaps were conditioned to listen to the message of hope. Little is known about the subsequent years of Ezekiel's exile. The last dated reference in his book extends his ministry down to the year 571 B.C. (29:17). Beyond the fact that he was married, nothing is known about his family. Since he was thirty at the time of his call he may not have lived to see the fall of Babylon and the return of the exiles under Cyrus, king of Persia.

The Book of Ezekiel

From a literary standpoint the Book of Ezekiel gains distinction along with Haggai and Zechariah as the best dated among the prophetical books.[8] The date lines throughout the book are chronological in order with the exception of 29:17, 32:1, and 17. These occur in the prophecies against the nations dated in 589 and 571 respectively. The rest of the dates are in chronological sequence, from 593 B.C. in 1:1 down to 585 B.C. in 33:21, when

[8] Howie, *op. cit.*, p. 46, recognizes the individual dates throughout the book as correct even though not all the material between two given dates must necessarily belong there chronologically.

the news of Jerusalem's fate reaches him. The final date line is noted in 40:1, placing the vision of the restored state of Israel in the year 573 B.C.

The Book of Ezekiel is logically divided into three main parts. Chapters 1–24 elaborate on the pending doom of Jerusalem. The next section (25–32) is devoted to the prophecies against foreign nations. The remaining chapters (33–48) mark a complete change in emphasis since the crisis anticipated in the first section occurred in the destruction of Jerusalem. The new theme is the revival and restoration of Israelites to their own land. For a more detailed analysis of this book the following subdivisions may be used:

I.	The call and commission of Ezekiel	1:1–3:21
II.	The doom of Jerusalem	3:22–7:27
III.	The Temple abandoned by God	8:1–11:25
IV.	The leaders condemned	12:1–15:8
V.	God's chosen people condemned	16:1–19:14
VI.	The last full measure	20:1–24:27
VII.	Foreign nations	25:1–32:32
VIII.	Hopes for restoration	33:1–39:29
IX.	The restored state	40:1–48:35

The content of this book as considered here is regarded as the literary composition of Ezekiel.[9] The setting for his ministry is in Babylon among his fellow exiles. Although Jerusalem is the focal point of discussion in 1–24, the context does not require the author to be in Palestine after Ezekiel's call to the prophetic ministry.[10] It is significant to note that he discusses the fate of Jerusalem with the exiles, and at no time indicates that he is addressing the residents of Jerusalem in person as did the prophet Jeremiah.

I. The call and commission of Ezekiel—1:1–3:21

Introduction	1:1–3
Vision of God's glory	1:3–28
The watchman of Israel	2:1–3:21

The date is 593 B.C. In their fifth year in Babylon the captives have no brighter prospects for a speedy return. They are restless and confused as they hear the false prophets counter Jeremiah's advice. The execution of two false prophets, Ahab and Zedekiah, by Nebuchadnezzar evidently did not dim their hopes for a return to Jerusalem in the near future. In the midst of this confusion Ezekiel is called to the prophetic ministry.

The call of Ezekiel is most impressive. Compared to the majestic setting

[9] For a summary of various theories of authorship see Whitley, *op. cit.*, pp. 82 ff.

[10] See Howie, *op. cit.*, Chap. I, "The Residence of Ezekiel," pp. 5–26, for a discussion of the various theories on the place of Ezekiel's ministry. Howie concludes that Ezekiel's entire ministry was in Babylon. Whitley, *op. cit.*, pp. 94 ff., also accepts this traditional view.

of Isaiah's vision and the simple communication to Jeremiah, the call of Ezekiel to prophetic service may be described as fantastic. The setting is by the river Chebar in the environs of Babylon. There is no temple in sight with which he could possibly associate God's presence. Great is the distance between him and Jerusalem, so that at best he has only memories of the sanctuary where God had manifested his presence since the days of Solomon. If Babylon was within view, Ezekiel could possibly see the great temples of Marduk and other Babylonian gods who were acknowledged by the triumphant conqueror Nebuchadnezzar. Here in this heathen environment Ezekiel receives a call to be a spokesman for God.

Ezekiel is made conscious of the presence of God through a vision (1:4–28). Initially his attention is arrested by a great cloud flashing with fire. Four living creatures elaborately described make their appearance, darting back and forth like a flash of lightning. These creatures appear to have both natural and supernatural features. Closely related to each creature is a wheel which is correlated to every movement. With the spirit of the creatures in the wheels the behavior is spectacular but orderly. By means of wings for each creature they move about under the firmament. Ezekiel also sees a throne above on which is seated an individual having the likeness of a human form surrounded by brightness similar to a rainbow. Without explaining or interpreting all these things Ezekiel labels the whole manifestation an appearance of the likeness of the glory of God. Here in a heathen country far from the Temple in Jerusalem Ezekiel is made conscious of the presence of God.[11]

Although he falls prostrate before this divine manifestation, God bids him rise as the Spirit fills him and enables him to obey. Addressed as a "son of man," he is commissioned to be a messenger to his own people who are disobedient, stubborn, and rebellious.[12] The message is given to him in symbolic picture. He is commanded to eat a scroll of lamentations, mourning, and woe which turns into the sweetness of honey in his mouth. Forewarned that the people will not listen to him or accept his message, Ezekiel is commanded not to fear them. As the glory of God departs, the Spirit makes Ezekiel conscious of the literal reality that he is among the exiles at Tel-abib by the river Chebar. Overwhelmed by all that he has seen, he reflects on these developments for seven days.

After a week's silence Ezekiel is commissioned as a watchman to the house of Israel (3:16–21). Living among his people he becomes aware of

[11] The presence of God with his people was vividly manifest in a cloud ever since their deliverance from Egypt. Cf. Ex. 14:19, 20, 24; Num. 10:11–12, 34, etc. When Solomon dedicated the Temple the visible presence of God in a cloud was identified as the glory of the Lord. Cf. II Chron. 5:14 and 7:3. Since Ezekiel was a priest, it may have surprised him to find this manifestation in a heathen environment so far from the Temple.

[12] This designation is exclusively used of Ezekiel in the Old Testament with the exception of Dan. 7:13. It emphasizes the fact that in the presence of God the prophet is human and merely a "child of man."

his own responsibility to warn them. If they perish in spite of his warning, he is not guilty. However, if he fails to warn them and they perish he is charged with their blood. Being a faithful watchman is a matter of life and death.

II. The doom of Jerusalem—3:22–7:27

Destruction portrayed	3:22–5:17
Idolatry brings judgment	6:1–7:27

By symbolic action Ezekiel not only arrests the attention of the exiles but vividly portrays the pending fate of Jerusalem. Under strict orders to pose dumbness and speak only to his audience as the Lord bids him, Ezekiel cuts a sketch of Jerusalem on a clay brick. Placing siegeworks and battering rams around it, the prophet demonstrates the immediate future lot of the city, so well known and loved by his audience. They need no verbal explanation, since they are fully familiar with every street in this city from which they have so recently been removed by the conquering Babylonians.

For a period of 390 days Ezekiel lies on his left side, representing the punishment of Israel, the Northern Kingdom. For 40 days he lies on his right side, signifying the judgment awaiting Judah, the Southern Kingdom. During this time Ezekiel's prescribed rations, normal to siege conditions, were limited to a daily allowance of about 12 ounces of bread and less than two pints of water. In baking his bread Ezekiel is instructed to use human excrement for fuel, depicting the uncleanness of Israel. This is so abhorrent to Ezekiel that God permits him to substitute the usual cow dung. A reasonable interpretation suggests that the prophet normally sleeps each night but during the day represents the fate of Jerusalem by lying on his side. He refuses to engage in ordinary conversation and speaks only as directed by God. Undoubtedly by this pattern of behavior the whole community of exiles come at one time or another to Ezekiel's home to see for themselves what the prophet is demonstrating.[13]

At the end of this period (5:1 ff.), when Ezekiel's peculiar behavior was known throughout the exilic colony, the people must have been shocked to see him shave his head and beard, carefully dividing his hair into three equal parts by weight. By burning one third, chopping one third into fine pieces with the sword, and scattering the rest to the wind, Ezekiel realistically demonstrates and announces what God will do to Jerusalem in judgment.

[13] See H. L. Ellison, *Ezekiel: The Man and His Message* (Grand Rapids: Eerdmans, 1956), pp. 31–35, for a logical interpretation. In view of the dates given in 1:1 and 8:1 which allow for a 413-day interval it seems reasonable to assume that the last 40 days of the 390-day period for Israel and the 40 days for Judah were concurrent, since both shared in the exile. For Israel the 390 years would extend from the division of the kingdom in 931 down to approximately 539 B.C., when Babylon fell. The LXX reads 190 instead of 390 in 4:5, 9.

One third of its population shall die of famine and pestilence, one third shall fall by the sword, and one third shall be scattered to the wind. God will not have pity on them. Time for judgment has come. The charge against them—they have defiled God's sanctuary with abominations and detestable things (5:11).

The details of the impending doom are clearly outlined in 6–7. Wherever the Israelites have worshiped idols the victims of famine, sword, and pestilence shall lie scattered throughout the land. Dead bodies before their idol altars will be the silent testimony that the gods they worshiped could not save. For emphasis Ezekiel is commanded to stamp his foot and clap his hands. By this severe judgment God will cause them to acknowledge him as Lord.[14]

Terrible destruction is near. God's sentence in all its dreadful aspects is about to be executed on Judah and Jerusalem. Injustice, violence, and pride are subject to God's wrath. Business is terminated. No one responds to the trumpet's blast that calls them to war. The sword surrounds them from without while famine prevails within the capital city. God is turning his face so that they may fully profane his sanctuary and allow robbers to plunder it. Because of their bloody crimes He is bringing the worst of nations upon them. The prophets, priests, elders, and king shall all fail them as this disaster becomes a reality in Judah. The Almighty is actually judging them on the basis of their terrible sins.

III. The Temple abandoned by God—8:1–11:25

The setting for the vision	8:1–4
Idolatry in Jerusalem	8:5–18
The judgment executed	9:1–10:22
God's mercy in judgment	11:1–25

In fourteen months' time the spectacular ministry of Ezekiel arouses popular interest and reaction among the exiles. The timely subject of Jerusalem's fate is of current concern to a people who have an intense desire to return to their native city at the earliest opportunity. They have the notion that God will not destroy his people, who are custodians of the law, nor his Temple, which represents his glory and presence with them (Jer. 7–12). In due time (592 B.C.) a delegation of elders comes to confer with the prophet. With the elders apparently waiting before him, Ezekiel has a vision of the conditions and pending developments in the Temple (8:1–11:25). This

[14] The expression "know that I am the Lord" occurs in this simple form 54 times and in expanded variations another 18 times. God made himself known in grace or judgment so that they realized that God was acting. For discussion see Ellison, *op. cit.*, pp. 37–39.

message he relates to them as indicated in the concluding statement of the passage.[15]

What is the analysis of the conditions in Jerusalem from God's standpoint as revealed to Ezekiel? The religious conditions are a far cry from conformance to the law and God's standards. Although the glory of God is still in Jerusalem, Ezekiel sees four horrible scenes of idolatrous practice in the shadows of the Temple. A reasonable interpretation is to recognize with Keil that not all of these practices actually prevailed in the Temple itself but that this vision represents the idolatrous conditions throughout Judah.[16]

Most conspicuous is the image of jealousy. Perhaps this is a man-made representation of Israel's God—an explicit violation of the first commandment. Whatever it signifies, the image of jealousy is a dreadful provocation to the holy God of Israel.[17] As representatives of Israel, the seventy elders worship idols in the Temple. Apparently they have humanistic conceptions devoid of an omniscient God. At the entry of the north gate to the Temple women are weeping for Tammuz, the god of vegetation who died in the summer heat and returned to life with the rainy season.[18] In the inner court between the porch and the altar twenty-five men are facing eastward worshiping the sun, which was explicitly forbidden (Deut. 4:19; 17:3).[19]

This provocation causes God to release his wrath in judgment. Executioners are summoned. The glory of God moves from the cherubim to the threshold of the Temple. Mercy, however, precedes judgment as a man dressed in linen marks all the individuals who deplore the idolatry in the Temple. Beginning with the elders at the Temple the six executioners proceed through Jerusalem killing all who do not have a mark on their foreheads. Overwhelmed with grief Ezekiel appeals to God for mercy but is reminded that Jerusalem is filled with blood and injustice. This is the time of wrath—God has forsaken the land.

When the man clothed in linen reports that he has identified and marked all the righteous throughout the city, Ezekiel sees the manifestation of the glory of God that he had seen at the time of his call. In this appearance the living creatures, standing on the south side of the Temple, are identified as cherubim. The man clothed in linen then receives the divine

[15] Ellison, *op. cit.,* p. 40, suggests that Ezekiel spoke intermittently to the elders before him.

[16] See C. F. Keil, *Commentary on Ezekiel,* at reference on 8:1–4.

[17] According to G. E. Wright, *The Old Testament against its Environment,* pp. 24 ff., no image of Jehovah has ever been found by archaeologists.

[18] For a fuller description see G. A. Cooke, *Ezekiel I,* pp. 96–97. This represents an ancient religious rite dating back to about 3000 B.C. in Babylon. In popular form this myth was common during Old Testament times from Canaan to Babylon.

[19] The position of these men seems to justify the inference that they represent the priesthood. Ellison, *op. cit.,* p. 43, and others identify this with the worship of Shamash the Babylonian sun-god, charging these 25 leaders with an acknowledgment that the Babylonian gods were defeating Jehovah God of Israel.

command to go in among the whirling wheels and the cherubim to obtain burning coals and scatter them over the city of Jerusalem. The divine glory now transfers from the court to the east gate of the Temple.

Ezekiel is brought by the Spirit to the east gate where twenty-five men responsible for the welfare of Jerusalem are assembled (11:1–13). Under the leadership of Jaazaniah and Pelatiah, two princes whose identity is uncertain, these men misinterpret the warnings and rest complacently in the hope that Jerusalem will protect them from the judgments of God.[20] The fallacy of this is evident to Ezekiel with the death of Pelatiah. Jerusalem will not be a caldron to protect them from the coming doom—they will be judged at the borders of Israel. God's people have disobeyed his commandments, conforming to the behavior pattern of surrounding nations.

Appalled, Ezekiel falls on his face before God, imploring him to save a remnant. In reply he is assured that God, who has scattered the people, will gather them back to their homeland. In the land of exile God will be a sanctuary to them. When they are brought back to the land of Israel, he will impart to them a new spirit and a heart of flesh conditioning them for obedience.

In conclusion Ezekiel sees in this vision the departure of God's presence. The glory of God which hovered over Jerusalem now moves to the mountain east of the city. Jerusalem with its Temple is abandoned for judgment. The pending destruction is only a matter of time.

This vision (8:11) reveals to Ezekiel the conditions in Jerusalem as seen by God. As a former citizen of Jerusalem Ezekiel was familiar with the prevailing idolatry but now, as a commissioned watchman for the house of Israel, he shares the divine perspective. Judah's cup of iniquity is almost filled. This divine revelation he shares with the exiles (11:25).

IV. The leaders condemned—12:1–15:8

Demonstration of the exile	12:1–20
The false leaders	12:21–14:11
The hopeless condition	14:12–15:8

By symbolic action Ezekiel enacts before his Israelite audience in Babylon the bitter experiences in store for the residents remaining in Jerusalem. Most pathetic is the last exit of a citizen who is forced to abandon his home, knowing that his city is doomed and that he is headed for exile. Ezekiel demonstrates this as he leaves his home through a hole in the wall, carrying on his shoulders a pack containing a few necessities. In a similar manner the

[20] Ellison, *op. cit.*, pp. 45–47, interprets this as a prediction of the conditions that existed during the siege a few years later. The pro-Egyptian leaders ignored Jeremiah's warnings and were confident that Jerusalem would stand, as their fanatical trust in the Temple indicates, Jer. 7:4. However, these leaders were executed at Riblah, II Kings 25:18–21.

prince in Jerusalem will make his final exit from the capital of Judah (12:1–16). Portraying the conditions in the last days of the siege Ezekiel eats anxiously his bread and drinks his water in fear and trembling (12:17–20).

Religious leaders are responsible for deluding the people by assuring them of peace, when the wrath of God is awaiting them. Women likewise have been guilty of causing the people to believe lies.[21] All who prophesy falsely are condemned for their evil speaking. Ezekiel boldly charges the elders, who appear before him to inquire of the Lord, with having idols in their hearts. He urges them to repent lest God's wrath come upon them.

Jerusalem is so sinful that no one can save it from destruction (14:12–15:8). Very likely the people believe that because of the righteous group in the city God will postpone his judgments as he has done in days past. In a final and solemn warning Ezekiel tells his audience that even if Noah, Daniel, or Job were in Jerusalem, God would not spare the city. They can only save themselves. As a vine in the forest ready to be burned so the inhabitants of Jerusalem await the judgment of God.

V. God's chosen people condemned—16:1–19:14

The spiritual history of Israel	16:1–63
The unfaithful king	17:1–24
Individual responsibility	18:1–32
Lamentation for princes of Israel	19:1–14

In allegorical language Ezekiel portrays the corruption of the Israelite religion. When Israel was as helpless as a newborn babe they were chosen by God and tenderly nurtured as the people of his choice. Enjoying these bountiful blessings Israel was as deliberate in her apostasy as a harlot is in her sinful ways. Instead of being devoted to God, she had misused the material things so abundantly provided for her. Parents had even offered their children in sacrifice to idols. In the course of time they curried the favor of heathen nations such as Egypt, Assyria, and Chaldea. The fall of Samaria should have been interpreted as a timely warning.[22] The indictment against Judah is concluded with a promise of restoration (16:53–63). God will remember his covenant with them in reconciliation after they have been duly punished for their sin.

In another allegory or riddle (17:1–24) Ezekiel presents the political doom of Judah, specifically illustrating the preceding chapter. The king of Babylon, like an eagle or a vulture that lops off the top of a cedar, has cut off the Davidic dynasty. The substitute king, obviously Zedekiah, will break

[21] "Sorceresses" would be a better modern term than "prophetesses" for the women described in 13:17–23, according to Ellison, *op. cit.*, pp. 56–57. The only other "prophetesses" mentioned in Scripture are Miriam, Deborah, Huldah, and Noadiah.

[22] Cf. Jer. 3:6–13.

his covenant with the Babylonian and turn to Egypt for help instead of trusting God. In consequence he will be taken captive to die in the land of exile.

Apparently the exiles had concluded that they were suffering for the sins of their fathers (18:1 ff.). Surely the exile was a place of corporate suffering (11:14–21) but in clearly defined terms Ezekiel draws a line of demarcation between the righteous and the unrighteous. Even though all must suffer for the present, the ultimate distinction between them is a matter of life and death. The unrighteous perish—the righteous shall live. As the basic laws of the Pentateuch are addressed to the individual, so Ezekiel here pinpoints the responsibility of each Israelite.

Having dealt with the problem of the individual, Ezekiel reverts to the theme of primary importance—the fate of Judah and Jerusalem. In a lamentation (19:1–14) he expresses the pathetic development picturing the prince of Judah as a lion caught with hooks and caged for deportation to Babylon. He laments that the destruction of the kingdom is so complete that not even a strong stem remains, not even a scepter for a ruler.[23]

VI. The last full measure—20:1–24:27

Israel's failure	20:1–44
Judgment in process	20:45–22:31
Consequences for unfaithfulness	23:1–49
Ezekiel tempered for judgment	24:1–27

For two years the prophet as a watchman has faithfully warned the people. Once more in the year 591 a delegation of elders is seated before him to inquire of the Lord. Zedekiah is still on the throne in Jerusalem.

Ezekiel once more reviews the history of Israel. This time he points out that God chose Israel in Egypt, gave them the law, and brought them into the land of Canaan but they have constantly provoked him with their idols, heathen rites, and sacrifices. In wrath God will scatter them and ultimately bring them back purified for his own name's sake (21:1–44).

The thrust of this review emphasizes the judgment which follows in natural sequence. God is kindling a fire to consume the Negeb (20:45–49). He is sharpening his sword, bringing the king of Babylon on Jerusalem in judgment (21–22). Princes have shed innocent blood, the people are guilty of social evils, breaking the law, and forgetting God. Jerusalem will become the melting pot or furnace to purify the people as God pours out his wrath.

The sin of foreign alliances is significantly developed in 23 as Samaria, named Oholah, and Jerusalem, named Oholibah, are charged with harlotry. Alliances with foreign nations which frequently involved the recognition of heathen gods constituted a serious offense against God.[24] Unfor-

[23] Cf. Is. 6:13.

[24] The request for a king in the days of Samuel (I Sam. 8:5) reflected the fact that

tunately Judah failed to take the fall of Samaria (722) as a warning. In view of her sins Jerusalem is warned that the Chaldean lovers are coming in to bring God's judgment upon them.[25] The cup of God's wrath is at hand.

On the very same day (January 15, 588) that the Babylonian armies surrounded Jerusalem Ezekiel was given another message (24).[26] Whether he dramatized this in symbolic action or conveyed it verbally as an allegory is not indicated. Having before him a choice lamb in the pot, representing Jerusalem, Ezekiel takes out the contents for destruction. The pot with rust spots depicting bloodstains is placed back on the fire until it melts. In the melting process the bloody spots are removed, clearly illustrating that the bloodstains of Jerusalem can be removed only by complete destruction. In the course of this portrayal Ezekiel's wife dies. As a significant sign to his audience Ezekiel is commanded not to mourn publicly. Neither are the people to mourn when they receive the news that the Temple in Jerusalem has been destroyed. The sovereign God does this so that they will know that he is the Lord. In conclusion God assures Ezekiel that when the news of Jerusalem's fate reaches him, his dumbness will be terminated.

VII. Foreign nations—25:1–32:32

Ammon, Moab, Edom, and Philistia	25:1–17
Phoenicia	26:1–28:26
Egypt	29:1–32:32

The dated prophecies in these chapters, with the exception of 29:17–21, occur during the tenth to twelfth years of Ezekiel's captivity. This approximates the period of Nebuchadnezzar's siege of Jerusalem, 588–586. With the capitulation of Jerusalem pending the question undoubtedly arose as to what place the other nations would have relative to God's plan for Judah. Would they also come in for judgment?

In the opening chapter of this passage the Ammonites, Moabites, Edomites, and Philistines are denounced for their pride and gleeful attitude toward Judah's fate. Although allied with Judah in plotting rebellion against Babylon (Jer. 27:3) they abandoned her to bear the brunt of Nebuchadnezzar's invasion. For their arrogance and hatred of Israel's religion they will be punished. Execution against them begins in the subsequent period but the

---

the people were impressed with heathen kings. Solomon made an alliance with Egypt, I Kings 3:1. In the Northern Kingdom Jehu paid tribute to the Assyrian king, Shalmaneser III, as depicted on the Black Obelisk, see Pritchard, *Ancient Near Eastern Texts,* p. 280. The Kingdom of Judah was most seriously involved with Assyria by Ahaz, II Kings 16:7 and Is. 7:1–17, who defied Isaiah by making a treaty with Tiglath-pileser III. Note also Hezekiah and the Babylonians in Is. 39:6.

[25] Note the warning of Jerusalem's doom as announced by Isaiah. Cf. Is. 39:6 and II Kings 20:17.

[26] The 9th year, the 10th month, the 10th day—January 15, 588 B.C. Cf. Parker and Dubberstein, *Babylonian Chronology,* p. 26, and Thiele, *The Mysterious Numbers of the Hebrew Kings,* p. 164. Note also Jer. 39:1 and II Kings 25:1.

complete fulfillment of this prediction awaits the ultimate establishment of Israel's supremacy in her own land. Through Israel God will bring vengeance upon Edom (25:14).

The longer passages are directed against the Phoenician cities of Tyre and Sidon and against Egypt. With the Babylonian armies concentrating on Jerusalem the exiles may have wondered why Phoenicia and Egypt escaped the vengeful thrust of Nebuchadnezzar.

In a more lengthy analysis Ezekiel treats the fate of Tyre and its prince with an appropriate lamentation for each (26:1–28:19). Sidon, which was of minor importance, receives only brief consideration (28:20–23). By contrast Israel will be restored (28:24–26). Tyre's doom is certain since God is bringing Nebuchadnezzar against her.[27] The lamentation over Tyre portrays the loss of glory and supremacy that she enjoyed in her strategic location, architectural beauty, military strength, and most of all her fabulous commercial wealth.[28] Neither will Sidon escape destruction (28:24–26).

To parallel the fall of Tyre Ezekiel takes up the fate of the prince who rules the city and kingdom of Tyre (28:1–10). Although a god in his own eyes the king of Tyre is only a man as far as God is concerned. For his vain aspirations he will be demoted.

Egypt, which usually played a vital part in the international relations of Judah, receives extensive consideration in these prophecies (29–32). In her associations with Israel the nation of Egypt has been like a reed, abandoning her to enemy conquest when expedient. She and her rulers are also charged with pride—Pharaoh boasts that the Nile River, on which Egypt depends for its existence, was made by him.

Conquest and plunder await Egypt. Even though she will be restored after a forty-year period of desolation she will never again resume her former position. Never again shall she provide false security for Israel. God will send Nebuchadnezzar into Egypt to spoil her wealth as evil men possess the land. The divine acts of judgment will be evident in the destruction of the idols in Memphis and the defeat of the multitudes at Thebes.

By way of warning Egypt is compared to Assyria, which towered as a cedar of Lebanon above all other trees (31:1–18).[29] Like the mighty kingdom of Assyria, Egypt will fall. Ezekiel likens the destruction to her descent into Hades. A year and two months later, after Ezekiel heard of Jerusalem's

[27] The siege of Tyre 586-573 B.C. ended as Ethbaal, king of Tyre, acknowledged Babylonian supremacy. The island city was not conquered until Alexander the Great built a causeway or mole in 332 B.C. to force complete submission.

[28] For a brief treatment of this prophecy see Ellison, *op. cit.*, pp. 99-116.

[29] This message is dated in May/June, 587 B.C. The exiles were hoping that Egypt would save Jerusalem from destruction by the Babylonians who had begun the siege in January, 588. On the use of "Assyria" as it occurs in the Hebrew text in Ezek. 31:3 compare the King James, American Standard, and Revised Standard versions.

fall, he once more lamented Egypt's pending humiliation (32:1–16). The funeral dirge (32:17–32), perhaps dated in the same month,[30] expands the lamentation, listing six nations already in Hades. Egypt in her fate will join such great world powers as Assyria, Elam, Meshech-Tubal, and the neighboring nations such as Edom, the Sidonions, and the princes of the north—undoubtedly a reference to the Syrian rulers. These will welcome Egypt to Hades in the day of her calamity.

VIII. Hopes for restoration—33:1–39:29

The watchman recommissioned	33:1–33
The shepherds of Israel	34:1–31
Contrast between Edom and Israel	35:1–36:38
Promise of restoration and triumph	37:1–39:29

Ezekiel's message is geared to the times in which he lives. Since the time of his call in 593 B.C. he has conveyed, by word and symbolic action, the fate of Jerusalem. During the actual siege of Jerusalem he was given a message concerning the place of foreign nations in the economy of Israel's God. With the destruction of Jerusalem accomplished Ezekiel once more directs his attention to Israel's national hopes.

A fugitive from Jerusalem reports to Ezekiel and the exiles in January, 585 B.C., that the city actually capitulated to the Babylonian army. Undoubtedly official reports in Babylon had previously announced the conquest of Judah. Very likely the given date (33:21–22) is closely related to the entire content of this chapter.[31] God, who had previously revealed to Ezekiel the fact of Jerusalem's fall on the eve of this messenger's arrival, now bids the prophet speak again. This termination of his period of dumbness is a sign of divine confirmation (24:27). God had already conditioned Ezekiel by reminding him that he is a watchman to the house of Israel (33:1–20). Addressed again as a son of man, he is responsible for warning his own people.

After the arrival of the fugitive Ezekiel is prepared for the transitional message (33:24–33). The unrepentant remnant in Palestine now transfer their confidence from the ruined Temple to the fact that they are Abraham's

[30] Keil, *op. cit.*, at reference suggests that this was composed 14 days later in the 12th month (cf. 32:1). Owing to a copyist's error the month was omitted here. RSV follows the Greek and inserts the first month. Since 32:1 is dated in the 12th month it seems reasonable to date this the same month, allowing for chronological sequence.

[31] Ellison, *op. cit.*, p. 118, reads "eleventh" in 33:21 on the basis of 8 Hebrew MSS, some LXX manuscripts and the Syriac identifying this date with August, 586 B.C. Cf. also Doederlein and Hitzig in commentaries at reference. G. A. Cooke, in *ICC ad loc.*, assumes a double system of dating. According to Thiele in his thorough study of chronology, *The Mysterious Numbers of the Hebrew Kings*, pp. 161-166, and the chart on pp. 74-75, Zedekiah fled from Jerusalem on July 19, 586, and the final destruction of Jerusalem began on August 15, 586. Although normally it was a three-month journey, this particular fugitive came to the exiles in January, 585 B.C.

seed.[32] With Jerusalem in ruins, surely none in Ezekiel's audience are foolish enough to think that they can stage a successful rebellion against Nebuchadnezzar. Ezekiel is warned that the people will be curious enough to listen to his message but will not obey it.

The theme of hope begins with a discussion of the shepherds of Israel (34:1–31). In contrast to the false shepherds, who are condemned for their selfishness, God is portrayed as the true Shepherd of Israel.[33] Looking far into the future the Israelites are assured of national restoration. Making a covenant of peace with them, God will establish them in their own land to enjoy unlimited blessings under the shepherd identified as "my servant David."[34] Since history has no record of the fulfillment of this promise to Israel, it seems reasonable to anticipate its realization in the future.

The thesis of Israel's restoration is developed (35:1–36:38) in contrast to the antithesis of Edom's destruction. Edom or Mount Seir is charged with enmity, bloody hatred, covetousness of Israel's land, and even blasphemy against God.[35] Edom, including all the nations (36:5), is earmarked for devastation. By contrast the Israelites will be gathered from all nations and once more enjoy God's favor in their own land. Israel has profaned God's name among the nations but he will act to bring them back for his own name's sake. By a transformation God will impart to them a new heart and a new spirit, purifying them in preparation for being his people.

No doubt both Ezekiel and his audience had questions as to how this could come to pass. With Jerusalem in ruins and the people in exile, prospects were dim. In 37:1–39:29 the restoration of Israel in triumph over all nations is developed and portrayed. By divine revelation Ezekiel comes to realize that this will be accomplished.

The Spirit of the Lord leads Ezekiel into the midst of a valley filled with dry bones. God bids the prophet to speak to these bones. To his utter amazement Ezekiel sees the bones take on life. This revival of dead bones signifies the revival and restoration of the whole house of Israel—including both the Northern and the Southern Kingdom. They will be reunited as the Israelites are regathered from among the nations with the specific promise that one king shall reign over them. The ruler or shepherd, again identified as "my servant David," shall be prince forever as the people conform to

[32] Cf. Jer. 40–43 for the attitude of the remnant in being unwilling to follow Jeremiah's advice.

[33] "Shepherd" is here used metaphorically meaning "king," according to Ellison, *op. cit.*, p. 121. See Ps. 23 for the perfect shepherd. Also John 10.

[34] See Ellison, *op. cit.*, pp. 119–122, for a summary of Israel's rulers past and present, indicating that under Persian and Greek and Roman rule no one of the Davidic line was ever recognized as king.

[35] Esau and his descendants, known as Edomites, settled in Mount Seir south of the Dead Sea, Gen. 36. Note the continuous animosity in the Old Testament between Israel and Edom. Cf. Num. 21, etc.

the statutes and ordinances of God. In the land of Israel God will once more establish his sanctuary so that all nations will know that he has sanctified and cleansed his nation Israel.

The establishment of Israel will not remain unnoticed or unchallenged. Nations from the uttermost parts of the north, notably Gog and Magog, will mass their armies to fight against Israel in the latter days. Living in unwalled villages and enjoying unprecedented prosperity, Israel will become the coveted object of the invading enemies from the north. This, however, will be a day of divine vindication. The forces of nature in the form of earthquake, rain, hail, fire, and brimstone will be released against this ferocious intruder. Confusion, bloodshed, and pestilence prevail as they fight each other. Birds of prey and wild beasts devour the armies of Gog and Magog and the enemy is rendered helpless, thus enabling Israel to gather the spoils of war. For seven months they will bury the dead and cleanse the land.

With all nations conscious of God's judgments Israel is assured of the restoration of her fortunes. They will dwell safely in the land with none to make them afraid. None will be left among the nations when God pours out his Spirit upon them.

IX. The restored state—40:1–48:35

The new Temple	40:1–43:12
Regulations for worship	43:13–46:24
The land of blessing	47:1–48:35

The Passover season during the month of Nisan (573) undoubtedly reminded the exiles of the greatest miracle that God had ever performed in behalf of Israel when he delivered them from Egyptian bondage. During the fourteen years that had elapsed since the destruction of Jerusalem the exiles probably adjusted to their new environment, having had no hope for an immediate return. At best, if they believed the prediction of Jeremiah concerning a seventy-year exilic period, only a few of the people who had been taken from Jerusalem would ever return. Undoubtedly Ezekiel's promise of ultimate restoration assured them of God's love and care for his nation Israel.

Ezekiel has another vision. Similar to the revelation in chapters 8–11 the prophet sees the reality of the restoration. Again the focal point is the Temple in Jerusalem, which symbolizes the actual presence of God with his people. An unnamed man, most likely an angel of the Lord, takes Ezekiel on a guided tour of the Temple, its environs, and the land of Palestine. The glory of God, which formerly abandoned the Temple to its doom, now returns to this holy sanctuary. Once more God dwells there among his people. Ezekiel is instructed to be observant on this tour of restored Israel. All that he sees and hears he shares with his fellow exiles (40:4).

From the vantage point of a high mountain Ezekiel sees a citylike structure representing the Temple and its surroundings.[36] The guide with a measuring reed in his hand carefully surveys the walls of the temple area and the various buildings while conducting Ezekiel on this most impressive tour. Climactic to the tour of the Temple is the reappearance of the glory of God, which Ezekiel identifies with the revelation he had at the canal Chebar (cf. 1 and 8–11). Ezekiel is now assured that in this new Temple God is establishing his eternal dwelling place with his people. No more shall they defile God's name with idolatry. To the penitent and contrite in Ezekiel's audience this message of the restored Temple offers hope. They are encouraged to conform their lives in obedience to God's requirements (43:10–13).

The new regulations for acceptable worship are carefully prescribed (43:13–46:24). Ezekiel sees the altar and takes note of the offerings and sacrifices which provide the people an acceptable basis for approaching God. As he comes into the temple itself he prostrates himself in recognition of God's glory which fills the sanctuary. Once more he is directed to mark well the instructions concerning the ordinances and the ones permitted to officiate in the new Temple. For breaking the covenant and profaning the Temple with idolatry the priesthood is subjected to severe punishment. God will bless Israel with a restored priesthood and a prince who shall teach the people, establish justice, and observe the feasts and seasons.

The vision culminates in Ezekiel's tours of the land of Israel (47:1–48:35). Beginning at the door of the Temple he sees a river issuing southward from below the threshold down to the Arabah, providing fresh water for abundant sea life and irrigating the land for the production of fruit. The whole area takes on new life as the fishing industry flourishes and fruit farms abound on every hand. The land of Canaan is carefully divided with allotments for each tribe, from the entrance of Hamath in the north to the brook of Egypt in the south. The prince and the Levites are allotted a portion adjoining the city in which the Temple is located.[37] This city in which the divine presence is manifest in the glory of God is identified as "The Lord is there."

Israel restored to the promised land—this is the hope Ezekiel has for his generation in the land of exile. God will regather his people in triumph and bless them once more.

[36] For a diagram of the Temple and its buildings as described here see F. Davidson, *The New Bible Commentary*, under article "Ezekiel," pp. 664–665.

[37] The basic theme of Ezek. 33–48 that Israel will be restored to her own land as supreme under the rule of a prince agrees with the theme in Isaiah that assures Israel of an absolute period of universal peace when Zion will be the focal point of all nations under the control of this ideal ruler who shall execute perfect righteousness. Cf. Is. 2, 4, 11, 35, and 65–66.

SELECTED READING

ALEXANDER, RALPH H. "Ezekiel" in *Expositor's Bible Commentary.* 6:735–996. Grand Rapids: Zondervan Publishing House, 1986.

BLACKWOOD, A. W., JR. *Ezekiel.* Grand Rapids: Baker Book House, 1965.

COOKE, G. A. *Ezekiel (ICC).* New York: Scribner's, 1937.

CRAIGIE, PETER C. *Ezekiel.* The Daily Study Bible. Edited by John L. Gibson. Philadelphia: Westminster Press, 1983.

DYER, CHARLES H. "Ezekiel" in *The Bible Knowledge Commentary.* Wheaton: Scripture Press, 1985.

ELLISON, H. L. *Ezekiel: The Man and His Message.* Grand Rapids: Wm. B. Eerdmans Publishing Co., 1956.

ENNS, PAUL. *Ezekiel.* Bible Study Commentary Series. Grand Rapids: Zondervan Publishing House, 1981.

FAIRBAIRN, P. *An Exposition of Ezekiel.* Grand Rapids: Zondervan Publishing House, 1960.

FEINBERG, CHARLES L. *The Prophecy of Ezekiel.* Chicago: Moody Press, 1969.

GAEBELEIN, A. C. *The Prophet Ezekiel.* New York: Our Hope Press, 1921.

HOWIE, C. G. *The Date and Composition of Ezekiel.* Philadelphia: Journal of Biblical Literature Monograph series, Vol. IV, 1950.

IRONSIDE, H. A. *Ezekiel.* New York: Loizeaux Brothers, 1953.

PAYNE, J. B. *Encyclopedia of Biblical Prophecy.* New York: Harper & Row, 1973.

TAYLOR, JOHN B. *Ezekiel: An Introduction and Commentary.* The Tyndale Old Testament Commentaries. Downers Grove: Inter-Varsity Press, 1969.

WHITLEY, C. F. *The Exilic Age.* London: Westminster Press, 1957.

WINWARD, A. S. *Guide to the Prophets.* Richmond: John Knox Press, 1969.

Chart VIII CHRONOLOGY FOR EZEKIEL

621—birth of Ezekiel
reforms of Josiah—ministry of Jeremiah
612—fall of Nineveh
609—death of Josiah
Jehoahaz rules three months—Jehoiakim made king
605—battle of Carchemish
hostages taken from Jerusalem to Babylon
601—Babylonian-Egyptian battle at borders of Egypt
598—Jehoiakim rebels against Babylon
597—Jehoiachin and some 10,000 people including Ezekiel taken captive
594—embassy sent by Zedekiah to Babylon—Jer. 29:3
Zedekiah appears in Babylon—Jer. 51:59
593—call of Ezekiel—1:1–2 and 3:16
592—tablet giving rations for Jehoiachin
elders confer with Ezekiel—8:1–11:25
591—elders confer with Ezekiel—20:1
588—siege of Jerusalem begins in January
message by Ezekiel—24:1
587—prophecies by Ezekiel—29:1; 30:20; 31:1
586—Babylonians enter Jerusalem—Zedekiah flees—July 19
Temple burned—August 15
prophecy against Tyre—26:1
585—fugitive arrives—January 8—Ezek. 33:21
lamentation over Egypt—32:1 and 17
573—Ezekiel's vision—40:1
571—Ezekiel's last dated prophecy—29:17
561—Jehoiachin released from prison—March 21, 561 B.C.—II Kings 25:27
(According to Thiele, a Nisan-to-Nisan reckoning is used in Ezekiel while Kings uses a Tishri-to-Tishri reckoning; the former begins in April, the latter in October)

Chapter XXI

Daniel—Statesman and Prophet

Eminent among the Jewish exiles in Babylon the man Daniel gained the dual distinction of politician and prophet. Rising from servitude to statesmanship he prospered in political leadership under Babylonian and Medo-Persian rulers for more than six decades. Interwoven in the book bearing his name are Daniel's personal experiences as well as prophetic revelations concerning future developments.[1]

Daniel was born in the kingdom of Judah during the reign of Josiah and was probably in his teens when taken captive in 605 B.C. In the opening chapter of his book he reflects the religious convictions of Josiah and Jeremiah, which certainly must have influenced him and other Jewish youth of his day.

Although Judah's hopes for continued independence may have risen with the fall of Nineveh, they were suddenly shattered when Josiah was killed at Megiddo (609). Judah became a subject of Egypt shortly thereafter, and the Pharaoh Necho placed Jehoiakim on the throne. With the battle of Carchemish (605) Egyptian domination yielded to Babylonian control. Jehoiakim's overtures of submission to Nebuchadnezzar must have come as a surprise to Daniel and his companions who were taken as hostages to the Babylonian capital.[2]

Daniel's familiarity with the Hebrew and Aramaic languages is appar-

[1] Two basic views prevail currently regarding the unity and authorship of this book: (1) For the viewpoint that it was written by Daniel himself in the sixth century B.C. or was compiled shortly thereafter see the extensive discussion by R. K. Harrison, *Introduction to the Old Testament* (Grand Rapids, 1969), pp. 1105–1134. (2) For the perspective that this book represents apocalyptic literature written or compiled during the Maccabean era in the second century B.C. see G. A. Larue, *Old Testament Life and Literature* (Boston: Allyn and Bacon, 1968), pp. 402–409. The former view is the basis for the interpretation offered in this analysis.

[2] See D. J. Wiseman, *Chronicles of Chaldean Kings,* p. 26. Cf. also Chap. XV in this volume.

ent in his writings.[3] Peculiar to this book is the most extensive Aramaic passage in the Old Testament canon.

A popular outline of Daniel is the twofold division designating the first six chapters as history and the last six as prophecy. It is noteworthy that in the former Daniel refers to himself in the third person and acts as the agent of revelation. In the latter he writes in the first person, recording predictive messages supernaturally revealed to him.

Emphasizing the prophetic aspects the Book of Daniel lends itself to the following analysis[4]:

A. Historical introduction	1:1–21
B. The Gentile kingdoms	2:1–7:28
C. The nation of Israel	8:1–12:13

This outline takes into account its bilingual composition. The Aramaic passage (2:4b–7:28) has a message of special interest to the heathen nations, indicating their order of succession, character, and destiny. The chapters written in Hebrew focus attention upon Israel's particular role in international developments.

For an initial study of the Book of Daniel historical perspective is essential. The various revelations that came to Daniel were consequential in the light of contemporary events. For placing the book in its historical setting the following chronological analysis may be helpful:

I. The reign of Nebuchadnezzar	
Jewish captives at the court	1:1–21
Daniel and the king's dream	2:1–49
The three friends on trial	3:1–30
The king's humiliation	4:1–37
II. The Nabonidus-Belshazzar era	
The bestial nature of the kingdoms	7:1–28
Kingdoms identified	8:1–27
On the eve of Babylon's fall	5:1–30
III. In Medo-Persian times	
Daniel's concern for his people	9:1–27
On trial for his religion	5:31–6:28
Daniel's final revelation	10:1–12:13

[3] Daniel may have learned Aramaic in Jerusalem before he was taken captive. As early as the seventh century Aramaic was used as the official international language in Egypt, Phoenicia, and Syria. R. A. Bowman, "Arameans, Aramaic, and the Bible," *Journal of Near Eastern Studies*, 7 (1948), 71–73.

[4] For a discussion of the prophetic passages in Daniel see R. D. Culver, *Daniel and the Latter Days* (Westwood, N.J.: Revell Co., 1954). For analysis and outline see pp. 98–104.

During the Reign of Nebuchadnezzar[5]

Among the hostages taken from Jerusalem were Daniel and his three friends, Hananiah, Mishael, and Azariah.[6] Selected for special training in the royal college these Jewish youths faced the problem of defilement when offered the lavish menu of the heathen court.

Daniel, as spokesman for the group, courageously but courteously appealed to the chief steward to provide them with a menu of their choice on a ten-day trial basis. At the end of this period the steward was pleased to find Daniel and his friends in better health than their fellow trainees. Before long it was obvious to the supervisors that these Hebrew youths were endowed with extraordinary skill and wisdom. When interviewed by the king Daniel and his three friends received highest honors and were recognized as far superior to all the other wise men at the royal court (1:17–21).

The affinity of religion and politics must have made an indelible impression on Daniel. At various times during the accession year of Nebuchadnezzar, which reached its climax in the celebration of the New Year's Day festival, the king acknowledged the gods Nabu and Marduk as he led them in the public procession ending at the Akitu temple.[7] Daniel may have been perplexed when he saw Nebuchadnezzar extend his conquests in the name of these heathen gods.

During the first year of his reign the triumphant Nebuchadnezzar again marched his armies westward and collected tribute from the kings in Syria and Palestine.[8] Of particular interest to Daniel must have been the notation of Jehoiakim in the list of tributary kings and the fact that Nebuchadnezzar had reduced Askelon to ruins before his return to Babylon early in 603 B.C.

The Babylonian chronicler reports little of Nebuchadnezzar's activity during his second year. For Daniel, however, the most eventful experience is his personal appearance before this greatest of Babylonian monarchs (2:1–49).

King Nebuchadnezzar has a perplexing dream. Calling all the wise men before him, he demands that they relate to him his dream and its interpretation.[9] Under the threat of death the wise men frantically but vainly implore the king to narrate his dream. Daniel, learning of the dilemma, re-

[5] The first ten years of Nebuchadnezzar's reign have been greatly illuminated by British Museum tablet 21946 as read and interpreted by D. J. Wiseman. See *op. cit.*, pp. 67–74 and 23–37.

[6] The Babylonian names for Daniel and his three friends were: Belteshazzar, Shadrach, Meshach, and Abednego.

[7] Wiseman, *op. cit.*, p. 27. Cf. S. A. Pallis, *The Antiquity of Iraq* (Copenhagen: Ejnar Munksgaard, 1956), Chap. XIII, "Sacrifices and Festivals," pp. 688–711.

[8] Wiseman, *op. cit.*, BM 21946, pp. 69 and 28. Cf. also II Kings 24:1.

[9] "The thing is gone from me," Dan. 2:5. The preferable interpretations is that this refers to the king's command and not to his dream. If they could tell him the content of his dream, then he could rely on their interpretation.

quests an appointment with Nebuchadnezzar. While arrangements are being made Daniel and his three companions earnestly appeal to God to reveal this mystery to them. In a night vision God makes known to Daniel the king's dream and its interpretation. Ushered in before Nebuchadnezzar, Daniel tells him that God has revealed the mysteries of the future to the king.

In his dream Nebuchadnezzar has seen a brilliant image with a head of gold, breast and arms of silver, belly and thighs of bronze, legs of iron, and feet of iron and clay. Before him this image is crushed by a stone, causing its complete disintegration.

Daniel informs Nebuchadnezzar that he is the head of gold to whom God has given this great empire. The second and third kingdoms will be inferior. The fourth kingdom represented by iron will crush all other kingdoms but the mixture of iron and clay in the legs and feet indicates its ultimate division. Eventually God will establish a kingdom which shall never be destroyed. Like the stone crushing the whole image, so this kingdom will terminate all previous kingdoms when it is permanently established.

Upon hearing this interpretation Nebuchadnezzar honors Daniel, acknowledging the One who has revealed this secret as the God of gods and the Lord of kings.[10] Daniel is made ruler over the province of Babylon and given the highest position among all wise men. At his request his three friends, whose Babylonian names were Shadrach, Meshach, and Abednego, are given responsible positions elsewhere in the province while Daniel himself remains at the king's court.

During the course of his reign Nebuchadnezzar erects a great image on the plain of Dura (Dan. 3:1).[11] This image may have had the form of an obelisk with a nine-foot base and towering ninety feet upward in a glitter of gold. At its dedication all people are expected, under the threat of death, to worship in prostration. When Daniel's three friends refused to conform, it is of course immediately noticeable.[12] Arrested and brought before the king they are cast into a fiery furnace. With great astonishment the heathen king observes that they are unharmed and accompanied by a fourth individual.[13]

[10] A reasonable interpretation is the recognition of the preceding protest, 2:27–28, by Daniel, giving all the credit to God. By honoring Daniel the king expressed his recognition of Daniel's God, 2:46–47. Cf. H. C. Leupold, *Exposition of Daniel* (Columbus, Ohio: Wartburg Press, 1949).

[11] The date is not given in the Hebrew text. If the Greek text is correct by inserting the 18th year of Nebuchadnezzar, then this exhibition of pride occurred in 586 B.C., the year in which Jerusalem was conquered by the Babylonians. That this was an image of Nebuchadnezzar seems to be a reasonable inference.

[12] Where Daniel was at this time is not indicated. Since the scriptural account does not mention him, his whereabouts is subject to conjecture. It is most unreasonable to infer, on the basis of Daniel's character as portrayed throughout the book, that he worshiped this image.

[13] Nebuchadnezzar uses heathen terminology to identify this supernatural being. For the translation "son of the gods," Dan. 3:25, see S. R. Driver, *The Book of Daniel* (Cambridge Bible Series, Cambridge University Press, 1900), at reference. Cf. also Leupold,

Bidding them to come out Nebuchadnezzar confesses that their God has delivered them and issues a public decree prohibiting anyone from speaking against the God of Shadrach, Meshach, and Abednego.

Nebuchadnezzar's humiliation and restoration (4:1–37) is so significant that he issues an official edict relating his experience.[14] Recognizing that God has humbled and restored him, he publicly acknowledges God as the ruler of an everlasting kingdom.

Nebuchadnezzar has another disturbing dream. Again he calls in the wise men, this time relating his dream to them. When they are unable to render an interpretation Daniel, also known as Belteshazzar, is called in for consultation. In this dream Nebuchadnezzar saw a tree extending upward to heaven. It was so gigantic and fruitful that it provided shade, food, and shelter for beasts and birds. In due time a holy guardian from heaven gave orders to chop down the tree, leaving merely a stump.

Daniel interprets this dream as follows: the tree represents Nebuchadnezzar as king of the great Babylonian Empire—as the tree was cut off, so Nebuchadnezzar will be demoted from his royal position to a bestial existence for seven periods of time, until he realizes that he is not supreme. Daniel informs the king that this decree comes from the Most High and warns him to right his ways so that his kingdom may be prolonged.

It appears that Nebuchadnezzar ignores this warning. Under his supervision the city of Babylon was made the most magnificent capital of ancient times. Massive walls with adjoining canal moats surround the capital enclosing the temples of Marduk and Ishtar. At the famous Ishtar gate lions and dragons of glazed tile mark the impressive beginning of the procession street leading to the luxurious royal palace. For his Median queen Nebuchadnezzar constructed the hanging gardens which the Greeks considered one of the seven wonders of the world. Boasting of all these accomplishments Nebuchadnezzar is suddenly stricken with lycanthropy in divine judgment,[15] deprived of his kingdom, and relegated to a life among the beasts of the field for a period designated as "seven times." When his reason returns to him he is reinstated as king. In an official proclamation he acknowledges that the Most High is omnipotent among the host of heaven as well as all the inhabitants of the earth, and in praise and honor he confesses that the King of heaven is just and right in all his ways and able to abase the proud.

---

op. cit., at reference, and E. J. Young, *The Prophecy of Daniel* (Grand Rapids: Eerdmans, 1949).

[14] Neither the date nor the exact length of time of Nebuchadnezzar's humiliation is given in Scripture. Presumably it occurred some time during the last two decades of his reign.

[15] For an acknowledgment of the historical accuracy of this see Pfeiffer, *op. cit.*, p. 758.

The Nabonidus-Belshazzar Era

Years of Babylonian history pass in silence as far as the Book of Daniel is concerned. Nebuchadnezzar's magnificent reign of forty-three years terminated upon his death in 562 B.C. After a two-year rule by Awel-Marduk and a four-year reign by Neriglissar the Babylonian empire came to an end under Nabonidus (556–539 B.C.). Belshazzar, a son of Nabonidus, whose identity as coregent and administrator of the Babylonian kingdom is established beyond dispute, is mentioned in three chapters of Daniel.[16] The events of chapter 5 are specifically related to the final days of Belshazzar when the city of Babylon is occupied by the Medo-Persian army (October, 539 B.C.). The exact date of chapters 7 and 8 depend on the year in which Daniel dated the beginning of Belshazzar's reign, since he was a coregent with Nabonidus. The contract tablets on which the name of Belshazzar appears are dated by the reign of Nabonidus. Based on examination of relevant cuneiform data, G. F. Hasel in his article "The First and Third Years of Belshazzar (Dan. 7:1; 8:1)" dates the beginning of his coregency in 550 B.C.[17] Consequently, Daniel's visions in chapters 7 and 8 can be dated respectively in 550 and 547 B.C.

The contemporary historical developments during the time of Belshazzar and Nabonidus are significant as background for the visions recorded in chapters 7 and 8. More than half a century has passed since Daniel clearly identified Nebuchadnezzar as the head of gold, after whose reign an inferior kingdom would arise (2). Surely Daniel was quite conscious of the rise of Cyrus, who after coming to the throne of Persia and Anshan in 559 B.C. had gained control of Media (550 B.C.), which in turn disturbed the balance of power to the point of endangering Babylon. By 547 Cyrus had marched his armies into the northwest, decisively defeating Croesus in Lydia. Because of his political experience Daniel must have been apprehensive of Persia's rise to power while the Babylonian kingdom disintegrated under Nebuchadnezzar's successors.

At this time Daniel has two visions within three years. In the first vision (7) he sees four great beasts rise out of the sea astir by the four winds of heaven. A lion with eagle's wings, which are plucked off as he stands erect on two feet, is given the mind of a man. The second is a bearlike beast—raised on one side with three ribs in his mouth—ordered to devour much flesh. Next comes a leopard with four wings and four heads. The fourth is a nondescript beast having iron teeth to devour and stamping the residue in destruction. Three of its ten horns are replaced by one horn with manlike eyes and a mouth that utters great things. Next appears a throne on which

[16] Cf. H. H. Rowley, *The Servant of the Lord and Other Essays on the Old Testament* (London, 1952), p. 262. Note Rowley's article "The Historicity of the Fifth Chapter of Daniel," in *Journal of Theological Studies,* XXXII (1930–31), 12–31.

[17] *Andrews University Seminary Studies 15* (1977), pp. 153–68.

is seated an individual dressed in white who is identified as the Ancient of Days. Books are opened—judgment is rendered. The body of this nondescript beast is marked for burning while the rest of the beasts are deprived of their power. The Ancient of Days then commits dominion over all kingdoms to one "like a son of man" and establishes this kingdom permanently.

Daniel is perturbed and seeks an explanation. In response he is informed that the four beasts represent four earthly kings. Eventually the Saints of the Most High will possess the everlasting kingdom. The fourth beast represents a fourth kingdom which shall extend over the whole world. The ten horns signify ten kings—three of these will be replaced by a king who defies the Most High, even attempting to change seasons and laws. After three and a half periods he is judged and destroyed. The Saints of the Most High take over the kingdom which shall last forever. Although Daniel is greatly perplexed by the dream and its interpretation he ponders these things in his mind—perhaps trying to relate them to current developments.

In the third year of Belshazzar Daniel has another vision (8:1-27). Although he does not give his own place of residence at this time, the setting for the vision is Susa, along the banks of the river Ulai.[18] This city was under Persian control and later became an important summer capital under Darius the Great (522-486 B.C.).

Before Daniel, on the banks of the river, appears a ram with two unequal horns. This ram has unchallenged control until he is attacked by a swift one-horned he-goat from the west. After the latter has destroyed the former the great horn of the he-goat is broken and replaced by four conspicuous horns. Out of these four comes a little horn which advances southward to trample underfoot the sanctuary for a period of 2,300 days.

Once more Daniel desires clarification. The angel Gabriel informs him that this vision is for the end time. The ram with two horns represents the kings of Medo-Persia. The he-goat is identified as Greece, with the great horn representing the first king. The four kingdoms emerging from Greece will not be strong until a mighty king of fierce countenance stands up. He will display vast destructive power against the holy people and the Prince of the host but will suddenly be cut off without human intervention.

Daniel is so disturbed by this vision that he is unable to resume the king's business for several days. Knowing that the Medo-Persians are about to absorb the Babylonian kingdom Daniel had reason to be concerned. The capacity in which Daniel served in the Babylonian government after the death of Nebuchadnezzar is not indicated, but Belshazzar turned to him on the eve of his death.

[18] The Ulai is identified as the Eulaeus which passed by Susa before joining the Choaspes River. See M. S. and J. S. Miller, *Harper's Bible Dictionary* (New York, 1952), p. 788.

The year is 539 B.C. Confident that Babylon was beyond conquest, Belshazzar assembled a thousand of his officials and their wives for a banquet. They drank their wine from gold and silver vessels which Nebuchadnezzar had confiscated from the Temple of Jerusalem. Simultaneously the heathen man-made gods were freely acknowledged. While drinking before his lords on a raised platform, according to Oriental custom, the king suddenly noticed a hand writing on the wall. Seized with terror Belshazzar called for the wise men of Babylon to read and interpret, offering as a reward a purple robe, a chain of gold, and the third place in the kingdom.[19]

Hearing of the king's predicament the queen rushed into the banquet hall. She reminded him that there was a man in his kingdom whom Nebuchadnezzar had appointed as chief of the wise men of Babylon.[20] Immediately Daniel was brought before Belshazzar. Not concerned with the reward Daniel assured the king that he would interpret the message on the wall. In simple language he reminded him that Nebuchadnezzar, whom God had entrusted with a great kingdom, was reduced to a bestial status until he acknowledged that the Most High God ruled in the kingdom of men. Although familiar with all this Belshazzar had failed to honor God. The hand and its writing were sent from God. The interpretation was clear. God terminated the kingdom and divided it between the Medes and the Persians. As for Belshazzar, he has been weighed in the balance and found wanting.

At the king's command royal honors were bestowed upon Daniel and he was acclaimed the third ruler in the kingdom. However, the closing hours of the Babylonian kingdom were fast slipping away. That very night Belshazzar was slain and the city of Babylon was occupied by the Medo-Persians.

In Medo-Persian Times

The Medo-Persians conquer and occupy the great Babylonian capital without destruction. By the end of October (539) Cyrus himself enters in triumph and remains in this noted city to celebrate the annual New Year festival.[21]

Darius the Mede, who conquers Babylon, apparently serves under Cyrus. Since not a single inscription or tablet has been found which bears his name, numerous theories have been advanced for his identification. Based on

[19] Since Belshazzar was coruler with Nabonidus, the third place in the kingdom was the best that he could offer as a reward.

[20] The queen refers to Nebuchadnezzar as the "father" of Belshazzar, Dan. 5:11. In Semitic languages this word is used in eight different ways. Here it may be used as a reference in the sense of ancestor. See the article "Daniel" by E. J. Young in *The New Bible Commentary* (F. Davidson, ed.), p. 674.

[21] Pritchard, *Ancient Near Eastern Texts,* pp. 315–316.

new facts, his identity with Gubaru the governor of Babylon under Cyrus warrants the conclusion that Darius the Mede can be regarded as a historical personage.[22] According to Daniel's account, Darius is in charge of the occupation of Babylon and is ruler of the Chaldean kingdom. Although a Mede by birth he governs under the laws of the Medes and Persians.

The personal experiences of Daniel recorded in chapters 6 and 9 are related to the reign of Darius. The concluding verse of 6 implies that subsequently Daniel was associated with Cyrus. His final revelation is dated in the third year of Cyrus. Perhaps by that time Darius had died or Daniel had been transferred, so that he was directly responsible to Cyrus. In the crisis of Babylon's occupation by the invaders Darius immediately recognized Daniel, appointing him one of the three presidents in his government. In all likelihood a period of time elapsed before the two fellow presidents took action against Daniel in an attempt to remove him (6:1–28). In the meantime Daniel may have had the experience recorded in chapter 9.

The fact that the Medo-Persians replace the Babylonians as the leading kingdom in the Near East does not come as a surprise to Daniel. Early in his life, in the second year of Nebuchadnezzar, about 603 B.C., Daniel clearly explained to the greatest of Babylonian kings that other kingdoms were to follow in the course of time. During Belshazzar's reign the identification of the next kingdom was revealed. When he stood before the trembling king on the eve of Babylon's fall, Daniel plainly stated that the Medes and Persians were taking over his kingdom.

When the crisis had actually occurred and the supremacy of the Medo-Persians is established, Daniel is eager to know what significance this has for his own people. In reading the prophecies of Jeremiah he carefully observes that a period of seventy years of captivity had been predicted.[23] Although he does not make mention of it he also may have read about Cyrus in the Book of Isaiah (44:28–45:1) where Cyrus is identified as the shepherd whom God would use to liberate his people for return to Jerusalem. Cyrus had already been on the international scene for several decades. Could it be possible that the Jews would now be allowed to return? Apparently the edict for their return had not yet been issued or publicized.

Daniel is greatly exercised about the prediction given by Jeremiah. Nearly seventy years have passed since the first group of Jews, including himself, had been taken from Jerusalem in 605 B.C. Realizing that the time for fulfillment was imminent, Daniel prays confessing the sins of Israel and acknowledging that God is righteous and just in all his judgments.

Gabriel enlightens Daniel concerning Israel's future. A general preview

[22] John C. Whitcomb, Jr., *Darius the Mede* (Grand Rapids: Eerdmans, 1959), 84 pp. Cf. also his examination of alternate theories in the light of biblical evidence.

[23] Cf. Jer. 25:11 and 29:10 with Dan. 9:1–2.

of a succession of world empires had already been given him. Here attention is focused upon the nation of Israel in the plan of God. Seventy weeks represent the period in which Israel shall see the fulfillment of God's promises.[24] Developments allotted to this period for Daniel's people and their holy city are as follows:

(1) to finish transgression
(2) to make an end of sins
(3) to make reconciliation for iniquity
(4) to bring in everlasting righteousness
(5) to seal up vision and prophecy
(6) to anoint the most holy.

Dividing the total period into smaller units, an era of seven plus sixty-two weeks allows for the appearance and cutting off of an individual identified as "anointed one." The city and the sanctuary are to be destroyed by a people from whom a prince shall emerge to make a covenant with many for one week. This covenant brings into focus the seventieth week as the time and duration of this relationship. However, in the middle of this week the prince will break the covenant, causing sacrifice and offering to cease and bringing in desolation until the destroyer is consumed.

Regardless of the varied interpretations of this somewhat ambiguous explanation as exemplified in numerous books written on these prophecies, Daniel himself receives the assurance that his nation, for whom he is praying, has a definite place in God's plan. Undoubtedly he is greatly encouraged as Cyrus, soon after he had subdued Babylon, issues a proclamation encouraging the Jews to return to their own land.

When Darius organizes his kingdom Daniel serves as one of the three presidents. Before long he distinguishes himself as such a wise administrator that his two associates become extremely jealous. Still failing to find any irregularities in his official duties they incriminate Daniel for his religious practice so that he is cast into the den of lions. When Darius finds Daniel unmolested he acknowledges in a public proclamation that God has delivered Daniel—the living God who works signs and wonders in heaven and earth as ruler of an everlasting kingdom.

Daniel's final revelation (10:1–12:13) is dated in the third year of Cyrus. By now the statesman-prophet was well established in the Medo-Persian government. If Daniel was in his teens when taken captive he would now be in his eighties. From the standpoint of his age and official responsi-

[24] For a summary of the evidence that each of these seventy weeks refers to a period of seven years see Alva J. McClain, *Daniel's Prophecy of the Seventy Weeks* (Grand Rapids: Zondervan, 1940). For a discussion of the prophecy of the seventy weeks, Dan. 9:24–27, see Culver, *op. cit.*, pp. 135–160. For a representative amillenniel interpretation see E. J. Young, *The Prophecy of Daniel,* at reference.

bilities in the government, it is not likely that he seriously considered joining the exodus of Jews for the return to Jerusalem. Nevertheless he had a genuine interest in the welfare and future hopes of his people.

Daniel spends three weeks in fasting and mourning. On the twenty-fourth day of the first month he is standing on the banks of the Tigris River when he becomes conscious of a man clothed in linen who has supernatural characteristics. When Daniel sees this vision and hears the sound of his words, he falls on his face in a deep sleep. The men who are with him flee.

Daniel is awakened and bidden to rise and this man assures him that his prayer has been heard. Owing to interference by the prince of Persia, the answer has been delayed. Since Daniel is a man greatly beloved, who humbled himself in prayer, this divine messenger has come with the aid of Michael, one of the chief princes, to reveal to him Israel's future. Though weak and fearful Daniel receives supernatural strength so that he is conditioned to receive the message. The messenger informs him that he is about to resume his conflict with the prince of Persia and subsequently to await an encounter with the prince of Greece. Before leaving he shares with Daniel the content of the book of truth.

Four kings will succeed Cyrus on the throne of Persia—the last of whom will arouse the Greeks by his excessive wealth. A most powerful king from Greece is coming to assert himself as he pleases but will suddenly be cut off. His kingdom divides into four (11:2–4). For some time a fierce conflict rages between the king of the north and the king of the south (11:5–20). After that a vile and contemptible person arises to challenge the king of the south in repeated battles. In his rage he profanes the Temple and causes the continual burnt offering to cease as many die in the conflict (11:21–35).

A willful king who is the most defiant of all exalts himself above all gods—even defying the God of gods (11:21–35). For a while he extends his control down to Egypt, Ethiopia, and Libya but ultimately meets his doom in a furious conflict.

What happens to Daniel's people? At the time of this terrible conflict Michael, the prince of Israel, arises to deliver them. A resurrection occurs when many are restored to everlasting life—others to everlasting contempt. With the assurance that those who are wise and turn to righteousness are the recipients of God's blessings Daniel is advised to seal the message revealed to him. In the end time many will read it to increase their knowledge (12:4).

Daniel sees two individuals, one on each bank of the river. Turning to the man clothed in white linen he inquires concerning the termination of these wonders. Raising his hands to heaven the man clothed in linen swears by "him who lives forever" that these wonders will end after three and a half periods of time. This also is the terminal point for shattering the power of the holy people. Daniel is still baffled. He hears the words but does not understand. Inquiring of the man clothed in linen he is advised to go his way—the words are closed and sealed until the time of the end. Many shall be purified and understand while others shall continue in excessive wickedness and shall not understand. Even though the coming events are not clear to Daniel he is promised rest and an allotted place at the end of time. With this personal hope and the assurance that his people will ultimately triumph Daniel is instructed to seal his book.

SELECTED READING

ANDERSON, R. *The Coming Prince.* London: Hodder & Stoughton, 1894.

ARCHER, G. L. "Daniel" in *Expositor's Bible Commentary.* Grand Rapids: Zondervan Publishing House, 1985.

———. *Jerome's Commentary on Daniel.* Grand Rapids: Baker Book House, 1958.

BALDWIN, JOYCE G. *Daniel: An Introduction and Commentary.* Downers Grove: Inter-Varsity Press, 1978.

CULVER, R. D. *Daniel and the Latter Days.* Rev. ed. Chicago: Moody Press, 1977.

KING, GEOFFREY R. *Daniel.* Grand Rapids: Wm. B. Eerdmans Publishing Co., 1967.

LEUPOLD, H. C. *Exposition of Daniel.* 1949. Reprint ed. Grand Rapids: Baker Book House, 1969.

MCCLAIN, ALVA J. *Daniel's Prophecy of the Seventy Weeks.* Grand Rapids: Zondervan Publishing House, 1940.

MCDOWELL, JOSH. *Daniel in the Critic's Den.* San Bernardino: Here's Life Publishers, 1979.

PENTECOST, J. DWIGHT. "Daniel" in *Bible Knowledge Commentary.* Wheaton: Scripture Press, 1985.

STRAUSS, LEHMAN. *The Prophecies of Daniel.* Neptune: Loizeaux, 1965.

WALVOORD, JOHN F. *Daniel, the Key to Prophetic Revelation.* Chicago: Moody Press, 1971.

WHITCOMB, J. C., JR. *Darius the Mede.* Grand Rapids: Wm. B. Eerdmans Publishing Co., 1959.

WILSON, R. D. *Studies in the Book of Daniel, Second Series.* New York: Revell, 1938; Grand Rapids: Baker Book House, 1979.

WISEMAN, D. J. et al. *Notes on Some Problems in the Book of Daniel.* Wheaton: Tyndale Press, 1965.

WOOD, LEON. *A Commentary on Daniel.* Grand Rapids: Zondervan Publishing House, 1973.

YAMAUCHI, E. *Greece and Babylon.* Grand Rapids: Baker Book House, 1966.

YOUNG, E. J. *The Prophecy of Daniel.* Grand Rapids: Wm. B. Eerdmans Publishing Co., 1949.

Chapter XXII

In Times of Prosperity

Political independence, expansion, and prosperity characterized Israel during the heyday of Jeroboam's success. From days of bloodshed and oppression in 841 B.C. the dynasty of Jehu eventually led the Northern Kingdom to the peak of economic and political prestige during the first half of the eighth century. Elisha continued his ministry, standing by as God's messenger during those early tumultuous years of Jehu's dynasty.

Blood marked Jehu's steps to the throne in Samaria. Not satisfied by slaying the kings of Judah and Israel, Jehu had shed blood freely as he exterminated the royal family. Spurred on by treacherous fanaticism he gathered together all the Baal zealots for a mass murder.

Jehu's local success was soon overshadowed by international problems. The gruesome death of Jezebel certainly did not induce the goodwill of Phoenicia. Jerusalem, with its king a victim of the revolution in Samaria, was thrown into a bloody turmoil under the terror of Athaliah. Moab rebelled against Israel. From Damascus Hazael ferociously pressed southward, seizing Israelite territory east of the Jordan. Jehu was helpless—too weak to save the people of Gilead and Bashan from Syrian oppression. Furthermore, he found it necessary to send tribute to Shalmaneser III in order to avert the ominous threat of an Assyrian invasion.[1]

Hazael came to be Israel's worst foe. As long as he ruled in Syria there was trouble for Jehu and his successors. Hazael not only invaded Bashan and Gilead but also advanced south into Palestine to capture Gath. Moreover, he threatened the conquest of Jerusalem (II Kings 12:17). Surrounded and oppressed by the Syrians, Israel seemed to have a hopeless future. Ap-

[1] J. B. Pritchard, *Ancient Near Eastern Texts Relating to the Old Testament* (2nd ed.), p. 280.
Cf. also chapters XII and XIII in this volume for further discussion.

parently neighboring states took advantage of Israel's impotency by repeated forays (Amos 1:6–12).

Shortly before the turn of the century prospects for Israel's relief began to dawn with the death of Hazael. With Assyria overpowering Damascus, Israel had the opportunity to emerge once more into the international limelight. Soon Jehoash had mustered a strong fighting force to challenge the new Syrian king, Benhadad, in his control of Israelite territory. In the wake of success the death of Elisha, the veteran prophet in Israel, came as a blow to Jehoash.

The army of Jehoash was so large that Amaziah, the king of Judah, hired from him a hundred thousand men to aid in the subjection of Edom. His success in this venture made Amaziah so arrogant that he returned the Israelite troops with a challenge to Jehoash to match the armies of Judah and Israel in battle. When his verbal warning was ignored Jehoash invaded Judah, broke down part of the wall of Jerusalem, plundered the palace and the Temple, and took hostages back to Samaria. With Judah as a vassal of Israel, Amaziah most likely was imprisoned, or at least dethroned, for an extended period.[2]

Jonah made his appearance about this time.[3] His prediction was timely and doubtless popular. He declared that Jeroboam was about to reclaim the territory lost to Hazael in days past. Indeed, it was not long before military success, territorial expansion, and economic prosperity became a reality under the energetic and aggressive leadership of Jeroboam II, 793–753 B.C. With Syria weakened by pressure from Adadnirari III, Jeroboam regained his nation's territory from the Dead Sea to "the entrance of Hamath" (the pass between the Lebanon range and Mount Hermon). Consequently Jeroboam II had under his control a domain larger than that of any of his predecessors.

Commercial relations were expanded. International trade flourished beyond any known to Israel since the days of Solomon. In this era of economic success and territorial expansion Samaria fortified itself against the day of foreign invasion.[4] With Syria as a buffer state, the Israelites complacently forgot about the danger of an Assyrian threat. Although Judah began to show signs of an economic and political revival, the Southern Kingdom was still the underdog and comparatively dormant, as long as Jeroboam continued to rule in Samaria.

With Israel in its heyday, two prophets made their appearance—Amos and Hosea. Each in turn tried to arouse the citizens of Israel out of their lethargy, but neither was successful in turning the people from apostasy.

[2] E. R. Thiele, *The Mysterious Numbers of the Hebrew Kings*, pp. 68–72.

[3] Jonah lived at Gath-hepher, about three miles north of Nazareth.

[4] Cf. André Parrot, *Samaria, the capital of the Kingdom of Israel* (London: SMC Press, 1958).

Jonah—The Nineveh Mission—1:1–4:11

As a servant of the God of Israel, Jonah may have attracted much publicity when he predicted that King Jeroboam would reclaim the territory east of the Jordan River that previously had been occupied by Hazael, the Aramaean king in Damascus. Very likely this enhanced his popularity in his homeland. There is no indication that he had a message of warning or judgment for his own people (II Kings 14:25).

Jonah's mission to Nineveh may have occurred during the reign of Assurdan III (773–756 B.C.), when the Assyrians suffered from international diplomatic and military losses, as well as from famine and popular uprisings domestically. After a plague swept Nineveh in 765, followed by an eclipse of the sun in 763 B.C., the city of Nineveh may have been psychologically prepared to respond favorably to Jonah's warning of divine judgment.

The Book of Jonah records the personal experience of the prophet Jonah, mentioned elsewhere only in II Kings 14:25. Classed with the prophets, it has a brief prophetic message but is unique in its focus on Jonah biographically. As a prophetic narrative, it is also didactic and shares similarities of style with the Elijah-Elisha accounts in the Book of Kings. As a sensational narrative, it also has some similarities to literature classified as parable and allegory. However, it is neither a parable nor an allegory. As a true story, it shares with the rest of the Bible miraculous events interwoven with its historical narrative.[5]

Whether Jonah himself or another narrator wrote this book cannot be ascertained from the text. Jonah and the sailors, knowing what happened while Jonah was asleep, could have supplied the details. News of his rescue and of his trip to Nineveh may have attracted considerable publicity for Jonah so that someone obtained all the material for writing this book from a personal interview with him. Since this narrative so often concentrates on "Jonah's improper attitudes and actions," it is quite possible that someone other than the prophet himself wrote the Book of Jonah.[6]

Observe the following analysis:

I. Jonah's experience in disobedience	1:1–17
God's commission	1:1–2
Jonah's flight	1:3
God's control	1:4–17

[5] For a discussion of Jonah as a *transition* prophet, "representing the shift from the preclassical model we have in Elijah and Elisha to that of Amos, Hosea, Micah, and Isaiah," see C.H. Bullock, *An Introduction to the Old Testament Prophetic Books* (Chicago: Moody Press, 1986), pp. 43–44.

[6] Cf. D. Stuart, *Hosea-Jonah* (Waco, Texas: Word Books, 1987), pp. 442–443.

II. Jonah's response to God's mercy	2:1–10
His distress	2:1–6
His appeal and promise	2:7–9
His deliverance	2:10
III. Jonah's mission to Nineveh	3:1–10
God's second call	3:1–3a
Preaching and repentance	3:3b–10
IV. Jonah's anger—God's corrective	4:1–11
Jonah's disgusting prayer	4:1–3
God's answer	4:4
God's object lesson	4:5–9
God's rebuke	4:10–11

Jonah is divinely commissioned to go to Nineveh—an unpleasant assignment for an Israelite. During Jehuan times Israel paid tribute to the Assyrian king Shalmaneser III. Jonah knew the suffering to which Aram was subjected in repelling the recent Assyrian attacks. Why should he expose himself to such a dangerous mission? The atrocities of the Assyrians, which later terrorized the nations into submission under Tiglath-pileser III, may already have been practiced at this time. From the human standpoint Assyria was the last place any Israeli would choose for a missionary venture.

Jonah, unique among God-called prophets, is disobedient. Deliberately, he runs away from God, going west instead of east to Nineveh. At Joppa he conveniently boards a ship heading for the distant Mediterranean coastlands equated with Tarshish.

En route, the sailors are frightened when a God-sent storm threatens to break up the ship. While alarm fills the hearts of the crew, Jonah is fast asleep in the hold. The mariners are so panic-stricken that they unload the ship and appeal to their gods. Jonah is bidden to rise and join in the prayer meeting. By casting lots, his fellow passengers decide that Jonah is responsible for their distress. Although fearful of divine wrath, they reluctantly throw him overboard. Immediately, the storm ceases, and a great calm prevails. As far as the mariners are concerned, their problem is solved. The awesome impression of this experience is expressed by the sailors in their vows and sacrifices after they come ashore.

As for Jonah, his problems have just begun. He has been swallowed by "a great fish" that was designated or provided by God to rescue him from death.[7] Enveloped by this sea monster, Jonah expresses his change of heart

[7] This "great fish" was not necessarily a whale. For a modern analogy to Jonah's experience note the account by John Ambrose Wilson, where a sperm whale near the Falkland Islands swallowed a ship's crew member, who was rescued three days later, was revived from unconsciousness, and subsequently lived in good health. Cf. *Princeton Theological Review*, "The Sign of the Prophet Jonah," XXV (1927), p. 636.

in a psalm, in which he conveys his realization that he has been rescued through God's grace and compassion. In profound gratitude Jonah recognizes that God's mercy has been extended to him in spite of his disobedience—a lesson that he needed to learn before God could use him in a mission to the Ninevites.

Brought to dry land by the fish, Jonah once more is bidden to go to Nineveh. Having learned the lesson that God's will cannot be ignored, he heads eastward to the land of Assyria, a distance of about eight hundred miles. Located on the bank of the Tigris, Nineveh is a large city with an administrative district of thirty to sixty miles across.[8] There Jonah begins his preaching mission. Sophisticated and sinful though they are, the people and the king listen to the prophet's warning: "Forty more days and Nineveh will be destroyed." Scarcely has Jonah begun his itinerary when the people respond. Throughout the city, the people repent in sackcloth, fast, and turn to God in faith.[9] No sooner does the message reach the palace than the king takes action. Exchanging his royal robes for sackcloth, he resorts to the ash heap. He issues to the citizens of Nineveh a royal proclamation admonishing them to turn in repentance from their sinful ways.

To Jonah's great surprise, his mission has been successful. To his disappointment, the city is not destroyed; it is spared, as God responds in mercy to a repentant populace.[10] In disgust and anger Jonah expresses his ardent nationalism; he cannot endure the fact that God has been merciful and gracious to Nineveh. His life did not end, as he expected, when the sailors threw him overboard, but now he, like Elijah under a broom tree (I Kings 19:4), asks God to take his life. "Rescue was all right for Jonah, but not for that important enemy city. A world in which God forgives even Israel's enemies is a world Jonah does not wish to live in," observes Douglas Stuart.[11]

In a flashback the author of this book returns to the point in Jonah's experience when Jonah does not know the outcome of his mission. Situated east of the city in a temporary shelter, Jonah anticipates seeing a Sodom-Gomorrah-style destruction. For this temporary shelter, God provides ("designates," as in 2:1) a gourd or vine to "ease his discomfort" (4:6, NIV). The next day God provides a worm, causing the vine to wither. God also

[8] "The great city of Nineveh" includes the city proper and its suburbs. From 1100 B.C. Nineveh was used as one of the royal residences. After 722 Sargon II made it his capital, and it continued to be the first city in Assyria until its fall in 612 B.C. D. Stuart, translating 3:1—"Now, Nineveh was a city important to God, requiring a three-day visit"—emphasizes God's concern for Nineveh and for the ancient oriental hospitality involved in a "visit" to a city (cf. op. cit., pp. 486–488).

[9] For a discussion of the "faith" of the Ninevites see E. B. Pusey, *The Minor Prophets*, Vol. I (New York: Funk and Wagnalls, 1885), p. 415.

[10] For a discussion of the reform—though not mentioned in secular history—see Aalders, op. cit., pp. 6–7.

[11] D. Stuart, op. cit., p. 503.

provides a "scorching east wind" (4:8, NIV). With the sun blazing on his head, Jonah becomes faint and petitions God to take his life.

Although Jonah knows that God is "'a gracious and compassionate God, slow to anger and abounding in love. . . .'" (4:2, NIV; cf. Ex. 34:6–7), and although he has experienced God's mercy in being divinely rescued at sea, he now is "'angry enough to die'" (4:9, NIV). He boldly asserts that he has the right to be angry in his unrepentant and stubborn attitude toward God over the loss of a single vine that has given him shelter. God's concern, by contrast, is to extend his compassion to the great city of Nineveh. Unfortunately, Jonah, who reluctantly fulfilled his mission after experiencing God's mercy, did not learn the basic lesson posed by Abraham centuries earlier in the question, "'Will not the Judge of all the earth do right?'" (Gen. 18:25, NIV). (Cf. also the teaching of Jesus, Matt. 18:33; Luke 15:11–31.)

What finally happened to Jonah? Very likely he returned to his homeland, where either he or another narrator provided us with the Book of Jonah without satisfying our curiosity.[12]

Amos—Sheep Breeder, Fig Slitter, and Prophet—1:1–9:15

In the latter years of Jeroboam's reign, Amos, the first among the writing prophets, proclaimed God's word to the Northern Kingdom. Living in Tekoa, about six miles south of Bethlehem, Amos earned his livelihood as a sheep breeder and cultivator of sycamore figs. He may have used his agricultural expertise as a fig slitter to support himself while traveling throughout the land.[13]

Preaching in Bethel, a royal sanctuary frequented by the monarchy, Amos boldly asserts that God has commissioned him, "'Go, prophesy to my people Israel'" (7:15, NIV; cf. also 3:8). His frequent references to Samaria (cf. 3:9, 12; 4:1; 6:1; 8:14) may reflect the presence of Samaritan citizens in his audience at Bethel or the possibility that he publicly addresses the residents in Israel's capital city.[14]

Basic in the message of Amos is the convenantal perspective given through Moses, especially as delineated in compact form in Deuteronomy 4:21–31. God is portrayed as sovereign over nature, all nations, and all

[12] The tradition that Jonah was buried on the Nebi Yunus mound, marked by a mosque on the site of Nineveh, lacks historical support. D. W. B. Robinson, in his article "Jonah," suggests that the book may have been written in the Northern Kingdom by Jonah before 721 B.C. Cf. *The New Bible Commentary*, p. 715.

[13] Cf. Stuart, op. cit., pp. 374–378, and Bullock, op. cit., pp. 55–57. To Stuart the most convincing translation of Amos's protest to Amaziah is, "'No, I am a prophet though I am not a professional prophet.'" Amos claims the prophetic office but denies the inference that he is making his living as a professional prophet.

[14] R. H. Pfeiffer, in *The Books of the Old Testament* (New York, 1957), p. 300, suggests that the ministry of Amos was limited to a few months after Amaziah reported that the land could not endure such hard words (Amos 7:10).

individuals, including Amos himself. God's implicit covenant extends to all nations, and in a special sense to Israel, so that all are accountable to God.

In his message Amos reflects the luxury and ease of Israel during Jeroboam's reign. Trade with Phoenicia, tolls on caravan traffic across Israel and Arabia, and the northward expansion at Aram's expense have fattened Jeroboam's coffers. The rapid rise in the standard of living among the wealthy has widened the cleavage between classes. Social evils prevail. With keen insight Amos has observed the moral corruption, selfish luxury, and oppression of the poor as the wealthy were ruthlessly accumulating more riches. In simple but forceful language, he boldly denounces the evils that permeate the social, economic, and political life of Israel. In religion, rituals are no substitute for righteousness, without which the nation of Israel cannot escape the judgments of a righteous God.

How long did Amos prophesy? Since he came from Judah into Jeroboam's domain to denounce the wealthy aristocracy, it is reasonable to assume that his ministry was tolerated for but a brief period. What happened to Amos after Amaziah reported him to Jeroboam is not recorded. He may have been imprisoned, expelled, or even martyred.

With literary brilliance and magnificent style, Amos sets forth the God-given message for his generation. In classical simplicity he portrays his encounter with the contemporary sinful generation. For a brief analysis of the Book of Amos, note the following:

I. Judgment oracles against the nations	1:1–2:16
II. God's charge against Israel expanded	3:1–6:14
Divine punishment for God's chosen people	3:1–15
Judgment for unrepentant people	4:1–13
Lament for fallen Israel	5:1–17
Exile for Israel in the day of the Lord	5:18–27
The certainty of God's judgment	6:1–14
III. Visions of doom	7:1–8:3
Locusts and fire—God relents	7:1–6
Tin—God does not relent	7:7–9
Amos-Amaziah interaction	7:10–17
The summer fruit basket	8:1–3
IV. God's wrath inescapable for Israel	8:4–9:10
Indictment for exploiting the poor	8:1–14
Destruction inevitable—a remnant saved	9:1–10
V. Restoration assured	9:11–15

Notice how Amos begins his preaching mission. By boldly announcing judgment for the surrounding nations he attracts the attention of the Israelites. The prophet's tirade likely provokes malicious joy in more than a few calloused hearts.

Damascus is the first to be arraigned. Surely some of the older Israelites remember how Hazael wrought havoc on them by invasion, occupation, and captivity during Jehu's reign. Others in Amos's audience are unpleasantly reminded of the Philistines, who have bartered captives in their trade with Edom. Tyre has been guilty of the same lucrative business. The Edomites, who have been notorious for their animosity and hatred toward Israel ever since the days of Jacob and Esau, could not escape punishment. Ammonite atrocities and Moab's treacherous deeds are likewise slated for judgment.

As the Israelites listen to these scathing denunciations by Amos, they doubtless rejoice in the fact that divine judgment is allotted to their sinful neighbors. These heathen deserve punishment. By this time Amos has circumvented Israel by indicting six surrounding nations. Seventh on the list is his own kingdom, Judah. Perhaps the people of Jerusalem have prided themselves on being custodians of the law and the Temple. Amos fearlessly condemns them for their disobedience and rejection of the law. In all likelihood this is most pleasing to the nationalistic Israelites, who resent Judah's religious pride.

Had Amos concluded his message here he might have been very popular, but such was not the case. Next on the docket are the Israelites to whom he is speaking. Social evils, oppression, immorality, profanity—these exist in Israel. God could not overlook such sins in the covenant people whom he redeemed out of Egypt. If other nations deserved punishment, how much more Israel. No, they could not escape the scrutiny of God.

Intimate indeed is the relationship between God and Israel (3:1–8). From all the nations of the earth God chose Israel to be his covenant people. But they have sinned. Only one alternative remains: God must punish them. Failure to measure up to greater privileges and more abundant blessings in turn brings God's visitation in judgment.

Does judgment come by chance? By a series of rhetorical questions, in which the answer is obviously "No," Amos expresses the climactic truth that evil or punishment does not come to a city without God's knowing about it. God reveals it to the prophets. And when God speaks to a prophet, who can help but prophesy? Consequently Amos has no alternative. God has spoken to him. He is under divine compulsion to speak God's word.

Appealing to the heathen neighbors as witnesses, Amos outlines his charges against Israel (3:9–6:14). In Samaria the wealthy have been drinking and carousing at the expense of the poor. Persisting in these evils, they have multiplied transgressions by ritual sacrifices. At the same time they hate reproof, resist the truth, accept bribes, neglect the needy, and afflict the righteous. They have in essence turned justice into poison. God's evaluation of conditions in Israel has left only one alternative. Mass exile is decreed for the Israelites.

Interspersed with these charges is the explicit delineation of coming doom. An adversary would surround the land. Neither religion nor politics would save Israel when the altars of Bethel and the ivory palaces crumble under the invaders. Like fish caught on hooks the citizens of Israel would be dragged away into exile. God is bringing a nation upon them in judgment to oppress the land from its northern boundary in Hamath down to the river of Egypt.

Mercy has preceded judgment. God has sent drought, plagues, and pestilence to shock Israel into repentance, but his people have not responded. Continuing on their impious course they anticipate that the day of the Lord would bring them blessing and victory. What a tragic delusion! Amos points out that for them this would be a day of darkness rather than light. Like a man who runs away from a lion only to meet a bear, so the Israelites will face an unavoidable calamity in the day of the Lord. God cannot tolerate their religious rituals, feasts, and sacrifices as long as they are guilty of sins toward their neighbors. Their only hope for life was to seek God, hate evil, love good, and demonstrate justice in their total pattern of living. Since they have not responded to repeated warnings, the judgment of God is irrevocable. God cannot be bribed by offerings and sacrifices to overlook justice. Utter ruin—not triumph—awaits them on the day of the Lord.

God's plan for Israel is clearly outlined. They have ignored his mercy. Judgment is now pending. In five visions Amos previews the developments providing him with a message of warning (7–9). Vividly these visions portray the coming doom. In orderly progression the first four visions—the locusts, the fire, the plumbline, and the basket of summer fruit—lead up to the climactic fifth, which signifies actual destruction.

When Amos sees the formation of locust swarms he is deeply moved with compassion for his people. Were they released on the land the people would be robbed of their sustenance, even though the king has his share from the spring herbage. Immediately Amos cries out, "O Lord God, forgive," and God's hand of judgment is stayed.

Next the prophet becomes conscious of a flaming fire which God is about to release in judgment on Israel. Amos cannot bear the thought of God's people being consumed by fire. Once more he intercedes, and in response God averts the judgment.

In the third vision Amos is informed that God will no longer withhold judgment from Israel, implying that intercession will not avail. In a recent reconstruction of this text (7:7–8, NIV), Douglas Stuart asserts that the Hebrew word *anak* should be translated *tin*, and not *plumb line*. Not used elsewhere in the Old Testament, the word occurs four times in this text. In this portrayal of God standing on a tin wall, which in one sense seems ridiculous, Amos acknowledges that the focal point is the word *anak*, or *tin*, which in Hebrew sounds almost exactly like *anaq*, a word sometimes used by prophets to express "moaning," in connection with coming miseries (Jer. 51:52; Ezek. 26:15). This play on words seems to be the real issue in this vision. The message is explicit: Israel, with its pilgrimage sanctuaries, will be "moaning" in the agony of destruction and exile.[15]

Apparently this message is too strong for some of the listeners at Bethel. Amaziah, who appears to be the chief priest at Bethel, is aroused in anger against Amos. Amaziah appeals, perhaps in the form of an official letter, to the king, who controls religion to a substantial degree. Claiming governmental authority as administrator at Bethel, Amaziah charges Amos with conspiracy and seeks to dismiss him. But Amos, with the firm conviction that God has called him, boldly announces Amaziah's doom. Not only would Amaziah be killed and his family exposed to suffering, but Israel would be uprooted and taken into exile (7:10–17).

A basket of summer fruit appears in the fourth vision (8:1–3). As in the preceding vision, the significance is focused on the sound of one word. Here the Hebrew word *qayis*, or *summer fruit*, is used in a play on words with *qes*, meaning *end*. Destruction is predicted and vividly protrayed in the wailing of temple songs and the piling of corpses.[16]

Israel is indicted for violating the basic requirement in the Mosaic covenant. Second to the commandment to love God, the Israelites were to love their neighbors (Ex. 23:6; Lev. 19:10, 13, 15; Deut. 15:7–11; 24:12–22). The land that God gave for all to enjoy is now controlled by the rich, so that injustice prevails in the oppression of the poor. Because of the exploiters, death and destruction await the Israelites. They would perish together with their idolatrous worship system.

While the fourth vision (8:1–3) indicates that the end is near (in that day), the fifth vision (9:1–4) vividly portrays the end. Without any dialogue or opportunity for intercession, Amos is informed that the process of destruction is virtually under way. The coming wrath is inescapable as God initiates the demolition of Israel, razing a sanctuary as a symbol of his rejection of Israel's idolatry. However, a remnant will be spared (9:9; cf. Zeph. 2:3, 9).

Amos concludes with a message of hope (9:11–15). The Davidic dynasty will be restored in a kingdom greater than the earthly monarchy, in which Gentiles will be included (cf. Acts 15:16–18). In the ultimate fulfillment of the restoration promise, they will possess the land, enjoying agricultural

[15] Cf. Stuart, op. cit., pp. 372–374.
[16] Cf. Stuart, op. cit., pp. 378–380.

bounty in absolutely peaceful conditions (Isa. 2:1–4; 11:1–12; Zech. 8:3–8). Brought back from exile, they have the divine assurance that they will "'never again . . . be uprooted from the land I have given them'. . ." (9:15, NIV; cf. Lev. 26:5, 42; Deut. 9:6–7; 28.10; 30.3–9).

Hosea—God's Love for a Prostituting Israel—1:1–14:9

Biographical information about Hosea is limited to chapters 1 and 3. Very likely he married Gomer about 760 B.C., since their marriage and their three children predated the downfall of Jehu's dynasty in the death of Jeroboam II in 753 B.C. (1:4). His second marriage (chap. 3) may have occurred as late as the last year of Hoshea's reign, 732–722 B.C. It is reasonable to associate the messages of Hosea with the developments that cast the lengthening shadows of Assyrian domination over the land of Palestine. For an analysis of his entire message, as recorded in the book bearing his name, consider the following:

I. Israel—a prostituting nation	1:1–3:5
Hosea's prophetic action	1:1–9
Covenant renewal promised	1:10–2:1
Lawsuit against Israel	2:2–15
Restoration assured	2:16–23
Prostitution cure portrayed	3:1–5
II. God's lawsuit against Israel	4:1–7:16
Failure to love and acknowledge God	4:1–9
Led by a spirit of prostitution	4:10–5:7
Indifferent to warning	5:8–15
Defiled by harlotry—covenant treason	6:1–7:1a
Toleration of civil and social injustice	7:1b–16
III. Warnings of divine judgment	8:1–10:15
Penalties for disregarding God	8:1–14
Covenant prostitution bringing rejection	9:1–17
War and exile terminating the kingdom	10:1–15
IV. God's love—a father-son relationship	11:1–11
God's love and grace—Israel's rebellion	11:1–7
Punishment limited—restoration assured	11:8–11
V. The broken covenant—judgment and restoration	12:1–14:9
God's legal case against Israel	12:1–14
Kingdom destruction delineated	13:1–16
Restoration in the new age	14:1–8
Wisdom—walking in God's way	14:9

Hosea's marriage and the naming of his children were prophetic acts commanded by God, symbolizing the unfaithfulness of the Israelites.[17] Gomer was called "a prostituting woman," and their children were called "prostituting children," metaphorically portraying the covenant infidelity that provoked God's wrath against Israel (1:2). With the birth of each child, the warning of impending judgment was presented with more forcefulness and exacting clarity.

The name *Jezreel*, for Hosea's first-born, stirs numerous memories of ominous import in the minds of the Israelites. As a royal city in Israel, Jezreel is associated with Jezebel's murder of Naboth. Currently it reminds the Israelites that the powerful dynasty of Jehu has marked its way to the throne in the murder of Joram (also known as Jehoram), king of Israel, and Ahaziah, king of Judah (II Kings 9–10). In this way Hosea warns his generation that the Northern Kingdom is nearing its end. Its power would be broken in the valley of Jezreel.

Another warning comes to Israel with the birth of Hosea's daughter, Lo-Ruhamah. The meaning of her name, *no compassion*, conveys the warning to the Israelites that God will withdraw his love and mercy. No longer will he fully forgive them.

Subsequently, the birth of the third child brings the climactic announcement that God is severing his intimate relations with Israel. In the covenant, a mutual bond exists between God and his people. Now Hosea is serving notice to Israel that this bond has been dissolved. No longer is Israel God's people; no longer is God the God of Israel. The covenant relationship has reached its breaking point.

With no reference to Gomer or her children, whose message-bearing names are symbolically significant, Hosea continues to focus on the divine-human relationship between God and his people in 1:10–2:23. After a brief promise of restoration (1:10–2:1), Hosea delineates God's legal accusation, or lawsuit, against Israel for its adultery and covenant prostitution (2:2–15). Once more he promises restoration, delineating the nature of the faithful relationship that will exist between God and his people Israel at that time (2:16–23).

In a prophetic autobiographical account, in which he notes a few events in his life, Hosea reports God's command to him to marry once more (3:1–5). He is divinely informed that in so doing he will be acting typologically, illustrating the metaphorical marriage between God and Israel. Since

[17] For detailed exegesis of Hosea 1–3 see D. Stuart, *Hosea–Jonah* (Waco, Texas: Word Books, 1987). The broken covenant relationship is the essence of Hosea's message. Information about Hosea, limited to chapters 1 and 3, merely gives those facts that serve this metaphorical-typological purpose. With no action ascribed to Gomer or her children they are designated as "prostituting" individuals, since they are Israelites, all of whom were "prostitutes" by breaking their covenant with God.

Gomer, not mentioned after chapter one, is a prostitute figuratively and this woman is sexually promiscuous and possibly a prostitute literally, it is likely that this woman is not Gomer. Through purchase and marriage, in which Hosea lives with this woman in a sexless relationship, Hosea actually stops this woman in her sinful ways (3:3). In like manner God will bestow his gracious love upon the Israelites so that they will "return and seek the Lord their God and David their king" and enjoy God's "blessings in the last days" (3:5, NIV).

Detailed charges are brought against the Israelites for violating the stipulations of the covenant that God made with them (4:1–7:1a).[18] The royal and priestly families, who inherited their authority and are exercising it in self-serving ways, must be held accountable and are summoned for judgment. Yielding to "a spirit of prostitution" (4:12, 5:4, NIV) instead of acknowledging God, they no longer are a kingdom of priests (cf. Ex. 19:6). Hosea sounds the alarm. They will lose their land and go into exile. With this announcement of the coming judgment on Ephraim (Israel) as well as Judah for its disloyalty to God comes the promise of healing for God's people. The people of both Judah and Israel will have their fortunes restored (6:1, 11; 7:1a).

In a series of laments expressing God's perspective of the religious and political conditions in the Northern Kingdom, Hosea portrays the frantic, hopeless political intrigue of the rulers in Samaria (7:1b–16). This portrayal may reflect the political instability after 733 B.C., when Pekah is assassinated. Three previous kings are assassinated after 753 B.C. (II Kings 15:8–26). The personal debauchery, political intrigue, and instability in international relations that permeate the rulers in Samaria will hasten the doom of the Israelite kingdom. In their scramble for power the rulers have failed to turn to God. In open rebellion and flagrance they continue to violate the God-Israel relationship established in the covenant.

In a new oracle Hosea portrays the nearness of judgment (8:1–14). The Israelites hope in vain to gain freedom from Assyria. Destruction awaits them. They have disregarded God's law by setting up "'kings without my consent'" (8:4, NIV), making idols, and looking to other nations for help. "'Israel has forgotten his Maker'. . . . " (8:14, NIV) is the basic charge against them. The palaces and fortified towns they have built will be destroyed.

Using the prostitution metaphor for the last time, Hosea charges his people with harlotry in their rituals on festival days (9:1–9). Because they have prostituted themselves, deprivation and divine judgment await them.

[18] The crimes detailed in this passage are related to the curses and blessings delineated by Moses in Deuteronomy 28–33. Exclusive devotion expressed in loyalty to God was more important than sacrifice or burnt offerings, 6:6. (Cf. also Ps. 51:16–17; Isa. 1:12–17; Amos 5:21–24; Micah 6:6–8; Matt. 9:13; 12:7.)

Retrospectively, the Israelites have been disloyal (9:10–17) and therefore can expect God's wrath and rejection. Their deceitfulness will bring divine retribution as they pray for mountains and hills to cover them (10:1–8). God's indictment and judgment is vividly expressed to his apostate people, indicating that the king of Israel will be completely destroyed (10:9–15). In 722 B.C. King Hoshea is captured and imprisoned by the Assyrians.

Hosea 11:1–11 constitutes a divine speech and a separate entity. God's profound love for his people is expressed at its best in the allegory in Hosea: Israel is a son. Although the Israelites spurned God's love expressed in bringing them out of Egypt and caring for them, God will restore them.

Through deceit, fraud, heterodox religion, and other crimes, Ephraim has broken the covenant between God and Israel (11:12–12:14). Judah is also guilty of this rebellious attitude toward God. With an intensity previously unmatched, Hosea here expresses God's wrath against God's covenant-breaking people (13:1–16). In making and worshiping idols, they have broken the basic commandment to "'acknowledge no God but me'" (13:4, NIV). Consequently, "'The people of Samaria must bear their guilt, because they have rebelled against their God. They will fall by the sword'" (13:16, NIV).

"Return" is the key word for Israel's hope and God's promise of restoration in the future (14:1–8, NIV). This covenant verb is used eight times by Hosea, reflecting its use by Moses seven times in his promise of prosperity for those who return to God (cf. Deut. 30:1–10). Forgiveness for "'all our sins'" (14:2, NIV) is assured for those who return. The only offering required is "'the fruit of our lips'"—not offerings and sacrifices (cf. Ps. 51:16). God will respond to their exclusive loyalty; He will "'love them freely'" (14:4, NIV). For the "wise" and "discerning," this is the way of the Lord (14:9, NIV).

SELECTED READING

AALDERS, G. *The Problem of the Book of Jonah.* London: Tyndale House, 1948.

ANDERSON, FRANCIS I., and DAVID NOEL FREEDMAN. *Hosea.* The Anchor Bible. Garden City: Doubleday, 1980.

ELLISON, H. L. *The Old Testament Prophets.* Grand Rapids: Zondervan Publishing House, 1966.

———. "Jonah" in *Expositor's Bible Commentary.* Vol. 7. Grand Rapids: Zondervan Publishing House, 1985.

HENDERSON, E. *The Twelve Minor Prophets.* Grand Rapids: Baker Book House, 1980.

MCCOMISKEY, THOMAS E. "Amos" in *Expositor's Bible Commentary.* Grand Rapids: Zondervan Publishing House, 1985.

STUART, DOUGLAS. "Hosea, Amos, Jonah" in *Word Biblical Commentary.* Vol. 31. Waco: Word Books, 1987.

WALTON, JOHN. "Jonah" in *Bible Study Commentary*. Grand Rapids: Zondervan Publishing House, 1982.

WOOD, LEON J. "Hosea" in *Expositor's Bible Commentary*. Vol. 7. Grand Rapids: Zondervan Publishing House, 1985.

Chapter XXIII

Warnings to Judah

Whom did God use to warn Judah's citizens of coming judgment? Distinguished among the major prophets were Isaiah and Jeremiah, each of whom served his respective generation for more than forty years. As minor prophets Joel, Micah, and Zephaniah emerge as leading voices in the Southern Kingdom. With a God-given responsibility to relate the prophetic message to contemporary developments, they came to grips with the problems facing their generation, concluding with a promise of restoration.

Joel—The Day of the Lord in Judgment and Restoration—1:1–3:21

Joel, like Jonah, limits his identification in giving only his father's name, Pethuel. His message reflects the environment of Judah and Jerusalem, each mentioned six times. Judah, with its capital (also identified as "Zion") constitutes the focal point in Joel's lamentation over the calamitous day of the Lord facing his generation (1:1–2:17) and the future day of the Lord bringing restoration (2:18–3:21).

Like Amos, Isaiah, Daniel, and the Psalter, Joel emphasizes universal monotheism, in which God exercises absolute authority over all the peoples of the earth. Although God uses invading nations as his army to punish Judah (2:11, 25), all nations are ultimately defeated in a cosmic battle and judged (3:12).

Dates for Joel range from the ninth century B.C., the reign of Joash (835–796 B.C.), to postexilic times.[1] With no datable historic events mentioned in the book, any dating can be only inferential and speculative. If the

[1] D. Stuart, *Hosea-Jonah* (Waco, Texas: Word Books, 1987), pp. 224–226. For other dates cf. L. Allen, *The Books of Joel, Obadiah, Jonah and Micah* (Grand Rapids, Michigan: Eerdmans, 1976), pp. 19–25; G. Archer, *A Survey of Old Testament Introduction* (Chicago: Moody Press, rev. ed., 1974), pp. 303–307; C. H. Bullock, *An Introduction to the Prophetic Books* (Chicago: Moody Press, 1986), pp. 328–330.

tragic conditions of drought and desolation portrayed by Joel reflect invading armies (locusts understood as figurative, symbols of the invaders), then Joel's message may reasonably be dated when Judah was invaded by Assyria (701 B.C.) or by Babylonia (598 or 588 B.C.).[2]

Note the development of Joel's message in the following outline:

I. Warnings to Judah	1:1–2:17
A call to lament—tragedy awaiting Judah	1:1–20
Sounding an alarm to repentance	2:1–17
II. Restoration blessings	2:18–32
Material bounties	2:18–27
An outpouring of God's Spirit	2:28–32
III. The day of the Lord	3:1–21
Nations in the valley of the verdict	3:1–16
God dwelling in Zion	3:17–21

Alarming the population of Judah to the need for lamentation, Joel appeals to the elders, the drunkards, the farmers, and the priests (1:1–20). The citizens of Judah and Jerusalem are facing three crises: (1) an invasion of either locusts, literally, or of an army, compared metaphorically to locusts; (2) a severe drought; and (3) desolation left in the wake of such an invasion, disrupting the way of life for all citizens.

In facing an unstoppable invasion, the only solution is repentance—an absolutely genuine repentance (2:1–7). God's appeal to them is "'Even now . . . return to me with all your heart, with fasting and weeping and mourning,'" with the assurance that the Lord God is "gracious and compassionate" (2:12–13, NIV).

Restoration blessings in abundance are assured. Abundant crops will be theirs to enjoy as the enemy is expelled from their land. God's people are assured that "'never again will my people be shamed. Then you will know that I am in Israel . . . '" (2:26–27, NIV).

Spiritually, their needs will be met in the manifestation of the presence and power of the Spirit of God (2:28–32).[3] This promise is not limited to a few individuals who are especially called or trained but is assured to all peo-

[2] Cf. D. Stuart, op. cit., pp. 232–234, 241–242, for identity of the invader. Note that "locusts" are actually mentioned only in 1:4 and 25. In simile or metaphor, human armies are sometimes compared to locusts (Jud. 6:5; 7:12; Nahum 3:15–16; Jer. 46:23). Locusts are also part of the Old Testament stereotypical imagery of judgment (Deut. 28:38; I Kings 8:37; Amos 7:1). Cf. also pp. 228–230 for thematic correspondence between Joel's message in chapters 1 and 2 with the curses in Deuteronomy 32 that brought the punishment of invasion, drought, and desolation upon the Israelites for their infidelity.

[3] While Peter emphasizes the initial clause (Acts 2:21) and the final clause (Acts 2:39) as applicable to "'everyone who calls'" (Acts 2:21, NIV), the phenomena of the sky, included in this passage (cf. also Joel 3:15), are associated with the final judgment in the day of the Lord (Isa. 13:9; 24:23; Matt. 24:29–30; Mark 13:24–26; Luke 21:25–27; Rev. 6:12–14).

ple, regardless of age, gender, or social status. Peter asserts that they are experiencing the initial fulfillment and that, until "'the great and glorious day of the Lord'" comes, "'everyone who calls on the name of the Lord will be saved'" (Acts 2:17–21, NIV).[4]

Ultimately, the day of the Lord will bring judgment to the enemies of Israel and restore Zion as God's dwelling place (3:1–21). As the people in Joel's time face destruction by the invading enemies, the God-fearing people are given the assurance that they will be vindicated. In the "'day of the Lord,'" when "'the sun and moon will be darkened and the stars no longer shine,'" the nations that oppose God's purposes and his people will be judged in "'the valley of decision'" (3:14–15, NIV). God will "'dwell in Zion, my holy hill. Jerusalem will be holy'" (3:17, NIV).

Micah—A Reformer in Turbulent Times—1:1–7:20

In the heyday of Assyria's domination of Syria and Palestine the prophet Micah appeared on the scene in Judah. From the days of Jotham (c. 740 B.C.) he continued his ministry down to the turn of the century. During the reign of Hezekiah he was overshadowed by his colleague, Isaiah.

The sun was setting on Judah's era of prosperity and international prestige when Micah stepped forth. Uzziah, whose commercial interests penetrated into Arabia and whose military might challenged the advancing armies of Assyria from the north, died in 740 B.C. Jotham maintained the *status quo* for several years more while Pekah developed an anti-Assyrian policy in Samaria. By 735 B.C. the pro-Assyrian party in Jerusalem had established Ahaz on the Davidic throne. Within a few years this young king sealed an alliance with Assyria which in essence made him a vassal of Tiglath-pileser III. During the two decades of this Judo-Assyrian bond the kingdoms of Syria and Israel toppled under the Assyrian advance.

In this hectic period—perhaps soon after Uzziah's death—Micah responds to the prophetic call. Repeated crises upset the balance of power among the nations in Palestine and Syria while the Assyrians extend their empire. Micah predicts the fall of Samaria as well as the destruction of Jerusalem in his introductory message to the citizens of the Southern Kingdom. Although the specific occasions for his preaching are not indicated, the book undoubtedly represents the essence of his messages during the reigns of Jotham, Ahaz, and Hezekiah. The prediction concerning Samaria may have been given as early as Jotham's reign. The corrupt and idolatrous conditions reflected throughout the book may be related to the low ebb of

[4] Cf. D. Stuart, op. cit., pp. 229–230, for discussion of "The Democratization of the Spirit." What Moses experienced when the Lord "'put his Spirit'" on the seventy elders so that "they prophesied" (Num. 11:26–29, NIV) is now promised to all of God's people throughout coming generations (Acts 2:39; 21:9; 22:16; Rom. 10:12–13; Titus 3:4–7).

morality and religious interest during the days of Ahaz. How long Micah continued in the reign of Hezekiah remains an uncertainty.

With the accession of Hezekiah in 716 B.C. a new era dawned in Judah. Tribute payments and heathen cult worship in the Temple, as promoted by Ahaz, had by this time become unpopular. The new king terminated the policy of Assyrian appeasement. It was advantageous that Sargon with his armies was busily engaged in other parts of his extensive empire. With a spirit of nationalism Hezekiah developed a strong defense program. Besides extending and fortifying the walls of Jerusalem (II Chron. 32:5) he secured an adequate water supply by constructing the Siloam tunnel—still a tourist attraction in our day. This tunnel's well-known inscription, at present in the museum in Istanbul, bears witness to Hezekiah's efforts.

Religious policies inaugurated by Hezekiah were so drastic and effective that they rightfully came to be viewed as the outstanding reforms in Judah's history (II Kings 18). Altars, sacred pillars, and the asherim were demolished. Even Nehushtan, the bronze serpent made by Moses, was destroyed since it had become an object of veneration and worship. In all likelihood the Assyrian cult objects also were removed from the Temple. Through these reforms the way was cleared for Israel to return to the worship of God as prescribed in the law.

In times such as these Micah lived in the land of Judah. His home town was the village of Moresheth-Gath, approximately twenty-five miles southwest of Jerusalem. It is possible that he saw his nation engulfed by the Assyrians under Sennacherib. The threat to Jerusalem in 701 was abruptly terminated by a remarkable deliverance recorded in Isaiah, Kings, and Chronicles. To what extent Micah became personally involved in these crucial developments is not known.

Beyond the limits of the book bearing his name the prophet Micah is noted only once in the Old Testament. Almost a century later Jeremiah bears testimony to Micah's pronouncement of doom (Jer. 26:18–19).

With repeated crises occurring in Judah and the surrounding nations Micah undoubtedly had numerous occasions to raise his voice as a prophet. The political and religious implications of the deliberate and firm expansion of Assyrian power into Palestine called for the bold ministry of courageous men like Micah and Isaiah. Although neither refers to the other, they undoubtedly were associated in their prophetic duties. So reasonable is this possibility that it is conjectured that Micah was a disciple of Isaiah. The classic passage of Zion's restoration is common to both books. It is also conjectured that Micah was a rustic prophet with a rural ministry while city-bred Isaiah devoted his prophetic efforts to the population and court of Jerusalem.

In the political and religious turbulence of this era, when Tiglath-pileser III initiated the domination of Palestine by Assyria, Micah begins his ministry. He fearlessly indicts the leaders, prophets, and priests with social and religious corruption. Unlike Amos, Hosea, and Isaiah, he does not call them to repentance. Rather, his imperatives subpoena them to the Lord's court of law—"'plead your case'" (6:1, NIV)—where the Lord is the key witness and judge (1:2–7). In Micah's oracles "his brevity is marked by deep insight into the social, religious, and political movements of the eighth century. His ability to grasp the essence of the Hebrew faith and to verbalize it in memorable form has gotten him the reputation of providing the 'golden rule' of the Old Testament (6:8)."[5]

Theologically, Micah's focus is on the Lord's kingdom and final universal rule. Consequently, Micah emphasizes the sovereignty of God. His "doctrine of the remnant is unique among the Prophets and is perhaps his most significant contribution to the prophetic theology of hope. The remnant is a force in the world, not simply a residue of people . . . that will ultimately conquer the world (4:11–13)." In his perspective of the Lord's kingdom, Micah portrays the messianic king as a powerful ruler from Bethlehem and "not as a redemptive figure as in Isaiah's Servant."[6]

Micah's message of judgment, hope, and promise may be outlined as follows:

I. God's case against Judah and Israel	1:1–2:13
Impending judgment	1:1–7
Micah's lament and warning	1:8–16
Oppression and false prophets	2:1–11
The promise of the restoration of Israel	2:12–13
II. Indictment of leaders	3:1–12
Injustice of rulers	3:1–4
Spirit-empowered Micah vs. religious leaders	3:5–8
Consequences for Zion	3:9–12
III. The Kingdom in Zion	4:1–5:15
Triumph of the messianic kingdom	4:1–8
Present realities in Jerusalem	4:9–13
The ruler from Bethlehem	5:1–6
Victory of the purified remnant	5:7–15
IV. God's controversy with his people	6:1–16
God's accusation	6:1–6
God's requirements	6:7–8
God's verdict	6:9–16

[5] Cf. C. H. Bullock, *An Introduction to the Old Testament Prophetic Books*, pp. 119 and 103.

[6] Thomas E. McComiskey, "Micah" in *Expositor's Bible Commentary* (Grand Rapids, MI: Zondervan, 1985), p. 399.

V. Micah's dilemma and triumph in hope	7:1–20
Lamentation over social evils	7:1–6
Determination to trust God	7:7–10
A bright future in God's kingdom	7:11–20

With a universal perspective, Micah alerts the "earth and all who are in it" (1:2, NIV) to witness the cosmic judgment that the Sovereign Lord has in store for Samaria and Jerusalem (1:1–7). The two cities are charged with idolatry, which God regards as spiritual fornication. Realizing the devastation that awaits these capital cities, Micah openly displays his grief by laying aside his robe, walking barefoot, and warning the people to prepare for exile (1:8–16).

Micah, like Amos, charges the rich with oppressing the poor. Captivity awaits them. In spite of protests by false prophets, he warns the rich that they are evoking God's anger by their blatant disregard for the social concerns demanded by the covenant (2:1–11). Although exile is inevitable, the remnant will be released by "'One who breaks open the way'" (the Breaker-King, who is one with them and emerges from them) and will form a procession with "their king" leading the way (2:12–13, NIV).[7]

Civil rulers are confronted with the devastating question, "'Should you not know justice?'" (3:1, NIV). Portraying them as treating the oppressed like animals, Micah warns them that God will not hear them (3:4). The day is coming when prophets, seers, and diviners will be disgraced because of their inability to obtain an answer from God. Micah, by contrast, is filled with the Spirit of God, rebuking and warning his generation of their sins.[8] In the meantime, judges render decisions for bribery, and priests teach for reward. Injustice prevails on every hand. For all this, Zion will be plowed as a field and Jerusalem reduced to a heap of ruins (3:1–12).

The mood changes from gloom to hope as Micah portrays the future glory of Zion "in the last days" (4:1–8, NIV).[9] The prophet's perspective of hope extends beyond a mere restoration from captivity to the messianic kingdom. From this mountain—condemned because of the sins of Judah—the law will have a universal outreach. From Zion righteous judgment will extend to all nations. Swords and spears will be turned into implements of agriculture. Israel will be free from fear as universal peace is established. The "lame" and "exiles," or outcasts, constituting the returning remnant,

[7] Cf. ibid., pp. 415 and 428. This king (4:13) seems to be the same as the Deliverer-King (5:2–4). In each context the remnant or returning Israelites are portrayed as a flock needing a shepherd or deliverer (2:12 and 4:4).

[8] See C. F. Keil, *The Twelve Minor Prophets*, Vol. I, at reference on Mic. 3:8.

[9] Ibid., p. 421, where McComiskey, aware of the difficulty of determining the origin of this oracle (4:1–4 and Isa. 2:1–4), suggests that "it seems likely that Micah was the original author. It is an integral part of his entire prophecy and follows logically from the preceding description of Jerusalem's doom. That the oracle is longer in the prophecy of Micah . . . may indicate that Isaiah adapted it for his own purposes."

will have their "former dominion" and "kingship" restored through the manifestation of God's power in Jerusalem.[10]

From this promise of a triumphant future, Micah turns to the present realities (4:9–13). Graphically he portrays for the people the exile and the loss of their king, who is considered God's anointed, resulting in their extreme distress, comparable to the anguish of a woman in childbirth. Although their doom is certain, the Lord will redeem them. They will bring the ill-gotten gains and the wealth of their enemies to "the Lord of all the earth" (4:13, NIV).

From the ignominy of "Israel's ruler," Micah now turns to the hope of Zion's victorious future vested in the ruler from Bethlehem (5:1–6). In vivid pictorial language Micah depicts the care and restoration of the flock by one who will 'be their peace' (5:5, NIV). This Breaker-King (cf. 2:13) will extend his authority, security, and peace universally.[11]

Metaphorically portraying the remnant as a lion overcoming his prey, Micah describes the triumph of Israel over the godless nations (5:7–15). Trusting in God, this remnant will be transformed from an insignificant group to one that will dominate the world. This dominance will not be accomplished through military might but through the remnant's purification and dedication in spiritual renewal. God's wrath will be upon "'the nations that have not obeyed me'" (5:15, NIV).

In the format of a legal controversy God confronts his people, asking them, "'What have I done to you?'" (6:3, NIV). Addressing them as "'my people'" (6:3, NIV), God reminds them of "'the righteous acts of the Lord'" (6:5, NIV) in redeeming them from slavery, sending Moses to lead them, and protecting them from Balak's curse.

This history recital ends abruptly as Micah, speaking for the people, asks God what their responsibility is to him (6:6–8). 'With what shall I come [into the presence of] . . . the exalted God?' (6:6, NIV). The implication is clear that the best that one could offer—even the firstborn, which is the most precious gift one could give—is not acceptable for the sin of one's soul.[12]

What does God require? Act justly, love mercy, walk humbly with your God; this is what God expects. In the context of God's love and mercy that

[10] This remnant that is regathered consists of the lame (those weakened through hardship and affliction) and the exiles (those disgraced through expulsion from their homeland), portraying their helplessness (4:6–7). They will be made into a strong force that will ultimately conquer the godless nations (5:8–15), with the Lord as their King in exalted Zion (4:8; cf. also Isa. 24:23; 52:7).

[11] Isaiah identifies this ruler as the "Prince of Peace" (9:6), coming in the lineage of David, ruling in a universal kingdom (9:7; 11:1–11), with the Israelites regathered from the distant parts of the earth.

[12] Sacrifice is not acceptable as a substitute for justice, acts of kindness and love, and an attitude of humble obedience Godward (Ex. 19:5–6). Sacrifice offered by the contrite in heart is acceptable (Ps. 51:17–19).

the Israelites experienced in their release from slavery, God expects them to act justly and to exercise love. What God did for them they are expected to do for others. This would be evidence that they are walking humbly with their God, therein reflecting God's justice and mercy. Maintaining their relationship with God would be expressed in acting justly and loving the exercise of mercy toward others. Moses, to whom God revealed what he expected of Israel, succinctly stated the essence of this basic requirement: Love God (Deut. 5:6; 10:12) and love the alien (Deut. 10:19), or neighbor (Lev. 19:18, 33–34).[13]

Dramatically, the voice of the Lord is introduced, sounding an alarm of coming disaster (6:9–16). Social sins and the idolatry of Omri and Ahab still prevail in society. For this God will not acquit them.

As Micah laments his lack of godly fellowship, he observes the behavior pattern in his generation (7:1–6). Aware of the disruption of the family unit, he concludes that there is no one that could be trusted. Speaking for the remnant, the prophet turns to God in prayer with a determination to look expectantly to him (7:7–10). Because of the societal sins, captivity will come as a just and holy God deals with corrupt society. In confessing their sins the Israelites anticipate exaltation while the enemy is humiliated.

The eventual triumph of the remnant is assured (7:11–20). Their kingdom will be extended as God's judgment brings desolation to the sinful world. In their relationship with God they are assured that through miraculous acts, similar to those of the Exodus, God will break the mighty power of nations that took them into captivity.

This prayer of the remnant concludes with a note of praise. In mercy God will forgive their sin and restore his people. Appropriate is the question, 'Who is a God like you[!] . . .' (7:18, NIV).

Zephaniah—The Day of Wrath and Blessing—1:1–3:20

True religion in Judah not only declined after Hezekiah's death but was replaced by gross idolatry. Manasseh erected altars to Baals, made asherim, and worshiped the host of heaven, even using the Temple for these idolatrous practices. By offering his sons in sacrificial rites, conforming to heathen customs, and shedding innocent blood in Jerusalem Manasseh led his people into such excessive sin that Judah was far worse than the nations God had expelled from Canaan in times past.

[13] God's requirement deals directly with the social evils of injustice and oppression, which give evidence that the people are not walking humbly with God and are ignoring the two basic commandments. Moses' command to love the aliens and one's neighbors is given in the context of reminding the Israelites that they had been enslaved and therefore should extend justice, mercy, and love to those about them (Ex. 22:21; 23:9; Lev. 19:33; Deut. 10:19; 24:17). Jesus and the religious leaders agreed that man's love for God and neighbor is the essence of God's requirements (Matt. 22:34–40).

Before long Isaiah's voice of warning was silenced. Whether he died a natural death or became a martyr under Manasseh's godless policies is not recorded in the biblical account. Neither does the Old Testament identify the prophets who had the courage to raise their voices in opposition to this wicked king of Judah. In any case, Judah's religion was so demoralized that the promised judgment was bound to be released in fury—especially when the king persisted in provoking God.

Divine judgment came upon Manasseh when he was taken captive to Babylon by the Assyrians. There he repented and in time was restored to his throne in Jerusalem. It is difficult to ascertain how effective he was in righting the wrong throughout Judah before his reign ended. Amon, his son, reverted to Manasseh's evil ways and thus incurred more and more guilt. In less than two years his reign abruptly ended with his assassination (*ca.* 740 B.C.).

Josiah, the heir to the throne, led Judah in a religious reformation as the Assyrian king, Ashurbanipal, devoted his efforts toward cultural interests and suppression of Babylonian uprisings. With the death of Assyria's king (*ca.* 633 B.C.) the spirit of restlessness throughout the Fertile Crescent erupted in open revolt, providing Josiah the opportunity to rid Judah of Assyrian influence. The premature death of Josiah in 609 suddenly changed Judah's political future.

Zephaniah's prophetic ministry is associated with Josian times (1:1). Beyond that a specific date is lacking but it seems likely that he was active before the beginning of the Josian reformation.[14] Apparently a descendant of Hezekiah, Zephaniah may have been reared under the influence of the same teachers who instructed and guided Josiah in the early years of his life. Certainly it is not beyond reason to credit this prophet with stimulating the reformation movement led by Josiah. Zephaniah's familiarity with Jerusalem suggests the probability that he was a citizen of Judah's capital. Speaking to his own people he sounds an alarm that should have stirred even the most self-satisfied to action.

Like a blaring trumpet Zephaniah raises his voice to shock the complacent citizens of Judah. The day of the Lord is at hand. It is a day of judgment. Most likely Zephaniah was familiar with Jerusalem's fate as predicted by Amos, Isaiah, and other preceding prophets. Over half a century had passed since Isaiah had explicitly warned Hezekiah that his descendants and the wealth of Jerusalem would be taken to Babylon. Besides indicting Judah for gross idolatry and bloodshed Zephaniah points up the porten-

[14] Cf. Bruce K. Waltke, "Zephaniah" in *Zondervan Pictorial Encyclopedia* (Grand Rapids: Zondervan, 1975). Also, E.J. Young, *Introduction to the Old Testament* (Grand Rapids: Eerdmans, 1949), pp. 265–267, and R.H. Pfeiffer, *Introduction to the Old Testament* (New York: Harper & Row, 1941), p. 275. For dating after 621 B.C. see John D. Hannah, "Zephaniah" in *The Bible Knowledge Commentary* (Wheaton, IL: Victor Books, 1985).

tous international stirrings in the Tigris-Euphrates area. Such a penetrating message should cause grave concern to every citizen in Jerusalem. With doom so near, the prophet not only sets forth the immediate implications but also warns of the final time of reckoning in the day of the Lord. In a brief message he covers the scope of judgments extending to the entire world.

The Book of Zephaniah may be outlined as follows:

I.	The impending doom of Jerusalem	1:1–18
II.	The scope of God's judgment	2:1–3:8
III.	Restoration and blessing	3:9–20

Fearlessly Zephaniah opens his prophetic ministry by announcing the day of final judgment upon the wicked (1:2–3). In that day man as well as beasts will be cut off from the face of the earth.

Speaking to his generation the prophet declares that Jerusalem is facing destruction. Baal nature-religion is doomed for extinction. Solemnly Zephaniah cautions his people to submit themselves humbly to the divine judgments in store for them. Vividly he portrays God as sacrificing the leaders of Judah who are responsible for fraud and violence. Included in this punishment are the people, who ignore God and spurn the law. There is no escape for Jerusalem or for the entire earth in God's day of wrath (1:17–18).

Zephaniah pleads with his people to seek righteousness and humility before this day of wrath comes (2:1–2). The warning itself is a sign of mercy, providing another opportunity for them to turn Godward in repentance.

In a panoramic view the prophet presents the judgments of God on the cities of Philistia. For taunting Judah the Moabites and Ammonites await the fate of Sodom and Gomorrah. Ethiopia also is earmarked for destruction. Even the proud Assyrian city of Nineveh is about to be reduced to ruins and abandoned to wild beasts. How much more is judgment due Jerusalem (3:1–8). Instead of trusting God, the officials, judges, prophets, and priests have led the people astray. Knowing God's decision to consume all nations in his jealous wrath Zephaniah once more seeks to arouse Jerusalem in the hope of averting God's pending judgment.

Against this dark background Zephaniah expresses the hopes for restoration. The time is coming when people from distant lands will call on the name of the Lord, when the proud and haughty will be banished from Jerusalem. The humble and lowly with the remnant of Israel will dwell in peace and safety under the rule of the Lord their King. Victoriously triumphant over all foes, the Israelites will once more enjoy the abundant blessing of God in their own land, with righteousness and peace prevailing.

SELECTED READING

ALLEN, LESLIE C. "The Books of Joel, Obadiah, Jonah and Micah" in *The New International Commentary on the Old Testament.* Grand Rapids: Wm. B. Eerdmans Publishing Co., 1976.

BULLOCK, C. HASSELL. *An Introduction to the Old Testament Prophetic Books.* Chicago: Moody Press, 1986.

CALVIN, JOHN. *The Minor Prophets.* Vol. 6. of *Calvin's Commentaries.* Grand Rapids: Baker Book House, 1979.

CARLSON, E. LESLIE. "Micah" in *The Wycliffe Bible Commentary.* Chicago: Moody Press, 1962.

HANKE, H. A. "Zephaniah" in *The Wycliffe Bible Commentary.* Chicago: Moody Press, 1962.

HANNAH, JOHN D. "Zephaniah" in *The Bible Knowledge Commentary.* Wheaton: Victor Books, 1985.

MAYS, J. *Micah: A Commentary.* Philadelphia: Westminster Press, 1976.

MCCOMISKEY, THOMAS E. "Micah" in *Expositor's Bible Commentary.* Grand Rapids: Zondervan Publishing House, 1985.

PATTERSON, RICHARD D. "Joel" in *Expositor's Bible Commentary.* Grand Rapids: Zondervan Publishing House, 1985.

PUSEY, E. B. *The Minor Prophets.* 2 vols. New York: Funk & Wagnalls, 1886.

SMITH, RALPH L. "Micah–Malachi" in *Word Biblical Commentary.* Vol. 32. Waco: Word Books, 1985.

STUART, DOUGLAS. "Joel" in *Word Biblical Commentary.* Vol. 31. Waco: Word Books, 1987.

THOMPSON, JOHN A. "Joel" in *Interpreter's Concise Commentary.* New York: Abingdon Press, 1956.

WALKER, LARRY. "Zephaniah" in *Expositor's Bible Commentary.* Grand Rapids: Zondervan Publishing House, 1985.

Chapter XXIV

Foreign Nations in Prophecy

Three minor prophets each focus attention upon one foreign nation: Obadiah on Edom, Nahum on Assyria, and Habakkuk on Chaldea, or Babylonia. Unlike Isaiah, Amos, and other prophets, the authors of these oracles hardly refer to other nations. They offer encouragement, assuring the righteous that those who oppose God await judgment, while the righteous, who have been oppressed, will be restored and exalted.

These three books, entirely undated, provide no information which would satisfy curiosity concerning the personal lives of the prophets. None of these three prophets gives their lineages, and only Nahum gives his native city. The limited references to contemporary events make it impossible to achieve certainty in dating their respective careers and messages.

Obadiah—The Pride of Edom—1–21

In this book, the shortest in the Old Testament, Obadiah delineates God's message concerning the downfall of Edom. Utter destruction is predicted for this nation because of the arrogance and pride of the Edomites.

The most identifiable event in this prophecy is the devastation of Jerusalem. Obadiah's graphic portrayal (10–14) of the condition of Jerusalem and Judah fits best into the early exile after the destruction of Jerusalem by the Babylonians. The accounts of the ninth-century relations between Edom and Judah in II Kings (8:20–22) and II Chronicles (21:16–17) offer little information for correlation with the account of Obadiah.[1] Some of the passages that reflect the sixth-century relations between Judah and Edom are Ps. 137:7; Jer. 9:25–26; Lam. 4:21; Ezek. 25:12–14; 35:11–15; and 36:2–6. It seems likely that the Edomites gradually appropriated land in southern Judah during the Babylonian invasions, 597–586 B.C. That they burned the Temple, as the

[1] Among scholars supporting the ninth-century date are G. Archer, R. Laetsch, M. Unger, and E. Young.

author of First Esdras (4:45) claimed, has not been verified from other sources. It is certain, however, that they did aid the Babylonians in destroying Jerusalem and in terminating the Davidic rule in Judah. Consequently, it seems reasonable to date Obadiah in the wake of Jerusalem's destruction in 586 B.C. However, any date for Obadiah must be held tentatively.[2]

The animosity between the Israelites and the Edomites began with Jacob and Esau (Gen. 27:41–45; 32:1–21; 33:1–17). Esau and his descendants settled in the land of Seir or Edom (36:1–43), an area extending about one hundred miles south from the Dead Sea to Elath on the Gulf of Aqaba. Israel under Moses had an unfriendly encounter with them en route to Canaan (Num. 20:14–21; Deut. 2:1–6; 23:7). King Saul defeated the Edomites (I Sam. 14:47). David conquered and subjected Edom, erecting garrisons throughout the land to control their abundant copper resources and trade routes (II Sam. 8:14). Edom successfully revolted under Jehoram of Judah (II Kings 14:7) and Ahaz (II Chron. 28:17). Between 700 and 600 B.C. Edom seems to have reached the zenith of its prosperity but very likely was destroyed during the latter half of the sixth century. Malachi corroborates this by referring to the "wasteland" of Edom (1:3–4, NIV).

Consider the following outline:

I.	Edom's pride bringing utter destruction	vv. 1–9
II.	The charge against Edom	vv. 10–14
III.	Israel's sovereignty restored	vv. 15–21

Edom's pride was grounded in its geographical location. With its center of civilization located in a mountain ridge towering over four thousand feet high in a region that was forbidding and inaccessible, the citizens of Edom had an unusual sense of security and self-sufficiency. Boastful and secure in their natural fortress, they also prided themselves on their wisdom. Virtually impregnable as far as human forces were concerned, the Edomites were vulnerable as God destroyed their wise men and released his power against them, reducing them in size and influence (1–9).

These verses (10–14) may well portray the participation of the Edomites in the destruction of Jerusalem by the Babylonians. Instead of helping their "'brother Jacob'" (v. 10, NIV), they stood by in anticipation of taking advantage of the refugees and sharing in the plunder. In a series of eight prohibitions, Obadiah portrays their attitudes and actions in mockery, violence, gloating, rejoicing, and boasting as the Judeans are subjected to misfortune, ruin, and distress.

[2] Among those supporting the sixth-century date are C. Armerding, in "Obadiah" in *Expositor's Bible Commentary* (Grand Rapids: Zondervan, 1985), 7:337; C. H. Bullock, in *An Introduction to the Old Testament Prophetic Books* (Chicago: Moody Press, 1986), p. 260; D. Stuart, in "Hosea-Jonah" in *Word Biblical Commentary* (Waco, Texas: Word Books, 1987), 31:403–404.

Obadiah predicts that the day of the Lord will bring doom to Edom (15–18). This will be executed by the Lord, who provides deliverance and restoration to "the house of Jacob" (the nation of Israel) on Mount Zion (18, NIV). The punishment for Edom will fit the crime (cf. Lev. 24:20; Deut. 19:21).

The returning exiles will not only occupy Jerusalem and the entire land of Israel but control the "mountains of Esau, . . . the land of the Philistines, . . . Gilead, . . . as far as Zarephath." Exiles will return from Sepharad,[3] indicating that Judeans will be brought back miraculously from even beyond the far reaches of the Babylonian empire. Occupying their own land, the Israelites will prosper. But "the mountains of Esau" will be governed from Mount Zion, the capital of the Lord's kingdom (19–20, NIV).

Nahum—The Fate of Nineveh—1:1–3:19

The prophet Nahum, known only by the book bearing his name, came from Elkosh, a city probably located southwest of Jerusalem. Speaking to a Judean audience (1:15), he was primarily preoccupied with God's judgment on Assyria, while assuring the restoration of Judah.

The message of Nahum is rooted in the Sinaitic revelation of God to the nation of Israel. Throughout the universe, God relates judicially as a God of wrath to those who oppose him and mercifully as a God of love to those who seek refuge in him.

Nahum vividly portrays Assyria as a strong power that has painfully oppressed Israel for a long time. While Assyria has been the agent of God's anger (Isa. 10:5) afflicting Israel, Nahum predicts that now judgment awaits the Assyrians.

As early as the ninth century, the Israelite king Jehu paid tribute to Shalmaneser III (858–824 B.C.). Beginning with Tiglath-pileser III (745–727), Assyrian armies advanced into Palestine, conquering Damascus (732), Samaria (722), and southwestern Judah and threatening the conquest of Jerusalem under Sennacherib (705–681). Under Esarhaddon (681–669) and Ashurbanipal (669–633), the Assyrians exercised dominion over Judah, even taking their king, Manasseh, captive to Babylon and restoring him later (cf. II Chron. 33:10–13).

Esarhaddon advanced into Egypt and captured Memphis in 671 B.C., with Thebes, about five hundred miles south, surrendering to the Assyrians.

[3] Possibly a reference to Shaparda, a district in Media to which Sargon exiled Israelites (II Kings 17:6). Cf. H. Bewer, "Obadiah" and "Joel" in *International Critical Commentary* (New York: Scribner's Sons, 1911), pp. 45–46. For identification with Sardis, *Cparda* in Persian monuments, the capital of Lydia in Asia Minor where a Jewish colony existed as early as the reign of Artaxerxes (464–424), see *The Interpreter's Bible* at reference (6:287). Cf. also C. Torrey, "The Bilingual Inscription from Sardis," *American Journal of Semitic Languages and Literature,* XXXIV (1917–1918), pp. 185–198.

Repeatedly, the Egyptians rebelled and, at times, successfully reclaimed Memphis. By 664 or 663 Ashurbanipal's patience was exhausted as he returned with a strong army. In vengeance he razed Thebes to the ground. Since then it has been largely a place of monuments to a glory and dominance long departed.

Nahum's reference to the destruction of Thebes makes 663 B.C. the *terminus a quo*, and the prediction of Nineveh's fall suggests 612 B.C. as the *terminus ad quem* for the period of his career. Within this range it seems impossible to fix a specific date, but the "formidable state of Assyrian power of the book itself requires that we date the prophecy prior to the decline of that kingdom after about 626 B.C."[4]

Noteworthy in the Book of Nahum are the many affinities with the Book of Isaiah. Carl Armerding asserts that in two themes—the language and imagery of redemption and the judgment on the oppressor—there is correlation between the Book of Nahum and Isaiah 51–52. "In view of the precision, uniqueness, and frequency of these correspondences, it seems evident, then, that Nahum's relationship to Isaiah 51–52 extends . . . to one of specific literary interdependence." The evidence for this interdependence . . . "is thus founded on unique, multiple verbal repetitions linking specific passages . . . reinforced by the extensive continuity of imagery in other related passages . . . corroborated to the point of virtual certainty by the shared pattern of oppression, deliverance, and judgment experienced specifically in relation to Assyria." Nahum in his dependency on Isaiah thus is "an outstanding example of OT prophetic interpretation and application within the OT itself."[5]

The following analysis suggests the leading themes as developed in the Book of Nahum:

I. Introduction	1:1
II. What God is like	1:2–2:2
His indignation and awesome power	1:2–8
His goodness and severity	1:9–2:2
III. Certainty of destruction	2:3–3:1
Siege and conquest portrayed	2:3–10
Interpretive analogy and verdict	2:11–3:1
IV. Prediction of Nineveh's total end	3:2–19
Conquest and utter ruination	3:2–7
Analogy to Thebes	3:8–11
God's sentence	3:12–19

[4] Cf. Carl Armerding, "Nahum" in *Expositor's Bible Commentary* (Grand Rapids: Zondervan, 1985), 7:452–453.

[5] Ibid., 7:453–456.

The majesty of God is the introductory theme of Nahum. Sovereign and omnipotent, God rules supreme in nature. The wicked—enemies of God by their deeds—are allowed to continue because God is slow to anger. In due time the vengeance of a jealous God will be released. Those who trust in him will be saved in the day of his wrath, but the enemy will be completely cut off (1:1–8).

This judgment is final. The enemy will afflict Israel no more. Announcing the judicial sentence more formally, the Lord assures Judah that the yoke of the Assyrians will be broken, their name will be barred from perpetuation, and the temple of their gods will be destroyed. To Judah comes the messenger with good news announcing peace. The people are to celebrate their festivals, renewing their religious devotion in gratitude for this deliverance. With a grave warning to Nineveh to brace themselves for an attack, the Lord assures the restoration of 'the splendor of Israel' (2:2, NIV). This is the final promise of salvation for God's people in Nahum (1:9–2:2).

Nahum vividly pictures the siege, conquest, and utter ruination of Nineveh. This proud city of the Assyrians, who plagued Jerusalem, is now subjected to the horrible ordeal of a siege in which complete confusion prevails. The enemy enters, plunders, and reduces Nineveh to ruins, leaving it utterly desolate (2:3–10).

In an extended metaphor that interprets the horror of the preceding verses, Nineveh is portrayed as ravaging Mesopotamia like a savage beast of prey. Now the people of Nineveh are called to account for their ruthlessness (cf. Isa. 5:29–30; 10:5–19; Jer. 50:17). Nineveh is condemned by the Lord Almighty (2:11–3:1). Its military power and political control will be eradicated. Even its messengers will be silenced. "Woe to the city of blood," is the divine verdict (3:1, NIV).

Nineveh's citizens have precipitated this catastrophe. They are charged with unscrupulous commercialism and ruthless plunder. Vividly describing one of the most dramatic battle scenes in Old Testament literature, Nahum portrays advancing chariots and charging horsemen as they crush the corpses of Nineveh's defenders. Using the simile of a harlot, he describes the shameful exposure of Nineveh before the nations she so ruthlessly oppressed. They will gaze at her in contempt, with no one lamenting her ruination (3:2–7).

The destruction of Thebes is cited by comparison. Despite its vast fortifications, this populous Egyptian city was conquered and plundered by the Assyrians in 663 B.C. Is Nineveh better than Thebes? Strong, fortified, and supported by Libya and Put, the city of Thebes could not withstand the Assyrian assault. Neither will Nineveh stand in the day of her attack. Her fortifications are ineffective under the crushing attack of the enemy, who advances as a consuming fire (3:8–11).

As ripe fruit falls from a tree, so Nineveh is ripe for destruction. It will be consumed from without by fire and within by its merchants, guards, and officials, compared to locusts that "strip the land and then fly away" (3:12–17, NIV).

The final verdict, addressed to the king of Assyria, predicts the scattering of the population accompanying Nineveh's end. Unlike Israel, the nation of Assyria has no hope for a remnant. Furthermore, everyone will rejoice over its destruction, for what people have been unscathed by the ravages of the Assyrian war machine?

Habakkuk—Justice in Universal Affairs—1:1–3:19

Unique among the prophets of Israel was Habakkuk in his dialogue with God. Instead of speaking for God to the people, he spoke with God about his people. His spiritual struggles reflect the period of apprehensiveness that prevailed in Judah as the powerful Assyrian Kingdom declined, ending with the destruction of Nineveh (612 B.C.) and the rise of the Chaldeans (626 B.C.) to establish the Babylonian Empire.[6]

Initially, Habakkuk is concerned with the spiritual decline and injustice he has observed among his own people. Turning to God in prayer, he asks some of the most penetrating questions in all literature. In God's answer (1:5–11), the prophecy is catapulted to the international and eschatological level and provides a proper view of God and of his relation to history.

The core of Habakkuk's message is expressed in 2:4: "'But the righteous will live by his faith'" (NIV). In the context the prophet is instructed to "'write down'" this revelation to preserve it for the future, even as Moses was bidden to do with what God revealed to him at Mount Sinai. The lasting relevance and importance of this verse is reflected in the New Testament. Paul quotes it when he argues in Romans (1:17) that salvation is by faith and not by works. Quoting it again in Galatians (3:11–12), he reasons that faith is the antithesis of law or legal salvation. In the Book of Hebrews (10:37–38) the author quotes Habakkuk 2:3–4, focusing upon the pending arrival of the fulfillment of Habakkuk's vision, in order to encourage those who have faith to persevere under pressure.

Habakkuk's message lends itself to the following outline as a guide for further consideration:

[6] Carl Armerding, "Habakkuk" in *Expositor's Bible Commentary* (Grand Rapids: Zondervan, 1985), 7:493.

I. The dialogue	1:1–2:20
Habakkuk's question for God: "Why?"	1:1–4
God's answer	1:5–11
More perplexing questions	1:12–2:1
God's response	2:2–20
II. Habakkuk's prayer—a psalm	3:1–19
Appeal to God's covenantal commitment	3:1–15
Confession of trust and joy	3:16–19

Lamenting the violence and destruction that is rampant in Judah, Habakkuk boldly asks God, "How long, O Lord, must I call for help, but you do not listen?" The ethical wrongs he sees—the "law is paralyzed" and "the wicked hem in the righteous, so that justice is perverted"—are beyond human control. Divine intervention alone can correct this imbalance (1:1–4, NIV).

In reply God assures Habakkuk that he is about to do something that is amazing and unbelievable. He is raising up the ruthless Babylonians. Compared to three predators—the leopard, the wolf, and the vulture—the invading hordes will gather "'prisoners like sand,'" with their kings and rulers. In their ruthless arrogance the Babylonians boast about their own strength as their god (1:5–11, NIV).

Expressing his confidence in God and addressing him in covenantal terms, Habakkuk continues his query. How can God be silent and continue to tolerate treacherous evil? How can God in his universal justice allow the wicked Babylonians to "swallow up those more righteous" (1:13, NIV), namely Judah? Can a God of justice tolerate injustice indefinitely and destroy nations without mercy? Revealing mature wisdom, Habakkuk determines that he will wait upon God for the answers to his questions (1:12–2:1).

Habakkuk is instructed to "'write down'" this revelation because it "'awaits'" fulfillment at "'the end,'" which in the context seems to refer to the Babylonian oppression (cf. vv. 4–20). A written copy is provided so that the one who reads it is assured that this revelation is certain to be fulfilled at "'an appointed time.'" For those in Judah who are about to experience the impending Babylonian invasion and captivity this assurance of fulfillment offers comfort (2:2–3, NIV).

The Lord answers Habakkuk's lament (1:12–2:1), identifying the Babylonions as "'puffed up'" with desires that are "'not upright.'" They are "'arrogant'" and "'as greedy as the grave'" in gathering captives from all nations for exile (2:4–5, NIV). In stark contrast to the "not upright" Babylonians the Lord informs Habakkuk about "'the righteous,'" or upright (cf. Ps. 32:11; 33:1). The former are under divine condemnation, while the latter are assured that they "'will live by . . . faith,'" or faithfulness, which entails a dependent trust and a steadfast commitment in vital relation to God (2:4, NIV). Governed by God's requirements, the righteous conduct issues from hearts that are new, humble, and contrite (Ezek. 36:25–27; Ps. 51:17).

With absolute finality the judgment implied previously (2:4–5; 1:5–17) is stated in a taunt-song. Each of the first four paragraphs begins with a "woe," introducing a judicial indictment in which the Babylonians are exposed as an object lesson (2:6–20). They are accused of aggression and intimidation (6–8), self-assertion and intemperance (9–11), violence and iniquity (12–14), and inhumanity and indignity (15–17). The last paragraph opens with a denunciation of idols portrayed as man-made objects that cannot breathe or speak. "Woe to him" who calls on lifeless idols. In contrast to such folly and absurdity is the reference to the Lord's presence in his holy "temple" or "palace" (18–20, NIV).[7]

The seductive, insidious futility of idols stands in contrast to the unique claim of a living God who shows love to those who love, obey, and trust him (Ex. 20:4; Lev. 26:1). The mere reference to the presence of God in this context constitutes an intimation of judgment, not only upon Babylon, but against all who fail to acknowledge him. Appropriate is the call for reverent submission to the Lord of history: "'Let all the earth be silent before him'" (2:20, NIV).

Habakkuk concludes with a psalm—a prayer for mercy (3:1–19).[8] In the central, focal passage of this prayer he implores God to make known once more his mighty acts. God manifested his glory and used nature to bring salvation to his people Israel when he brought them through the wilderness and established them in the promised land. Aware of the distress that the ruthless and impetuous invader (1:6) will bring to his people, Habakkuk is determined to "wait patiently" (3:16, NIV) and thereby demonstrates the greatness of his faith as he anticipates their final "day of calamity." Basing his faith on God's revealed word, Habakkuk recognizes that the same covenant that promises the devastating invasion (16–17) also promises God's restoration and favor (cf. Deut. 30:1–10). This hope is the basis for his rejoicing (3:18). In the midst of disaster Habakkuk stands as a noble example of a living faith in the blessings of Israel's God (Deut. 33:1), who is universally ruling and judging in sovereign power. For his times as well as for ours, Habakkuk offers a theology for life—a faith in God as our basic response to the unanswered problems in today's universe.

[7] Cf. *Theological Word Book of the Old Testament,* 1:214–215.

[8] Cf. Carl Armerding, op. cit., pp. 520–522, for an excursus on chapter 3 as closely related to the Psalms, especially Psalms 18, 68, and 77.

SELECTED READING

ARMERDING, CARL E. "Obadiah, Nahum, and Habakkuk" in *Expositor's Bible Commentary*. Grand Rapids: Zondervan Publishing House, 1985.

BENNETT, T. MILES. *The Books of Nahum and Zephaniah.* Grand Rapids: Baker Book House, 1968.

FEINBERG, CHARLES L. *The Minor Prophets.* Chicago: Moody Press, 1973.

LAETSCH, THEODORE. *The Minor Prophets.* St. Louis: Concordia Publishing House, 1956.

MAIER, WALTER A. *The Book of Nahum.* 1959. Reprint. Grand Rapids: Baker Book House, 1980.

STOLL, JOHN H. *The Book of Habakkuk.* Grand Rapids: Baker Book House, 1972.

STUART, DOUGLAS. "Obadiah" in *Word Biblical Commentary.* Vol. 31, "Hosea–Jonah." Waco: Word Books, 1987.

Chapter XXV

Beyond the Exile

After the nationalistic hopes of Judah were shattered with the burning of Jerusalem in 586, the prophet Jeremiah accompanied a remnant of the Jews to Egypt and there concluded his ministry. Ezekiel, a prophet among the exiles in Babylonia, devoted his message to the prospects of an ultimate restoration to the homeland. His prophetic ministry probably terminated around 570 B.C. With the return of the Jews to their native land, Haggai and Zechariah began to exercise an effective influence, stimulating the Jews in their efforts to rebuild the Temple. Before the lapse of another century, Malachi would step forth in Judah as a prophet of the Lord.

The Times of Rebuilding Jerusalem[1]

Jeremiah's written prediction regarding a seventy-year period of Jewish captivity was in circulation among the exiles in Babylon (Jer. 25:11; 29:10; Dan. 9:1–2). As long as the Babylonian rulers continued in power the hopes for a return to the homeland were dim. For those familiar with Isaiah's message (44:28–45:1) a new hope must have dawned when Cyrus, the Persian, emerged in political and military leadership (559 B.C.). With his conquest of Babylon in 539 the prophecy of Jeremiah aroused renewed interest among the pious and devout (Dan. 9:1–2).

Momentous days were ahead for the Jews. Shortly after the fall of Babylon Cyrus issued a pertinent decree. Reversing the policy of uprooting conquered peoples from their homeland—a practice of the Assyrians and Babylonians for over two centuries—Cyrus favored the Jews and other captive peoples with a proclamation allowing them to return to their native

[1] For a fuller discussion of the times of Zechariah and Haggai see chapter XVI.

lands. Approximately fifty thousand Jews joined in the trek from Babylon to Jerusalem to restore their national fortunes under the leadership of such men as Zerubbabel and Joshua (Ezra 1–3).

Optimistically the returning Jews began the tremendous task of rebuilding their national home. They erected an altar and reinstituted worship in Jerusalem according to the law of Moses. With enthusiasm they renewed the observance of the prescribed feasts and offerings. They courageously tackled the rebuilding of the Temple in the second year after their return. While many shouted with joy, others wept as they reflected on the beautiful Solomonic structure that had been utterly reduced to ruins by the Babylonian armies some five decades earlier.

Optimism soon gave way to discouragement. By refusing the aid of the mixed population in the province of Samaria, the Jews became the victims of hatred. So hostile were the neighbors to the north that the building project was completely abandoned for about eighteen years.

Not until the second year of Darius (520 B.C.) were the Jews able to renew their efforts. At that time the prophets Haggai and Zechariah stirred up zeal and patriotism in a new generation.[2] Less than a month after Haggai made his first public appearance the people resumed the building program. Their incentive was heightened a few weeks later when Zechariah joined Haggai in messages of rebuke, comfort, and encouragement. Zerubbabel and Joshua gave their people courageous leadership in this noble effort despite the opposition of Tattenai (Ezra 4–6). When the latter appealed to the Persian king, Darius made an investigation and issued a verdict in favor of the Jews. In five years' time the people of Judah saw their hopes fulfilled in the dedication of the new Temple.

Haggai and Zechariah are barely mentioned in Ezra (5:1–2 and 6:14) as prophets who aided Zerubbabel and Joshua. The effectiveness of their prophetic ministry and the impact they made on the people of Judah are seen more clearly in their writings.

Haggai—Promoter of the Building Program—1:1–2:23

Little is known about Haggai beyond his identification as a prophet. Very likely he was born in Babylon and returned in the migration to Jerusalem in 539–538 B.C. His specific task was to induce the Jews to renew their work on the Temple.

[2] Widespread revolutions occurred during the early years of the reign of Darius. Whether or not they had any bearing on the activities of these two prophets is not indicated in their writings, although Pfeiffer, *Introduction to the Old Testament*, pp. 602–607, interprets Hag. 2:6–9 and Zech. 2:6 ff. as references to the unsettled conditions of this time. Cf. also Albright, *The Biblical Period*, p. 50. Certainly Ezra 5 represents Darius as most favorably inclined toward the Jews.

Beginning in late August of 520 B.C. Haggai delivered four messages to the people before the end of the year. The brevity of his book may indicate that he recorded but a summary of his oral messages. The following outline of the book is based on the four oracles:

I.	Haggai's activation of the Temple rebuilding	1:1–15
II.	The greater glory of the new Temple	2:1–9
III.	Oral interpretation and assurance of blessing	2:10–19
IV.	Zerubbabel's signet ring	2:20–23

The second decade since a stone has been added to the Temple is rapidly slipping by. The religious enthusiasm expressed when the foundation was laid has been decisively squelched by the hostile Samaritans. In the meantime the people have become occupied with the building of their own homes.

Haggai addresses his opening words to Zerubbabel, the governor, and to Joshua, the high priest. Boldly he declares that it is not right for the people to delay the building of the Temple. Turning to the laity he reminds them that the Lord of hosts is the source and controller of all material blessings. Instead of devoting their efforts to the holy project, they have built paneled houses for themselves. Consequently drought and crop failures have been their lot (1:1–11).

Hitherto no prophet has enjoyed such speedy results in Judah. Enthusiastically the people respond to Haggai's exhortation. Within twenty-four days Haggai has the satisfaction of seeing building activity renewed (1:12–15).

Construction of the new Temple goes on apace for nearly a month before Haggai delivers another message. The occasion is the last day of the Feast of Tabernacles. Since there has been a meager harvest, this celebration is markedly mediocre in comparison to the elaborate festivities in the Temple court in pre-exilic times. Probably there are still a few among the elders who saw the former Temple—fewer in number, however, than in 538 B.C. when the new foundation was laid. Comparing the current prospects with the glory of the Solomonic structure, they become pessimistic and discouraged. The work lags as a spirit of despondency begins to permeate the whole group.

To counter this discouraging situation Haggai assures them (2:1–5) that the "Lord Almighty," who brought them out of Egypt, has covenanted with them that "'my Spirit remains among you. Do not fear.'" God will "'shake all nations . . . and . . . fill this house with glory'" so that the "'glory of this present house will be greater than the glory of the former'" (2:5–9, NIV). God's glory was manifested in their exodus experience (cf. Ex. 13:21–22; 14:19–20; 16:10; 24:15–18). The tabernacle was built at God's request as a sanctuary for

God to dwell among his people. There he manifested his glory and his presence (Ex. 25:8–9; 40:34–38; Lev. 9:23–24). Although the departure of God's glory was recognized in the days of Eli (I Sam. 4:21–22), a greater manifestation of God's glory occurred when Solomon dedicated the Temple (I Kings 8:10–11; II Chron. 7:1–2). Most awesome, however, was Ezekiel's portrayal of the departure of God's glory from the Temple in Jerusalem before its destruction in 586 B.C. (Ezek. 8–11).

Haggai's announcement of a "greater glory" must have brought excitement, hope, and encouragement to the builders.[3] Isaiah had already associated God's glory with the coming of the Messiah (40:5; 60:1–3). Simeon, "moved by the Spirit" (Luke 2:25–32, NIV), and the disciples (John 1:14) recognized God's glory in Jesus Christ, whose ministry was associated with this Temple.

Two months later, Haggai comes with another message (2:10–19). By this time the prophet Zechariah (1:1–6) has earnestly warned the people that they should not be like their forefathers, who ignored the word of the prophets.[4] Raising questions about defilement and consecration as prescribed in the law (2:10–14), Haggai teaches his audience that crop failure at this time—when they are dilatory in building the Temple—is God's way of reminding them of their duty to him. Now that they have repented (Zech. 1:6), God's word of assurance is "'From this day on I will bless you'" (2:19, NIV).

Haggai's fourth message, on that same day (Dec. 18, 520 B.C.), is directed personally to Zerubbabel, the governor of Judah (2:20–23). In cosmic language the shaking of the heavens and the earth portrays the overthrow and destruction of Gentile dominion but interprets it as referring to the ultimate final establishment of the universal kingdom at the second advent of Christ (cf. Isa. 2:1–4; 9:7; 11:1–11; Zech. 14). The signet ring, a token of authority taken away from Jehoiachin, king of Judah, is given to "'my servant Zerubbabel'" (2:23, NIV), who represents the resumption of the messianic line interrupted by the exile (cf. Matt. 1:11–12).

[3] Cf. Robert L. Alden, "Haggai" in *Expositor's Bible Commentary*, pp. 586–587.

[4] Note the chronology for these two prophets:

Haggai's first message (1:1–11; Ezra 5:1)	—29 August 520
Rebuilding begun (1:12–15; Ezra 5:2)	—21 September 520
Haggai's second message (2:1–9)	—17 October 520
Zechariah's first message (1:1–6)	—October/November 520
Haggai's third and fourth messages (2:10–19, 20–23)	—18 December 520
Tattnai's letter to Darius (Ezra 5:3–6:14)	—519–518
Zechariah's eight night-visions (1:7–6:8)	—15 February 519
Zechariah and the Bethel delegation (7–8)	—7 December 518
Dedication of the Temple (Ezra 6:15–18)	—12 March 516
Zechariah's final prophecy (9–14)	—ca. 480 or later

Zechariah—Israel in a Universal Setting—1:1–14:21

Jerusalem was buzzing with activity and excitement when Zechariah enunciated his apocalyptic utterances. In the days of hesitation following Haggai's second message, Zechariah lent further inspiration to the struggling band of Jews. In all likelihood he was of the priestly lineage of Iddo, who had returned to Palestine (Neh. 12:1, 4, 16). If he is the priest noted in Neh. 12:16, he was still a young man in 520 B.C., when he began his ministry as a prophet.

The messages of Zechariah in chapters 1–8 are definitely related to the time of the rebuilding of the Temple. The remaining chapters (9–14) can also reasonably be credited to him but dated in the latter years of his life, probably 480 B.C.[5] Observe the following analysis of the Book of Zechariah:

I.	A call to repentance	1:1–6
II.	Eight night-visions	1:7–6:8
III.	The coronation of Joshua	6:9–15
IV.	The problem of fasting	7:1–8:23
V.	Messiah and the shepherd-king	9:1–11:17
VI.	God's universal rule established	12:1–14:21

Zechariah's opening words follow in the wake of Haggai's message of encouragement at the Feast of Tabernacles. Citing the disobedience of their forefathers by way of warning, Zechariah supports his colleague's effort to activate the Jews. Only an active change of heart will evoke God's favor (1:1–6).

Within a few months, on February 19, 519 B.C., Zechariah has a series of prophetic (dream) visions, through which God reveals the future of Judah and Jerusalem.[6] Kingdom hopes, dormant during the seventy-year exile, are now revived as the revelatory events are seen and recorded by Zechariah. Explained by a divine interpreter, the theological content is primarily eschatological and provides encouragement for God's people in rebuilding the Temple because of the promise of a glorious future.

In the opening vision four horsemen return from patrol duty reporting that they "'found the whole world at rest and in peace.'" God is "very angry with the nations," but Jerusalem will be restored. This is the general theme of the whole series (1:7–17, NIV).

Four horns and four craftsmen appear in the second vision (1:18–21). The destruction of the former by the latter signifies the ruination of the nations responsible for the dispersion of Judah, Israel, and Jerusalem.

[5] Cf. Kenneth L. Barker, "Zechariah" in *Expositor's Bible Commentary*, pp. 596–597, for discussion of the unity of Zechariah.

[6] Cf. op. cit., pp. 610–642, for exposition of these visions.

In the third vision a surveyor comes into view before Zechariah (2:1–13). Restored Jerusalem will be so populous and prosperous that it will be necessary to expand beyond the walls—a prediction not realized in the days of Nehemiah (7:4 and 11:1–2). This awaits fulfillment when the Lord "'will be its glory within'" and "'a wall of fire around it'" (2:5, NIV). In regathering Israel the Lord will terrify the nations so that they will become a spoil to the people they once held captive. Judah will again be God's inheritance when the Lord Almighty once more chooses Jerusalem as his habitation.

In the fourth vision Zechariah sees Joshua clothed in filthy garments. Satan, the accuser of Israel's high priest, is rebuked by the Lord, who has chosen Jerusalem. Expeditiously, Joshua is then clothed in festive garments. Conditioned by his obedience, Joshua is assured that before God he can now acceptably represent his people—a condition in which the Israelites have failed to become "'a kingdom of priests and a holy nation'" (Ex. 19:6, NIV). This promise for the future is vested in the servant identified as the Branch. In a single day the Lord of hosts will clear away the guilt of the land in preparation for the return of peace and prosperity (3:1–10).

Especially noteworthy is the vision of the gold lampstand with its seven-spouted bowl between two olive trees that apparently provide a continuous supply of oil (4:1–14). Zechariah is awakened to its importance by an angel. Through this vision comes the assurance that God by his Spirit will accomplish his purpose in completing the building of the Temple. Keeping vigil, the Lord of the whole earth is supported by two anointed ones who obviously are Joshua (3:1–10) and Zerubbabel (Hag. 2:20–23).

Dramatic indeed is the sixth vision. Zechariah sees a flying scroll, fantastic in size (ca. fifteen by thirty feet), announcing a curse against stealing and perjury (5:1–4). Lawbreakers are condemned by the law they have broken.

Vividly depicted in the next vision is the removal of wickedness. A woman, representing the sin of the people of Palestine, is removed to Babylonia in a measuring basket (5:5–11).

In the final vision chariots depart to the four points of the compass to patrol the earth. The Temple builders are assured once more that the Lord of all the earth exercises universal control (6:1–8).

Coming five months after the Jews resumed building activity, Zechariah's night-vision messages must have met a crucial need as Tattnai and other Persian officials investigate developments and complain to Darius, king of Persia (cf. Ezra 5:3–6:14). During these days of anxiety concerning the verdict of Darius, the builders' faith is tested as they listen to Zechariah's assurance that they are involved in the work of "'the Lord of the whole world'" (6:5, NIV).

Climactic as well as predictive is the prophet's symbolic act (6:9–15). With the gold crown on Joshua's head comes the promise vested in the Branch, who, as "'a priest on his throne'" (6:13, NIV), will build the Temple with nations from afar lending their aid. This unique combination of royalty and priesthood was not realized in Joshua. The symbolic crown was placed in the Temple for a memorial. How soon the favorable verdict from Darius comes is not indicated. Zechariah's message is certified as Tattnai and his fellow governors are ordered to aid the Jews with material supplies and revenue (Ezra 6:6–15).

Two years later, December 7, 518 B.C., a delegation from Bethel comes with an inquiry about fasting.[7] Should they continue to fast in the fifth and seventh months—fasts instituted by the Jews to commemorate the fall of Jerusalem? Zechariah reminds them that God scattered them and made the land desolate because their forefathers had not heeded the warnings of the prophets (7:1–14; cf. Isa. 65:11–12). Once more they are assured that the Lord "'will return to Zion and dwell in Jerusalem'" (8:3, NIV), where God's regathered people will live in security and peace (8:1–8; cf. Isa. 59:15a–63:6).

The immediate application to his audience is given in 8:9–19. The builders who were present when the foundation of the Temple was laid about two decades earlier are admonished to redouble their efforts. The Lord Almighty, who "'had determined to bring disaster,'" has now "'determined to do good again to Jerusalem and Judah'" (8:14–15, NIV). Let truth, justice, and peace prevail among them. Let fastings be changed into seasons of gladness and joy.

The glorious promise for the future is once more brought into focus for the encouragement of the Temple builders (8:20–23). When the nations hear that God is with his people, "'many peoples and powerful nations will come to Jerusalem to seek the Lord Almighty . . . '" (8:22, NIV).

The kingdom of God anticipated in the previous section is the theme of chapters 9–14.[8] While surrounding nations are subjected to God's wrath (9:1–8), Jerusalem and Zion are admonished to jubilate in the prospects of a King who is righteous and who brings salvation, even though he is humble and lowly in appearance (9:9; cf. Matt. 21:1–9; Mark 11:1–10; Luke 19:28–38; John 12:12–15). This King will establish universal peace, removing military weapons (9:10; cf. Isa. 2:4; 9:5–7; 11:1–10; Mic. 5:10–15). God's covenant people will be victorious over all their enemies when the "Lord their God" saves them "as the flock of his people" (9:16, NIV) so that they can enjoy his abundant provisions (9:11–10:1). The Lord Almighty will punish the selfish cor-

[7] Cf. C. Hassell Bullock, *An Introduction to the Old Testament Prophetic Books*, p. 320, for discussion of the fast days observed during the exile.

[8] For a messianic exposition of these chapters see K. L. Barker, op. cit., pp. 656–697.

rupt leaders and gather his people from the distant lands to restore the nations of Judah and Ephraim (10:2–12).

The faithless shepherds of Israel are about to be consumed in a fearful judgment (10:1–3). Through a second symbolic act Zechariah is bidden to become the shepherd of Israel. In acting out this role he becomes a type of the messianic Shepherd-King. Detested by the flock, this Good Shepherd terminates his providential care and withdraws his favor—revoking his covenant of restraint—so that the other nations will be permitted to overrun them (11:4–14).

Next Zechariah is instructed to act out the role of the foolish shepherd (11:15–17). Pathetic is the lot of the flock abandoned to a morally deficient shepherd, who deserts and destroys them. The divine imprecation calls for the arm of this "worthless shepherd" to be "'completely withered'" and his right eye to be "'totally blinded'" (11:17, NIV). This judgment against him for his diabolical deeds may still await fulfillment in the final destruction of Israel's enemy (cf. Ezek. 34:1–4; Dan. 11:36–39; Rev. 13:1–8).

The Kingdom of God is the theme of Zechariah's final message (12–14). The nation of Israel is assured of full restoration by the Lord, who is the creator of the universe and of humanity (12:1; cf. Gen. 1–2). Though abandoned to the nations for judgment, the day is coming when Israel will become an "'immovable rock for all the nations'" (12:3, NIV). Judah will emerge in victory over all nations that come against it (12:2–9).

Moved by God's "'spirit of grace and supplication'" (12:10, NIV), the Israelites will turn to the One whom they once rejected (12:10–14). The people of Jerusalem will avail themselves of a fountain for cleansing from sin and impurity—one that will purify them as well as the land. Idols will be banished from memory, and false prophets will be ostracized (13:1–6).

The smiting of the true shepherd, apparently by the Lord Almighty, results in the scattering of the sheep. Although two-thirds of the people will perish, a remnant will survive the refining fires. These will turn to God and acknowledge that the Lord is God (13:7–9).

In that "day of the Lord" (14:1, NIV) all nations will be gathered to Jerusalem for battle (14:1–21). From the Mount of Olives the Lord will withstand all the enemies and become king over the whole earth. Jerusalem, with a supernatural water supply, will be securely established. Panic-stricken, the opposition will disintegrate so that the wealth of all the nations will be collected without interference. All survivors will go up to Jerusalem "to worship the King, the Lord Almighty, and to celebrate the Feast of Tabernacles" (14:16, NIV). With Jerusalem established as the focal point of all nations, the worship of God will then be purged of every impure element so that all of life, universally, may redound to his magnification.

Malachi—The Final Prophetic Warning—1:1–4:6

The only occurrence of the name *Malachi* is in the opening verse of this book. Since Malachi means *my messenger,* the Septuagint renders it as a common noun. The fact that all the other books in this group are associated with the names of the prophets favors the recognition of Malachi as a proper name.

It is difficult to ascertain the time of Malachi's ministry. The second Temple was standing, the altar of sacrifice was in use, and the Jewish community was under the jurisdiction of a Persian governor (cf. 1:8). This places Malachi's activity subsequent to the times of Haggai and Zechariah, when the Temple was rebuilt.

How is Malachi's ministry related to the time of Ezra (ca. 457 B.C.) or the times of Nehemiah (ca. 444–432 B.C.)? With no specific references to either, did Malachi precede the arrival of Ezra, or did he follow the times of Nehemiah?[9] Gary V. Smith suggests 420 B.C. as a probable date for Malachi's activity.[10] This allows time for the serious reforms of Nehemiah to wear thin and the need for a prophetic voice when the Israelites had become lax in their relationship with God. Malachi and Nehemiah had basic concerns in common, such as mixed marriages (2:11–14 and Neh. 13:23–27), the tithe (3:8–10 and Neh. 13:10–14), and social ills (Mal. 3:5 and Neh. 5:1–13). However, it is by no means certain that these prophets refer to the same time and circumstances.

Malachi has the distinction of being the last of the Hebrew prophets. He speaks to the common problems facing his community, especially economic depression and the lack of theological teaching. In his dialogue pattern, somewhat similar to Haggai's style, he reflects his community's misunderstanding of God's character in a series of questions, such as,

"How have you loved us?" (1:2, NIV)
"Where is the honor due me?" (1:6, NIV)
"Have we not all one father?" (2:10, NIV)
"Where is the God of justice?" (2:17, NIV)
"Who can endure the day of his coming?" (3:2, NIV)
"Will a man rob God?" (3:8, NIV)

Aware of the failure of the priests to instruct the people, Malachi emphasizes the lordship of God, identifying him as "the Lord Almighty" or "the Lord of hosts" twenty-four times. The people should recognize God

[9] For dating Malachi before Ezra's return in 457 B.C., cf. Joyce Baldwin, "Haggai, Zechariah, Malachi," p. 213; also, C. H. Bullock, op. cit., pp. 338–339.

[10] Cf. G. V. Smith, "Malachi" in *The New Standard Bible Encyclopedia* (Grand Rapids: Eerdmans), Vol. III, 1986.

as father and master (1:6), as a great king (1:16), as creator (2:10, 15), as the one who loves those who fear him (3:16–17), and as the judge of the wicked (3:18).

With six oracles this book lends itself to the following outline:

I.	Superscription	1:1
II.	God's love for Israel	1:2–5
III.	Disrespect for God in worship	1:6–2:9
IV.	Rebuke for unfaithfulness in marriage	2:10–16
V.	Divine justice	2:17–3:5
VI.	God's challenge and assurance	3:6–12
VII.	God-fearing people on God's scroll	3:13–4:3
VIII.	Moses and Elijah	4:4–6

God's love for the Israelites reaches back in history to the time of the patriarchs. In countering their skepticism, God says that the mystery and significance of his love is evident in the fact that he chose Jacob, contrary to custom, in which Esau would have been preferred (cf. Gen. 12:1–3; Ex. 19:5–6; Rom. 9:10–13).

The priests have failed to provide proper moral and religious leadership. By offering imperfect or stolen animals in sacrifice, the people have demonstrated their disrespect for God. They would not dare treat their governor in this way. God's name is revered among the nations but not in Israel. He will not be treated in this manner by his chosen people. Such deceit warrants God's curse (1:14).

The priests are singled out for retribution. They have been unfaithful as messengers of the Lord Almighty to provide the people with knowledge and instruction. Consequently, God's pronouncement is this: "'So I have caused you to be despised and humiliated before all the people . . .'" (2:9, NIV).

By marriage to heathen women and by divorce, the people of Judah have profaned the sanctuary. These are faithless acts that have destroyed the natural and spiritual unity between God and his people. He could not accept their offerings (2:10–16).

Beyond all this, Malachi brusquely reminds his audience that they have wearied God by their failure to seek the right ways. God is about to send his messenger to his Temple to judge, refine, and purify his people. The charges against them are sorcery: adultery, false swearing, failure to tithe, and social injustice toward hirelings, widows, orphans, and strangers (2:17–3:5).

God expects his people to acknowledge him in giving one-tenth of what he has given them (Num. 18:21; Lev. 27:30). "'Return to me, and I will return to you'" (3:7, NIV) is God's condition for them to enjoy the productivity of the land (3:6–12).

God is cognizant of those who fear him; they are his special possession. Recorded in a scroll of remembrance, the righteous are designated for salvation in the day of God's wrath. Those who have been presumptuous and have promoted wickedness—"all the arrogant and every evildoer" (4:1, NIV)—will perish as stubble in a burning field after the harvest. The God-fearing, however, will wax strong (3:13–4:3).

In conclusion, Malachi exhorts his own generation to obey the Mosaic law (4:4–6). With the terrible day of the Lord pending, he reminds his audience that this judgment will be preceded by a period of mercy ushered in with the coming of Elijah. Predictive in import, the name *Elijah* suggests a time of revival through a God-sent individual. Such a one has already been promised (3:1). Some four centuries later this messenger is identified (Matt. 11:10, 14).

SELECTED READING

ALDEN, ROBERT L. "Haggai" and "Malachi" in *Expositor's Bible Commentary.* Grand Rapids: Zondervan Publishing House, 1985.

BALDWIN, JOYCE C. "Haggai, Zechariah, Malachi." *Tyndale Old Testament Commentaries.* Downers Grove: Inter-Varsity Press, 1972.

BARKER, KENNETH L. "Zechariah" in *Expositor's Bible Commentary.* Grand Rapids: Zondervan Publishing House, 1985.

LEUPOLD, H. C. *Exposition of Zechariah.* Columbus: Wartburg Press, 1956.

SMITH, G. V. "Malachi" in *The New Standard Bible Encyclopedia.* Vol. 3. Grand Rapids: Wm. B. Eerdmans Publishing Co., 1986.

SMITH, RALPH L. "Micah–Malachi" in *Word Biblical Commentary.* Vol. 32. Waco: Word Books, 1984.

UNGER, M. F. *Commentary on Zechariah.* Grand Rapids: Zondervan Publishing House, 1962.

VERHOEFF, PIETER A. *The Books of Haggai and Malachi.* Grand Rapids: Wm. B. Eerdmans Publishing Co., 1987.

WOLF, HERBERT. *Haggai and Malachi.* Chicago: Moody Press, 1976.

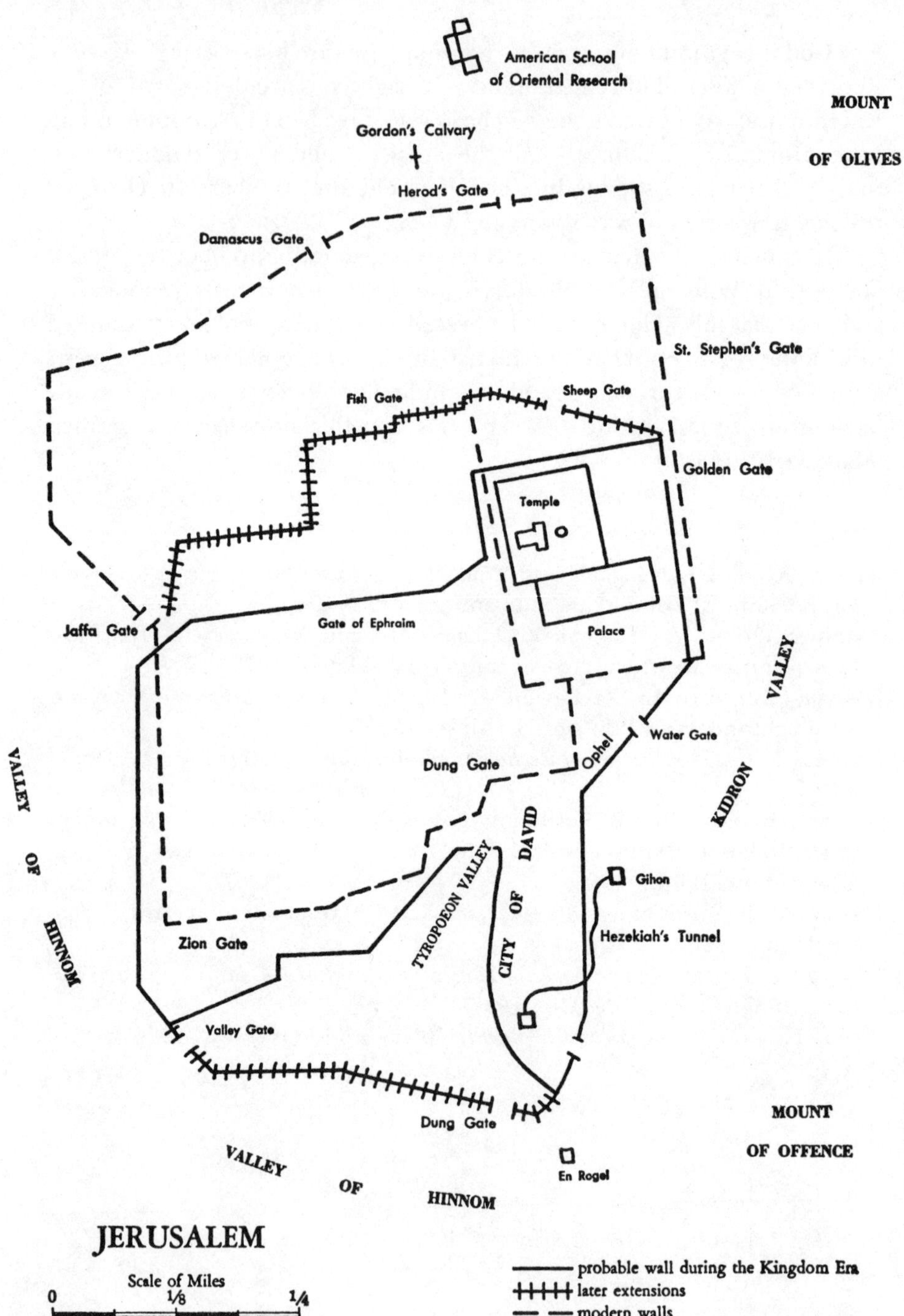
American School
of Oriental Research
MOUNT
OF OLIVES
Gordon's Calvary
Herod's Gate
Damascus Gate
St. Stephen's Gate
Fish Gate
Sheep Gate
Golden Gate
Temple
Palace
Jaffa Gate
Gate of Ephraim
VALLEY
Water Gate
Ophel
Dung Gate
KIDRON
VALLEY
OF
HINNOM
TYROPOEON VALLEY
CITY OF DAVID
Gihon
Hezekiah's Tunnel
Zion Gate
Valley Gate
Dung Gate
MOUNT
OF OFFENCE
En Rogel
VALLEY
OF
HINNOM
JERUSALEM
Scale of Miles
0
1/8
1/4
probable wall during the Kingdom Era
later extensions
modern walls

Index of Biblical References

OLD TESTAMENT

Index of Maps

Index of Names and Subjects

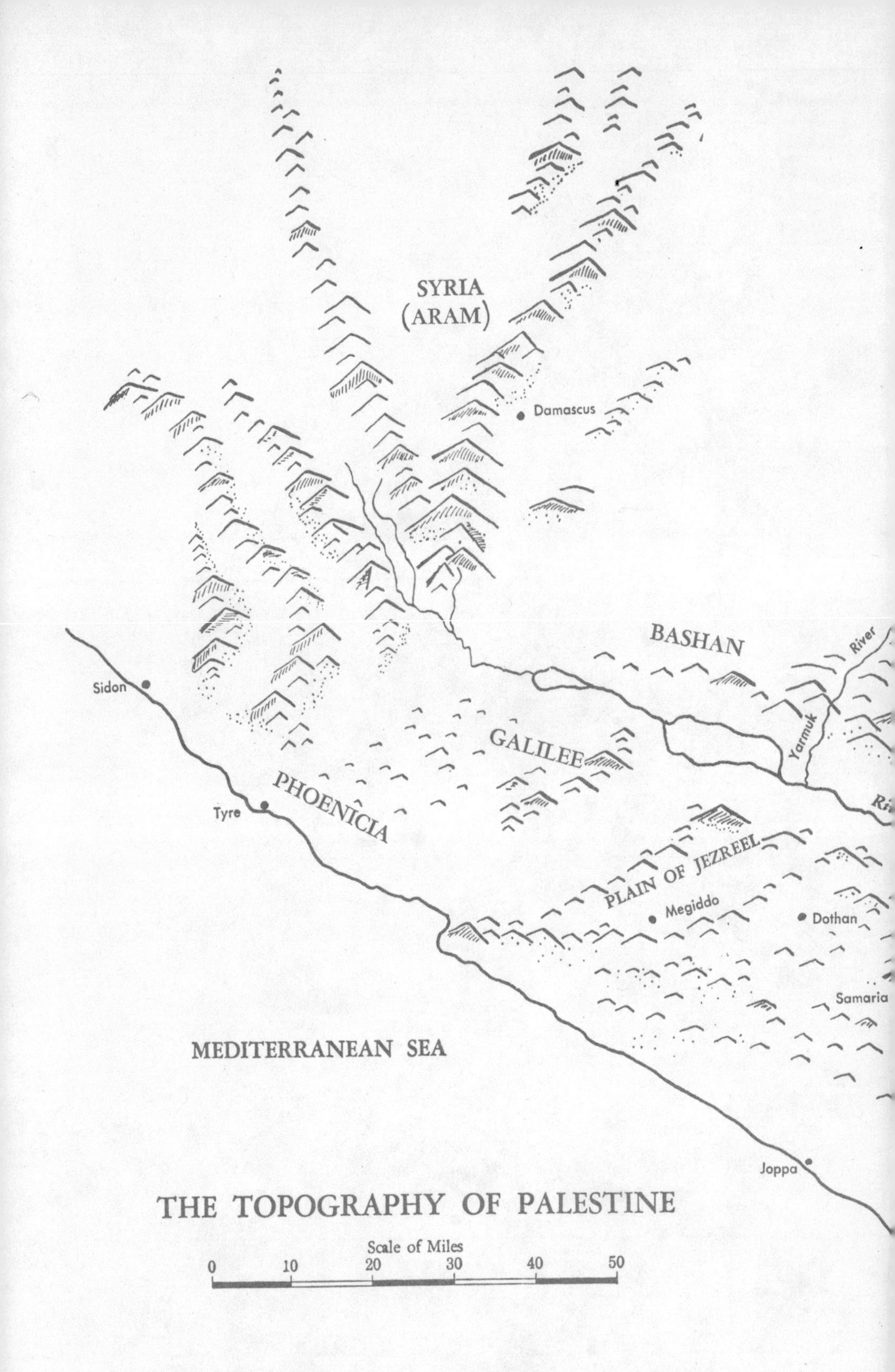

THE TOPOGRAPHY OF PALESTINE